STALIN'S GAMBLE

Stalin's Gamble

The Search for Allies against Hitler, 1930–1936

MICHAEL JABARA CARLEY

UNIVERSITY OF TORONTO PRESS
Toronto Buffalo London

Toronto Buffalo London
utorontopress.com

ISBN 978-1-4875-4441-6 (cloth) ISBN 978-1-4875-4591-8 (EPUB)
ISBN 978-1-4875-4593-2 (PDF)

Library and Archives Canada Cataloguing in Publication

Title: Stalin's gamble : the search for allies against Hitler, 1930–1936 / Michael Jabara Carley.
Names: Carley, Michael Jabara, 1945– author.
Description: Includes bibliographical references and index.
Identifiers: Canadiana (print) 20230208452 | Canadiana (ebook) 20230208495 | ISBN 9781487544416 (cloth) | ISBN 9781487545932 (PDF) | ISBN 9781487545918 (EPUB)
Subjects: LCSH: World War, 1939–1945 – Diplomatic history. | LCSH: World War, 1939–1945 – Causes. | LCSH: Soviet Union – Foreign relations – 1917–1945.
Classification: LCC D754.S65 C37 2023 | DDC 940.53/2–dc23

Cover design: Val Cooke
Cover image: Sebastian Frye

We wish to acknowledge the land on which the University of Toronto Press operates. This land is the traditional territory of the Wendat, the Anishnaabeg, the Haudenosaunee, the Métis, and the Mississaugas of the Credit First Nation.

This book has been published with the help of a grant from the Federation for the Humanities and Social Sciences, through the Awards to Scholarly Publications Program, using funds provided by the Social Sciences and Humanities Research Council of Canada.

University of Toronto Press acknowledges the financial support of the Government of Canada, the Canada Council for the Arts, and the Ontario Arts Council, an agency of the Government of Ontario, for its publishing activities.

Canada Council for the Arts | Conseil des Arts du Canada

Funded by the Government of Canada | Financé par le gouvernement du Canada

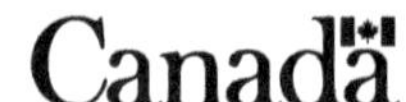

Contents

List of Illustrations and Maps vii

Acknowledgments ix

List of Abbreviations and Acronyms xiii

Biographical Notes xv

1 Introduction: Prologue to Crisis 3
2 A Dimly Lit Night Lamp: Early Attempts at Détente in Paris and Warsaw, 1929–1932 11
3 A Steep Hill: The Soviet Quest for US Recognition, 1930–1933 35
4 Setback: The Metro-Vickers Affair, 1933 65
5 Rapallo or Not? Soviet Relations with Germany and Poland, 1933 105
6 "Strike while the Iron Is Hot": Strengthening Relations with France, 1933 123
7 Shadows of Doubt over Moscow: Consolidating Collective Security, 1933–1934 144
8 "One Step Back, Two Steps Forward": Ups and Downs in Soviet Relations in the West, 1934 168
9 Nobody Wants "the Bolo Baby": The Failure of US-Soviet Relations, 1933–1935 194
10 *Koshmar*: The Agonizing Turn in Relations with France, 1934–1935 245
11 Bridging the Gap: The Anglo-Soviet Rapprochement, 1934–1935 262
12 Showdown: Negotiating the Franco-Soviet Pact, 1935 334
13 No Bridging the Gap: Erosion of the Anglo-Soviet Rapprochement, 1935 393
14 The Weak Hinge: France and Its East European Allies, 1935–1936 424
15 Collapse in London: The Failure of the Anglo-Soviet Rapprochement, 1936 455

16 Good News, Bad News: The Fall of Laval and the Abdication of France, 1936 476
17 Epilogue 505

Notes 517

Bibliography 581

Index 593

Illustrations and Maps

Illustrations

1.1 The odd couple: Georgii V. Chicherin and Maksim M. Litvinov, 10 April 1922, Genoa 5
2.1 Maksim Maksimovich Litvinov, ca. 1920s 12
2.2 Iosif Vissarionovich Stalin, 1932 22
2.3 Boris Spirodonovich Stomoniakov, ca. 1930s 33
5.1 Nikolai Nikolaievich Krestinskii, ca. 1930s 108
6.1 Marcel' Izrailevich Rozenberg, ca. mid-1930s 128
7.1 Litvinov and Józef Beck meeting in Moscow, 13 February 1934 158
8.1 Litvinov making a speech in Geneva, 1934 188
10.1 Vladimir Petrovich Potemkin, ca. 1930s 248
11.1 Ivan Mikhailovich Maiskii, ca. 1930s 278
11.2 Eden's arrival in Moscow, 28 March 1935 317
11.3 Eden meeting with Litvinov in Moscow, 28 March 1935 318
12.1 Meeting in Geneva between Litvinov and Nicolae Titulescu, June 1934 338
12.2 Pierre Laval and Litvinov in Geneva, 1935 341
12.3 Potemkin and Laval in Paris sign the Franco-Soviet pact with officials looking on, 2 May 1935 383
12.4 Stalin and Laval meeting in Moscow with Charles Alphand, Alexis Léger, Litvinov, Potemkin, and Viacheslav Mikhailovich Molotov, May 1935 391
14.1 Litvinov and Eduard Beneš exchange ratification documents in Moscow, 8 June 1935 426
14.2 Mikhail Semenovich Ostrovskii and embassy staff in Bucharest, ca. 1936 438

Maps

0.1 Europe, 1930s xx
9.1 Maritime provinces, Manchuria, China, interwar years 199
14.1 Eastern Europe, 1930s 428
16.1 France and the Rhineland frontiers, 1930s 494

Acknowledgments

This work is the sequel to my book *Silent Conflict*, which focuses on Soviet relations with the Western powers during the 1920s.[1] The present study is the first volume of a trilogy on the foreign policy of the Soviet Union in Europe during the lead-up to the Second World War and the Great Patriotic War in 1941. It is a narrative history, based on extensive multinational archival research. Old files of papers kept in archives across Europe and in the United States, written by people who died long ago, bring back to life their struggles to deal with the international crises of the 1930s. Soviet foreign policy, Iosif V. Stalin's foreign policy in effect, aimed to find European allies, great and small powers, to contain the rising danger of Nazi Germany, or to defeat it in war if containment failed.

My study has been a long time in gestation. I opened my first files on the 1930s at the Quai d'Orsay and other archives in Paris around 1990. I then moved on to the National Archives in Kew, Surrey, and to Moscow where files gradually became available after 1992. In the Russian foreign policy archives (AVPRF), files were opened and closed, and then opened again. One supposes that archivists were not sure of what was in the files and therefore were reluctant to release them. It is always exhilarating when new records are declassified. I will not get too personal about working in Moscow, but I remember the first time I received a dozen or so *dela* (files) to start my research. It was twenty-six years ago. I was elated. Of course, there were ups and downs in the archives as there are in life. The downs came when I did not obtain access to the files I requested. I remember an archivist at the AVPRF became cross with me because I was too persistent in my quest for files. "Who does he think he is?" she wondered aloud outside the reading room. Everyone could hear her. "I am only after the files," I might have replied. "Just the files, ma'am" (to borrow a phrase from LA police sergeant Joe Friday in the American television series *Dragnet*). Sometimes one needs a sense of humour when dealing with archivists.

I am not complaining, mind you, but I am a digger rather than a skimmer – a *rat des archives*, the French would say – and am not satisfied until I have got to the bottom of my mysteries … if I can. As readers may surmise, my approach is empirical. I have never been much interested in "theories" of history. I mean intellectual constructs unsupported by legitimate forms of evidence, or an archival base when apposite. This is just to say that I have read many files, but of course, it is never enough. I should add that in recent years the Russian authorities have helped by putting a great number of files or selections of documents online. This has allowed me to continue research in Moscow from my study in Pierrefonds, Quebec. During the COVID-19 pandemic, it has made a difference. In Moscow, as elsewhere, the keys to success of archival research are patience, persistence, courtesy, and good luck.

The extensive study of Soviet foreign policy files makes my work different from that of many of my colleagues. The new material permits fresh interpretations of Soviet relations with the Western powers in Europe and the United States, which, in this book, focuses on 1930 to 1936. Following volumes will examine the periods 1936 to 1939 and 1939 to 1941. My emphasis is on Soviet relations with the Western powers, and on the origins and early conduct of the Second World War and Great Patriotic War. Readers will meet familiar and not-so-familiar characters. They played their roles in the unfolding of tragic events, which led to civil war in Spain in 1936, to a European war in 1939, and to the Nazi invasion of the Soviet Union in 1941.

I have incurred debts to people who have helped me in various ways during the course of my research in European archives. Archivists were and are the first indispensable guides. I have been at work so long that the first generation of archivists I met during my trips abroad, have retired or are no longer with us. I remember them for their assistance and kindnesses over the years, in fact five decades now. For the present, I thank Ms. Anna Nikolaevna Zaleeva, the long-standing chief of the AVPRF, for her helpfulness. I remember having a meeting with her in the lounge area outside the reading room. She looked me over and then cracked a smile to which, naturally, I responded in kind. She authorized the granting of rights to publish the photographs of Soviet and European diplomats and politicians found in the pages of this book. I would be remiss if I did not also thank the legendary Sergei Vitalievich Pavlov, retired now from the AVPRF. For more than a generation he was often a patient intermediary between researchers who wanted access to more files and archivists who perhaps wanted to offer less.

I also wish to acknowledge the support of the Social Sciences and Humanities Research Council of Canada (SSHRC) in Ottawa. It has supported my research off and on since the 1980s, most recently through a generous "Insight Grant" in 2016.

Thanks are also due to the University of Toronto Press and to UTP editor Stephen Shapiro who invested in this large volume and took it through the evaluation process. The Awards to Scholarly Publications Program in Ottawa provided a publishing grant to defer production costs.

Colleagues and friends have helped me along the way. I mention in this regard, Geoffrey Roberts, with whom I have exchanged ideas about Stalin, Soviet foreign policy, and the origins of the Second World War for nearly thirty years. Also special to me is the late Zara Steiner. We often discussed war origins in correspondence, or when I visited her in Cambridge during my research stints at the National Archives in Kew. She followed my progress in writing the manuscript and she pushed me to let no distraction or obstacle get in the way of finishing the work. I regret that she could not see the end result of my labours.

Other colleagues who have helped me over the years are Aleksei M. Filitov, Veronika Iu. Krasheninnikova, Sergei V. Kudryashov, Vladimir O. Pechatnov, Vladimir V. Simindei (and his colleague Aleksandr A. Dyukov), and Dmitrii V. Surzhik. Messrs. Simindei and Dyukov have published translations of some of my essays.[2] Kudryashov and Krasheninnikova oversaw, among other things, the Russian translation of *Silent Conflict*.[3] We have often met in Moscow to share a meal and to discuss the great and tragic figures of the history of the Second World War and the Great Patriotic War.

To tell the stories of my historic characters has been lonely work, sitting at my desk year after year writing a long manuscript without any immediate impacts or positive results. Yet, it has been a way of making friends with people, historical ancestors, who probably did not imagine that they would come to life again in a distant future. I am glad to have gotten to know them and to be able to share their successes and tragedies with readers who turn the pages of this book. An author must have tenacity, and must rely on the encouragement of friends and colleagues. “Keep going, don’t let up,” Zara used to say to me, and then she would remind me of other colleagues who intended to write big books and never did. Tragedies, she might have said.

Finally, I would also like to thank Liia R. Levitskaia, who served as my assistant-typist in Moscow, and Samuel Allard and especially Louis Vallières, who worked with me as research assistants. Mike Bechthold and Arthur de Robert provided the maps. Finally, I must recognize my spouse, Irina Borisovna, for putting up, most of the time, with my long, exhausting days at work on the manuscript.

MJC
Université de Montréal
January 2023

Abbreviations and Acronyms

AFL	American Federation of Labor
Auswärtiges Amt	German ministry of foreign affairs, Berlin
AVPRF	Archive of Foreign Policy of the Russian Federation
Bolsh/Bolshies (British), Bolos (American), Bolchos (French)	Western slang for the Bolsheviks
Comintern	Communist (Third) International
Die-Hards	Far-right, anti-Soviet members of the British Conservative Party
Entente	Bolshevik terminology for the Allied powers, Britain, France, and the United States
FO	Foreign Office, London
Gensek	Secretary general of the Politburo, I.V. Stalin
Gosbank	Soviet State Bank
HMG	His Majesty's Government
IKKI	Executive Committee of the Communist International
ILP	International Labour Party
Instantsiia	The Politburo, in effect Stalin
Kollegiia	The executive committee of the Commissariat for Foreign Affairs (until 1934)
Kulaks	"Rich" or relatively prosperous Russian peasants
Narkom	People's Commissar
NKID (Narkomindel)	People's Commissariat for Foreign Affairs
NKVD	People's Commissariat for Internal Affairs
NKVT (Narkomvneshtorg)	People's Commissariat for External Trade
NSDAP	National Socialist German Workers' Party
OGPU	Soviet Joint State Political Directorate (secret police)

Politburo	Governing body of the Russian Communist Party, the Soviet government, and the Comintern
Polpred	Soviet ambassador or plenipotentiary representative
Quai d'Orsay	French Ministry of Foreign Affairs, Paris
The Quartet	Stalin, Molotov, Voroshilov, Kaganovich
Razvedchik	Soviet intelligence agent
RKP	Russian Communist Party
SIS	British Secret Intelligence Service
Torgpredstvo	Soviet trade mission abroad
Torgpred	Soviet foreign trade representative
The Troika	Molotov, Voroshilov, Kaganovich
TsIK	All-Union Central Executive Committee
TsK	Central Committee
VKP(b)	All-Union Communist Party (Bolsheviks)
Vozhd'	Also *khoziain*, the chief or boss, i.e., Stalin
VTsIK	All Russian Central Executive Committee, VKP(b)
Whites, or White Guards	Anti-Bolshevik forces during the Civil War against the Soviet government (1917–21)
Zamnarkom	Deputy People's Commissar

Biographical Notes

Sergei Sergeievich Aleksandrovskii, polpred, Prague, 1934–9.
Charles Alphand, French ambassador, Moscow, 1933–6.
Vladimir Aleksandrovich Antonov-Ovseenko, polpred, Warsaw, 1930–4.
Mirosław Arciszewski, Polish minister, Bucharest, 1932–8.
Frank Ashton-Gwatkin, counsellor, British embassy, Moscow, 1929–30; head, Economic Relations Department, Foreign Office, 1934–9.
Stanley Baldwin, British prime minister, 1922–4, 1924–9, 1935–7.
Louis Barthou, French foreign minister, 1934.
Józef Beck, Polish foreign minister, 1932–9.
Eduard Beneš, foreign minister, 1918–35; president, Czechoslovakia, 1935–8.
Philippe Berthelot, secretary general of the French foreign ministry, 1920–2, 1925–32.
Léon Blum, député, 1919–40; leader of the French Socialist Party; président du Conseil, 1936–7, 1938.
Aristide Briand, président du Conseil, 1921–2, 1925–6; foreign minister, 1925–32.
Fernand de Brinon, French journalist, *Journal des débats*, 1920–32; *Le Matin*, 1930s; close to Daladier and Laval, go-between with Nazi Germany, 1930s.
Nikolai Ivanovich Bukharin, head of Comintern, 1926–9; member, Politburo, 1924–9; editor, *Izvestiia*, 1934–6.
William C. Bullitt, US ambassador, Moscow, 1933–6; Paris, 1936–40.
Neville Chamberlain, British Chancellor of the Exchequer, 1931–7; prime minister, 1937–40.
Camille Chautemps, many times French cabinet minister, 1930s; président du Conseil, 1937–8.
Aretas Akers-Douglas Lord Chilston, British ambassador, Moscow, 1933–8.
Winston S. Churchill, MP, House of Commons, 1930s, Conservative gadfly; prime minister, 1940–5.
Laurence Collier, Far Eastern Department, 1924–5; Northern Department, 1926–32; head, Northern Department, Foreign Office, 1932–41.
Charles Corbin, French ambassador, London, 1933–40.

Pierre Cot, French Aviation Minister, 1933–4, 1936–8.

Robert Coulondre, French ambassador, Moscow, 1936–8; Berlin, 1938–9.

Édouard Daladier, président du Conseil, 1933, 1934, 1938–40; Minister of War, 1932–4, 1936–40; foreign minister, 1939–40.

Iakov Khristoforovich Davtian, polpred, Warsaw, 1934–7.

Yvon Delbos, French foreign minister, 1936–8.

Anatole de Monzie, French minister and centre-right politician, 1930s.

Valerian Savel'evich Dovgalevskii, polpred, Paris, 1928–34.

Anthony Eden, Lord Privy Seal, 1934–5; Foreign Secretary, 1935–8, 1940–5; Dominions Secretary, 1939–40.

Aleksandr Il'ich Egorov, Marshal of the USSR, 1935; Soviet chief of staff, 1935–7; zamnarkom, defence, 1937–9.

Walter Elliot, British minister of agriculture, 1932–6; Secretary of State for Scotland, 1936–8; minister of health, 1938–40.

Pierre-Étienne Flandin, French commerce minister 1929–30; finance minister, 1931–2; public works minister, 1934; président du Conseil, 1934–5; ministre d'État, 1935–6; foreign minister, 1936.

General Maurice Gamelin, chief of the French general staff, 1931–40; commander-in-chief of the French Army, 1939–40.

Evgenii Vladimirovich Girshfel'd, Soviet chargé d'affaires, Paris, 1934–8.

Edward Lord Halifax, Lord President of the Council, 1937–8; Foreign Secretary, 1938–40.

Jean Herbette, journalist at *Le Temps*, 1918–24; French ambassador, Moscow, 1925–31.

Édouard Herriot, député, 1919–40; leader of the Radical-Socialist Party, 1919–36; French président du Conseil and foreign minister, 1924–5, 1932; many times a cabinet minister, 1926–36.

Sir Samuel Hoare, Foreign Secretary, 1935; First Lord of the Admiralty, 1936–7; Home Secretary, 1937–9; Lord Privy Seal, 1939–40.

Herbert Hoover, US Secretary of Commerce, 1922–9; president, 1929–3.

Cordell Hull, US Secretary of State, 1933–44.

Lazar Moiseevich Kaganovich, secretary, Central Committee, 1928–39.

Lev Mikhailovich Karakhan, Soviet polpred in Warsaw, 1920–1; head, Eastern Department, NKID, 1922–3; member, NKID kollegiia, 1922–3; Soviet polpred, Peking, 1923–6; zamnarkom, NKID, 1926–4; polpred, Ankara, 1934–7.

Robert F. Kelley, chief, Division of East European Affairs, US Department of State, 1926–37.

Lt. Colonel Jan Kowalewski, Polish intelligence officer and military attaché, Moscow, 1929–33; Bucharest, 1933–7.

Nikolai Nikolaievich Krestinskii, narkom, finances, 1919–21; member, Politburo, 1919–21; polpred, Berlin, 1922–30; zamnarkom, NKID, 1930–7.

Jules Laroche, French ambassador, Warsaw, 1925–35.

Pierre Laval, président du Conseil, 1931, 1932, 1935–6; minister for colonies, 1934; foreign minister, 1934–6.

Sir Reginald A. Leeper, Central Department, 1920; Northern Department, Foreign Office, 1921–3; head, News Department, 1935–9; head, Political Intelligence Department, 1938–41.

Alexis Léger, sous-directeur d'Asie, Quai d'Orsay, 1925–7; sous-directeur des Affaires politiques, 1927–9; directeur des Affaires politiques, 1929–32 ; secrétaire-général, 1933–40.

Maksim Maksimovich Litvinov, zamnarkom, NKID, 1920–30; narkom, 1930–9.

David Lloyd George, British prime minister, 1916–22; MP, House of Commons to 1945.

Juliusz Łukasiewicz, Polish ambassador, Moscow, 1934–6; Paris, 1936–9.

Ramsay Macdonald, British prime minister, 1924, 1929–35.

Ivan Mikhailovich Maiskii, Soviet counselor, Soviet embassy in London, 1925–7; polpred, Helsinki, 1929–32; London, 1932–43.

Georges Mandel, French minister of communications (post, telegraph, and telephone), 1934–6; colonies, 1938–40.

Jan Masaryk, Czechoslovak minister, London, 1925–38.

Colonel Edmond Mendras, French military attaché, Moscow, 1933–4.

Anastas Ivanovich Mikoian, narkom, external and internal trade, 1926–30; supply 1930–4; member, Politburo, 1935–66; narkom, food industry, 1934–8; external trade, 1938–49.

Viacheslav Mikhailovich Molotov, secretary, Politburo, 1921–30; member, Politburo, 1926–57; narkom, NKID, 1939–49.

R. Walton Moore, US Assistant Secretary of State, 1933–7.

George A. Mounsey, Assistant Permanent Undersecretary, Foreign Office, 1929–39.

Benito Mussolini, *Il Duce*, head of the Italian government and prime minister, 1922–43.

Rudolf Nadolny, German ambassador, Moscow, 1933–4.

Léon Noël, French ambassador, Warsaw, 1935–9.

Mikhail Semenovich Ostrovskii, torgpred, Paris, 1933–4; polpred, Bucharest, 1934–8.

Štefan Osuský, Czechoslovak minister, Paris, 1921–38.

Edmond Ovey, British ambassador, Moscow, 1929–33.

Joseph Paul-Boncour, French war minister, 1932; président du Conseil, 1932–3; foreign minister, 1932–4, 1938; ministre d'État, 1936.

Jean Payart, French chargé d'affaires, Moscow, 1931–7, 1938–40; conseiller d'ambassade, Spain, 1937–8.

Gabriel Péri, député, member of the French Communist Party, journalist for *L'Humanité*, 1930s.

Pertinax (André Géraud), French journalist, notably for *L'Écho de Paris*, interwar years.

Eric Phipps, British ambassador, Berlin, 1933–7; Paris, 1937–9.

Józef Piłsudski, generalissimo of Polish armies, 1919–20; head of state, 1926–35.

Raymond Poincaré, président du Conseil, 1922–4, 1927–9.

Vladimir Petrovich Potemkin, polpred, Paris, 1934–7; zamnarkom, NKID, 1937–40.

Karl Berngardovich Radek, member, IKKI, Comintern, 1920–4; later, journalist for *Izvestiia* and *Pravda*, 1930s.

Paul Reynaud, French justice minister, 1932, 1938; finance minister, 1938–40; président du Conseil, 1940.

Marcel' Izrailevich Rozenberg, Soviet first secretary, Paris, 1931–4; Soviet representative in Geneva, 1934–6; polpred, Madrid, 1936–7.

Arkadii Pavlovich Rozengol'ts, narkom, foreign trade, 1930–7.

Evgenii Vladimirovich Rubinin, NKID department head, 1928–35; polpred, Brussels, 1935–40.

Sir Orme Garton Sargent, head, Central Department, Foreign Office, 1926–33; Assistant Permanent Undersecretary, 1933–9.

Albert Sarraut, Radical politician; minister of the interior, 1934; président du Conseil, 1936.

General Victor-Henri Schweisguth, French deputy chief of staff, 1935–7.

General Nikolai Aleksandrovich Semenov, Soviet military attaché, Warsaw, 1933–6; Paris, 1936–7.

Horace James Seymour, head, Northern Department, Foreign Office, 1929–32.

Sir John Simon, British Foreign Secretary, 1932–5; Home Secretary, 1935–7; Chancellor of the Exchequer, 1937–40.

Boris Efimovich Shtein, Soviet polpred, Helsinki, 1933–4; Rome, 1934–8; at the same time a member of the Soviet delegation at the League of Nations, Geneva.

David Grigorievich Shtern, bureau chief, NKID, 1931–7.

Boris Evseevich Skvirskii, unofficial Soviet representative, Washington, 1922–33; chargé d'affaires, Washington, 1933–6; polpred, Kabul, 1936–7.

Gregorii Iakovlevich Sokolnikov, narkom, finances, 1922–6; deputy director, Gosplan, 1926–8; polpred, London, 1929–32; zamnarkom, NKID, 1932–4.

Iosif Vissarionovich Stalin, general secretary (gensek) of the Communist Party of the Soviet Union, 1922–53; member, Politburo, 1919–53.

Boris Spiridonovich Stomoniakov, torgpred, Berlin, 1920–5; member, NKID *kollegiia*, 1926–34; zamnarkom, NKID, 1934–8.

William Strang, Far Eastern Department, Foreign Office, 1927–9; councilor, British embassy, Moscow, 1930–3; adviser on League of Nations Affairs, 1934–7; head, Central Department, 1937–9; head, Western Department, 1939; Assistant Permanent Undersecretary, 1939–43.

Iakov Zakharovich Surits, polpred, Berlin, 1934–7; Paris, 1937–40.

Geneviève Tabouis, French journalist, 1930s.

Gheorghe I. Tătărescu, Romanian prime minister, 1934–7.

Nicolae Titulescu, Romanian foreign minister 1932–6.

Aleksandr Antonovich Troianovskii, polpred, Washington, 1933–8.

Lev Davidovich Trotskii, narkom for foreign affairs, 1917–18; narkom, war, 1918–25; member, Politburo, 1919–26; exiled from the USSR, 1929; assassinated in Mexico, 1940.

Mikhail Nikolaevich Tukhachevskii, Marshal of the USSR, 1935; zamnarkom, defence, 1931–7.

Sir Robert Gilbert Vansittart, Permanent Undersecretary of State, Foreign Office, 1930–7; chief diplomatic adviser, Foreign Office, 1938–40.

General Semen Ivanovich Ventsov, Soviet military attaché, Paris, 1933–6.

Boris Dmitrievich Vinogradov, first secretary and razvedchik, Soviet embassy, Berlin, 1930–5; Bucharest, 1935–6; Warsaw, 1937–8.

Friedrich Werner von der Schulenburg, German ambassador, Moscow, 1934–41.

Herbert von Dirksen, head, East European Desk, Auswärtiges Amt, 1928; German ambassador in Moscow, 1928–33; Tokyo, 1933–8; London, 1938–9.

Joachim von Ribbentrop, German ambassador, London, 1936–8, foreign minister, 1938–45.

Kliment Efremovich Voroshilov, Marshal of the USSR, 1935; narkom, defence, 1925–40; member, Politburo, 1926–60.

John Wiley, US chargé d'affaires, Moscow, 1933–6.

Jean Zay, French minister of education, 1936–9.

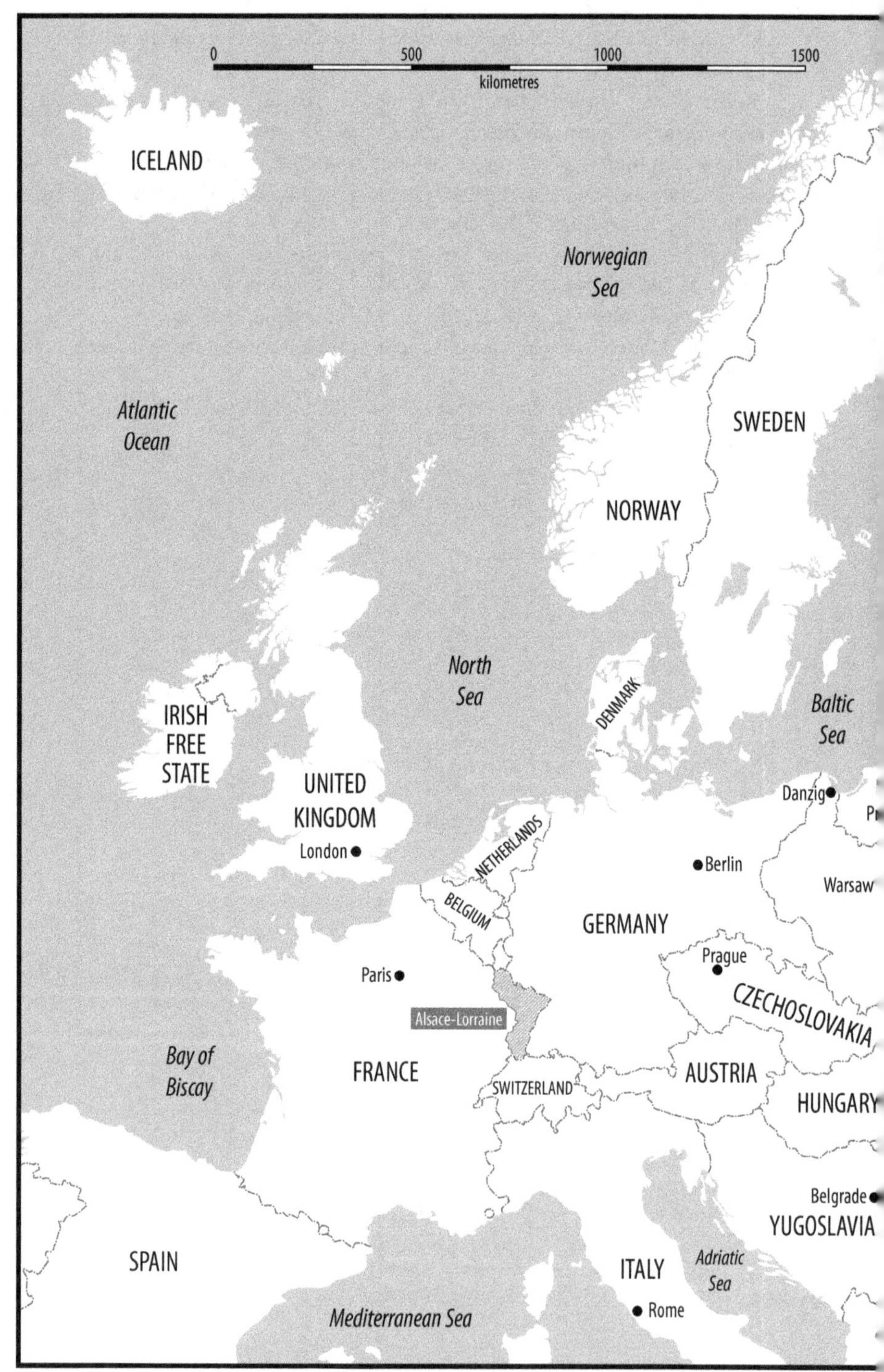

Map 0.1. Europe, 1930s.

Barents Sea
Murmansk
White Sea
Arkhangelsk
URAL MOUNTAINS
N
W
E
S
FINLAND
Leningrad
UNION OF SOVIET SOCIALIST REPUBLICS
Moscow
Tula
Smolensk
Orel
Minsk
Byelorussian SSR
Stalingrad
Kiev
Ukrainian SSR
Bessarabia
Odessa
ROMANIA
Sevastopol
Sochi
Caspian Sea
Bucharest
Black Sea
Gori
Tbilsi
GeorgianSSR
Baku
Batum
Azerbaijan SSR
BULGARIA
Armenian SSR
Istanbul
TURKEY
PERSIA

STALIN'S GAMBLE

Chapter One

Introduction: Prologue to Crisis

On 1 January 1930, few Europeans worried about the outbreak of a Second World War. Parisian fortune tellers might have ventured such a sensational prediction on their advertising coupons. The French, of course, worried instinctively about a new war with a revanchist Germany. In fifteen years, predicted the French politician Édouard Herriot. That was in 1922, and he was not a fortune teller. The Soviet commissar, or *narkom* for foreign affairs, Maksim Maksimovich Litvinov, sometimes speculated about such possibilities. Marxist ideologues thought of world war as the inevitable result of capitalist and imperialist rivalries. Litvinov opined that with the possible exceptions of the Italian fascist leader, Benito Mussolini, and Józef Piłsudski, the Polish generalissimo, no government in Europe wanted war. Sure, there was a "war scare" in the Soviet Union in 1927, but Litvinov did not make much of it. Apparently, many rank-and-file communists did not take the war scare too seriously either, considering it "a tool of social agitation," which undoubtedly it was.[1]

Besides the Italian *Duce* Mussolini, another fascist leader was emerging in Germany. This was Adolf Hitler, who headed a fringe party, the National Socialist German Workers' Party (NSDAP) or Nazi Party, who had ideas about a German renaissance of power relying on war as a means of achieving it. He even published a long book, *Mein Kampf*, in 1925, where he elaborated his plans for the future domination of Europe. It was hard to read *Mein Kampf* to the end, but you did not have to read every page to understand the message. The Nazi Party did not win a great many votes in the Reichstag elections during the 1920s, and thus did not appear to be a threat to European peace. In January 1930, it is unlikely that Litvinov or anyone else among the Soviet leadership worried much about Hitler.

As the new decade opened, it was more or less business as usual at the People's Commissariat for Foreign Affairs in Moscow, or the NKID. The principal objective was normalization of relations with the Western powers and the United States. A new world war was not an agenda item. In the autumn of 1929, the British government renewed diplomatic relations with the USSR, which it had broken off more than two years before on a wave of anti-communist hysteria. This was a victory for Soviet diplomacy. The NKID remained alert for Western attempts to organize an anti-Soviet bloc. Litvinov did not consider it a likely possibility, however, since capitalist political and economic rivalries would prevent the Western powers from ganging up on the USSR.[2]

The Soviet Union and Weimar Germany had reasonably functional relations at the beginning of the 1930s. It certainly did not look in Moscow as if they would be at war a decade later. At the beginning of the 1920s Soviet Russia and Germany were pariahs, the one a proscribed revolutionary socialist state and the other condemned to take the blame for provoking the Great War, even though a democratic Weimar Republic had been established in November 1918. The Treaty of Versailles, concluded in June 1919, was supposed to settle the problem of German power, but did not do so. The German government passed the decade attempting to loosen the constraints of Versailles; and the Soviet government, to break out of its diplomatic isolation. What could have been more natural than these two pariah states joining together to escape isolation? In April 1922 they signed an agreement at Rapallo, Italy, to renounce prewar debts and obligations and to re-establish diplomatic and economic relations. The Entente Powers, France and Britain, were furious, realizing that the two outcasts had slipped out of their control. The pressure, both political and economic, would now be on the Entente Powers to come to terms with Weimar Germany and Soviet Russia.

The pattern of relations in Europe was thus set for the decade of the 1920s with attempts at rapprochement with Britain and France more successful on the German side than on the Soviet. If the Entente Powers succeeded in defeating Wilhelmine Germany during the Great War, they failed to overthrow Soviet power after the Bolshevik Revolution. They tried though as much as they dared. The West's *bête noire* in Moscow was the Communist International, or Comintern, established in 1919 not only to pursue the cause of world revolution, but also to defend Soviet Russia against foreign intervention. During the 1920s there were ups and downs in Soviet-Western relations, a crisis now and again, but no danger of another world war.

Western Europe appeared more or less stable and prosperous. It was the Roaring Twenties: the European bourgeoisie had money for leisure and conspicuous consumption. In capital cities like Paris and Berlin, men in tuxedos and women in sleek evening dresses rocked to the beat of big band music and American jazz at nightclubs and cabarets. The menus offered expensive cuisine that went down well with wine and champagne, while dancers perspired on the dance floor. Nor were the slick and well-to-do absent from the *terrasses* of popular cafés where they rubbed shoulders with American expats, painters, writers, and socialists. "It's class fraternization," a Marxist ideologue might have joked.

Figure 1.1. The odd couple: Georgii V. Chicherin and Maksim M. Litvinov, 10 April 1922, Genoa. Photographer: Walter Gireke. Ullstein Bild, Granger Collection, NY.

Politically, France and Britain were often at odds; in fact, their wartime alliance appeared to dissolve on 11 November 1918, the day the Great War ended. This allowed room for both Germany and the Soviet Union to manoeuvre. Germany had the better of the diplomacy. The Red Scare of the 1920s and lingering Soviet revolutionary ambitions hampered efforts to normalize relations in the West. After the premature death in January 1924 of Soviet leader Vladimir Il'ich Lenin, a struggle for power erupted between Iosif Vissarionovich Stalin and Lev Davidovich Trotskii. Hatred is the first word that comes to mind in describing relations between these two Soviet leaders. This conflict had its effects on both Soviet domestic and foreign policy. At the end of the decade, the struggle for power was settled. Stalin established himself as the new, indisputable Soviet leader. Trotskii was sent into exile. Stalin calmed the Bolshevik itch to pursue world revolution and launched a five-year plan for industrialization and collectivization of agricultural lands. The troubles created by these domestic policies were an additional incentive to maintain correct relations with the Western powers.

The architects of Soviet foreign policy in the 1920s were Georgii Vasilievich Chicherin, the narkom for foreign affairs, and his principal deputy, *zamnarkom* Litvinov.

These two were an odd couple, one descended from the Russian aristocracy, and the other from a rather peculiar middle-class Jewish family. They often differed among themselves, both because of personal rivalries and jealousies and because of differences in temperament. Historians have said they pursued conflicting policies, Chicherin being pro-German, and Litvinov, pro-British. This is untrue, they were not pro this or that Western government, they were pro-Soviet. They sought to protect what they defined as the national interests of the Soviet state. In the northwest that meant the Baltic frontiers; in the south, it meant the borders in Central Asia. On the big issues like Rapallo or better relations with other Western powers, or difficulties with the Comintern, they saw eye to eye. It was on tactics rather than on strategy that their personal rivalries played themselves out. If Chicherin argued white, Litvinov would argue black, and vice versa. This rivalry continued until 1928 when an ailing Chicherin went on leave, never to resume his duties. Litvinov became the acting and then formal narkom of the NKID.

Soviet foreign policy was a complicated business. The NKID had to cope not only with hostile Western governments but also with politics in Moscow where foreign policy was often a stake in the struggle for power between Stalin and Trotskii and then other rivals. There were many arenas where the struggle to succeed Lenin unfolded, but none more important than in the Politburo, which was in effect the cabinet of the Soviet government. In most cabinets, the minister of foreign affairs is a high-ranking member. In the Politburo, Chicherin was not a member. He and Litvinov were invited consultants when foreign policy was discussed. On the other hand, during the 1920s, the Comintern, the nemesis of the NKID as well as of the West, was represented in succession by two of Stalin's provisional allies, Grigorii Evseievich Zinoviev and Nikolai Ivanovich Bukharin. These two Bolshevik politicians not only represented the Comintern, but used it as a platform for influence and power in the Politburo where Stalin sometimes gave them leeway as he manoeuvred for power. Politburo members tended to think they knew more about foreign policy than the NKID, which exasperated Chicherin and Litvinov. Zinoviev and Bukharin, they complained, talked too much, did not think enough, and irritated Western governments for nothing. The NKID often played the unwanted roll of concierge cleaning up their messes. Litvinov let it slip from time to time with foreign diplomats that he was fed up with the Comintern. Of course Stalin could not say that.

A persistent idea survives that the Comintern conducted Soviet foreign policy during the interwar years, or that the priorities of world revolution dominated it. "National interest" was not a concept much in use in Moscow.[3] Such assertions do not stand up well in a close examination of Soviet archives. After

Stalin consolidated his power, the Comintern faded into the background. It still functioned, still sought to direct the business of foreign communist parties, and still annoyed the Western powers, though less than before. If there was local resistance to French or British colonialism, the Quai d'Orsay or Foreign Office blamed it on the Comintern. When Litvinov heard such complaints, his stock reply was that indigenous resistance to Western colonialism flourished without any help from the Comintern. What was the USSR supposed to do? Should it become an advocate of colonial empires? This question came up, as readers will see, when Italy invaded Abyssinia in October 1935. Even capitalists were getting used to the Comintern. It was, like a stone in your rubber boot, which you could not take off until you stepped out of the bog. Among the Western powers, the said and unsaid idea was that the Soviet Union should abandon socialism and embrace capitalism, thus behaving like every other state. Why should Stalin and his colleagues do that? Would capitalists ever abandon capitalism?

In the 1930s the Comintern, at times, played a role in support of Soviet national interests, in Spain, for example, during the civil war, although that was a point debated inside the NKID. There were sometimes residual tensions left over from the 1920s, but it was the NKID that formulated foreign policy most of the time and the Politburo (but in reality, Stalin) that approved or modified it.

Stalin sometimes told the Comintern leadership, Georgi Dimitrov, for example, to develop policy without him. I was too busy, he would say: "Decide by yourselves."[4] He never said that to Litvinov or his deputies in the NKID. Stalin's involvement in foreign policymaking began after Lenin took ill in 1922–3. The narkom proposed and most of the time the *vozhd'*, who was Stalin, approved. Occasionally there were clashes. A pervasive Western view holds that there were two Soviet foreign policies, Litvinov's, pro-Western, and Stalin's, pro-German, even after Hitler's rise to power in 1933.[5] The German orientation was Stalin's preference, but he let Litvinov "talk him into something" in abandoning Rapallo.[6] One often hears the argument, yes, collective security was Litvinov's policy, but what about Stalin's real preferences? This view is widespread among Western historians, seeking to explain away Litvinov and the policy of collective security. The fact is there were no personal policies, no duality of policies, only one policy that was Soviet and, perforce, Stalin's.

It is widely believed in the West that Stalin was a confidence man just waiting for an opportunity to trick the Western powers and to return to the "old" Rapallo policy with Nazi Germany. In the meantime, he would string them along. Collective security and mutual assistance against Nazi Germany were a sham. Stalin was a would-be conqueror, a kind of red Genghis Khan, just waiting for opportunities to strike.[7] The Soviet archival evidence upon which this narrative is based demonstrates that the Soviet leadership was serious about collective security and that Britain and France were not. In the case of France, one can make a partial exception for the period 1933–4. This revelation may come as a surprise to some readers, or others may simply not believe it, sticking to preconceived ideas. There is little evidence to substantiate Stalin's clandestine pro-German policy, risible in any case because composition with Hitler during 1930s was not a sin, or if it was, everyone was being sinful. Britain and France, not to mention Poland, led the way. Some historians in the West might argue that the Western states had their "liberal scruples" about dealing with "arch-enemies." The trouble was that for many European conservatives, Stalin was the arch-enemy, not Hitler.

Two could play at who loves me, who loves me not. Even the narkom Litvinov argued that a minimum of relations with Hitler, mostly economic, should be maintained in order to avoid a diplomatic rupture. Litvinov feared Soviet isolation, which could facilitate Anglo-French security arrangements with Hitler.

The view of Stalin as trickster, "Germanophile," and "ally" of Hitler has been around for a long time and originates in the anti-communism and Sovietphobia of the interwar years and the second stage of the Cold War after 1945. A.J.P. Taylor, the great British historian of the mid-twentieth century, commented in 1981 that detached study of Soviet foreign policy was unlikely in his lifetime. "Most of my historical colleagues," he said, "are so corrupted and blinded by their obsession with the Cold War that it is quite impossible for them to see clearly or to speak honestly about Soviet policies." The same was true of their Soviet counterparts.[8] Taylor was trying to be "balanced." The Cold War ended in 1991 – at least many people hoped it had – after the dismemberment and disappearance of the Soviet Union. The immense Soviet archives began to open. It was the most extraordinary experience for historians to go to Moscow for the first time and hold in their hands freshly declassified *dela*, or files, that no one, apart from archivists and a few Soviet historians, had ever before read, let alone explored. Maybe we should talk about "History BC," before the opening of the Soviet archives, and "History AD," after the opening. I would respectfully contend that historians cannot study the origins of the Second World War without reference to the Soviet archival sources. Now that we have those files, or a great many of them, it should be possible to get to the bottom of the big questions that divided Taylor's generation.

Yet here we are, and so far, it has not been possible. A new generation of English-language writers, seemingly disdainful of their predecessors, has resumed old habits. One evokes "memory" to justify not going to the archival records.[9] Another goes to the files, cherry-picking evidence. He uses that part of the archival record which suits his strong ideological objectives and ignores that part which does not. It is dust in the eyes. Such *modi operandi*, writes one reviewer, "undermine confidence" in the author. Yet even when reviewers catch an author red-handed, it does not appear to bother either author or publisher.[10]

In the early 1980s, an untenured "Marxist historian" at Princeton University was drummed out of the profession for mistakes of documentation. Senior historians accused him "of systematically distorting evidence"; he was "called a 'liar' and a 'faker.'"[11] Now, forty years later, those very words, but not the punishment, might apply to certain academics or politicians of a new generation. As politicians go, the prime minister of Canada, Justin Trudeau, comes to mind, or delegates at the European Parliament in Strasbourg.[12]

In the flurry of such Western ideas, it goes against the grain to propose that Soviet foreign policy functioned more or less as it did in other states, I mean based on perceptions of national interest. In fact, in the Politburo there existed considerable animosity towards Germany and towards the Rapallo policy, though it continued with ups and downs throughout the 1920s and into the beginning of the 1930s. Germany was the only Western power with which the Soviet Union had tolerable relations. It was the only foothold in Europe and had to be protected lest the USSR risk dangerous isolation. All the better, Litvinov argued, if relations with other powers could be improved, but not at the risk of damaging Rapallo. Litvinov was under no illusions about the permanency of Rapallo. Eventually, Germany and the USSR would part company.[13] Other options, therefore, had to be cultivated, but for the time being such options were "music of the future."

Western-Soviet tensions came and went like bad weather. Trade turnover rose and fell according to Soviet economic and political needs. Moscow used trade as bait to obtain better political relations, though this strategy never really worked except in Weimar Germany, and even there, bilateral relations were often strained. It was not trade per se but political calculations of national interest on both sides, which kept Rapallo going.

By the end of the 1920s, the Soviet government managed to achieve prewar production levels. It was slow going, too slow for the Bolsheviks, for they were all industrializers and modernizers whatever the disagreements between them on how fast to proceed. The USSR was burdened with millions of peasant smallholdings, which produced only enough grain and other foodstuffs to sustain the peasant producers. Sometimes it did not, and the poorest peasants had to hire themselves out as labourers to the more prosperous so-called *kulaks*, to make ends meet. There was not enough agricultural surplus to feed the cities, at reasonable prices, in order to support industrialization or to sell in the West to obtain vital foreign exchange. Something had to be done. Having won the conflict to succeed Lenin, Stalin clenched his fists and smashed all the obstacles to industrialization by launching the First Five-Year Plan in 1928 and by forcing at the same time the collectivization of small peasant holdings, grouping them into large collective farms. Forced collectivization provoked a peasant "Luddite" rebellion (a turn of phrase coined by the late Isaac Deutscher), which along with drought and insect infestations, led in 1932–3 to a disastrous concatenation of circumstances, a famine in the Soviet wheat belt.[14] These developments did not affect Soviet foreign policy or the Soviet need to trade. If anything, industrialization increased the need to buy capital goods and to sell agricultural products, lumber, oil, and manganese in the West.

In the 1930s the stakes in Soviet relations with the West changed rapidly. In October 1929, the stock market crashed in New York, setting off what became the Great Depression, which spread from the United States to Europe. The deceptive political and economic stability of the 1920s was shattered. Credit dried up, banks and businesses went broke, industrial production fell, international trade declined, commodity prices plummeted, and unemployment rose to calamitous levels.

The Roaring Twenties became a memory. One imagines that many prized tuxedos and evening gowns collected dust in the closet or ended up in second-hand shops. American expats still flocked to Paris, and jazz men still played the cabarets, but in reality, everything had changed. The music sounded the same, but people were not. The legions of unemployed worried about making ends meet. People were desperate and angry. The far-right leagues (or *ligues*) in France and the Nazi Brownshirts in Germany went out into the streets looking for trouble, fighting with communists and unionists. There were casualties. It was war, not all-out, but war all the same.

The Depression thus brought renewed political instability, especially in Germany, where the Nazi Party under Hitler made impressive gains in federal elections in September 1930, rising from 12 seats in the Reichstag to 107. Hitler was no longer a fringe politician. Nazi power increased rapidly until Hitler became chancellor in January 1933. This should have set off alarm bells in European capitals and in Washington, and it should have led to changes in policy. Sometimes it did and sometimes not. It certainly did in Moscow. The threat of war, which had largely been a theoretical discussion, became a real, tangible danger. As a result, major changes in foreign policy and in relations with the Western powers took place in the Soviet Union as it turned to face the menace to European peace and security posed by Hitlerite Germany. Sooner or later, Litvinov had said in 1927, Germany and the USSR were bound to go their separate ways. That time had come.

Chapter Two

A Dimly Lit Night Lamp: Early Attempts at Détente in Paris and Warsaw, 1929–1932

If developments in Germany began to cause alarm, it would only have been natural in Paris to think about improving relations with the USSR as a counterweight to a resurgent, hostile German state. At first, this did not happen. In France it was business as usual with the USSR in spite of efforts by Soviet diplomats to test the possibilities of détente. Relations continued to be abysmal. At the end of 1928 Litvinov reckoned that any agreement in Paris was "unrealizable" even if it benefited France alone.[1] The French wanted to maintain the "policy of the night lamp" (*politika nochnoi lampochkoi*). Keep the lamp of relations with Moscow lit, but only dimly so. The French ambassador in Moscow, Jean Herbette, was hostile to the Soviet government. It's "open war" with him, Litvinov said in 1928, his conduct "is intolerable."[2] Only the fear of French retaliation prevented his recall. Meetings with Herbette were frequent and often tested the limits of Litvinov's patience. The ambassador regularly complained about Soviet press hostility towards France. Talk about the pot calling the kettle black! If he were to complain about the *French* press, Litvinov replied in so many words, he would be summoning Herbette almost every day. And still Litvinov left the door open for an improvement of relations.[3]

Maksim Maksimovich Litvinov

Maksim Maksimovich Litvinov is an interesting personality whom readers will encounter many, many times in the course of this narrative. He was born in Bialystok in tsarist Poland in 1876 into an unstable, disputatious Jewish family. His father was a minor bank official and "businessman."

Unlike many of his colleagues, Litvinov did not have a formal university education, which was difficult to obtain as a Jew in tsarist Poland. He joined the army, became a gunner, and began to read Karl Marx and Friedrich Engels, and other revolutionary writers. In 1901 he was arrested for the first time as a Kiev member of the Russian Social Democratic Workers' Party. His given name was

Figure 2.1. Maksim Maksimovich Litvinov, ca. 1920s, AVPRF, Moscow.

Maks Vallakh, but he went by many revolutionary pseudonyms to confuse the tsarist police: among them were Papasha, Feliks, Graf, and Nits. He escaped from a tsarist jail in 1902 and made his way to Europe returning to Russia in 1905, to St. Petersburg, to join the first revolution to overthrow the tsar. He helped to edit the Bolshevik newspaper *Novaia Zhizn*, and then moved on to gunrunning and money laundering in Europe for the Bolshevik Party.

Maksim Maksimovich was a polyglot, an adventurer, and a secret agent. In an early photograph, he is seen wearing a Cossack-style blouse; he has a walrus moustache and long dark curly hair. He looks formidable, like a bandit, and in those days the walrus moustache was a symbol of the alpha male. Litvinov's early years as a Bolshevik gunrunner would make a good adventure novel or Hollywood film. In 1908 he was arrested in France on a tsarist extradition warrant, and sent out of the country, not to Russia but to Great Britain. When he settled in Britain, he gave up the gunrunning, but not the revolution, for he continued to speak publicly for the Bolshevik Party based on instructions from Lenin. He needed a job, however, and went to work for a London publisher. In 1916 at the age of forty, he married a twenty-seven-year-old English woman, Ivy Low, descended from a British middle-class family of writers and intellectuals and already a talented novelist. They at once had two children, and but for the revolution, Maksim Maksimovich might have become an eccentric London publisher and salon intellectual.

That was not his fate, however, for revolution broke out in 1917 and the Bolsheviks seized power in November of that same year. In 1918, Litvinov became the unofficial Soviet representative in London. His first telegrams back and forth to the Soviet government were *en clair* and sometimes in English. In September 1918 he was arrested and later exchanged for the British diplomat in Russia, R.H. Bruce Lockhart. He left Ivy and the two kids in London for safety and went back to Soviet Russia, by then a blockaded, encircled, hungry, cold, and very dangerous place, to defend the revolution.

The US, British, and French governments aimed to overthrow the Bolsheviks and would have hanged them all if they had gotten the chance. It was a hard job to represent Soviet Russia in the West. You had to have a strong will, and this Litvinov had in spades. His adversaries called him mulish, stubborn, and inflexible. Compliments really, though they were not intended as such. Litvinov had to sell the idea of better relations on the practical terms of mutual benefit, namely trade, economic development, and some resolution of the tsarist foreign debt in exchange for coexistence. The West, of course, would never have allowed the Bolsheviks to survive, if they had been able, but revolution was contagious after the end of the Great War. Elites were ready for the fight from the comfort of their armchairs and posh clubs in various European capitals. *Fini les Boches, voilà les Bolchos* was their war cry … from their clubs and government offices. The Everyman and especially soldiers who had survived more than four years in the abattoir had no interest in risking life and limb fighting the "Bolsh" in Russia. If pushed too hard, those soldiers might have gone over to the side of the revolution. There were noteworthy examples of what could happen. French soldiers and sailors sent to fight against Soviet authority in the Ukraine and Crimea mutinied and threatened to take their guns and ships over to the Bolsheviks. These events had a sobering effect on the armchair interventionists.

Western elites eventually reconciled themselves to a grudging "live and let live" relationship with the Soviet government, not because they wanted to but because there was no other option. Litvinov played an important role in the 1920s trying to obtain diplomatic recognition and establish trade with the West under difficult circumstances. He was no longer the handsome bandit and gunrunner. The walrus moustache and the mass of dark hair were gone, along with the young man's flat belly. He was developing a slight double chin and losing his hair, but he looked like he might be a diplomat even though his hair was sometimes mussed and his suits a little wrinkled and not always a perfect fit. From the beginning, he was a Soviet pragmatist, a polyglot salesman for the idea of rapprochement both in the West and at home. It was a hard sell in the West but also in Moscow where many of his colleagues – "our orators," Litvinov called them – still advocated for world revolution. For them, relations with the West were a temporary expedient; for Litvinov and his NKID colleagues, pragmatism was the only viable policy.

A Little Scandal

French ambassador Herbette was not Litvinov's only problem. In October 1929 a police station in the chic 7th arrondissement of Paris received a call from a Soviet diplomat asking for help. Grigorii Z. Besedovskii, the counsellor at the embassy on the rue de Grenelle, told police that he had had to flee the premises. A Cheka agent was after him. According to the police report, Besedovskii was in some alarm because his wife and son were being held at the embassy. Even a Bolshevik could have family, as it turned out. Besedovskii asked the police to return with him in order to free them from the clutches of his former colleagues. Force could be necessary.

The police officers listening to Besedovskii, looked at each other not knowing what to think, but agreed to accompany him back to the embassy. Before leaving, they asked him to hand over a Browning revolver he had in his coat pocket. "I had to use it to protect myself," he replied (if I may paraphrase). "You don't know what I am up against. Believe me, I know better than anyone what goes on there." Arriving at the embassy, Besedovskii telephoned his wife from the concierge's lodging and asked her to come there with their son. Maybe she was not being held hostage, after all, the police surmised. Two embassy officials got into a loud argument in Russian with Besedovskii in front of the police. Again the police looked at one another, not knowing what to think. "He's crazy, *fou*," said an official, "this has been going on for several days." The police acknowledged the official's statement without replying.

Just to demonstrate that no one had been kidnapped, the official showed the police officers Besedovskii's baggage that was ready to be taken away. Another more senior official came out, repeating that Besedovskii was *fou*. He could not say what the consequences would be of a colleague gone "crazy." The police explained to the Soviet diplomat that they had come to the embassy at Besedovskii's request "to avoid a violent incident." While this conversation was going on, Besedovskii quickly moved "his numerous suitcases" to the sidewalk in front of the embassy, and he, his family, and the police left without incident. The whole business had not lasted more than thirty minutes.[4]

The *affaire*, which was minor by French standards but more serious for the Soviet side, made the Moscow press a week later. A *Pravda* editorial asserted that Besedovskii was a swindler who had stolen public funds. He was a malcontent, acting commissar Litvinov told Ambassador Herbette: he was not doing his job and had stolen $5,000 in embassy funds.[5] The Soviet *polpred*, or ambassador in Paris, V.S. Dovgalevskii, who had been absent in London negotiating with the British at the time of Besedovskii's departure, eventually discussed the affair with Philippe Berthelot, the secretary-general of the Quai d'Orsay. He's "half-crazy," said the ambassador, and an intriguer. After further observations, Dovgalevskii, a former electrical engineer who had been educated in France, agreed that the police had not acted improperly, and that he considered the matter closed.[6] Of course the matter was not closed since the station head of the British Secret Intelligence Service (the MI6) in Paris interviewed Besedovskii within two days of his departure from the embassy. "Extremely talkative and indiscreet," concluded the MI6 man, much to his pleasure and amusement. Besedovskii would make his living as a journalist and book author. It was he, who apparently published Litvinov's bogus *dnevnik*, entitled *Notes for a Journal*. The forgery was not good enough to fool historians. The NKID was well rid of Besedovskii. He was too small a fish to merit intense attention from the OGPU, the Soviet secret police, and he survived the Second World War. There are reports that he even worked for the OGPU in the post-war period.[7]

This was not the only case of "defection" of a Soviet official in 1929. A former commissar and deputy commissar, A.L. Sheinmann, got himself into trouble in the spring of 1929 and refused to return to Moscow. This was much more embarrassing than the Besedovskii affair for Sheinmann was a senior Soviet official. The Politburo even sent a delegate and close friend to talk to him in Berlin but he was adamant, he was not going back. "I won't commit the folly of returning to Moscow," he said (to paraphrase him), "where I would undoubtedly be shot." Eventually, a deal was struck where Sheinmann agreed *inter alia* to hand over secret funds in exchange for being left in peace. In the late 1930s he ended up running an Intourist office, a Soviet-based travel agency, in London.[8] It was a strange affair.

A Big Scandal

By Parisian standards, the Besedovskii scandal was a passing matter, a brief amusement to read about in the Sunday papers while enjoying a *petit déjeuner*. The bigger issues of Franco-Soviet relations, however, continued unresolved. These were exacerbated three months later by a sensational kidnapping in downtown Paris. The White Guard General Aleksandr Pavlovich Kutepov disappeared on 28 January 1930, and was never seen or heard of again. It was assumed that OGPU agents were responsible, and it raised a storm in the Parisian press, which called for the rupture of diplomatic relations with Moscow. Dovgalevskii wrote officially to the Paris police to say the embassy and Soviet authorities had had nothing to do with Kutepov's disappearance, and he complained about the press campaign to the French foreign minister, Aristide Briand.

Briand was curious to know what had happened to General Kutepov. "Tell me please, what did you do with the General? How did you manage to kidnap such an important fellow in the heart of Paris? Did you do this for a movie scenario?" Dovgalevskii did not want to go into details about the disappearance of Kutepov, and as he reported to Moscow, "I tried to adopt Briand's tone, and escape with some jokes." But Briand would not let it go, and wanted to know how the ambassador could explain the kidnapping. Readers may wonder what Dovgalevskii really knew. He did not tell Briand, if he did know something, escaping the subject by reviewing press speculations about who had carried out the abduction. The OGPU was not the only suspect. The Paris press speculated that the kidnapping could have been a settlement of accounts between rival anti-Bolshevik groups. Briand did not make much of the press campaign, but he raised the perennial subject of "propaganda," which could not be so easily dismissed. Dovgalevskii finally turned the discussion to the problems of Franco-Soviet trade, and Briand promised to get back to him. The problems remained the same: a split between bankers and Sovietphobes who opposed credit for Soviet trade ventures and businessmen who wanted to increase trade with the USSR. Soviet diplomats held out the possibility of richer contracts, hoping thus to create pressure on the government and the banks to offer credit and insurance for Franco-Soviet trade.

To no avail, for Paris had become a magnet for White Russian émigrés attracted by a legal system all too ready to rule against Soviet interests. The so-called Hertzfeld affair was a case in point. Harry Hertzfeld was a White Russian who had sought damages in British courts for alleged financial losses arising from the revolution. He came to Paris to obtain a seizure of assets of the Soviet trade mission in France, which the French courts at first were willing to grant him. The Soviet trade mission was ready to move all its assets out of France in order to prevent their seizure. This would have been catastrophic for French manufacturers who wanted to do business in the USSR.[9] Eventually, Hertzfeld's case failed in the courts.

The same old abysmal relations thus continued between Paris and Moscow. The Kutepov affair dragged on well into the spring. The embassy, Dovgalevskii reported, was "surrounded by an atmosphere of hostility and wariness." Everybody was talking about the "secret kidnapping of Kutepov." Everybody. "In the best of all worlds," he noted, "we are suspects, but generally we are blamed." The situation was dangerous. "We are trying to maintain our composure, but we are ready for any eventuality."[10]

In March, spring was beginning in Paris and the pressure seemed to ease off: the "*Kutepovshchina*" was turning into a farce, according to Dovgalevskii: it's "now obvious to all" that the "White emigration" in Paris has had close ties with the Paris police and with government authorities. Monarchist groups had gotten into "completely open fights," much to the dismay of their French patrons. Dovgalevskii was not sure what would happen next. Who knew if some scoundrel would not pull out of his sleeve some proof of direct or indirect involvement of "GPU agents" in the "kidnapping" of Kutepov?[11]

In the spring of 1930, Herbette went on leave to Paris. His last meeting with Litvinov before he left was along the usual lines. The press campaign in Paris was a subject of conversation. The ambassador commented that the Soviet government needed to make proposals. "We already have," Litvinov retorted, "in 1927, to which the French government has never responded." Relations between states, Litvinov added, could not be settled by unilateralism or by one-sided proposals. Normally there were negotiations, but until now the French government had avoided them. On his way out the door, Herbette asked, rather awkwardly, if he could be exempted from customs duties for personal items he had acquired in Moscow. Litvinov noted sarcastically that customs duties had been waived for fear of exciting the press campaign in Paris over Kutepov.[12] It was any concession to get Herbette out of Moscow.

In Paris, Dovgalevskii instructed his wife, Nadezhda Ivanovna, to query Mme Herbette discreetly to discover if her husband planned to return to Moscow. The two spouses were getting together for a social visit. That was diplomacy in those days: sometimes wives could break the ice even when their husbands could not manage it. Nadezhda Ivanovna did not learn anything definite, Dovgalevskii reported to Moscow.[13] Litvinov must have been disappointed. So was Dovgalevskii.

An Autumn Crisis

A fresh crisis erupted in the autumn of 1930. In late September, Litvinov got wind of a possible Western gang-up against "so-called Soviet dumping," selling goods at below costs of production. Any government drawn into such an "anti-Soviet movement," Litvinov proposed, should be warned that we will take measures against their exports.[14] Sure enough two days later, on 1 October, the French government imposed restrictions on Soviet imports and accused Moscow of "dumping." Soviet officials denied it and retaliated three weeks later by placing an embargo on French imports to the USSR. This action appears to have taken French officials by surprise, and they soon had to deal with angry manufacturers denied access to the Soviet market. The Great Depression came late to France, but even so, manufacturers could see they needed new clients and contracts to avert layoffs and shutdowns. It made no sense to cut oneself out of a profitable market – unless shooting oneself in the foot made sense.

The crisis nevertheless dragged on until the spring of 1931. The French were the first to blink. In March, Herbette called on Litvinov to advise that he was leaving soon for Paris; he asked if Litvinov had any messages to convey to Briand. This seemed like an opening, and Litvinov took full advantage of it. Soviet opinion, he replied, was not quite sure who was the greater adversary of the USSR, was it Britain or was it France? France had been "more active" during the foreign intervention, but the Soviet leadership held Britain responsible as the main aggressor. Of course, Soviet opinion was influenced by the "legacy of past Anglo-Russian antagonism." Litvinov reminded him of the Russian adage, "The English Queen fouls (*anglichanka gadit*)." The phrase meant the various ways that Britain had sought to oppose Russian interests before the Great War. And he rhymed off a long list of crises during the 1920s to emphasize his point. But public animosity against Britain was now giving way to animosity against France. And again Litvinov rhymed off a long list of recent French provocations against the USSR, as though France wanted to pick a fight. If it did, then there was not much to talk about. On the other hand, if France wanted to pursue a different policy, "then we," said Litvinov, "are willing to meet it halfway." Herbette "shook my hand warmly," Litvinov recorded, saying he would do what he could to facilitate negotiations.[15] Litvinov probably doubted the ambassador could play a positive role in improving Franco-Soviet relations, and Dovgalevskii let it be known in Paris that the NKID did not want him involved. "Of course, there will be no benefits from Herbette in negotiations, but I don't think he will cause any great harm," Dovgalevskii joked, "except perhaps to me personally, some unnecessary damage to my nerves."[16] No doubt to everyone's relief in Moscow, the Quai d'Orsay did not insist on retaining Herbette as ambassador in Moscow.

On 20 April, Berthelot, still secretary-general of the Quai d'Orsay, paid a call to an ailing Dovgalevskii at the embassy on the rue de Grenelle. Readers may have encountered Berthelot in *Silent Conflict*.[17] Suffice it to say, that he was an influential diplomat, the *éminence grise* of French diplomacy for most of the period after 1914. In 1918 Berthelot played an important role in sealing French hostility against the new Soviet government. He mellowed somewhat during the 1920s and was even cordial with Dovgalevskii, but when he talked to his British counterparts, he still brimmed over with scorn when it came to the Bolsheviks.

Patching Up Franco-Soviet Relations

On that day in April 1931, Berthelot proposed to Dovgalevskii a settlement of the economic dispute by the conclusion of a trade agreement and of a non-aggression pact. These were not new issues. They had been part of discussions in 1926–7 when Raymond Poincaré, then *président du Conseil*, had scuttled Franco-Soviet negotiations to support an anti-communist electoral campaign against the centre-left *Cartel des gauches*. Poincaré resigned during the summer of 1929 and was out of the way. The current président du Conseil, Pierre Laval, an unfrocked socialist – and never much of one at that – was under pressure from French manufacturers who were angry at being cut out of the Soviet market. Wanting to get them off his back, Laval sent Berthelot to see Dovgalevskii to deflate the crisis. The non-aggression pact was supposed to cover the French retreat in the trade war.[18] Given past French duplicity, Soviet diplomats were sceptical of Berthelot's démarche. As well they might have been, for the French government was not of one mind on dealing with Moscow. While the commerce ministry was sensitive to angry manufacturers, the finance ministry and the Banque de France were openly hostile to Moscow and unwilling to approve credit or insurance facilities for trade with the Soviet Union. It was the traditional split between bankers thinking of unpaid debts and manufacturers looking to fill empty order books.

Meetings between Berthelot and Dovgalevskii continued into the beginning of May. Moscow accepted Berthelot's proposals. Litvinov, now officially named commissar for foreign affairs, suggested that the French and Soviet October decrees be abrogated to create a positive atmosphere for negotiations. The two sides finally agreed on this step after two or three meetings of the trade delegations. Negotiations would start in June.

Each side mistrusted the other; neither wanted to be too anxious to conclude or to appear to be the supplicant in the negotiations. In early May, Dovgalevskii commented that Berthelot was already backing away from commitments to the negotiations: French promises – even in the presence of stenographers – were unreliable, French officials often reversing themselves.[19] They, the French, mistrusted their Soviet counterparts just as vehemently. Quai d'Orsay officials doubted if the USSR really wanted better relations with France. More likely, Moscow was only seeking "to divide and rule" the capitalist powers and to gain a favourable press in the West.[20] Were the French missing Soviet signals, or were they too blind to see them?

The British ambassador in Moscow, Sir Edmond Ovey, reported that there was a new "tendency" in Soviet policy "toward cooperation with foreign countries." Litvinov even confirmed confidentially that there had been a shift in policy, though if news of it leaked into the press, he would issue a *démenti*.[21] Herbette apparently missed the boat on the changes in Soviet policy, and so did most clerks at the Quai d'Orsay. It was not going to be easy to obtain an agreement in Paris.

Berthelot's retreat, as Dovgalevskii saw it, was caused by the hostility of the finance ministry and the Banque de France. Finance was adamant: no credits and no credit insurance for trade with the USSR. According to the finance minister, Pierre-Étienne Flandin, Soviet demands for credit were "clearly excessive." Dovgalevskii would have to be brought back to earth: until the settlement of the debts question, the parameters of any agreement with the USSR would be limited.[22] Only private arrangements for credit would be acceptable, and even here, the Banque de France was "very reserved."[23] The bankers forgot, one supposes, that it was the Poincaré government that rejected Soviet offers in 1927 to settle the tsarist debts. Those offers were as generous as those the Soviet side ever made during the interwar years. If there was then no settlement, the French had only themselves to blame.

The Quai d'Orsay itself appears to have been divided about pursuing a détente with Moscow. Berthelot told Dovgalevskii that he was principally responsible for the change in French policy. Later on, Briand said to Litvinov that he had pressed for the new initiative and that Berthelot had not always favoured better relations, though he seemed to be coming around.[24] Berthelot sometimes boasted of spiking relations with Moscow; perhaps Briand was more to be believed.

Both Briand and Berthelot tried to assure Soviet diplomats of French good will, but given past experience, the Soviet side was highly sceptical. Briand told Litvinov at the end of May that the rupture of talks in 1927 had been Poincaré's mistake, but he hoped now that political and economic relations would improve. To demonstrate goodwill, Briand asked if the Soviet government would object to the continuation of Herbette as ambassador. Litvinov was startled. He reminded Briand of long-standing Soviet concerns about the trouble-making Herbette. Briand said he would look for a replacement.[25] *Slava Bogu*, thank God, Litvinov must have said to himself.

Dovgalevskii expected the negotiations to be difficult and they were. The first meeting took place in early June 1931 when the two sides laid out their principal objectives. The French wanted a substantial improvement in the balance of trade and an eventual settlement of the debts question without which parliamentary ratification of a long-term trade agreement would be impossible. Soviet representatives wanted a provisional trade agreement; were agreeable to increasing industrial orders in France, but on condition of appropriate credit and the resolution of the legal status of the Soviet trade mission in France.[26] Progress was sufficient to lead to the simultaneous abrogation on 16 July of the October decrees, but continuing talks through the summer and autumn were inconclusive because of difficulties over the credit issue. However, Briand kept his word about Herbette; he was sent off to Madrid and replaced by a career diplomat, François Dejean.

On the political side, Berthelot and Dovgalevskii discussed the conclusion of a non-aggression pact and they initialled a draft text in August. The document – which provided for neutrality in the case of aggression by a third party – was unremarkable, but it was leaked to the press raising a hubbub on the French right. To avoid criticism, Berthelot put off on the Soviet side the responsibility for the initiative to begin negotiations.[27] It was often thus in Soviet-Western relations that each side sought to avoid giving the appearance of having ceded to the other. In this case, the French offer of the non-aggression pact was bait to the Soviet side to get them talking about more important economic issues.

Complications

There were other complications. Two of France's allies, Poland and Romania, were hostile to and fearful of the Soviet Union. Both held territories claimed by the Soviet Union. Both were part of France's eastern alliance system and sentinels of the anti-Soviet *cordon sanitaire*. So if the USSR wanted a non-aggression pact with France, it needed to offer similar agreements to Poland and Romania.

Slow negotiations with the Poles prompted Stalin, who was on annual holidays in the south at Sochi, to ask what was going on. "This is a very important business, nearly the decisive question of peace during the last two to three years. I fear Litvinov, having succumbed to the pressure of so-called 'public opinion' will pursue it with a pacifier." The Politburo needs to get more involved, Stalin instructed: "Try to carry it through by all possible means."

"It would be ridiculous," he added, "if we succumbed in this business to the general philistine epidemic of 'anti-Polandism' [*sic*], forgetting even for a minute the basic interests of the revolution and the construction of socialism." Stalin also wanted to push the negotiations in Paris for a trade agreement. "What's holding things up?" he asked. "Why are all the orders going to Germany and England, and we don't want to give orders to the French?"[28]

French negotiators tied a trade deal to a debts settlement that was unacceptable to *anyone* in Moscow. The Politburo instructed its negotiators to try concluding specific contracts with French manufacturers.[29] Lazar M. Kaganovich, who was the secretary to the TsIK, the Bolshevik Central Executive Committee, and close to Stalin, continued to criticize the NKID for timidity. "Our diplomats started from the necessity of calming the Germans and as you foresaw in your letter, succumbed to the howling of so-called public opinion, jumping back hastily, not trying anything."[30] Readers should not think Stalin had gone soft on the French. He was getting impatient. "We obtain," he observed, "better credit terms in Germany, Italy, and England. Either the French agree to Italo-German terms of credit, or they can go to hell." But then Stalin suggested a "last concession," British terms where credits were offered on acceptable conditions, though without "direct British government guarantee."[31] This was not the first time that Stalin had jumped on Litvinov. In the most notorious known case in 1927, Stalin had written a five-page, handwritten memorandum denouncing Litvinov for daring to question Politburo policy.[32] That was often Stalin's way, venting his spleen, and then thinking practically. Stalin was a great cynic. This modus operandi explains Stalin's relationship with Litvinov, sometimes his whipping boy, but whose policy recommendations he largely accepted. They were fellow realists, though internal politics often required Stalin to hide his practical side with nastiness and sarcasm.

Iosif Vissarionovich Stalin

Here something more should be said about Stalin, the *vozhd* or "boss" of the USSR, whose word was final on both small and large questions of the Soviet state. Many people have written about him over the generations starting in the 1930s with critics Trotskii and Boris Souvarine. One might wonder if everything that can be said about Stalin has already been said, but of course the historian's curiosity is rarely quenched.

Figure 2.2. Iosif Vissarionovich Stalin, 1932, Klimbim, Moscow.

Stalin was born Iosif Vissarionovich Dzhugashvili in Gori, Georgia, in December 1878. His father was a cobbler; his mother, a peasant's daughter. Both were the offspring of serfs. The young Dzhugashvili grew up poor unlike many of his Bolshevik colleagues who came from comfortable bourgeois families. Poverty breeds violence and sorrow, and the Dzhugashvilis were not spared either. Their first two sons died not long after birth. The father, Vissarion, made a living as a shoe maker, and for a time did fairly well at it. He was also an alcoholic, and, it is said, beat his wife, Ekaterina, in front of their only surviving son. The couple eventually separated. One of Stalin's early biographers, the late Issac Deutscher, reckoned that the father could not have been all bad. He and his wife sent their son to the local church school to be educated. Like most fathers, Vissarion, who died in 1890, apparently wanted more for his son than he had. At age fifteen, Iosif Vissarionovich obtained a scholarship to go to a seminary in Tiflis where he was a good student. Like Lenin and Trotskii, he ran into trouble, as a rebellious teenager, and did not graduate. The revolutionary movement intercepted him as it did so many others of his generation.

If Litvinov was a money-launderer and gunrunner, Dzhugashvili became a rougher Georgian variant: a bandit, itinerant propagandist, and union organizer, all in the cause of the revolution in the Caucasus. He soon ran afoul of the police in Baku and did time in tsarist jails. Like Trotskii, he escaped from Siberian exile only to be sent back again. His pseudonyms, among others, were Koba and Ivanovich before he settled on Stalin, or *stal'*, being the Russian word for steel. Stalin was an alpha male, bearded when young, clean shaven later in life, except for a well-tended, abundant moustache. As a young man, he was attracted to women and pursued them freely. Women were attracted to him, even though physically he was handicapped and his face pockmarked by smallpox. He was married twice, and twice widowed. His second wife, Nadezhda Sergeevna, committed suicide. He had two legitimate sons, Iakov and Vasilii, and a daughter, Svetlana, and two bastards, whom he never acknowledged as his.

Stalin's most recent biographer, Stephen Kotkin, wrote that he was "a human-being."[33] Well, of course, he was. He liked women and tobacco, was sociable, could drink hard and banquet into the early hours. He enjoyed music and film and liked to go to the theatre. He was good at billiards, read voraciously, collected watches, and enjoyed gardening. That was his normal side, but there was another side, not so normal and not at all attractive. He was a workaholic, knew his files backwards and forwards. He had few friends, being completely taken up with the revolution and then the Soviet state. He could be affectionate with colleagues, but he could also turn on them in a heartbeat. He was given to vulgarity and cynicism and had a propensity for pitiless violence, which first showed itself in 1918 during the Civil War. Human life counted for little to him except during the Great Patriotic War, when even he was appalled by the horrendous losses of the Red Army and by profligate Nazi violence against the Soviet civilian population. In the meantime, the tribunal, labour camps, and capital punishment were freely used to eliminate real or perceived rivals and enemies of the Soviet state. On a bad day, *anyone* could fall afoul of Stalin's police. Some 700,000 people perished during the height of the Purges, from the most loyal servants of the Soviet state to anonymous, unlucky nobodies. "You can't yawn and sleep," Stalin once wrote, "when you are in power!"[34] Power was something to be watched constantly for otherwise someone would take it away from you. Russia of course had a violent history. Serfdom was a form of slavery and over three centuries or more provoked peasant uprisings, violently repressed. In the latter part of the nineteenth century, a crude form of capitalism developed, factories, mines, and industrial centres operated like forced labour camps, where violence was endemic.

When revolution erupted in March 1917 Stalin was in Siberia, but he and other Bolshevik exiles quickly made their way back to Petrograd. During 1917, Stalin rose to prominence becoming a member of the inner circle of Bolshevik leaders. During the Civil War, he was in the south at Tsaritsyn, later called Stalingrad, on the west bank of the Volga River. It was here that many of the first clashes with Trotskii took place, with an impatient Lenin in the middle, calming hot tempers.

Stalin was a pedestrian orator, theorist, and pamphleteer. Trotskii called his language "soporific." But Stalin was a smart, capable organizer, a talent which Lenin noticed and appreciated. In all of these activities, he nevertheless found time to attack Trotskii, attacks which Lenin either ignored or diverted. In the summer of 1920, during the war against Poland, Stalin's hostility to Trotskii and his insubordination left open the Red Army's southern flank, which the Polish general and Soviet nemesis Józef Piłsudski stove in to prevent the fall of Warsaw. Here was a consequence of Stalin's grudge against Trotskii. Bad tempered, moody, vengeful, and intolerant of dissent, Stalin never forgot or forgave political opposition. A vote for Trotskii at a party meeting years before or an ill-considered remark were all it took. Like the English Die-Hards, Stalin was a good hater. Once dirty, always dirty was his view of adversaries. He could bide his time, wait for years, before exacting retribution on oppositionists, or on anyone who looked at him the wrong way. It is doubtful that his comrades could ever have imagined the lengths to which he would go in pursuit of his "enemies."

Stalin's "mistake" during the summer counteroffensive against Poland in 1920 did not do long-term damage to his reputation. In April 1922, Lenin sponsored Stalin for the post of general secretary, or *gensek,* of the Communist Party, less than two months before Lenin fell ill. Stalin thus obtained control of government appointments and began to place his allies in key positions. Trotskii said the choice of Stalin as gensek went against Lenin's better judgment. It was not long before Lenin regretted his decision, apparently, but by then it was too late.[35]

Lenin suffered a first stroke in May 1922 and died in January 1924. A struggle for leadership ensued. Stalin swept away his rivals, Trotskii for starters, then all others, followed by his former allies, one after the other, until by the end of the 1920s, he was the uncontested leader of the Soviet state. If he eliminated rivals, he also developed a small entourage of loyalists who survived with him until his death in 1953. These were Viacheslav Mikhailovich Molotov, Kliment Efimovich Voroshilov, and Lazar M. Kaganovich. While others came and went during the 1930s, for various reasons, these three remained, becoming a *troika* at the centre of policymaking. After 1933, they received copies of important NKID telegrams, many of Litvinov's briefing papers to Stalin, and various other dispatches from Soviet embassies. When Stalin took holidays in Sochi or in Abkhaziia, it was Molotov and Kaganovich who most of the time held the fort in Moscow and consulted him on important policy issues. No policy, important or not, could proceed through the Politburo without Stalin's approval. No one had personal policies which they pursued on the side, least of all Litvinov. NKID policy was Stalin's policy. During the 1920s, Litvinov got into the habit of writing notes and briefing papers for Stalin and he continued to do so until he was sacked in 1939. The vozhd' was just as interested in foreign policy as he was in domestic and party issues. He had his hand in everything.

Stalin and Litvinov on Foreign Policy

Litvinov wanted the speedy conclusion of economic and political agreements with France. "This is dictated by new developments in Europe."[36] He did not say what developments, but in Germany, Nazi power was on the rise. It was July 1931. Stalin too was impatient and continued to complain about what he saw as mishandling of the discussions with Poland about a non-aggression pact. This time his ire was directed against zamnarkom, deputy commissar Lev M. Karakhan, who had been conducting negotiations with the Polish ambassador Stanisław Patek. A dispute had arisen over who had taken the initiative to begin discussions. Everybody is touchy about this question, Stalin noted, for fear of provoking political opposition. Who cared who took the initiative? "By stupidity," Karakhan had irritated Patek and "spoilt the file." Unable to resist, he also blamed Litvinov for the "blunder."[37] The problem is, Kaganovich responded, that the *NKIDovtsy*, that is, Soviet diplomats, were too accommodating to Germany; they did not want to cause offence in Berlin over Poland. "They can't see that we don't have any reasons, which would oblige us to run after Germany, it's rather the case that it [Germany] needs us most of all."[38] Litvinov resisted the pressure, which he obviously felt from Kaganovich, prompting the latter to write again about Poland. "I must tell you," Kaganovich informed Stalin, "that from conversations with Litvinov, I am even more convinced of his peculiar 'Germanophilia.' We, he says, 'are now dancing on German feet,' since from the French we still have nothing. He does not understand that we cannot subordinate our diplomacy solely to relations with Germany." Litvinov is "too narcissistic ... believing too much in his 'greatness,' but let it pass, the main thing essentially is his mistake."[39] Kaganovich played dirty, grossly oversimplifying Litvinov's position, as Stalin would surely have recognized. On 15 September, Litvinov returned to the charge, with detailed papers arguing that the NKID did not know what "tricks" Poland was playing. The Polish government remained hostile to the USSR and had territorial ambitions in Soviet Byelorussia and the Ukraine. Poland would like nothing better than to break up Rapallo and itself come to terms with Germany. That was a good call in the autumn of 1931.

Let Litvinov continue his argument addressed to Stalin. The idea would then be to draw Germany into a rapprochement with France and Poland, leaving the USSR isolated. Germany was the only country in the West with which the USSR had tolerable relations, Litvinov argued, and not for the first time. Italy was unreliable and, if the Conservative Party returned to power in Britain, there would be no hope of a rapprochement with London. Germany was all that the Union had, Litvinov argued, and to lose it without definite gains elsewhere was unthinkable. Discussions must have become heated. According to Kaganovich's account, Litvinov said, "I know better, and you here know nothing." In Stalin's absence, this was more than likely true, but you can see why Kaganovich accused Litvinov of "narcissism." Pushed by Stalin, the Politburo rejected Litvinov's position during a meeting on 20 September 1931 and directed the NKID to return with proposals to pursue a non-aggression pact with Poland. In his report to Stalin, Kaganovich indicated – this time without abusive comments – that Litvinov was sticking to his guns.[40]

Negotiations in Paris

The Polish issue was on the Politburo agenda twice during that autumn of 1931. After much discussion – and French diplomatic manoeuvres – negotiations began with Polish ambassador Patek in Moscow about a non-aggression pact.[41] As Litvinov had predicted, the negotiations were prolonged and without positive result. Franco-Soviet negotiations did not go anywhere either and were suspended in October 1931, although it was no fault of the NKID or of Litvinov. French political divisions and instability blocked any progress until the spring of 1932 when there were new parliamentary elections. Soviet diplomats reckoned nevertheless that the time was right to try for an improvement of relations. Unfortunately, French cabinet ministers lacked nerve, according to one Quai d'Orsay official, who told Soviet counterparts that the minister responsible for trade negotiations was frightened by incessant right-wing attacks against him. Dovgalevskii explained that the trade minister was caught between two fires: for and against trade with the USSR. The minister was therefore sensitive to press attacks, the more so, because he did not want journalists delving too closely into his past.[42] It was always thus in France of the interwar years. Scandals were commonplace and offered perverse amusement to the Everyman and Everywoman, glad to see big shots being taken down a peg or two.

There was more to Soviet problems in France. Governments changed in dizzying succession. The momentary président du Conseil, ex-socialist Laval, reminded Dovgalevskii of his exasperation with the Comintern and its support of the French Communist Party. "Moscow then and now finances revolution and strikes," Laval commented. Dovgalevskii protested that his government had nothing to do with the Comintern. "Unfortunately," replied Laval, "the line drawn by you is not so clear."

This was an old complaint and Litvinov had earlier explained to Dovgalevskii how to respond to it:

> We of course firmly deny any financial ties whatsoever between the [Soviet] government and foreign communist parties, but it is impossible nevertheless to deny the fact that communist parties receive money from Moscow. We always explain the business thus: that communist parties pay certain subscription fees to the Comintern, but since the Russian Communist Party is the largest party, its fees constitute a substantial part of the Comintern budget which is shared out between

> other parties. Thus, we by no means deny that the Comintern from Moscow sends money to the French Communist Party, but we insist that this money does not come from the [Soviet] government or from government agencies … You cannot entirely deny the receipt of money from Moscow by communist parties because on this point you cannot know.[43]

Here was a disingenuous argument, and you can see why Laval had a point. But Litvinov did not have the power to close the Comintern, any more than he could control Bolshevik rhetoric in Moscow, although he tried. The narkom hoped that his Western interlocutors would listen to what he and his ambassadors had to say *in private* and discount what Bolshevik "orators" were saying *in public*. In the West this was a hard thing to do.

The NKID wanted to press the French to sign the Franco-Soviet non-aggression pact, but did not know quite how to go about it. Litvinov tried André Tardieu, who for most of the period between November 1929 and May 1932 shared the présidence du Conseil with Laval. Tardieu was a traditional French nationalist on the right, hostile to Germany *and* to the Soviet Union. In March 1932 Litvinov complained to him that, after nine months, the French government was still deferring signature of the Franco-Soviet non-aggression pact. Tardieu shrugged his shoulders and made a joke about the delay. Litvinov then complained about a lack of progress in trade negotiations, but Tardieu could not see why France should trade with the Soviet Union in order to help it – according to the Soviet press – to achieve "supremacy over the capitalist world." Tardieu listed French grievances against the Soviet government: the Treaty of Rapallo with Germany, the non-payment of debts, the Comintern's activities in French colonies, and the French Communist Party. Litvinov riposted by listing Soviet grievances against France: the nasty "bourgeois" press and the hostile activities of tsarist émigrés in France. On the Comintern, Litvinov replied along lines similar to those he laid out for Dovgalevskii, though with less flimflam, for Tardieu was not one to fall for it.

More importantly, Litvinov laid out the essential argument in favour of better relations. It was basic realpolitik: the Soviet government had no major conflicts with France. "We look for cooperation with other countries, and we take this cooperation where we find it. We are free from any national prejudice, we would like to have friendly relations with France, and it is not our fault if this has not come to pass until now," wrote Litvinov. At the time of Rapallo and long afterward, "we were alone and isolated and we would have been idiots if we had refused collaboration, on which only Germany then agreed. Any government in our place would have done exactly the same thing." Even though their systems were different, it did not mean the USSR and France could not trade on mutually profitable terms. Tardieu was "very friendly," observed Litvinov, and said he would think things over.[44] He most certainly did so, but his ruminations would have been of little use for his government, yet another, fell in May 1932.

Parliamentary elections in the spring of 1932 moved the French government slightly to the left and put the centrist politician Édouard Herriot back in power as président du Conseil and foreign minister. Nevertheless, the guard was changing: Tardieu did not again lead the government. Poincaré, Briand, and Berthelot retired from the scene; all were dead by the end of 1934. Herriot kept to what he called his *idée fixe* on Franco-Soviet relations. This was to re-establish in some form the pre–First World War Franco-Soviet alliance against Germany. In 1924, Herriot's first government had re-established diplomatic relations with the USSR. For Herriot, Germany represented an existential threat to France, and this conviction was only reinforced by the growing strength of Nazism in Germany. In the spring of 1932, Hitler came second in presidential elections. Even in 1922, long before the Nazis became dangerous, Herriot feared a German resurgence. "In fifteen years Germany will attack us again," Herriot had said at the time, and he was not that far off the mark: in the end, it was less than two years.

Who Is Enemy No. 1?

During the 1930s one often heard the question, "Who is enemy No. 1, Nazi Germany or the Soviet Union?" Herriot had no trouble with the answer, but moving the government towards a rapprochement with Moscow was easier said than done. Herriot admitted to Dovgalevskii that he did not trust hostile Quai d'Orsay officials.[45] Soviet diplomats did not trust them either. They were also uncertain of Herriot's determination to conclude the non-aggression pact and trade agreement. According to the deputy commissar, zamnarkom Nikolai Nikolaevich Krestinskii, Herriot had been up and down with the Soviet diplomats and they should not count on "great friendliness" from him, though better Herriot than Tardieu.[46]

Krestinskii might have thought his scepticism justified, had he known that Herriot would meet Franz von Papen, then German chancellor, in Lausanne in mid-June. Papen proposed an anti-Soviet Franco-German *bloc*. The NKID eventually heard about Papen's proposals. Herriot waved them off, they were just a ruse anyway, but Moscow was concerned about German policy. In November, Litvinov asked for an explanation from the German ambassador in Moscow, Herbert von Dirksen. "Public opinion," Litvinov said, "had read in the press about Papen's proposals and had justifiably developed 'a certain scepticism in regard to Soviet-German relations.'" The ambassador replied that these "so-called suggestions" to the French had been denied. In form, not in substance, Litvinov retorted, adding that Germany ought not to take umbrage if the French "informed us about unfriendly suggestions coming from the Germans."

In fact, in December, Litvinov learned from the Italian ambassador in Moscow that Papen's proposals had been repeated in more concrete form to Berthelot in Paris.[47] It was always thus in European politics, wheels turning inside wheels, knives all the time ready to be unsheathed, to stab another in the back. That was what passed for diplomacy during the 1930s.

Litvinov was not the only one worried about Germany, Molotov and Kaganovich, Stalin's trusted lieutenants, were also alarmed by increasing Nazi violence and hooliganism against unions and workers' organizations. They proposed, and Stalin approved, a united front of workers' organizations under communist direction to resist the Nazis.[48] It was July 1932. These ideas were passed on through the Comintern executive. Well, so what, Stalin might have thought to himself, if we provide a little advice to German communists.

Events in Germany increased Litvinov's impatience to sign the non-aggression pact with France. And speak of the devil, who turned up if not Anatole de Monzie who was the chief French negotiator with the Soviet delegation in the 1920s. Monzie was a politician with a big ego who did not always get along with his Soviet counterparts. He accused Ambassador Dovgalevskii of avoiding him. Untrue, Dovgalevskii explained to Krestinskii, but "our relations were practically broken off because of the insolent, bullying tone of this *monsieur* – who permitted himself attacks and offensive epithets against Chicherin, you, and other people – turned my stomach."[49] Like him or not, Monzie sometimes got the attention of Soviet diplomats during the 1930s. He told the highly competent Soviet chargé d'affaires in Paris, Marcel' Israilevich Rozenberg, that "the German danger" made a Franco-Soviet rapprochement essential.[50] This was also Herriot's view.

The non-aggression pact was finally signed in late November 1932, just before the fall of Herriot's government. Governments did not last long in Paris during the interwar years. Herriot's six months in power were not a record, but not bad for the 1930s. In January 1933, his successor, Joseph Paul-Boncour, a socialist in and out of the Socialist Party, lasted six weeks. Historians need to keep lists of who was in and out of power in France during the interwar years. Paul-Boncour was also reported to be in a hurry to strengthen Franco-Soviet relations. This was true. Dovgalevskii worried about ratification of the non-aggression pact, but Paul-Boncour remained foreign minister in the subsequent government of Radical Party politician Édouard Daladier, which put minds more at ease in Moscow.[51]

Joseph Paul-Boncour

Joseph Paul-Boncour was born in Saint-Aignan (Loir-et-Cher), southwest of Paris, in 1873. His father, Louis, was a physician, and Joseph, like many others of his class and generation, studied law at the Université de Paris. He became involved in the labour movement before the First World War and thus leaned left, but not too far. He became a minister for the first time in 1911, and then not again until 1932 when he was Minister of War in Herriot's cabinet before himself becoming président du Conseil. He was a handsome man, indeed he looked like a dashing fellow, small in stature with great locks of long grey hair in the 1930s. His contemporaries said he did not know his files and was better talking than doing. He knew his Soviet files, however, and read the telegrams from the embassy in Moscow without any summaries. He got on well with Dovgalevskii and Litvinov and continued Herriot's policy of Franco-Soviet rapprochement. In fact, Paul-Boncour went further than Herriot; he was aggressive in pursuing better relations with the USSR. He tried to control, with modest success, the Quai d'Orsay "clerks" who thought ministers were passers-by in their offices and that *they* decided policy. Sometimes he drew the ire and contempt of Foreign Office officials who did not like to see France drawing close to the USSR. Criticism from the Foreign Office should have been and sometimes was regarded in Paris as a badge of honour.

Litvinov was impatient for ratification of the non-aggression pact. "I attach great importance to the early ratification of the pact," he wrote to Dovgalevskii, "and it seems to me that it would be possible to push Boncour gently to ratify in a simplified way without the chambers [i.e., the Assemblée nationale]. Otherwise, delays are inevitable, and, possibly, failure."[52] In French politics, one often did not know what was going to happen next. What might be the policy of the French government today, Litvinov observed to French ambassador Dejean, might not be tomorrow. "The Franco-Soviet rapprochement is an expression of the policy of the government now in power in France," he reiterated, "but it is impossible to count on the continuation of that policy in the case of the arrival in power of the parties of the right."[53] In mid-May 1933, the Assemblée nationale voted to approve the non-aggression pact (technically the exchange of instruments of ratification). Herriot then presided over the Commission des Affaires étrangères in the Chamber of Deputies. During the debate he evoked the memory of the sixteenth-century alliance of the French Catholic king Francis I and the Ottoman sultan Suleiman the Magnificent against a common Habsburg foe. It was an elegant way to endorse the principle of the enemy of my enemy is my ally. In the Chamber of Deputies there were 554 in favour, forty-one abstentions, and only one vote against, that of Tardieu.[54] Tardieu had a reputation for obstinacy, and well deserved too. Litvinov did not hold a grudge. The weak point of a rapprochement with France was always the future: would the arrival in power of governments of the right put an end to it? "I would recommend," Litvinov wrote to the Soviet chargé d'affaires in Paris, "taking advantage of the present mood, to strengthen ties with Tardieu and with his politically liked-minded people and in general with the right-wing parties."[55]

The Importance of Poland

While NKID worked to improve relations with France, it did not neglect relations with Poland. In fact, the two issues were inter-related. A rapprochement with France went hand in hand with a rapprochement with Poland. While Poland was often a subject in Stalin's correspondence with Molotov and Kaganovich in 1931, it barely rates a mention in 1932. This could only mean that Stalin was satisfied with the way the NKID was handling the Polish file. Litvinov always preferred getting along with Western neighbours and Poland was no exception. A non-aggression pact was signed on 25 July 1932, and did not rate a mention either by Stalin or by Molotov and Kaganovich in Moscow.

In early 1933, as relations with France improved, so also did those with Poland, or so it seemed. At the end of January, Hitler became chancellor of Germany. That got people's attention. Even so, there were ups and downs with Poland, affected by Polish relations with France and Germany. When relations with Germany were strained, Polish interest in relations with the Soviet Union appeared to intensify.[56] Boris Spiridonovich Stomoniakov, a member of the NKID *kollegiia*, stressed this point to Vladimir Aleksandrovich Antonov-Ovseenko, the polpred in Warsaw. "Hitler's triumph in Germany and the developing offensive of revisionist elements in Europe continues to strengthen opinion in favour of a rapprochement with us in Poland and has led the Polish government to exaggerate in the wider world the improvement of relations with the USSR." It is a systematic propaganda campaign, pushing untrue rumours from Polish sources of a further Polish-Soviet agreement for a "united front … against Hitler." This was alright, Stomoniakov advised: the NKID did not have any interest in exposing the exaggerations, for they could exert "a useful influence on the policy of the German government." Soviet diplomats were as cagey and sophisticated as any in the West. Stomoniakov instructed Antonov-Ovseenko to see what he could find out, as it was an opportunity to break down the walls of isolation around the Soviet embassy. Talk to people, left and right, figure out what is going on.[57]

Of course, it occurred to the NKID that the Polish government was trying to interest Berlin in rethinking relations with Poland. In fact, in April 1933, Marshal Piłsudski, head of state, and his foreign minister, Józef Beck, were already sounding out German authorities about a "stabilisation of relations."[58] It was a double game, but the same one that the NKID and France were playing. All the same, Stomoniakov was encouraged by developments. Because of Hitler's policies, the Polish government was seeking to strengthen its ties with France and with the Little Entente of French allies, Czechoslovakia, Romania, and Yugoslavia.

Then, Stomoniakov had this to say: "If even a few months ago in France there were illusions concerning the possibility of coming to terms with Germany, making concessions to it on matters of rearmament and sacrificing certain interests of its allies, then now, thanks to Hitler's policy, this illusion has vanished, and we have in fact a united front from the far right up to and including the socialists." These developments suited Soviet interests, Stomoniakov continued: "We have therefore decided on all current issues of our relations, where it is consistent with our interests, to meet Polish proposals and strive not only to strengthen our relations with Poland, but also to publicize their improvement to the outside world."[59]

Boris Spiridonovich Stomoniakov

Boris Spiridonovich Stomoniakov would soon rise in rank to zamnarkom with the reorganization of the NKID in 1934. He was responsible for Polish and Baltic affairs, very important files within the larger dossier of European collective security and mutual assistance. Stomoniakov was born in Odessa, a port city on the Black Sea, in 1882. His family was Bulgarian. His father, Spiridon Ivanov, was a Bulgarian merchant. We do not know much about his parents, but his father had resources enough to send his son to study at the St. Petersburg Mining Institute between 1900 and 1904. Stomoniakov is often referred to as a Bulgarian, but he was born in Odessa; if he had a Bulgarian passport, it was by virtue of his father's nationality.

At eighteen, the young Stomoniakov became a member of the Russian Social Democratic Workers' Party. It was the usual path to the revolution. In 1905, he was in Belgium where he ran guns to Russia. He returned to Russia in 1906 and was arrested but not long imprisoned. In the doldrums and repression that followed 1905, he dropped out of the revolutionary movement. Perhaps for family reasons, Stomoniakov went to Bulgaria in 1912; his father died there in the following year. Eventually, he joined the Bulgarian army which entered the war against Russia in October 1915. In 1917, Stomoniakov made his way to Moscow. In 1921 he went to Berlin as a Soviet *torgpred* or trade representative. He was involved in the various trade negotiations with Weimar Germany during the 1920s. In the existing photographs of Stomoniakov, he is dressed in a suit and tie, he is partially bald, and has a moustache and chin whiskers. His gaze is rather benign. In fact, he looks like a Soviet *kupets*, a businessman, as indeed he was. We do not know much about his personal life, but he could be temperamental and strong willed. In 1928, he complained directly to Stalin about the Politburo being in too much of a hurry to conclude a new trade agreement in Berlin. We are giving too much away, he complained. Essentially, he was criticizing the NKID's policy recommendations, which put Stomoniakov at odds with Litvinov. He was so disgusted that he asked to be reassigned. At the time he was already a member of the NKID *kollegiia*, the executive committee of the Commissariat, until it

Figure 2.3. Boris Spirodonovich Stomoniakov, ca. 1930s, AVPRF.

was abolished in a government reorganization in 1934. Later on, it is said that he got on well with Litvinov.

The Soviet-Polish Rapprochement

Stomoniakov was good at his job and kept a firm hand on Soviet policy on Poland. His dispatch to polpred Antonov-Ovseenko was a clear statement of Soviet intentions. There was some hope in the spring of 1933 that Poland might want to improve relations with the Soviet Union. Karl Radek, an old Bolshevik and journalist for *Izvestiia*, reported a conversation with Boguslaw Miedziński, who was the director of the *Gazeta Polska*, a semi-official newspaper in Warsaw. Miedziński was a go-between, acting unofficially and wanting to talk to Radek about sensitive questions, which were not yet "ripe" for official diplomatic discussions. He was close to the leading *pilsudchiki*, had fought under Piłsudski during the war, and offered to be an unofficial conduit for any questions that the Soviet side might like to raise. Soviet concerns would be passed to all the principal Polish leaders and not just the foreign minister Beck. Conversations between the two journalists could be conducted with more frankness than in formal diplomatic exchanges. According to Miedziński, the Polish leadership "was convinced that Germany would go to war with them [with Poland], but they do not want to rush events." Nor did they think that the Soviet Union was interested in seeing Poland weakened vis-à-vis Germany. Poland did not wish to serve as a "weapon of foreign interests" against the USSR. Miedziński was convinced, Radek reported, that the Germans would try "to create complications between us and Poland, reinforcing tendencies in Romania directed against the USSR." Germany's next move, according to Miedziński, would be in the Baltics. Baltic farmers would be attracted by higher agricultural prices resulting from a customs union and the British government might support German expansion in that direction. Such expansion would permit the preparation of a *place d'armes* against Leningrad. Poland did not want the Germans in the Baltics and this would create a common interest between the USSR and Poland. Miedziński was thus offering to facilitate a Polish-Soviet rapprochement.[60] In the opening moves to counter Hitlerite Germany, wheels turned within wheels once again and many people became involved openly or clandestinely. Their names will be unfamiliar to readers, but not for long. Many actors in this narrative will become old friends as the 1930s unfold.

Would Poland hold to its apparent new line? Would France? Was the Soviet analysis of a "united front" premature? A fortnight later Stomoniakov began to wonder: the Polish government had reverted to a "certain reserve" with regard to the rapprochement "in large and small matters."[61] As tensions subsided between Poland and Nazi Germany, so also did Poland's interest in a rapprochement with the USSR. On 1 May, Piłsudski met Antonov-Ovseenko, but the conversation was limited to the Marshal's personal chit-chat.[62] Stomoniakov thought the message was clear: "The contents of Piłsudski's conversation with you confirm our assumptions that, in inviting you, Piłsudski had in mind not the further development of Polish-Soviet relations, but exclusively its effect in other countries, and especially in Germany." This was alright, Stomoniakov observed, for we are doing the same thing. Let the Germans worry "about the prospects for further rapprochement of the USSR with Poland and France." Two could play a double game. Stomoniakov reckoned that Polish policy was calculated on a lack of confidence in the strength of Anglo-French "anti-Hitlerite" opinion.[63] Litvinov also worried about this.

Chapter Three

A Steep Hill: The Soviet Quest for US Recognition, 1930–1933

In the United States, the evolution of policy towards the USSR was slower than in Europe. During the 1920s, Republican administrations refused to grant diplomatic recognition to the Soviet Union, but they did permit trade to be conducted with ups and downs. Under the administration of Herbert Hoover, the policy of non-recognition continued unchanged. Trade relations improved, but this took pressure off the government from business lobbies to recognize the Soviet Union. As in France, as in the United States, there were periodic outbursts of anti-communist propaganda anytime the question of recognition got the attention of the press. In 1930, a series of counterfeit documents that were published by the *Daily News* and other New York papers accused agents working for the Amtorg Trading Corporation, the Soviet trade agency in the United States, of maintaining ties with revolutionary organizations and spreading revolutionary propaganda. Litvinov called it an anti-communist "crusade."[1] The use of bogus documents was a proven method of anti-communist propaganda, which had worked with spectacular success in the 1924 British election campaign. The publication of the so-called Zinoviev letter contributed, with the connivance of British intelligence services and the Conservative Party, to the defeat of the minority Labour government in October 1924. What worked in Britain and France also worked in the United States where anti-communism flourished. Counterfeit documents were an important weapon in the struggle against the Soviet state.

The Fish Committee

In the House of Representatives, Hamilton Fish, a fervent anti-communist Republican, organized a House committee to investigate communist activities in the United States. Boris Evseevich Skvirskii, the unofficial Soviet representative in Washington, sent detailed reports to Moscow about the debates in the House of Representatives on the resolution to form the committee.

Most congressmen present for the debate – apparently there were not many – supported it. Skvirskii mentioned one exception, a congressman who called the committee a "witch hunt." Given the economic crisis, the congressman added, the House ought to be more concerned with unemployment, instead of trying to divert public opinion from real problems. It's worth mentioning the congressman's name – Christian William Ramseyer, an Ohio Republican. It took courage to speak out against the anti-communist mob.[2]

According to Skvirskii, it was expected that the economic crisis would slacken off, but the optimism had not been justified. All indications were, in fact, that the crisis was going to get worse. The deteriorating economic situation led to attacks on any competitive imports. The USSR was selling lumber, coal, and matches in the United States, Skvirskii noted, but these imports did not amount to much in the US marketplace of "astronomical figures," a mere $12 million per annum. Nevertheless, they were a target worth shooting at in the present crisis and resulting state of public opinion. Politicians exaggerated the importance of Soviet trade for political purposes as did Soviet "enemies" in the American Federation of Labor (AFL) who "defended the interests of workers" allegedly put out of work by Soviet imports. In these circumstances any tool in the shed would do: accusations of dumping and the use of "convict" or "forced labour" were the main points of attack. Skvirskii went into considerable detail to explain what Amtorg was doing to defend its commercial interests. If US manufacturers wanted to sell to the USSR then one had to expect that Soviet agencies would also want to sell in the US market.[3] Naturally, in the anti-communist tumult, damage to US business interests often went unnoticed.

In late July 1930, Congressman Fish called before his committee Petr Alekseevich Bogdanov, the head of Amtorg in New York, and later called Skvirskii. The Politburo was caught off guard by Bogdanov's appearance and asked for detailed information on his testimony. Anastas Ivanovich Mikoian, then commissar for external trade and Bogdanov's boss, was indignant and demanded to know why Bogdanov had voluntarily testified before the committee.[4] Here was an astonishing breakdown in communication between Moscow and the New York office of Amtorg, and not the first in Soviet-American relations.

Bogdanov defended himself as best he could. His interrogation was spread over three days and eleven hours. The atmosphere was hostile, and he had difficulty even in reading a prepared statement. Bogdanov reported that he was compelled "to answer questions with one word replies: yes, no, or I don't know." Refusal to answer prompted committee warnings that he could be jailed. A "White Guard," who was present, in fact a document counterfeiter, suggested questions to one committee member. It was a set-up. The committee demanded copies of all Amtorg's encrypted cables to Moscow, at the latest in two weeks. Clearly that was not going to be acceptable. Bogdanov asked for instructions, though perhaps he should have done so *before* going to the Fish Committee.

"Personally I would suggest," he cabled, "refusal [of the cables] even at the risk of prison."[5] It was a circus.

The way it looked to Litvinov, Bogdanov, Amtorg, and the USSR had been smeared. Why didn't Bogdanov refuse to answer "political" questions having nothing to do with Amtorg, Litvinov demanded to know from Skvirskii, why had he submitted to the Committee's "provocations"? Skvirskii replied that Bogdanov did not have much choice. When he refused to answer inappropriate questions, committee members threatened him with contempt and imprisonment. It was that or attempt "to manoeuvre or claim lack of knowledge." When Bogdanov tried "to manoeuvre," committee members "rudely" demanded yes or no answers. The bullying and abuse infuriated Moscow. Mikoian confirmed that under no circumstances was Bogdanov to turn over Amtorg's encrypted cables to the Fish Committee; and the Politburo forbade him to make any further public statements without authorization from Moscow.[6] Bogdanov had walked into a trap. The Fish Committee rattled him, provoking criticism from Soviet colleagues in the United States and from the NKID. Bogdanov cabled Mikoian to say that he was at his wit's end and needed holidays.[7]

According to Skvirskii, the Fish Committee expected Western Union Telegraph to hand over the encrypted telegrams between Moscow and Amtorg, and intended to give them to its experts for decryption. Since even British code breakers were then having trouble with the decryption of Soviet cables, one wonders whether the Politburo worried much about the Fish Committee's "experts." The committee "put on display those forces which were waging a systematically hostile campaign against the USSR and Amtorg. These were all the AFL leaders, patriotic organizations, and Catholics. To them were joined the politicians, attempting 'politically' to capitalize on the struggle against 'the red peril.' Among these were large and small scale politicians." Skvirskii mentioned the names of some local New York politicians to which he added Republican bosses who needed "'the red peril' to draw voters' attention away from the economic crisis and the unemployed on the eve of the November elections when a third of the Senate and all of the House of Representatives will be elected." Skvirskii went on in some detail about the various economic interests looking for the support of senators and congressmen. AFL leaders picked up on these cries for help and declared a "trade war" on the USSR. The Fish Committee supported the movement, "forgetting for a while about communism and focusing on the USSR as a future economic competitor." Skvirskii also went into some detail about Bogdanov's testimony before the Fish Committee and the dirty tricks used against him, for example, exploiting his lack of understanding of English. Fish and his committee appeared to pull out all the stops. These circumstances provoked the irritation of the Hoover administration itself and of important economic groups doing business in the USSR. Even elements of the press, according to Skvirskii, criticized the Fish Committee for being bent upon the disruption of Soviet-American trade.[8] It was the old split between ideologues and businessmen in search of contracts in the USSR and a demonstration of the difficulties in dealing with the United States without diplomatic recognition. Even government departments, State and Commerce, for example, disliked the Fish Committee's abusive interrogations and went to the defence of Soviet-American trade.

The Del'gas Affair

Bogdanov had other troubles during that summer of 1930. One of his subordinates, Vasilii Vasil'evich Del'gas, an Amtorg vice-president and an OGPU agent no less, informed him that he would remain in the United States. He planned to move to California and work as an engineer-consultant on Russian affairs. "I ask you to cable Moscow," Del'gas wrote, "so that they do not publicly shoot me." Given all Bogdanov's troubles, this was not a welcome development. He tried to find out why Del'gas wanted to remain in the States.[9] Ten days later, Bogdanov informed Moscow that Del'gas had definitively broken with the USSR, that he was going to ask for US citizenship, and was going to work for a company that supplied the USSR with petroleum equipment. Del'gas, it appeared, wanted to chase "the American dream." He was living among "White Guard circles." Bogdanov reported that they would be sacking people in Amtorg connected to his work.

The more Bogdanov dug into the affair, the more he was obliged to report disagreeable news to Moscow. Del'gas was afraid of facing bribery charges in Moscow if he returned home. He nevertheless promised to keep quiet if Amtorg did not bother him. He let it be known that he would "never" walk down "Besedovskii's road." Readers will remember that Besedovskii was the pistol-packing Soviet chargé d'affaires in Paris, who had defected, allegedly with $5,000 in embassy funds. Bogdanov did not believe Del'gas, suspecting that he had given information to the Fish Committee. Moscow was not so sure but considered any "defector" (*nevozvrashchenets*) as an "enemy." Any statement by such persons that they would not "walk down Besedovskii's road" could scarcely be taken at face value. "All defectors always went down Besedovskii's road."[10]

The Del'gas case made it all the way to the Politburo where the matter was referred to committee and to the Soviet Supreme Court. Del'gas was judged an outlaw and his property confiscated, a light sentence by Soviet standards. The surmise that Del'gas might end up before the Fish Committee proved correct. It was one fiasco after the other.

The Fish Committee resumed hearings in the autumn, and Bogdanov, who must have worried about being jailed for failure to comply with committee subpoenas, proposed the wacky idea to Moscow of paraphrasing telegrams. This was too much for Moscow. The Politburo ordered Bogdanov not to appear again before the Fish Committee and not under any circumstances to communicate the contents of cyphered cables.[11] You can see why Moscow wanted its trade representatives protected by diplomatic status.

At the end of November, Skvirskii cabled Moscow to advise that he too had been subpoenaed to appear before the committee. "I did not succeed in dodging them," Skvirskii reported, "for they would have come looking for me. And Fish would have made a 'sensation' of my attempt to avoid them." The previous day, Del'gas had provided the "sensation," by testifying before the committee, thus proving Moscow right. Skvirskii reckoned that he had two choices: refuse to appear and risk arrest and the closing of our offices or appear and "protect the dignity of the USSR." He reported that Republican Senator William E. Borah, who favoured Soviet recognition, had advised him to go and answer questions, being careful but trying to win opinion over to his side. The NKID grudgingly agreed, directing Skvirskii to refute the "defamatory claims" made against the USSR and its US offices.[12]

Skvirskii and Fish

Judging by Skvirskii's report of his testimony, which went on for about five hours, he gave a good account of himself, no doubt profiting from Bogdanov's experience. State Department official Robert Kelley, a good hater of the USSR, encouraged Skvirskii to appear before the committee, saying it would only be routine. It was far from being so: Skvirskii was aggressively cross-examined on relations between the Comintern and the Soviet government. The interrogation began with his swearing in. Skvirskii refused, explaining that he was an atheist. Instead, he had "to swear solemnly" to tell the truth. Imagine the reaction of Fish and his colleagues to Skvirskii's avowal that he was an atheist, and then later that he was a communist and a member of the Russian Communist Party. Skvirskii meant to go right at the committee, and he did, sparring at length with Fish and his colleagues who kept returning one way or another to the Comintern. And Fish asked again for Soviet telegrams, which Skvirskii refused to hand over.

"You have something to hide then?" Fish asked.

I have been in the United States for nine years, Skvirskii replied in effect. He had had dealings with many government departments, and did not think that any of them could say that he was involved during that time in any "suspicious" activities.

Fish then asked again if Amtorg would hand over its telegrams.

Skvirskii replied that he would not, and Fish let the matter drop.

He then tried to drag Skvirskii into a discussion of the American Communist Party and its program and activities. Skvirskii refused to be drawn in. "I imagine," he replied in a matter of fact way, "that its program is like that of other communist parties."

"Doesn't every communist work for the overthrow of capitalism?" asked Fish.

In Russia, as Skvirskii pointed out in his response, there had been a socialist revolution and capitalism was overthrown. The task of each Soviet citizen working abroad was to strengthen the Soviet state. The sparring with Fish continued. Skvirskii handled it with aplomb.

Fish kept returning to Comintern activities. Skvirskii offered some comments about the history of the International.

"Are you a member of the Comintern?" Fish wanted to know.

"I am not," Skvirskii replied. He said that he worked for the Narkomindel, that is, for the Soviet government. "*Molodets*, well done," Litvinov must have thought to himself; Comrade Skvirskii doesn't need coaching.

And then Skvirskii went further, as Litvinov might have done: "I categorically denied Soviet government participation in propaganda, observing that no one could accuse it of sending troops to overthrow a foreign government whereas Soviet Russia can accuse many governments, among which the American government, for attempting to overthrow it by means of armed intervention." There was indeed the small matter of "Allied" intervention to strangle the enfant Soviet state, which Congressman Fish failed to mention in his remarks.

Skvirskii continued: "I pointed out the abnormal situation in which each Soviet citizen is suspected of not eating or drinking, but only of overthrowing the American government; if we followed this example, we would have to suspect each American or generally each foreigner in the USSR of wanting to overthrow the Soviet government … We however do not think this." Well, here unfortunately, Skvirskii overpleaded the case, since OGPU *did* regard all foreigners with suspicion.

When Skvirskii was finally permitted to speak about Soviet-American trade, he pointed out that while business was increasing, the balance of trade was highly unfavourable to the USSR. "This trade could be five times higher if we had the necessary bank credits," he said. The USSR and United States had common interests to trade with one another, Soviet-US interests were complementary. Why did the United States want to shoot itself in the foot by not trading with the USSR during a time of mass unemployment? This was a standard Soviet argument in favour of better trade relations.

At the end of his testimony, Skvirskii reported sarcastically that Fish thanked him for his "collaboration" with the committee.[13] Nevertheless, there was no improvement in Soviet-American relations. Bogdanov reported that there was a concerted effort to stop Soviet imports into the United States. The Fish Committee attempted to demonstrate that Amtorg was conducting political propaganda and that it was "dumping" Soviet goods in the United States. Bogdanov held out hope nevertheless that those manufacturers, who wanted to increase foreign trade as a means of escaping the Depression, would eventually take the upper hand.[14] Skvirskii did his best in the Fish Committee to underline this point.

The Fish Committee made its report to the House in mid-January 1931 and recommended, *inter alia*, the tightening of immigration regulations to keep communists out of the country; banning the use of coded messages to governments not recognized by the United States; banning lumber imports in the case where the USSR did not allow onsite inspections by US officials for verification of the use of forced labour; and so on. This was not so bad, Bogdanov reported, as there was likely to be a battle in Congress over the actual implementation of the Fish Committee's recommendations.[15]

By the end of January, it looked to Skvirskii as though the Fish Committee had failed to obtain implementation of its main recommendations. There was considerable opposition from business circles that wanted to trade with the USSR. Congressman Fish, sensing that his anti-Soviet campaign was not producing the desired results, went looking for allies in the House. Fish was still pushing for a committee of inspectors to be sent to the USSR to investigate accusations of forced labour, knowing full well that the Soviet government would never approve such a proposal. This would then serve as a pretext for Fish to push for an embargo on Soviet goods. On the "political" side, Fish planned a series of bills to counter the "Red peril," including a demand for the deportation of Bogdanov and other Amtorg officials. Although curiously, as Skvirskii added, he was not one of them. One member of the Fish Committee had gone into a minority position finding the final report to be "hysterical." A lot of "serious people in Washington and in other places" were laughing at Fish and his colleagues. To add to its embarrassment, the Fish Committee had not succeeded in decrypting the Amtorg cables obtained from Western Union. All in all, Skvirskii concluded, Fish had not gotten very far with his agenda, prompting him to complain publicly about unfair treatment in certain sectors of the press. Skvirskii's assessment was confirmed by an influential American go-between, Ivy Ledbetter Lee, who told a Soviet diplomat in London that Fish's attempt to ban Soviet imports had failed, at least for the time being.[16]

The struggle in Washington continued. Fish and his allies pursued their agenda, which was resisted by Senator Borah, friendly journalists, and certain business elements. The battle swayed this way and that during 1931. Soviet objectives remained unchanged: gain access to cheaper, long-term credit and diplomatic recognition. In this regard, Bogdanov reported the views of an unidentified go-between who had seen President Hoover and concluded that no changes in American policy were likely in the near future. In American business circles, non-recognition was perceived to be the biggest obstacle to better trade relations.[17] Of course the "Black Hundreds," as Skvirskii called the AFL, and various other associations continued to lobby for a complete embargo on Soviet imports. The unfortunate French attempt to embargo Soviet imports thus appears to have entirely escaped the notice of these anti-Soviet groups. The New York Chamber of Commerce voted to support an embargo of all trade, imports and exports, with the USSR. In some ways, the heated debates about the USSR were an American tempest in a teapot. According to Skvirskii, Soviet imports to the United States were an insignificant percentage of its total imports from abroad while US exports to the Soviet Union represented only 16 per cent of total Soviet foreign imports. It was the absence of "normal relations" with the United States and debt claims against the USSR that blocked Soviet access to financial markets. The USSR could not even import gold, Skvirskii reported, because the assay offices would not accept it. Nor would most US banks discount Soviet bills of exchange or promissory notes – with some notable exceptions – because the Federal Reserve would not rediscount them. So Soviet business was a "big risk." The situation had only worsened after another stock market crash in mid-1931. Amtorg tried to establish new ties to other important New York banks, but without success. Because of the scarcity of bank credit, companies wanting Soviet business were obliged to offer credit themselves, but it was extremely dear, reaching as high as 53 per cent in some cases. The costs of doing business in the United States were thus exorbitant, in addition to the fact that the balance of trade was highly adverse. In spite of the relative insignificance of Soviet imports, ferocious agitation continued against them, caused by the gravity of the economic crisis, but exacerbated by the AFL and its sectorial business allies and by the "general position of Washington," which was encouraged and inspired by Congressman Fish and his friends.[18]

Stalin was informed of all these developments and intervened. "In view of exchange difficulties and the unacceptable terms of credit in America, I am against any new orders whatsoever in America." Current negotiations should be broken off, according to Stalin, and where possible previous orders, cancelled. Soviet business should be transferred to Europe, or to Soviet plants. "No exceptions."[19] The "Yankee Trader" had finally met his match.

The situation did not look promising, as the commissar for foreign trade, Arkadii Pavlovich Rozengol'ts, reported to the Politburo in September 1931. He had sharply reduced US orders. Bogdanov, back in the United States, confirmed the worsening situation, due especially to the deepening economic crisis. During the first nine months of 1931, more than a thousand US banks declared bankruptcy. Others were barely afloat. Gold was flowing out of the country. The mood in business circles was pessimistic. These circumstances simply added to the already considerable difficulties that Amtorg faced in obtaining credit. "Our friends" in banking circles, Bogdanov added, do not see any encouraging signs of opportunities to obtain better credit arrangements. Anti-Soviet hostility in Washington, especially from Hoover, continued as before, but in other places in political and business circles there were signs of change in the air. The USSR would have to continue to improve its relations with these elements to establish "normal trade relations." As the go-between Ivy Ledbetter Lee told Bogdanov, he had never seen in his life the banks in such difficult straits. Don't take bank refusals to provide credit, Lee said, as particularly directed against Amtorg. "No one is getting credit; no one is giving credit in this country."[20]

Friends and Foes

The news from the United States was not all bad. US diplomats were not discouraging trade with the USSR. Take the business if it's offered, seems to have been the message. Russia had stabilized for the time being, they were saying, and Soviet trade agencies respected their credit obligations; they were paying their bills.[21] In December 1931, a new session of Congress opened. "Again the 'friends' and 'foes' of the [Soviet] Union began to stir," as Skvirskii so nicely put it. "Friends" offered a resolution on diplomatic recognition of the USSR; "foes," a resolution for banning all Soviet imports into the United States. Congressman Fish introduced a resolution to fund, on an annual basis, investigations of "revolutionary propaganda and the activities of communists and other groups advocating the violent overthrow of the government of the United States." According to Skvirskii, there were fresh rumours circulating in the press that the USSR was on the brink of financial collapse and that the USSR could not pay its bills abroad. He thought it best to publish a statement denying such rumours.[22] The irony should not escape readers' notice: the United States and countries in Europe were on the brink of financial collapse, not the Soviet Union.

It was a very difficult period nevertheless for the USSR, both at home and abroad. At home, the Soviet government had to cope with unforeseen consequences of industrialization and forced collectivization of agricultural lands. Industrialization went at breakneck speed, so did collectivization, which met the determined resistance of large sectors of the peasantry. Peasants burned their grain, slaughtered their livestock, destroyed their machinery to keep it out of the hands of the Soviet collectivizers. It was a new civil war in the countryside, which led to widespread destruction, famine, deportations, and violence before peasant resistance was put down. At the same time, the Soviet international situation was precarious. Relations with France and the United States continued to be bad. Anti-communism and hatred of the USSR flourished, as indeed it did in Eastern Europe. "One continuous forest of hostility, Russophobia and Sovietphobia, in which there is no glimmer of light," was how the *polpred* in Helsingfors (Helsinki), Ivan Mikhailovich Maiskii, put it in a letter to a friend.[23]

Still, Litvinov seemed to be gaining respect in the West. He was a "smart guy," according to one American diplomat. Maiskii wrote to Litvinov in 1931 that his "personal authority" was growing. Stalin had approved the appointment of Litvinov as narkom in July 1930, though one wonders why, for "the boss" was quick to criticize him. Stalin's amanuensis, Kaganovich, secretary of the

Communist Party Central Committee, did not like Litvinov either and often attacked him. The narkom nevertheless stayed on the job, defying serial annual rumours that he would soon be sacked. By 1932, Stalin seemed to have come around, as much as he ever did. "Get Litvinov's opinion," Stalin told Kaganovich, when a question of foreign policy came up. It was the French and Romanian non-aggression pacts; important business for Stalin.[24] Did Kaganovich gulp? He might have.

Stalin as Businessman

Soviet-American relations continued to stumble along, at least that is the way it looked in January 1932. The Politburo monitored them closely, motivated by trade considerations based on information from Bogdanov and on recommendations from Rozengol'ts. When the New York National City Bank offered credit in exchange for a claims settlement, Stalin perked up. It was not the first time this bank had made offers.[25] When the terms were not good enough, Stalin proposed others, a low bid, completely unrealistic in view of the economic crisis in the United States. "We might consider a settlement with the bank," he said, "in exchange for a big loan.'"[26] Stalin haggled like a kulak when it came to business, but even a kulak would close the deal on acceptable terms. If he had really wanted a deal, it would have been better to let Litvinov, or Rozengol'ts handle it.

When American go-betweens came to Moscow looking for business, Stalin could be interested but also cynical. Even the most important arrivals got rough treatment. Take for example Colonel Hugh L. Cooper, a civil engineer who worked on the Dniepr dam, which was completed in 1932. For his role in the construction of the then largest dam in the world, Cooper received the "Order of the Red Banner of Labour." This order was no trinket; it was given by the Supreme Soviet for great services to the USSR. Cooper's a "big smart guy (*nakhal*)," Stalin wrote from Sochi (where he was on his annual holiday), "and spoilt by easy access to Soviet leaders." He wanted to meet with the Politburo, indicating that he represented important business circles in the United States. He doesn't appear to have concrete proposals, Stalin wrote: Cooper was just looking for new business for himself. "We shouldn't pamper him," Stalin instructed. "Nevertheless, we have to receive him politely, listen attentively, write down every word, reporting everything to the TsK."[27] It turned out that Cooper did have a proposal for Moscow, from General Motors: 100–200,000 used trucks and cars, with a guarantee that they would run for at least 150,000 kilometres, "fully equipped" with new tires, average price around $200 on ten years credit. Kaganovich and his colleagues in Moscow asked Stalin what he thought.[28]

"The deal on the used vehicles from General Motors is very suspicious," Stalin replied. "They can cheat and foist off the trash on us." Readers might laugh here, remembering jokes about used car salesmen and especially about poorly made American cars. At least they were not Fords. "Moreover, our middlemen have never distinguished themselves by conscientiousness and vigilance." And then the irrepressible Georgian kulak in Stalin emerged again: "Nevertheless we should try to buy not more than fifty thousand units, if the price is much lower, let's say, one hundred dollars, and not less than ten years credit. If the first deal gave good results, Stalin added, we could buy some more, of course with spare parts. We need mostly trucks, say forty-five thousand trucks, and five thousand cars."[29]

When another American arrived in Moscow to make proposals, Stalin sneered. This time it was Lester Barlow who proposed business to Bogdanov – the sale of blueprints for a bomb, which was sufficiently interesting for Amtorg to cover his expenses. Stalin was interested too, but the cynicism was irrepressible. "I would not advise," Stalin wrote from Sochi, "simply and 'politely' seeing Barlow out of Moscow. *All* [emphasis in the original] bourgeois foreign experts (*spetsy*) are or can be spies. But this still does not mean that we must 'politely' see him off. No, it does not mean that. I suggest: do not break off relations with Barlow, be attentive to him, toss him some money, take the blueprints, but don't show him our achievements (you can say that we are backward people and ready to learn from Barlow, of course, – of course! – for money)."[30] It was the same old Stalin modus operandi: cynicism and vulgarity in private and then the Georgian kulak's desire to conclude a deal if on favourable terms.

There was more to Barlow, by the way, than just blueprints for a bomb. He had ties with Franklin D. Roosevelt (FDR), a Democratic politician and the then governor of New York, who was running for the US presidency. When Barlow returned to the United States, FDR called him in to talk about his meetings in the USSR. According to Barlow, Roosevelt had said he would not make the "Russian question" a campaign issue, but if elected, he would "take measures to resolve it quickly."[31] It sometimes paid dividends to be "polite" with foreign *spetsy*.

The grim, dark relations of the previous two years now gave way to some glimpses of light ahead. Stalin was feeling more upbeat as he surveyed the world scene. In the Far East, the Japanese had occupied Manchuria the previous year, a development that raised anxieties in Washington. And developments in Germany were becoming more unstable and disquieting. The last Weimar government of Henrich Brüning fell at the end of May 1932. Franz von Papen, a rather nasty, Bolshevik-hating aristocrat took his place. Stalin saw these developments as positive in the sense that they would disquiet the US government, and, as he put it, make them more disposed "to look for ties with the USSR."[32] The numerous visits of bankers and businessmen to Moscow that summer encouraged him and his colleagues to think that a break might be coming. Kaganovich agreed with Stalin, as he usually did.

Ups and Downs

Ivy Ledbetter Lee, the American "journalist," was back in Moscow that same summer and had a long talk with Krestinskii. Two factors favoured a rapprochement, Lee said, the first was business. "American businessmen are more and more asking the question why all other governments have renewed normal relations with the USSR, and the United States can't do this." The second factor was Japan's conduct in the Far East. As in France, security threats were beginning to encourage pragmatism in the West when dealing with Moscow.

What about the "propaganda" issue? Krestinskii wanted to know. Where was the problem, with the governing elites or the broad masses?

"With the broad masses," Lee replied, "the AFL especially is working against you. Their leaders fear losing their influence and their cushy jobs/advantages after the renewal of American-Soviet relations." And then, said Lee, there was the Catholic Church, which had a lot of influence in the United States.

Krestinskii brought the conversation back to events in the Far East. Lee replied that most people in the United States were preoccupied with domestic issues. Maybe one hundred people are well informed and worried about events in the Far East. Lee considered himself one of the one hundred people. For example, say if the Japanese were to occupy Vladivostok, Lee proposed hypothetically, such a development would lead the United States to enter into closer relations with the USSR.

Would it take the Japanese occupation of Vladivostok to activate Soviet-American relations? Krestinskii asked, rather surprised. What would happen if the Japanese attacked the US Pacific fleet, would the US look to the USSR?

Lee could not say. He reckoned, nevertheless, that war in the Far East would lead to "a gradual reorientation of American public opinion in favour of the USSR." Anyway, he added, "business circles in the United States don't fear communist propaganda, and in these business circles is a growing desire to work with the USSR and to normalize relations with the Soviet Union."

"In foreign political relations," Krestinskii replied, "we need restraint and patience. And we remain patient waiting while the question of normalization of relations ripens."

"This waiting," Lee said in so many words, might pay off in the end.[33]

The issue of "propaganda" was more sensitive than Lee made out, though it may have been that US businesses were not going to let it interfere with Soviet contracts. Colonel Cooper had also been making the rounds in New York. He had a different message about "propaganda," though it appears to have been motivated by personal irritation with Moscow. "Take me, for example," he said to an Amtorg clerk in Moscow, "a person who has worked tirelessly for the last five years on the business of recognition. It costs me at least twelve thousand a year since I keep two people who specially take care of the recognition file.

Nevertheless, the Russian government does not pay me for this, and I would refuse payment, even if it proposed to do so. And even so, all my work is for nothing."[34] Clearly, Cooper was irritated that he was *not* paid for this work, though he was for his work on the Dniepr dam.

Black and White

Cooper went on to complain about "those Negroes who you ordered from here for the production of an anti-American film, depicting the persecution of Negroes in America. Do you know who these Negroes are?" The Russian word used by his Soviet interlocutor was *negry*, but it might not have been the word which Cooper used. "They are quite often rapists, who violate American white women, and we for this beat them, lynch them and will lynch them." It is true, Cooper admitted, that there are fewer examples of Negro rape, but this is because they fear what will happen to them afterward. And you solicit here "these beasts" to make a film depicting "the persecution of Negroes in America."

Cooper was talking about the film project entitled *Black and White*, which was intended to depict racism and labour conflicts in Montgomery, Alabama, in Jim Crow America. Twenty-one Black Americans, including the poet Langston Hughes, were invited to Moscow to participate in the project.

"This is outrageous," Cooper opined. "And I am not saying this confidentially, but completely openly, and you can circulate it." Imagine, he went on, if "the American people" hired a couple of dozen kulaks and made a film about Soviet persecution of them. "How would you like it?"[35]

Cooper's Soviet interlocutor responded calmly that there was nothing particularly "frightful" about the arrival of American "Negroes" in Moscow. "Our country," he added, "is not driven by racism or other such prejudices." The Amtorg clerk then asked if Cooper had spoken to Molotov about his complaint.

"I didn't think it necessary," Cooper replied, "to speak about such matters to the head of government, who is not clever enough to know himself about the undesirability of such a venture. I am simply amazed by the juxtaposition of these bosses' geniality with their unspeakable stupidity. They don't understand anything about what is going on in America. They don't know that such a venture will without a doubt arouse the American people against the idea of recognition and all the past work until now will have been in vain."

"Are you for or against Negroes?" Cooper then asked.

"I am not against them in any way," the Amtorg agent responded.

"That means you are for Negroes," Cooper retorted: "If that is the case, then it will be impossible for you to interact with Americans. In any way. When I get to New York, I will explain all of this, and you will be isolated from any relations with Americans. You get out of here."

The Amtorg agent added a postscript: "He showed me out of the room in front of his interpreter, a Russian citizen, whose surname I don't know."[36] Obviously, Cooper was bullying a junior Amtorg official. Had he spoken like that to Molotov, it would have been Molotov who showed Cooper the door, escorted to the frontier by OGPU policemen. Stalin's cynicism would seem to have been justified. Cooper's flagrant racism is a reminder of how it was for "Negroes" in Jim Crow America.

Nor did American complaints about *Black and White* stop with Cooper. The State Department brought up the subject with Frederick Pope, another American engineer and businessman working in the USSR. He was the president of the Nitrogen Engineering Corporation and was in Washington in October to see State Department officials. Pope was in Moscow in the June 1932 where he had been wined and dined by Soviet officials. He had said that the US government would be prepared to send an unofficial representative to Moscow, if Comintern propaganda stopped. The Politburo approved a message saying simply that the Soviet government would receive such a representative on the basis of reciprocity. No mention was made of propaganda.[37]

Nothing came of this June exchange. But propaganda returned to the agenda when Pope was back to see Kelley in October. In a belligerent mood, Kelley brought up the "Negro film which the Bolsheviks were going to stage in Moscow." He instanced this film as an example of Soviet interference in US domestic affairs, and he then commenced a long monologue about the Comintern and the American Communist Party. The latter could not function a single day on its own resources. "There can be no question of recognition," Kelley said, "until such time as … they [the Bolsheviks] stop propaganda in the USA."[38]

The Secretary of State Henry Stimson also talked with Pope about "the Negro film." "What induced the Bolsheviks to invite these Negroes for the making of a Negro film?" Stimson wanted to know. "Who are they, these Negroes? Not one of them was ever in a Negro district; not one of them is a real Negro and knows Negro problems. They are night club habitués, bribe takers and degenerates. The fact of the making of this film shows how much one can invest in the promises of the Bolsheviks not to interfere in our affairs." Stimson then repeated Kelley's statement that there would be no recognition until the "propaganda" stopped.

Pope was no Cooper, for he asked Stimson, if he, Pope, should return to Moscow to tell the Bolsheviks how they should run their party? This sounded like a question trying to corner Stimson who refused to be baited. No, he replied in so many words, let them worry about their own affairs.

Pope concluded that Stimson, Kelley, and others were less well-disposed than they had been earlier in the summer. Nevertheless, Pope also had some good news for Amtorg agent, G.I. Andreichin. "I had a meeting with Roosevelt, who I have known since 1902 when he was in the law firm 'Roosevelt and Marvin'. Marvin is my old college friend and my cousin Robert Pope is also a close friend of Roosevelt. There are nothing like family and business ties to grease the wheels of progress. Learning of my return from the USSR, Roosevelt wrote to me and invited me to Albany." They were together for the entire day, Pope went on to say, and that Roosevelt was "very sympathetic to the USSR." He considered trade discrimination against Soviet goods to be "scandalous." He knew these laws were made by Democrats, Roosevelt said, but he intend to change them. That would be his first order of business regarding Russia. Obviously, Roosevelt expected to win the coming elections. Pope concluded that more Soviet-American trade would improve the situation.[39]

Litvinov, who hated Western go-betweens, was sceptical of Pope's activities. "I personally think that we should not organise meetings for Pope either before or after 10 November [US election day]. He is sufficiently exposed already as Khlestakov [the self-important Gogol character], trying with our help to create publicity for himself in the United States without any advantage for us. His conversations … bring more harm than good. I do not recommend by any means pushing Pope away, but, having listened to his stories, we should not give him any encouragement and information nor arrange any meetings for him."[40] That was Litvinov's opinion, but not the Politburo's, which authorized meetings, hospitality, and a message for Pope to pass on to Washington. Whenever Litvinov spoke of his "personal" opinion, it meant *his* opinion, not Politburo policy.

One has to wonder whether *Black and White* and Cooper's racist rants set back the campaign for recognition. Racism was not limited to Cooper; Stimson's characterization of the Black Americans who went to Moscow as lounge lizards and "degenerates" was as bad as Cooper's of "Negro" rapists of white women who merited lynching. Readers may suspect that another word exited easily from Cooper's mouth. Cooper was born in Minnesota, and Stimson was born in New York City. They were not Southern crackers. But that was America of the 1930s. Racism was everywhere. After Cooper returned to the United States in late autumn, he went to see Bogdanov. There he talked again about the "Negro film," though without the same racist vulgarity he had used in Moscow. He told Bogdanov that he had appealed to Molotov to stop the film, but when no satisfactory reply was forthcoming, he had issued an ultimatum. Either the production of the film would stop or Cooper would leave the Soviet Union and abandon further work there. Authorities then promised to comply, Cooper told Bogdanov, and he considered the matter closed. Apparently, Soviet officials did not, for he was cold shouldered afterward while he remained in Moscow. Soviet authorities had offered another general contract to Cooper, but he demanded twice the money they offered, and he would not discuss lowering his price. As a result, Gosplan, the Soviet planning agency, broke off discussions.[41] Cooper had blotted his escutcheon.

President Roosevelt and the Clean Slate

On 10 November 1932, Roosevelt was elected president. According to Bogdanov, Roosevelt's election meant a fresh start. Although he had not said anything about the Soviet Union during the election campaign, Roosevelt's private conversations with various people, which had got back to Bogdanov, suggested that the new government would re-examine the "question of the Soviet Union." Since Roosevelt had campaigned on economic issues, the first matter to be raised would probably be Soviet-American trade and how it might profit US interests. Roosevelt was not Hoover, Bogdanov observed. He was a person of broader horizons, without Hoover's hatred of the USSR. That was true.

There was a lot of speculation about what would happen next, and the usual issues came up: debts, "propaganda," Japan, China, insecurity in the Far East. American journalists in Europe were free with their advice to Soviet diplomats. "Roosevelt has said neither yes nor no," opined one newsman in Warsaw. "He is free." The Soviet government should give him a helping hand for he was under pressure from "reactionary elements." There had been a definite swing towards the USSR, even before Roosevelt took office, opined another American journalist in London. The Department of Defense was favourable to the resumption of diplomatic relations, not so much the Department of State. It was anyone's guess what Roosevelt would do, but one thing was for certain, he would not pursue Hoover's anti-Soviet line. He had no personal animus towards the USSR, but no definite policy either. On the "Russian question," Roosevelt was like a "clean slate." The next few months would tell.[42]

We can expect a change in policy, Skvirskii reported from Washington. The only question was whether the new administration would be able to assess correctly the overblown opposition to recognition, and disregarding it, determine a new policy without intermediaries or delays.[43] Intermediaries were quick to appear in New York. One was Senator Robert LaFollette Jr., a progressive Republican, who proposed informal talks. Roosevelt, he said, did not want any premature publicity about Soviet-American relations. Litvinov immediately shut down this channel, being against any negotiations on prior conditions for recognition.[44]

Two other familiar faces also turned up, those of Cooper and Pope. Cooper actually met with Roosevelt, as well as with State Department officials in April 1933. President Roosevelt considered "desirable" normal Soviet-American relations "not only in the interests of both countries, but also for the establishment of international peace." For the moment, however, important domestic opposition to recognition prevented action. Cooper presumed to give advice to Bogdanov, and Litvinov once again reacted quickly. It was not clear to Litvinov what if any proposals Cooper was making. So he advised Skvirskii about what the Soviet government would do and not do. It would enter into direct discussions with the US government in one form or another, but not through the intermediary of Cooper who could propose his own ideas rather than those of Roosevelt or even the USSR. Skvirskii was to inform Bogdanov at once, Litvinov directed, so that there would be no confusion.[45]

Pope too had some wacky ideas in spite of having met directly with Roosevelt and with the new Secretary of State, Cordell Hull. One such idea was that the Soviet Union would agree to take any person convicted in the United States of being a communist. This would be a good preliminary step to ease the way to recognition. Valerii Ivanovich Mezhlauk, the deputy director of Gosplan, and Pope's interlocutor, must have tried hard not to laugh. It's an "unusually amusing and completely unrealistic" idea, Mezhlauk told Pope; it will never work. It was Cooper's idea, replied Pope, as if to exonerate himself.[46]

The manoeuvring, lobbying, and vying for the attention of public opinion continued through the summer of 1933. In August, Bogdanov reported that Roosevelt was promoting trade relations with the USSR independently from any timetable for diplomatic recognition. Trade relations were a "political trump," even credits for trade were being contemplated. The USSR needed to get the idea into the press, Bogdanov concluded, that trade relations could not develop without the establishment of "normal diplomatic relations."

The Dam Breaks

The dam broke three months later. The "final battle" against recognition was taking place, Skvirskii reported in early October. In business circles and in the press, there was much talk about recognition. The American Legion renewed its opposition. Mathew Woll of the AFL, the long-time oppositionist to recognition, published an open letter to Roosevelt. The New York Chamber of Commerce, notorious "professional" oppositionists and backers of the Fish Committee, returned to the charge. It was the final paroxysm of fury against recognition. Skvirskii reported that oppositionists were not the only ones speaking out. The AFL leadership, closer to the Roosevelt administration, muted its previous opposition contrary to Woll's position. Business circles wanted contracts in the USSR and the American-Russian Chamber of Commerce was campaigning for recognition.[47]

Four days after sending his report to Moscow, Svirskii followed up with an urgent cable. He reported having met with officials Morgenthau Jr. and Bullitt, on Roosevelt's instructions. Henry Morgenthau Jr. was a close, long-time associate of Roosevelt and soon to be Secretary of the Treasury, and William C. Bullitt had worked for US president Woodrow Wilson at the Paris Peace Conference and gone to Moscow to negotiate with the Bolsheviks. Now he worked for Roosevelt. "In a few hours," Skvirskii wrote, "I will send you the translation of a draft letter from Roosevelt to [Soviet president Mikhail Ivanovich]

Kalinin proposing the naming of a representative to discuss personally with the American president the question of American-Soviet relations."[48] Skvirskii sent other cables with more detailed information on what was afoot. If Roosevelt's draft was acceptable to the Soviet side, he would sign it for delivery to Kalinin. Skvirskii pointed out to Bullitt that the letter proposed, in effect, preliminary discussions, which the Soviet government on principle always opposed. The letter meant "much more," Bullitt replied, it's an official letter signed by Roosevelt inviting the Soviet government to send representatives for "personal discussions" with the president.

"I of course agreed to complete secrecy," Skvirskii reported, "and to the forwarding of the text of the letter to Moscow … I would recommend the sending of Litvinov for discussions with Roosevelt. It would strengthen our position." Skvirskii asked for an urgent reply.[49]

Molotov and Kaganovich signed a telegram to Stalin, who was on holidays in Abkhaziia, forwarding Skvirskii's cables and Roosevelt's draft. They recommended sticking to standard Soviet policy, that is, no preliminary negotiations before formal recognition and rejecting the draft. Instead they proposed a formulation used before with the British in 1929 on prior procedural discussions.[50]

Stalin did not agree. "We think that it is necessary to agree to Roosevelt's letter and then upon receipt of his official letter to Kalinin, answer that we are sending our people for discussions with Roosevelt. It will be best to send Litvinov."[51]

Litvinov, he said. Times had changed. Stalin was not sneering now at his narkom for foreign affairs. When Litvinov replied that it was inexpedient for him to go to Washington and that someone else should go in his place, Stalin demurred. "We insist on the dispatch of Litvinov. Act boldly without delay for now the situation is favourable."[52]

On 14 October, the Politburo approved the Roosevelt draft. Bullitt asked to see the Soviet draft reply and suggested some minor revisions accepted in Moscow. "Hurry up with the response to Roosevelt," Stalin cabled from the south.[53] When he said hurry, he meant hurry, and things moved quickly. On 17 October, the Politburo formally approved a Soviet reply and named Litvinov to go to Washington for talks with Roosevelt.[54] A last-minute, minor word change was made to the text in Washington by Skvirskii after talking to Bullitt. Roosevelt wanted to publish the letters first in the American press. The exchange of letters was published in the Soviet and American papers a few days later. Some news agencies in the United States jumped the gun on the specified time of publication, though they quickly denied breaking the embargo.[55] It was only a tempest in a teapot, smoothed over by the enormity of the breakthrough for Soviet diplomacy.

Litvinov proposed guidelines for the negotiations, which Stalin approved. The big issues had not changed: debt claims, propaganda, trade opportunities.

Maybe religious issues, Litvinov added. Some questions were going to be difficult to resolve like a debts settlement and should not be linked to formal recognition. And what if Roosevelt wanted to talk about Japan? Kaganovich and Molotov recommended sticking to generalities, but Stalin did not agree. "I think," he wrote, "that Litvinov should not avoid concrete discussions about relations with Japan. I think that if, in discussions with Litvinov, Roosevelt will seek some kind of rapprochement with us or even a provisional rapprochement against Japan, Litvinov must respond to it favourably." If Roosevelt wanted to deal, Stalin was ready to accommodate him. Politburo approval was quickly forthcoming.[56]

Litvinov Goes to Washington

One wonders what Litvinov was thinking as he set out for Washington. On 7 November, he met Roosevelt for the first time. Mrs. Eleanor Roosevelt was present and so was the Secretary of State, Cordell Hull. Was Hull the State Department's minder? FDR was charming, it seems, trying to put Litvinov at his ease. There was a lunch, said Litvinov, and afterward Roosevelt went over all the issues with him. "There won't be difficulties here," Roosevelt said, "since we speak the same language, although I've been warned that you apparently are the one diplomat in the world who gets everything you want." The flattery must have put Litvinov on his guard. But Roosevelt continued, mentioning *Mein Kampf*, Hitler's published blueprint for conquest. This was a sure way to get Litvinov's attention, and he reported it in his telegram to Moscow. As we shall see, Litvinov often raised *Mein Kampf* with foreign diplomats, Germans included, when he wanted to discuss the potential danger of Nazi Germany.

"I notice," Roosevelt said, "that in the English translation the most offensive sections of Hitler's book have disappeared ... No doubt the Germans themselves were responsible for this." Litvinov did not record his reply, if he made one. He must have been on his guard. "Bullitt said to me," Litvinov noted, "that he hopes for a successful outcome of the negotiations, though in a very uncertain tone."[57]

Next day Litvinov met Hull in the morning. The issue which Litvinov thought *might* come up, religion, was the first on Hull's list. There was no further mention of *Mein Kampf*. Hull advised Litvinov not to be fooled by press opinion in favour of recognition, for Litvinov did not know about the numerous appeals received by the government against it. Hull pointed out that the president was in a difficult position, and had to be mindful of future elections and could not ignore an important part of the electorate. Right or not, American opinion had the impression that religion in the USSR was persecuted. Hull wanted to know what guarantees the Soviet government could offer. Such matters, Litvinov responded, were a domestic affair, though stories of religious persecution were "one-sided propaganda, disinformation, and slander." Not exactly an honest reply, for Litvinov himself had written to Stalin in the past, urging him to rein in the OGPU. It made for bad publicity abroad.[58] "After a long argument," Litvinov reported, Hull laid out his bottom line, a guarantee for Americans to practise religion freely in the USSR. If there was no guarantee, he added, the establishment of relations would be "impossible." Litvinov repeated that everyone in the USSR, citizens and foreign nationals alike, had the right to practise their religion – which he knew not to be true – but came to his main point that the Soviet government would not accord special privileges to foreigners.

Hull then moved on to the question of the right of American citizens living in Russia in case of arrest. Would they have the right to counsel and bail? Litvinov replied that everyone was treated equally and that the Soviet government would not accord special privileges to foreigners. And then, finally, at the end of their discussion, the issue of financial claims and "propaganda" came up. Litvinov did not go into much detail about these issues, though he was well practised in responding to them.[59]

Apparently Litvinov and Hull also discussed security issues for the subject came up again at a meeting later that morning with Roosevelt. Litvinov had referred to "two sources of military danger" without naming any particular culprits. Hull had apparently briefed the president, because as Litvinov put it, Roosevelt didn't mind being less subtle; he "decrypted" my statement to mean Japan and Germany. We face the same danger, Roosevelt repeated, and "together … we might be able to counter these dangers." After lunch, Roosevelt politely thanked his guests for coming, but asked Hull to stay. Litvinov reported that he and Hull both explained what they had discussed that morning. FDR defended Hull and repeated that he faced pressures from all sides, notably the Catholic Church and evangelicals. Litvinov had little patience with Catholics, as readers will know. From the way Litvinov reported Roosevelt's comments, the president did not either, but he had to contend with them "pouring out their tears" and making trouble in Congress. The president agreed that the United States could not interfere in Soviet internal affairs, and that the American intervention in northern Russia could not be justified. Confidentially, Roosevelt complained about the British. They and the French had profited from the war and therefore could pay their war debts, whereas the USSR had come out of the war with nothing, besides ruin. Roosevelt urged Litvinov to try to come to an agreement on a formula that would satisfy the opponents of Soviet recognition. A formula on the Comintern was also necessary for the same reason. Roosevelt recognized that the Soviet government could not simply expel the Comintern from the Soviet Union, but he thought sending it to Geneva to keep company with the League of Nations would be the best solution. All these questions were insignificant, Litvinov responded, compared to the international importance of Soviet-American cooperation. Roosevelt recognized the "importance of the question," which could "possibly [mean] the difference between war and peace for fifty years."[60]

Hull and Litvinov met again that afternoon. They talked about financial claims, but then Hull "again unexpectedly returned to the question of religion." He "suddenly" handed Litvinov a written text on the subject, which enumerated the rights that the United States guaranteed. "I am not asking from America any religious guarantees," Litvinov replied. There then ensued a half-hour argument on this question, which led nowhere. Litvinov reluctantly concluded that some kind of minimal written reply to Hull should be contemplated, stating that existing Soviet laws would give Americans in the USSR the right to practise their religious beliefs. If we do not offer this minimal gesture, Litvinov reported, "it will be difficult to continue negotiations." The narkom also expected a demand that US consuls be informed of the arrest of American citizens, and suggested using the same formula established with Germany. "I ask for an immediate reply on these two questions," Litvinov telegraphed to Moscow. "The dragging out of negotiations will have a harmful impact on them." He also suggested dropping claims for the US intervention in the Far East in exchange for the US dropping claims for the tsarist debts. This would offer some satisfaction to Roosevelt and permit discussion of remaining financial claims after formal recognition.[61]

There was yet another discussion on the following day with Hull, going over the same issues and some new ones. Hull seemed ready to accept Litvinov's proposal on the religious question, but on other issues there were some prickly exchanges. "The session ended," Litvinov noted, "with the recognition of disagreement on all issues." Bullitt, who had been present at the meeting, "characterized the situation as hopeless." Litvinov advised that there would be further meetings on the following day, one with Hull and Roosevelt. In the meantime Stalin, without any sneering, agreed to Litvinov's proposals for compromise.[62]

Litvinov reported yet another meeting with Roosevelt, Hull, Bullitt, and William Phillips, Under Secretary of State. Roosevelt indicated that he would like to move to bigger questions, but before that was possible, he had to quiet down the opposition to recognition. So, for example, he needed to be able to assure public opinion that Americans in Russia would have special rights to practise their religion. There must also be guarantees against propaganda. Nor could the debts question be left open. Roosevelt handed Litvinov some written proposals and advised him to look them over and consult Moscow if he needed to. Then they could discuss them, eye to eye, without formality, in order to be able to cuss each other a little (*porugat'sia nemnogo*). Litvinov responded that he had not come to Washington to settle every question but to lay the ground work to discuss them on the basis of equality and without pressure, that is, after the establishment of diplomatic relations. He was ready to discuss the big issues, which Roosevelt had already noted and before which the questions thus far debated paled in comparison. In fact, Litvinov had Stalin's approval for a rapprochement based on cooperation against Japan. Litvinov passed over the various outstanding questions again, and he wanted to put off the complicated financial issues not thinking an agreement possible. He also reminded Roosevelt that the Soviet Union would not admit special privileges, or "capitulations," for American citizens. The Soviet leadership had refused this kind of proposition ten years ago, and would not accept it now when the USSR was much stronger. That was out. The discussion went on without resolution. "My impression," Litvinov reported, "is that Roosevelt bought the silence of hostile organizations with imprudent promises about religion and propaganda, and that in this lays the root of the encountered difficulties."[63]

Litvinov forwarded to Moscow Roosevelt's drafts, which Stalin rejected. No further concessions on religion or propaganda were to be made. Stalin then went into details of a Soviet program of orders in the United States if credit on acceptable terms were offered. On 11 November, there was another three-hour long meeting with Roosevelt and Bullitt, in which religion and propaganda dominated discussions. But Roosevelt also handed to Litvinov a list of eleven other issues that he wanted to resolve. Among these was recognition of the so-called Kerenskii debt, the loans made by the United States to the Russian Provisional Government which was headed briefly by A.F. Kerenskii in 1917. Litvinov seemed discouraged. "Obviously Roosevelt and the State Department were exaggerating their disinterest in recognition and the consequences of the failure of my mission and will be obstinate until the end. The question, however, is do they have enough sense … not to cut off a path of retreat, in order to give way at the last moment? I am having lunch alone with Bullitt today," Litvinov advised, "I have already warned him of the possibility of a rupture of negotiations."[64]

On Roosevelt's eleven points, Litvinov reported that he did not think Moscow could reject them all. And he indicated where ground could be given. He asked for instructions on where further concessions, if any, might be made. "I have informed Bullitt," Litvinov advised, "that I reject almost all the new proposals and that if Roosevelt insists on them, I can take my leave, not even asking Moscow." So two could threaten a rupture of negotiations, if the other demanded too much. Litvinov reported that he might have gotten Bullitt's attention and Bullitt promised to discuss the points of contention with Roosevelt before their next meeting. On other issues, Bullitt smiled at Litvinov's proposal to swap claims for damages from the Far Eastern intervention in exchange for the Kerenskii debt, but Bullitt promised to try to get the debt reduced to "a symbolic figure" in exchange for the dropping of Soviet damage claims against the US intervention in northern Russia. Roosevelt himself had spoken to Litvinov about reducing the debt "to the minimum."[65]

Stalin again rejected any special rights for American citizens in the USSR, but he suggested some ideas for concessions to Roosevelt on points where fundamental Soviet principles were not put into question. There was no sneering, nor any unrealistic counteroffers. It was just business; it was just trying to come to terms with Roosevelt.[66] The discussions in Washington passed directly into Roosevelt's hands. Hull was out. Soviet-American disagreements were being leaked to the press, Litvinov reported: "The cardinal point is the question of claims." Religious and legal rights seemed to be settled more or less based on already existing agreements with other countries or existing Soviet laws. Litvinov preferred to delay any immediate decision on mutual claims and pass off the dossier to financial experts. This was an old Soviet strategy to delay decisions until the Greek calends. Roosevelt wanted an immediate settlement. "I have little hope for an agreement," Litvinov cabled Moscow.[67]

Bullitt and Roosevelt remained insistent and Litvinov cabled again for instructions. There was another two-hour meeting with Roosevelt and Bullitt on the various issues. Now it was Bullitt who threatened to break off negotiations. "I turned a deaf ear," Litvinov noted in his report of the meeting. Roosevelt "argued hotly," according to Litvinov, for a debts settlement. It must have been a stormy meeting, a real merchants' quarrel, as Roosevelt had anticipated. The president proposed a reduced, global sum to settle all claims. Obviously, they were exaggerated, he admitted. They started talking real money. Bullitt proposed that a sum of around $150 million could discharge the Kerenskii debt in order to avoid creating precedents, another Soviet preoccupation. Litvinov tried to stall. There were "constitutional restraints." Roosevelt felt this could be settled in a few days, and of course Litvinov should write to Moscow for instructions. The quid pro quo was also discussed. The United States had frozen assets in Germany, debts owed by the German government. The idea was that these could be passed on to the USSR at no additional cost to the US Department of the Treasury. Litvinov began to show some interest, but he still recommended delay. "Although the present moment would indeed permit us to escape from all American claims for the negligible sum of $100 million, and to receive some loans on profitable terms, I suggest not agreeing on negotiations now and promising to begin them soon after the exchange of ambassadors. The question is complicated and will require considerable time." But Litvinov hesitated a little. In the event of a risk of the breakdown of negotiations, we (in Washington) could agree to discussions of claims but only for a few days. "I think that if we agree on recognition of the Kerenskii debt, then Roosevelt will not insist on immediate negotiations, but I will only do this as a last resort." Litvinov telegraphed Moscow for immediate instructions. Was a deal possible after all? "Roosevelt again mentioned that he wanted to discuss with me the big problems and about peace, and also about private subjects, but he did not fix a meeting. Obviously, he wants first to get disagreements out of the way."[68]

The Politburo ordered the creation of a subcommittee composed of Stalin, Molotov, Kaganovich, and Krestinskii to resolve "all the questions" related to the negotiations in Washington. In two telegrams, Stalin approved all of Litvinov's recommendations and gave him authority to come to terms with Roosevelt "on all questions" based on those recommendations. Don't forget, Stalin wrote, that a Soviet agreement to pay on the Kerenskii debt is conditional on an American cash loan. "In our telegrams we are giving you the possibility to manoeuvre. It depends on your skills (*iskusstva*), to give to the Americans the minimum and not to sell cheaply."[69] Now there was the Georgian *kulak* talking, but showing confidence in Litvinov to pull off a deal at the lowest possible cost to the Soviet treasury.

Here was an opportunity to close a deal with the United States. It was always the "red thread" of Soviet policy to get on good terms with Washington. Could Litvinov pull it off without demanding too much and offering too little, as was Stalin's habit? Litvinov reported another meeting with Bullitt. It was 13 November. The negotiations had been going on for a week now. There were still differences on religious and legal rights and on propaganda. Litvinov advised that he was giving little ground on differences. Litvinov was going to have to make some concessions on debt claims. He wrote: "Bullitt explained Roosevelt's position thus, that after the failure to resolve debts issues with other countries he wants to achieve this even if with us, even at the price of big concessions. Besides that, Roosevelt wants himself to take care of these questions, but this he can do only with me, since he cannot so often receive ambassadors and other delegates, as he does me, and will have to pass the file to the State Department or the Treasury." Bullitt appeared to be in good spirits, as he thought a deal could be done. He "half-joked," said Litvinov, that as part of the deal to clear US claims, the Soviet government could not only build but also decorate a new US embassy in Moscow. Litvinov was almost as tight fisted as Stalin and did not comment on Bullitt's "joke."[70]

Stalin responded quickly to Litvinov's latest telegram. He gave a little more ground on religious rights. On the rights of arrested US citizens, he offered most favoured nation, in effect the same consular rights offered to German citizens. "On propaganda, you can offer anything already conceded in previous agreements," Stalin underlined, "but do not offer larger concessions."[71]

On 14 November, Litvinov again saw Bullitt. It was day eight of the negotiations. "Litvinov and I continued to argue for two hours on the subject of debts and claims," Bullitt reported. "I finally managed to shake him a bit by telling him that the Johnson Bill, forbidding loans to countries in default on their indebtedness to the … United States, was certain to be passed in January and that if the Soviet Government should make any absurd offer of settlement such an offer would surely be turned down by Congress and the Soviet Government would be unable to obtain one penny of credit."[72] That was the Yankee trader for you, hard bargaining, but Litvinov could handle it. He was a Bolshevik. Roosevelt was busy all that day, but would see Litvinov on the morrow. Bullitt again stressed Roosevelt's desire to close a deal. The president was leaving Washington for therapy for his polio in Warm Springs, Georgia. He invited Litvinov to go with him to settle the deal. Roosevelt would have more time for discussions than he had in Washington. Litvinov responded that he could do so only after the formal renewal of diplomatic relations. Bullitt raised the subject of a loan in connection with the recognition of the Kerenskii debt, again referring to frozen US "credits" in Germany. Litvinov seemed open to this idea, and asked Stalin for further instructions.[73]

On 15 November, Litvinov saw Roosevelt again. It was day nine of the negotiations. "I just now shook hands with Roosevelt," Litvinov cabled Moscow, "to mark agreement in order tomorrow to prepare all documents and sign them on Friday."[74] "We were a bit too gentle with him this morning," Bullitt later commented to FDR.[75] The clerks were always out for a tougher deal. After nine days of hard bargaining, they had got an agreement, but even after FDR's handshake, Litvinov had his doubts. "I am not at all confident that, before the signing, new unexpected difficulties will not arise or that at the insistence of his colleagues Roosevelt does not try to change points of the agreement." This comment was redolent of Dovgalevskii's observation about the difficulty of obtaining an agreement with the French even in the presence of stenographers. Roosevelt was not that bad, Litvinov might have mused. I suggest complete secrecy, he cabled to Stalin, until receipt of the telegrams confirming the signature of the agreement. Then Litvinov summarized the settling of the difficult issues. He started off with debts. "I will not make any announcement on recognition of any debts whatsoever. The press will say that there was an exchange of opinions on ways to resolve questions of claims and counterclaims that permit hope of rapid resolution of these issues." Litvinov would remain in Washington for some little time after the signing of the agreement to try to come to a final agreement with Bullitt and Morgenthau to extinguish mutual claims in exchange for recognition of the Kerenskii debt or some other name the final sums to be paid through additional interest on an American loan. "I gave, however, my gentleman's word that I will undertake to convince my government to propose not less than $75 million with a maximum American demand of $150 million, though about my promise Roosevelt will publicly say nothing." The difference between these two limits, interest rates, amount, and length of loan was to be the subject of his negotiations with Bullitt and Morgenthau. Litvinov then passed over the other issues resolved along the lines he had explained to Stalin and had proposed to Roosevelt.

Litvinov concluded his report with a warning: "I suggest that judging from the circumstances and course of negotiations that we should anticipate the possibility of new difficulties. The negotiations were extremely tough and I did not even inform you of the various demands which I succeeded in liquidating immediately." He mentioned, as an example, the continuation of the recognition of Armenian independence. Roosevelt joked that when he reported to Congress on this question he would say, "I plugged my ears and refused even to listen."[76]

In the meantime Stalin sent further instructions on the debt-loan negotiations, suggesting sums, interest rates, and payment schedules. The interest rates were on the low side, but not completely unreasonable. On the amount of the debt to be paid, Stalin offered no suggestions. This cable crossed with Litvinov's announcing the handshake with Roosevelt, and another going into more detail about negotiations. Litvinov asked for detailed instructions on the upcoming debt-loan negotiations. Congress would consider a bill in January, Litvinov advised, which would refuse credit to any country that had not settled its debts with the United States. After the passing of this bill, the United States would not be able to offer credit to the USSR before settlement of American claims. The agreement concluded in Washington would then become impossible to carry out. That was why Roosevelt was in a hurry to close a deal in order to seek approval in early January. Roosevelt anticipated considerable opposition, but reckoned that the agreement would pass if the Soviet government accepted to pay $150 million. Litvinov reckoned that he would have to raise the Soviet offer to $100 million during negotiations, for which, Litvinov added, "I have your authorization." There was more talk of pulling foreign exchange out of the frozen German credits, though Stalin was sceptical about this idea.[77]

Litvinov wrote a number of telegrams on 15 November, the last one offered more details on the final negotiations with Roosevelt. It was only at the last minute of the second and last session of the day that Roosevelt finally agreed "very reluctantly" to the agreement with the debts-loan negotiations still unsettled. "He proved to be a wiry (*zhilistyi*) person, the newspapers incited him, lending to his negotiations with me a sporting character, which someone wins (*kto kogo*)."[78]

On 16 November, day ten of the negotiations, problems came up. "As I expected," Litvinov reported, "Bullitt brought today the documents corrected by Roosevelt, somewhat changing and broadening the agreement." It was not only the French, then, who attempted such manoeuvres with Soviet diplomats. FDR tried to slip into the text all his desiderata on religious rights to which Litvinov had agreed. More importantly, he also tried to increase the debt to be discharged by the Soviet government to $150 million. In what Litvinov called their "gentleman's agreement," which was *not* to be publicized, he had agreed to a sum of no less than $75 million. Roosevelt considered that $75 million would never pass the Congress, and therefore that Litvinov should "plead" in Moscow for $100 million. "In this way he gave to understand that he also agreed to $100 million, whereas yesterday he said that he cannot propose to Congress less than $150 million." Litvinov had been negotiating with the Western powers since 1918 and had given as good as he had got on many occasions. But, even though on guard, he was not pleased by FDR's attempted legerdemain. "I indignantly rejected these new demands," Litvinov reported to Moscow. "Bullitt went to report to the president. Tomorrow Roosevelt is leaving, and if [I] have to choose between my chasing after him on his cure and immediately signing even if with some concessions, I will choose the latter, in as much as the concessions keep within your instructions. I am seeing Roosevelt at 22h00 local time."[79]

That evening Litvinov got Roosevelt to back up a little on some points. On the big issue of Soviet indebtedness, Litvinov promised to make the case for $100 million though without any commitment on the part of the Soviet government. In fact, Roosevelt would not accept less, he noted, and we will not agree to more. Litvinov reckoned that in the end the agreement was favourable to Soviet interests. He met Roosevelt again on Friday, day eleven of the negotiations, for a farewell visit. Litvinov agreed to the naming of Bullitt as the ambassador and to a building for the embassy. The building was respectable, Litvinov noted, but it needed renovation and furniture.[80]

Stalin's latest instructions crossed with Litvinov's last telegram. Basically, the deal was agreement on a maximum of $100 million in debt for $200 million in a long-term loan at 7 or 8 per cent annual interest, 4 per cent on the loan, and 3 or 4 per cent for the payment of the debt. The Georgian *kulak* urged Litvinov to try for 7 per cent and use 8 per cent only as a last resort. Nor did Stalin like the German option, of obtaining American credits in Germany, assuming this was even possible. It could worsen Soviet relations with Germany, which were already bad. Another complication was that Stalin did not want to make any commitment to new orders in Germany in 1934. On other matters, Stalin gave Litvinov the authority to propose Aleksandr Antonovich Troianovskii as Soviet ambassador in Washington. "We suggest that you pursue the negotiations to the very end even if you have to stay in Washington for this until the end of the month."[81]

On Saturday, 18 November, day twelve of the negotiations, Litvinov met with Morgenthau and Bullitt about the debt-loan negotiations. Litvinov reminded his American interlocutors that he would stay in Washington only to "establish sums," in accordance with the "gentleman's agreement." Litvinov proposed to leave Washington on 25 November. If they could obtain agreement before his departure, all the better, if not, the new ambassador would carry on negotiations. Morgenthau and Bullitt did not object but insisted that agreement be achieved before January. They then got down to the business of interest rates. Litvinov proposed his "maximum" of 7 per cent with 2–3 per cent for payment on the debt. Readers will notice that this was less than what Stalin had approved, but Litvinov needed to keep a little in his pocket to concede later if agreement was near. Morgenthau proposed 10 per cent, for which 6 per cent was for amortization of the loan. They were not that far apart, if one considered Stalin's 8 per cent. Could they split the difference at 9 per cent, or 8.5 per cent with 5 per cent for amortization? The next meeting would be on the morrow, Sunday. Litvinov asked Bogdanov to attend since he knew better what the going interest rates were. Litvinov had his doubts about achieving an agreement. The press was closely scrutinizing the negotiations, and was being briefed on each session and demanding results. Negotiations with Troianovskii would draw less press scrutiny. "It's more advantageous for us," Litvinov observed, "to conduct negotiations in the presence of the president who will be, as experience has shown, more flexible than his advisors." Litvinov reported that the day before he had asked Bullitt why Roosevelt had been so insistent on the religious question. Bullitt had been frank in his reply, saying it was strictly a question of domestic politics; the documents on religion would give Roosevelt another fifty votes in Congress, which he needed for his economic reforms. Religion per se had nothing to do with relations with the USSR.[82] It also became obvious to Litvinov during a later discussion with a State Department official that Roosevelt had not kept State informed of their discussions. There are "very hostile relations between the State Department and Bullitt," Litvinov added, "but he is close to Roosevelt, with whom he will likely communicate directly."[83]

After settling on the terms of recognition, Roosevelt and Litvinov finally had a discussion about political issues. Leaving Roosevelt's platitudes aside, he spoke of Germany and Japan as the main threats to peace. The United States and the Soviet Union, according to FDR, "had to put themselves at the head of the movement for peace." He saw the movement of Germany toward the east as a real possibility. He hoped, however that Hitler would not last but would "burst." The Japanese military represented, according to Roosevelt, a "serious danger." He did not fear attack, but Japan was forcing the United States to spend "hundreds of millions of dollars on armaments." He noted that the US could build three warships for every one that Japan built and wondered whether Japan could stand the financial strain. Roosevelt came quickly to his point. It would take the USSR ten years to bring Siberia to an appropriate state of development. Litvinov reported that "America is ready to do everything it can in order to ward off the Japanese danger. America will not go to war, for not one American wants that, but Roosevelt is 100 per cent ready to provide us with moral and diplomatic support." The two governments could exchange information about Japan, for example. Roosevelt suggested a non-aggression pact on which Litvinov hastened to agree. Roosevelt said he had asked Bullitt to look into these questions and report back to him. Litvinov attempted to see how far FDR was willing to go in this direction. What would the president think about bilateral security cooperation with the USSR? Here FDR backed off, saying that he preferred unilateral declarations when necessary. "From my many conversations with Roosevelt, I took away the impression that if we can settle the debts question and in the absence of incidents with Americans in the Union, we could establish with Roosevelt very friendly relations." Public opinion also seemed favourable, Litvinov added.[84]

Could this be done? Roosevelt seemed willing, and Stalin too. He dropped his cynical Georgian *kulak* low-bidding during the exchanges with Litvinov in Washington. On interest rates there was a 2 per cent difference of opinion with Morgenthau. On total indebtedness, the difference at the opening of negotiations was between $75 and $150 million, not great sums either for the United States or the USSR. The amount of the loan was not really discussed. Stalin aimed for $200 million. The haggling over religious and legal rights of a handful of Americans puzzled Litvinov for he considered these to be issues of little importance. Roosevelt had his political reasons, as he and Bullitt explained. It might seem somewhat ironic that the United States would be so insistent on the legal rights of Americans in the USSR while at home Black Americans were subjected to lynch laws and Jim Crow. Readers will find equally implausible Litvinov's references to the protections of Soviet law when collectivization had provoked destructive peasant resistance and widespread famine, while in a few years Stalin would embark on the mass executions of the purges. The main question nevertheless, was whether the differences could be bridged on the economic issues. Would the normally hostile State Department cooperate? Was the danger of Nazi Germany and Japan great enough to overcome other obstacles to cooperation? The following year would tell the tale.

Litvinov spoke freely with his US counterparts while he was in Washington. He talked a lot about the Japanese threat to Soviet security. Fortunately, he said to the undersecretary of state, William Phillips, the Red Army had been building up its defences on the Manchurian frontier. They "were sufficient to hold the Japanese in check for the time being." Litvinov also dropped a big hint to Phillips about what was important and what was not. Relations with France were better, said the narkom, "largely because of the political situation; politically, it was of advantage for France to be on good terms with Russia." Then, there was this comment: "This entente cordiale had been accomplished in spite of the fact that the French people were holders of Russian securities in vast numbers … the fact they were not getting satisfaction from these securities did not militate against the growing friendship between France and Russia, *which was based on the need for security* [emphasis added]." That was the whole point, wasn't it? Phillips concluded: "Hitler and his regime were very evidently not in favour with Litvinov, who spoke strongly against the Nazi campaign against the Jews."[85]

Soviet diplomacy had nevertheless made gains in both Paris and Washington. It is clear from the existing correspondence that Litvinov had earned Stalin's respect. The sneering, for the time being anyway, disappeared from Stalin's correspondence with Kaganovich and Molotov. This was a good thing because the dangers to Soviet security were mounting in both the West and the East.

Chapter Four

Setback: The Metro-Vickers Affair, 1933

While the Soviet government had some success in improving relations with France and the United States, Britain was going to be a tougher nut to crack. During the 1920s, Soviet relations with Britain were even worse than those with France. There were some efforts to improve relations, notably during a brief interlude in 1924 under a minority Labour government. The Conservatives won fresh elections in October 1924, assisted in the last week of the campaign by the publication of the so-called Zinoviev Letter, a fake document purporting to show Soviet interference in British domestic affairs. The British government eventually broke off diplomatic relations with Moscow in May 1927.[1]

The growth of Anglo-Soviet trade in the 1920s hampered the Conservative Party's "Die-Hard" agenda against the USSR. At first, British merchants, like Arthur G. Marshall of Becos Traders, who conducted business in Soviet Russia, were poorly received at the Foreign Office, where officials considered trade with the Bolsheviks to be unseemly for "reputable" Englishmen. As Anglo-Soviet trade increased in the 1920s, so did the pressure for pragmatism in relations with the USSR. Anti-Bolshevism was one thing; business, quite another. Such pragmatism was not strong enough to overcome fear of Comintern "propaganda" and subversion in the British Empire.

In 1929, a second Labour minority government renewed diplomatic relations with the USSR. British merchants wanted the Russian business and were encouraged by the Soviet government, which promised rich contracts. Even the Tories, who did not want themselves to renew relations with the Bolsheviks, were glad to see Labour take the responsibility.[2] In 1929–30, the Labour government opened up credit guarantee facilities to Russian trade and signed a commercial agreement with the USSR, but it could go no further because of Tory red-baiting in the House of Commons and in the press. "I imagine," recorded one Foreign Office clerk in his minutes, that if the British anti-communist press called "a truce in the long range bombardment of Moscow … half their 'copy' would go."[3]

In 1931 a Tory-dominated National Government was formed. The Foreign Office prepared a briefing paper for the new Liberal foreign secretary, Sir John Simon:

> It is one of the unfortunate legacies of the War that Anglo-Soviet relations have become a subject of the most acute internal political controversy …
>
> From being a pre-war enigma Russia has become a post-war obsession … a matter of party strife at most of the post-war appeals to the British electorate. So long as one section of opinion, even if a small one, hitches its wagon to the Soviet star, and another longs for nothing so much as the star's eclipse, the task of reducing Anglo-Soviet relations to normal remains hopeless.[4]

Subsequent events proved out the Foreign Office analysis. In 1932, the British government negotiated trade agreements with the Commonwealth Dominions providing to them tariff and other trade preferences and discriminating against other countries. As a result of Canadian pressure from timber and wheat interests, the British government abrogated the 1930 Anglo-Soviet trade agreement in October 1932. This set off fresh negotiations for a new agreement that continued into the winter months of 1933. Soviet officials were none too pleased by these developments, but had to agree to the negotiations. As these talks were underway, a crisis erupted in March 1933.

Arrests in Moscow

On Saturday evening, 11 March, a posse of GPU agents raided the compound of Metro-Vickers near Moscow, a British electrical engineering company employed by the Soviet government to set up various plants and factories. Other offices and flats of Metro-Vickers employees were also raided. The GPU eventually arrested six British citizens working for the company and confiscated boxes of documents. They were looking for evidence of espionage, sabotage, or "wrecking" of Soviet plants where the Metro-Vickers engineers were working. The incident was eerily similar to the Shakhty affair in 1928, which included the arrest of six German citizens and created a serious row with the German government. It was the same charge of sabotage of an industrial plant. In one Politburo resolution in March 1928, the name Metro-Vickers turns up along with an order to handle British citizens with care, but to investigate thoroughly the Metro-Vickers establishment in the USSR.[5] The "handle with care" order was lifted five years later.

The news of the arrests quickly reached the British embassy in Moscow. William Strang, then the first secretary, immediately made telephone inquiries at the NKID. It was Sunday, a day off, and only a skeleton crew was on duty. Strang obtained the home phone number of Lev B. Gel'fand, an assistant department head for Western Europe, and succeeded in reaching him at around noon. Gel'fand listened to Strang's account of the arrests. Strang wanted to know why the Metro-Vickers men were arrested, where there were being held, and when the embassy could send someone to see them. Gel'fand knew nothing about the arrests – Strang's news was the first he'd heard of it. There was nothing he could do on Sunday, but he would make inquiries first thing in the morning. Strang nevertheless asked for a face-to-face meeting that day to which Gel'fand grudgingly agreed, not happy to give up his Sunday off. At a meeting that afternoon Strang indicated "privately" that "the embassy … was obliged to telegraph to London about what had happened, where, undoubtedly, this message would make 'a very painful impression.'"[6]

All hell was about to break loose. The following afternoon, Strang telephoned again, and again Gel'fand had to respond that he had not yet received any information. Then Strang, prompted by Ambassador Sir Edmond Ovey, who was listening in on the conversation, asked for an immediate meeting with Litvinov. The narkom indicated to staff that he was booked up for the day, but Ovey insisted and Litvinov asked Krestinskii to meet the ambassador. When Ovey arrived, Krestinskii wrote in his journal, "I said to him that after Gel'fand told me this morning about Strang's visit yesterday, I immediately contacted the investigating authorities for information, but I have not as yet received an answer." This was *not* what Ovey wanted to hear. He was, according to Krestinskii, "very agitated" but trying to control his emotions. There was not much the zamnarkom could say until he had information from the OGPU. Krestinskii had been in the thick of the Shakhty affair in 1928, and had crossed swords with Stalin.[7] Did he remember, as he drafted his record of conversation? Ovey repeated that British opinion was likely to react badly to the arrest of Metro-Vickers engineers. As Strang had done, the ambassador asked what charges were filed and where the arrested men were being held. In the interests of Anglo-Soviet relations, Ovey said, he hoped the charges proved to be the result of some "misunderstanding" and that the arrested men would quickly be released. According to Krestinskii, Ovey had laid it on pretty thick but apparently not beyond instructions from London.[8]

Those instructions came from the Permanent Undersecretary of State, Sir Robert Vansittart. He sent out his first telegram on Monday, 13 March, in which he agreed with Ovey's description of the arrests as "an act of folly which had produced the gravest impression" in London. Any allegations would "command no credence whatsoever" and would lead to the conclusion that "reputable" British citizens could not work in the USSR without risk. If this was so, there was no point to negotiating a new trade agreement.[9] Hence, the Foreign Office agreed with Ovey: Soviet charges against British citizens could not possibly have any legitimacy even if no one, either in London or the British embassy in Moscow, knew as yet what charges had been laid. The immediate reaction therefore was to fire off threats.

Later during the evening of 13 March, the NKID received information about the arrests. Gel'fand telephoned Strang and asked him to come to the NKID at 12:30 a.m. When he arrived, Gel'fand read to him a prepared statement concerning the arrested men. Two British and three Soviet citizens had been released. The other British nationals were being held in Moscow and arrangements were being made to allow a consular meeting with the arrested men. After making some notes, Strang asked to use the phone to call the ambassador. It was then that a little comedy unfolded.

Let Gel'fand explain.

> Very agitated and nervous, Strang added that the ambassador wanted immediately by telephone to make to me some kind of statement. Strang's look told me that the communication would be 'unpleasant.' So, I said to him, that it was already very late, I only had authority to make to the embassy a written communication and that it made no sense to make any statement to me now by telephone because I could not in any case forward the statement to anyone today. Hence, I asked Strang to explain this to the Ambassador and to recommend that any messages, if there is a need for them, be put off until tomorrow.

Gel'fand obviously did not want to receive and have to pass on to his superiors an "unpleasant" communication from the British ambassador. Strang, who appeared to sympathize with Gel'fand, replied that Ovey was likely to insist on an immediate conversation over the telephone. "It became obvious to me," Gel'fand wrote in his record of conversation, "that either the statement was really urgent (which is unlikely), or it would be much more difficult to deliver it tomorrow." According to Gel'fand, Strang tried to indicate by his gestures that he did not agree with the ambassador's insistence on an immediate communication, but that he was only following the ambassador's instructions. So Gel'fand gave Strang access to a telephone and went into the next office to ring up Krestinskii to decide what to do. They finally decided that to refuse a telephone conversation with Ovey would be "inconvenient and impossible." Gel'fand returned to his office where Strang was reading to the ambassador the NKID statement about the arrested Metro-Vickers engineers. Ovey asked Strang to pass the phone to Gel'fand.

> Ovey began in an irritated and rather impudent tone which in the course of the conversation my firm answers gradually moderated. He said that he had just received instructions from his government to bring to our attention the following (here he lied that the instructions were received after Strang left to see me at the

> Commissariat, whereas Strang two minutes before had warned me that Ovey had a special communication for us).

Then Gel'fand wrote down the rather long statement from the ambassador who seemed to have trouble keeping his temper. British public opinion is indignant at the arrests, Ovey stated, and trade negotiations might be affected. Here was a first threat against the Soviet government. A second was that the British government would halt trade with the USSR. Ovey declared that British opinion did not believe the charges against the arrested men. HM Government wanted a detailed explanation.

"We have given you one to the best of our ability," replied Gel'fand in so many words, "please forward it to your government." Ovey was not satisfied, and asked further questions. Gel'fand repeated what he had said to Strang and reassured the ambassador that he would obtain answers to his further questions.

"Ah, no," Ovey replied, "I must report this to my government immediately. I must point out that the arrested men are threatened with death, that they are thrown into prison on absurd charges. We strive to improve relations between our countries, Mr. Gel'fand, you and I, we are both diplomats and you understand what this means!" Gel'fand gave as good as he got from Ovey, not responding well to what sounded like a veiled threat to break off diplomatic relations. "Why, if Ovey had such pressing questions that he could not wait for an answer, did he not put them [earlier] in conversation with Comrade Krestinskii, but remembered to ask them to me at half past one at night?" This was a reminder to Ovey that it was getting late, and the meeting soon ended. For a desk officer, Gel'fand held his own against an angry British ambassador. His general impression was that Ovey wanted to pick a fight. "In my opinion, it is advisable to respond quickly to Ovey's latest questions in order to limit his hostile activity and the possibility of provocative messages to London."[10]

A Crisis Erupts

On the following day, which was Tuesday, Ovey was getting the wind in his sails, expatiating in a telegram to London on Soviet "folly" and declaring that the Soviet government had "gone off the deep end." From a British point of view, it was impossible to imagine that the Soviet authorities could have any valid reason to arrest a British citizen. The only language understood in Moscow was tough talk, according to Ovey, "nothing will have any effect short of a threat that, in the event of decision of the courts or the enquiry being a mere travesty, we shall break off negotiations or even diplomatic relations." Ovey was therefore going beyond one threat to add another, a possible rupture of diplomatic relations. The Foreign Office had already broken off relations in 1927 without any noticeable effect on Moscow. But threats it was to be. "This may seem to be going far," Ovey continued, "but I think this alone will bring them to their senses." Unless of course, the ambassador went on, the Soviet government intended to expel British companies.[11] Gerald Fitzmaurice, a legal advisor in the Foreign Office, had his doubts and advised against going off half-cocked.[12] Vansittart did not at first show any signs of wanting to listen to legal advice or to issue more cautious instructions for Ovey.

Ovey returned to the charge on the next day, 15 March, this time with Gel'fand's boss, Evgenii V. Rubinin. The row was creeping up the chain of command in the NKID. Litvinov was apparently hoping to keep the problem off his desk. Ovey again asked the same questions over the telephone that he had put to Gel'fand the night before. Rubinin tried to answer as best he could with the information the NKID had received. "Ovey made an effort to maintain a calm demeanor during the conversation," Rubinin noted, "and only once failed." Again, Ovey said that British public opinion was aroused and that this could lead to another Arcos (All-Russian Co-operative Society) affair, when the Soviet trade offices were raided in 1927. That sounded like yet another threat. Why did Western states have so much difficulty understanding that threats did not work well at the NKID or with Stalin? "I replied dryly," Rubinin noted, "that I really could not understand the meaning of such analogies and would not recommend giving a direction to the conversation which I could not follow."[13] That was a very diplomatic way of saying, "please do not threaten me."

Not satisfied with the answers he had obtained from Rubinin, Ovey telephoned Gel'fand to pursue the same questions about the fate of the British prisoners, whether there would be a trial, whether it would be open or closed to the public, and who would preside over the proceedings. According to Ovey, he had received instructions to obtain answers to these questions before a session of the House of Commons that same day. The ambassador read out a London telegram and pressed hard for satisfaction. He asked that Litvinov be informed of "the impossible position" of Anglo-Soviet relations when British citizens were accused of treason [*sic*] and subjected to a show trial organized for internal policy purposes. These were lines that Vansittart had sent to Ovey as additional instructions.[14] This is "serious business," Ovey said to Gel'fand, which represented a "colossal danger to relations between the USSR and England." Again there was a threat. Gel'fand replied that the NKID itself did not have all the answers to the ambassador's questions, but when they had them he would be informed. After getting off the phone with Ovey, Gel'fand reported to Litvinov who refused to listen to the full text of the British telegram and instructed Gel'fand to so inform the ambassador.[15] Tempers were growing short.

Ovey continued to badger, this time Rubinin, in spite of his efforts to provide all the necessary information concerning the incarceration, treatment, and prosecution of the Metro-Vickers personnel. The ambassador wanted to know why Litvinov refused to listen to the report of the British telegram. Rubinin replied that Litvinov would not legitimize any British statement implying interference in Soviet internal affairs. Ovey seemed to pay no attention as he continued to insist that there was no evidence to convict the Metro-Vickers men, and questioned whether Rubinin did not agree with him. How could the ambassador assume innocence without imputing illegitimacy to the OGPU investigation? That was the point, and Rubinin declined any competence to respond.[16] According to Ovey's account to Vansittart, "I spoke to him [Rubinin] very strongly" about answers to questions not yet received. Rubinin's voice is scarcely heard in the ambassador's report of the meeting. According to Ovey, the Soviet government did not understand the "seriousness" of the situation.[17]

Litvinov appears to have wanted to keep the Metro-Vickers affair from becoming a noisy scandal, which would explain his initial refusal to meet Ovey and to let Gel'fand and Rubinin deal with him. On 16 March, five days after the arrests, Litvinov realized that this strategy was not going to work and he met the ambassador for a long discussion. Given the frantic, repeated meetings and telephone calls with Gel'fand, Rubinin, and Krestinskii, readers may anticipate that Litvinov would give Ovey a hard time. He certainly knew how to do that when it came to governments and their diplomats unfriendly to the USSR. In this case, however, he heard out a very agitated Ovey, and listened to his lines already repeated many times to Gel'fand and Rubinin about the risk to Anglo-Soviet political and trade relations. There had been some government speeches in the House of Commons, and Litvinov had to listen to Ovey read one from the acting prime minister Stanley Baldwin, while Ramsay MacDonald was in Geneva.

When Litvinov finally took his turn to react to the ambassador's remarks, he had a lot to say. Boiled down, it came to this: the British government seemed to think that its citizens should be exempt from Soviet laws and immune to arrest and prosecution. That was not possible, nor was it possible to release them simply on the British government's say-so that they were innocent. It happened that foreign nationals ran afoul of the laws of countries where they were residing and this caused frictions between states. But these kinds of situations took place in other countries and not just in the Soviet Union. They were episodes in international relations, but they were resolved one way or another and then consigned to the archives. "International relations," Litvinov said, "are affected by, and must be determined by higher and more important considerations than such episodes." Ovey, still very nervous, according to Litvinov, asked a series of questions about various aspects of the case, and, in most cases Litvinov, if he did not know the answer, said he would inquire and let Ovey know when he had further information. Ovey then seemed to calm down a little and he asked Litvinov what he might advise in dealing with the arrests. Litvinov agreed to respond "unofficially." "I think," he said, "that not only the ambassador but also his government were showing too much nervousness in this affair and making too much noise. This was not in the interests of resolution of the case. On the one hand, Baldwin and the ambassador were convinced of the absolute innocence of the prisoners, and on the other, at the same time, reasoned that since the guilt of all the prisoners would be demonstrated beyond a doubt and they would all inevitably be shot."

These assumptions were contradictory and too categorical, according to Litvinov – although an external observer might be forgiven for having doubts. In any case, the narkom advised the ambassador to calm down; two of the arrested had already been provisionally released. Strong language and threats would not help the prisoners or facilitate Anglo-Soviet relations. In fact, the opposite might certainly be true. The Soviet government would not knuckle under to threats. Exactly. "The more calm the British government retained about the case, the better for the prisoners and for our relations." On minor questions, Litvinov advised Ovey, to contact his subordinates in order to speed up matters, for he (the narkom) was not always available, but the appropriate NKID bureau was always open. Litvinov recorded in his notes that Ovey at the end seemed reassured.[18] If he was reassured, it was not for long.

Ovey made his own report of the meeting for the Foreign Office. It was far more what Ovey said to Litvinov than what Litvinov said to Ovey. Litvinov's comments were reduced to two paragraphs and understated. The narkom was an "irritable and in some respects good-natured boor." This meant, one supposes, that Litvinov was not up to the standards of the British elite, and that one did not have to pay too much attention to what he had to say. The meeting "was in no way hectic," Ovey continued, though according to Litvinov, Ovey was on edge throughout most of their conversation.

> I suspect that in particular Jewish element in Commissariat for Foreign Affairs, where it is predominant, and everywhere else, is sufficiently permeated with bourgeois and intelligentsia sentiment to realise the dangerous direction which Stalin is now following. The signs of immediate sinking the ship are not sufficiently obvious to cause these rats yet to make a move to safety. I feel that such of them as retain any genuine loyalty to party would positively welcome action on the part of Great Britain which would prevent Stalin from sinking his own ship by quarrelling with Great Britain.

According to Ovey, Litvinov was "forced to play a game, [but] in his innermost heart disapproves, I feel, the orders which he had been given." So Ovey recommended "the strongest possible action" lest Great Britain lose "all prestige" in the Soviet Union. He recommended demands for immediate release of the prisoners "with apologies." That the ambassador could write such comments and recommend such policy to London after meeting with Litvinov means that he did not hear the narkom's message at all.[19]

Litvinov suspected as much. He wrote a note to Stalin to warn him that events were going in the wrong direction since "the English" were raising a storm in Parliament and in the press and "the English ambassador" was talking daily to foreign correspondents, "giving them a one-sided account of the discussions with us" while we have remained "completely silent." This would not do. "I fear that Ovey is misleading not only the correspondents but also his own government, distorting the discussions with us and transmitting from them only that which he considers useful for him, in order to show his energy and the superiority of his arguments." Litvinov was correct. He recommended publishing a résumé of his discussion with Ovey, a draft of which he included for Stalin's approval.[20]

Given Ovey's telegrams to London, Litvinov was on the right track. On the evening of 16 March, still Wednesday, Rubinin was at home in his flat when the phone rang. He no doubt looked at his watch, it was 11 p.m. Ovey was on the line; he wanted to see Litvinov at once. "What now?" Rubinin must have thought. It was like babysitting. "Can I be of assistance?" Rubinin replied. Ovey asked him to come at once to the embassy for he could not go to the NKID. His chauffeur was ill, and his wife had gone out somewhere for dinner and he was waiting for her to return. Again, Rubinin did not want to be drawn into the ambassador's game, so he made excuses that it was late and that following day was a day off. He would have to prepare a report to send to Litvinov and Krestinskii, but they would not read it until they returned to work on the morrow. "After a rather prolonged discussion on this theme," Ovey finally got around to explaining why he was in such a hurry to see Litvinov, or *in extremis*, Rubinin. He had heard that there would be some kind of communiqué published in the Moscow press about his meeting that day with Litvinov. He was afraid there could be something in the communiqué "which might have an unfortunate effect on the course of events." In view of Ovey's "extraordinary insistence," Rubinin agreed to look into the matter and get back to him.

This narrative is becoming rocambolesque, but let Rubinin explain what happened next.

> After discussing with Comrade Litvinov, I called Ovey and told him that I, unfortunately, was unable to leave home now. However, I added that I was able to contact our Press Department and found out that the communiqué about Ovey's conversation with Comrade Litvinov had already gone to press. I noted at the same time that we naturally could not postpone any longer informing the press about the Soviet Government's response to British démarches, in as much as the British Government had released a number of public statements on this issue, and the ambassador informed foreign correspondents about every step he took.
>
> Ovey then asked what was in the communiqué. Nothing "very sharp," he hoped. "It is difficult for me to remember …," Rubinin replied evasively, but it is a report of

conversation and Litvinov would be the one to elaborate since he knew best what had been said.

"Well, if so," replied Ovey, "then all is in order, our conversation was quite correct."

Except that their respective reports of meeting were out of sync. That was what worried Ovey, although he worried for nothing. The conversation was not quite over for Ovey again returned to the charge asking Rubinin to come to the embassy first thing in the morning. "After many attempts to persuade him of the pointlessness of such a meeting on our day off," Rubinin concluded, "I agreed to meet him at 9h.30."[21]

In the meantime, Vansittart backed off a little from his original aggressive position on the Moscow arrests. He did not like the ambassador's proposal for demanding apologies from the Soviet government, but Vansittart did give Ovey wide leeway to offer a revised formula without referring it back to London and he approved of the ambassador's language to Litvinov.[22] What he did not understand was that Ovey had failed to give an accurate report of the narkom's comments and advice.

After Rubinin returned from the British embassy, he drafted yet another record of conversation with Ovey over breakfast. The ambassador started by complaining that he was working now only on the Metro-Vickers affair every day until four in the morning. Litvinov had said to him that he looked ill. To which Ovey agreed: he was looking for sympathy, one supposes. He said to Rubinin that he had been working for three and a half years to improve Anglo-Soviet relations and now everything had blown up. "I know," Ovey went on, "that people were now saying about him that he had deliberately complicated the case, that he was attempting to take the role of colonial administrator. This is absolutely untrue. I am your best friend. In England some people accuse me of being pro-Bolshevism." About all this, according to Rubinin, Ovey went on at some length. He then returned to more familiar lines, *inter alia*, about the indignation of British public opinion. He also alluded to the possibility of a deterioration in present Anglo-Soviet relations. Rubinin tried to interrupt several times to ask why Ovey continued to repeat things he had already said and to ask questions to which he had already received answers. Although he worried about Litvinov's communiqué, Ovey agreed that it was "entirely correct," even if the NKID press *otdel* was a little over the top. Then the ambassador finally got around to his main idea that the British government, while respecting the right of the Soviet Union to apply its own laws, asked for the immediate release of the British prisoners. The Soviet government should also, "if possible," express regret over the mistakes made and the "troubles" to which they, the prisoners, had been subjected. On this point, Ovey had received Vansittart's latest telegram prior to the meeting with Rubinin so that the "if possible" Soviet regrets were a sufficient revision to try out on the NKID. Rubinin refused to be drawn into discussion about Ovey's proposal, saying only that he would forward it to Litvinov, though he could not swear that the narkom would even consider such a proposition.[23]

Rubinin was only being diplomatic, he knew Litvinov's mind on this point all too well. Ovey saw Litvinov briefly at a Swedish reception that same evening and asked to meet with him. Litvinov agreed but told Ovey he was wasting his time on the new proposal for freeing the prisoners and expressing regrets. This idea was not up for discussion. "I do not understand," Litvinov wrote in his journal, "why the ambassador wants to repeat to me again this proposal, knowing in advance my answer." There was nothing else to add. Ovey said he had instructions from his government, and Litvinov replied that he would receive him so that he could carry out his instructions, but that he should not expect anything to come of the conversation. Ovey tried to draw Ivy Low, Litvinov's English wife, into the conversation. The ambassador was looking for her sympathy for fellow citizens. That was a mistake. "My wife dryly replied to him," Litvinov noted, "that she supposed he was in sufficient measure English, in order to know how to conduct a correct conversation and on correct topics."[24]

Ovey made his own record of conversation. "From the few minutes he gave me, it is possible to measure the cynical indifference or calculated obstinacy of the Soviet Government … I asked whether he had read the most recent declarations and speeches in England. He had the effrontery to assert that it was these which were the root of the existing trouble."[25] Here was a classic case of two diplomats talking past one another. Ovey did not mention his brief conversation with Ivy Low.

The Clash of the *Posol* and the *Narkom*

As promised, Litvinov met Ovey on the following day. It was Sunday, 19 March, eight days after the arrests. The ambassador carried out his instructions proposing the immediate release of the British prisoners. They, Ovey and Litvinov, could work out a jointly agreed upon formula announcing the release. However, the Soviet side would have to declare to the British government that "such incidents will not be repeated." Litvinov responded as he had warned Ovey that he would. "I observed to O.," the narkom wrote in his journal, "that he is proceeding from a completely invalid assumption about our decision to free the prisoners and to end the entire affair and that we apparently only wish to save face, a gesture with which he is kindly ready to help us. I must entirely dispel this illusion." That was not going to happen, Litvinov continued, the case file had been transferred to prosecutors who would decide on any future course of action. Ovey then asked some questions about the likely decisions of the prosecutors. Litvinov was not encouraging.

The narkom then proceeded to offer a lesson in diplomacy.

> The NKID looks at this affair from the point of view of our relations with England, but ... we cannot, however, lose sight of general interests of state. We are trying as much as possible to mitigate the situation, we obtained for the embassy a first meeting [with the prisoners], sped up the investigation and so on. Unfortunately, the storm which immediately followed in the English press, the imprudent declaration of Baldwin in the House of Commons and the intemperate declarations of Vansittart to the [Soviet polpred Ivan M.] Maiskii and Ovey to me including veiled threats, weakened and neutralized the influence of the NKID. I fear that if the conduct of the English press and the government itself do not change I could scarcely be of any use to Ovey in the present case and my assistance, for which the ambassador had asked, would lead to nothing.

Litvinov then went into some detail about the actions he had taken to ease the handling of the case, but said his actions would not be of any use unless the British government practised some restraint in its public statements.

Ovey did not move off his position that the only way to resolve the impasse was the unconditional release of the prisoners. The British government could not control the press, and was itself under the pressure of public opinion. Nor could Ovey say to his government that its own actions were making matters worse for the prisoners. In response, Litvinov reiterated his own position and he asked Ovey to convey it to London. The Soviet government did not need British agreement to conduct a trial. Ovey responded that if the arrest of such important people, as the accused, was considered by the Soviet government to be a normal situation, then it would be more difficult to have economic relations with Britain. Ovey began to repeat that in England people were "utterly convinced that the entire case was staged." At which point Litvinov cut off the ambassador. "I suggested to him not to continue to express such ideas, if he did not want to compel me to say to him all that I thought about his government." This was thus a conversation about to close. "Ovey bit his lip," Litvinov noted and changed the subject. The conversation quickly ended. As Ovey was leaving, he commented that he was not sure the Soviet government appreciated "the seriousness of the situation." Oh, we do, Litvinov replied in effect, "we have sufficient imagination to foresee all scenarios and to take them into account."[26]

Ovey also made a record of the conversation, which did and did not reflect the contents of Litvinov's entry in his *dnevnik*. Ovey tried to persuade Litvinov that they were close to coming to terms; just a little nudge would get them to agreement. "Whatever M. Litvinov may say, and I smoothed him down in every way," Ovey noted, "it would seem that only a delicate but emphatic push may perhaps now be required to achieve immediate liberation,"[27] If Litvinov's record of conservation is accurate, readers may wonder how Ovey could have drawn such a conclusion. Just how was Ovey "smoothing down" the narkom? You would not know it from reading Litvinov's record. Was it two diplomats again talking past one another?

Ovey suggested making an approach to Maiskii to obtain the final nudge. Litvinov must have been thinking the same thing. The NKID did not trust Ovey to convey Litvinov's views to London, and so Krestinskii sent instructions to Maiskii, who had only been on job for a few months, to advise the Foreign Office that British tactics were self-defeating and "could only harm their case." He reiterated what Litvinov had said to Ovey.

> No sovereign government can halt an investigation and release arrested foreigners suspected of committing a crime simply because the foreign government expresses its confidence that those arrested are innocent or because this foreign government demands the release of its citizens. The satisfaction of the British demand would signify our acceptance of a regime of capitulations, which we, of course, will not accept, and for which, as the English government cannot but understand, there are no grounds in the current political situation.

Krestinskii gave Maiskii further information about the case, and further leads to pursue with British interlocutors along the lines of those Litvinov had developed with Ovey. "We are aware," Krestinskii wrote, "that this case will for some time spoil our relations with the English government, but we nevertheless cannot, under the pressure of a foreign government, stop the investigation and release those for whose guilt there is substantive evidence."[28]

The NKID thought Ovey was overplaying his hand, but until 19 March, he had followed Vansittart's instructions. After the meeting with Litvinov, Ovey sent recommendations to London to obtain the release of the prisoners, concluding with the recommendation of a rupture of diplomatic relations if nothing else worked. Laurence Collier, head of the Northern Department, and Sir Lancelot Oliphant, Assistant Permanent Undersecretary, were against this. Collier opined that the Soviet side cared more about business than diplomatic relations. "I think Sir E. Ovey is going too far and too fast," noted Vansittart in the minutes. He opposed the recall of the ambassador or the breaking off of diplomatic relations.[29] Ovey did not let go of his option for the rupture of diplomatic relations. He continued to think that the British government could obtain a Soviet "surrender," but on this point he was dead wrong. He had misread the signs. "The enemy are in full retreat," he advised Vansittart. "They have got to yield somewhere. The sooner, the better."[30] Ovey was not for turning, and sent yet another telegram recommending the rupture of diplomatic relations if the Metro-Vickers prisoners were not freed. The Foreign Office deputy legal counsel Fitzmaurice thought Ovey was going too far: "Already questions are being asked as to why we do not take similar action in regard to British subjects arrested in Germany, and though the cases may not be parallel, it is awkward." Fitzmaurice's boss also advised caution. What if the tables were turned, he asked, and the Soviet government made similar demands to London?[31] Ovey stopped telephoning Rubinin and instead asked for another meeting with Litvinov after receiving instructions from Vansittart for further pressure short of diplomatic rupture. Ovey was to say that Parliament would soon consider a bill giving the government powers to impose an embargo against Soviet trade.[32]

Once again, Ovey saw Litvinov on 28 March, now seventeen days after the arrests. The meeting did not go well and was not long. Ovey asked if there was any news. On what subject? Litvinov replied facetiously, knowing full well what news the ambassador wanted. Now Ovey got a taste of the acidic Litvinov when his back was up. Ovey eventually tried to inform the narkom of the bill which was to be put before Parliament, but Litvinov cut him short. "I expressed my astonishment," Litvinov wrote in his journal, "that the English government graciously considered it necessary to inform me of its draft bills before introducing them in Parliament." Ovey took out a piece of paper from his pocket and started to read what amounted to a threat to impose an economic embargo on the USSR unless it immediately released Metro-Vickers prisoners. Litvinov cut him off in mid-sentence. He had had enough of English threats. "I stopped Ovey, saying that I could spare him the time and immediately declare that according to the prosecutor, there will be a trial and this trial in no case will be halted whatever the English ambassador might say to me, that if then what Ovey wanted to read to me had the objective of influencing our decision, then I could not see the need to hear this communication for it could have no influence whatsoever on my government."

Some further but brief sparring ensued. Ovey tried to speak about "consequences," but again Litvinov cut him off. "Permit me, Sir Edmond, to say that if such methods of diplomacy can work successfully in such a country as Mexico, then they are destined to complete failure in the USSR. We do not barter our independence." Litvinov recorded one last exchange of fire: "Blushing, Ovey asked who used such methods in Mexico. I reminded him that I said conditionally – 'if such methods were used in Mexico by anyone.'" According to Litvinov's record of meeting, Ovey was "completely taken aback," and, "embarrassed," took his leave. The meeting had not lasted more than ten minutes. Litvinov scrawled out a footnote to the effect that Ovey, before coming to Moscow, had been the British minister in Mexico.[33]

Yes, of course, in case you, the reader, are wondering, Ovey provided his version of the meeting to London. It did not *quite* confirm Litvinov's record. After the opening exchange, Ovey noted, "I got Litvinov a little quieter towards the end." Then there was this:

> Litvinov was nervous and excitable. The news came to him evidently as an unpleasant, but I venture to think, not entirely unexpected shock. In other words he, I still

> think, cannot have entirely shared the optimistic theories about indifference of HMG [His Majesty's Government] which Stalin himself presumably holds and has instructed Litvinov to express.
>
> On leaving I informed him that if he had anything more to add I was entirely at his disposal at any time. He retorted: "There will be nothing more." Interview could not have lasted more than some seven or eight minutes.[34]

Ovey was "completely taken aback," said Litvinov. Litvinov was "nervous and excitable," said Ovey. The one point on which they agreed – well, more or less – was the brief exchange about Mexico. Ovey did not mention it in his initial report, but TASS published a communiqué on the meeting closely following Litvinov's record in which the subject of Mexico is included. Ovey felt compelled to say something to London. "I did not report this typical *boutade* at the time partly because I am used to such outbursts and partly because I felt I had rather neatly dealt with it by replying very calmly and with a puzzled expression 'I do not quite understand, M. Litvinov, your reference to Mexico. Do you mean that someone or some country is in the habit of applying such methods to Mexico? If so, who?' to which he, evidently repenting his words, somewhat feebly replied, 'Oh, any country.'" These lines sounded so like those of a caricatured member of the British elite, thick, arrogant, nose raised high in the air. No petit bourgeois Polish Jew could get the better of Sir E. Ovey, a man of many honours and only recently knighted by His Majesty George V. Press correspondents in Moscow encouraged him to give a public account of what had occurred, but the ambassador had replied that he did not intend to be drawn "into a polemic" with Litvinov.[35] This was just as well for the narkom was not one to tangle with in a public fight. On that same day Simon recalled Ovey to London.[36] The clash of the *posol* (ambassador) and the narkom was over. Ovey left Moscow on the following evening, 30 March, never to return. His tenure as ambassador was much like that of Jean Herbette – full of optimism at the beginning, and conceited hostility at the end – except that Litvinov did not have to wait four years to be rid of him.

It was not immediately obvious that the British ambassador had left Moscow for good. On 29 March, the day after the last meeting with Ovey, Litvinov wrote to Stalin to ask for authorization to publish a further TASS communiqué. "I believe that we cannot avoid retaliatory (*repressivnykh*) measures on the part of the British government and that therefore our communiqué will not hurt the case, but it will nevertheless be a lesson for Ovey and for other ambassadors."[37] Litvinov continued to believe that Ovey was misrepresenting Soviet policy in London, and that his record of meeting would demonstrate it. He was not the first ambassador to embellish his reports from Moscow. Herbette had also pursued this strategy, although the Quai d'Orsay never appeared to understand, or perhaps was ideologically incapable of understanding. In fact, Ovey failed to report accurately Litvinov's views to London. He was thus not the first and would not be the last to do so.

Zamnarkom Karakhan also intervened, which was unusual since Western Europe was not his area of responsibility. "In connection with the departure of Ovey and the campaign which he and the English press will lead against us, portraying Ovey as the Lamb of God, we ought to do something to discredit him." He continued:

> From various sources, we know that Ovey insisted on breaking off relations with us and that this was not met with sympathy in London. Having failed in this, he wanted to be recalled, leaving Strang as chargé; he was not allowed to do so at the time. It is also known that he received instructions to be more restrained in his reports in order, in case of need, to be able to publish them, for the publication of his telegrams demanding the rupture of relations would be a scandal for the English government.

This was sound information. Karakhan recommended informing the British press of Ovey's activities, or better yet, Labour people sympathetic to the USSR who could raise a scandal in Parliament. "It seems to me," Karakhan wrote, "that we should act in this direction and at once."[38]

Given that Litvinov and Karakhan were former rivals, the narkom may have failed to appreciate his deputy's advice, though he would have agreed with the assessment of Ovey, in effect, a British Herbette without Herbette's staying power. A few days later, Krestinskii sent to Maiskii an unflattering assessment of Ovey as a troublemaker who was stirring up animosity after his return to London.

> He is very proud, very stubborn and vindictive. In addition, he is a conceited, arrogant person who wants to pursue a policy of the strong hand, and has not managed to understand for all these three years that with us this policy does not work. At first, he may have hoped that with the help of fierce pressure we could be forced to retreat, to release the English [prisoners], without referring the case to the courts. Then he understood that this would not happen, though he deliberately advised his government along the lines that if we press, they will give in. By doing this, he pushed and he continues to push the English government to such steps, which, in their logical development, in his opinion, will lead first to the rupture of trade and then of diplomatic relations. He is now striving for this, he would regard this as his victory and as his revenge.[39]

Was the NKID reading Ovey's telegrams, or just guessing? Or was the information taken "from various sources," as Karakhan said? Krestinskii's assessment of the ambassador's strategy, spelled out in his telegrams to London, was correct. Apparently accepting Karakhan's advice, Litvinov also confirmed it in a conversation with the young British journalist Gareth Jones: "Ovey has been too tactless, and too bullying. He is seeking a quarrel, and has as his aim the breaking off of diplomatic relations … We cannot have his bullying, tactless way. He is a very unfortunate representative."[40] If Litvinov said this to a British journalist, it was because he wanted his view of Ovey to circulate.

Ovey Recalled. Now What?

At the beginning of April, Litvinov was none too optimistic about Anglo-Soviet relations. He had familiarized himself with the indictments, Litvinov wrote to Maiskii, "they make me afraid of a rather harsh penalty against some of the British [accused]." Trade and trade negotiations with the British would be frozen. Would diplomatic relations be broken off? "It is difficult to guess about the prospects of our relations with England. However, I am inclined to think that, no matter how hard Ovey tries in London, with the assistance of the Die-Hards, the English government will not resort to a complete break of relations, where its concern for the fate of the convicted British will play a significant role. It is possible to carry out an embargo on our imports and a more or less long hitch in our trade relations." Litvinov did not think that Ovey would return to Moscow, and the British might see this as a form of "punishment." In fact, it would be all to the good, Litvinov noted: "Our relations with England will benefit from the absence of Ovey in Moscow." Maybe, the Foreign Office would ask for the recall of Maiskii, but Litvinov did not think reprisals would go any further.[41]

Litvinov met Stalin six times in March and eleven times in April – more than usual for him – often with Krestinskii and in April with Karakhan as well. In particular, he saw Stalin on 16 and 19 March, the same days he met Ovey, and again on 27 March, before seeing Ovey at the Swedish reception in the evening and before meeting him for the last time on the following day. The timing of the meetings suggests close coordination of policy with Stalin and the latter's acceptance of Litvinov's recommendations. Litvinov and Stalin sometimes clashed, occasionally fiercely, but more often than not they agreed on policy even if Stalin grumbled about the narkom with Molotov and Kaganovich.

Ovey returned to London on Sunday, 2 April, and met with the inner cabinet on the next day. But after that date, he was not in the paper loop at the Foreign Office on the Metro-Vickers crisis or the USSR. He disappeared from the files with the exception of Vansittart's passing reference to him on 8 April.[42] Just to make a point, Litvinov's records of conversation with Ovey, with interesting deletions, were published in *Izvestiia* on 16 April. They were translated into English and circulated in the Foreign Office.[43] No one left any marginal notes or long minutes. No one seemed to care. Ovey was past history; he was not going to get "revenge," although perhaps he thought he would. Strang took over as chargé d'affaires in Moscow, holding to a slightly more dispassionate approach to dealing with the Soviet side, while Maiskii began to play a role in London in trying to find a way out of the crisis. He was of course no better informed than the NKID of the Metro-Vickers arrests, and he complained about being blindsided by the crisis. The first news he received about the arrests came from Metro-Vickers in London whose agents called on him to find out what had happened in Moscow. "The news fell on us," Maiskii wrote to Krestinskii, "like a bolt out of the blue." We could say nothing about the arrests except to promise to make the necessary inquiries in Moscow. "I do not think that such a situation served to enhance the authority and prestige of the embassy." Certainly not in the Foreign Office, where the clerks reckoned that Maiskii was not informed and not in a position to exert influence in Moscow. In fact, the embassy received no news from the NKID for five days, neither information nor directives. When Maiskii was called to the Foreign Office on 16 March, he had no directives and found himself in an uncomfortable situation. "I was compelled, at my risks and perils," he noted, "to improvise points of defence and counter-attack against a fierce campaign underway in England, while not quite sure that our actions corresponded with the actions being undertaken in Moscow."

In the circumstances, Maiskii did well anticipating the points that Litvinov had made to Ovey: *inter alia*, that the British authorities should keep their composure and "not lose their heads." Except for diplomatic personnel, British citizens were not exempt from Soviet laws, and that "threats to break trade and diplomatic relations not only would not facilitate, but would only complicate the situation." These were Litvinov's lines to Ovey. As the narkom had done, Maiskii warned his British interlocutors that the Soviet government would not knuckle under to threats, quite the opposite. Assertions that the charges against the Metro-Vickers men were groundless constituted an attempt to short circuit Soviet laws, and was in effect an attempt to interfere in Soviet domestic affairs. Such claims – for example, Baldwin's statement in the House of Commons – could only lead to one result: "to compel the Soviet government to emphasize its sovereignty to the maximum."[44]

At the meeting on 16 March, Vansittart recorded mostly his comments to Maiskii and not the polpred's to him: "the Ambassador … of course contested my statement throughout the interview." Vansittart's statement resembled Ovey's to Litvinov. "I was using no threats," Vansittart told Maiskii, "but it was my duty to make sure that the Soviet Government were proceeding with their eyes open." That, of course, was a threat.[45]

If Vansittart would not give voice to Maiskii's comments, then Maiskii should be allowed to give his own account of the meeting. Without instructions from Moscow, he emphasized that he had stayed away from details of the case and improvised with generalities. "I was obliged," he noted, "to observe the greatest caution." One can only imagine. Maiskii tried unsuccessfully to separate the trade talks from the Moscow arrests and to attack the British assumption that the accused engineers could possibly be guilty of anything. On what basis, on what evidence, he asked, could the British government claim that the Soviet indictments were bogus? Here, according to Maiskii, he forced Vansittart into a tactical retreat, the latter stating that he was only describing the views of public opinion.[46]

In his report to Krestinskii, Maiskii said the British press had become unhinged. "From the very first moment of the arrests, the press launched an absolutely fierce campaign. I have seen in my lifetime more than one anti-Soviet campaign in the press and in more than one country, but the campaign that unfolded between March 12 and 20 surpassed anything I have until now observed. Firstly, it developed with lightning speed, and, secondly, it literally covered all the press, with the exception of the communist papers." The right wing *Daily Mail* was as one with the *Manchester Guardian*. With MacDonald and Simon abroad, and Baldwin replacing them, the government was vulnerable to pressure from the "Die-Hard" wing of the Conservative Party. According to Maiskii, this pressure explained Baldwin's "imprudent" declaration in the House of Commons on 15 March. The situation became so grave during the course of 16–17 March that "pressure from the 'Die-Hards' and the press created such a situation in the cabinet that a number of its members ([Lord] Hailsham, [J.H.] Thomas, and others) began overtly to raise the question of breaking economic and even diplomatic relations with us." Only the TASS communiqué concerning Litvinov's meeting with Ovey on 16 March "sobered" a little public opinion.

Maiskii also turned his mind to the question of Ovey and his role in the crisis. "You, in Moscow apparently have the impression that Ovey on all contentious issues always takes a more intransigent position than his London superiors. It seems to me that this is not quite true … One of two things – either Ovey entirely reflects the point of view of the Foreign Office, or the Foreign Office is too easily amenable to Ovey's ideas." In fact, Maiskii had the impression that the Foreign Office took the "most intransigent position" in the cabinet. This appears to have been true in the early days, but as of 21 March, Vansittart tried to slow down the movement towards a diplomatic rupture. So Maiskii appears to have been right at least in the early days of the crisis. He warned that the cabinet might impose a trade embargo. His basic position was that the Soviet government must hold the line on points of principle, that is, on Soviet sovereignty, while offering concessions, for example, on the issue of bail, which did not call into question Soviet sovereign rights. "Such manoeuvring would undoubtedly strengthen the more moderate wing in the government and at the same time provide less material for anti-Soviet demagogy in the press."[47]

From his "window seat" as he put it, Maiskii sent a "personal" dispatch to Litvinov, making so bold as to suggest ways of ending the crisis with a "minimum of unpleasantness for us." There was, of course, no use fooling ourselves, he added in so many words, that the affair was going to leave a "serious imprint" on Anglo-Soviet relations for some time to come. So Moscow should get a trial over with as quickly as possible. There should be no delays. "Once surgery becomes inevitable, it is better to do it sooner so that the process of gradual post-operative healing of the wound can begin earlier." Furthermore, the trial should be conducted against the Metro-Vickers engineers and not against the company itself. According to the company director, Sir Felix Pole, Metro-Vickers wished to continue to work in the USSR, and "as a last resort, would be willing to make peace in recognizing the guilt of one or another individual company employee." If the trial aimed to convict the company, then the company would quite naturally, in its own defence, turn against the Soviet government. "This is a very serious thing," Maiskii added: evidence against the accused should be persuasive and if there are convictions, sentences should not be severe. There were other suggestions as well with the same objective of calming British opinion and getting past the crisis.[48]

Litvinov forwarded Maiskii's letter to Stalin with a cautious endorsement. He thought Maiskii was at times "too optimistic," but on the key issues of getting past the crisis with as little damage as possible, he certainly agreed.[49] He also recommended visas for British correspondents. As Maiskii was getting inquiries, they needed to decide, Litvinov wrote to Stalin, if they would admit journalists and in what numbers. "The NKID kollegiia, having discussed this issue, came to the conclusion that, since we are talking about the openness of the process and the presentation of serious prosecutorial evidence that should convince all impartial people of the guilt of the defendants, a major refusal would be misinterpreted." Since the trial was approaching, a rapid decision was necessary.[50]

On the same day that Litvinov met Ovey for the last time, Maiskii received a visit from George A. Macmillan, Conservative MP and publisher, and Arthur Marshall of Becos Traders. Macmillan was apparently a newcomer to the Soviet embassy, but Marshall was an *habitué* dating back to the early 1920s. He was a businessman, had had economic interests in Russia before the Revolution, and sought contracts with the Soviet government. In pursuit of his interests, he had become a go-between for Soviet diplomats and the Foreign Office. Vansittart did not want to deal with intermediaries on the Metro-Vickers affair because one could not be sure of obtaining accurate information. "Moreover," he added, "we could not possibly at this stage attempt a settlement out of court behind Sir E. Ovey's back & by this rather devious method."[51] On this point Vansittart and Litvinov saw eye to eye both on the principle and on Marshall. The narkom hated dealing with go-betweens for they rarely got anything right or were looking out for contracts with the Soviet government. "My experience at the NKID has convinced me of the harmfulness of all sorts of intermediaries," Litvinov explained to Maiskii. "Exceptions are so rare and random that for the sake of them one should not violate the general principle of their undesirability."[52]

Nevertheless, there seemed no better option than Marshall, and a go-between might be better for both sides. Tempers were frayed in Moscow and London. The Foreign Office had to deal with an angry press and the ticklish problem of Ambassador Ovey. Why the problem of Ovey was so sensitive is another question. In Moscow there was no budging on the principles of Soviet sovereignty. The British would get no regime of capitulations, and the knife was out for Ovey.

Hence, Maiskii welcomed Macmillan and Marshall at the embassy and he made a record of their conversation. Macmillan began by saying that he represented those Conservatives who opposed a rupture of relations with the USSR and who were for the development of trade relations. He added that he had recently travelled to the USSR and he considered himself a "friend." "In fairly colourful language," according to Maiskii, "he described the mood prevailing now in the Conservative Party. This mood is extremely dangerous and threatening. Before the Moscow arrests, most Conservatives were generally calm about the USSR. A comparatively large group of die-hard people was angry about the 'Russian question,' but did not have any serious influence." After the arrests, all hell broke loose.

> Events in Moscow gave a perfect trump card into the hands of the Die-Hards. It was as if it fell to them directly "from heaven." They could never have ever dreamed of a scenario so advantageous to them. It is not surprising that the Die-Hards are going all out and trying to use this favourable situation to the maximum. Thus the task is to impose an embargo on Soviet goods, but if they succeed in achieving their goal, then the next step will be a break in diplomatic relations.

According to Macmillan, it was not just the Die-Hards who were on the rampage; almost the entire Conservative leadership was stirred up. "There are relatively few people like him in the Conservative Party who have kept a sober head and are keeping an eye on the future. If the government came to Parliament tomorrow and declared a rupture of relations with the USSR, the entire House (with the exception of the Labour Party and maybe a dozen other Liberals) would receive such a statement with deafening applause." So what could be done? Macmillan asked: "I am ready to help in every way possible … to resolve the conflict." As a quid pro quo, he asked for a "gesture" from the Soviet side, releasing the four remaining prisoners on parole without having to pay bail. Such a gesture might break the momentum towards the rupture of relations. Macmillan and Marshall both said they would try to use their influence in Conservative circles to find a way out of the crisis.

Maiskii did not record his reaction to Macmillan's suggestion, but he reported that Marshall came back to see him the afternoon of the following day, 29 March. Marshall had talked to Collier that morning at the Foreign Office:

> According to Marshall, Collier spoke in the sense that Ovey's negotiations with Comrade Litvinov in Moscow were at a dead-end, that the F.O. can plainly not understand wherein lies the problem there and why Ovey was getting nowhere, although it acknowledged the fact that the situation in Moscow is bad. Therefore, in the F.O. is developing a desire to transfer negotiations from Moscow to London and to try to achieve something from this end.

Again, Maiskii did not record his reaction to Marshall's information. The latter left and returned in the early evening. He had spoken again to Collier. "This time he came up with a kind of 'proposal': if I asked for a meeting with Collier or Vansittart, they would be willing to talk with me about the situation and, perhaps together, we could find some way out acceptable to both parties." Maiskii replied that he could not see the point of such a meeting in that the papers had announced that on the following day the government was going to introduce a bill in Parliament to embargo trade with the Soviet Union. If this were the case, Maiskii told Marshall, it would indicate that the government did not want to mitigate the situation but rather preferred to exacerbate the conflict. In that case what was there to talk about?

Marshall returned the following morning, 30 March. He told Maiskii that he had been to the Foreign Office the previous evening to see Collier and another unnamed official, probably Oliphant, though Marshall did not want to say. They said that the bill would not be presented in the House in order to avoid obstructing an attempt to settle the conflict. On the following morning, yet again at the Foreign Office, Marshall learned that the bill was indeed going to be introduced in Parliament, the reason being the publication of the TASS communiqué summarizing the last meeting between Litvinov and Ovey. The communiqué caused "great indignation" and was interpreted to be a sign of Soviet obduracy. As a result, it was decided in the Foreign Office to go ahead with the introduction of the bill in Parliament. Marshall added that Vansittart intended to summon the polpred to the Foreign Office. Maiskii repeated that such a meeting would be pointless if the embargo bill went forward. Marshall then again returned to the Foreign Office. He telephoned Maiskii to say that the introduction of the bill would be delayed until Ovey's return to London for "consultations." Simon added this clarification in order to quell rumours that the government was preparing to break off relations with Moscow.

All this occurred on the morning of 30 March. At noon that day Collier called the embassy to invite Maiskii to come to the Foreign Office. He declined thinking that Collier had insufficient authority to decide anything and that he could only serve as a conduit for information. At the same time that Maiskii was on the phone with Collier, Marshall reappeared at the embassy to say that the "mood" was "much better" in the Foreign Office. Everything was looking up, according to Marshall, and Maiskii really ought to accept Collier's invitation. Macmillan had been lobbying. Parole of the prisoners without bail would make a "great impression" in London, Marshall reported: in the Foreign Office they believed that such a "gesture" would change the "mood of influential circles" and would be interpreted as an indication of Soviet wishes to find a way out of the crisis. Marshall urged a sceptical Maiskii to make the recommendation to Moscow. "I told Marshall," Maiskii wrote in a report to Moscow, "that I still do not see any concrete manifestations of goodwill on the part of the British government – on the contrary, I hear all the time from various business sources talk about a supposed rupture of economic and even diplomatic relations with our country. I cannot make any proposal to Moscow to resolve the conflict, because in this situation, nothing might come out of it."

Maiskii was also suspicious of an invitation to see the subaltern Collier instead of the permanent undersecretary Vansittart. We are not discussing second or third level issues, he told Marshall, but important political questions. These should be discussed with the minister or his deputy. While respecting Collier, Maiskii recorded, he could not be the one with whom to discuss a way out of the present crisis. The problem was that Simon said he could do nothing until he met with Ovey. So nothing would happen for several days. Whether Maiskii actually said all the above to Marshall, or whether he was recording for the NKID, is not clear. In any case, Maiskii decided to send his first secretary, Samuil Betsianovich Kagan, to see Collier. That was a safe move. Marshall then left for the Foreign Office, and a half hour later Collier called Kagan to invite him in for a conversation. Kagan left at once. The upshot of that meeting, according to Maiskii, was that Collier said he was speaking on the authority of Simon to say that the British government had no intention of rupturing economic or diplomatic relations nor was it looking for a pretext to impose a Soviet trade embargo. Well, that sounded promising, though Maiskii was careful not to comment in his report.[53]

The reader may wonder if Collier or his colleagues left any records of these goings-on. It happens that they did. Bail or release on parole was the question that prompted the flurry of activity in London. The Metro-Vickers director, Pole, had not at first liked the idea, but then reconsidered and wanted Marshall to pursue the issue with Maiskii. Pole conveyed this information to Collier who passed it on to Marshall during the afternoon of 29 March who then went to see Maiskii. It was after the meeting with Macmillan and Marshall on 28 March, Maiskii picked up the story of his discussions with Marshall. In Maiskii's narrative, Marshall had learned that the Foreign Office wanted to try moving discussions to London, the Ovey-Litvinov exchanges having led to a dead end.

Apparently, it was considered inappropriate in the Foreign Office to criticize Ovey on paper, and so Collier did not mention any of this in his account of discussions with Marshall. Here is how he put it:

> Mr. Marshall called again to-day [30 March] and told me that M. Maisky, though much troubled by the "TASS" communiqué [on the Litvinov-Ovey meeting of 28 March] and the impending statement in the House of Commons, was nevertheless willing to recommend to Moscow that the remaining British prisoners should be released on surety as proposed, "with a view to the ultimate liquidation of the whole case," if only he could have an assurance from the F.O., which he could pass on to his Government, that H.M.G. were not seeking an excuse for an embargo or a breach of relations but genuinely desired a settlement. I replied that M. Maisky surely knew this already – to which Mr. Marshall retorted: "Oh yes, he does: but he thinks Stalin doesn't."

According to Marshall, the idea was that the Foreign Office would invite Maiskii in for a discussion, and would ask if he could see his way clear to recommend to Moscow that the remaining Metro-Vickers prisoners be released on parole. The ambassador would then ask, as a quid pro quo, "whether he could assure his Government that we were not seeking a breach; and, on receiving an affirmative rely, he would telegraph or telephone to Moscow stating that he had received this assurance and that, in view of it, he was recommending their release on parole with a view to discussing an ultimate settlement." Collier thought this approach was a rather complicated way of going about making a simple arrangement. "Yes, it is," Marshall replied. "But Maisky has to save both his Government's face and his own face with his Government." Interesting silences, a reader might think. Collier did not mention loss of confidence in Ovey, and Maiskii said nothing about "face," although one can see how Marshall might have so interpreted Maiskii's remarks. That was always the trouble with go-betweens, Vansittart or Litvinov might have rejoined, they rarely got the story right. The deal was clear enough to both sides, nevertheless, and Collier said he would recommend it to his "chiefs." There was nothing to lose in trying it. The trouble was that Maiskii did not speak of "saving face" and Litvinov had plainly stated to Ovey that the Soviet government was not seeking such a solution. This message had not passed to Collier, a perceptive analyst of Soviet policy. Oliphant proposed to wait on Ovey's return to London, but Vansittart overruled him and Simon gave his authorization to pursue the negotiations.[54]

According to Collier's minutes, Kagan duly came to the Foreign Office and Collier passed on the message about not rupturing relations or looking for a pretext for an embargo. Kagan replied that he would inform Maiskii, which he did.[55] Collier reported that Maiskii wanted not only a guarantee of no embargo but also a modus vivendi extending the Anglo-Soviet trade agreement for one month to give time for trade negotiations to be resumed. With regard to bail, it would be up to Metro-Vickers to come to an agreement with the Soviet authorities for the parole of the remaining prisoners. "The scheme … seems worth trying," Collier opined. "If it succeeds I think we shall have got all we could reasonably expect to get … and if it fails we shall be no worse off than we were before."[56] Then Simon clarified the Foreign Office position: the British government "is not 'seeking' a breach of relations or an 'excuse' for an embargo, but of course M. Maisky must not be told that if the prisoners are bailed no powers will be taken. His Majesty's Government is not making a bargain on the subject of bail at all." Bail was an issue for Metro-Vickers, not for the Foreign Office. We are not "bargaining," Simon noted, or "tying are our hands."[57] Maiskii thought *he* was bargaining. In any negotiation the principal was, as he put it, *daiu, chtoby ty dal* (I give so that you may give).[58] The Soviet side would be giving something for nothing in return. Stalin would have suspected as much; it is not clear whether Maiskii understood that he had been had.

Returning to the polpred's chronology of events, he (Maiskii) indicated that Marshall came to see him again during the afternoon of 3 April. He had earlier been to talk to Collier who was in a radiant mood, hoping that "finally, the conflict was entering on to the grounds of a gradual settlement." Marshall started to reminisce about helping the late L.B. Krasin through the Curzon crisis in 1923. "I listened to Marshall," Maiskii wrote, "and asked what he was so happy about." He (Maiskii) had received a phone call advising that the prime minister had just announced in the House that the government would on the morrow introduce an embargo bill. Maiskii wrote:

> Marshall was shocked. His whole face darkened, he said that it was absolutely impossible, and that he would immediately go to F.O. to clarify the question of what happened. After 2 hours, Marshall reappeared before me. His mood was quite depressed. He said irritably that in cabinet some kind of unexpected development had occurred. Only at 12 o'clock in the afternoon, he had spoken with Collier and Collier at that moment did not even suspect that three hours later the Prime Minister would announce in Parliament the introduction of an embargo bill.

Marshall managed to learn that the "sudden shift" had occurred during the morning. The cabinet heard that the Soviet government would not release the Metro-Vickers engineers on parole (although three of the four would get bail on the following day, 4 April), but, as Simon pointed out, that was no affair of the British government. Furthermore, Strang had cabled the previous day that all the engineers would be charged. It was also on that morning that Ovey met with the inner cabinet. He would after all obtain some "revenge" as Krestinskii had speculated that he wanted. Both Strang and Ovey used tough and sometimes inflammatory language to describe the situation in Moscow and the

Soviet government. The "fantastic nature of charges," Strang wrote, "make it plain beyond doubt that HMG are right in contending that the whole thing is a frame-up." According to Ovey, the Metro-Vickers men were "the victims of … heretic witch hunts in stage trials." The USSR, he implied, was not "a normal civilized country." The least that His Majesty's Government (HMG) could do, according to Strang, was to impose an embargo and "to visit their displeasure upon Soviet Government in the fullest possible measure."[59]

So there was not much Marshall or Maiskii could do. "That's the way it was," Maiskii noted, "and Marshall was very discouraged and left me in complete despondency."[60] It did not take long before Maiskii obtained more detailed information about what had transpired at the end of March and the beginning of April. First, on Ovey, Maiskii had this to report to Moscow:

> The conversation with comrade Litvinov on 28.III not only ended the career of Ovey in Moscow – he will no longer be the ambassador in the USSR – it also produced an extraordinarily powerful impression in the Foreign Office. Even before this conversation [Ovey] felt that in Moscow things were not going well, but, apparently, he did not see clearly enough the problem, that is, where lay the reason for the Moscow difficulties. The discussion of 28.III and following publication of it in the Soviet papers immediately opened the eyes of the F.O. Simon understood that it was impossible to keep Ovey any longer in Moscow, and therefore already on 29.III he recalled Ovey "for consultations" to London. At the same time some signs of frustration (*rasteriannost'*) began to be noticed in the Foreign Office. As now, it is entirely clear from the contents of the "White Book," that Ovey was the initiator of that policy of the "big stick," which the British government adopted and continues to apply in the present conflict. The Foreign Office supported Ovey's initiative, blessing his aggressive actions.

The White Book, to which Maiskii referred, was a collection of documents published by the Foreign Office. Maiskii duly noted that Vansittart had taken a somewhat more cautious approach, and that if Ovey had himself been more careful and less "anti-Soviet," the situation would have turned out differently. This was not a very Marxist approach, but might have been true. "However, Ovey is Ovey," Maiskii noted, and he took the Foreign Office for a ride further than it might have wanted to go. Then the Foreign Office "remembered" that there was a Soviet ambassador in London and it tried through Marshall to find a way out of the Metro-Vickers crisis. As Maiskii noted, this démarche failed for several reasons, the most important being Ovey's return to London. Even though it was Sunday, 2 April, Ovey saw Collier for a long meeting and Simon that evening. The following morning the "Big Seven" (*bol'shaia semerka*), as Maiskii called the inner cabinet of the prime minister – Simon, Neville Chamberlain, Walter Runciman, Lord Hailsham, J.H. Thomas, and Baldwin – met with Ovey. The meeting lasted for "around two hours" and Ovey pressed for a hard line towards the USSR and in particular the immediate introduction in Parliament of an embargo bill. According to Maiskii, there was some disagreement among the "Big Seven" about future tactics. MacDonald, Simon, and Runciman were for a more careful policy; Hailsham, Thomas, and Chamberlain for a hard line. Maiskii did not mention Baldwin. Ovey apparently pushed the argument – from where he got it, who could say – that the Soviet government intended to condemn and shoot the British prisoners. The only way to save them was the embargo and the threat of ending Soviet exports to Britain.

According to Maiskii, Hailsham and Thomas made the most of Ovey's argument; the wobbly (*miagkaia dusha*) MacDonald could not hold out against such pressure and the "Big Seven" lined up behind Ovey's recommendation. The bill passed easily in the House of Commons. How Maiskii came by the inside cabinet information is anyone's guess. Collier to Marshall to him, perhaps. Maiskii perceived the British government to be in "a difficult situation." He noted, "Thanks to Ovey's zeal (*userdie*), [the British government] from considerations of prestige and necessity to support its ambassador went further than it wanted." It was "undoubtedly" looking for a way out of the crisis without "losing face," which is what the British perceived to be the Soviet objective.[61]

The Trial

In fact, in April there was never the chance of a deal because Simon was not interested in a deal on the terms agreeable to Maiskii, not to speak of Moscow. The trial would go ahead. It began on 12 April. Even so, Maiskii did not give up on finding a solution to end the crisis. Through Marshall, he passed on the message that he would like to meet Simon. This meeting occurred on 13 April. Each side kept a record of conversation, though Maiskii's is more detailed and interesting than Simon's. According to Maiskii, he received a telephone call from Simon's office saying that the Foreign Secretary would like to see him in forty-five minutes, that is, with forty-five-minutes' notice. Maiskii did not appreciate the short notice and took it amiss, but nevertheless put on his hat and coat and left for the Foreign Office. When he arrived in Simon's office, he immediately noticed that Runciman was also present. "Both ministers very emphatically greeted me, as if wanting to underline that that the meeting had a particular importance." The Foreign Secretary did most of the talking. "Simon tried always to be very polite, but behind this courtesy one could clearly feel the cat's claws." Maiskii was therefore on his guard. After some "trifles" were discussed, the meeting turned to the essentials. The trial was underway in Moscow. The Foreign Office wanted the Metro-Vickers men freed one way or another. Simon suggested that it would be "not bad" to discuss some subjects of interest to both sides. Maiskii said he had no instructions from his government to seek a meeting, but he was ready to discuss those issues of interest to the minister. Simon gestured "vaguely" and began to lay out what was on his mind. It was not hard to guess the minister's agenda. First, it was the trade agreement that would expire in a few days. Then there was the matter of the trade delegation and its status. The British government would have its hands free to close the trade mission and expel its personnel. But, as Simon put it, the government did not have such actions in mind; on the contrary, it valued Anglo-Soviet trade and good relations in general and would facilitate the work of the trade mission. Simon went on in this vein for some minutes, Maiskii noted, and then turned to Runciman for confirmation. "Having been listening to Simon's verbal graces with a look of utter boredom, he then abandoned his passivity briefly to reply: 'Yes, of course, we want to trade. On this point all the government is agreed.'"

Simon then let Runciman return to his role as silent witness and again took charge. "His smooth advocate's speech," as Maiskii observed, "poured forth in an endless stream." While the British government valued good relations with the USSR, it faced the unfortunate situation arising from the arrests in Moscow. Maiskii had heard many times before all of what Simon was going to say about the innocence of the incarcerated engineers, the indignation of British public opinion, and so on. It appears that Maiskii listened politely waiting his turn. Simon spoke about the embargo; its sole purpose, he emphasized, was to secure the freedom of the prisoners in Moscow. Simon repeated himself on this point to make it clear that the British government was not trying to blackmail the Soviet government on matters of trade. On this point, Maiskii thought he noticed a difference in emphasis between Simon and Runciman. And Simon continued: "I do not want in any way to make threats. It is far from my mind to put pressure in any way on the Soviet government. But I, as Foreign Secretary of Great Britain, consider it my duty simply to inform you, as ambassador of the USSR, to my profound regret what in all likelihood will occur if the legal proceedings now underway, conclude in guilty verdicts." Of course, the British government would never contemplate interfering in Soviet domestic legal proceedings; it recognized the sovereign rights of the Soviet government. And on and on Simon went, Maiskii recording all the details highlighted with a slight but unmistakable ironic tone. Of course, if the prisoners were exonerated or simply expelled, then relations would rapidly return to order, and Lord Runciman would be all too glad to resume trade negotiations. At this moment, as Maiskii noted, "Runciman then again showed some signs of life and again briefly commented: 'Oh, of course, of course, I was very happy with the pace of our negotiations and would very much like to see their prompt resumption.'"

That terminated Simon's remarks. "My turn came to speak," Maiskii noted. Having listened to the Foreign Secretary's comments, he concluded that British policy had not changed. It was still "the big stick." Simon cut Maiskii off in mid-sentence and "somewhat heatedly" asserted that he was not an advocate of the "big stick."

"I continued however," Maiskii wrote, "with my counter-offensive." He reminded Simon of Ovey's conduct in Moscow and the public declarations of Baldwin and other cabinet ministers. He referenced the threats to halt trade and to enact a trade embargo. How else could one describe British policy except as a "big stick"?

"If I translated into simple language all that I have heard said today," Maiskii continued, "then the case can be reduced to the following: if you acquit the English engineers then we will not put into effect the embargo bill … if on the other hand, you convict even one of the Englishmen, then we will hit you with an embargo on Soviet exports. In other words, it is again a threat." Simon again interrupted Maiskii claiming that he had not made nor was he making any threats, he was stating what "fatally" would occur, in spite of his own wishes in case of guilty verdicts in Moscow. Maiskii retorted that Simon's clarification changed nothing. "In effect, we are talking about a threat, about a policy of the 'big stick,' which is condemned in advance to failure in the USSR." There followed an exchange of barbs, Maiskii saying that the Foreign Office ought to know better than trying to threaten a great, independent state, even he (Maiskii) with his limited diplomatic experience knew better. "I do not doubt," Simon interjected with a put-on "especially kind face," "that His Excellency has a very rich diplomatic experience." The exchange went on for yet a while. Maiskii commented that if the British government really wanted good relations with the USSR, it would need to change "its methods."

Simon responded by asking what the ambassador had in mind. First of all, put down the "big stick," Maiskii replied, and try "the method of friendly negotiations." And then Maiskii had this to say: "If Simon wants to go down this path, I believe that we will succeed in finding some acceptable exit from the situation, for both sides." Maiskii advised that they should not prejudge the verdicts, but wait and see what they would be and then go from there. Simon listened politely but then returned to his "stick": if anyone was found guilty in Moscow, the embargo would immediately go into effect. "Isn't that so," he said in effect, turning again for support to Runciman, who "somewhat apathetically nodded his head in a sign of agreement." Then Maiskii turned the tables saying that, in his personal opinion, Soviet "public opinion" would react adversely to an embargo, and then the Soviet government would be able to do nothing for the "alleviation of the plight of the English prisoners." That was a new element on the table, but then both sides reverted to a repetition of their previous positions. The meeting came to an end to the relief, perhaps, of Runciman.[62]

The Foreign Office account of the meeting with Maiskii is shorter and not as lively as the Soviet account. Naturally, Runciman's somnolent boredom is absent. Simon's threat in the event of a Moscow conviction is less overt. Maiskii's voice is not so often heard, his views more summarily presented. The ambassador's suggestion about a diplomatic resolution of the conflict is not underlined in the Foreign Office account but rather focused on what would happen after the trial. Maiskii said that "after conviction and sentence, there would be the opportunity for negotiations as the sentence would not necessarily be the end of the legal procedure." Maiskii's warning about the reaction of Soviet "public opinion" to an embargo is not present in the Foreign Office account.[63]

In Moscow, Strang had his own ideas for acceptable terms, but he was not buying any of Maiskii's plea for a "diplomatic" solution to the case. Whether there were acquittals for some of the men or expulsions for others did not matter to Strang. The Soviet government had gone too far. He wrote:

> It may be that HMG with their larger views and higher responsibilities may regard this as a conclusion not necessitating the imposition of an embargo which cannot fail to be of disadvantage to certain British commercial and financial interests.
>
> But (if I have permission to speak frankly) to all of us here whose passions have been touched by sight of savage persecution of these men, acceptance of such conclusion would be intolerable.
>
> Unless some reparation or apology were exacted failing this some sanction actually applied, Soviet authorities would have been allowed to organise a gigantic frame-up of these six completely innocent (if occasionally indiscreet) British subjects, based on "confessions" of agents provocateurs or terrorized Russian colleagues; to subject them to the rigours of a secret interrogation nature of which they themselves have described to us … to subject them to a farcical trial with every disadvantage of procedure before a bullying President and a gloating audience; to convict them of crimes which they have not committed; and then to close incident (as they may think) by flinging their bodies contemptuously back to us.[64]

Strang's plea would have been impossible to resist in London even if Simon had ever contemplated not having recourse to an embargo. But for the time being, there was not much to do in London, but await the result of the trial, which ended on 17 April. OGPU officers had put the accused through long periods of interrogation and succeeded to some degree in turning one accused against another. Strang tried to buck them up and to coach them as much as he could. They were sometimes shaky during the trial, which did not make a good impression on the Western journalists present. "I still think they are all innocent," Strang cabled, "but skillful use of a cruel and all powerful machine has been able to present some of them, even to the outside world, as not only guilty but unheroic."[65] In fact, two of the accused had signed confessions. It looked at times in court like the accused were indeed accusing one another. Some outside observers wondered whether there might be something behind the Soviet charges. There were questions about payments made to Russian employees, bonuses according Metro-Vickers, bribes according to the OGPU; and damaged turbines, defective and repaired according to Metro-Vickers, and deliberately sabotaged according to the Soviet prosecution. There was also apparently loose talk among the engineers with Russian colleagues critical of the Soviet government.

One can see how the OGPU would have bored in on that. Maiskii asserted at his meeting with Simon and Runciman that the Soviet judiciary was independent, but this would not have persuaded the British side. In fact, during March and April, Litvinov met Stalin nine times in the presence of Andrei Ia. Vyshinskii, the prosecutor in the case against the Metro-Vickers engineers. On 15 and 17 April, they met twice each day. There are no records of the conversations but one can imagine that the case against the British engineers was a topic of discussion, and that strategies for dealing with it were worked out. There is no doubt that Litvinov was looking for ways to lower the intensity of the crisis, a desire which Ovey failed to report to London. It was also not a secret around the diplomatic community in Moscow that Litvinov "greatly desires … a victory over the OGPU."[66] With Vyshinskii, who was said to have greater respect for legal forms and procedures, Litvinov would have wanted to know the basics of the case and whether there were legitimate grounds for a trial. There is, in the NKID files, a long report outlining the indictments.[67] At about this time, Litvinov "confidentially" informed the British journalist, Gareth Jones, what he had said to Ovey on 16 March: "The greater the pressure the less chance that is of my helping because we cannot give way to pressure … The men will not be shot. There will be a trial. The matter has been taken out of the hands of the OGPU and will be dealt with by the Supreme Court."[68] Again, he would have wanted this information to leak out in order to calm British anger.

It was a no-holds-barred fight played out in the Soviet courtroom, with diplomatic cudgels, and working the press behind the scenes. "Foreigners here are glad that at last somebody has had the guts to do something to hit the Soviet Government, and they hope we shan't weaken," Strang wrote to Collier. "We have done our best to keep the foreign press correspondents right, but some of them have gone astray. [Arthur J.] Cummings [*News Chronicle*] hasn't been nearly so bad as I feared. Reuters has been very wobbly. The F.O. New Department have done wonders with the diplomatic correspondents. What with all that, and the two White Papers [in London], we have for once given the Soviet Government a taste of their own propaganda medicine."[69]

The trial concluded on 17 April. One of the six engineers was acquitted, three were expelled from the USSR, and two were sentenced to two and three year sentences. According to Cummings, the *News Chronicle* reporter, the mildness of the sentences came as a surprise to those observing the trial and apparently to the accused as well, judging from their obvious expressions of relief in the court room. Strang thought that it was the pressure from London that had led to the lenient sentences. Foreign observers in Moscow thought so as well. The British government, nevertheless, invoked the embargo on Soviet imports and the Soviet government retaliated with its own British trade embargo.

Remediation

There followed a period in the spring of 1933 during which the two sides tried to settle the crisis. In the aftermath of the trial, Krestinskii was irritated with Maiskii's pressing for a settlement. "After all," he wrote, "we are not going to capitulate to the British." And continued:

> If we considered it possible to give in to the demands of the English, it would have been more rational to do this at the very beginning, without bringing the matter to court. If we did not yield to pressure, brought the arrested Englishmen to court and the court passed a sentence, then obviously all this was done not to enter into negotiations with the British immediately after the trial to mitigate the fate of those convicted for this or that compensation in regard to Anglo-Soviet trade.

The decision of the court was going to be carried out, Krestinskii advised, and after all the sentences were "extraordinarily light." If the British government was interested in a settlement, it would not be imposing an embargo. Judging from the Reuters reports, he noted, the embargo was inevitable and the Soviet leadership would soon see what that entailed.

> There is nothing you can do about it; you have to accept and endure the struggle. If the introduction of the embargo becomes a fact and the scope of it is known, then we will discuss what countermeasures we can take. No special decisions have as yet been taken. This is the opinion of Maksim Maksimovich and it is mine, which coincides, in our opinion, with the point of view of all the leading comrades.[70]

Given the number of meetings with Stalin in March and April, Krestinskii's statement to Maiskii is not surprising.

The Soviet reaction to the British embargo was immediate, as the Foreign Office should have expected based on the French experience in 1930. If the British wanted a fight, they would get it. Reciprocity was always a Soviet principle, and it was applied quickly. Litvinov advised Maiskii that, for the time being, there could be no question of discussing the release of the prisoners. "We have no, and cannot have any, solutions on this score," as Litvinov put it, "and it would hardly be timely even to raise this question now." Everything depended on the British. If they calmed down, the embargo was put on hold, and so on, the question could be raised about "the fate of the convicts." If, on the other hand, the press campaign continues and the embargo goes into effect, "a very complicated situation will arise, and we will probably have to think about economic countermeasures." Litvinov laid out some positions regarding the *torgpredstvo*, the Soviet trade mission. We can live without it, if necessary; it was a stake for bargaining. "In conversations with friends, we need at every opportunity to demonstrate that after the statements by Baldwin and Thomas [in March], and especially after Ovey's well-known conduct in Moscow … with threats and intimidation, the case could not go in any other direction."[71]

Litvinov was not a soft touch when it came to a diplomat or government trying to ride roughshod over the USSR. This was a trait of character that would have drawn Stalin's respect, as indeed it did during this period. If someone hits you on the head, hit them back. On 21 April, the Soviet government retaliated against the British embargo by imposing its own on Britain. Litvinov approved and recommended publicity for the Soviet decree. Moreover, the NKID kollegiia did not foresee an early end to the crisis and therefore recommended cancelling previous orders where there was no risk of lawsuits.[72]

In London, Maiskii retreated from trying to find a solution on the spot, though he complained again about a lack of information from Moscow. "The hardest thing about my situation throughout the conflict was that I never knew, never even had a clear idea of how and what we were supposed to do tomorrow. I usually received reports only of already accomplished facts. Meanwhile, it is to the highest degree important for me to know at least more or less what our next steps are likely to be in the near future."[73]

Litvinov was getting a little tired of Maiskii's whining. "I ask you please to remember what cannot be demanded from the most beautiful woman. One cannot write about decisions when they do not exist or before they are made. Assumptions, especially personal ones, can only be misleading." Having got that point out of the way, Litvinov briefed Maiskii on the situation in Moscow. The two convicted Metro-Vickers engineers had submitted petitions for commutation of their sentences. The commission to evaluate the petitions had instructions not to examine the files before six months of each sentence had passed, unless there were special circumstances. The instructions were not going to be published "in order not to tie our hands." Litvinov noted, that at the present time,

> clemency would be interpreted as a concession to the pressure of the embargo and as our capitulation, and from this point of view the later comes this decision, if there is such a decision, the better for us. In order to dispel Embassy and London illusions, where they are awaiting a pardon from day to day, Rubinin, on my instructions, sent a message to Strang, about which I telegraphed you. Thus, no changes in the situation are to be anticipated in the near future.

Litvinov then went on to discuss Maiskii's ideas about a "scheme" to end the crisis, the idea being to grant clemency but not release the prisoners until the embargo had been withdrawn. This approach would amount to hostage-taking, and would be a dream-come-true for the Die-Hards who would exploit it to the hilt. There could be no link between clemency and the embargo. Litvinov was dead right on this point, the Foreign Office having already prepared for such an eventuality.[74]

But Litvinov proposed a subtle line that Maiskii could use to draw the link without seeming to do so. The British would get the point. The problem was, as Maiskii himself had noted, the British had gone too far to be able to reverse course without "losing face." It was ironic that both combatants brought up "face" as an obstacle to a settlement. In any case, Litvinov said that Moscow would leave the initiative for the next step to the British. Maiskii thought that Simon was in no hurry for a solution, thinking that the embargo would force a Soviet surrender and thus a British diplomatic success. But this did not make any sense to Litvinov since the Soviet government had no intention of hurrying clemency. Hence, the longer the convicted men spent in prison, the less success Simon would be able to claim. It must be, therefore, that Simon and the cabinet would want a rapid solution to the conflict.[75]

Litvinov's assumptions about British policy were essentially correct, but what Litvinov did not say was that he was just as anxious to end the conflict. It was only a question of how to get the process started. As it turned out, the British took the first steps. On 24 April, Strang made the suggestion that the British government take the initiative by indicating that, upon the release of the two British citizens, the embargo would be raised. Strang reckoned that for both governments the affair had become a question of "prestige," but that somehow the process of negotiations had to be initiated. This could be done by a public statement from London declaring that the embargo would be lifted once the Metro-Vickers men were released.[76] Hailsham and Simon made statements to this effect in Parliament on 26 and 27 April, and Strang so informed Rubinin on the following day. Rubinin offered no comments apart from confirming that the two prisoners had made appeals for clemency which could take two to three months or more to resolve.[77]

The NKID put this information out to some foreign correspondents in Moscow who had sent reports to their papers, but Litvinov advised Maiskii that he did not know if the British press had picked up the information. Maiskii persisted in thinking that Simon was stalling on a resolution of the conflict, but Litvinov stuck to his view that Simon could only claim victory through a prompt freeing of the prisoners. It would appear that both Litvinov and Maiskii were right and wrong. When Strang recommended another démarche in early May, the Foreign Office advised him to wait and let the Soviet side take the initiative. "If we nibble … the only result will be to indicate our anxiety and to encourage Soviet Government to ask for more. I agree that we should avoid provocative answers in Parliament but I consider that our only line is to show that we can wait."[78] The problem thus remained of who would take the first step: the Soviet side freeing the prisoners, or the British side lifting the blockade? The obvious answer would be simultaneous steps, but it took another six weeks before so obvious a solution became clear to both sides.[79]

Epiphany

The epiphany occurred in London during the World Economic Conference, which began in mid-June and continued until the end of July. Litvinov made the argument to Stalin that a delegation should be sent in spite of hesitation in the Politburo. The conference would provide the Soviet government with the opportunity to showcase its plans for economic development and necessarily for imports in the context of an international plan to cope with the "world crisis." It was not to be expected that the conference would produce any concrete results, but it could lay the groundwork for subsequent negotiations with other countries or groups of countries on Soviet proposals made at the conference.[80]

Litvinov joked with the Italian ambassador, who was trying to pump him for information, that he would have preferred the conference to have been held anywhere but in London. The Italian ambassador had the impression that Litvinov was "working for a settlement but [was] meeting with difficulties." That would not have been surprising, but another Soviet informant in Moscow, the somewhat mysterious Soviet go-between Boris Sergeevich Steiger, advised Strang that "matters were 'developing smoothly'" and that "Litvinov was going to London with 'very clear ideas on the subject.'"[81] The negotiations were thus passing from Moscow and Strang and Rubinin to London and Litvinov and his British interlocutors.

The discussions in London began on 15 June with a meeting between the Metro-Vickers director, Sir Felix Pole, and Litvinov. According to Litvinov, Pole inquired about what it would take to free his men in Moscow. He came quickly to the point, proposing a simultaneous amnesty in exchange for the dropping of the embargo. Litvinov stuck to his position that the status of the two British engineers was a legal matter; they could be freed by amnesty, but there could be no amnesty "without, among other things, the elimination of the unfavourable atmosphere that had been created." It was for the British government to make the first move in lifting the embargo. The British started the "economic war," so they could end it. The Soviet government was not offering a quid pro quo for this action. "We do not bargain with people." This was Litvinov's line established in Moscow and he was writing to Stalin, so it was the hard line. According to Litvinov,

> Pole replied that he did not see any way out of the situation, because whether his government had done the right thing or not, it was already so engaged that it

> would not be able to lift the embargo before the deportation of the convicted men. He, Pole, and other industrialists are extremely unhappy with the situation, but there are people in England who are triumphant. When Pole asked if I wanted to meet Simon, I said that I had nothing to offer him and nothing to ask, and that I could only repeat what I had said to Pole.

This was a line that would not fly for a single moment in the Foreign Office at any level. Pole said he was leaving Litvinov in "complete despair" because he thought the conflict could drag on for months. The embargo had to be renewed in six weeks, Litvinov replied, or the government could let it lapse. Litvinov advised that he had received no calls from the Foreign Office, but he did not seem to care. At a state dinner, MacDonald and Simon had both expressed their desire to talk, but Litvinov refused to respond. All sorts of intermediaries had also introduced themselves. Litvinov was not interested. "The situation for me is as clear as it was in Moscow: for the British government to lift the embargo without the promise of a quid pro quo is impossible without losing face." Litvinov had made a proposal during the conference for an "economic truce," which might include the lifting of the embargo, but he did not think this idea would be acceptable to the Foreign Office. So the Soviet government should wait, Litvinov advised Stalin, and stick to the policy already laid out in Moscow of no bartering. Pole's record of conversation closely resembled that of Litvinov.[82]

Pole was not the only one to sound out Litvinov. Rex Leeper, who was then a Foreign Office senior clerk in the News Department, paid a call to Litvinov at the Soviet embassy. He wanted to sound him out about a settlement. Leeper had known Litvinov in 1918 when the narkom was serving as an unofficial Soviet ambassador in London. "It was understood on both sides," Leeper wrote in a long, handwritten record of conversation, "that the visit was of a purely personal character to renew acquaintances after 15 years." Leeper wrote an interesting characterization of Litvinov to which we shall return further on. This was not the purpose, however, of Leeper's visit. He wanted to discover whether a deal could be struck to free the Metro-Vickers engineers. Litvinov stuck to the position he had laid out to Stalin, and declined to make any suggestions to resolve the conflict. Leeper then backed off, not encouraged by what he had heard.

> He [Litvinov] is probably convinced that there was something in the charges … as he shares to the full the suspicions of his fellow-Bolsheviks … He will try to drive a hard bargain with us for the very reasons that he thinks his efforts to bring about satisfactory working relations with us have met with little response here … though a moderate man according to Soviet standards & at bottom perhaps quite benevolent, he is an out-and-out Communist of the Lenin school & will be quite unyielding on anything that he regards as a question of principle.[83]

Vansittart was not encouraged by Leeper's report. "I think you will have to let Litvinoff alone for ten days or so now. This is the second time he has been sounded here; and Mr Leeper thinks he is unlikely to make any advance himself. We cannot make a 3rd advance too quickly."[84] It was still the Alphonse and Gaston routine, but not for much longer. British businessmen were putting pressure on the Foreign Office to resolve the impasse. The pressure came, for example, in the form of a resolution of the Federation of British Industries, calling for the release of the Metro-Vickers engineers and the resumption of trade relations. The resolution appears to have led Simon to take the initiative of a meeting with Litvinov without waiting for a phone call from the Soviet embassy.[85] There also appeared to be a feeler in the *News Chronicle*, from Cummings, "the very pro-Russian correspondent of the paper who was recently in Moscow and is now in close touch with the Soviet Embassy [this according to Collier], suggesting that Litvinov was ready to move forward."[86]

The feeler may well have come from the Soviet embassy. Three days later, on 24 June, Litvinov wrote to Krestinskii much less certain of his way forward.

> I just want to add that we in Moscow had no idea about the impact of the Metro-Vickers case on public opinion in England. In this regard, we have returned here to the time before the resumption of relations [i.e., before 1929]. The British of the VOKS [Soviet cultural] organisations say that all their work over the years has gone down the drain. The embassy finds itself in a state of semi-boycott. We endure insults at every step of the way. Despite the best efforts of the English to show our delegation every courtesy, there have been not a few unpleasant moments in our interactions with them. Our enemies are working all out, using the favourable mood, while the industrialists are inactive and helpless in the face of serious political intrigues. Even "friends" do not understand our current position in the conflict and accuse us of exaggerating prestige issues. "Our [British] government has done a lot of stupid things, but it has already committed itself and cut off its way to retreat. You have to be smarter and get us out of the impasse" – that's what their reasoning comes down to.[87]

Solution

In face of this situation, and to avoid letting the situation drag out, Litvinov moved his position and asked for approval from Moscow for a modified, "minimum" proposal to take to the British.[88] He advised Stalin that Simon had invited him to the Foreign Office for discussions. As far as Litvinov knew, the British position was a simultaneous lifting of the embargo in exchange for the freeing of the Metro-Vickers prisoners. So Litvinov moved his red lines, but not by much. The narkom proposed that the British government end the embargo *and* permit the resumption of trade *for a week* at which point the Soviet government would accord amnesty and deport the prisoners. A further concession at the limit would be *a promise* from the Soviet government or the NKID to support amnesty after the lifting the embargo. In any case, Litvinov asked Stalin for plenipotentiary powers to resolve the dispute.[89] Litvinov had moved but not by much. It is surprising that he thought that the British government would accept such a proposal. In any case, Leeper's assessment appears to have been close to the mark. Litvinov was not some Western-oriented pussy cat.

A first meeting between Simon and Litvinov took place on 26 June. Litvinov tried out his proposals, which Simon, not unexpectedly, rejected. It was simultaneous concessions or no deal. The embargo would continue. Matters were left at that. Litvinov asked for time to mull over the options and then, he said to Simon, he would ask for a further meeting. The narkom at once wrote to Moscow for instructions. Prior removal of the embargo was not likely, he advised, nor was it likely that Simon would make any further suggestions. So Litvinov proposed accepting Simon's idea of simultaneous concessions: lifting of the embargo and the Soviet countermeasures and, on the same day, commuting the sentences of the two Metro-Vickers engineers. The one twist was that the embargo and countermeasures would go first and the commutation would follow it during the course of the same day. The response from Moscow was prompt. "As a last and penultimate concession," Stalin agreed to Litvinov's recommendations.[90] There were three further meetings that week between Simon and Litvinov and another between Simon and Maiskii to settle the details and to make sure that each side would respect its commitments.[91] The agreements were thus carried out on the weekend, and the prisoners set free on the evening of 1 July. They crossed into Poland two days later.

The English patrician and the Polish-born Bolshevik were able finally to establish sufficient mutual trust to come to terms and carry out their agreements without a hitch. What had changed to induce the two sides to agree so quickly to end the conflict? On the British side, business was lobbying the government to find a solution to the crisis so that trade with the USSR would not be disrupted. The Foreign Office was not the only interested party in this question; the Board of Trade and Runciman were also looking for a solution. The strength of the business lobby came to light in a conversation, which Maiskii reported, between Aleksandr V. Ozerskii, torgpred, and F.H. Nixon of the Export Credits Guarantee Department. Apparently under the influence of alcohol, Nixon opened up about the Metro-Vickers conflict, saying that "during the conflict and, in particular, after [the imposition of] the embargo, the Foreign Office all the time sought to break diplomatic relations with the USSR."

> It met, however, strong resistance from the Board of Trade, as well as from some other members of the government. In addition, it was extremely inconvenient for the British cabinet to sever relations with the USSR just before the convening of a

> world economic conference. When the latter gathered, the Board of Trade insisted on the need to profit from Comrade Litvinov's stay in London to eliminate the conflict. The Foreign Office resisted desperately. Then [David John] Colville [secretary of the Department of Overseas Trade] in a very insistent way raised the question of lifting the embargo with Runciman … [who] backed Colville. Together they went to MacDonald and raised a great scandal. MacDonald summoned Simon and suggested that he begin negotiations with comrade Litvinov.

According to Nixon, it was only then that Simon invited Litvinov to the Foreign Office to discuss a resolution of the conflict with Colville present as *politkom* (political commissar) to make sure nothing went amiss. Maiskii was convinced that this information was sound since it coincided with details he had picked up at the time of the crisis.[92] Readers should be grateful therefore for Nixon's indiscretions under the influence of alcohol and Maiskii's record keeping.

On the Soviet side, Litvinov was clearly disturbed by the Nazi danger, saying as much in his letters to Krestinskii and Stalin. "With Germany, obviously," Litvinov wrote to Krestinskii, "we will not be able to get along. We must therefore look for support wherever we can." That meant settling the Metro-Vickers affair, which Litvinov had never considered to be worth a serious row. In his letter to Stalin, Litvinov mentioned the so-called Alfred Hugenberg memorandum promoting German eastern expansion, and recommended strengthening ties with France.[93] The Foreign Office picked up on the shift in Soviet policy. It was getting hard to miss. Journalist Karl Radek had been publishing articles about Soviet policy, which caught the notice of the Foreign Office.[94] Steiger, the shadowy Soviet informant in Moscow, mentioned to Strang the Hugenberg speech in London and opined that it "had given a definite impulse in favour of a settlement" of the Metro-Vickers conflict. "Everything seems to point to the Soviet Government," Collier noted, "being so preoccupied by the menace of Hitler that they will not quarrel with anyone else while it lasts." Although Litvinov could not say it in his dispatches from London, Steiger hinted "that there is a marked disposition on the part of the governing authorities here to favour the establishment of calm and stable relations with … [Britain]."[95] It did not seem to occur to Foreign Office officials, at least not in the context of the Metro-Vickers affair, that Britain too ought to be "preoccupied," as Collier put it, with "the menace of Hitler."

It was nevertheless true that the Foreign Office was interested in calm in Anglo-Soviet relations. When Collier showed some interest in stirring up the controversy again after the release of the prisoners, he found no support. "I am firmly of the opinion," Oliphant noted, "that we shd. damp down & not blow up the dying embers into any form of flame." When Collier asked about the proofs of a third White Paper, both Oliphant and Vansittart opposed publication. It was "applying sand in the machinery," according to Oliphant. Vansittart did not think the last two Metro-Vickers engineers deserved more attention: "These men have little to reveal except their own selfish cowardice. They were innocent but gave way under a minimum of pressure to save – as they thought – their own skins, without ever thinking of their fellows. I am indeed surprised to find how much less the pressure was than I had expected. We did the right thing, and scored a very considerable success: but we did for poor stuff, and I don't think we need prolong the story, which culminated with their exit from Russia."[96] It was time to move on, although to what remained to be seen.

The Metro-Vickers affair is a good example of how Soviet-Western quarrels could be settled. It shows also that the decisions inside the Soviet government, where relations with other states arose, did not always pass by the NKID. This was especially dangerous as awareness arose in Moscow of the Nazi menace and the need for allies in the West. In June, Litvinov clearly recognized the danger and warned Stalin. Relations with Britain needed to be put right, and the two British engineers were not worth the trouble in the larger context of rising instability in Europe. As it was, the Metro-Vickers affair delayed by a year Soviet efforts to launch a rapprochement with Britain. A cooling off period would be necessary. In the meantime, Soviet diplomacy became focused elsewhere.

Chapter Five

Rapallo or Not? Soviet Relations with Germany and Poland, 1933

In Germany political developments were happening fast. In 1932, governments in Berlin changed almost as quickly as those in Paris. That all stopped in January 1933. Hitler became chancellor and immediately set about to establish a Nazi dictatorship, making illegal first the Communist and then the Socialist Parties. Hitler made no secret of his intentions; he published them in 1925, in a book entitled *Mein Kampf*. It was his blueprint for the German domination of Europe and territorial expansion far into Eastern Europe to the Ural Mountains, and it often drew the attention of Litvinov and his NKID colleagues.

Could Rapallo Survive in Nazi Germany?

In mid-February 1933, the Soviet polpred in Rome, Vladimir Petrovich Potemkin, commented to his German counterpart that belligerent statements by Nazi leaders were raising doubts about the future of Soviet-German relations.[1] In late February 1933, not quite a month after Hitler became chancellor, zamnarkom Krestinskii, met the German ambassador, Herbert von Dirksen. The ambassador got along pretty well with his Soviet counterparts. German policy towards the USSR, said Dirksen, would continue as before. The German government's internal "struggle with communism" could proceed while at the same time preserving good relations with the Soviet Union. "We do not want and we are not making any change in our policy toward Germany," Krestinskii replied in a long conversation, "but we cannot fail to be concerned about the proposals of the former Chancellor and the present vice-Chancellor von Papen made to the French government." Under the circumstances, friendly declarations made privately to Soviet diplomats, "eye to eye," by representatives of the German government are insufficient. Such declarations are unknown to public opinion and do not prevent parallel, contrary declarations from being made. Dirksen tried to be reassuring.[2]

Two days later Litvinov met the German foreign minister, Konstantin von Neurath, in Berlin for a similar conversation. A change in government, Neurath repeated in what was already a familiar line, did not mean a change in policy towards the USSR. Litvinov was not so sure.[3] Words were not enough to reassure the Soviet government, the narkom often replied to German interlocutors. Only actions count. "I do not know," Litvinov wrote to Potemkin, "if it is widely known abroad about the numerous cases of unfriendly and offensive acts on the part of the new German authorities against Soviet citizens and establishments."[4] Ironically, back in 1927 Litvinov and Dirksen, independently from one another, had concluded that Rapallo would not last forever. It was only a matter of time and interests.[5]

In the campaign against German communists, Nazi hooligans rousted Soviet citizens working for various Soviet enterprises. "All our protests against the provocative actions of the German fascists," Litvinov reported to Stalin, "have until now produced no results." One could only conclude that a cooling or even a crisis in Soviet-German relations was in the cards. The only option Litvinov saw to pressure the Germans was to play a Polish card, that is, to send a business delegation to Poland and give it a high level of publicity.[6] Proposing a Polish option, given Warsaw's doubtful policy, underscored the weakness of Litvinov's pressure point, but what else could he do?

Words and Deeds

The Soviet counsellor in Berlin observed that public statements by Nazi Party officials corresponded with the main lines of *Mein Kampf*.[7] On 3 April, the same day Litvinov wrote to Stalin, Krestinskii again met Dirksen to talk about the deterioration of German-Soviet relations. They had never been more difficult than now, Krestinskii said. Hitler's reassurances during a speech in the Reichstag on 23 March were not enough. Actions spoke louder than words, and based on this criterium, abuse on the streets against Soviet establishments continued. "Our public opinion" – which essentially meant Stalin and his close associates in the Politburo – was worried. The chancellor said one thing, but his colleagues did otherwise. What was it to be? Dirksen and the German military attaché, who was with him, tried to be reassuring. The troubles would pass.[8] Litvinov had his doubts and seemed to pick up on the warning from the Berlin embassy about *Mein Kampf*. He drew Stalin's attention to anxieties in the Baltic countries resulting from Hitler's rise to power and also to his well-known proposals (from *Mein Kampf*) for *Lebensraum* in the east.[9]

Having talked to Krestinskii, Dirksen also met with Litvinov. The conversation passed much as it had with Krestinskii, except the tone of it seemed a little blunter. Dirksen tried to explain away attacks in Germany on Soviet citizens and establishments as "isolated" events that would pass, but Litvinov was not buying it. "I responded," the narkom wrote in his journal, "that we were really alarmed by the arrival in power in Germany of people whose political credo could not inspire in us optimism about the fate of our mutual relations." "We,"

Litvinov said. The ambassador "needed to understand the public indignation and resentment which events [in Germany] had provoked." In fact, comments in the press did "not reflect to the remotest degree the feelings of our public." On and on Litvinov went. Dirksen might speak of isolated events, "but the fact is that in Germany we now are facing not isolated, local events, but mass baiting of everything which carries the name soviet. This is about an organised campaign, directed from a single centre … against which the [German] government is taking no measures to stop." This cannot continue, Litvinov said, "our public" (*obshchestvennost'*) was demanding reciprocal measures. Dirksen responded lamely that the Soviet press might refrain from publishing news from Germany. "The question," Litvinov responded, "still needs to be resolved by the government."[10] Dirksen definitely got the message. "It is my conviction," he wrote to Berlin, "that a serious crisis has been reached in our mutual relations." If the crisis could not be resolved, the USSR could reverse policy towards Germany.[11]

Dirksen was alarmed by the downward plunge of Soviet-German relations, though Hitler not so much. Dirksen stressed to the Auswärtiges Amt, the German foreign ministry, that the extension of the treaty of Berlin was the only way to stabilize relations with Moscow. This was done in early May, but it had little positive effect. Krestinskii noted that treaty renewal was just a ruse to disrupt improving relations between the USSR and France and Poland. Still, Krestinskii was cautiously hopeful about a change for the better in German policy, though, as he said, "we must not lessen our vigilance."[12] So the Soviet government launched a public shot across the German bow; Litvinov hoped that France and Poland would notice. It was an article by Karl Radek in *Pravda* that argued against the revision of the Treaty of Versailles. "Revision," he wrote, was just another word for a new world war. Litvinov noted that Radek's article had drawn a protest from Dirksen and approval from Polish sources. What about the French? Litvinov asked Dovgalevskii.[13] The French embassy did not appear to have reported the article to Paris.

Litvinov agreed with Krestinskii that Germany was looking for a way out of its isolation, though he spoke less about the desirability of repairing Soviet-German relations and more about pursuing the rapprochement with France.[14] Krestinskii seemed a little more positive than Litvinov about maintaining the "Rapallo policy." But maybe not. Although the NKID distanced itself from the Radek article in conversation with Dirksen, Krestinskii thought it "absolutely correct" on the Treaty of Versailles.[15] Keep in mind that the worsening of Soviet-German relations was taking place at the same time as the Metro-Vickers crisis.

Nikolai Nikolaievich Krestinskii

Krestinskii was the first deputy commissar in the NKID, and a sympathetic Soviet personality with whom readers should become acquainted. He joined the Russian Social Democratic Workers' Party in 1903, and after the split in the

Figure 5.1. Nikolai Nikolaievich Krestinskii, ca. 1930s, AVPRF.

party, opted for the Bolsheviks. He was born in 1883 in the provincial town of Mogilev; he was seven years younger than Litvinov. Nikolai Nikolaievich was a good student in *gimnaziia*, as one might perhaps expect from a son born into a family of teachers. Eventually he completed a degree in law at the University of St. Petersburg. Krestinskii was a member of the first Politburo, and the narkom of finance. Close to Lenin, he was the Central Committee's secretary until he was sacked in 1921, according to Molotov, for not paying attention to "politics." He then went to Berlin as polpred; at the time, it was the most important Soviet posting abroad. Multilingual and pragmatic like Litvinov, he was the right person for the job of dealing with the middle class, social democrats, and Prussian conservatives of Weimar Germany. Krestinskii knew how to make his way among the German elite. If you look at his photographs, Krestinskii did not look like a steely eyed, hard-bitten Bolshevik. None of the Soviet diplomats did, of course; the few wild cards were weeded out early on. Krestinskii had a kindly look about him, with a subtle smile, wearing round, gold-rimmed spectacles, balding, but with a Van Dyke moustache and beard in his younger days. He was smooth in his dealings with Berlin business circles, which irritated some German diplomats, but was just what was needed in pursuing Soviet trade policy. The French ambassador in Berlin said Krestinskii knew how to avoid drawing unwanted attention and trouble to himself. In politics, he sided with Trotskii during the leadership struggle with Stalin, though more quietly and discretely than other colleagues. Molotov accused him of being a "Trotskyist." It is true he did not much like Stalin, and Stalin did not much like him. In 1928, Stalin rounded sharply on Krestinskii, still the polpred in Berlin, for not following Politiburo directives closely enough. The language of Stalin's letter was chilling; Krestinskii retreated. Even in 1928, it was not a good idea to tangle with Stalin. In 1930, Krestinskii returned to Moscow to become the zamnarkom in the NKID. Some say that he wanted Litvinov's job, but in the NKID correspondence, it does not show. Perhaps Krestinskii was a little more minded to save Rapallo. This was understandable, since he had invested so much time in smoothing over Soviet-German relations, but if so, it was only a passing nuance, for in the end his position corresponded to that of Litvinov.

Litvinov and Dirksen

In Moscow, the sparring and probing between the German ambassador and his NKID interlocutors continued. Litvinov saw Dirksen again in mid-May. "Fascism per se, as also with any other social-political ideology of bourgeois governments," he noted, "is not an obstacle to the establishment and development of good relationships." Unlike Italy, however, the Nazi government seemed to go out of its way to exacerbate relations with the Soviet Union. The ratification of the renewal of the Berlin treaty was well received, especially "by our governmental circles," but strong doubts remained. "We have people at home," he wrote, who think Hitler is hiding his real intentions towards the Soviet Union and that plans are being formulated to worsen Soviet relations with France and Britain, "or other governments." Litvinov was remarkably blunt with Dirksen. "It seems to me," he said, "there is not one Soviet or quasi-Soviet establishment in Germany, which has not been subjected to searches or vandalism." The exchange with Dirksen went as before. "We would like nothing better than to continue those relations with Germany which existed between us and [Walther] Rathenau, [Gustav] Stresemann and [Julius] Curtius [*inter alia* German foreign ministers]. The possibility of this, however, depends not on us, but on the German government." Then Litvinov added sarcastically, that any improvement in relations with Berlin would be facilitated by "our policy of rapprochement with France, Poland and other governments."[16] He confirmed this message two weeks later with Neurath.[17] Salvaging the Rapallo policy was for the moment still Soviet policy and continued thus through the summer months while Litvinov settled the Metro-Vickers affair.

Krestinskii summarized the Soviet position to the Soviet polpred in Berlin, Lev Mikhailovich Khinchuk. The National Socialist foreign policy was "sharply anti-Soviet," and since Hitler's rise to power, Nazi Brownshirts (*Braunhemden*) "have struck one blow after the other against us." If there had been a softening of Nazi policy, it was because Germany was trying to break out of diplomatic isolation created by its maladroit foreign policy. "The greater part of our public thinks it is only a temporary, contrived tactic," said Krestinskii, "the basic line of foreign policy of the Nazi government remains as before to extend its control in the east at the expense of the Soviet Union." The Soviet public saw the proof of these intentions in the statements of Nazi officials, supported by White Guard Russian immigrants, who had a definite influence on German foreign policy. "In this case, neither Litvinov, nor I, nor [David Grigor'evich] Shtern [NKID department head] share the mood of our public, though we defend the legitimacy of such views … to Dirksen."

The Soviet government was pursuing a cautious line, hoping for the best with Germany while at the same time improving relations with France and Poland, there too, hoping for the best. "We do not wish by virtue of putting unnecessary public emphasis on friendship with Germany to prevent an improvement of our relations with France and Poland." But, according to Krestinskii, "at the same time we want in effect to improve our relations with Germany, we want to resolve all conflicts having occurred during the last several months, in a word, we want our relations to return to their former calm waters." Essentially, Krestinskii hoped a "respite" in German hostility would serve Soviet interests, and the longer the better. If it developed, Krestinskii cautioned.[18] One wonders about the zamnarkom's recollections of Rapallo. Soviet-German relations during the 1920s were often difficult, and rarely in "calm waters."

Krestinskii told Khinchuk that he and Litvinov saw eye to eye on the desirability of preserving the old policy, but perhaps not entirely. "With Germany, obviously," Litvinov observed in June, "we will not be able to get along. It is necessary therefore to look elsewhere for support wherever possible." That meant France. But it also meant improving relations with the Little Entente in Central and Eastern Europe (Czechoslovakia, Romania, Yugoslavia), which in turn would benefit Soviet relations with France and Poland.[19]

In mid-June Alfred Hugenberg, then the economics minister in Hitler's government and head of the German delegation to the World Economic Conference in London, gave a speech making reference, among other topics, to Germany's need for new living space and "for new territories at the expense of the USSR." In his so-called memorandum, Hugenberg was speaking on his own responsibility, but his central theme was a reflection of Hitler's ideas articulated in *Mein Kampf.* This was the same speech that aroused Litvinov's alarm when he was in London trying to ease Anglo-Soviet relations. One way or another, it set off the fire alarms in Moscow. The Soviet embassy in Berlin lodged an official protest.[20] Litvinov wrote to Krestinskii that the Hugenberg speech, as readers will remember, was yet another warning, which "must induce us to strengthen our activities in Paris."[21] And calm the troubled waters in London, he might have added.

Litvinov did not mention Poland in that particular letter, perhaps because in the summer of 1933 the NKID remained suspicious of the Polish government's intentions. These suspicions were only increased by Polish attempts to undermine Litvinov's proposals for the definition of an aggressor, which he saw as a supplement to the conclusion of various Soviet non-aggression pacts. He first made these proposals in February 1933 in the context of the World Disarmament Conference, which had begun in 1932 but was now deadlocked. Germany aimed for "equal rights" on rearmament and France wanted to maintain the advantages it had obtained as a victor in the Great War. Litvinov considered the disarmament conference to be a "fiasco" and the League of Nations to be "disintegrating." The idea, however, was to participate and be visible in order to strengthen the Soviet "international position."[22]

Would the Soviet-Polish Rapprochement Continue?

There was a problem, amongst others, regarding Soviet-Polish relations. Poland could not admit any "strengthening of the international influence and authority of the USSR," Stomoniakov observed (he was responsible for the Polish file): "The backroom conduct of Poland demonstrates that Poland is pursuing a very complicated diplomatic game, which anticipates not only the possibility of a further improvement of Soviet-Polish relations but also the possibility of a worsening of them. That is why all the history of negotiations on the convention [defining the aggressor] obliges us to be very cautious in relation to Poland and very wary of Polish policy." Stomoniakov was also doubtful about Polish relations with Germany. There were many indications both in Poland and Germany of efforts to avoid straining of relations. One could see in the press, for example, that the two sides were holding their fire. There were also rumours, which could not simply be discounted as disinformation, of German-Polish negotiations. Édouard Daladier and Joseph Paul-Boncour had twice drawn Litvinov's attention to these negotiations from which they had dissociated themselves. Charles Alphand, French ambassador in Moscow, also remarked upon the recent "strange" behaviour of Poland. A Polish-German agreement could therefore not be ruled out. "We must see clearly the danger" of such a turn in Polish policy, Stomoniakov said. The French had already put out an inspired comment in the Paris papers. The Poles have two options for and against us. We have to strengthen those political forces in Poland favourable to the USSR and "to strive by all means to strengthen, develop and deepen our relations with Poland."[23]

To that end, Karl Radek, the old Bolshevik of Polish origin, was sent on a two-week tour of Poland in July to talk to Polish counterparts about better

Soviet-Polish relations.[24] It was a highly publicized affair, with Radek even paying a visit to his mother in Tarnow, Galicia, where he was born. In Warsaw, the Polish go-between Bogusław Miedziński was there to facilitate contacts. Among others, Radek met with Józef Beck, Polish foreign minister, and General Edward Rydz-Śmigły, inspector general of the Polish armed forces. Radek thought these meetings were a step forward, signalling a "complete change of mood." He repeated some of the ideas that Miedziński had already passed to him in their earlier discussions. The Poles had no illusions and understood that Germany wanted to transform Poland into a "vassal" for use in a future campaign against the USSR. "They believe that Hitler wants to play for a lot of time possibly to delay war." War, however, could break out in the Far East or in the Balkans; if a clash occurred between Japan and the USSR, Germany might exploit it to attack from the west.

These were speculations with which the Soviet side was all too familiar. Soviet relations with Japan were strained. The Polish position was to play the game with Hitler, "peaceful manoeuvre" against peaceful manoeuvre, but the Poles would fight to defend the Polish Corridor, which divided East Prussia from the rest of Germany. "Everyone said that it was necessary to go further along the path of rapprochement," Radek noted. Even Beck, but could that be true? The quid pro quo would be Soviet help to Poland to defend the corridor and Polish cooperation to obstruct a German advance in the northeast towards Leningrad. Radek wanted to try for agreement on all questions "from the Black Sea to the Baltics." Beck was a dreamer and he dreamed big, but there was certainly room for discussion about security in the Baltic area. Along with Polish dreams came the nightmares, one being that "France might sell them [Poland] to the Germans." They (the Poles) knew, however, that the more Poland could look to its own defences, the more France would rely on it. That was true. Radek noted that Beck also alluded to Polish concerns about the Rapallo policy, fearing the influence of the German army and the "German tradition in the NKID."[25]

Who could say how to evaluate Beck's statements? The French ambassador in Warsaw, Jules Laroche, took note of Radek's visit, reporting to Paris that it was yet another sign of improving Soviet-Polish relations, or so it seemed. Beck *prend des airs mystérieux*, Laroche reported, hinting to a colleague that something was up, which, *forcément*, did not mean with the USSR.[26] Laroche had been in Warsaw for a long time; he knew Beck well, better than Radek knew him. The Polish minister might have been using Radek as bait to encourage German interest. Stalin did not annotate or circulate Radek's first report, but he did annotate a second report that went into details about how a deepening of a Soviet-Polish rapprochement might look.[27] Radek's visit was largely, though not entirely, an exercise in publicity and had no lasting effect. The Miedziński channel stayed open for a while longer but proved barren.

Antonov-Ovseenko Complains

There was, however, another reaction in Warsaw from the polpred Vladimir Aleksandrovich Antonov-Ovseenko, who was encouraged by Radek's discussions and felt that the NKID was not doing enough to solidify a Polish-Soviet rapprochement. It was still locked into the Rapallo policy. "It is not the Poles, but us," he wrote to Stomoniakov, "who are proving unready for a 'rapprochement' with Poland."[28] Krestinskii intervened, alarmed by what appeared to be a polemic between Antonov-Ovseenko and Stomoniakov. He wrote a long dispatch to Antonov-Ovseenko arguing that his position and that of Stomoniakov were not so far apart. More than that, he disputed Antonov-Ovseenko's belief that intelligence from Daladier and Paul-Boncour about Polish secret discussions with the Germans was disinformation. There were other indications that confirmed the French information, the most important of which was the absence of a strong Polish reaction to the Hugenberg memorandum that threatened Poland as much as it did the USSR. "We must therefore be extremely vigilant," Krestinskii wrote, "and react against that tendency in Polish policies which inhibit our rapprochement with it [i.e., Poland]." This is why *Pravda* had published an editorial, he continued, to indicate to "our enemies in Germany and in Poland that we have caught on to their game."[29]

In the autumn, it became clear that Poland was moving towards some kind of agreement with Germany. In early October, Stomoniakov again reported the latest developments to the embassy in Warsaw. Franco-Polish relations were marked by animosity and mistrust, although they continued as before, Beck having visited Paris, to underline that both sides still valued the Franco-Polish alliance. It's a "marriage of convenience," Stonomiakov concluded. He also advised Antonov-Ovseenko that the Polish government was supporting anti-Soviet activities in the western Ukraine and that the campaign had spilled over into other countries.[30] A fortnight later a Soviet official working in the consulate in Lvov was assassinated by a Ukrainian "nationalist." In fact, in mid-October, Polish and German diplomats talked about settling outstanding issues. On 15 November, the Polish foreign ministry informed Ambassador Laroche of a meeting that the Polish ambassador Józef Lipski had just had with Hitler.[31] That courtesy was not extended to Antonov-Ovseenko. A joint communiqué was issued on the following day. Stomoniakov called in the Polish ambassador, Juliusz Łukasiewicz, to ask for an explanation. The ambassador had to admit, red-faced, according to Stomoniakov, that a Polish-German non-aggression pact looked to be in the cards.[32]

Stomoniakov nevertheless affirmed to Antonov-Ovseenko that the NKID would pursue its rapprochement with Poland and that Polish-German negotiations would not affect Soviet policy. The object remained to strengthen those Polish elements that supported "friendship with the USSR against Germany."

The only circumstance that would oblige a change of policy would be a direct Polish-German agreement against the USSR. Such an option was not to be envisaged without a prior Japanese attack in the Far East. Stomoniakov added that improved relations with the United States facilitated a continuation of Soviet policy towards Poland. Every part of Soviet policy fit together as in a large puzzle. "The single practical lesson which we must draw from the most recent events in our relations with Poland," Stomoniakov noted, "is the need to exercise great caution and great vigilance in regard to our Polish partners. It is impossible to overestimate the meaning of those declarations that are made to us by Polish politicians; impossible, under the influence of the spring time of our relations, to accept at face value 'outpourings,' which are made sometimes with the direct objective of disinformation." Stomoniakov was still trying to calm down Antonov-Ovseenko's leaning towards over-optimism about the prospects for Soviet-Polish relations.[33]

In a meeting with Beck, Antonov-Ovseenko accused the Polish foreign ministry news department of "direct disinformation," if not bald-faced lying, since it denied to the Warsaw TASS correspondent that any negotiations were underway between Germany and Poland. As Antonov-Ovseenko put it, such behaviour was not likely to inspire confidence in Moscow. That was certainly an understatement. A red-faced Beck declined to reply. He tried to explain Polish policy as basically *sauve qui peut*. "Geneva institutions have collapsed; so has the disarmament conference," he said. Hence, the Polish government was trying to take advantage of opportunities outside of Geneva. Nevertheless, Beck still proposed "close contact" on disarmament and other issues.[34]

Antonov-Ovseenko offered an explanation of Polish policy negotiations with Germany. It came down to this: that Poland could only depend on itself to protect its national interests. A united anti-German front did not exist. Poland could not count on France, nor the Little Entente, still less Britain or Italy as "reliable" allies against Germany. It was surrounded by states ready to sell it to save themselves from conflict with Germany. In fact, it was Poland, not Germany, which faced isolation. According to Antonov-Ovseenko, Poland could escape isolation by strengthening relations with the USSR in conjunction with the liquidation of the Rapallo policy. Since "preventative war" against Germany was not conceivable, Poland had to reduce tensions with Berlin, "playing for time," while also assuring for itself a place at the table of the other European powers. Antonov-Ovseenko apparently thought Rapallo was still considered an option in Moscow, when in fact it was moribund. He warned that the spectre of Rapallo played into German hands.[35]

The TASS correspondent in Warsaw wrote that the Poles were not giving up their Soviet cards. They reinforced the Polish position in Berlin. Everybody had cards to play. The Poles were playing for time, say three years. Beck was not pursuing a "pro-German" policy, he was pursuing a pro-Polish policy and "manoeuvring very carefully."[36] Except that Nazi Germany was not just any other great power. Poland thought it could ride on the tiger's back, but so did the other European powers. They were all wrong, including the USSR, as we shall see.

Radek Meddles

Radek must have thought he was a Polish expert because he injected himself into the discussion of Polish-Soviet relations. He knew he was meddling by writing to Stalin and admitted as much. "Very much now depends," Radek wrote, "on the arrangement of people. Comrade Antonov-Ovseenko is fainthearted and he does not say to you what he says to me." And with this, Radek took sides in what he saw as the conflict between the NKID and Antonov-Ovseenko over Soviet policy towards Poland. The polpred and Stomoniakov were "constantly exchanging polemical letters." The NKID *apparat*, brought up on Rapallo, had taken one line against another represented by Antonov-Ovseenko. Radek was ill-informed, the Rapallo line was dying, Stomoniakov represented caution in the pursuit of the rapprochement with Poland, not opposition. Radek saw it as a whispering campaign inside the NKID. The head of the press bureau, for example, passing from Litvinov to the press office in the Warsaw embassy, opined that all the talk of Polish rapprochement was nothing but Radek's (*radekovskoe*) enthusiasm. Thus, Radek was defending his own policy views, not those of the Soviet embassy in Warsaw. He saw rivalries inside rivalries impeding the policy of rapprochement with Poland. The NKID correspondence does not reflect Radek's view of things, but who can say what the correspondence was hiding? "If you consider it useful to call me for sorting out relations with the Poles," Radek wrote to Stalin, "I would be grateful."[37]

Krestinskii was cold-blooded. The NKID did not need to say anything to Germany or to Poland about their emerging rapprochement, Krestinskii advised the Berlin embassy: "As before the Hitler-Lipski meeting and after it, we have maintained and we will maintain caution and restraint."[38] One unnamed Bolshevik put it more acidly to the French military attaché Colonel Edmond Mendras in a private conversation, "When the Poles make pleasantries … I always wonder what dirty trick they are going to play on me."[39] But, of course, the Poles always had similar things to say about Russians. That's the way it was between Poles and Russians, for several centuries at least.

In mid-December, Antonov-Ovseenko wrote directly to Stalin without sending copies to the NKID. "No matter how you evaluate the Polish-German game – my evaluation, you know – one thing is certain, we need to oppose the strengthening of Germanophile tendencies in Poland. Germany is putting unprecedented pressure on Poland. We would facilitate the anti-Soviet work of the Germans and Japanese if we do not continue the already launched line of rapprochement with Poland." No one in the NKID was telling Antonov-Ovseenko that the rapprochement was being suspended, but he remained sceptical and therefore pressed Stalin directly. He made a series of recommendations, including the upgrading of the Polish legation in Moscow to embassy status and "obliging" Litvinov to make a stop in Warsaw to meet Beck on his next trip abroad. Stalin underlined the dispatch and indicated that it should be filed in his archives.[40]

Also in mid-December, Litvinov met Łukasiewicz to ask for clarifications on Beck's statements to Antonov-Ovseenko. Was it contemplated to turn the German-Polish "declaration" into a written pact? The ambassador responded negatively. Litvinov did not sound convinced. He nevertheless turned the discussion to a joint Polish-Soviet draft declaration endorsing peace and security in the Baltic and consultation in the event of a threat to the independence of the Baltic states. This was an idea from Antonov-Ovseenko. Łukasiewicz did not appear enthusiastic, but Litvinov asked him to forward the draft to Beck.[41] What was the narkom thinking? Was it an attempt to keep the Poles in play, or to test their intentions? Łukasiewicz returned a few days later with Beck's reply. In effect, he agreed in principle, but supposed that draft was subject to revision and consultation with others. Litvinov suggested that Beck visit Moscow for a face-to-face discussion. The ambassador agreed, of course, but wondered about a suitable date.[42] That same day, Stomoniakov reported difficulties with Łukasiewicz who had raised an old dispute last discussed ten years before.[43] What were the Poles up to?

Beck revealed his hand a few days later in a conversation with Antonov-Ovseenko, as if understanding Litvinov's démarche. He himself brought up the question that had not been posed directly. There was no inconsistency, he said, between negotiations with Germany and the rapprochement with the Soviet Union. They're related questions. He was in no hurry about Litvinov's draft, but was agreeable to the visit to Moscow. Antonov-Ovseenko wanted to talk about the Polish démarche in Berlin. The secrecy which surrounded it, said the polpred, continued to prompt "bewilderment" (*nedoumenie*) in Moscow. Beck did not react directly to this observation, but said, that "in principle" the conclusion of a pact of non-aggression with Germany was possible. Economic negotiations were not going well, Beck added: "But Poland has completed its own manoeuvre in Berlin and achieved something different: it articulated and defended its international position … Poland wants questions concerning it[s interests] not to be decided without it." This was, of course, an honest explanation of Polish policy; the only question was whether Poland had the power to achieve it. Beck talked about France and other subjects, and he asked about Litvinov's negotiations in the United States. There were hints, he remarked, of a closer rapprochement between the United States and the Soviet Union. Roosevelt and Litvinov also discussed, the polpred replied, a "triple alliance" (*o troistvennom soiuze*) of Poland, France, and the Soviet Union. To this observation, Beck did not respond.[44] All would become clear in the coming weeks.

Józef Beck

Józef Beck was not a very popular personality among his diplomatic interlocutors. He was young for his high position, born in 1894 in Warsaw, thus only in his late thirties when he became foreign minister. His father was a lawyer and Polish nationalist who ran afoul of the tsarist police prior to the Great War. The family eventually ended up in Austria-Hungary. In 1914, Beck had just finished his university studies when war broke out. He joined Józef Piłsudski's Polish legion raised by the government in Vienna to fight the Russians. At the end of the war, Beck was an officer in the Polish army and served as military attaché in Paris where he was widely despised. These circumstances may actually have spoken well of Beck since the French behaved like arrogant orientalists after the war and often treated Poland as a dependency and the Poles as interns. The Polish elite was not short on arrogance, either, aspiring to re-establish Poland as the great power it had been during the Late Middle Ages. Neither the French nor the Poles were as strong as they thought themselves to be. A cynic would say they deserved one another. Photographs of Beck show a strong looking, arrogant individual with receding, slicked back hair and a nose that was too large for his face. He was married but philandered. Like many of his contemporaries, he was an alpha heterosexual male with a fondness, so it was said, for young girls. It was not that, however, which caused him to be hated and mistrusted. It was his conniving and double-dealing which did that, embellished by his belief that Poland stood as a great power. He was the kind of personality about which one might say "there are none so blind as those who will not see."

Antonov-Ovseenko Still at Odds with Moscow

Soviet military intelligence reported information originating from the German embassy in Warsaw that the Poles had put the question to the German side of a non-aggression pact.[45] Germany was said to have agreed. Intelligence reports always had to be assessed carefully, but Beck himself had confirmed the movement towards a non-aggression pact. Antonov-Ovseenko's suggestions to Stalin would not change matters if the Poles had already decided to move towards Germany. There was another meeting with journalists Miedziński and Ignacy Matuszewski, but that channel seemed about played out. They were not privy to the details of the discussions with the Germans. Miedziński tried to be reassuring about the Polish-Soviet rapprochement, but that was not a good sign.[46]

Antonov-Ovseenko remained unhappy with his colleagues in the NKID. In a handwritten letter to Radek, he was triumphant over Beck's agreement to meet

Litvinov in Moscow (the visit would take place in February). This was an "anti-German demonstration which should shut the mouths of those who shouted about the failure of the 'Radek line.'" According to Antonov-Ovseenko, Beck was playing for time with the Germans in order to strengthen Poland's position. This was also Miedziński's view. Of course, what did that mean? The NKID was not prepared to accept at face value Antonov-Ovseenko's confidence in the Poles. He, however, saw matters differently: an "overabundance of mistrust towards the Poles" led the NKID to distort Beck's statements. "I am afraid that the serious political act [not clear which one, but perhaps a bilateral guarantee of Baltic security] conceived by the owner of the NKID [i.e., Litvinov], who understands it only as a test manoeuvre and will therefore act carelessly and arrogantly (towards the Poles), unwittingly upsetting it." Antonov-Ovseenko returned to recommendations he had made earlier to Stalin. He needed help from Moscow. "Support me, friend, in this." There were lots of possibilities in Warsaw, Antonov-Ovseenko added, "but means (people, money) I do not have. We should strengthen [our ties with I.A.] Koval'skii [TASS correspondent in Warsaw]."[47] He should have asked Stomoniakov or Krestinskii for help. They might have been willing. Radek could do nothing. He was a journalist, not a diplomat, and he was not close to Stalin.

Krestinskii and Dirksen

While the discussions between Poland and the Soviet Union continued, so also did the conversations between Dirksen and Krestinskii during the summer and autumn of 1933. All the top leadership in Berlin, Dirksen liked to say, had told him that they favoured a continuation of good relations with the Soviet Union. He and they wanted to know if the Soviet leadership intended to abandon its previous policy towards Germany. Reading the French or Polish press, for example, one might draw that conclusion. Dirksen was playing the aggrieved party, but that did not work in Moscow. Krestinskii gave the by-then stock reply that the Soviet leadership did not want to change its policy towards Germany but could not ignore German conduct towards the Soviet Union. And there was the usual reference to the Soviet "public" and its suspicions of Nazi promotion of an "anti-Soviet bloc." The Soviet government could only wait prudently as it faced the "zig-zags" of German policy, while at the same time being responsive to gestures from other places. Nevertheless, the disposition remained to continue the old policy.[48]

Two weeks later there was another meeting. It was mid-June. This time the discussion was about the Hugenberg speech. Dirksen had come for another problem, but Krestinskii then changed the subject. "During the twelve years of my work on the line of Soviet-German relations – nine years in Berlin and already almost three years here," Krestinskii observed, "I have never had to speak about such an unpleasant occasion – I mean the glaringly anti-Soviet speech of the German delegation in London." He mentioned some highlights of the speech to Dirksen: colonization of southern Russia and Eastern Europe, in general, and putting an end to the USSR and its Revolution. The German delegation in London disavowed Hugenberg's speech, but Krestinskii was not persuaded by this hollow gesture. The ideas came from other Nazi leaders, though Hugenberg did not mention Hitler or *Mein Kampf*. The speech was so at odds with the Treaty of Berlin and "friendly relations" between Germany and the USSR, that an explanation was required from Berlin. Dirksen replied that he had only just heard about the London speech, and cabled to Berlin for an explanation. Then Dirksen brought up a "current question," a railroad line from Leningrad to Stettin and Hamburg. "I replied," Krestinskii wrote in his journal, "that the Soviet decision to discontinue the exploitation of this line was 'final.'" Although the zamnarkom did not say so, it was also at this time that the Soviet government closed down military training programs with Germany and cancelled officer exchanges. It was only the end of June and already the Soviet government was shutting down Rapallo. Dirksen tried to balance things out by a reference to negative comments about Germany in the Soviet press, but Krestinskii was not buying that line. The reality of the situation in Germany was ten times worse than the most pessimistic comments about it in the Soviet press. He felt as though his work of the last twelve years had been thrown out the window. The Hugenberg memorandum was just too much to swallow.[49]

A few days later, Dirksen went again to meet Krestinskii. It was the usual dialogue except this time Dirksen complained about demonstrations the previous day during the funeral in Moscow of exiled German communist Clara Zetkin. It was 22 June. All the important Soviet leaders, including Stalin, Molotov, and Voroshilov, were present along with a crowd of ten thousand people. "You are entirely correct," Krestinskii responded after Dirksen had finished his observations:

> The broad masses not only of our party, but of all the Soviet Union are reacting very nervously to what is going on in Germany not only in relation to the USSR, but also in relation to communists, workers, Jews and to the progressive intelligentsia in Germany. But the authority of our party leadership is so great that, of course, it would be able to conduct the necessary external political line in relation to Germany.

If the right conditions existed, of course, but the party leadership needed to be convinced of German goodwill and it was that conviction which "unfortunately" did not exist.[50]

Dirksen returned to the NKID in July, although Krestinskii was not quite so indulgent. The zamnarkom complained about a new anti-Soviet press campaign in Germany, which appeared to have government backing. "Our public," again the usual reference, would perceive these expressions of hostility as a "declaration of war by German political circles and the German public." At the end of his report, Krestinskii noted that he had offered no "soothing words" to Dirksen about continuing the Rapallo policy.[51]

Deeds, Not Words

Three weeks later, Dirksen again met Krestinskii, this time to tell him that he was moving to the German embassy in Tokyo. The NKID would be sorry to see him go, Krestinskii replied, according to his record of the meeting. It would be hard to leave Moscow, Dirksen admitted, but the conditions of work had changed so much during the last few months that he found it difficult to adapt. This was Dirksen's way to get back to business and to pursue his usual line about restoring good Soviet-German relations. He jabbed at Krestinskii: "Obviously, the Soviet government cannot adjust to the fundamental change in the political structure of Germany and is changing its foreign policy."

Krestinskii responded with a comment that Dirksen had heard before. "I replied," he wrote in his journal, "that our wariness towards Germany is not at all explained by our views on the internal political structure of Germany. It is a reaction to the foreign policy of Germany. Until Germany, through deeds and not words, proves its desire to continue the old policy, as long as anti-Soviet statements continue to be made from the German side, until then we cannot give up our expectant watchfulness." Dirksen went through all his usual lines: I've talked to people in Berlin: I am convinced that they want to maintain the "previous policy." "The German government has made a number of steps to this end," insisted Dirksen. "Now, in my opinion, the next word must come from the USSR, not from Germany."[52] These lines were often heard when describing relationships between the Western powers and the USSR: "After you, Alphonse. No, you first, my dear Gaston."

The German chargé d'affaires, Fritz von Twardowski, called on Krestinskii two days later to replay the same music about improving relations. "We consider," Krestinskii said, "that the German government should demonstrate not only with words, but with action, its good will and its sincerity regarding the continuation of previous policy." This was no ordinary conversation, apparently, because Krestinskii sent a record of it to Stalin.[53]

Dirksen also returned to the charge. Not satisfied with the feedback he was getting from Krestinskii, the ambassador asked for a meeting with Molotov. He was too busy, the zamnarkom replied, but all the same Molotov found time to see him a few days later. Krestinskii advised the Soviet embassy in Berlin that it was a replay of his discussions with Dirksen and Twardowski. Molotov reassured Dirksen that the Soviet Rapallo policy remained in force, but that recent events in Germany had raised doubts. Molotov instanced a recent speech by the propaganda minister Joseph Goebbels, where he condemned the Rapallo treaty. Krestinskii reported to the embassy in Berlin that Dirksen had come away from the meeting saying he was in a stronger position to make representations in Berlin.[54]

"A Lack of Discipline"

At the beginning of September, there was a "new series of cases of disloyalty and unfriendliness of the German authorities." Litvinov directed the embassy in Berlin to take up these matters with the German foreign ministry as yet another affirmation of the change of German policy. Twardowski went to see Litvinov to talk about the usual subject of a "normalization of relations." No explanations or declarations would help to do that, Litvinov commented, as long as the German government officially or unofficially pursued its present line of policy.[55]

Twardowski returned to see Litvinov at the end of September; it was still the same music and the same role as the offended party. Relations were worsening, Twardowski said, "in spite of the fact that ruling circles in Germany sincerely want again to restore these relations and to correct all the defects and reasons for complaint." One can only imagine Litvinov raising his eyes to the ceiling, thinking here we go again, don't take us for idiots. But Twardowski continued: "We've noticed the increasing shift of [Soviet] policy to France. It has come to the point, they say, that the envoy of a friendly power communicated to his government, that apparently the Soviet authorities forwarded to Paris detailed information on German … armaments." Then the discussion passed to other subjects, the treatment of Soviet journalists, for example. It's a new government, Twardowski replied, there has been a certain lack of discipline by the new authorities. "I enumerated," Litvinov replied, "the anti-Soviet excesses of the German authorities about which we have protested though utterly barren of producing any results. The Auswärtiges Amt [the German foreign ministry] politely accepts our protests, expresses regret, offers apologies, promises to take measures, but on the next day anti-Soviet tricks resume. It seems to me that in Germany they overestimate our patience."

It was a lack of discipline, Twardowski repeated.

"The German government," replied Litvinov, "has become as if already accustomed to our protests as if they were a completely normal event and has ceased to be receptive to them. Obviously, more energetic means are needed in order to compel the German government to understand that our patience has limits."

Twardowski's reference to Soviet authorities passing information to the French was a "complete fiction from some idle or malicious diplomat," according to Litvinov. And he repeated another warning: "When Germany disregards our friendship, and other countries seek it, we, naturally, will move closer to these other countries, but from this it does not follow any sort of hostility to Germany or any desire to harm it." So the door was still open, if Germany wanted to walk through it. Twardowski understood and off the record asked Litvinov what might be done to back out of the existing dead end. This has not been discussed, Litvinov replied, but the least that needed to be done was to "remove those reasons which have provoked the given conflict."[56]

Litvinov in Berlin

As the autumn unfolded, the exchanges continued along the same lines. Readers should remember that this was at the same time that Polish-German negotiations were underway and Antonov-Ovseenko was lobbying for his policy of rapprochement with Warsaw. A lot was going on during that autumn of 1933. Litvinov sent fresh instructions to the Berlin embassy in early October repeating what he had said to Twardowski. Litvinov also killed the idea of Krestinskii meeting with Hitler in Berlin at the end of October, especially inappropriate, he judged, after the German withdrawal from the League of Nations and from the World Disarmament Conference, both of which had just then occurred.[57] On holidays in the south, Stalin questioned this decision. "What do we care about the League of Nations and why should we mount a demonstration in honour of the insulted League and against Germany which has offended it?" This was typical Stalin cynicism, but then he conceded he might not be privy to all the necessary information. The decision stood on Krestinskii, but the Politburo authorized Litvinov, who was en route to Washington to discuss the re-establishment of diplomatic relations, to stop in Berlin to meet Neurath or Hitler should he so desire. The Soviet government was still disposed to "a restoration of previous relations."[58]

Litvinov met with Neurath for half an hour in Berlin. They settled a row over journalists, but there was no serious discussion of Soviet-German relations. The issue of relations with Poland and France came up as it often had with Dirksen. "I noted," Litvinov wrote in his *dnevnik*, "that we also, like Germany, will strive towards a further rapprochement with these two countries. I added as a joke, that our relations with France and Poland will increase as Germany's love for them grows. Neurath replied that he was not against that sort of 'competition.'" Jokes aside, how could a half-hour meeting resolve the breakdown of Soviet-German relations? Neurath wished Litvinov good luck in the United States.[59] As it turned out, the success of Litvinov's mission in Washington appears to have had an impact on Soviet policy towards Germany. Back in Moscow, Dirksen made farewell calls at the NKID, where he offered his usual comments. Krestinskii wrote in his journal that he listened politely but chose not to take up the usual Soviet replies.[60] What was the point?

Chapter Six

"Strike while the Iron Is Hot": Strengthening Relations with France, 1933

Soviet diplomats were active in Paris while discussions with the Germans and Poles went on. At first, the French seemed more interested in solidifying Franco-Soviet relations than the Soviet side. It was January 1933. The Soviet embassy sensed the French interest in better relations. Pierre Cot, the young Radical Party politician and Undersecretary of State for Aviation, offered help in trying to advance various issues at the Quai d'Orsay.[1]

An Exchange of Military Attachés

"We should strike while the iron is hot," Dovgalevskii advised, so as not to miss the favourable "conjuncture" to establish "direct and serious links with the French military and the general staff and the arms industry." He proposed moving forward on the exchange of military and naval attachés. The French did not want to take the initiative, which would be too much like going down the road to Canossa. "I managed in a private conversation to interest Pierre Cot … in this question without showing that I myself was interested in it." Dovgalevskii asked for authorization to raise the issue "unofficially" with the Quai d'Orsay. This could be done, he suggested, without any risk of losing face ("our prestige") over a rejection of the proposal. How touching; it was like two young lovers not wanting to make the first move. No more slapstick Alphonse and Gaston. Dovgalevskii asked for immediate instructions.[2] Caution was unnecessary, however, since Ambassador Dejean had already, in November 1932, recommended the naming of a military attaché. In February, the French and Soviet governments agreed: Colonel Edmund Mendras went to Moscow and General Semen Ivanovich Ventsov, to Paris.[3]

The heat turned up after Hitler became chancellor on 30 January. It was time to throw away the dimly lit night lamp. "The arrival in power of Hitler, like nothing else could," the Soviet chargé d'affaires Rozenberg observed, "has strengthened here the mood of quiet anxiety."[4] Krestinskii was sceptical. A "temporary manoeuvre," he opined, dictated by events in Germany and elsewhere and facilitated by "our response" to them. "We are doing this," Krestinskii advised, "since the Sovietophile demonstrations in France are water to our mill."[5]

Rozenberg was not sure what to think. The circumstances had created an "interesting situation" where the general staff was actively seeking closer contacts with the Soviet high command. This development had been ripening for several months, according to Rozenberg, but had encountered opposition from General Maurice Gamelin, the chief of staff. Rozenberg was astonished, apparently, for there were discussions about resurrecting a military alliance and even the granting of a loan. The "most ardent supporters of a rapprochement" in the general staff were talking about both. "I draw all this to your attention because these moods, I repeat, characterize the political atmosphere in Paris which preoccupies Herriot." France was anxious, feeling isolated and looking for a way out. "In my opinion there is no harm in this … we can wait for a further crystallization of these conversations, not encouraging them directly, but also not pouring buckets of cold water on the heads of zealous Frenchmen."[6]

In reaction to Krestinskii's comment that it was all a "manoeuvre," Rozenberg, who was on the spot, thought it was more than that.

> You tend to regard the change in the local moods as a great manoeuvre. A big manoeuvre is also not bad, if it is in accordance with the manoeuvres that we ourselves need at the present time. I am personally inclined, however, to think that we are dealing with a clear turn in French politics, a turn the solidity of which it is certainly difficult to measure, but is still a turn. It was possible to talk about a certain shift in moods before Hitler came to power, but the last event gave these moods a more definite form and direction.

The Paris daily, *Le Journal*, ran an article stating that "a Franco-Soviet military alliance is in the air." It was being talked about, Rozenberg advised: "Manoeuvre or shift [in policy], there is no doubt that a lot of pressure for a rapprochement with us has recently come from the general staff."[7]

Mikhail Semenovich Ostrovskii

Rozenberg's information was confirmed by his colleague in Paris, Mikhail Semenovich Ostrovskii, who was the head of the *Soiuznefteksport* (the Soviet petroleum syndicate) in Paris. Ostrovskii is someone who will play an important role in this narrative especially after he was named polpred in Bucharest in 1934. He was a Francophile and spoke French well. In fact, he liked to use French turns of phrase in his reports to Moscow. Like Rozenberg, he got on well with his French counterparts, which helped in the continuing improvement in Franco-Soviet relations. Given his responsibilities, he had close ties with the defence ministry and with the Compagnie française des pétroles (CFP), notably with Colonel Jean de Lattre de Tassigny and with Robert Cayrol, vice-president of the CFP. According to Ostrovskii, de Lattre, "my colonel," as he liked to say, was the *éminence grise* of General Maxime Weygand, then *vice-président* of the *Conseil supérieur de la guerre*, a very senior post in the military bureaucracy. Ostrovskii established close ties with de Lattre in the effort to strengthen Franco-Soviet relations. His relations with Cayrol served the same cause. As a result, he picked up inside information, for example, about a row caused by Pierre Cot, the new Minister of Aviation, who made a controversial speech in Geneva about European security. Weygand resigned in protest, but the *président du Conseil,* Daladier, refused to accept it. Weygand then went to the president of the Republic, Albert Lebrun, who advised him to take back his resignation and to keep his composure. Wait for "better times," Lebrun said, they will not be long in coming, "prepare for 'great events,' but for the time being remain patient and get the army ready." De Lattre did not think Weygand could cope and was "getting ready to go" for he was "sick of these political bastards (*politicaille*)."

From the reports by Rozenberg and Ostrovskii, one could see that the mood in Paris was changing, even at the defence ministry. Weygand sent de Lattre to see Émile Buré at the Parisian daily *Ordre*. This was the newspaper of the *Comité des forges*, the influential lobby group for the iron and steel industries. The general staff wanted the *Ordre* to change its hostile line towards the USSR, and Buré had started to carry out this directive. You can see how things worked in Paris. Another journalist, one Pierre Dominic, published a nasty article about the USSR in *République*, a Radical Socialist paper. De Lattre called him on the carpet. He was ordered to change his line – this was according to what Ostrovskii had heard – or documents would be published which linked Dominic with the "cash box" of the Italian ambassador in Paris. "I set my sights," Cayrol said, "on converting the general staff and our politicians to the pro-Soviet faith. I consider my mission at this stage completed, and not badly completed at that." The next step, according to Ostrovskii was to bring around the big banks. "I will start with [Horace] Finaly, the man to know at the Banque de Paris et des Pays-Bas, 'the most anti-Soviet bank in Paris.'" This should be easier than bringing around the general staff and politicians, Ostrovskii boasted. It was early 1933. The weather vane was fluttering and seemed to be changing direction.

Ostrovskii also reported that Charles Alphand was going to Moscow as ambassador. He had been a member of Anatole de Monzie's "kindergarten" during the 1920s at the time of the first failed attempt to improve relations. Alphand was known to be favourable to a rapprochement with the Soviet Union. Colonel Mendras, the new military attaché, was also known to be "pro-Soviet." Ostrovskii lunched with Mendras before he left for Moscow. He made a good impression. Mendras was a professor of artillery at the general staff "academy."

He spoke decent Russian, Ostrovskii noted, and was in Russia before the war. In fact, according to Cayrol, Mendras had a long-standing reputation for Sovietophilia among his peers. In 1919, he filed a report against French military intervention in southern Russia. It proved to be a fiasco. Mendras produced the impression of a "modest, thoughtful individual, who weighed each word, and was very reserved." He spoke a great deal about his commitment to advance the Franco-Soviet rapprochement "though without the usual French pathos and high-sounding phrases."

Ostrovskii added a jovial postscript to his letter to the defence commissar, Voroshilov, about a recent lunch with senior officers: "If the month of May goes well, there will be no war this year."[8] Talk of war was already in the air. It was late February 1933. Ostrovskii was someone who knew his way around Paris and was buoyant over the successes of Soviet diplomats in advancing the Franco-Soviet rapprochement. Was it all too good to be true?[9]

It is hard to say if there were more political gossips in Paris than in other capitals ready to talk to Soviet diplomats, but there were a great many French politicians and salon hangers-on more than ready to talk. The Paris hotel Lutetia in the 6ᵉ arrondissement was a good place to meet them. One heard all sorts of stories, for example, about where the *Surêté générale* was getting its "Kremlin lowdown." Apparently from "a people's commissar who frequently visited Paris," or so boasted an expert on Russian affairs, "a certain Alec." Surely it was not Litvinov, though he did sometimes speak rather freely to foreign diplomats. Then there was lots of gossip about the Soviet colony in Paris and all sorts of Russian émigrés from a well-informed clerk at the *Préfecture de police*, named Lagerie. The "main advocate" in the general staff of a Franco-Soviet rapprochement was General Weygand; the main opponent was General Henri Albert Niessel, a Sovietphobe from the earliest days of the Bolshevik Revolution. Freemasons in the military establishment and the police acted as informants who secretly kept an eye on "reactionaries" like Weygand. Good stories of uncertain value for the historian, but interesting enough to pass on to Moscow.[10]

Pierre Cot was also a good source of information. His name turns up frequently in reports to Moscow. In late January, he became the aviation minister in the new Daladier government. In April, he told Dovgalevskii that he wanted to send an air attaché to Moscow.[11] In May, he was again in touch with the Soviet embassy promoting better Franco-Soviet relations generally and talking, indiscreetly, about discussions in the Council of Ministers. He was not the first or last cabinet minister to do so. The military attaché, General Ventsov, having just arrived in Paris, met with General Gamelin who evoked "memories of the Franco-Russian military alliance." That was getting carried away for Gamelin. According to Rozenberg, the rapprochement was encountering less opposition on the right. As an example, he mentioned Paul Reynaud, a former finance minister, and "one of the most intelligent people among political personalities on the right." People were saying, according to Rozenberg, that even Tardieu was taking a "more respectable position," although this was yet to be confirmed.[12]

Marcel' Izrailevich Rozenberg

Marcel' Izrailevich Rozenberg was a Pole, born in Warsaw in 1896. His family was Jewish and his father was a merchant of modest means. Before the age of ten, Marcel' Izrailevich spoke only Polish; he learned Russian to gain admission to a vocational school. However, the family soon left Warsaw for Koenigsberg, and there Rozenberg entered the local *gimnaziia*. At the age of seventeen, he moved again, this time to Berlin to stay with relatives who had emigrated from Russia. In Germany he became interested in Marxism, read Karl Marx's *Das Capital*, a formidable undertaking, and in Berlin rubbed shoulders with German social democrats. The following year, in the spring of 1914, the young Rozenberg set out for England, to learn English, he later said, the better to find a job. Rozenberg was already a polyglot. On the move again in the following year, he went to New York where he found work as a translator for an arms manufacturer supplying the tsarist government. It is not known how Rozenberg, age nineteen, managed to escape English recruiting sergeants on the alert for conscription-age men. He could not find steady employment in New York, however, and returned to Russia after the outbreak of revolution in the winter of 1917.

Now twenty-one, Rozenberg's background was not at all like that of the typical Bolshevik revolutionary, but his knowledge of languages would serve him in good stead in Soviet Russia. And what young man of Rozenberg's background could fail to rally to the call of revolution? In 1918, he joined the Bolshevik Party, and in April, he returned to Berlin with Soviet diplomat Adol'f A. Ioffe to become head of the press office of the Soviet embassy. The future foreign intelligence chief, Viacheslav R. Menzhenskii, also a Pole, made friends with Rozenberg and took him under his wing. Back in Moscow in 1920, he became private secretary to narkom Chicherin. Later during the 1920s, not yet thirty years old, he served in Soviet embassies across Europe and in Turkey and Afghanistan. In the late 1920s, he was back in Moscow charged at the NKID with the coordination of intelligence work, working again with Menzhenskii, who was then head of the OGPU. In the few existing photographs of Rozenberg, one sees a man of small stature, with a receding hairline and a moustache. He was married to a sculptress, Marianna Emel'ianovna Iaroslavkaia. Rozenberg looks, in fact, a little like Léger. In 1931, at age thirty-five, he went to Paris as first secretary where he soon found himself in the thick of the negotiations to strengthen Franco-Soviet relations. Two years later, like Ostrovskii, he knew his way around Paris.

Figure 6.1. Marcel' Izrailevich Rozenberg, ca. mid-1930s, AVPRF.

All the rumours of a Franco-Soviet rapprochement, Gamelin's reminiscences of the Franco-Russian alliance, and Cot's statements attracted Krestinskii's attention. He thought the rapprochement should be pursued. Remembering his own experience as ambassador in Berlin, Krestinskii recommended that relations with the French military establishment should not be limited to Ventsov, but should also include Dovgalevskii and Rozenberg. However, he cautioned against making commitments about military support in the case of conflict between France and its allies and third parties. Such commitments would not, said Krestinskii, "correspond to our real intentions, and then, being passed on to German governmental military circles (and moreover they will be transmitted to them in a distorted form of course), they would undermine, to a large extent, the confidence in us from the side of Germany."[13] It was May 1933, and Krestinskii and the Soviet government were still thinking in terms of saving "the old policy" towards Germany. Still, the weather vane was fluttering.

Could the Rapprochement with France Move Forward?

Litvinov was disappointed that the rapprochement with France had not moved beyond the non-aggression pact. Not from the French side, where there had been numerous public statements made by Herriot and others, but from Moscow, where the press response until then had been low key. "We are now thinking about some concrete manifestations of rapprochement," Litvinov advised. Unfortunately, not in the Chambre des députés where "friends" had raised the unhelpful issue of the prewar debts.[14] It sounded like gears were grinding in Moscow and Paris as policy began to change.

Momentum was nevertheless building for a change in Soviet policy: first, because Soviet-German relations were going the wrong way, and second, because there was French support for stronger ties. Alphand arrived in Moscow in June 1933. He was keen for pushing ahead with a rapprochement and knew a thing or two about Franco-Soviet relations. He was in the thick of negotiations in the 1920s. In 1932, he was Herriot's chef de cabinet. He had good credentials for getting on better with Moscow. Not all the ranking clerks in the Quai d'Orsay opposed better Franco-Soviet relations.

On 5 July, Alphand met with Stomoniakov; Litvinov was still abroad. Alphand talked about various subjects – Poland, Romania, the rotten French press – but what he really wanted to discuss was a further extension of the Franco-Soviet rapprochement. The USSR needed to play a greater role in international politics. Alphand remembered listening to Litvinov in Geneva the first time he spoke there, "and the ironic attitude towards him in the audience." Now the times had changed and delegates at the League of Nations were listening to Litvinov. The importance of the USSR had grown and was growing stronger. "Normalization of relations with France is only the beginning. We have to aim for agreement (an entente) between France, the USSR and England." Alphand even referred to the pre–First World War Entente cordiale as an example to pursue. Remember, it was only July 1933. To deepen Franco-Soviet relations, according to Alphand, required an improvement in Anglo-Soviet relations. This was true. Litvinov had only just settled the Metro-Vickers crisis.

Stomoniakov wrote in his journal,

> Since the conversation was conducted in a very friendly manner, with the utmost caution, I agreed in certain places with Alphand, but then observed that, given the importance of little things, we must at the same time not lose sight of the differences in regimes in the USSR and France, because of which it is sometimes impossible here to take a positive decision on any issue, which in France is self-evident. But, first of all, I added, apart from the little things, we should not lose sight of the great interests which tie our countries together.

Try to be flexible on "the little things," which mattered in Paris, Alphand replied in so many words: that will make it easier to advance "the big issues." Stomoniakov said that Alphand could count on "the very friendly attitude of the NKID."[15]

Although the gears were grinding, Soviet policy was still officially to save the "old policy" with Germany while at the same time pursuing better relations with

France and Poland. On the following day, Litvinov met Daladier and Paul-Boncour in Paris. This was the same meeting that had aroused Antonov-Ovseenko's suspicions about disinformation. Litvinov was looking for those "concrete manifestations of rapprochement." One idea was to persuade the French government to sign Litvinov's convention on the definition of the aggressor. The other was "a gentleman's agreement" on the exchange of secret information of interest to both countries.[16]

Poland also came up in Litvinov's discussions with Daladier. It was over lunch two days later, on 8 July:

> Daladier again spoke about the strange policy of Poland and about his mistrust of Beck. I have the impression that he wanted to dissociate himself in advance from a possible Polish adventure known to him. It would not hurt to publish a report of some correspondent of TASS or *Pravda* about Polish-German schemes. It would be wrong, however, to run a campaign in our papers in such a way as *to give the impression in Germany that we have irrevocably broken with it and are finally reorienting ourselves* [emphasis added].[17]

Already in the summer of 1933, Litvinov was pursuing a subtle policy towards Germany. All was not as it seemed. Wheels within wheels were turning.

Nor were relations with France as they seemed. In spite of confidential lunches with Daladier, the French *apparat* had its own policy towards the USSR. Soviet neighbours signed the Litvinov convention on the definition of the aggressor, but Léger considered French adhesion to be premature and did "not want to cause trouble with England."[18] Ah, Alexis Léger, a name that readers should not forget.

The "gentleman's agreement" also failed. The *Directeur politique* of the Quai d'Orsay killed it on the pretext that it would be secret and that it could prove to be "a spear's point (*une pointe*) against England, the entente with which remains at the base of any French policy."[19] Paul-Boncour, still foreign minister, tried to guild the lily with Dovgalevskii, saying that the Litvinov convention was essentially regional and that the "gentleman's agreement" was unnecessary since the French and Soviet governments did not need it to exchange information.[20] These were minor setbacks but they were indications of the obstacles to be expected in the process of deepening Franco-Soviet relations. In the meantime, however, trips to Moscow were organized for Herriot and Cot, both of whom were strong advocates of better Soviet relations. In August, the French government agreed to the exchange of air and naval attachés.[21] That was a step forward.

The Herriot and Cot visits went well, from both the French and Soviet points of view. According to Alphand, Herriot received a welcome reserved for a head of government. He made a tour of the Ukraine where he did not notice the effects of the famine that had struck the entire Soviet wheat belt and was then coming to an end.[22] In Moscow, he was feted at a banquet of 150. The Russians knew how to throw a party to make someone feel welcome. People were in their cups. There were the obligatory toasts. The enthusiasm, well lubricated with vodka, was infectious. Someone evoked the idea of an eventual Franco-Soviet alliance. *Vive la France* came the collective, boisterous reply.[23] Herriot told Litvinov that he would do all in his power to deepen the Franco-Soviet rapprochement. Litvinov responded in a like manner, speaking of "our firm decision and our wish to pursue a further rapprochement with France." "Our," Litvinov wrote in his record of the meeting, meaning it was Soviet policy. Remember, it was September 1933 and the Politburo had not yet officially abandoned the "old policy" towards Germany. Litvinov's "our" might have been a little premature, maybe not. The narkom did not hide from Herriot that he had noticed a certain reticence on the French side, instancing the convention on the definition of the aggression and the "gentleman's agreement." The latter proposal caught Herriot's ear and he promised to support it.

While Herriot was out of power, Cot was aviation minister and he had very definite ideas about Franco-Soviet aeronautical cooperation.[24] Litvinov met Cot the day after he saw Herriot. The conversation remained largely one of generalities. Cot said he was greatly impressed by Soviet air power, both present and potential. The members of his delegation were of a similar opinion. Again Litvinov raised his recurring fear of a change of government to the right, which could halt the rapprochement. Cot proposed organizing visits from members of the *Assemblée nationale*, of all the parties, to see for themselves Soviet developments. French visitors could not help but become attuned to the rapprochement.[25]

Alphand followed up two days later. He was full of enthusiasm about the Herriot and Cot visits, according to Litvinov's record, but he also asked some frank questions about the "gentleman's agreement." Daladier had not liked Litvinov's proposal, wondering how it would fit in with similar obligations to Germany. We do not have any formal obligations with Germany, Litvinov responded, or with any other government except Turkey. Then, Litvinov brought up the Papen-Herriot conversation in 1932 that proposed Franco-German cooperation against the USSR. This event came up often in Soviet correspondence and clearly bothered Litvinov and his colleagues. Dirksen also reported on this point to Berlin. Their information, Litvinov said to Alphand, did not come from the German side; in fact, it came from Herriot himself. Litvinov defended his proposal and Alphand replied that he understood and was "sympathetic" to it. Then the narkom spoke of his "bewilderment" over French indecision about the rapprochement. Of course with new "friendships," old ones were sometimes lost or weakened. Then Litvinov brought up *again* an issue that was clearly bothering him. "We are at ease now, dealing with the current French government, but we do not have any certainty that its political line will continue in case of a change of government, especially after the coming to power of people like Tardieu." Alphand responded that the Soviet leadership had to win over "the government *apparat*," which was easier said than done. The Franco-Soviet rapprochement was also hindered, Alphand added, by "third countries," which among them included Germany, Italy, Poland, and the Little Entente. "And England?" Litvinov asked. England was not waging any anti-Soviet campaign in France, Alphand responded, but he mentioned Poland twice.[26] Ah yes, Poland and its "strange policy."

All of this information flowed back to Paris, especially after Cot and Herriot returned home.[27] Cot reported to the Council of Ministers about the "dispositions … among several Soviet leaders (*dirigeants*) concerning the possibilities of security agreements." He had spoken about these possibilities with Paul-Boncour. Léger wrote to Alphand for his reactions and recommendations. There were always some misgivings in the Quai d'Orsay about the rapprochement, for Léger worried that a deepening of relations might draw France into trouble with Japan. Remember, the last time Léger looked for a pretext, it was Britain. Was the Soviet side thinking of pulling France into commitments in Asia?[28] Alphand responded quickly: "Litvinov has repeated to us on various occasions that he was persuaded that Germany would make war in two years." Alphand sent Léger several recommendations for better relations, among which acceptance of the convention on the definition of the aggressor, though he did not mention the "gentleman's agreement." He also proposed the exchange of technical missions for collaboration in railroads and aviation, among other areas. Closer cooperation with Moscow, he opined, would not trouble Franco-Japanese relations.[29] Litvinov must have been quite open in making his prediction of war to Alphand because the military attaché, Colonel Mendras, had also reported it to Paris a few weeks earlier.[30] At that point in time, Litvinov does not appear to have informed Stalin of his view, at least not in writing. The narkom was not wrong in forecasting war, although he was off by four years on its start date. Ironically, in 1922 Herriot had made a similar prediction while meeting with Soviet officials in Moscow: Germany will strike us again in fifteen years.[31] He was closer to the mark than Litvinov; both proved correct about German intentions. Mendras opined that the Soviet authorities were ready to move forward "resolutely" on "an effective rapprochement" as soon as they had the certitude that France was of a like mind.[32]

In Paris, Rozenberg quickly heard the echoes of the two missions to the Soviet Union from Cot himself. The "resonance" of the visits of Herriot and Cot "surpassed, as it seems to me, all expectations." I was worried, Rozenberg wrote to Litvinov, that "antagonism" between Daladier and Herriot might "hinder business," but that had not occurred. "With extraordinary aplomb, Herriot led the campaign for us, and an indirect indicator of the weight he has retained in the political life of the country is the fact that even hostile newspapers like

Matin and others reproduced in a prominent place his statement." Rozenberg praised Cot "as a more practical person [than Herriot] and only gradually gaining political capital, [he] acted with more restraint and exclusively in coordination with Daladier. He submitted to the Council of Ministers a dry factual report on the state of our aviation, etc." Cot told Rozenberg that his report was "a big success." He mentioned the names of several ministers who had reacted positively. "Concerning Daladier himself, Cot assures [me] that he has agreed to a pact of mutual assistance, and on like matters, going even further."[33] Was Cot exaggerating? Daladier was believed to be more interested in a rapprochement with Germany than with the USSR, but that was also said about Stalin. At least, official Soviet policy was still to try to patch up the "old relationship" even if Litvinov thought it was dead.

As Litvinov set off for the United States, readers will remember that he had instructions from the Politburo to talk to Neurath in Berlin or even Hitler, should he wish to meet. The meeting with Neurath led to no breakthroughs and Litvinov went on to Paris where he saw Paul-Boncour. At this meeting, which as Litvinov put it, was more cordial than any previous encounter, Paul-Boncour raised the issue of a pact of mutual assistance; he had alluded to the idea with Dovgalevski a week earlier. "Boncour again spoke about the necessity to think, us and France, about countermeasures in case of the rearmament and the preparations of Germany for war, of which he mentioned several times mutual assistance in addition to the pact of non-aggression." And unlike the Quai d'Orsay, Litvinov thought mutual assistance should mean "not only in the west but also in the east so that we do not have complications in the east." They agreed, according to Litvinov's telegram, "that he and I will think about the possible means of collaboration (*sotrudnichestva*)."[34] They also discussed the exchange of technical missions, which Cot had raised in Moscow, and they talked about ongoing trade negotiations that dragged on endlessly.

Remember, these trade talks started during the summer of 1931. The French wanted a more advantageous balance of trade; the Soviet side, selling a good deal more than it was buying in France. The French also wanted a settlement of the pre-war debts, but there they had no case since then président du Conseil Poincaré and his government had negotiated in bad faith and sabotaged a Soviet offer on the tsarist bonds considered acceptable by senior officials in the finance ministry. Electoral considerations of the governing centre-right Bloc national against the Cartel des gauches, took precedence over a debts settlement in the interests of middleclass French investors.[35] The Soviet government also wanted advantageous terms of credit, as it had from its earliest days. As one British Treasury official put it in 1931, "credit is Russia's God." If the USSR had had a God, credit might well have been it. The more Soviet trade agencies were willing to buy, the more interesting their offers appeared to French and other Western industrialists who were anxious to fill their order books, as the Great

Depression bit into the European economy. French banks, and especially the Banque de France, opposed credit or credit insurance for Soviet trade agencies until the pre-war debts had been settled. After the failed negotiations of 1926–7, however, this was not going to happen. The Soviet government reckoned it had made its best offer, to which the French never responded. It was not going to bid against itself.[36]

Trade was important in itself, but it was also important as a major step towards better political relations. From its first days, trade offers were always the Soviet government's opening bid for better relations with the West. Paul-Boncour understood the principle perfectly well, and he himself adopted it in trying to advance the Soviet rapprochement. As minister, he pushed hard for agreement. "Boncour agreed," Litvinov wrote to the NKID, "that it was necessary to hurry and to conclude the negotiations."[37] What Paul-Boncour said to Litvinov, he said to his officials. His message was "hurry." You can see it in the margins of the documents that came to his desk. On one report, he wrote, "we must succeed"; on another, "*aboutir vite*"; and yet another, "*aboutir, aboutir*." Paul-Boncour was a minister in a hurry. He survived four changes of government in 1933, but who knew how long he would remain at the Quai d'Orsay. He was already beating the odds. In Moscow, who could say if the rapprochement with France would survive the next change of government? That question was ever on Litvinov's mind. The trade talks nearly broke down in November, and there were problems over the technical missions. The French side was more interested in aviation under Cot's pushing, but the exchange of naval missions was less interesting to the admirals in Paris who reckoned they had nothing to learn from their Soviet counterparts.[38] Stalin had caught on early on. From the south, on holiday, he cabled to Kaganovich: "The French are sending their *razvedchiki*, intelligence agents, to investigate us. They are interested in our aviation because it is well-established and we are strong in this field. Aviation cooperation is acceptable, but it should be conditioned on cooperation in the construction of naval ships, especially submarines, destroyers, where we are rather weak." It was all or nothing, said Stalin.[39] Voroshilov was inclined against the exchange of aviation experts, but recognized that after Cot's visit, saying no was impossible given the "political minus" it would entail.[40]

Daladier's cabinet fell in October, but he remained as war minister. He did not get on with either Paul-Boncour or Herriot. In fact, Daladier would have liked to sack Paul-Boncour who also remained in the new cabinet.[41] Alphand pressed the Quai d'Orsay for action to consolidate relations with Moscow. All the circumstances – but especially the "aggressive nationalism" of Nazi Germany – militated in favour of "a real political union with the Soviets." "The USSR," Alphand wrote, "is a power with which one has to reckon in Europe."[42]

"*Absolument d'accord*," replied Paul-Boncour, "with your dispatch … read attentively by me as with all that you send." The Russia dossier was important.

Circulation of Aphand's letter was limited to the Council of Ministers and to Léger. The latter must have been watching uncomfortably the rapid movement to embrace Red Moscow, even though Rozenberg had heard that he was "favourably disposed to us."[43] That was untrue.

Alexis Léger

Alexis Léger was Philippe Berthelot's successor as secrétaire-général of the Quai d'Orsay. He was born into a wealthy family in Pointe-à-Pitre, Guadaloupe, in 1887. His father and grandfather were lawyers and plantation owners. Léger thus descended from the French grande bourgeoisie. He gained a degree in law, and studied at the elite École des Hautes études commerciales in Paris. He married late in life and had no children. His first postings in the diplomatic service were in China between 1916 and 1921. He returned to Paris where he rose quickly from sous-chef de bureau to sous directeur d'Asie, to directeur des affaires politiques, until he succeeded Berthelot in 1933. In photographs he is not physically imposing, showing a receding hair line and a thin, meticulously trimmed moustache. The walrus moustache was then out of fashion for alpha males, although it is true that Léger was not an alpha male. He apparently liked bow ties for he was often wearing them in photographs and he was rarely depicted smiling except when he won the Nobel Prize for Literature in 1960, long after he left the Quai d'Orsay. He was a far better poet under his penname of Saint-John Perse than he was a diplomat as Léger. He was no Berthelot and he was wrong in just about every idea he had about relations with the USSR and about how to deal with the Nazi menace.

Léger was a saboteur of relations with Moscow, a role he accomplished with Gallic arrogance and accents of orientalism. Like Berthelot he looked to London, but without his predecessor's confident and engaging smile, and without the aplomb. No one would have said of Berthelot that he curried favour with *perfide Albion*. In fact, many of Léger's Foreign Office counterparts – we will meet them anon – were just as wrong as he was about how to deal with Hitler, and that right up to 1939. This latter comment by the way is no historian's simple "aftermindedness" or hindsight. As we shall see, Léger obstinately pursued the wrong policies in spite of hearing from many sources that the road to French security ran through Moscow. There were many people in France like Léger; they seemed confused or dead wrong about how to confront the menace of Hitlerite Germany.

Ostrovskii Has Dinner with de Lattre and Cayrol

However, this is getting a little ahead of our narrative. We are still in the autumn of 1933. Information from Paris flowed into Moscow from many different sources. One was Ostrovskii who continued to meet with de Lattre and Cayrol.

On 20 October, they dined together a few days before Litvinov passed through Paris to meet with Paul-Boncour. The conversation focused on events in Geneva and the recent German withdrawal from the League of Nations and disarmament negotiations as well as the political crises in Paris. Daladier's government was about to fall. It was hard to govern in Paris and to pursue firm policies. According to de Lattre, Franco-German negotiations were not to be excluded. Weygand thought such talks impossible without a strong majority government. In that case, they would not be without usefulness in demonstrating Hitler's interest in rearmament, not peace, and in playing for time to rearm. Everything would become clear to everyone. Unfortunately, no such strong majority government was possible and any Franco-German negotiations would lead to "concessions" dangerous for France. There was some talk of a united front of France, England, Italy, and the United States, but that idea was illusory and dangerous for various reasons. This was still de Lattre explaining to Ostrovskii Weygand's views.

The subject inevitably turned to Franco-Soviet relations and Litvinov's worries about French political instability and thus policy instability. On that point, de Lattre had this to say: "One of the main factors in the stability of French foreign policy is the French army. The French general staff overwhelmingly consider – and this I declare to you, said de Lattre, in the name of General Weygand – that its Russian policy is calculated not in connection with the arrival in power of a left majority and left cabinet, but wholly on the precise danger of war, menacing France from the direction of one enemy, which, in the opinion of the French general staff, equally threatens the Soviet Union. This enemy is Hitler." De Lattre referred to previous conversations and stressed that unfortunately the French general staff could not help lower tensions in the Far East between Japan and the USSR, but it nevertheless pursued with "complete loyalty its policy of rapprochement and cooperation in all three services: land, sea, and air."

The day before, on 19 October, de Lattre said, this policy was confirmed at a meeting between Weygand and the chiefs of staff of the navy and air force. Even the naval high command was embarrassed by the delays in the launching of military exchanges, apparently due to officials at the Quay d'Orsay. De Lattre went out of his way to re-emphasize the "loyalty" of the general staff to Franco-Soviet cooperation. Still, not all his news was reassuring. He advised that in Radical Party circles, especially those of Herriot there were rumours that Daladier was a proponent of a bilateral agreement with Germany. There were, however, all sorts of rumours going around, according to Ostrovskii, some of which were contradictory. Finally, de Lattre offered the comment that trying to get things done only through "ministers" without the general staff would be a waste of time or would only "delay decisions." The dinner nevertheless finished on a high note. De Lattre affirmed that Weygand thought Franco-Soviet relations were on the right path and that cooperation of the two general staffs was "strong guarantee of peace in Europe."[44]

Time to Get Moving

The Soviet chargé d'affaires Rozenberg was another conduit of information to Moscow. He often spoke privately with Herriot and Cot, among other French politicians, and was well informed about the politics of the French government. He worried about policy differences between Daladier and Herriot. "Daladier is the proponent of direct negotiations with Germany," Rozenberg wrote to Krestinskii, "moreover he proceeds from the possibility that these negotiations will lead to some sort of agreement. They say that in particular Daladier would not be opposed to 'Anschluss' since its implementation would cause Germany and Italy to butt heads." As for Herriot, he had "no illusions" about any agreement with Germany, even if, from a tactical point of view, Daladier's approach might "bring clarity to the situation," that is, expose Germany's true intentions. This information confirmed what Ostrovskii was hearing from de Lattre. According to Rozenberg, Daladier saw relations with the USSR as an insurance policy in the event that "Germany began … to manifest aggressive tendencies." This is ironic since Soviet policy had a similar objective.

For Rozenberg, the portrait of relations with France was generally positive, but there were dark spots. Certain groups of industrialists, the Comité des forges, for example, wanted a "general agreement" with Germany that would only be possible by agreeing to a free hand in Eastern Europe. Any foot dragging in Paris to Cot's proposals, for example, would be "water to the mill" for those elements who wanted to deal with Germany and not the USSR or who were looking for proof that the Soviet government was all talk and no action. In fact, Cot could not understand why it was taking so long for Moscow to act on his proposals. "No one needs to tell me," Rozenberg wrote, "that policymakers are living human beings, and that this same Cot is a very ardent supporter of the rapprochement with us. We receive information from a wide variety of sources that Cot has in this respect shown really tireless energy." Rozenberg added:

> We also know that Cot violently cursed the director of the Political Department at the Quai d'Orsay, [Paul] Bargeton, who tried to slow up the passage of naval questions. Therefore, I would like to emphasize as insistently as I can that it is not in our best interests to pour a tub of cold water onto the head of this ardent supporter of a rapprochement with us. We would thereby, in my opinion, demagnetize it [the rapprochement] and give arguments to our opponents, for, I repeat once again, the adversaries here of a rotten deal with Germany argue, essentially, in favour of the opportunity to rely on us and, it seems to me, that we should not disavow them.

Rozenberg emphasized the urgency of the situation. "It seems to me that if Comrade Litvinov, on the way back [from Washington], passes through Paris, it will be unfortunate to elude with general phrases Boncour's proposal, which he promised to 'think over.'"[45]

In the meantime, Rozenberg received the records of Dovgalevskii's conversations in Geneva with Paul-Boncour where the latter explained the fragility and urgency of the political situation in France, thus confirming Rozenberg's views. French public opinion was far from united on the German question, Paul-Boncour said it was becoming harder to hold the line against recognition of German rearmament that was being pushed by Britain and Italy. There were also "influential political and commercial and industrial circles striving for agreement with Germany." He added and this was "strictly confidential," that but for his (Paul-Boncour's) opposition Daladier "would already be undertaking direct negotiations with Germany." He raised again the subject of the Soviet entry into the League of Nations, which would help exit a "dead-end situation" in dealing with a resurgent Germany. France could no longer defend a "purely negative" line. If public opinion could be persuaded to support "a positive foreign policy based on the creation of a solid barrier against the onslaught of Hitlerite Germany … it would take a weapon from the hands of those who insist on an agreement with Germany." According to the Soviet record, Paul-Boncour was "thinking of a barrier in the form of a treaty of mutual assistance."[46]

So there it was out in the open, the minister had taken the bull by the horns. Rozenberg fully understood the importance of Paul-Boncour's conversations with Dovgalevskii for he added a postscript to his original report:

> When I wrote this letter yesterday, I did not yet know the content of Comrade Dovgalevskii's conversations with Boncour. These conversations are an incomparable more weighty argument than all of my suppositions. They fully confirm that any delay on our part, will disarm supporters of a rapprochement with us. I am personally least of all an advocate of running after anyone but when we are dealing with concrete proposals, we cannot freeze them. There is a fierce struggle between different [political] movements and we need to manoeuvre more quickly when this is required.[47]

Rozenberg's dispatches drew a prompt response from Krestinskii, who wrote that they in Moscow agreed to Boncour's proposal for entry into the League of Nations. On mutual assistance, it was something to discuss, "we do not mind listening to concrete proposals … You can start discussions with Boncour. Communicate results."[48]

On 1 December, Dovgalevskii, who was ill, invited Paul-Boncour to the Soviet embassy. Everyone seemed to be in a hurry now, both Soviet and French. Paul-Boncour promised to move from generalizations to specifics on both the

League of Nations and mutual assistance. He repeated much of what he had said to Rozenberg in November. Krestinskii replied that Dovgalevskii could say that the Soviet government was opposed to German rearmament because it constituted a threat to "world peace."[49]

This rapid Soviet change in policy occurred in November and early December while Litvinov was abroad. In fact, the Politburo authorized him to return from the United States via *paquebot* to Rome in order to enlist Mussolini's support against Germany.[50] Krestinskii had made the recommendation in this sense to the Politburo. Litvinov indicated that he thought he should go. It was only three months after the signature of a Soviet-Italian pact of friendship and non-aggression. "I personally believe," Krestinskii wrote, "that we should not shy away from a meeting. Italy will play now in international affairs an ever increasing role. My conviction is growing that relations with Germany will not improve. This makes it all the more important to befriend (*druzhit'*) Italy."[51] The Politburo approved Krestinskii's recommend on 10 November, as the negotiations in Washington were drawing to a close.

Everything was falling into place to justify a Soviet policy shift abandoning Rapallo. In Washington, the negotiations had gone well. Roosevelt and Litvinov had discussed mutual assistance against the two potential common enemies. The news from Ostrovskii and Rozenberg in Paris was encouraging. In late October, Mendras had reported that the Soviet leadership feared a Nazi-Japanese combination aimed at the USSR.[52]

Litvinov met Mussolini on 4 December. He told Mussolini that the Soviet leadership would like to have good relations with Germany, which was the standard Soviet line. But they could not ignore various expressions of German hostility, among which was Hitler's *Mein Kampf* and its discussion of "expansion to the east." The rapprochement with France was intended to prevent a Franco-German alliance aimed against the Soviet Union.[53] "Our relations with France," Krestinskii advised Dovgalevskii, "are beginning to intensify in a number of directions."[54] It was 4 December, the same day Litvinov was in Rome talking to Mussolini. In a further letter to Dovgalevskii on that day, Krestinskii was blunt without any pushing from his boss. Earlier in the year, one might have noticed nuances in the positions of Krestinskii and Litvinov. Not now. "We are decisively against the augmentation of German armaments since in the foreign policy setting of the present German government these additional armaments sooner or later will be turned against us."[55] The Italian, Polish, and British governments might not oppose German rearmament. Even in France there was no unified position.

> It is therefore important for us to support those members of the present government, and those candidates for leadership in future French governments, who are opponents of not only separate negotiations with Germany, but also of the

expansion of the German army. Such politicians are Boncour and Herriot. Our agreement in principle to enter the League of Nations and to conclude an agreement on mutual assistance give to Boncour the possibility in the conflicts with his adversaries in cabinet who oppose a closer rapprochement with us by means of a proposal to yield in part to Germany on the question of rearmament. That is why we decided to respond positively to Boncour's proposal.

After the exit of Japan (in March 1933) and Germany from the League of Nations, Krestinskii added, "we would play in the League one of the leading roles and, to a certain extent, could use the League in the interests of our own security." It was Krestinskii's personal idea that the Soviet government should propose to the United States that it enter the League of Nations at the same time. Not an attractive proposal in Washington, but in principle, it was a good idea. Then Krestinskii made this important statement: "If our agreement to enter the League of Nations proves insufficient to oppose the growth of German rearmament aimed against us, we are ready to take the next step and to go to a direct agreement with all opponents of German expansion." Krestinskii cautioned that there had been no detailed discussion in Moscow of these issues, and that his letter represented to a large degree his "personal commentaries" on the Politburo's directives, which Dovgalevskii had received by telegram.[56]

From Moscow it seemed urgent to act, the more so since Paul-Boncour was pressing the issue. Rozenberg reported on the worsening internal situation in France. A mood of panic was growing and so was "a tendency in favour of dictatorship." Inflation, budget deficits, and devaluation of the franc were causing governmental instability. In foreign policy, the "Herriot tendency" still challenged the "Daladier tendency." Rozenberg had already reported on Daladier's inclination to make concessions to Nazi Germany: "[André] François Poncet [the French ambassador in Berlin], allegedly, three months ago put forward a fantastic sounding proposal about a private meeting between Hitler and Daladier on the Franco-German border, to which each of them had to fly by airplane to the venue." Rozenberg did not quite say it but he implied that Daladier was becoming Hitler's Boy Friday in Paris, even if the meeting proposed by François Poncet did not come off.[57]

The Decision for Collective Security

It was into this atmosphere of "hurry" that Litvinov returned to Moscow, his credibility and prestige lustrous after obtaining US diplomatic recognition. The narkom must have had the wind in his sails. I am "deeply attached" to the rapprochement with France, he told Alphand shortly after his return to Moscow.[58]

Litvinov had wanted to keep the League of Nations as a separate issue, but Paul-Boncour insisted on the connection between the League and mutual assistance. As for the latter issue, Paul-Boncour was proposing mutual assistance "limited to" Belgium, France, Czechoslovakia, Poland, the USSR, and the Baltics, even Finland, or some combination thereof with obligatory participation of France and Poland.[59] It was 15 December 1933. Four days later, Litvinov made formal proposals to the Politburo. He wrote to Stalin describing the recent French démarches for a mutual assistance pact against Germany. Paul-Boncour had raised the subject in October. "I promised him, of course, to think about it and to discuss [it] with Moscow." The French did not wait for Litvinov's reply, and Paul-Boncour again broached the subject with Dovgalevskii on 26 November. For France, he said, the conclusion of a treaty of mutual assistance would be impossible without Soviet entry into the League. Litvinov then recommended various steps to Stalin, responding positively to Paul-Boncour's initiative. The Politburo approved these propositions, as submitted, on 19 December 1933. On Stalin's copy of Litvinov's briefing note is Stalin's annotation "*za*" (for or in favour of), and the approval of all other Politburo members, as if to underline the importance of the shift in Soviet policy.[60] Rapallo was finished.

The build-up of momentum for the change in policy occurred during Litvinov's absence from Moscow. No doubt his success in Washington contributed to Soviet confidence that the shift in policy was worth the risk. Alphand was also pressing, although Paul-Boncour needed no persuasion to move ahead. In Paris, Dovgalevskii and especially Rozenberg likewise pressed for action. Everyone, Soviet and French, seemed to be in a hurry. Collective security was not just a Litvinov project. Momentum in both Moscow and Paris pushed it ahead.

In fact, Paul-Boncour first broached the subject of mutual assistance. He wrote to Alphand that he had taken the initiative to speak with the Soviet ambassador in Paris, "very discreetly" about forms of Franco-Soviet mutual assistance, but he gave no details. Greater detail on Paul-Boncour's proposals is to be found in the NKID correspondence. Litvinov appears to have dispensed with discretion with Western interlocutors when speaking about the danger of Nazi Germany. In meetings with Roosevelt and Mussolini, the Italian Duce, Litvinov remarked to Alphand, that "the two war powers" (*les deux puissances de guerre*) were Germany and Japan.[61] Mussolini of course had not yet thrown in his lot with Hitler, and Litvinov hoped that Italy might be part of an anti-Nazi pact of mutual assistance. But this is getting ahead of the story.

Mendras reported a conversation at a French embassy luncheon in December between chargé d'affaires Jean Payart and the Soviet ambassador in Warsaw, Antonov-Ovseenko, who was home for consultations. Soviet policy is "very simple," the ambassador declared. "It is dictated by the fact that all that reinforces Germany, we are against, and all that reinforces France, we are for." Mendras also reported on Litvinov's speech to the Communist Party's Central Committee on 29 December where he spoke about the new Soviet foreign policy. We are not interested in old style "military alliances," the narkom declared, but we are ready to "collaborate in a common project of legitimate defence of all those who do not have an interest in disturbing the peace. From its side, the USSR is ready to participate in the realisation of this idea." However, Litvinov also spoke of his recurring worry, the instability of "capitalist states" – of course, he was thinking of France – where governments "change constantly." This circumstance opens the possibility of the arrival in power of groups or personalities animated by "class hatred" intense enough "to blind them to such a point that they would sacrifice the interests of their own country." Litvinov praised the rapid development of Franco-Soviet relations. "I want to believe," he stated, "I am persuaded that ['the upward march' of these relations] will intensify as the dangers to peace increase."[62] That was the gamble, which the Politburo had just decided to take.

A Huge Risk

It was a huge risk. Quickly, all too quickly, there were signs of trouble. On 28 December, Dovgalevskii went to see Paul-Boncour. The first topic of discussion was mutual assistance. Paul-Boncour approved the list of potential participants, discussed earlier, but already there was trouble. Belgium would not join without Britain. Dovgalevskii argued for the inclusion of Romania and Czechoslovakia. Paul-Boncour was "not against my arguments," Dovgalevskii advised, "although he welcomed the idea of the inclusion of the Baltics, he added that in the end the most important [signatories] would be the USSR, Poland, France, and Czechoslovakia." Paul-Boncour also "did not like the point about assistance in the case of other conflicts." He also objected to "material assistance, arguing that the supply of war *matériel* could create the presumption of participation in a conflict." Then the subject of the press came up, although, according to Paul-Boncour, its influence might only be "minimal." Who was he kidding? The Paris papers were hired guns available to the highest bidder. It all sounded like backtracking. In a pact of mutual assistance, Britain was a non-starter and so was Belgium. The Baltics were going to be a touchy subject, already that was becoming clear, and Poland, who knew about Poland? Paul-Boncour suggested that Dovgalevskii sit down with Léger to pursue the discussion.[63]

Was this the kiss of death, given Léger's lack of enthusiasm for mutual assistance? What had happened to Paul-Boncour? This telegram must have caused Litvinov to grimace as he read it. It was Rozenberg's bucket of cold water only this time it had been poured over Litvinov's head. However, the Politburo had approved talks with France on mutual security. It was too late for reversing course; and anyway mutual assistance was the only way forward against Nazi Germany. Solutions would have to be found. Léger did summon Dovgalevskii to the Quai d'Orsay in early January to follow up on the conversation of 28

December. The resulting French note discusses both the Soviet entry into the League of Nations and mutual assistance. Reading the note one might suppose that the initiative for mutual assistance came from the Soviet side and not from Paul-Boncour. It concludes that once the department has undertaken an adequate study (*une étude suffisante*) of the issues, it would again summon Dovgalevskii.[64] It appears, therefore, that Paul-Boncour's enthusiasm for mutual assistance had met up with the Quai d'Orsay *apparat*.

It was a setback to overcome. The Politburo had made a formal decision to adopt a new policy pivoting on France. It was a long-term policy. Accordingly, in mid-January 1934, Litvinov proposed to Stalin the creation of a new weekly newspaper in the French language to replace the *Moskauer Rundschau*, in German, which had recently ceased publication. Litvinov aimed at an "authoritative" voice to discuss Soviet foreign policy and to get a Soviet view of international relations out to a wider audience, but in particular to "political circles of the countries essential to us." This meant France, the Little Entente, and Poland. To begin, it would be six to eight pages with a print run of two to three thousand copies. The newspaper would not be an "official" organ of the Soviet government, but would be edited and produced in the NKID. It would thus be an "unofficial" organ for NKID opinion:

> In addition to its own leading foreign policy articles, the newspaper should regularly provide an overview of the Soviet press, especially in the field of foreign policy, along with information treated from the point of view of a foreign audience on the internal life and construction of the USSR. The newspaper should devote special attention to the issues of foreign trade and the artistic and scientific life of the USSR.

Litvinov asked for and obtained Politburo approval of the new publication.[65] It would be called the *Journal de Moscou*. The switch from the German to the French language as a medium to communicate with the external world underlined the change in direction of Soviet foreign policy.

Chapter Seven

Shadows of Doubt over Moscow: Consolidating Collective Security, 1933–1934

The new German ambassador in Moscow sensed the shift in Soviet policy. This was Rudolf Nadolny, who came from the German embassy in Turkey. Like Dirksen, he was a proponent of Rapallo, the "old" or "former policy," and hoped to put it back on the rails. He arrived in Moscow on 16 November 1933 as Soviet policy was swinging towards collective security. Litvinov still being in the United States, Krestinskii welcomed the new ambassador to Moscow. There was the usual polite exchange that one might expect with a new ambassador. Krestinskii thought Nadolny would have a more difficult time than his predecessor. The ambassador replied that he hoped to re-establish good Soviet-German relations; differences in political systems had led to "misunderstandings" but these should be overcome. This point of view, Krestinskii replied, was shared by many German politicians and diplomats, but not by the present German leaders who for a long time had spoken against Rapallo. That is why Nadolny was likely to run into difficulties in Moscow, the zamnarkom continued, "though not from our side." Politicians criticize their predecessors before taking power, Nadolny replied, then once in power, they have to resume the very same policies of their political adversaries. Krestinskii replied that the Soviet side had never wanted to change the previous relations, and if Nadolny could turn things around, then he could count on a positive Soviet reaction.[1] Nadolny saw Krestinskii again a week later for a longer conversation along the lines of his predecessor. The zamnarkom's stock response had not changed either: the German government's actions belied the ambassador's words. Nadolny requested a meeting with Molotov. He was too busy at the moment, came the reply. The ambassador was treated on a personal level with every courtesy, but the lunch in his honour was limited to embassy officials and their NKID counterparts.[2]

Mein Kampf

The next time Nadolny came to the NKID was to meet Litvinov after his return from the United States and Italy. The narkom dropped Krestinskii's personal courtesies, at least from his record of the conversation. It was Litvinov's first day back on the job and he had a string of appointments with ambassadors, so he did not have much time for Nadolny. It was the usual "the pot calling kettle black" kind of conversation. Litvinov gave the ambassador the whole list of Soviet grievances. Nadolny responded that it was the Soviet government's fault that relations with Germany had gone bad even before Hitler's arrival in power. The conversation resumed two days later, on 13 December, as Litvinov was preparing policy papers for Stalin and the Politburo on solidifying the rapprochement with France. At this second meeting Litvinov fired back with an impressive accounting of German policy from the time of German foreign minister Stresemann onward, a policy which could be interpreted as repeatedly going behind the Soviet back. But the narkom dismissed all these events with a wave of the hand. The real problems started with Franz von Papen and then Hitler. You could tell Litvinov was out of patience because he brought up *Mein Kampf*. Dirksen had not been subjected to *that* interrogation. What about "Hitler's literary works?" Litvinov asked bluntly. But that was just the beginning of a long indictment of German anti-Soviet activities. "I could not admit," he wrote to his journal, "that Nadolny can seriously talk about our guilt in the worsening of relations with Germany. If he says this seriously, then I am afraid that it will not be easy for him and me to talk."

"Nadolny resorted to the usual justifications," Litvinov observed. As for *Mein Kampf*, or "Hitler's book," the ambassador said it "belongs to the past." Litvinov, of course, did not believe him. As for the rest, it was the whole basket of dirty laundry thrown onto the pages of Litvinov's journal from Papen's attempt to attract Herriot into an anti-Soviet coalition, to Nazi ideologue Alfred Rosenberg's rants about seizing the Ukraine, to more barbs about *Mein Kampf*. Nadolny was despondent as the narkom described the scene. "He threw up his hands in great distress and declared that my words left him in utter despair, for if he forwarded what I said to Berlin, it would create the impression of a complete hopelessness in relations." Nadolny proposed some general principles for re-establishing better relations, notably to calm down the mudslinging in the press and the mutual recriminations and mistrust. "I have nothing against these principles," Litvinov replied, though he doubted that the mutual trust existed for all that the ambassador proposed.[3] Litvinov did not copy his record to Stalin and the Politburo, an indication that Nadolny's intervention was too little, too late to stop the shift in Soviet policy. Nadolny's report of the meeting indicates that it went on for two-and-a-half hours and led to "a very sharp dispute, but finally ended on a friendly note." The usual accusations were exchanged. *Mein Kampf* received more attention in Litvinov's report than it did in Nadolny's where it was scarely more than an etcetera.[4]

At the end of December 1933, Khinchuk, the Soviet polpred in Berlin, sent Litvinov a detailed résumé of a new edition of *Mein Kampf*. These details included Hitler's views on the Jews and on Austria. His "so-called 'eastern policy'" also drew Khinchuk's attention. It is, he noted, "the policy of extending German borders towards the East, by means of war, at the expense of the border states and the Soviet Union."[5] Having Khinchuk's dispatch to hand, Litvinov raised the subject with the French ambassador Alphand in early January 1934. Has the French government, he asked facetiously, called Berlin's attention to the continued dissemination of *Mein Kampf* in which Hitler promotes *revanche* against France, the "age-old enemy" of Germany? Alphand also made a record of this meeting, skipping over the narkom's sarcasm. Germany, Litvinov said, "needs two or three years to get organized before it attacks us. In order to obtain it [the respite], she will sign all the treaties and pacts you want without attaching any more importance to them than formerly [Theobald von] Bethmann-Hollweg [German chancellor in 1914] had done."[6] Khinchuk had obviously got Litvinov's attention.

Mendras also noticed. He reported the same conversation to Paris, and he noticed a remarkably prophetic article by Radek to mark the beginning of the New Year. "Wherever it breaks out, war will be a world war and will draw all the powers into its whirlwind. Today there is no other alternative than to coordinate all efforts against it or let the avalanche begin, which no one will have the power to stop." Mendras was equally prophetic: "Against the German advance, the Soviets understand very well that there is only one sure and certain barrier with us. Here, all the foreign diplomats see clearly this situation and our enemies, past or future, watch anxiously the least signs of collaboration between France and the Soviet Union … one could be tempted to see there yet another reason to persevere [towards that goal]."[7] Yes, this was the realist's argument. The enemy of my enemy is my ally.

German Ears in Moscow

It is interesting that the German embassy in Moscow picked up on a French offer to conclude "a regional pact." "An American journalist who is well disposed towards Germany," Twardowski reported, "informed me on the night of 21 December that, in the last few days, France made the Soviet Union an offer to conclude a pact for mutual assistance in case the European territory of one of the two partners should be attacked by a third party." The Soviet government was more inclined now than before, especially because of the situation in the Far East "to respond to the French proposal." The unnamed journalist had done a story; he considered the news to be "a political sensation of the first order." The Soviet censor had blocked the dispatch, Twardowski indicated, saying his report was "premature" and so on. Twardowski speculated on the source of the information: maybe it was Mr. Bullitt, the new US ambassador in Moscow. The date of Twardowski's dispatch is 26 December 1933. Paul-Boncour had repeated his offer to Dovgalevskii on 26 November, the same that he had made to Litvinov in late October on his way to Washington. It was also seven days after the Politiburo had approved Litvinov's new policy recommendations, and two days before Dovgalevskii had a new meeting with Paul-Boncour on 28 December. The unnamed American journalist did not quite have the story right, but was close enough to draw a veto from the Soviet censor.

Twardowski did a follow-up with "a local diplomat who is a close friend of ours." He was "exceedingly surprised" but thought the information possible. He spoke with Litvinov just before Christmas, and the narkom was "nervous" and not very forthcoming. The diplomat pressed after listening to some generalities, but Litvinov "only shrugged his shoulders" and said nothing more. Twardowski thought the story was very likely true, some kind of "defensive alliance" could develop from the French offer.[8] This was just what Paul-Boncour had in mind, if he could pull it off. The Quai d'Orsay "clerks," as readers will know, were already trying to sabotage their minister's plan. A day later, Twardowski sent another telegram which noted "that a French offer, or at least a French proposal, has been made to the Soviet Union can hardly be doubted any more."[9] Who leaked the information? Would Nadolny raise the subject with Litvinov?

The Italian ambassador threw a New Year's Eve party and almost everybody who was somebody in the Moscow diplomatic community was there. Twardowski cornered Litvinov for a conversation. He opened with a query about Litvinov's speech on 29 December on which Mendras had reported. Litvinov hoped his speech would attract attention in Berlin. Twardowski replied that his accusations against Germany were "laughable." And so it went. "The conversation was ended," Twardowski recorded, "by the approach of the French ambassador, who greeted Litvinov with both hands and told him many flattering things about his speech."[10] That was to rub it into Twardowski.

Nadolny vs. Litvinov

There was no rest for the weary as the Near Year began, at least not for the NKID. Nadolny asked for a meeting with Litvinov. An old Bolshevik and former people's commissar, Anatolii Vasilievich Lunarcharskii, had died and Nadolny expressed his regrets, but "then immediately passed to political questions." The ambassador was upset by Litvinov's late December speech to the Central Committee. Why the public speech, he wanted to know, which made him look like a fool in Berlin after their agreement, so Nadolny thought, to calm down public opinion. It looked like he, Litvinov, had "disavowed" him. Litvinov replied with a long explanation about how he was obliged to inform Soviet opinion about the state of relations with Germany. This was mere courtesy; the narkom was announcing publicly a shift in policy. Rapallo was dead. Nadolny was no fool; he sensed it. The conversation went on for some time if one is to judge from the length of Litvinov's record of the conversation. He was sarcastic and sharp tongued. His comments on Soviet-German relations were less "harsh" than those of Hitler and other Nazi leaders, said the narkom. "Can you correct the effect of your speech?" Nadolny asked. "There is nothing to correct," Litvinov replied.

At the end of their conversation, Nadolny wanted to talk about Soviet relations with France. There had been articles in the press about the French offers of a defensive alliance that Twardowski had reported earlier to Berlin. When Litvinov declined, the ambassador lost his composure, exclaiming that Moscow was pursuing a "dishonourable" policy, an *Unehrliche Politik*. "I said to Nadolny that he was forgetting himself, that I could not permit him to speak with me in that tone, and that if he did not immediately take back his words and apologize, I would terminate the conversation. I closed my notebook and got up. Nadolny begged me not to end the conversation on this note, but I insisted strongly that he immediately excuse himself. Nadolny, apologizing, extended his hand to me and excused his outburst as a 'patriotic' reaction." Litvinov again took his seat and the conversation quickly ended.[11] Alphand heard about the meeting the next day. "Nadolny was very upset," according to Litvinov, "by the news of the Franco-Russian alliance reported in the press."[12] The gloves were off with the Germans.

Nadolny reported having spent two hours with Litvinov. It must have been gruelling. The conversation was "very unsatisfactory." Litvinov was "exceedingly reserved and in part actually unfriendly." It was not the first time that German diplomats complained about Litvinov's cold shoulder. Ironically, Nadolny strongly objected to Litvinov's speech and his characterization of Germany as "a disturber of world peace." It is a "provocation," he said. Nadolny left out of his account the moment where Litvinov got up from his chair to offer the door to his interlocutor and the apology that followed. Then, according to Nadolny, there was Litvinov's indifferent "shrug of the shoulders" in response to the ambassador's observation, threat really, that there would be "consequences" resulting from Soviet hostility.[13] The narkom's shrug was becoming habitual.

Nadolny returned to the NKID two days later to see Krestinskii and Karakhan, still zamnarkom in the NKID. Nadolny wanted to re-establish contact after his holiday leave in Berlin, or so he said, but what he really wanted to do was determine if his unfortunate meeting two days earlier with Litvinov was only the latter's personal outburst or an expression of Soviet policy. He took the same line that the German leadership wanted better relations with Moscow but that Litvinov's speech to the Central Committee had been "a heavy blow" to his hopes. "He [Nadolny] told me that he had seen comrade Litvinov with whom he had had a very difficult discussion." Karakhan feigned not to know about the conversation, though he had read Litvinov's record of it.

Nadolny began to give an account of the discussion, starting with the German observation that "we lent too much importance to the book that was written ten years ago." The ambassador of course meant *Mein Kampf*. It was as though Nadolny was trying to look for a breach in the position of the NKID leadership. Karakhan was too smart to fall for that ruse. "Litvinov's speech, in his opinion [Nadolny's], had again aggravated the situation." Karakhan listened politely and then replied much as Litvinov had. Nadolny "tried to trick me," Karakhan reported, "by stating that Litvinov, allegedly, talked to him about ongoing discussions with the French for developing agreements on mutual assistance, etc., etc." Karakhan noted that the ambassador changed the subject after he saw that "his cunning" had not worked, resuming his complaints about the conversation with Litvinov, which indicated that the USSR was siding with the enemies of Germany, notably France.

Karakhan finally interrupted: "I explained to him that he simply did not understand our policy. In the present international situation, the basic question is the question of war." The ambassador could not deny this "basic danger," and according to Karakhan, he did not try to do so. It was normal, Karakhan said, that the USSR was ready to cooperate with any powers opposed to war, France for example. Nadolny insisted "hotly" that Germany did not want war and he complained again about Soviet relations with France, which made it too late to return to better Soviet-German relations. "It is never too late to change the present line of the German government," Karakhan replied. Nadolny insisted that as ambassador he wanted to improve relations. The solution to the problem was not to deny present German policy, the zamnarkom replied, but to work for a change of policy in Berlin and "a return to the old position of the German government." Karakhan asked Nadolny to talk in future to Litvinov and Krestinskii who were responsible for German affairs, and he sent Stalin, Molotov, and others in the Politburo a copy of his conversation.[14]

This is an interesting detail since Litvinov did not send a copy of his 3 January conversation to the Politburo. Was this an insignificant fact, or was Karakhan covering himself for having spoken to Nadolny? Or was it the old personal rivalry stirring for a last time, drawing Stalin's attention to Litvinov's rough treatment of the German ambassador? It is impossible to say. What is noteworthy is that the explanations of the NKID leadership and of Litvinov, Krestinskii, and Karakhan were in tune. Nadolny followed up his meetings at the NKID with a long memorandum to Berlin proposing measures "to take the wind out of Litvinov's sails." This meant controlling German press outbursts and those of Alfred Rosenberg, and putting *Mein Kampf* on a back shelf. He had heard from unnamed Soviet sources that Litvinov had gone "too far" in his language about German intentions. German authorities should treat Litvinov more respectfully, Nadolny recommended, as that might have some positive results.[15]

Nadolny was still making his rounds in Moscow. On 11 January, he met with one of Stalin's key supporters, War Commissar Voroshilov for an hour-long conversation. Voroshilov talked about all the issues raised by Litvinov. *Mein Kampf* was again a major topic of conversation. Litvinov's line, according to Nadolny, had made a strong impression on Voroshilov, but he at least was open to better German-Soviet relations.[16] The next day Twardowski had a long chat with the Soviet chief of staff, Aleksandr Il'ich Egorov, who stuck to Litvinov's line, noting that the cooling of relations had naturally affected relations between the two armies. We don't want to send our officers to Germany, Egorov said, to risk having them rousted or beaten by Nazi Brownshirts. "Change your policy," he said, "and everything will be alright again."[17]

Franco-Soviet Trade Talks

The NKID understanding of the international situation was precocious compared to many Soviet counterparts in the West. Litvinov became the best-known spokesperson for Soviet policy, but he was not the only advocate for the policy that gelled after his departure for Washington while Krestinskii was acting head of the department. Judging from Krestinskii's correspondence, the shift originated in the Politburo under Stalin's direction. What is also clear in the Soviet papers, though not as clear in the French papers is that Paul-Boncour took the initiative to advance mutual assistance with the support of Herriot out of government and Cot in government. His efforts led finally to the signature of a trade agreement on 11 January 1934.[18] Here, ironically, the French government was working against itself because the Ministry of Finance and the Banque de France obstructed the negotiations by refusing to approve competitive credit arrangements to finance Franco-Soviet trade. The provisional trade agreement was modest, guaranteeing, *inter alia*, 250 million francs per annum in Soviet orders. The haggling was intense, like two merchants in a bazaar, and continued until the last minute. The Soviet side wanted to reduce the value of Soviet orders in France from 250 to 200 million francs, but the French held the line at 250 million.[19]

Judging from the asperity of the negotiations, one might not have known that the importance of the agreement was more political than economic. Both Paul-Boncour and Litvinov underlined the agreement's political significance.[20] *Izvestiia* and *Pravda* gave the agreement favourable notice, stressing that it fit into the larger context of improved Franco-Soviet relations. "It is a link in the chain of strengthening relations between the two countries," Litvinov said to Alphand.[21] Back in Paris, the bankers were not so happy, but they ought not to have blamed Moscow for the failure to get a settlement of tsarist bonds. That responsibility lay squarely in the hands of the Poincaré government.[22]

Nadolny and Litvinov Again

Nadolny, no doubt having read about the trade agreement, went back to see Litvinov on 15 January. Consistent with his recommendations to Berlin, he took a softer approach than at the earlier meeting, first raising less difficult subjects before asking again about negotiations with France for a pact of mutual assistance. "Our recent discussions with France," replied Litvinov, "have been limited to negotiations on the trade agreement." This was true, only if one omitted Dovgalevskii's discussions with Paul-Boncour and Léger, but the narkom left out his strong belief that the trade agreement was key to the general improvement of Franco-Soviet relations. The subject eventually turned to the Baltic area. If Litvinov had any "suspicions" about German intentions there, Nadolny proposed they discuss them. That sortie provoked Litvinov's irritation. If the Soviet leadership had suspicions, he replied, "they are prompted by the rants in the German press of politicians and journalists on the theme of expansion in the East." Here was another indirect reference to *Mein Kampf* and Alfred Rosenberg, though Litvinov did not mention either the book or the person. Still Litvinov tried to be polite and, at the end of the conversation, was even conciliatory though not without a mild dose of sarcasm.[23]

In response to Nadolny's policy recommendations, Foreign Minister Neurath in Berlin responded with a damp squib. He wrote to Nadolny not to run after Litvinov and not to take any initiative in conversations with "important persons" in Moscow. "There is no purpose in making attempts which are hopeless from the very start to change the attitude of the dominant statesmen of the Soviet Union."[24] In reaction to these instructions, Nadolny rejoined and then retreated.

Judging from Litvinov's record of the conversation, he sounded confident and did not need to pay too much attention to Nadolny's spurious complaints about the Soviet misunderstanding of German policy. Not quite a month earlier, the Politburo had dumped Rapallo for the rapprochement with France and some kind of mutual assistance, yet to be determined, among all those states worried about Nazi Germany. With all the publicity about the signature of the provisional trade agreement, maybe Litvinov had not been paying enough attention to internal French politics, especially for someone who worried about the steadiness of French foreign policy. There were four cabinets in 1933, the longest surviving, that of Daladier, lasted a little less than nine months, which was not bad by French standards. The changes of governments might normally have given pause in Moscow, except for the fact that Paul-Boncour remained foreign minister throughout the year and that he had aggressively pursued the rapprochement with the Soviet Union, going as far as proposing a pact of mutual assistance in October. Paul-Boncour might have made Litvinov and his colleagues a little more confident than perhaps they should have been, but the success in Washington must also have added to Soviet aplomb.

A Little Scandal in a Small French Town

On 24 December 1933, five days after the Politburo had approved the shift in policy to collective security, the police in Bayonne, a town in the far distant southwestern corner of France, near Biarritz, arrested the director of the Crédit municipal de Bayonne, a Monsieur Tissier, for fraud worth 200 million francs. One could not blame Litvinov for failing to notice the news of this event. Bayonne was a long way from Paris, and who had ever heard of Monsieur Tissier outside of Bayonne? Moreover, scandals in France during the interwar years were a dime a dozen, which was another reason not to pay much attention to the news on Christmas Eve. Under police interrogation, Monsieur Tissier started "to sing," incriminating a Monsieur Garat, the député-maire of Bayonne who was arrested on 7 January, for crimes including embezzlement and fraud. This was four days before the signature of the trade agreement in Paris. Again, who could blame Litvinov or the Soviet embassy for not paying attention to events in distant Bayonne?

The following day, 8 January, the French press announced the sensational news that Alexandre Stavisky, a well-known fraudster and celebrity of the French yellow press, had committed suicide in Chamonix, a French mountain resort near the borders with Italy and Switzerland. The police said it was suicide; many citizens and pundits suspected that it was murder by the French police to prevent him from "singing." Stavisky was a friend of Monsieur Garat from Bayonne, and also a generous contributor to the Radical Party of Messieurs Herriot and Daladier. He might have had a lot to say. Moreover, his defence lawyer was the brother of the then président du Conseil, Camile Chautemps. It also happened that the brother-in-law of Chautemps, Monsieur Georges Pressard, was the head of the Paris parquet, or chief prosecutor's office, which had postponed nineteen times a case for fraud opened against Stavisky in 1928. You begin perhaps to see the problem. The story became more and more phantasmagorical with every passing day.

At some point, the Soviet embassy in Paris must have reported the news to the NKID, which was, no doubt, too busy to have noticed given the hustle and bustle to conclude the trade agreement. On 9 January, two days before the signature of the agreement, the minister of colonies, Monsieur Albert Dalimier, a Radical-Socialist, resigned. There were also several other high-profile arrests. In little more than a fortnight, the scandal had reached from Bayonne into the Council of Ministers in Paris. On 12 January, the scandal reached the floor of the Chambre des députés. The government won a vote of confidence after the debate, and then another a few days later, but the scandal would not go away. By the end of the month, on 26 January, after more revelations in the press about the police protection offered to Stavisky, alias "Monsieur Alexandre," the justice minister resigned. That was the coup de grâce. The Chautemps cabinet resigned the following day.

Was It to Be a *Koshmar* Then?

Was Litvinov's worst *koshmar* about to come true? Daladier formed a new government and he took over the Quai d'Orsay. Paul-Boncour was out; Daladier had finally got rid of him, it seemed. On 28 January, two days before leaving office, Paul-Boncour called in Dovgalevskii to assure him that the "essence" of French policy would remain unchanged, only the "style" might differ.[25] Notwithstanding Paul-Boncour's assertion, did the change in government mean the Daladier line would now take precedence over the Herriot line? Litvinov must have allowed himself some doubts. Stalin must have had them as well, even if the Politburo had approved the new policy barely a month before. In a speech on 26 January at the 17th Party Congress, Stalin warned the West, in effect, not to take the USSR for granted:

> Some German politicians say that the USSR has now taken an orientation towards France and Poland; that from an opponent of Versailles it has become a supporter of it ... That is not true ... It is not for us to sing the praises of the Versailles treaty. We merely do not agree to the world being flung into a new war because of this treaty. The same must be said of the alleged new orientation taken by the USSR. We never had any orientation towards Germany, nor have we any orientation towards Poland and France. Our orientation in the past and our orientation at the present is towards the USSR and towards the USSR alone. And if the interests of the USSR demand rapprochement with one country or another which is not interested in disturbing the peace, we adopt this course without hesitation.
>
> No, that is not the point. The point is that Germany's policy has changed.[26]

Yes, of course, Stalin was quite right about the Soviet Union looking after its own interests – all independent states do that – but the Politburo had in fact reoriented its policy towards France and the United States. Poland was a large question mark. Nadolny was encouraged by Stalin's remarks in comparison with those made by Litvinov, and he sold the speech to Berlin as an open door to Germany through which to make some statement "respecting Russian fears." There is no indication in Soviet papers that it was. It is interesting to note that Nadolny considered Litvinov to be one of "the four most important men of the Soviet Union" along with Stalin, Molotov, and Kaganovich. Silence from Berlin in response to Stalin's remarks would only confirm Soviet suspicions of German policy.[27]

And Poland?

What then about Poland? The indications were not encouraging. Polpred Antonov-Ovseenko tried to draw out Foreign Minister Beck at a meeting on 5 January. It was the new year and a good time to review the international situation. The polpred turned the discussion to Germany. Soviet relations with Germany were "clearly defined," Antonov-Ovseenko said, but Poland's, not so much. There was, for example, a lack of clarity in the Polish position on German rearmament. The Polish government had informed Paris, Beck replied, that Warsaw was against it, and was ready to align with Paris on the rearmament question and to oppose any weakening of France. The Polish government entered into negotiations with Germany and "an alignment of relations with it because we did not want a repetition of Locarno [where the interests of Poland were not fully addressed and protected]." There have been some successes, continued Beck. "We did not intend and we do not intend to break with France, but it [France] must properly respect (*otsenivat'*) us." Beck was quick to add that he approved of the French position against separate negotiations with Germany. "And what about us?" responded Antonov-Ovseenko. "Will we again be placed before some political surprise?" Beck reiterated that Poland wanted to maintain "present cooperation" with the Soviet Union on rearmament issues.[28]

Litvinov had a conversation with Polish ambassador Łukasiewicz a week later, again to feel out Polish intentions. It was 11 January. The conversation eventually turned to the negotiations with Germany and to rumours of a non-aggression pact. "Łukasiewicz said to me confidentially that Poland had received from Germany a formal proposal for the conclusion of such a pact." The proposal had been discussed at length in Warsaw and Józef Lipski, the Polish ambassador in Berlin, had been instructed to enter into negotiations with the German government. Łukasiewicz did not know how long it would take to conclude an agreement: it could be only one day or it could be that discussions would drag out. Litvinov asked the ambassador to thank Beck for this information and then suavely, according to the narkom's account, turned to another subject.[29]

The Nazi-Polish non-aggression pact was signed on 26 January 1934. It was on that same day that Stalin made his speech to the Party Congress. Apparently unaware of the signature of the non-aggression pact, Stalin had this to say about Poland:

> Surprises and zigzags in policy, for example in Poland, where anti-Soviet sentiments are still strong, can as yet by no means be regarded as out of the question. But the change for the better in our relations, irrespective of its results in the future, is a fact worthy of being noted and emphasized as a factor in the advancement of the cause of peace.

Whatever scepticism existed in Moscow about Polish intentions, Soviet policy was still a rapprochement with Warsaw. This intention was now tested.

On 26 January, the Polish foreign ministry summoned Antonov-Ovseenko to inform him of the conclusion of the agreement. Beck asked to see him again, three days later to complain about Stalin's speech. "We have established with you," Beck said, "the appropriate understanding." He continued, "I was astonished by the expression of mistrust in the stability of our policy in relation to you which featured in one place in Mr. Stalin's speech. On what is this [mistrust] based?" Antonov-Ovseenko appeared to be caught off guard. "I answered," he noted, "that I did not yet have the full text of the speech, but speaking personally I also think that the given tactics of Poland in relation to Germany cannot fail to raise doubts. Any strengthening of Germany is harmful to the affairs of peace, the given agreement undoubtedly will strengthen Hitler's regime, increase his credit worthiness abroad." Antonov-Ovseenko enumerated a fairly long list of negative impacts. The polpred must have been disappointed given his attempts to establish better Soviet-Polish relations. Beck was argumentative and, as Antonov-Ovseenko noted, he gave as good as he got on various subjects.[30] It was a fair assumption that in Moscow there would be some unhappiness over Poland's deal with the devil. Antonov-Ovseenko warned that the Germans hoped the non-aggression pact would worsen Polish relations with France and the USSR.[31] So, the Germans were trying to spring a trap: worsening Polish relations with France and the USSR would lead to greater Polish dependency on Germany.

On 28 January, Litvinov asked Stalin for authorization to publish a commentary in the Soviet press on the Nazi-Polish non-aggression pact. "We cannot not welcome the conclusion of the Polish-German pact agreement ... in as much as it will serve the reinforcement of peace in general and in Eastern Europe in particular. We are not interested in the continuation of strain in relations between our neighbours and Germany or with other countries." Some press commentaries, Litvinov noted, had observed that the accord was "something like an Eastern Locarno." During Foreign Minister Stresemann's time in office, the German government resisted any such agreement. Least of all could one expect such an agreement from Hitler who had accused Weimar governments of excessive concessionism and who had called for a policy of *revanche* and the re-establishment by force of pre-war German borders. So why had he agreed to the pact with Poland? It was a manoeuvre – and a successful one at that – to escape from diplomatic isolation. So had Hitler "capitulated," made major, unreciprocated concessions, and changed his policies? Governments across Europe, opined Litvinov, must be asking these very questions.

Other questions arose. How would the non-aggression impact on Franco-Polish relations? Polish security was a major source of conflict between France and Germany. In France, there were not a few politicians who had earlier proposed to sacrifice Polish interests in order to obtain an agreement with Germany. The "separate agreement" with Germany would only strengthen these ideas and leave Poland "completely isolated." it was not enough simply to offer a blanket guarantee of the security of Polish borders. "It is completely obvious," Litvinov concluded, "that this agreement does not resolve the problem of the Polish Corridor and Polish-German frontiers."[32]

French Ambassador Laroche told Antonov-Ovseenko that "Poland had morally tied itself to Germany." A Polish press campaign about Těšín (a Czechoslovak district with a large Polish population) indicated that Marshal Piłsudski was looking to expand Polish frontiers. It was his dream.[33] By distancing itself from France and moving closer to Germany, Poland, so it was believed in Warsaw, could pursue its own more modest territorial ambitions. Modest ambitions, certainly, but also dangerous.

Litvinov soon had to contend with an irate Polish ambassador in a heated meeting over Soviet press comments. "Łukasiewicz at once spoke in an aggressive tone about the dissatisfaction provoked in Poland by the declaration of comrade Stalin on the zigzags of Polish policy." And the ambassador had other complaints to make, in particular, about comments in *Izvestiia*. Stalin had obviously approved the publication of Litvinov's "theses." The narkom did not attempt to argue. "I calmly listened to Łukasiewicz," Litvinov wrote in his journal. How interesting that the Polish ambassador obtained a "calm" reply while the German ambassador was hauled on the carpet for tempestuous remarks he had made only a month before. On that occasion, Litvinov had demanded an apology, but not this time. He dealt politely with all the Polish ambassador's complaints, occasionally it must be said rather disingenuously, but it was clear that unlike the Germans, the NKID, whatever Stomoniakov's doubts, was desirous of maintaining and deepening the Polish rapprochement. Beck was expected in Moscow, and Litvinov did not want that meeting called off, as Łukasiewicz apparently hinted might happen. It was a masterful diplomatic performance, if one wants to believe Litvinov's account of the meeting. Łukasiewicz was rude, and even interrupted the narkom, who took it all patiently, continuing his explanations when the ambassador let him speak. Patience sometimes has its own reward, for Łukasiewicz eventually admitted that he was speaking on his own initiative about Beck's trip to Moscow, to which comment Litvinov expressed his "astonishment." After a brief lecture on diplomatic protocol, Litvinov let the conversation end.[34]

The Polish ambassador was sufficiently worried by the clash with Litvinov that he went to see Stomoniakov a week later to clear the air before Beck arrived in Moscow on a three-day visit. "I have come," he said, "on my own personal initiative to talk in a completely private capacity." He was still worried about the reaction in Moscow to the "Polish-German agreement" and Stalin's speech to the Party Congress. He had expected that there would be a public calming of the waters, but nothing of the sort had occurred. If anything, the atmosphere in Moscow had worsened. I do not have the impression, Łukasiewicz continued, that Beck was to be welcomed as an "honoured guest." After listening to a long monologue, Stomoniakov made an equally long reply, the details of which do not need to be related. But the long and the short of it was that Stomoniakov assured Łukasiewicz that Beck would be a "welcomed guest." The ambassador calmed down, but still appeared to be worried even as he walked out the door of Stomoniakov's office.[35]

Beck in Moscow

Beck's visit did after all occur as planned and without disagreeable incident. The tiff over Stalin's speech was forgotten. The meetings between Litvinov and Beck were spread over three days. Conversation was "eye to eye," according to the narkom's record. Topics of conversation ranged from the League of Nations, to Nazi Germany, the Baltics, and other issues concerning European peace and security. Beck opened with concerns about the League of Nations and its "weakness" in dealing with international problems. This was producing "nervousness" and instability. For Beck, the solution to the League's irrelevance was the conclusion of bilateral agreements like the agreement with Germany on "the non-use of force."

"I expressed the opinion," Litvinov wrote in his journal, "that the existing nervousness … was caused not by the absence of [international] institutions … but by the presence of real dangers of a breach of the peace for the prevention of which effective means have not been found, and not only because they do not exist but because not everyone is looking for them and wants to find them." A long discussion then ensued about the Nazi-Polish non-aggression pact. Litvinov questioned Beck's assumptions about why the Nazi government had agreed to the pact when various Weimar ministers had declined to do so. Internal weakness explained it, replied Beck, and Prussia had ceased to exist. Hitler had realized that Poland was not some "trifling, fair-weather government" which could easily be disregarded.

Litvinov challenged Beck's assumptions. Hitler was a unifying force whose platform included non-recognition of the Polish Corridor and *revanche*. The non-aggression pact went against these elements of his platform and created dissent inside Germany and inside the Nazi Party. Nor had Prussia disappeared. On the contrary, "Germany is now one continuous Prussia." Beck had horribly miscalculated was Litvinov's essential reply. But he continued:

> Prussian utterances about the necessity to find its place under the sun, about excess population, for which it is necessary to find new territories for colonization, about the glorification of the martial spirit and military conquests find their most passionate expression in Nazi ideology. On Hitlerite aspirations we judge by the old Hitlerite literature, and not by the political speeches which Hitler now pronounces, switching to pacifist phraseology. These speeches are prompted by tactical considerations. The Nazis, like the Japanese, are convinced that sabre rattling and loud conversations about the necessity and inevitability of war and preparations for it would mobilize public opinion everywhere against them. Learning this lesson, the Hitlerites, like the Japanese, having by no means renounced the basic principles of their foreign policy and from preparations to bring to life these principles, deem it necessary temporarily to persuade the world of their peaceful intentions.

Figure 7.1. Litvinov and Beck meeting in Moscow, 13 February 1934, AVPRF.

Do not be confused, Litvinov added, by distinctions between anticipated new conquests of territory and the recovery of old territories lost because of the Great War. It was only a question of tactics about when, what, and where to strike first. This is why many countries were concerned; the Polish-German agreement played into Hitler's plans. They worried even more because of the absence in the pact of a customary termination clause in the event of aggression against a third state by one of the contracting parties.

Beck appeared to listen politely to what Litvinov had to say and then demurred. There was no "danger from the side of Germany or in general the danger of war in Europe." It seemed to him that the Soviet government was "looking too far forward." Beck was thinking in "smaller segments of time and evaluates from the perspective of the present day." If Poland could guarantee its security in the short term (*na segodniashnego dnia*), then that was good enough. On the issue of the absence of a "termination clause," Beck brushed it off. Litvinov did not insist on the issue of the termination clause but pointed out that there was such a clause in the Soviet-Polish pact. Nothing seemed to bother Beck until Litvinov, apparently in gest, but really not, brought up the point – in a fit of "jealousy," Beck said – that the pact with Germany was good for ten years while the Soviet pact was only good for three years. "Beck was clearly embarrassed," Litvinov noted, "the only time during all of our conversations and he even fidgeted in his chair and said indistinctly that this can be corrected." Beck also insisted on the Polish commitment to the rapprochement with the Soviet Union. Litvinov then brought up his idea for a joint Polish-Soviet statement endorsing the independence of the Baltic states.

For Litvinov, the security of the Baltic states was an important matter. "Recent events," he wrote to Stalin, "demand an energetic activation of our policy vis-à-vis the Baltic governments. Their great importance, as a possible *place d'armes* in a future war against the USSR has grown all the more for us after Hitler's rise to power in Germany." Poland and Britain were also active in the area. The Soviet government needed to project more "influence," not just political, but political and economic in the Baltic countries "to develop friendly relations." He made a series of recommendations approved by the Politburo.[36] In a subsequent note, Litvinov warned Stalin that the proposal for a Baltic guarantee was not going well. The NKID informed the Baltic governments of Litvinov's proposal, but Finland replied that it did not feel threatened and was therefore not interested in a guarantee. "As we expected, the Finns immediately made public our proposal with the objective of sabotaging it."[37]

Beck was not any more favourable than the Finns to Litvinov's idea, although the discussion of it was long. Conversation eventually turned to other subjects, but for Litvinov, it was clear that the Soviet-Polish rapprochement, whatever the appearances, was dead in the water. At the end of his record of conversations, Litvinov composed some conclusions. First of all, cooperation with Poland in regard to Germany in the near future had "disappeared." In fact, it seemed worse than that. "Beck not only in his categorical declaration closed the road to such collaboration at the present time, but did not even make any reservations about the possibility of returning later to this subject. One has to conclude that Poland considers itself for the time being guaranteed from the side of Germany." Litvinov did not think there were any secret agreements with Germany, but these were not excluded in the future in the event of a Soviet "collision" with Japan. Also dead was any Soviet-Polish guarantee of the independence of the Baltic states. Poland might cover its new German orientation by maintaining the semblance of a rapprochement with the Soviet Union. The Soviet government should take advantage of this situation, Litvinov thought, to prevent the worst by at least pursuing cultural ties.[38]

The once promising, if briefly so, rapprochement with Poland was dead. Beck was playing the short game, as he told Litvinov, and in that game, he saw no danger from Germany. Litvinov tried to warn Beck that he was making a terrible mistake, that Hitler was covering his preparations for war and territorial expansion with sweet words about peace. In the end, however, it was going to be war, and Beck should not think that the non-aggression pact would protect Poland when Hitler decided the time was right to attack. Litvinov's analysis was so to the point that his record of conversation was declassified in 1965 and published in the years thereafter. You can see why.

Alphand also signalled the danger to Paris. There had been "a modification of the Polish attitude vis-à-vis France as well as the USSR." According to Alphand, Beck was even boasting of his accomplishments. "We do not fear," he was reported to have said, "attacks on the part of Germany." For Alphand as for Litvinov, Beck had blundered. "That Poland is mistaken, there can be no doubt; the history of its previous partitions is the result of these sorts of errors, of these games of manoeuvre between its competitors."[39] The ambassador was evoking the eighteenth-century partitions of Poland leading to its disappearance in 1795. One wonders whether Beck remembered his conversations with Litvinov a little more than five years later, as he fled Warsaw on 4 September 1939 with the Wehrmacht closing in on the capital. He had been so sure that he was right and Litvinov, wrong.

Stomoniakov sent a summary of Soviet views on the Beck visit to the Warsaw embassy. "The basic meaning of Beck's arrival in Moscow may be summed up thus: he brought great clarity to our relations with Poland. The conversations of comrade Litvinov with Beck revealed that Poland, moving from a rapprochement with us, is attempting first of all to keep a free hand, and that at this stage it does not want to enter into any cooperation with us against Germany." Hence, from earlier ideas about Polish cooperation with the USSR against Germany, "nothing remained." Stomoniakov could not have been blunter, but he added that the Soviet government would continue to promote a multifaceted rapprochement with Poland. "We are by no means interested in showing any kind of disappointment at the results of Beck's visit and in general at the state of our relations with Poland after her conclusion of a treaty with Germany." We are counting on Polish cooperation *with* the USSR against Germany being more popular with Poles than cooperation with Germany *against* the USSR. In the meantime, the "clarification of the Polish position in relation to the USSR underscores the necessity for maximum vigilance from our side in all that concerns Polish-German relations."[40] This remained Soviet policy with ups and downs until Stalin decided to turn the tables on the Poles in August 1939 and to conclude his own non-aggression pact with Hitlerite Germany. Two could play Beck's game, but in the end not any better than Beck.

This is getting ahead of the narrative. For the time being, Litvinov still sought to pursue the rapprochement with Poland in spite of Polish opposition. Stomoniakov thus continued his conversations with Łukasiewicz asking for an explanation of recent public expressions of hostility towards the USSR, notably in two speeches by Prince Janusz F. Radziwiłł, an influential conservative politician. "According to Radziwiłł, it turns out that while he expects the further development of relations with Germany, he seems to find that the rapprochement with the USSR has already gone too far and that it should not be developed further, but rather slowed down." The speeches were not as bad as that, Łukasiewicz said, trying to guild the lily. That was hard to do with Soviet diplomats. The conversation eventually turned to the "Austrian question," and there, Łukasiewicz said in so many words that he considered Anschluss to be inevitable. "Poland was not so interested in the Austrian question and so powerful that it could prevent Anschluss." This was an unusual statement from a Polish diplomat; normally, the Poles were prickly about their status as a major European power. It could hardly have been encouraging to Litvinov.

The conversation was not quite over, however, for there was a cultural exchange underway. Performances in Warsaw by the Soviet Vakhtangov Theatre Company were being discussed. Stomoniakov had his doubts whether this was a good idea because of the company's sometimes revolutionary plays. These might not go down well with Polish nationalists and Russian *émigrés*. Łukasiewicz opined that performances would go alright if one particular play was not performed. A discussion of pros and cons ensued about particular shows. Stomoniakov wondered about the play concerning the defeat of the French intervention in the Ukraine and Crimea. A discussion ensued.

> STOMONIAKOV: "Well, what about the play which shows the French military in a very unfavourable light?"
>
> ŁUKASIEWICZ: (*with astonishment*): "Well, so – what of it?"
>
> STOMONIAKOV: "Well, you are allies. Perhaps [the play] could provoke annoyance? Maybe someone will be offended."
>
> ŁUKASIEWICZ: (*greatly agitated, hesitating at first, then blurting out emotionally*): "Well, with this [performance] you will bring only pleasure in Warsaw."[41]

Readers should appreciate the irony of this exchange. The Poles were fed up with the French and their superior ways, and the Soviet side, long suffering at French hands, now was intent on solidifying relations with them. Was there on this one rare occasion some empathy between the Soviet and the Pole?

Meanwhile, a Polish response to Litvinov's idea of an extension of the Soviet-Polish non-aggression pact was slow in coming. It was the middle of March, a month after Beck's visit to Moscow. You might wonder whether it was really worth the bother. The Radziwiłł speeches were not forgotten; on the contrary, they appeared to reflect "the Piłsudski line." The NKID western bureau was reporting a string of anti-Soviet articles in the official Polish press that was close to the government while at the same time being very careful in commenting about the rapprochement with Germany. The Polish delay in responding to Litvinov's proposal was irritating. In instructions to Antonov-Ovseenko, Stomoniakov advised not to show any interest in the file. The news, in fact, from Poland seemed uniformly bad. There were rumours about the Nazi propaganda minister Joseph Goebbels visiting Warsaw. No one in Warsaw was objecting to German rearmament. The Polish government persisted in stirring up trouble with Czechoslovakia over the Těšín district.[42] Still, the NKID continued to pursue the policy of rapprochement with Poland. It was always thus when the Soviet government wanted to improve relations with France. Antonov-Ovseenko must have felt rather foolish going out of channels for the now-dead rapprochement. Maybe the NKID also thought so, for he would soon be recalled to Moscow.

Litvinov advised Stalin that the news, or rather rumours, from Warsaw about the prolongation of the non-aggression pact was not encouraging. Łukasiewicz, who had been recalled to Warsaw, was expected back in a few days. Unofficially, it was being said, Litvinov continued, that Poland would condition its response to those of the Baltic states to which the NKID had made similar proposals for prolongation of the existing non-aggression pacts. "I would not consider it opportune," Litvinov wrote, "that our relations with the Baltic countries should be based on directives from Poland."[43]

At the end of March, Litvinov finally received an official response from the Polish government rejecting the ten-year prolongation of the non-aggression pact, but countering with periodic two-year prolongations. It seemed like a trivial dispute, but wasn't. For Litvinov, Poland was playing games, keeping its options open in the event of a Soviet-Japanese war. For a cynical realist like Litvinov, he had a naïve side, as if a non-aggression pact would stop Poland from attacking the Soviet Union in a moment of crisis. Poland wanted to keep open the possibility, Litvinov advised Stalin, of denouncing the pact in 1935. Tit for tat, Litvinov recommended delaying a response to Łukasiewicz until all the Baltic governments had replied to Soviet proposals. Indications were they would accept extensions that would put the Poles on the spot. The Politburo approved Litvinov's recommendation on the following day.[44] Litvinov's strategy worked like a charm. In late March, all four Baltic states, even Finland, accepted the Soviet proposals for prolongation of the non-aggression pacts, and eventually after Beck dragged his feet, the Polish non-aggression pact was also extended to ten years. Not exactly a big win for Soviet diplomacy, but when relations with Warsaw were bad, negotiations could grind over trifles.

Iakov Khristoforovich Davtian

The Politburo also approved the upgrading of the Polish mission to the status of embassy and thus Łukasiewicz to the rank of ambassador. This was one of Antonov-Ovseenko's ideas, but he had already been recalled. The NKID asked for Polish acceptance of a new Soviet ambassador in Warsaw. This was Iakov Khristoforovich Davtian who was then polpred in Athens. Like many of his colleagues, Davtian was a polyglot. He spoke French and German and knew some English.[45] He was born in 1888 in Azerbaijan. His father was Armenian and a merchant of modest means who could nevertheless afford to send his son to the *gimnaziia* in Tbilisi. He was an "old Bolshevik," having joined the party in 1905, at age seventeen. He moved to St. Petersburg in 1907 – he was only nineteen – and was involved in various aspects of party work for the Bolsheviks until the tsarist police arrested him. In the following year, he went into exile in Belgium where he graduated from university with a degree in engineering. He stayed in Belgium to do party work. At the beginning of the Great War, he did not or could not escape the German invasion and was arrested by German occupation authorities in 1915 and sent to different internment camps after repeated escape attempts.

He must have been quite a daring fellow. The earlier photographs of Davtian show a young man with a rich shock of black hair, a modest moustache, and some carefully trimmed chin whiskers. In a later photograph, Davtian is heavier, but he still has the rich, dark hair and moustache. After the conclusion of the treaty of Brest-Litovsk, Ioffe, the polpred in Berlin, obtained Davtian's release and he returned to Russia in the summer of 1918. He was already a hardened Bolshevik. He worked for a time in Soviet counter-intelligence during the civil war and foreign intervention. From 1919 onward, he served in Soviet posts in the Baltic states, China, France, Persia, and Greece. In France, he was in the thick of the unsuccessful negotiations to obtain a debts settlement. In Warsaw, he immediately jumped into the fray, earning the approval of Stomoniakov in Moscow.

Stomoniakov's Instructions

Stomoniakov advised Davtian that the prolongation of the non-aggression pact had been signed in Moscow on 5 May. The Poles, he wrote, were trying to exploit the new agreement as a sign that the USSR was leaving isolated, neighbouring Lithuania to its fate against Poland and Germany, both of them eyeing parcels of Lithuanian territory. Stomoniakov gave Davtian instructions to counter the Polish line when talking to journalists and diplomats. But here was his main point: "The prolongation of the [non-aggression] pact, for all the significance of this act, still cannot change the situation wherein the Soviet-Polish rapprochement at this stage can be considered basically ended. Everyone says that Piłsudski does not want to pursue further the rapprochement with the USSR. We will, of course, continue to strive, as before, to expand steadily and systematically ties in all areas, but we must also take into account the given prospects." Stomoniakov stressed, nevertheless, that the Polish governing elite was not entirely with Piłsudski. Some influential Poles saw the sole means of protecting Polish security in cooperation with France and the USSR against Germany.[46] One wonders how he drew this conclusion since, unlike Paris or London, for example, oppositionists did not often call at the Soviet embassy in Warsaw.

A week later, Litvinov sent a briefing paper to Stalin that basically repeated what Stomoniakov had written to Davtian. His estimate of the situation in Poland was surprisingly positive given the circumstances. "The most important genuine result of our policy of rapprochement over the past two years has been the undoubted change in the attitude of the Polish public towards the USSR. Interest in a rapprochement with the USSR in Poland is incomparably greater than for rapprochement with Germany. This applies especially to our achievements on the cultural and economic fronts." We ought not to lose the momentum that the present situation seemed to offer, Litvinov argued. He therefore proposed to Stalin a detailed program in all spheres to deepen Soviet-Polish ties.[47] It is ironic that both in France and in the USSR there was a shared desire to bring Poland onside. Could their efforts overcome the opposition of Piłsudski and his circle? Or put another way, more cynically, could Poles stop being Poles in order to strengthen the security of their country?

A Little Scandal Becomes an Attempted Coup d'État

While the NKID was endeavouring to advance its policy of rapprochement with Poland, events in France had taken a serious turn for the worse. Stalin's public comments in January about Polish "zig zags" had provoked Polish irritation, but his comments about political instability in France elicited no French protests and were almost immediately shown to be apposite. All hell was about to break loose in the "Republic of Pals." Readers may not know, but this was the France "where rigorously honest men were on good terms with fairly honest men, who were on good terms with shady men, who were on good terms with despicable crooks." On 25 January, the day before Stalin's speech and the resignation of the justice minister, Dovgalevskii telegraphed Litvinov that neither Paul-Boncour nor Léger had called him in to talk about League of Nations entry or "mutual defence." "I am taking a wait and see position," he wrote, "because I do not want it to seem as if we are more interested than the French." Paul-Boncour's slowness to act can be attributed to the "struggle in France and even in the cabinet itself of two doctrines: pro-Soviet and pro-German." This was going further than the previous explanation of a struggle between a Herriot line and a Daladier line.[48]

In his cipher cable to Litvinov, Dovgalevskii made no mention of the governmental crisis which was about to bring down the cabinet; perhaps he did in other correspondence. It would have been hard to miss. Daladier took over as président du Conseil on the morning of 30 January. There was no time for relations with Moscow; he had to act on the Stavisky scandal or see his government stillborn. "*Petit air de Vaudeville,*" one historian called Daladier's efforts. On 3 February, three days after the formation of the government, two right-wing ministers resigned, not happy over the sacking of a kindred soul, the Paris prefect of police, Jean Chiappe. He was fired because, as a favour to a Radical politician, he had turned a blind eye to a certain file gone missing on Stavisky's alleged crooked dealings. Politics were always a balancing act, especially in Paris during the interwar years, and apparently Daladier was trying to offer Chiappe's sacking as a *petite satisfaction* to the socialists. Also interesting, no sooner had Daladier gotten rid of Paul-Boncour as foreign minister than he took him back as war minister to replace one of those right-wing colleagues who had resigned the previous day. "I need the left now more than I need the right," Daladier must have thought. And it was Daladier's old job. In politics after all, one should never quarrel with an adversary so much that one could not on the morrow become allies with that very same adversary. This rule of conduct was especially necessary in France where governments changed on average every three to four months. If potential ministers held a grudge for very long, it would become impossible to organize a new cabinet. So Paul-Boncour was back, but it did little good for the new government.

It was Sunday, 4 February, and the Paris press had a field day over the latest comings and goings in the government, no doubt to amuse Parisians as they took their morning *café* and *petit déjeuner*. On that day, Daladier issued a communiqué to the effect that the new government was determined to get to the bottom of the Stavisky *affaire*. It was one thing for the Parisian press to mock the government, however, it was quite another when the numerous right-wing leagues called their members into the streets.

On Tuesday afternoon, 6 February, the Chambre des députés voted confidence in the new government, just as the right-wing leagues and many other discontented souls converged on the place de la Concorde across the Seine from the Assemblée nationale, there to raise holy hell. There also was hell to pay in the Chambre des députés where members on at least two occasions almost came to blows, with squads of *huissiers* intervening to prevent fisticuffs and the spilling of blood. Communist and allied deputies, there were about twenty in all, sang "The Internationale"; the right, more numerous, sang "La Marseillaise." Outside on the *place*, it was war, an attempted "fascist coup," said one American journalist, William Shirer, who was there. He watched from a hotel balcony overlooking the *place*. It was not a safe vantage point: a woman standing near Shirer slumped over dead with a bullet wound in her forehead. "If they get across the bridge [over the Seine]," Shirer wrote in his journal, "they'll kill every deputy in the Chamber."[49] In the street fighting, fifteen people died and 1,500 were injured.

On the following day, Daladier resigned. His government had lasted one week. A new cabinet was organized, headed by the former president of the Republic, retired, septuagenarian "Papa" Doumergue, and composed of former présidents du Conseil and chefs de parti. In this government of the centre-right, Daladier was out and so was Paul-Boncour. Cot was also out, but

Herriot was back in as a minister without portfolio, balanced on his right by André Tardieu, Litvinov's worrisome nemesis. Louis Barthou, an old guard conservative nationalist, became foreign minister. Litvinov had observed the events in Paris from Moscow, no doubt wondering whether the rapprochement with France was already on the rocks. The narkom remembered Barthou from the Genoa conference in 1922, just as Barthou remembered him.[50] In a report a few days later to the newly arrived polpred in Washington, Aleksandr Antonovich Troianovskii, Litvinov referred to the "impending fascization of France," which he concluded would bring "new changes, although perhaps not very drastic, in our relations" with Paris.[51] That was the thing in dealing with France, there were going to be ups and downs. One had to expect the worst, and hope for the best.

"So far we have not had to make adjustments to our latest projections, in particular regarding the viability of the current government," Rozenberg reported to the NKID. If there were no exacerbations of the financial situation and no new scandals compromising members of the present government, the cabinet could survive until the summer or perhaps even longer. That meant perhaps six months, but who knew for certain? Six months was not bad. Rozenberg continued his observations:

> The atmosphere in Paris is characterized, with a few exceptions, by a situation in which the most prominent political figures, as much from the left as from the right, directly or indirectly, are compromised by the Stavitsky case, this talented *Monsieur*, who in all of his adventuristic career, tried to "protect" himself by involving in his network the most prominent representatives of Parliament, the government, the courts, the press, not to mention the police. It is characteristic that a former minister remarked in a conversation with me that the mere fact that he was a member of the government, in the current Parisian atmosphere, turns him into some kind of a suspect person, and this was said by someone the least tainted in all these scandalous affairs.

That was bad enough, but Rozenberg then began to talk about fascism in France. He mentioned Anatole de Monzie, who in the 1920s had worked in favour of a Franco-Soviet rapprochement.

> People like de Monzie, who themselves have praised fascism, now shudder at the thought of the fate that fascist military gangs are preparing for them, and de Monzie, like many others, wants to influence us to achieve a change in the tactics of the Communist Party, which predicts that the French fascists will immediately conclude an alliance with Hitler. Of all my interlocutors, only Albert Millau, the general-secretary of the Radical Party and an ardent French patriot, has convinced me that French fascists would remain opponents of Germany.

That might have been so before the events on the place de la Concorde, but after it, a somewhat less realistic scenario. "I have had many people implore us to advise 'Moscow' of the evil of Communist Party tactics, which, by rejecting joint action with social democracy, contributes to the success of fascism … Withstanding this siege, we, of course, explain to these people that they are turning to the wrong address, etc." Nor did Rozenberg have any good news about the Radical Party, in the past a bastion of support for a Franco-Soviet rapprochement. The party seemed to be "decomposing," there are no leaders who retained their "authority," not excluding Herriot, "about whom they say that he has given up."[52]

Considering that Moscow, just a few months before, had committed to a major policy change pivoting on France, Rozenberg's report could not have been good news. It was considered to be important enough to send to Stalin, who underlined noteworthy passages in it, including details about the French communist policy against "social democracy." In July, on the initiative of the French communists, that policy was abandoned when the communist and socialist parties formed the *Front commun*. It was intended to oppose fascism in France and was the first step in the organization of the *Front populaire* in 1935 when the Radical-Socialist Party joined the coalition to fight parliamentary elections in the following year. Whether these developments would strengthen the Franco-Soviet rapprochement remained to be seen.

Chapter Eight

"One Step Back, Two Steps Forward": Ups and Downs in Soviet Relations in the West, 1934

Assessing the Damage

The riots, or failed coup d'état on the place de la Concorde, was bound to come up in conversations between Soviet and French diplomats. A week after the formation of the Doumergue government, Stomoniakov met Alphand at a diplomatic reception and dinner for Polish Foreign Minister Beck and made a record of the conversation. "He [Alphand] invited me to sit aside [from the crowd] on a sofa, and we had a rather interesting conversation." They talked about various subjects, most importantly about French domestic politics and how to influence foreign policy. Alphand said he "did not think" French policy would change, but Stomoniakov had his doubts, especially with Tardieu and Barthou as ministers. "They are even more anti-German than anti-Soviet," Alphand responded, and Doumergue had made a favourable reference to the rapprochement in a radio address. Stomoniakov asked about a French agreement with Germany, saying that some people around Tardieu were in favour of it. Alphand waved off this idea "with Barthou as minister." Stomoniakov asked about the general staff: some were against the Soviet rapprochement and some were in favour of an agreement with Germany. "This is true," Alphand replied, "but they do not decide the question, and Weygand is not badly disposed to relations with the USSR." One of those close to Weygand, Alphand added confidentially, "played a big role" in his posting to Moscow. These were questions that had come up constantly during the previous year when Paul-Boncour kept the momentum going in Paris.

Then Alphand complained about some "little affairs" like delays in a French naval mission to Moscow. There was slowness in Paris too, Stomoniakov responded, referring to Dovgalevskii's complaint about Paul-Boncour. That did not seem like a fair comment, and Alphand responded emotionally saying frankly that there was opposition in the government bureaucracy, and outside of it, to the rapprochement. For one thing, "our capitalists are afraid of you." For another, more important, there was fear in the government of a Soviet-Japanese war. Overly friendly relations with the USSR could lead Japan to seize French colonial possessions in Indochina. France did not have the means to defend them. Alphand mentioned Léger in this regard. Others, like Albert Sarraut, the interior minister, feared the spread of communism in Indochina.[1]

Alphand could also have mentioned the *fonctionnaires* of the Quai d'Orsay. At the beginning of January 1934, Léger had said an *étude suffisante* would be undertaken looking at Soviet entry into the League of Nations and into mutual assistance. Entry into the League was not the main issue; it was mutual assistance that was the key to solidifying Franco-Soviet relations. That "study" was circulated at the end of January by the Quai d'Orsay's Direction politique. It was Paul Bargeton's office, and he was known to dislike the rapprochement with Moscow. The report shows how a legal argument was built against mutual assistance, that is, the argument ran against the 1925 Locarno accords. Mutual assistance offered by France to the USSR was dismissed in a single sentence. "It is without doubt by error that it was said that M. Paul-Boncour had envisaged a convention of mutual assistance including France." The report does not indicate *who* said that Paul-Boncour envisaged mutual assistance, although in reading the Soviet correspondence, Litvinov's, for example, it is certain that he did. The report further noted that the "Rhine pact would scarcely permit us [France] (not more by the way than for Belgium) to give direct assistance to Russia." Then there was the problem of Japan: "the political situation of France" would not permit it.[2] Of course, it was for politicians, not *fonctionnaires*, to make calculations about "the political situation" in France. Essentially, this Quai d'Orsay document, dated 26 January, the day before the collapse of the Chautemps government, killed the very idea that mattered most to the Soviet government, genuine mutual assistance against Hitlerite Germany and also against Japan, a subject that Litvinov and Roosevelt had discussed in Washington. Judging from Paul-Boncour's apparent retreat at the end of December in talking to Dovgalevskii, the Quai d'Orsay's permanent officials had "got to" the minister.

Soviet officials continued to have their doubts, although they did not seem to have understood that Quai d'Orsay officials had come out against mutual assistance. Colonel Mendras confirmed what Stomoniakov had told Alphand. The Soviet government was hesitant to engage fully with Paris in view of French political instability. There was a widespread fear that sworn enemies of the USSR could return to power. This was Litvinov's *koshmar*. "The most authorized voices have said it to us quite plainly," Mendras noted. "On several occasions they have expressed to us their disquiet over the sudden disappearance of Pierre Cot." The leadership had been following recent events in Paris, he continued, paying close attention to events and not without a little anxiety.[3]

A New Minister of Foreign Affairs

Barthou must have picked up the echoes of Soviet disquiet for he received Dovgalevskii on 24 February to assure him of his personal good will. "My relations with the German ambassador," he said to Dovgalevskii, "were polite but nothing more." Barthou mentioned his "difficult past at Genoa [in 1922]," but stated unambiguously that he supported the rapprochement initiated by his predecessors, mentioning among other points, his support for the exchange of air force technical missions. The meeting was cut short by another meeting scheduled with the German ambassador, but it nevertheless seemed like a good beginning with the new minister.[4] Maybe Alphand was right about Barthou. Time would tell.

Herriot also wanted to assure Litvinov. He wrote privately to Alphand, his former chef de cabinet, to convey to Litvinov that "although his cabinet colleagues are not at the same stage of support (*zhelanie*) for a rapprochement with the USSR, about which they are not well informed, he, Herriot, will defend his ideas with insistence." For Herriot, Soviet entry into the League of Nations was crucial. The next step would be up to the French government, Litvinov had replied.[5] That was a sure sign of Soviet misgivings. A few days earlier, there had been a cabinet meeting in Paris. Herriot noted that Barthou had said he was favourable to an improvement of relations with the USSR.[6] It was not going to be that easy.

There were hesitations inside the French cabinet. On 27 March, Herriot told the Soviet chargé d'affaires Rozenberg that the cabinet was "better disposed to us" than the Daladier government. Naval and air missions were being exchanged, and they (cabinet ministers) say that "general negotiations are advancing satisfactorily." Rozenberg replied that they were not. Léger was causing problems over Japan, and Barthou was not active enough. Herriot said he would speak with Doumergue.[7] How could general negotiations advance when the Quai d'Orsay opposed mutual assistance? There were cabinet meetings on the following two days, and in his notes Herriot confirmed that Barthou did not seem interested in mutual assistance, at least he did not speak about it.[8] Barthou left the cabinet meeting early on 28 March to meet with Rozenberg. Having been briefed by Herriot – obviously, noted Rozenberg – Barthou asked about the pace of negotiations, if they were going satisfactorily. Rozenberg answered that they were not. Barthou pleaded that he was overwhelmed with less important questions than the negotiations with the USSR, but urgent nonetheless, even showing Rozenberg his schedule. Barthou promised to "study" the files during the Easter holidays and then get back to Rozenberg, who noted, "He asked me to give him some 'credit' for a short time, assuring me that he stands for the development of friendship and the like."[9] This sounded like an honest plea that Rozenberg could not refuse.

Three days later, Rozenberg had a conversation lasting more than three hours with Herriot. According to Rozenberg, Herriot insisted that the current government was better disposed to the USSR than some of its predecessors, and that Doumergue, the aviation minister Victor Denain, the war minister Marshal Pétain, and Barthou were all for the rapprochement. Even Tardieu was not speaking openly against it.[10] Still, there were problems at the cabinet meeting on 10 April. Doumergue and Barthou seemed to hesitate, or were ready to accept a postponement of any decision on the Soviet rapprochement. "Obviously, there is hidden opposition," Herriot wrote in his notes. Tardieu is "favourable" to Japan. The labour minister, a socialist, Adrien Marquet, was openly hostile, and according to Herriot, influenced by domestic politics and an intense "anti-Marxism." He denied the "exterior" (i.e., offensive) value of the Red Army.[11] It was always thus with the Sovietphobes – and none could be more *acharné* than a socialist – they could always find a pretext for not allying with the USSR. The only factor that should have counted, however, was French national security.

On 17 April, there was another cabinet meeting in Paris. The Quai d'Orsay prepared a discussion paper, which is noteworthy for making no mention of Paul-Boncour's initiative in proposing mutual assistance and for appearing to reverse position on that policy, noting only that the applicability of an accord to cover Japan was not acceptable.[12] Barthou called in Rozenberg to advise that the government had given him authority "to continue negotiations with us." Rozenberg asked for a clarification. "Does that mean the Doumergue government has decided to continue negotiations based on the proposals made to us by Paul-Boncour?" Barthou answered in the affirmative. He then said he had not wanted to discuss the issue before being briefed on the state of disarmament negotiations in Geneva and on the position of French allies towards the USSR. Barthou said to talk to Léger about details and then they could meet again. Ah, Léger, head of the Quai d'Orsay *apparat*. "I will ask to see him," Rozenberg telegraphed to Moscow.[13]

That meeting took place on 24 April. Rozenberg made a long record of conversation, which must have disquieted Litvinov when he read it. Léger insisted that Franco-Soviet negotiations should remain rigorously confidential. Rozenberg replied that others – he mentioned Czechoslovak and Romanian diplomats – were already informed, and by the French themselves. The Czechoslovak ambassador in Paris had also been talking to the press. Léger acknowledged that the broad terms of their negotiations were known to "a wider circle of people" since they had been discussed in the Council of Ministers. In the Quai d'Orsay, only he and Bargeton were fully informed. As for Barthou, he likely would not have leaked anything "since he, as Léger added condescendingly, is not on top of all questions." He needed a "cheat sheet" for cabinet meetings. This is what Alphand meant when he spoke of the *apparat* and about Léger. The secretary-general could not be trusted. Mutual assistance was an important subject of the ensuing conversation. Léger gave the impression of doubting that Paul-Boncour had initiated the discussions of mutual assistance. He was also reluctant to talk about details, since he claimed not to have clear instructions from the government even if earlier he had given the impression of not needing them. At the end of the conversation, Léger assured Rozenberg of his "complete loyalty" and that in order to avoid any "inaccurate impressions" in Moscow, he thought it appropriate to meet before Barthou's return to Paris from a trip to Eastern Europe.[14]

Léger's rather odd comments prompted Rozenberg to write to Litvinov on the following day that he was not so sure of the French position. Léger "gave me to understand that there is not yet clarity regarding the extent (*ob"em*) of negotiations and that the government did not, he says, give the initiative to the ministry of foreign affairs." Rozenberg had reacted sceptically to this assertion. He went on to quote what Barthou had said to him earlier about receiving the delegation from the cabinet to continue negotiations.[15] Obviously something was amiss.

On 28 April, Litvinov responded by telegram after having read Rozenberg's dispatch. "In conversation with Barthou, you should reaffirm to him, even in the case of the renunciation of Paul-Boncour's suggestions, as a result of Poland's position, the immutability of our desire for rapprochement and cooperation with France in the strengthening of peace."[16] It is not clear whether Rozenberg received this telegram before his next meeting with Léger on that same day.

It was as Litvinov anticipated. Léger called in Rozenberg for another discussion. He proposed an "Eastern Locarno," a security arrangement that included Germany, Czechoslovakia, Poland, the Baltic states, but *without* France. Belgium was also out. That was not what Paul-Boncour had in mind or what the Soviet side wanted. All the signatories would agree to the renunciation of force and to the obligation to go to the support of the contiguous neighbours in the event of aggression. This pact would be "ancilliary" to a "Franco-Soviet convention" along the following lines: "Considering the importance for the preservation of peace of the regional pact (Eastern) and also the Locarno pact, the USSR and France promise to offer one another assistance in the event they would be subjected to attack following the disturbance of the above mentioned agreements by any of those participants." Léger added that the formula could be adjusted with respect to Locarno to target only Germany. "He said that his predominant thought was to find the most effective formula for cooperation between the USSR and France against Germany."

Rozenberg reacted unenthusiastically to Léger's proposals, which were a sea-change from Paul-Boncour's. But he declined to comment further because he had no instructions from Moscow. He did ask for some clarifications for his report to the NKID. Why was France unwilling to join the Eastern Pact? Why did French obligations not cover the Baltic states, which could serve "as the gateway for an attack on us"? Léger's explanations rang hollow and his formulation of mutual assistance struck Rozenberg as too vague and lacking the specificity of Soviet ideas. Léger offered some willingness to be flexible. Rozenberg proposed to Litvinov to pursue discussions with Léger and Barthou *ad referendum*, subject to approval of his positions by Moscow. In fact, if one reads the French *aide-mémoire*, which was not given to Rozenberg, it is even less encouraging than the Soviet account of the meeting with Léger. The French position was to limit as much as possible its obligations, as if it was the Soviet Union that needed mutual assistance and not France.[17]

It turns out that Léger had proposed his ideas to Barthou two weeks before and that the minister had subsequently agreed to them.[18] That would explain Léger's evasive behaviour during his previous meeting with Rozenberg. Léger and Bargeton appear to have sidetracked Paul-Boncour's original ideas and then adjusted to the new minister who was at first uncertain of his position. The Soviet side feared that Poland would interfere in the negotiations with France, Barthou having visited Warsaw in the latter part of April. Poland was causing trouble, but the real trouble was "hidden opposition" in the Quai d'Orsay and Council of Ministers, which could not always be uncovered. Was Léger acting constructively, or was he part of the "hidden opposition"? That depends on who you talk to. His recent biographer, Renaud Meltz, thinks he was acting in good faith. He wanted to persuade Barthou "to play the Russian card."[19] Léger insisted to Rozenberg that he was acting with "complete loyalty." Maybe he was. Or maybe the cards he wanted to play were sixes and sevens and not the aces of the deck.

It was 1 May, three days after Rozenberg's meeting with Léger. On that day he met with Barthou. Rozenberg asked if Barthou identified with Léger's proposals, and noted: "Barthou twice unconditionally declared that he had accepted Léger's scheme, presented to us, to his own account, but he added that he could not engage his government." Barthou said it was too soon to go to the cabinet: "A report to the Council of Ministers would provoke unnecessary friction, for not all ministers relate to us like Herriot, and besides, it would attract superfluous publicity. The government authorized him to conduct negotiations, but he did not want either to ventilate the question prematurely, or to create a *fait accompli*." So the "hidden opposition" was still to be reckoned with. Barthou also agreed that the negotiations should henceforth be "rigorously confidential." He asked that the Soviet embassy not go into the details of the negotiations with Herriot but to "say to him that our confidence has been restored." Then Barthou went into the details of the proposals for an Eastern Locarno, repeating what Léger had said, and the details about his trip to Poland. Davtian had cabled a few days before to report on the results of Barthou's discussions in Warsaw, having heard from Laroche. Barthou had wanted to calm Franco-Polish relations, and according to Laroche, he had done this. Piłsudski and Beck had given assurances. Of course, all the news was not good. Polish relations with Nazi Germany were not reassuring. Piłsudski thought, for example, that information about German rearmament was "exaggerated." Beck was "less definite" about Anschluss and about Soviet entry into the League of Nations. On Soviet-Polish relations, Barthou either did nothing or achieved nothing. The Poles, after all, remained Poles. One had to live with that: not only France but also the USSR. In Paris, Rozenberg appeared satisfied with the meeting with Barthou. It seemed like a step forward.[20] Litvinov thought so and advised that he considered the Léger proposal to be acceptable, although not all aspects of it were sufficiently clear. These questions should be the subject of negotiations.[21]

Litvinov and Barthou Talk It Over in Geneva

On 19 May, Litvinov and Barthou met in Geneva. According to the narkom's account, the meeting went well. For the Soviet side, the security of the Baltic area was a high priority. Barthou agreed to look at the question "of extending French assistance (*pomoch'*) to the Baltics, saying that this was by no means excluded." He also made some other concessions regarding the inclusion of Finland in the larger Baltic area, as a single entity for the purposes of mutual assistance. "Barthou again confirmed his favourable disposition to us and that of his government, using a phrase about 'friendship up to a military alliance.'" Entry into the League of Nations also came up, and Barthou agreed that the Soviet Union should not be put into the position of soliciting entry. All this suited Litvinov.[22] There is also a much longer French record of the conversation that appears consistent with Litvinov's telegrams to Moscow. What if Germany did not agree to these proposals? Litvinov asked. "If Germany refuses, we would be authorized to conclude the pact without it. But we must not show ourselves to be in a hurry. We must do nothing which can appear to be directed against it. If [Germany] enters into the system of security, all the better. If it does not enter, it will be putting itself in the wrong." Poland took up a large part of the conversation, Litvinov was concerned about Polish double dealing, Barthou tried to be reassuring.[23] All in all, whether based on the Soviet or French reports of the meeting, the results were positive. The meeting appeared to be a step forward.

It was not going to be as easy as all that. On 4 June, Litvinov, along with Rozenberg this time, again met Barthou in Geneva, and with him, Bargeton. They were attending a disarmament commission meeting. Litvinov pressed Barthou for confirmation of the French cabinet's agreement in principle to the Eastern Locarno pact. "We cannot go on forever," Litvinov said, "conducting negotiations only in the name of Barthou and me." Barthou agreed to send Bargeton to Paris to report to Doumergue and then to return to Geneva on the morrow with the answer. Readers will remember that Barthou had not wanted to go to the Council of Ministers prematurely to provoke opposition needlessly, but here was Litvinov pressing him. There were other subjects of conversation. On French assistance to the Baltics, Barthou admitted the persuasiveness of Soviet arguments, but he did not give a definite reply. Litvinov raised another concern: what if Germany and Poland did not agree to the Eastern Locarno, did Barthou think "personally" that "some kind of agreement between us was possible?" Barthou answered in the affirmative. Litvinov feared that Poland would "sabotage" the negotiations. Behind the scenes, Beck was waging a "fierce agitation against our entry into the League and against the pacts suggested by us."[24]

Litvinov and Beck

Litvinov was never one to let the Poles get away with anything without calling them out. He had dinner with Beck that same day. "What do you think of the French proposals?" he asked. In reply, Beck railed against the League and anything coming out of Geneva. He reamed off reasons for not liking the French proposal.

Litvinov knew how to come to the point: "Did you give Barthou a negative answer?"

"The government is discussing it," Beck replied.

"My impression," Litvinov continued, "is such that without Germany, Poland would probably reject the pact, but even with the agreement of Germany it is also not likely that she [Poland] would accept it." Poland might also encourage Germany to reject the pact, if Germany needed any persuading. Such was Litvinov's opinion of the Poles. "Beck cursed in every way possible the League of Nations and Geneva and immediately assured me that rumours about Polish agitation against our entry into the League are incorrect."[25]

Barthou to Paris and Back to Geneva

Barthou must have decided to return to Paris with Bargeton to talk to Doumergue. According to Herriot, at a cabinet meeting on 5 June, Barthou asked for authorization to pursue negotiations for a regional assistance pact. "The Russians have even proposed to take on a commitment similar to that which we had with England before 1914, it is just what Litvinov has offered to me." This might have been so in some private conversation, but it does not appear to have been official Soviet policy. Herriot also recorded that Barthou was still "very reserved." Was he just being cautious? The "hidden opposition" erupted into the open. This time it was Laval, minister for colonies, who argued in favour of "an accord with Germany," the "Daladier line," and against the rapprochement with the USSR. Laval was nothing if not consistent. For him the rapprochement meant bringing to France "the International and the Red Flag." But Herriot speculated that Laval's emotional intervention was due to a recent clash with communists in Aubervilliers where he was mayor. *Petites causes, grands effets* (petty causes, large effects), wrote Herriot, but it was more than that.[26] Laval hated the French communists who were his principal electoral rivals in Aubervilliers.

Barthou returned to Geneva to see Litvinov again on the following day. According to the narkom, "The French government chaired by the president [Doumergue] approved yesterday his negotiations with me and the proposals concerning the pact." On French assistance for the Baltics, however, the government could not agree. Litvinov continued to worry about the Poles:

> I will have one more conversation with Barthou before leaving ... to insist on speeding up negotiations with Germany before Poland has time to work on her ... The French are more and more expressing doubt about the position of Poland. From all sides there is pressure on France in order to draw it away from us and to return it to the path of Franco-English and Franco-German agreements. Essentially the struggle here at the conference is the struggle between us and Germany.[27]

Litvinov was nothing if not tenacious. He persisted with Barthou at another meeting two days later. He raised again the Baltic issue and the importance of French "assistance." "Barthou said that although the Council of Ministers had so far decided negatively, he did not consider this to be the final answer and he was ready to discuss again my opinion on that account, which I promised to spell out in written form." Barthou also promised to pursue discussions with Poland and to put pressure on the Baltics.[28]

Meantime, at the French Embassy in Moscow

In Moscow, and without knowing about the problems in Geneva, Mendras was cautious about not-always-easy bilateral relations. "The Russians have always been far removed from us," he wrote, "and today in addition, they are communists." There existed a "barrier" between foreigners and Soviets; the conversation was not as easy as between, say, French and British interlocutors. The Communist International made a difference even if it was under a tight rein. The riots in Paris in February had stirred "the flames of revolution," according to Mendras, which explained Laval's rough ride at the hands of communists in Aubervilliers mobilizing against fascism. Still the Comintern had to "yield the field to the realist Litvinov." I am not saying, Mendras said in effect, that we should abandon "the rapprochement with the Bolsheviks," but the best way to overcome difficulties is to know them well. "I remain persuaded that the USSR represents a definite force, growing, which we can and we must bring into our game."[29]

The French chargé d'affaires Payart noticed that Litvinov's position had been strengthened. After some uncertainty caused by "countercurrents," Litvinov's "policy of national defence" had prevailed. "[His] personal position has been consolidated, even reinforced, [a development] which we can only welcome."[30] In parsing Stalin's summertime correspondence with Molotov and Kaganovich, one will notice that mutual assistance and the rapprochement with France do not come up. If Stalin and his close associates in Moscow had not liked, or were worried about foreign policy, they would certainly have said so.

During that summer of 1934 the anti-communist Laval was not in a position to impede the Franco-Soviet rapprochement. The meetings in Geneva between Barthou and Litvinov had a positive effect. Alphand spoke of it with Litvinov in Moscow a few weeks later. He had personally noticed a change for the better in Barthou before and after Geneva. The tone of the press was also better, and so too were attitudes among the Quai d'Orsay *apparat*. Even the "earlier hostility" of Léger had abated. Attention to the *apparat* was Alphand's old saw because, as he said, "ministers go, but the *apparat* remains."[31] One needed to maintain close, cordial contact with them. Soviet diplomats did that very well, though it seldom led to better bilateral relations.

In Moscow, Alphand often socialized with commissars and officials. It was a normal, less formal way of exchanging information and discussing problems. Stalin, a "veritable oriental *souverain*," was "invisible" to foreign diplomats, so that one had to establish relations with his subordinates. It should be added that Alphand had excellent sources of information. He had established good relations with Commissar Voroshilov having often organized dinners at the French embassy. This time, Voroshilov considered it his turn to host a dinner at his *dacha* outside Moscow. It was a personal way to solidify relations and build up mutual confidence. The week before, Alphand reported, Litvinov had invited him to lunch and a day *en famille* at his *dacha* on the road to Leningrad. As for the dinner at Voroshilov's *dacha*, Alphand offered a detailed description of the residence, which was far more luxurious than Litvinov's and set in a park of forty hectares. And the dinner was sumptuous. Krestinskii was there along with two other NKID officials, so was Mikhail Nikolaevich Tukhachevskii, Voroshilov's deputy commissar, and Egorov, his chief of staff. On the French side, it was Mendras, his deputy, and Alphand, and their wives. After dinner, the men enjoyed a game of Russian billiards in their shirt sleeves while the women danced. Around midnight, Voroshilov and Alphand had a two-hour-long conversation in the presence of Krestinskii, Mendras, and one of the other NKID people present. Alphand brought up the Eastern Pact; Voroshilov talked about Soviet security concerns in the Far East against Japan. The Soviet government still hoped for French support there. *Pas possible* was Alphand's reply. Voroshilov then brought up Poland's disquieting relations with Germany, and his conviction that only French pressure could put a stop to them. He hoped that the Poles would eventually "come to their senses." Mendras lauded military contacts between the two sides; Voroshilov agreed but noted that they seemed to be stalled and not going further. Alphand had touched upon, ever so lightly, the enduring French complaint about "propaganda." That drew an emotional reply from Voroshilov. "Give us credit," he replied, "not to think us so stupid as to meddle in the matters of other countries that do not concern us." Alphand and Mendras were both pleased by the cordiality of the discussions. From all this, Mendras opined, that "the conversation allowed us to note once again the value that the Soviet government attaches to the entente with France with a view to the safeguard of its western frontiers."[32]

Germany Again (January–June 1934)

Readers may be wondering, with all the Soviet attention going to the French, if the German ambassador Nadolny had been left to brood, isolated in his embassy during the winter of 1934. He saw little of Litvinov and Krestinskii after the meetings of early January, but Nazi Germany was never far from Litvinov's mind. Nadolny still promoted a return to the "old policy" and talked about it with Stomoniakov during a dinner party at the ambassador's residence. It was Nadolny's usual line about early Nazi mistakes and the desire to get things back on the right track. Stomoniakov was unpersuaded: "The basic reason for the mistrust of our public lies in the sharp anti-Soviet ideology of the Nazi Party. You can only remove the mistrust by removing the reasons for it, that is, Hitler's renunciation of his earlier stated anti-Soviet exhortations." Without some public reversal, and Stomoniakov said it was only his personal opinion, the mistrust of the Soviet public would not disappear. "Such a declaration from Hitler is impossible. Hitler considers himself an apostle," Nadolny said with sly smile, "and he, Hitler, cannot, especially now after his rise to power, recognize publicly that he made a mistake." For Nadolny, the solution was for the Soviet government to reign in the press – everyone knew, he said, that the Soviet press was controlled by the government – and he reamed off a stream of concrete complaints about anti-German articles.[33]

On the very same day Litvinov had written to Stalin once again about the Baltics. He wanted to increase Soviet influence there and keep out the influence of other states. He was worried most of all by Germany and Poland. Litvinov recommended making a proposal to Germany for a joint guarantee of the independence of the Baltic countries. The proposal would improve Soviet relations with the Baltic states and with Germany, if approved, or would further expose Nazi intentions, if rejected. It would also serve as a "nice lesson" for Poland. He asked for authorization to participate in Politburo discussions on this issue.[34] Having failed to get a joint declaration from Poland, Litvinov thus proposed a similar device to Nadolny on 28 March 1934. Nadolny asked many questions about the text of the draft protocol. He did not think it would be acceptable to the German government because of the German-populated city of Memel, then under Lithuanian sovereignty. Nadolny thought the Soviet proposition would be a "first step" towards better relations, notwithstanding the likely response from Berlin. The ambassador did not say in his telegram to Berlin that he expected a negative reply. On the contrary, he opined that rejection was "hardly possible."[35]

That same day, Nadolny organized a dinner in honour of Voroshilov. Krestinskii, Karakhan, and military and civilian officials were present. Nadolny was in a good mood, pleased, as he said, that Voroshilov had accepted his invitation and pleased also that a trade agreement had been recently concluded in Berlin. Nadolny, half joking, half serious, commented that the German side had given too much away, but that the trade agreement also represented a "first glimmer of light" in otherwise poor Soviet-German relations. He had obviously come from the meeting with Litvinov and was also encouraged by the proposed Baltic protocol even if he did not expect a positive reply from Berlin. Krestinskii and others present replied that a German rejection would be perceived by world public opinion as proof that Berlin had "aggressive intentions" in the Baltic states. The main problem was Lithuania and Memel, replied Nadolny. Does Germany have "to cling to this trifling bit of its former territory?" came the Soviet reply. The conversation then turned to the more general question of Soviet-German relations, and there it followed along familiar lines of previous conversations that are already familiar to readers. There was discussion back and forth on arcane points about the Comintern and the White Guards in Germany leading nowhere. It must have been a pretty good party all the same, fuelled with wine and vodka and without any heated exchanges. As Krestinskii noted, the discussion was good in parts and even friendly, but of course changed nothing.[36]

On 14 April, Nadolny visited Litvinov ostensibly to talk about the Baltic protocol, which was actually a preface to raising objections to a Radek article entitled "The Hissing of Fascist Vermin." You can see why Nadolny would complain, but Litvinov was as usual unsympathetic. "I recommended that he ask to see comrade Shtern who would present him with a dossier of anti-Soviet attacks of the German press." They finally got around to Litvinov's proposed protocol. Nadolny did not have good news. Berlin's answer was no, and the narkom was not going to change anyone's mind in Berlin.[37] Krestinskii wrote to Khinchuk that Nadolny was surprised by the negative reply from Berlin, but in fact the ambassador had told Krestinskii and Voroshilov at dinner that he did not expect the protocol to be accepted.[38] Maybe Krestinskii should have reread his *dnevnik*.

Litvinov reckoned the German rejection to be a clear sign of aggressive intentions in the Baltic, and he authorized the Soviet polpred in Riga to say as much in unofficial conversations. "You can even draw attention to the … cynical

[German] attitude to pacts, permitting Hitler to prepare for war and at the same time to offer pacts of non-aggression to everyone and even to sign a pact with Poland, while Hitler refuses to give a paper obligation in relation to the Baltics. This means that action against Poland is postponed for a certain time in the course of which the impression from the signed German-Polish agreement can evaporate and lose its meaning." According to Litvinov, his proposal would have committed Germany to obligations to the Baltic states and to the Soviet Union. This argument is hard to follow since the Litvinov protocol would have had no more value than the non-aggression pact with Poland. It was, however, a way to play for time. After the Polish and German refusals to agree to Baltic guarantees, Litvinov was resigned. The "sole real guardian of the independence of the Baltics," the narkom asserted, "is the USSR."[39] Readers of course would be justified in doubting whether the Baltic governments saw matters in the same way. Nor would events prove out Litvinov's view of the USSR as "guardian" of Baltic independence. Those events were, however, more than six years into the future and under very different circumstances.

On 21 April, Nadolny saw Litvinov again. The first topic of conversation was the German government's rejection of the protocol on Baltic independence. Obviously, Litvinov was irritated, but readers might wonder why. Hitler's pactomania was only a screen to lull his future victims, including Poland and the USSR, before he struck at them. Litvinov saw more clearly than many of his contemporaries. So why get upset and take it out on Nadolny except as a cathartic venting of spleen? Nadolny offered the comment, strictly personal and off the record, that it was a "big mistake" for the German government not to disavow *Mein Kampf*. The ambassador was still looking for a way forward. Litvinov did not respond directly to Nadolny's comment about "Hitler's book" or to an idea of eliciting new German proposals. Nadolny left out of his report the personal view of *Mein Kampf* and attributed Litvinov's attitude to "sensitivity on account of rejection."[40]

In what world did Nadolny live? As if Litvinov did not have his own sources of information, coming from the Soviet embassy in Berlin. When he saw Nadolny, he had in hand a report from Khinchuk. "In the centre of Hitler's foreign policy is the question of the rearmament of Germany." To rearm and build up the armed forces, time and money were necessary, and for that Hitler had to pursue his "well-known pacifist manoeuvres." He was talking to the English, counting on Conservative Party support for his anti-Soviet plans, and trying to use those contacts as intermediaries to reach the French. This information would have raised a red flag in Moscow, and Khinchuk went on at some length about the French ambassador François-Poncet and his various efforts to find terms with Berlin. In effect, Hitler was sowing the seeds of division and discord everywhere in Europe. Everyone was talking to the Germans. The Poles, Khinchuk noted, were placing cards all over the poker table with Germany, France, and the USSR. The German agreement with Poland had allowed Hitler to break the international isolation of Germany and had broken out of the French array of allies the most important Polish link. As for relations with the USSR, Khinchuk described them "at the stage of hidden or open tension." Nazi policy towards the USSR remained what it had always been: the *Drang nach Osten* and the struggle with world Bolshevism. "Since then, as it has become clear, that intervention against us is not an easy business, that it requires serious economic, military and diplomatic preparations, the Nazis have moved from the tactics of direct assault to more clever manoeuvres." Here Khinchuk was preaching to the converted. He stressed that the Nazis were also using the Soviet "card" as a means of pressure in negotiations with the French and Poles; indeed the French and Poles were themselves using it. This game was complicated, wheels turning within wheels. The German situation was "very difficult" (*ochen' tiazhelo*), Khinchuk noted, and therefore Hitler could not risk new strains in relations with the USSR.[41]

Hitler rejected, nevertheless, the Litvinov protocol and this led to Nadolny's resignation in June. At that time, Mendras noted that Nadolny, after failing to get Litvinov's support for the "old policy," had gone over his head to Voroshilov to get a hearing for better relations with Berlin. Voroshilov must have informed Stalin, for he had urged Litvinov to "soften" his policy towards Germany while Japan remained a danger in the East. Litvinov was highly irritated by Nadolny's attempt to go around him, though in the end it mattered only as a point of curiosity since the ambassador failed to get Hitler's support for better Soviet relations. Nadolny reported on his January conversation with Voroshilov, which gave credence to Mendras's report. The ambassador found himself, as Mendras put it, caught between Berlin, which disapproved of his advances, and Moscow, which rejected them. His departure was thus "inevitable." According to Mendras, there was a lesson to be learned in what had happened, that is, that the bridges between Moscow and Berlin were not completely down and that a sudden shift of policy remained possible. The French government should therefore see to its own bridges to Moscow, so as to take the place vacated by Germany.[42] Like so much other good advice arriving in Paris, it was filed.

Litvinov met Neurath in Berlin in mid-June to discuss the German reaction to the Eastern Pact or Eastern Locarno. The narkom tried to promote the accord as a means of relieving popular anxieties about European security. Neurath said he was aware of Soviet apprehensions but that as far as Germany was concerned there was no basis for concern. It was true that "a few idiots" (*neskol'ko gluptsov*) in Germany "dreamed about expansion in the East, about colonization, and so on, but the German government is not thinking about this." The proposal for the new pact, Neurath continued, was "unacceptable for Germany," uninteresting, and impractical. To all this Litvinov replied that it was not "a few idiots" who had written about expansion in the East but also the "present 'boss' of the country. He has never distanced himself, but, on the contrary, has permitted until now the dissemination in Germany [of the book] in which this program is outlined. On this program, consequently, the German people are being educated, which accustoms them to the idea about the necessity and inevitability of expansion in the East." Among other points, Litvinov noted that the present Nazi government appeared to be undertaking a series of measures to realize the objectives laid out in "the book." Then there were the statements of people like Hugenberg, Alfred Rosenberg, and others who promoted these ideas. "If we even believed 99 per cent of the declarations about the absence of aggressive intentions among some right-wing German circles and doubted only 1 per cent, then in that case, we, as a government, would have to undertake all possible measures of precaution."

Neurath listened to Litvinov's long declaration and said at the end of it, "smiling a little," that the German reply would be as he had communicated it. Germany was not looking to expand anywhere, it had an interest only in the Polish Corridor but on this point had given a ten-year guarantee. "In spite of everything," Neurath said at the end of their discussion, he hoped that "our personal relations would remain as before." In Neurath's account of the meeting, the reference to "a few idiots" was left out, as were Litvinov's extensive comments in reply. There were other nuances in the two accounts of the meeting, but the essential message was that Germany was not interested in the Eastern Locarno.[43]

Neurath observed that Litvinov appeared "less self-assured than usual," but according to the Soviet embassy in Berlin, the German press was in a "panicky mood" over Litvinov's meetings with Barthou in Geneva. Because of this "panic," and to oppose Litvinov's plan, the German press opened a new campaign of "baiting" against the USSR.[44] The new press campaign seemed to belie Neurath's assurances. The news travelled quickly of the Litvinov-Neurath meeting. On the same day, François-Poncet reported on Neurath's opposition to an Eastern Pact. Litvinov had the impression that Beck or the Polish ambassador Lipski had been in touch with the German foreign ministry to coordinate their positions, while leaving to the German side the responsibility of scuttling the French proposals.[45] On the following day, 14 June, Beck informed the French ambassador Laroche that he was unenthusiastic about an Eastern Locarno. France needed to get used to the idea that Poland had finally established "normal" relations with Germany. Beck declared his confidence in Hitler's commitment "to maintain good relations with Poland." That might be, Laroche replied dryly, because Germany is preoccupied with problems in the west as important for us as those in the east are important for Poland.[46]

And Britain?

When things were going badly, the French usually turned to London. Barthou pressed the case for an Eastern Locarno. Failure to keep the USSR on side could lead to a Soviet reversion to an "exclusively Asiatic" policy.[47] Barthou went to

London on 9 July looking for British support of an Eastern Pact. He obtained it on the condition that Germany be brought into any system of guarantees. Litvinov first heard of the French policy through the press, reporting that France had agreed to guarantee an Eastern Pact. At first Litvinov did not understand that this would mean a French guarantee of Germany in the event of Soviet aggression against Germany. Imagine, a guarantee of security to Hitlerite Germany. Always preoccupied with the Baltic, Litvinov wanted to know if the French guarantee would cover it. The Politburo decided not to oppose the German guarantee, but Litvinov tried again to obtain inclusion of the Baltic states in the new security agreements.[48] Baltic security was a key to Soviet security.

British support for an Eastern Pact changed nothing for Poland. In a conversation with Laroche on 13 July, Beck continued to be sceptical. British support was purely "platonic"; France could guarantee the pact, but Britain would not. It changed nothing for Germany, which would remain "negative." It was easy for the Polish foreign minister to find reasons why the pact would not work. Davtian, the new Soviet polpred in Warsaw, put it this way: "The position of Poland to the pact is clear – it does not want it. The Polish government will do everything possible to drag out negotiations, looking for any 'clarifications' to cause the failure of the pact." The British position was key. If Britain were strongly in favour of the pact, Poland would have to go along, but they, the British, were trying to emasculate its contents. In a meeting with Davtian a few days later, the French ambassador drew the same conclusion: "[Beck] is largely against the pact."[49]

At the end of that second week in July, there was a great deal of correspondence going back and forth between Paris and Moscow. On 13 July, Alphand met Litvinov to hand him, on Barthou's orders, a statement on the Anglo-French discussions in London. "I expressed doubt as to Germany's agreement to sign the pact," the narkom wrote, "even after the English démarche and said that the sole means to incline Germany to sign … would be pressure on Warsaw. When Germany is faced with the threat of the conclusion of a pact with the participation of Poland even without Germany, the latter will prefer to be included … And France has sufficient means of pressure on Warsaw." Alphand said he entirely agreed with Litvinov's conclusions.[50]

On the following day, 14 July, it was the French national holiday, Bastille Day. At the Soviet embassy, there must have been some sadness. Dovgalevskii, who was in a Paris clinic being treated for cancer, died that day. He had been the Soviet ambassador in Paris for more than six years. In Moscow a few weeks later, Dovgalevskii's ashes were carried to the Kremlin wall for interment by Stalin, Kalinin, and Molotov, among others. Not a bad farewell for a polpred of the USSR.

On the day Dovgalevskii died, Litvinov reported to Stalin on news from London: Britain had given its approval to a regional pact, but was also attempting to prevent the conclusion of a Franco-Soviet pact of guarantee. The Foreign Office would favour strengthening a connection between the proposed Eastern Pact and the existing stipulations of the Locarno accords. It is possible, Litvinov wrote, that Britain was pursuing this line knowing full well that Germany and Poland would refuse to agree to the Eastern Pact. "Undoubtedly, England was influenced by France's somewhat intimidating signals, saying in every direction that it would conclude a military alliance with the USSR, in the event of the failure of the pact." As Litvinov put it, "Before us now stands a question, not foreseen in my negotiations with Barthou." The options ranged from a bilateral Franco-Soviet pact to a pact of guarantee between Germany, France, and the USSR. Litvinov preferred the latter, since "we earlier had put forward the idea of a general pact with the participation of France, in which case a guarantee would also be given to Germany."[51] This preference may surprise readers since Litvinov thought it unlikely that Poland or Germany would agree to any such general pact.

These were not the only obstacles to reaching an agreement on an Eastern Pact or a bilateral Franco-Soviet agreement. Britain would be another, as we shall see. It was nothing new. The Foreign Office had constrained Franco-Soviet relations during the 1920s. During the early 1930s, the British did not need to restrain French interest in better relations with the USSR, because there was no serious interest until Herriot again became président du Conseil. Then came Hitler's arrival in power, and the increasing French interest in relations with Moscow, which were pursued by Paul-Boncour and Barthou. The British government began to pay closer attention. "The Conservatives and religious organizations, especially the Catholics," wrote the French councilor in London, Roger Cambon, "are very mistrustful of the USSR." He continued:

> Each time a rapprochement between it and another state arises, these milieux have the feeling of an enlarging of the zone of danger ... The great majority of English Conservatives attribute to the communist peril an importance which only recent events in Germany have succeeded in slightly diminishing. Until then, they were sympathetic to the ideas of order which inspire the Nazis and to the anti-Bolshevik services rendered by Hitler simply from his arrival in power. To the [Conservative] mind, even the most stable nations, are exposed to fearful perils, in getting closer to the Soviets.

Liberals and Labourites, Cambon continued, took a somewhat different view of the USSR, not embracing it, but being sympathetic to the Franco-Soviet rapprochement. The Foreign Office also recognized the justification for the rapprochement, but quite understood the French desire "to avoid too much intimacy with the [Soviet] Union."

Then there was this comment. "Individually, my Foreign Office colleagues in general consider the Russians to be very gifted from the point of view of imagination and intellectual speculations. On the other hand, they have reservations about the political, economic, and even simple organizational capabilities of Soviet personnel. They consider that left to himself, [the Soviet] ends up getting wrong or rendering inoperable the most advanced mechanisms, especially in matters of production and transport."

That sounded like traditional British orientalism, but there was more to Cambon's dispatch. As we see when we let him finish his comments. "In the eyes of English diplomats, Russia, present day or future, especially risks becoming a real international danger, if it is taken in hand by foreign elements … The Germans, having already demonstrated it, are particularly well suited to play this role. However, a Francophile policy pursued by Moscow constitutes the best antidote against the German danger." We ought not to be surprised, Cambon concluded, to see the Foreign Secretary, Sir John Simon, support French efforts to bring about an Eastern Pact.[52] Unfortunately, Cambon was wrong. The British government was not going to be very indulgent towards later French efforts to consolidate relations with Moscow. But this is getting ahead of our story.

And Poland?

In that summer of 1934, Poland was becoming the spoiler of collective security. One had to wonder, Laroche advised Paris, if every French step towards Moscow would lead to a Polish step towards Germany.[53] The Latvian minister in Warsaw, Olgerd Grosvald, told Laroche that the Baltic countries were uneasy over the prospect of a Franco-Soviet alliance. Germany was separated from the USSR by other states, Grosvald observed: "We would not like to let Soviet troops pass through our territory, and he doubts that this idea would be any more attractive to Poland." The spectre of a Franco-Soviet alliance "haunted" the Poles.[54] Polish diplomats soon passed on their own opposition to such a possibility. The Red Army, they say, would never leave Polish territory, while others added that they would "foment revolution." The Polish deputy secretary in the Ministry of Foreign Affairs in Warsaw, Jan Szembek, was vehement on this point: it would lead to the partition of Poland.[55] This was the passage issue. It came up repeatedly between 1934 and 1939, and remained an obstacle to Soviet-Polish cooperation against Germany right up to the outbreak of war in September 1939. Even the Germans were not particularly worried. "The present Russian flirting with France does not concern us very much," said one German embassy report intercepted by Soviet intelligence. "Russia is not our neighbour. At the present time, the Red Army is difficult to employ outside the country, not to mention that not one of the neighbouring governments will allow it to pass across their territory."[56]

In mid-1934, Soviet military intelligence reports on Poland were consistently negative. According to one such report, Laroche's relatively positive information about Barthou's visit to Warsaw that was conveyed to Davtian at the end of April was gilding the lily. The meetings had not gone as well as Laroche had suggested. Barthou succeeded, however, in playing to Polish "pride" (*samoliubie*), so that the discussions went from cool to lukewarm. Barthou had after all raised the issue of Polish-Soviet relations. These "left much to be desired," according to Barthou, "and in case of misunderstandings with Germany, Poland would also have to reckon with the enmity of the USSR." Again, according to a Soviet source in Paris with ties to the Quai d'Orsay, when Beck had been in Moscow, he was warned against the policy of "betting on two horses," France and Nazi Germany. Barthou had strongly recommended to the Poles to improve relations with the USSR. To this Piłsudski had responded that he did not believe in "the Moscow government," that "the Soviet army was extremely weak," and the Soviet "regime" unstable, "fragile." Thus, Barthou's efforts to improve Soviet-Polish relations had failed.[57]

A Soviet report from a Polish source with ties to Beck and others in the Polish government remarked, among other items, that Poland and Germany intended to act together to prevent an alliance between France, the Little Entente, and the USSR. If such an alliance were to be concluded, Poland would break its alliance with France and side openly with Germany. Germany and Poland would cooperate to prevent an alliance of the Baltic states and prevent Soviet, French, or British influence from gaining a foothold. Germany and Poland would together oppose the signature of an Eastern Pact. These lines are underlined in a report annotated by Stalin and sent by his direction to other Politburo members.[58]

By the end of July, Barthou was losing patience with Poland and its stalling over an Eastern Pact: "There are in Monsieur Beck's reply some objections and reservations that merit discussion if they do not conceal a real hostility against even the principle of a pact. Everything is there. Without upsetting Poland, we will need it to take a position on the principle and to abandon a diplomacy which is really too dilatory."[59] Formal instructions in this sense were sent to Laroche, and he put forward the case in Warsaw, though Beck continued to stall.[60]

Soviet Entry into the League of Nations

In the meantime, the issue of Soviet entry into the League of Nations was coming to the fore because of the annual League meetings in September. At the beginning of July, the Soviet position had not yet been decided. Litvinov sent a briefing paper to Stalin explaining where matters stood. The main opposition to Soviet entry into the League came from the two powers that had quit it, Germany and Japan, and from Poland, of course, settling into its role as spoiler of European collective security. One French report, however, indicated that Beck had resigned himself to Soviet entry. This subject had come up many times in Geneva, Litvinov advised: France and the Little Entente were pressing. "I emphasized," he wrote, "that we had not ourselves discussed this question and that it could only be discussed in the event of agreement on the pact of mutual assistance."[61] In July 1934 that did not seem a likely possibility. Litvinov wrote to Stalin again three weeks later. France and other states expected the USSR to apply for entry into the League in September. League entry was linked to mutual assistance. Delays could mean putting off entry until 1935. Whatever was to be the position of the Soviet government, France needed to be informed. Litvinov therefore proposed a meeting before the summer holidays.[62] Four days later, the Politburo approved Soviet entry into the League, abandoning its previous position on prior acceptance of a regional mutual security pact, on condition of a formal invitation, and on approval of a permanent place on the League council.[63] Litvinov warned against Beck's sabotage of mutual assistance. It was the usual wheels turning inside wheels. "For some reason the Germans were spreading rumours," Litvinov advised Rozenberg, "about an allegedly anticipated change of Soviet policy in the direction of a rapprochement with Germany. Obviously, this is being done with the objective of undermining confidence in us in France and Czechoslovakia. There are no indications which would point to the possibility of a new rapprochement with Germany."[64] In early September there was more manoeuvring, especially on the part of Poland. Litvinov worried that things were headed for "a dead end." "Obstacles grow with each new day," he cabled from across the border in France, waiting for the decision in Geneva. Foreign Secretary Sir John Simon was stalling, hiding behind the backs of the Dominions and of Beck.[65] At the last moment, Beck dropped his reservations, pressured by Barthou and reassured by Litvinov. On 18 September, the Soviet Union officially became a member of the League.[66]

While Litvinov was in France nursing Soviet entry into the League, US Ambassador Bullitt conversed with Radek, who was still working with Stalin as a journalist and publicist for Soviet policy. His newspaper columns often caught the attention of embassies in Moscow. Here is what he said to Bullitt about Stalin's view of Soviet foreign policy:

> (One) that he [Stalin] agreed ... that removal of all obstacles to close cooperation between the US and the Soviet Union was of prime importance for the maintenance of peace in the Far East, (two) that at the moment however it was even more important to arrange for the protection of the rear of the Soviet Union in case of Japanese attack by putting through the understanding with France and establishing a friendly relationship with England, (three) that therefore nothing should be done at the moment which might anger France and England.[67]

Figure 8.1. Litvinov making a speech in Geneva, 1934, AVPRF.

Radek's description of Soviet policy sounds about right. Stalin had set the priorities.

After his return to Moscow, Litvinov had a conversation with Bullitt about the League and the general situation in Europe. Bullitt found Litvinov in a sour mood, "chastened and pessimistic," was how he put it. Geneva had not made a good impression. Participation in League business had discouraged the narkom. He had returned home, as Bullitt put it, "convinced that ultimate war in Europe was inevitable; that there was not one government in Europe, even the French, which was ready to do anything real to preserve peace; and that he felt that there was nothing for the Soviet Union to do except to strengthen the Red Army in every way possible and rely on the army to protect the Soviet Union from attack." Still, Litvinov's idea was to mobilize the League to protect European security, and with this in mind, to get the United States involved in Geneva in some form or another.[68]

Readers may remember that this was a variation of Krestinskii's idea at the end of 1933. Publicly, Litvinov always talked peace, and in the past he had promoted disarmament on a grand scale. In the circumstances, peace was the best language to use because the European right was quick to accuse the USSR of plotting war to spread world revolution. What Litvinov meant was certainly peace, if it could be preserved by restraining or containing Hitlerite Germany, and war if necessary in the event containment failed. Litvinov considered the disarmament conference to be a "fiasco," and, according to one US diplomat, he was embarrassed by discussions of it in view of the previous "radical" Soviet position on that topic. The Soviet government had no intention of disarming given the perceived danger from Germany and Japan; quite the contrary, it was rearming at breakneck speed.[69]

Barthou Talks to Beck

Soviet entry into the League did not resolve the question of an Eastern Locarno. In June, Neurath had told Litvinov that Germany would not agree to collective security. In Geneva, Barthou (as did Litvinov) continued to press Beck for Polish agreement to the pact. Beck responded with conditions: that mutual security would not vitiate the non-aggression pact with Germany, while Lithuania and Czechoslovakia would be excluded from the pact.

"I observed to Monsieur Beck," wrote Barthou, "that he was draining the pact of a large part of its substance." Then Barthou put a hypothetical question to Beck: What would he think of an alliance between Russia and France?

"That is your business; you are free," Beck responded.

"*Non*," Barthou retorted, "that is your business also. First, because we will not sign a new treaty without advising a friendly country and ally, and secondly, because you are a directly interested party." Barthou referred to a Polish démarche to Romania, proposing its entry into the Eastern Pact. It was a setup. "A trick to sabotage the pact," Litvinov had earlier called the Polish initiative. Barthou was of a similar opinion, obviously, imputing bad faith to Beck. We made a simple communication to Romania, Beck responded: the Romanian government would make of it what it would. Barthou was far from satisfied with Beck's comments, and noted in his record of the conversation that the Polish minister was ill at ease throughout their meeting.[70]

Two days later, on 9 September, the German government announced its rejection of the proposed Eastern Pact, and Poland did the same later that month. The French chargé d'affaires in Warsaw warned that the Franco-Polish alliance was menaced – it was "undergoing a crisis." This was for many reasons, which the chargé d'affaires, Pierre Bressy, outlined in a long dispatch. The Poles generally believed that the USSR would collapse, either because of a bad harvest or because of war with Japan. Some even believed that in such a situation, Poland should intervene in an alliance with other powers, but certainly with Germany. Even the Poles who did not believe in such fantasies, feared a Soviet intrusion into European affairs and "intrigues at Polish expense."[71] The Polish chargé d'affaires in Moscow, remarked to his US counterpart, chargé d'affaires John Wiley, that "Russian troops as allies either fail to come to one's aid or, if they come, they arrive after the battle – and then are more difficult to get rid of than the enemy." The Pole thought that was funny, but it wasn't really.[72]

In Moscow, Alphand advised of the already habitual fear of the Red Army's transit across Poland, Łukasiewicz having raised the subject during a reception at the French embassy. The Soviet side also worried about Poland, throwing in little by little with Germany. Nevertheless, Stomoniakov said to Alphand that the Soviet government was "very satisfied" with developments in Geneva and elsewhere and was obliged to Barthou for his handling of the League of Nations issue. "They understand," Alphand wrote, "that with this first stage accomplished, the most delicate work for the organization of peace remains to be achieved, on which the USSR continues to want to work in full agreement with France."[73] This was Stomoniakov's view, and Litvinov's also. It was 8 October 1934. On the following day, the Soviet side saw its worst *koshmar* begin to play out in France.

Koshmar in France

Barthou took the night train to Marseille that evening of 8 October and would not have read Alphand's last telegram relating Stomoniakov's thanks to the minister. Barthou travelled to Marseille to welcome King Alexander I of Yugoslavia as part of the French effort to strengthen its relations with the Little Entente. No sooner had the king and Barthou got into their open car to drive into the city than a man with a pistol, an assassin, rushed at them opening fire on the king. He was hit three times and did not survive. Barthou was wounded, almost certainly by a stray police bullet. He was hit in the arm, not a grave wound, except that the bullet severed a humeral artery, causing him to hemorrhage. Security was not good enough to prevent the assassination but an iconic contemporary photograph shows a mounted gendarme about to cut down the assassin with his saber. Incredibly, Barthou was left to make his way to hospital in a taxi. His wound was not properly treated and he died in the operating room. It was a senseless, avoidable death, the result of bungled security and bungled first aid.[74]

Stalin thought the assassination of the Yugoslav king was the work of "German-Polish agents." Assassinations in Austria and Romania were also the work of "German-fascist agents" intended to change policy in those countries. The Marseille assassination had the same objective. "For me, this is clear," Stalin advised.[75] Soviet intelligence agencies were producing one report after the other noting Polish conniving with Germany and Japan, banking on war in the Far East, and reporting on German rearmament. These reports no doubt contributed to Stalin's view of things. If Germany was a potential enemy, so was Poland.

If Barthou had survived his wound, it is perhaps doubtful whether he would have remained foreign minister for much longer, given the frequent changes of government in Paris. Who can say whether Barthou might have made a difference in consolidating relations with Moscow? "Cemeteries," according to the French proverb, "are full of indispensable people." What is certain is that in Moscow, the narkom and his colleagues were shocked by Barthou's death. Litvinov's old nightmares about a change of government in Paris and therefore a change in French policy returned to haunt the NKID. Alphand rang the alarm bells in Paris, noting that the events in Marseille had provoked deep concerns about a potential change in French policy less favourable to the Soviet Union. There were already accusations in the French press that the Comintern was implicated in Barthou's death.[76] In fact, the assassin was a Bulgarian in the employ of the Croatian fascist organization Ustashe, behind which stood Italy.

The February riots in the place de la Concorde had set off a movement to unify the left against a fascist takeover of power in France. The Socialist and Communist Parties formed an alliance, a Front commun, in July 1934, which in turn disturbed the French right and called into question support in that quarter among French nationalists for the Franco-Soviet rapprochement. Events in Marseille further destabilized the domestic political situation. It was on 13 October, only four days after the death of Barthou, that Alphand called on Litvinov to discuss the political situation in France. Alphand mentioned a confidential letter to Payart from the right-wing journalist Henri de Kerillis concerning French internal politics. The political situation in France had "completely changed," he said, since his return from Moscow. "Right circles" feared the political alliance of the Socialist and Communist Parties, which in turn influenced their views about foreign policy. Having reluctantly supported cooperation with the USSR in view of the German danger, the right had reversed position. The "communist danger," not the German one, was now considered the greater peril. According to Kerillis, the socialist-communist political alliance was a mistake, which had undermined support on the right for the Franco-Soviet rapprochement. Kerillis had promised Payart to support Barthou's policies in his columns, but when he returned to France, he changed his mind. He wrote to Payart to explain why he had not kept his promise.

Readers may imagine Litvinov's reaction to Alphand's account of the Kerillis letter four days after Barthou's death. It seemed to be the sudden realization of his worst fears. "I thanked Alphand for his information," Litvinov wrote in his *dnevnik*, "expressing regret that internal political questions can influence foreign policy in France, against which, however, we are powerless to do anything whatever." This seemed a rather naïve comment, since Litvinov knew as well as anyone in Moscow that domestic policy almost always influenced foreign policy. Nor was the Politburo without means to influence French public opinion, that is to say, without funds which the Soviet embassy in Paris invested as "allowances" to French newspapers and journalists. The Soviet government had used such funds since the early 1920s to influence the French press without positive result. The idea was to get the French papers to offer a more favourable view of the USSR, though as one Soviet diplomat had remarked during the 1920s, it was tough to buy a favourable front-page leader. It was also hard, as Litvinov had often noted, to compete with other governments and indeed with the Quai d'Orsay, all of which had greater sums to pay journalists for hire. The French security services were well aware of Soviet "allowances" and Alphand certainly knew about them, having raised the subject with Litvinov in the past. It was doubly discreet that neither man mentioned the obvious.

The narkom had of course more to say about the situation in France. "We do not dictate policy to either the Socialist or Communist Party." Readers may know that this was certainly true about the socialists, but everyone in France who was not a communist thought the French Communist Party took its orders from the Comintern, in other words, from Moscow. But here I have interrupted Litvinov on the subject at hand. Let him finish what he had to say to Alphand. "Just as the Franco-Soviet rapprochement was prompted by the danger of German aggression, so also was the Front commun most certainly dictated by the danger of fascism, and fascism and aggression are different sides of one and the same coin." Soviet propaganda underlined this point: *fashizm, eto voina,* "fascism means war."

Once he had finished sharing his laments with Alphand, the narkom turned to a question of the highest priority. Who was going to succeed Barthou? Alphand speculated on the possibilities, but one point was certain, the foreign policy of France would not change. If only Litvinov could have been sure of that. He was not so sure, however, and mentioned the name of François-Poncet, the ambassador in Berlin and a known partisan of a Franco-German agreement, as one particularly undesirable candidate. He had no chance, Alphand replied, but he admitted that a Franco-German agreement had more and more partisans in Paris. Here was the argument they employed: France had earlier declined to pursue an agreement with Germany for the sake of which it would have to abandon its alliance with Poland. Now when Poland had itself abandoned France, or so it seemed, why not come to terms with Germany and let it feed on Poland? The British government too, or at least some British Conservatives, were also pushing this idea, Alphand added, as if Litvinov did not know already.

The Soviet leadership was familiar with this argument, Litvinov replied, but there was a counterargument to the effect that France should not leave itself in a situation where it had to face Germany "eye to eye," but rather it should seek to insure its security by drawing in the USSR. Alphand interjected that he had put this very idea to Daladier when he was leaning towards a rapprochement with Germany. The ambassador thought Germany would go for such a combination with France and he wondered how the Soviet government would react to it. "I answered," wrote Litvinov, "that such a thought has never entered our minds, and that any possible combination we shall evaluate from the point of view of the best guarantee of peace."[77] Of course, such ideas had *always* entered Soviet minds, but the last part of Litvinov's comment is enigmatic. What did it mean? Alphand apparently did not make a record of this conversation, so we cannot compare notes. In November, Iakov Zakharovich Surits, the new polpred in Berlin, reported on various inclinations in France and elsewhere to improve relations with Germany. "While our relations with France are not yet fully formed," he opined, "it is not in our interest to create confidence in the French camp that our relations with Germany are hopelessly spoiled." Yes, exactly. On Stalin's copy of this report, these last lines are underlined in blue pencil.[78]

One name that did not come up in the conversation between Alphand and Litvinov was Pierre Laval. He had three times been président du Conseil, and he was Minister of Colonies in the Doumergue government. He was part of the "hidden opposition" to the Franco-Soviet rapprochement and to mutual assistance. The Comintern and the red flag haunted him. During a cabinet meeting in June, he went on a rant against the rapprochement with Moscow, provoked by militant communists in the electoral district of Aubervilliers where Laval was mayor and held a seat in the Senate. If Litvinov had been thinking of Laval, he would have thought the choice a catastrophe. He knew him, had met him in Paris, and had listened to his complaints about the French Communist Party and the Comintern interfering in French domestic affairs and in Indochina. *Bozhe moi*, oh my, was it possible?

Chapter Nine

Nobody Wants "the Bolo Baby": The Failure of US-Soviet Relations, 1933–1935

The establishment of Soviet-US relations got off to a fast start. The new Secretary of the Treasury, Henry Morgenthau Jr., wanted an agreement by January 1934. State Department officials began to look at ways of implementing the "gentleman's agreement" between Litvinov and Roosevelt. Litvinov was also in a hurry; delays in negotiations could only be "harmful." But we have to back up in time, more than a year. It was the autumn of 1933.

Aleksandr Antonovich Troianovskii

On 19 November 1933, the Politburo approved Aleksandr Antonovich Troianovskii as polpred in Washington, and he was approved that same day by the State Department. Skvirskii would remain in Washington as councillor. Litvinov had discussed Troianovskii's appointment with Molotov and Kaganovich.[1] He was born in 1882 in Tula, located south of Moscow, a fortress in defence of the revolution during the civil war. His father was a tsarist officer and the family was well-to-do. There was nothing unusual about that; many Bolsheviks came from the tsarist elite. Troianovskii followed his father into the army, which is where the revolution caught up with him. In 1908, he was arrested; two years later, he went abroad living in Vienna and Paris. He floated between the Bolsheviks and the Mensheviks, depending on the issue. When the revolution broke out in 1917, like so many others, he returned home, more Menshevik than Bolshevik. During the civil war, he served in the Red Army as a teacher. In the mid-1920s, he worked in the Commissariat for foreign trade. Anastas Ivanovich Mikoian, who was the narkom, said Troianovskii was at his best the equal of any American businessman. A Bolshevik was necessarily a jack of all trades. In 1927, Troianovskii was named polpred in Tokyo where he served for six years. He was thus well informed on Japanese foreign policy. He also spoke English and German. The English-language skills would have been essential in dealing with US counterparts. In the available photographs of Troanovskii in

Washington, his hair is greying, carefully parted and combed. He looked like a businessman, dressed for work in expensive suits or a tux for evening receptions and dinners. His ability to speak in English, and his conservative looks seemed to suit him for the Soviet embassy in Washington. He had shortcomings, however. He was an arrogant fellow and thought he knew better than the NKID on how to deal with the Americans. It was not long before he crossed swords with Litvinov.

William C. Bullitt

Also in November 1933, the Soviet government agreed to receive William C. Bullitt as US ambassador in Moscow. He had made a good impression on Skvirskii who thought he favoured the establishment of US-Soviet relations. Meeting in Washington, Litvinov viewed him as a kind of pilot and adviser on achieving recognition. Bullitt had a history with the USSR. President Wilson sent him to Moscow in 1919 to negotiate with the Bolsheviks. He was an impetuous fellow, only twenty-seven when he embarked on the dangerous trip to Soviet Russia. Lenin made his acquaintance and gained a good opinion of him, or at least so it was said. Bullitt tried to sell a peace deal with the Bolsheviks to Wilson and David Lloyd George, then British prime minister. That did not work out. Lloyd George explained to Bullitt that Winston Churchill, then Secretary of State for War, was dead set against peace with Soviet Russia. The White Guards, it was widely believed, would eventually defeat and hang all the Bolsheviks. Is it not interesting how the paths of important actors in this narrative cross from time to time?

Bullitt descended from the old guard American elite and a wealthy Philadelphia family. He was educated at Yale University and dabbled in radical ideas. When his father died, he inherited the family fortune. His pathway was not so different from young Bolsheviks of his generation, except that Bullitt flirted with radical ideas. He was talented, however, and rose rapidly as a journalist working in Washington. If you look at photographs of Bullitt, you will see an attractive young man, clean-shaven and well dressed, who eventually began balding and whose face hardened over the years. He looked like what he became, a mean, arrogant descendant of the old-money American elite. In the 1920s, he divorced his high-society first wife to marry Louise Bryant, the widow of the American journalist John Reed, author of *Ten Days that Shook the World.* Bryant was a well-known journalist in her own right, but after she married Bullitt, he apparently discouraged her journalism and she became a rich man's wife. She must have seemed hot to Bullitt, sexually independent, sensuous, and free-spirited. They had a daughter, Anne, shortly after they married. Bullitt appeared to be something of a rake and ran with a fast crowd in the 1920s, spending time in Paris like many other wealthy American expats.

If you could afford it, the French capital was the place to be. You could mingle with all sorts of writers, artists, wannabes, and eccentric people, and it helped if you liked to dance and to dine elegantly. Bullitt published a satirical novel in 1926, about the Philadelphia elite, which became a bestseller. This was someone who seemed to excel at whatever he took up. Well, except marriage, he divorced Bryant in 1930, so he said, because of a lesbian affair. That was Paris for you, wild and free, but the lesbian *affaire* was enough for Bullitt to give up his chic bohemian ways at age thirty-nine. He emerged unscathed from the bitter divorce with sole custody of Anne. Not so Bryant. She became gravely ill, an alcoholic, prematurely old, and short of funds. She never saw her daughter again. Bullitt was not a total cad, however, and apparently sent money to Bryant that helped her get by. In January 1936, she died in Paris of a cerebral hemorrhage, at age fifty. Later that year, Bullitt went to Paris as the US ambassador.[2]

Bullitt met Roosevelt briefly during Wilson's presidency and then began to work for him as an informal adviser, backing him during the 1932 presidential campaign before being appointed to the State Department as a special assistant undersecretary. It was no surprise that Roosevelt brought him into his negotiations with the USSR and then named him US ambassador. He was cock sure of himself as he set out for Moscow in December 1933, rather too sure of himself. He thought the Soviet leadership was so desperate for good relations with the United States that it would agree to almost anything to get them. Bullitt was not the first to have such notions in dealing with the Soviet government. Those people did not fare well with their Soviet interlocutors; you could not just "handle" them. In that regard the French were the worst of the lot. In 1927, they had waved off the best offer the Soviet government would ever make to any foreign government to settle the tsarist debts. Would Bullitt and the State Department make the same blunder?[3]

Bullitt Takes the Train for Moscow

At the outset, it did not look that way. The Soviet authorities rolled out the red carpet for Bullitt. On 10 December, an NKID delegation met Bullitt at the frontier rail station Negoreloe, headed by Ia. S. Il'inskii, the NKID polpred in Belorussia, and a TASS correspondent, both of whom wrote reports of their discussions with the new US ambassador. It was early evening and cold when he crossed into Soviet territory. The railway commissariat even sent a newly refurbished VIP railcar to take Bullitt to Moscow. Before they left, there was an "improvised" dinner in the railroad station. Not an everyday event, the station restaurant had to be warmed up for such distinguished company. It was quite an event apparently, almost a banquet, according to Il'inskii, well-watered with wine and even champagne. There were American journalists and their wives and Bullitt's officials present, and the ambassador had with him his young

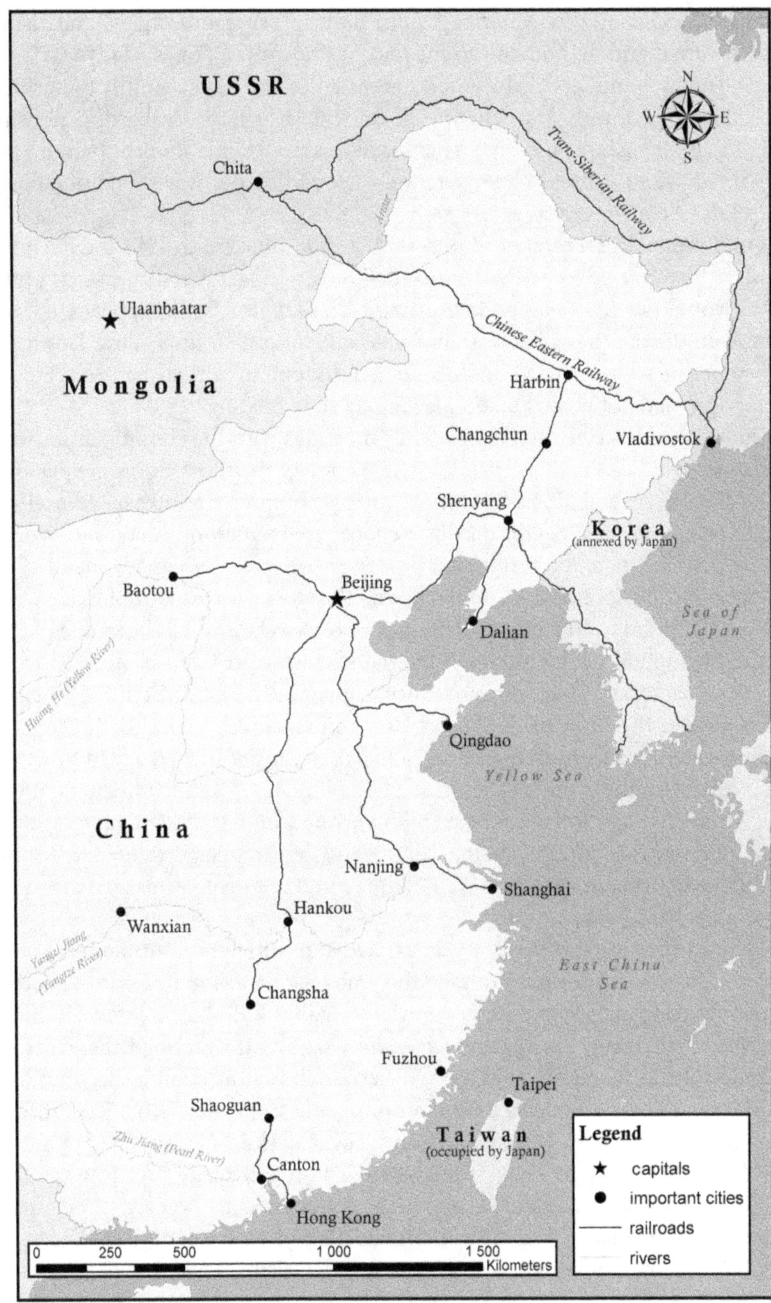

Map 9.1. Maritime provinces, Manchuria, China, interwar years.

quality that no one in America would dare to serve nowadays, and many toasts were drunk to you and to me and to the United States." This was only one of many banquets and dinners intended to introduce Bullitt to various officials and commissars with whom he would have to deal. Alphand had been treated to a large banquet when he had arrived some months before Bullitt. If the USSR wanted better relations, the red carpet was rolled out along with lots of caviar and spirits.

On Sunday, 17 December, Bullitt took a little time off to visit the Kremlin Wall, as he reported to FDR. "I put some flowers on Jack Reed's grave, as I told you I would do." This was an interesting comment, for Bullitt appears to have met Reed during the Great War and then taken up with his widow. Destinies are sometimes star-crossed. Bullitt seemed disappointed that the press, Soviet or foreign, had not picked up on his Sunday showboating.

Bullitt also described to Roosevelt his meetings with the commissar for war. "I had several talks with Voroshilov, who is one of the most charming persons that I have ever met. He has an immense sense of humor and keeps himself in such perfect physical condition that he looks like a man of thirty-five." Voroshilov invited the ambassador to a dinner at the Kremlin. Stalin intended to be present. This looked like pulling out all the stops. No other diplomats were getting that kind of treatment. "This lack of close relations has been due partly to the inclination of the foreign diplomatists to regard themselves as spies in an enemy country." They were also boring apparently. Unlike Bullitt, of course. "The men at the head of the Soviet Government today are really intelligent, sophisticated, vigorous human beings and they cannot be persuaded to waste their time with the ordinary conventional diplomatist. On the other hand, they are extremely eager to have contact with anyone who has first-rate intelligence and dimensions as a human being. They were, for example, delighted by young Kennan who went in with me." Well, Bullitt could not say to Roosevelt that they were "delighted" with *him*.

"The dinner at Voroshilov's was carried out with great formality." Voroshilov's car was sent around to take the ambassador to the Kremlin. "There I found awaiting me Mr. and Mrs. Voroshilov, Stalin, Kalinin, Molotov, Litvinov, Egorov, … Piatakov, … Kaganovich." The way Bullitt described the event, it sounded like the beginning of a high-society affair in Philadelphia, except it was in Moscow. There were also a number of people from the NKID: Krestinskii, Karakhan, Sokolnikov, Troianovskii, and Dovgalevskii. "Litvinov said to me as I looked over the room, 'This is the whole "gang" that really runs things – the inside directorate.'" The ambassador was introduced to everyone, including Stalin, with handshakes all around. Bullitt offered FDR a long description of Stalin: "The first impression Stalin made was surprising. I had thought from his pictures that he was a very big man with a face of iron and a booming voice. On the contrary, he is rather short … and of ordinary physique, wiry rather than powerful. He was dressed in a common soldier's uniform, with boots, black trousers and a gray-green coat without marks or decorations of any kind."

This was a banquet where the hors d'oeuvres would have been enough to satisfy the appetites of most ordinary human beings: caviar, crab, "and every conceivable kind of vodka." Bullitt was seated in the centre of a long-sided table near all the bigwigs. As soon as everyone was seated, the toasts began. Stalin led off: "To President Roosevelt, who in spite of the mute growls of the Fishes dared to recognize the Soviet Union." Bullitt explained that the reference was to the Sovietphobe Hamilton Fish (the Republican critic), though FDR would not have needed the explanation, although readers certainly will now. Bullitt responded with a toast to President Kalinin, and thereupon began a salvo of toasts that continued to the end of the evening. "After the tenth toast or so, I began to consider it discreet to take merely a sip rather than drain my glass." Litvinov noticed, however, and replied that the one who proposed the toast would be insulted if Bullitt did not drain his glass. Russians are a mischievous lot and know that most Westerners cannot keep up with them when it comes to vodka. Bullitt said he hung on until the end. "There were perhaps fifty toasts and I have never before so thanked God for the possession of a head impervious to any quantity of liquor." Still, fifty shots of vodka is staggering even for Russians. People must have been barely able to stand at the end.

"Discretion was conspicuous by its absence," Bullitt advised. There was a good deal of talk about the prospects of a Japanese attack in the east. Stalin introduced chief of staff Egorov as the man who would beat the Japanese. Then Stalin, over the table, said to Bullitt that the USSR needed a quarter million tons of US rails, used would be fine, he said, for the double-tracking of the Trans-Siberian Railway. It would help with the supply of Soviet armed forces in the Far East. This was serious business being watered by vodka. After dinner, everyone moved to an adjoining drawing room. Stalin got hold of Iurii Leonidovich Piatakov to play some tunes on the piano. Stalin stood behind him, "from time to time putting his arm around Piatakov's neck and squeezing him affectionately." Piatakov was then zamnarkom of heavy industry and good at his job. Of course, Stalin would not always be so affectionate. Most of the people at that banquet would be shot or sent to labour camps five years later. This is getting a little ahead of the narrative, but Stalin's arm around the neck was often *not* to show affection.

Stalin eventually went round to talk to Bullitt to emphasize how much the Soviet leadership desired close relations with the United States, referring to the need to preserve peace in the Far East. "Stalin was feeling extremely gay, as we all were, but he gave me the feeling that he was speaking honestly." Bullitt was laying it on pretty thick for Roosevelt, but there is no reason to think that Stalin was not serious. Bullitt took advantage to get the building he wanted for the US embassy. Stalin at once agreed to it.[10] Ever since 1918, the Bolsheviks had sought better relations with the United States, and now it looked as though *finally* they had got them.

On 21 December, just before his departure, Bullitt met Litvinov for a long discussion. He advised Roosevelt that the narkom had talked a lot about Soviet entry into the League of Nations. France was putting on the pressure. In fact, two days before the Politburo had approved a new policy based on the League and collective security to rein in Nazi Germany. Readers should remember that we have backed up a little in time. The USSR would only enter the League some nine months later. Japan was a threat, and the Soviet government needed to secure its western frontiers. Germany and Poland were not an immediate threat, but they might become one if the USSR was pulled into a long war with Japan. Litvinov said that they knew Poland and Germany had held "conversations … looking towards an eventual attack on the Soviet Union" in the event of a long Soviet war in the Far East. Poland had it sights set on the Ukraine and Germany, on the Baltic states. A month later, in January 1934, Poland and Nazi Germany concluded a non-aggression pact. So while Bullitt was a little surprised by the Polish angle, he might soon have been less so. Without mentioning the conversations with Paul-Boncour, Litvinov said that "France had offered to make a defensive alliance with the Soviet Union providing that if either party were attacked by Germany the other party should at once declare war on Germany." The essential condition was Soviet entry into the League. Readers will, of course, know that while Paul-Boncour was keen on this idea, his officials in the Quai d'Orsay were not. Litvinov had just got Politburo approval for a new foreign policy in the West and he must have been feeling sure of himself. Bullitt brought up the point that the USSR had no common frontier with Germany, but Litvinov seemed unperturbed. Did that mean, Bullitt asked, "that the Red Army would march against Germany to support France?"

"That would be easy," Litvinov replied, "compared with the difficulty of getting the French Army to march against Germany to support the Soviet Union." Litvinov had a sharp sense of humour; he had just put his finger on the central problem of Franco-Soviet relations during the coming years. But let's not get too far ahead of our narrative.

For the Soviet Union, security in the West was tied to security in the East. The conversation turned back to the situation with Japan. Litvinov had no idea whether Japan would pick a fight or not, and he opined that the Japanese did not know either. "We discussed," Bullitt wrote, "ways and means of preventing such an attack." Apart from steel rails, Litvinov suggested a series of non-aggression pacts between the United States, the Soviet Union, China, and Japan. Bullitt thought that idea would raise "difficulties." Even the impression of Soviet-US cooperation, however, would be valuable in discouraging Japanese aggression. In this regard, Litvinov suggested the visit of a US squadron or warship to

Vladivostok or Leningrad in the spring of 1934. Bullitt agreed to propose the idea to Roosevelt.

The conversation then moved on to trade issues, though not to the "gentleman's agreement." Litvinov said that the Soviet policy looked to economic self-sufficiency, but that if the Soviet government could obtain long-term credits, it would continue to buy from the United States. "Litvinov's entire preoccupation at the present time," Bullitt concluded, "is the preservation of peace in the Far East. I am convinced that there is almost nothing that the Soviet Union will not give us in the way of commercial agreements, or anything else, in return for our moral support in preserving peace." Here was the beginning of Bullitt's overestimation of the US position vis-à-vis the USSR.

Bullitt added some interesting details in a telegram he sent to Washington on his way home. There was again the issue of Franco-Soviet relations and the fear of war with Japan in league with Germany and Poland. Litvinov said that "the Soviet Union considered an attack by Japan this spring so probable that it felt it must secure its western frontier in every way." As for an agreement with France, Litvinov hoped there would soon be "a definite binding contract." Then he added: "The entire agreement might fall through as Daladier was opposed to it and the British were opposed but that Herriot and the majority of the French Government were in favour of it." Thus, for the time being Daladier's Germanophilia had been checked. Rising dangers from Germany and Japan increased the Soviet government's interest in obtaining better relations with the United States. "It is difficult," Bullitt wrote, "to exaggerate the cordiality with which I was received by all members of the Government including Kalinin, Molotov, Voroshilov, and Stalin." In a covering message to FDR, Phillips underscored Litvinov's reference to a possible joint German-Polish attack on the USSR in concert with Japan. This is "something so new and unexpected that I thought it worth while [*sic*] to make sure that you had noted it."[11]

Bullitt left Moscow on the evening of 21 December, stopping off in Berlin and Paris. He talked to Paul-Boncour, among others, who discouraged him from thinking France could pay its debts to the United States. Bullitt huffed and puffed, but without any effect on the French. The Soviet Union was not the only one with a debt problem with the United States. Bullitt asked Paul-Boncour about a possible war in the Far East, to which he responded that he thought it was likely. But then he added, that "many wars which one expects to break out do not break out."[12]

Litvinov also made an entry in his *dnevnik* for the conversation with Bullitt and it was much more matter of fact. The narkom's record begins with the question of US rails raised by Stalin at Voroshilov's banquet. Bullitt expressed his regret that Troianovskii could not accompany him back to the United States for he was thinking of the renewal of debt negotiations. He mentioned the Johnson Debt Default bill that was before Congress and which would forbid credits or loans being made to debtor nations which had not settled prior financial obligations to the United States. If there were no deals by 15 January, Roosevelt could encounter political "serious difficulties." Trade issues also came up and Litvinov warned Bullitt of the obstacles and limits involved in developing Soviet-US trade. The question of a US fleet visit was likewise a point of discussion, but on Bullitt's initiative, not Litvinov's. Litvinov advised of the difficulties of a non-aggression pact in the Far East, consistent with Bullitt's note. There was nothing in Litvinov's report suggesting worries of imminent war with Japan that Bullitt could use as leverage on Moscow to pay its debts, but France and Britain, among other nations, were not paying their debts, either.[13] In point of fact, Roosevelt was just as worried about Japan as Litvinov. Would security interests therefore take precedence over debts that no one else (well, except Finland) was paying?

Litvinov forwarded his record to Stalin, drawing his attention to the fact that Bullitt lent considerable importance to the conclusion of debt negotiations by 15 January. He therefore asked Stalin "to put pressure" on Troianovskii not to delay his departure for Washington any longer because of "organizational trifles." He needed to get moving if he wanted to catch the next American steamship leaving France on 28 January.[14] What was going on with Troianovskii? Was there a problem?

Troianovskii

There was indeed a problem as Litvinov explained to Stalin in a briefing paper on the following day. "I just received a statement about the staff for the embassy in America. I do not know whether you have been informed that the NKID strongly objects to some of Troyanovskii's candidacies and of our considerations. You have repeatedly and just the other day reproached me for not using my authority as narkom in my relations with the polpreds. You will probably agree that the narkom cannot have this authority when, in his conflict with the polpred on a matter in which the polpred can understand nothing, the Central Committee resolves the dispute entirely in his favour." There was thus a row underway between Litvinov and Troianovskii. Had the appointment to Washington gone to the new polpred's head? It appears as though it had.

"I just want to draw your attention to the political side of the matter," Litvinov continued: "I found Skvirskii in Washington with a well-established apparatus which has worked for 11 years … to establish relations. Throwing people out of this machine on the second day after the restoration of relations will make a very negative impression not only among our employees in America, but also on American public opinion and in the American press." Skvirskii had done a good job in very adverse conditions. He worked to establish and cultivate good relations with the press and indeed with American officials. He had handled the Fish Committee with aplomb. This job description was not for everyone and not easy to accomplish for an unofficial Soviet representative, especially in the wasps' nest of anti-Soviet officials at the State Department. Litvinov did not want Skvirskii and his colleagues cast out like old socks. Let Troianovskii *first* have a look around Washington to get the lay of the land before reorganizing everything, or throwing a monkey wrench into a well-functioning apparatus. The narkom was obviously irritated with Troianovskii's presumption and wanted to take him down a peg. He therefore asked that certain appointments to the Washington embassy be withdrawn and that Troianovskii be sent on his way without further delay. "If Troianovskii leaves Moscow on the 26th, he will not get the [next] American passenger steamship, as Bullitt advised him to do … [and] the following American *paquebot* leaves Cherbourg only on 25 January. There is no business reason why Troianovskii cannot leave on the 23rd or 24th to go with Bullitt on the American steamship leaving Le Havre on the 28th." Apparently the new polpred wanted to do some sightseeing in Paris or impress the local Soviet community as an important official in transit.[15] Something was amiss. Haste was of the first order but Troianovskii seemed in no rush. Important questions sometimes get fouled up in trifles and pride of place.

That last week in Moscow before Christmas took on the appearance of a farce. Litvinov was uncertain whether Troianovskii had any instructions or had even studied the NKID files on Soviet-US relations. So he advised Stalin, which the latter understood to be a complaint. Litvinov therefore wrote up instructions himself and sent them to Stalin for approval. These directives basically outlined the "gentleman's agreement" with Roosevelt (without parameters for negotiations), the possibility of a non-aggression pact, and other more routine issues. The instructions were at once approved by the Politburo.[16]

Litvinov *still* had trouble getting Troianovskii on his way. What was the problem? The Politburo intervened finally, and that did the trick. Troianovskii took the steamship SS *Washington* from Le Havre and made the crossing with Bullitt along with staff for the Washington embassy.[17] There is no record that the two ambassadors had any important discussions on board the *Washington*. Everyone arrived safely in New York on 6 January to be met by Skvirskii and other Soviet officials. A State Department official was also on hand. A special cutter took them, as well as Bullitt, his secretary, and his daughter from Ellis Island into the city, quite a different place than the border village of Negoreloe. Troianovskii presented his credentials to Roosevelt on 8 January. Under the circumstances, this was an accomplishment.

"Wheels within Wheels"

Even before Troianovskii's arrival in Washington problems began to crop up in obtaining credits for Soviet trade as part of the "gentleman's agreement." "I am beginning to feel like a second Ponzi," State Department official John Wiley wrote to Bullitt in mid-December. The reference was to the notorious Boston swindler Carlo Ponzi. What Wiley meant was that he was chasing after money, borrowing money from Peter to pay Paul in order to fund US-Soviet trade. The US government did not want to lend money directly to the USSR or act as a guarantor, and so sought other ways to make the "gentleman's agreement" work.

The first big idea, as readers will remember, was to turn over to the USSR German obligations held in the United States in exchange for Soviet long-term obligations. The German obligations would be used to pay Soviet bills coming due in Germany. Once this arrangement had been secured, a revolving credit would be set up to fund US-Soviet trade. Wiley opined that some sort of solution could thus be found without engaging the government apart from "a lot of moral responsibility." Wiley advised that there had been some changes in government personnel, which would not necessarily help to find solutions to fund trade with the USSR. "There are wheels within wheels and this new turn of events may be somewhat unfortunate." Wiley had the feeling that Secretary of the Treasury Morgenthau would "only be too delighted to find a convenient doorstep on which to deposit the Bolo baby." There was also a time element involved other than Congressional deliberations on the Johnson Debt Default bill. The Soviet government had invoices coming due in Germany in February, and there were "self-appointed impresarios" and US businesses looking to sign contracts with the Soviet government. So, time was pressing. Wiley thought a government-supported export-import bank was the best way forward and presented "no inseparable obstacles."[18] Could it be pulled off?

The original idea was to send Troianovskii to Washington as soon as possible to start negotiations to finalize the "gentleman's agreement" and to settle on a final sum of indebtedness: $75 million was the opening Soviet position, in exchange for a large long-term loan. But that did not happen. In fact, there were signs in early February of slippage in positions in Washington, which prompted Litvinov to write to Troianovskii reminding him of what the Soviet government deemed to be acceptable terms. Of course, that was not all; Litvinov wanted to know if Troianovskii had made any progress about a fleet visit to the USSR and on an agreement in principle for the sale of rails.[19] It seemed as though matters were off to a slow start.

On 20 February, long-time State Department Sovietphobe Robert Kelley handed Troianovskii US proposals to settle the "gentleman's agreement." The State Department was upping its demands on debts and interest rates and talking credits, not a long-term loan. It looked like a hostile bait-and-switch operation. Troianovskii noticed the changes, to which Kelley responded, that Bullitt had approved the proposals. What about the president? Troianovskii suggested that negotiations should take place in Moscow between Litvinov and Bullitt and not in Washington as originally intended. He met Roosevelt two days later and suggested that the debt negotiations were presenting "large difficulties" and that it would be better if they were conducted in Moscow. "I wanted to keep this file in my own hands," FDR replied, but he did not object to the change of venue.[20] It is not hard to see why; the negotiations looked to be turning into a dossier to pass on to someone else.

Negotiations with Bullitt

Bullitt was back in Moscow in early March 1934 and, of course, began to make the rounds. Litvinov was sick in hospital with the flu, so he met Ivan Anatol'evich Divil'kovskii, NKID secretary general, and Krestinskii, who he had not met officially during his visit to Moscow in December. He had some interesting tidbits to pass on to Divil'kovskii. Assistant Secretary of State R. Walton Moore, was made responsible for Russia policy in the State Department. Moore would read all incoming and outgoing telegrams from and to Moscow. Kelley, who headed the Eastern European Division, was a "minor clerk" (*malen'kii chinovnik*), a "bureaucrat," according to Bullitt, whose relations with the USSR would be defined by the line of the US government. He had pushed a hostile line, however, towards the USSR and had to be reined in. Also interesting, Bullitt thought Soviet-Japanese relations were easing. The Japanese were persuaded that, during Bullitt's first visit to Moscow, an agreement had been reached for US military help in the event of a clash of arms between the USSR and Japan. En route to Moscow, Bullitt had by chance met a Japanese minister in The Hague, who had previously been chargé d'affaires in Washington. He said that the Japanese foreign minister had declared that in so far as it depended on him and the present cabinet, there would be no war with the USSR, certainly not decided by some hotheaded Japanese colonel sitting on the banks of the Amur River.[21] Bullitt went back to see Divil'kovskii a few days later to ask when he would be able to meet Litvinov, who was quite ill. That would depend on the doctors, Divil'kovskii replied, adding that Krestinskii was handling day-to-day business, if the ambassador wished to see him. Bullitt replied that matters discussed in Washington with FDR could only be taken up with Litvinov.[22]

Bullitt saw Krestinskii on the following day to go over, more or less, the same issues discussed with Divil'kovskii. According to Krestinskii, it was a long conversation but with little substance. Bullitt passed on information he had picked up in Paris and Warsaw on his way to Moscow about Polish-German relations. The non-aggression pact had been signed only six weeks before and was causing "extraordinary" concern within the French government. There was talk in Paris, as readers will remember, of learning to get along without Poland. Beck had been in Moscow only a few weeks before. Rumour had it that there was a *written* agreement on several points, Polish disinterest in Anschluss; a Polish promise not to conclude any "pact" with Czechoslovakia; and if Japan attacked the USSR, Germany and Poland agreed to join the war from the west. Poland would help itself to Byelorussia, and Germany would take the Ukraine. Relations with Poland were of course a matter of importance to the NKID and a source of frustration. In Warsaw, Bullitt met with Beck and other Polish government officials. He had drawn the impression, according to Krestinskii, that Germany and Poland had *not* signed written or made verbal agreements along the lines circulating in Paris, but that there had "probably" been an "exchange of opinions."[23] This would have been nothing new to Krestinskii who offered no comments.

Bullitt finally met a convalescing Litvinov on the following day, 9 March. It was their first meeting. From Litvinov's point of view, that meeting produced no concrete results. On Japan, Bullitt repeated what he had said earlier, that he did not think there was any danger of the Japanese picking a fight. Litvinov asked about his idea of a non-aggression pact. Bullitt's reply was evasive and Litvinov concluded that the US government would take no initiative in this regard. On the sale of rails to the USSR, Bullitt said it would have to wait for the setting up of new a bank along the lines suggested by Wiley. From there the discussion passed to the "gentleman's agreement." Bullitt was not aware of Kelley's proposals to Troianovskii in Washington. Litvinov, therefore, gave him a copy to read. Obviously, it looked like sabotage. The narkom rhymed off the problems. The Soviet government did not want any agreement that could serve as a precedent for other governments to come asking for similar settlements. That was why there was the focus on the Kerenskii debt, which excluded any reference to debts of the tsar. Then there was the question of the amount of the debt; Litvinov had proposed $75 million and, at the limit, $100 million. The State Department wanted $150 million. The loan to the Kerenskii government had largely gone to finance the White Guard armies, and the USSR felt no obligation to pay one cent, as Litvinov put it, on account of those debts. The Kelley document spoke about an indebtedness in gold dollars, but Litvinov had only agreed to a debt denominated in paper dollars on which the Soviet government was now expected to pay interest. It was too much for Litvinov, but he was not finished with an enumeration of Kelley's legerdemain. The idea of a "loan" to the USSR had now become commercial credits. "On this we cannot agree," Litvinov said. Essentially, the State Department was proposing to tax Soviet exports. This was not profitable for either side, and it made trade with the United States uncompetitive.[24] Were US-Soviet relations reduced to a business deal profiting the United States, or were they to be motivated by the recognition of common enemies and important common security interests?

Bullitt went again to see Litvinov, still in hospital, to discuss the issues in question. On the main issue, there was no movement at all. Litvinov reported that Bullitt replied that if there were no resolution, the Johnson Act would apply and all US-Soviet trade based on credit would stop.[25] Bullitt telegraphed his record of the conversation to Hull. He told Litvinov no loan was on the table. It was credit through the Export-Import Bank, established in early February, or nothing. "I then expressed the hope that in the absence of trade our relations might nevertheless remain friendly. Litvinov answered 'We could remain on friendly terms with the United States without mutual trade but I fear that the United States would not remain on friendly terms with the Soviet Union." In Litvinov's version of the conversation, Bullitt said friendly relations might continue without trade, *but* that "such a situation would provoke disappointment in many circles." Litvinov replied that friendly relations could continue without trade, but he suggested separating trade from the settlement of debts. Bullitt recommended "that the Johnson bill be passed as soon as possible and that the Department should adopt a firm attitude with Troyanovsky and bring to his attention the revulsion of feeling which would be likely to take place in the United States if the Soviet should so soon after recognition fail to continue the policy of cooperation between our two countries." Wait a minute; that is not what Litvinov said. On the contrary, he said he would take the matter up with Stalin when he was released from hospital. "Previous negotiations with Litvinov have led me to observe," so Bullitt concluded, "that his decisive negotiations are often followed by acquiescence and I do not consider the present problem insoluble."[26]

As promised, Litvinov followed up with a counterproposal approved by the Politburo, rejecting the Kelley propositions, but proposing that the US Export-Import Bank put at the disposition of the USSR $150–200 million in credit for twenty years at 7 per cent interest per annum. This was Litvinov's original proposal. Three per cent would go to pay off the Kerenskii debt of $75 to $100 million. The $100 million represented an important Soviet concession, considering how tight-fisted Stalin was. Litvinov himself was no rube. The sum of credits should be two times the sum of indebtedness.[27]

At the same time, the NKID decided to send Rubinin, whom readers will remember from the Metro-Vickers affair, to get the lay of the land in Washington and to brief Troianovskii on Soviet policy. This seemed to indicate that the NKID was still looking for a way forward. Bullitt liked Rubinin and thought his visit might prove helpful. As he put it to Assistant Secretary of State Moore, "Mr. Rubinin is in a position to be enormously helpful or harmful to us here, and I trust that you will receive him with more than the usual courtesies. He is a delightful young fellow. His French is perfect and he has a working knowledge of English."[28] Bullitt eventually obtained more information on Rubinin's purposes in Washington. "I am informed unofficially but I think reliably that Troyanovsky has reported that he is in a helpless position being unable to successfully interpret the assurances which Litvinov gave in Washington or to contest the position taken by the Department."[29]

In the meantime, on 8 April, Bullitt met Litvinov again. The Soviet counteroffer was unacceptable, and if the USSR did not accept the original State

Department proposal (Kelley's) the Johnson Act would apply. The Soviet compromise was thus for naught. Litvinov's temper began to fray. The narkom accused the State Department of blackmail, as it surely was. Bullitt suggested the export of large supplies of Soviet platinum for example to soften the position of the State Department. He could not say if it would cause the State Department to change its position, but it might "sweeten the pill." Litvinov was unimpressed. The Export-Import Bank was exempted from the Johnson Act. On whose "unfortunate advice," Litvinov asked, "was it decided to tie the hands of the bank?" He answered his own question:

> Such advice could be given only by someone completely unversed in our positions and in the history of our relations with the outside world. If he thought this advice frightens us and pressures us, in order to force us in one way or another to settle the old debts, then he can expect a bitter disappointment. Such pressure on us came from all sides in the course of a decade from European countries and they had to be persuaded of the ineffectiveness of such means and rejection of them.

The Soviet Union was trading with other countries with larger claims than the United States, without any conditions. The State Department attempt to tax Soviet orders would not succeed. Forget it. We will trade with other countries, said Litvinov, if the United States wants to tax our business. That was laying it on the line. "Bullitt was very confused," Litvinov wrote in his journal, "for he clearly came to check the impression of the measures of intimidation, of which he himself is the author." So that is why the narkom put his question about the instigator of the State Department measures. He wanted to flush out Bullitt. "A firm tone," Litvinov concluded, would be necessary in the future.[30] Bullitt wanted to play hard ball; Litvinov also knew how to play that game.

Bullitt also reported on the meeting with Litvinov. The US was playing hardball, all right. Bullitt rejected the Soviet proposal outright, refusing even to consider it. "I had a completely unsatisfactory discussion with Litvinov this afternoon. He was angry and adamant." The narkom would not take the Kelley draft "as a basis for discussion either now or hereafter." It was an impasse. Bullitt tried to wheedle more Soviet concessions, in effect encouraging the Soviet government to bid up its own proposals without any movement from the US side. Bullitt ought to have known, if he knew anything at all, that the Soviet side would never fall into that trap – not under Chicherin and not under Litvinov. "He [Litvinov] said that he had said his last word and made his maximum offer … and so far as he was concerned the matter was closed." There was a heated exchange of accusations. Clearly the American side was falling into the same strategy as the French in 1926–7. It did not work then and it would not work now, as Litvinov said in so many words. And the result would be that instead of obtaining the half loaf, the US would get no loaf at all.

When Bullitt raised the threat of cutting off US-Soviet trade, per the Johnson Act, Litvinov shrugged and waved him off. "He said that he was fully aware of this and was not disturbed. He added that the Johnson bill presumably applied to England, France and Italy, as well as the Soviet Union and said 'we shall be in very good company.'" Litvinov raised a good question in effect: why was the United States indulging in hard ball with the USSR, something it would not dream of doing with its former western allies? This was a good question. The State Department had never warmed to FDR's policy of recognition and this was its way of sabotaging the "gentleman's agreement" and the US-Soviet rapprochement. In view of the rising danger of war provoked by Japan and Nazi Germany, the State Department was thus pursuing the policy of shooting oneself in the foot. The United States could bully Central American states or overthrow their governments if bullying did not work, but that policy would not work against the USSR. It had already been tried. Foreign intervention had failed, and bullying had not worked when the Soviet government was weak, it would certainly not work when the USSR was stronger. As a member of the US elite, Bullitt thought he knew better. He was against further discussions with Litvinov "until he has had time to be impressed by an attitude of complete negation on our part."[31] So, it would be no loaf at all.

The United States was trying to pressure the Soviet government, Litvinov advised Troianovskii. The US thinks that we were so interested in trade that threatening to cut it off was the sole means of pressure to bring us around. The Johnson Act was their weapon of choice. Even in Washington, Bullitt used it as a cudgel. Litvinov explained:

> There is no doubt that Bullitt was always a proponent of the establishment of relations and played not a little positive role in this business, but at the same time, he set out to get as much out of us as possible in favour of America, and so even in my negotiations with the president, he played a negative role, sharpening the controversial issues and taking a more irreconcilable position than Roosevelt. He does this, obviously, either in order to divert reproaches of excessive Sovietophilia, or to prove to the State Department and to Roosevelt that, despite his Sovietophilia, or even thanks to it, he is able firmly to protect American interests. We must defeat Bullitt's attempts at blackmail, and this we can only do with self-control and serenity. We have to demonstrate that the cessation of trade with America does not produce the effect on us expected by Bullitt, that it does not hit us, but only hits Americans interested in trade.

Litvinov made clear that he was not proposing a boycott of US trade. On the contrary, if the Amtorg Trading Corporation could negotiate advantageous contracts with US firms, it should go ahead and do so. However, if the United States obstructed trade, the USSR could live without it. Go see Roosevelt, Litvinov instructed, since he could not, and try to bring him around to our positions.[32] Krestinskii also wrote to Troianovskii at the same time on more day-to-day issues about the acquisition of rubles, housing for American embassy staff, and so on. In these cases, the Soviet government tried in so far as possible to meet the Americans half way.[33] There was thus some movement in Soviet policy, but none on the US side.

End of the Honeymoon

Bullitt did not see it that way. Soon after the meeting on 8 April with Litvinov, he wrote to Roosevelt to warn him that things had turned sour:

> The honeymoon atmosphere had evaporated completely before I arrived. As Wiley says, "The Japanese have let us down badly." The Russians are convinced that Japan will not attack this spring or summer and, as they no longer feel that they need our immediate help, their underlying hostility to all capitalist countries now shows through the veneer of intimate friendship. We shall have to deal with them according to Claudel's formula of the donkey, the carrot, and the club.

Had Litvinov seen this letter, he would have replied, as he did on 8 April that the USSR was not a donkey and that the stick would not work on it. As for the "carrots," let's see it. With FDR, Bullitt brought up "misunderstandings" (his usage), on various topics, but including "extra interest on credits." The Soviet reaction to the Kelley proposals was predictable, but no one seemed to get it on the American side. "The only effective way of dealing with this general attitude, I believe," Bullitt continued, "is to maintain the friendliest possible personal relations with the Russians but to let them know clearly that if they are unwilling to move forward and take the carrot they will receive the club on the behind." This was a formula for certain failure. "The next time I discuss the payment of debts and claims with Litvinov, I shall allow him to derive the impression that if the Soviet Union does not wish to use the facilities of the Export-Import Bank the Japanese Government will be eager to use the facilities of the Bank to finance large purchases from certain American heavy industries."[34]

Would Roosevelt agree? Bullitt missed the point completely and misrepresented the problem. Litvinov denounced the Kelley propositions but proposed a compromise position. The US side stuck with its opening proposal. This position would not fly in Moscow and had nothing to do with "hostility to all capitalist countries." FDR did not take matters too seriously: "I get a lot of chuckles out of the scraps that you and Litvinov have. Keep up the good work!"[35] Maybe he should have.

Hull fully supported Bullitt's position and drew the impression that Litvinov was "repudiating" his agreements with Roosevelt. If a trade agreement fell through, Hull advised Bullitt, the Japanese might be encouraged. "It would seem that Litvinov should appreciate the necessity of doing everything possible to retain the advantage he obtained by recognition and the prospect of active trade."[36] Hull appeared to think that the United States was doing the USSR a favour and that the US government would derive no benefit from better US-Soviet relations. Litvinov had thus correctly understood the US negotiating position; Hull's views, and those of Bullitt, were formulas for failure. That was not a problem for the State Department. On 16 April, Troianovskii met Hull to explain the Soviet position on the debt. Litvinov had not repudiated any agreement with Roosevelt, he said. Hull seemed to back up a little admitting there had been a misunderstanding in the State Department.[37]

The US-Soviet row on a debts settlement and other issues concerning the US diplomatic establishment in Russia had nothing to do with the more important questions of international security. A week after Litvinov sent his instructions to Troianovskii, these issues came to the fore again, thanks to Japanese belligerence in China. On 17 April, the Japanese foreign ministry issued a statement to the effect that relations between Japan and China were the business only of those two countries and no one else. In other words, the US and the USSR should butt out. In Moscow, Bullitt went to see Litvinov. This time there were no arguments. Bullitt opined that the Japanese statement was a declaration of a protectorate over all of China. Litvinov agreed. "This was to be expected," he said, "in as much as Japan had not met up to now any opposition to its aggressive plans." Bullitt asked what could be done. That question was less a concern to the USSR, Litvinov replied, since it has no capital investments there or military obligations. The only action likely to draw Japanese attention would be a collective declaration of all the Pacific Basin powers. Bullitt had his doubts and suggested that Japan would not have made such a démarche without prior agreement from Britain. Litvinov did not think so.[38]

"Soviet reaction to Japan's announcement in regard to China," Bullitt cabled to Hull, "is one of unalloyed delight. The position of the Soviet Union is regarded as greatly improved since it is considered likely that the United States and Great Britain now will have to oppose Japan openly whereas the Soviet Union will be able to remain discreetly in the background." According to Bullitt, Litvinov was in a good mood, "grinning broadly."

"Perhaps your Government," this was Bullitt reporting Litvinov's words, "will realize now that there is no limit to which Japan will not go. Any concession whatever leads merely to further demands. This is equivalent to proclamation of a protectorate over China." Wait a minute, didn't Bullitt say that, according to Litvinov's record of the conversation? It was often thus in Soviet and Western records of conversations. It was best to let the other person speak of sensitive issues.

Bullitt asked Litvinov why a joint declaration should not come from the League of Nations.

"The League would take no action," Litvinov replied.

Would "words be of any use," Bullitt asked, "unless we were ready to back them up by acts which none of us were anxious to perform?"

"Thus far Japan had only used words," Litvinov observed, "and that at the moment words were a fitting reply."[39]

Unfortunately, for the "gentleman's agreement," the Japanese declaration was a flash in the pan. The US ambassador in Poland, John Cudahy, explained the position to polpred Davtian. In the United States there was no leader then capable of leading the United States into war. Roosevelt was "very influential," but he was beset with "too many large internal difficulties." Americans, Cudahy said, were too "provincial" and not easily focused on larger issues.[40]

So, it was back to the dead-end debt-credit negotiations. Troianovskii confirmed Cudahy's view that FDR was wavering on the Soviet file because of internal difficulties. The Republicans were ready to attack him from all sides. The president seemed to be losing momentum. He could not, therefore, make any decisive move towards the USSR. The fate of Soviet relations with the United States, Troianovskii noted, was tied to the fate of Roosevelt. Troianovskii recommended patience, which might have irritated Litvinov, because US businessmen wanted to trade with the USSR and would put pressure not on the USSR but on the US government to loosen up the Johnson Act and lift the prohibition on the Export-Import Bank. Therefore, the situation was not hopeless and negotiations were still possible.[41]

Troianovskii was being too optimistic, but he thought he could pull off a deal, if only Litvinov would let him. Moore went to see Roosevelt to secure a negotiating position. Troianovskii speculated that there might be differences between the president and the State Department. If there were, Moore straightened them out. FDR approved Bullitt's handling of negotiations with Litvinov. If the Soviet side offered further concessions, then FDR might also "indicate some modifications." That was one thing. The other was that Troianovskii wished to meet the president without Rubinin.[42] Ah yes, Rubinin was sent to Washington to help Troianovskii who did not seem to want it. What was going on? Rubinin went back to Moscow without having influenced the conduct of negotiations in Washington.

Troianovskii finally did meet the president along with Hull and Moore on 30 April. The meeting was not a great success. Hull and Moore must have been along to make sure FDR did not stray from the agreed upon course laid out earlier by Moore, and that is the way it turned out. There were no breakthroughs and Roosevelt indicated that he preferred negotiations to continue in Moscow. Troianovskii thought he might have more success taking the lead in Washington, but Roosevelt seemed to brush off that idea.[43]

Hull drafted a record of the meeting with Troianovskii. It confirmed the Soviet account and notably that Roosevelt wanted negotiations to be conducted in Moscow. Hull seemed to suggest however that Troianovskii might be easier to handle even if a proposal made in Washington would have to pass through Moscow to both Litvinov and Bullitt.[44]

Litvinov was not happy with the results of this meeting. "Unfortunately, in conversation with Roosevelt, you did not stick to instructions …" There were more and more indications that Litvinov and Troianovksii did not see eye to eye. Troianovskii had not even broached the subject of a loan, had not raised the question of figures, or long term credits as Litvinov had proposed to Bullitt. For the narkom, the meeting was a bust. "We are not going to escape this dead-end until the State Department gives Bullitt new instructions on the central points of disagreement. Explain this immediately to the State Department." You are focusing on details, Litvinov concluded, missing what is most important.[45]

On 9 May, Bullitt saw Litvinov again to discuss various issues, but not the main question of debts and credit. As Bullitt got up to leave, Litvinov mentioned that he had received a telegram from Troianovskii, indicating that the State Department had apparently sent him (Bullitt) further instructions. Litvinov described conversations with Roosevelt and Moore. Bullitt expressed surprise saying that he had only received a telegram from Washington indicating that Litvinov wanted to see him. At that point they both laughed at seeming to need mediation from Washington to get over the rough spots in their relations. A good laugh allowed them to have a constructive conversation about the main points of disagreement, much as Litvinov had signalled to Troianovskii. He even mentioned Troianovskii's omissions in his discussion with Roosevelt. After a long discussion, Bullitt conceded that Litvinov's proposals and the sweetener of an additional $25 million for the Kerenskii debt might offer a way out of the impasse.[46] Nevertheless, the priorities, as Litvinov pointed out, were all wrong. Twenty-five million dollars was a trifle when Europe and Asia looked to be on the point of exploding.

There were some minor gestures on each side to try to keep relations from blowing up. Litvinov sent a collection of Soviet stamps to FDR, who was a stamp collector, and the president agreed to receive Litvinov's son on a visit to Washington. Bullitt saw Litvinov again three days later. Bullitt seemed a little less adamant than usual having cabled Washington for clarifications on the State Department's position. He was still waiting for a reply. The meeting was without rancour or argument, but rather an elucidation of each side's position. Litvinov indicated that he was leaving Moscow for Geneva and that Krestinskii along with Rubinin, who was back in Moscow, would carry on discussions.[47] "Litvinov was most amiable throughout our conversation," Bullitt reported, "I derive the impression that the absence of his usual belligerency was due in part to the desire of the Soviet Government to reach agreement and the conviction that we are adamant, but in larger measure to the fact that he was about to be absolved from the necessity of making concessions personally."[48]

On 16 May, Bullitt met Krestinskii and Rubinin. The meeting did not advance negotiations. Bullitt gave Krestinskii a copy of the original State Department proposal, Kelley's, which meant there had been no movement in the US position although there had been on the Soviet side. Krestinskii refused to discuss it, or to accept it as the basis of discussion. Bullitt replied that he only wanted to give him a history of the negotiations. Krestinskii stated that he was fully aware of the course of negotiations, and then he asked if there had been any new ideas from Washington. Nothing new, was Bullitt's reply. In other words, the Soviet side had made two important concessions, which were the additional $25 million of indebtedness and the acceptance of the Export-Import Bank as the intermediary to provide credits (a loan, in other words) to the Soviet government to buy US goods. Bullitt then suggested that negotiations be shifted to Washington. Krestinskii referred to Roosevelt's own view of the matter, and opined that they should continue in Moscow. It appears that the State Department officials were beginning to form the view that they might get further with Troianovskii than with Litvinov. Bullitt considered Litvinov to be obdurate, but it was the Soviet side that made concessions and the US side that made none. There then occurred an exchange of views of their respective positions that led nowhere. Krestinskii said that the US proposals were unacceptable, which was Litvinov's position all along. Essentially what Krestinskii said was that the Soviet Union conducted trade in its own interests and not the interests of others. That was the rub, since it was just what the State Department did not wish to concede. If it kept its thumb on Soviet trade, it could control prices, interest rates, and money paid on account to the Kerenskii debt. Krestinskii concluded by saying that the State Department should accept the Soviet offer, which represented concessions to the US position. Bullitt asked if this was the last word from the Soviet government, and Krestinskii replied that it was and that he, Bullitt, should advise Roosevelt. With that the meeting ended. Krestinskii added to his record of the conversation, that although he gave no ground, the conversation had been conducted in a friendly manner.[49]

Bullitt discovered that Krestinskii could be just as tough as Litvinov. He described the meeting as "fruitless." Krestinskii's offer was essentially this: let the Export-Import Bank discount Amtorg orders by 100 per cent, thus in effect making a loan of $200 million to the USSR, "and we," said Krestinskii, "will pay $100 million on indebtedness and the matter will be settled. We will make no agreement unless it places us in a position to buy for cash and not on credit." Bullitt replied that such a proposal would not be acceptable in Washington, and it would be "a waste of time" to continue conversations. Bullitt suggested that the State Department should prepare a document with its minimum position to be handed to Troianovskii, "so that both governments might cease to cherish illusions." Krestinskii replied that "he preferred infinitely to continue conversations here." Such statements do not appear in Krestinskii's record. "Rubinin

… for an hour tried to persuade me to recommend acceptance of the [Soviet] proposal." Bullitt replied that this was "impossible."[50]

Rubinin made a record of the conversation with Bullitt, which covered several topics. When they finally got around to talking about debts and credits, Rubinin did try to persuade Bullitt that it was in US interests to accept the Soviet proposal because it would provide orders for US companies. Of course, it would. Rubinin also allowed himself a personal comment. He said to Bullitt that he had before him a "very important task." He "was writing himself into the history of Soviet-American relations as the active and courageous fighter for the normalization of these relations." This was laying it on pretty thick, but there was more. The normal sort of career diplomat followed instructions from his government, mechanically delivered messages, and so on. "The task of a political figure such as Bullitt" was to interpret the public opinion of the government to which he was accredited. This was, Rubinin conceded, a tough job in Washington where everyone was not always ready to understand Soviet points of view or to contribute to the resolution of issues. Bullitt became wary and asked Rubinin if he shared the view of some of his colleagues about the hostility of Kelley to the USSR. Rubinin offered an evasive reply. Bullitt then commented that while Roosevelt was in power, he would work for Roosevelt. Afterward, beyond that he had not given it much thought. Bullitt added that one could not ignore US public opinion but, from Moscow, it was hard to judge the mood of US public opinion and that he would ask the president for detailed proposals to present to the NKID. Rubinin then concluded his report with this comment:

> Bullitt gave me the impression of great confusion. It is not at all obvious that he is seriously engaged in his work or studying the USSR. The only thing he does with zeal is to learn the Russian language. He seems determined to fulfill his commitment to Roosevelt, to learn Russian in three or six months. Judging by his own words and the stories of some of his comrades, he leads a rather absurd, idle way of life, and does not cultivate ties even with those [Soviet] comrades whom he has long known … One cannot see if he is interested in any serious issues. This is the manifest result of the almost fifteen-year life of *bonvivantism*, in which Bullitt immersed himself after his break with Wilson [in 1919].[51]

What an unexpected comment. Rubinin was someone Bullitt liked and respected; he was a "delightful young fellow." And Rubinin seems to have gotten along well with the ambassador, well enough to speak with him in rather personal ways. This was not what one might expect from the usual clichéd characterizations of relations between Soviet and Western counterparts. Readers will notice other such relationships elsewhere as this narrative unfolds.

The State Department approved Bullitt's rejection of Krestinskii's proposals: it was "practically … an unconditional loan of two hundred million dollars."

Right, it was in effect a loan, the $200 million would be paid back in full with interest, with the difference above market rates used to pay off $100 million of the Kerenskii debt. Hence, at the end of the period of twenty years, the Export-Import Bank would have its money back *with* interest, *plus* interest to pay off the Kerenskii debt. What could be wrong with that? It was a win-win situation, and US manufacturers would have $200 million in new business, and US workers would have new jobs. This was basically Rubinin's line to Bullitt. Here was the problem: "Since all credit transactions would be placed under the control of Amtorg with power to decide terms, class of goods purchased, and choice of producers, it would to a large extent place [US] business at the will of Amtorg, and the Export-Import Bank would really pass out of the picture."[52] But hold on, since the USSR was the buyer, didn't Amtorg decide what goods it wanted and what prices in cash it wanted to pay? According to the State Department, the answer was no, the Export-Import Bank would have a say in these matters. It wanted to keep a thumb on the flow of US-Soviet trade, to control it in effect. Tax it, Litvinov said. This was exactly the reason, among others, why the NKID refused the US proposal.

Negotiations Going Nowhere

The meeting with Krestinskii put a halt to discussions, which had reached an impasse. At the beginning of June, Hull asked Bullitt whether the negotiations should be transferred to Washington. "From what he says, Troyanovsky realizes importance of action since he is fully informed of many credit transactions of probable advantage to both countries which await agreement on debts being reached."[53] Hull drew an immediate reply from Moscow. Bullitt had a scheduled meeting with Krestinskii, Litvinov was still in Geneva. "Until I can report Krestinskii's views I believe that it would be inadvisable for the Department to negotiate with Troyanovsky who may or may not represent the point of view of his Government."[54] So, did Troianovskii think he could do better than his bosses in Moscow? That remained to be seen.

Krestinskii made a record of his meeting with Bullitt on 9 June. There was a discussion of day-to-day issues about the organization of the consulate general in Moscow and the leasing of the embassy building, and then they turned to the debt-credit negotiations, "which, according to the press," said Bullitt, "either are being conducted, or they are not being conducted at all." A curious way of putting a question to Krestinskii, but what Bullitt wanted to know was whether they should agree that both sides had reached the point where they would not move from irreconcilable positions and that they should therefore agree to end discussions, or whether they could move to concrete negotiations about what products to buy, at what price, and with what credit arrangements. If agreement could be reached on the basis of a "procurement program," it might be a way out of the dead-end. "I replied to Bullitt, that the compromise which he offered is the actual implementation of their position." It was to impose a tax on Soviet procurement in the United States in favour of the US government and in favour of US creditors. That was not an improvement over what had previously been discussed, but worse.

Then they turned to a discussion of what the "gentleman's agreement" was supposed to mean, not the first time they had gone over that issue. Essentially, Krestinskii said that the Soviet government had made concessions, which was true, and that it would not make any more. "All the same, I cannot understand," Krestinskii said, "the stubbornness which the American government manifests on this question, the material significance of which for the American government is nothing." Exactly. Bullitt agreed that the sums in question were derisory in comparison with British and French debts, but it was as he always said a question of "public opinion." And then Bullitt railed against the British, to which Krestinskii and Rubinin, who was also present, must have been amused spectators. The meeting led nowhere and Bullitt did not apparently raise the question of a change of venue for continued negotiations.[55]

Bullitt took up the conversation again with his favourite NKID clerk, Rubinin, five days later, on 14 June, after a lunch with Krestinskii. The two sides battled but could still sit down to a meal together.

"We had such hopes for an improvement of relations," Bullitt said, "but we have gotten nowhere."

"For this, you yourselves are completely responsible," Rubinin said. That was being blunt.

"Who? Me personally?" Bullitt replied.

"I said," Rubinin wrote in his journal, "that I was not concerned now with the personal role of Bullitt himself but in general with the American line of conduct, very hard to understand with regard to the USSR."

Rubinin raised the issue that Krestinskii had broached at their last meeting, that is, the "complete insignificance" of the disputed sum of money in comparison with the billions of dollars which the US government was spending to deal with the economic depression. Why had the American government turned this issue into a boulder lying across the road of better Soviet-American relations?

Rubinin recorded a surprising response. "Bullitt said that perhaps he himself bears a significant share of the responsibility for creating the impasse; he should have at the time brought more clarity to the issue of debt and credit. He now thinks day and night about how to get out of this situation. He can't think of anything except what he last suggested to Krestinskii." Bullitt then repeated more or less his idea about putting before the president a pragmatic proposal: repayment of so much debt for so much credit under such-and-such terms for the purchase of such-and-such US goods. Rubinin responded that he did not see how that formula would work without some agreement on basic principles.

When it came down to it, although Rubinin did not say it, but Krestinskii had, the USSR wanted a long-term loan one way or another to pay cash for goods, which it found useful for Soviet economic development without being overseen by the United States. In exchange, the USSR was willing to cover $100 million of the Kerenskii debt. What the United States did with that money was no concern of the Soviet government. Bullitt retreated a little, saying the idea was his own, and he did not know whether it would fly in Washington. In the United States, when one talked about credit for foreign governments, it raised a hue and cry. You had to put it in terms of US goods purchased. Cotton, for example, to guarantee the support of a senator from the South, and so much copper to guarantee the support of a senator from the North. Then you had to talk about railway equipment for Pennsylvania and Ohio. That was how to demonstrate the practical value of business with the USSR and how to present it to the president.[56]

The trouble was that Bullitt spoke one way with Krestinskii and Rubinin, and another way with the State Department. "I am under constant pressure," Bullitt advised Hull, "from American correspondents for information regarding negotiations with the Soviet Government particularly with respect to debt settlement. Thus far I have consistently maintained that no negotiations worthy of the name were being conducted here *as the Soviet Government had refused to accept any basis for negotiations*" [italics added]."[57] As readers will immediately understand, the latter part of the sentence is untrue. At least Bullitt, or his office, asked for instructions about what line, his or another, he should take in Moscow. Hull's reply is interesting. "American businessmen" were making "constant inquiries" as to the prospects for success of the Moscow negotiations. "We have not interpreted temporary cessation as meaning abandonment." And there was this comment: "We have no thought of taking up matters with Troyanovsky until we hear from you."[58]

Litvinov was back in Moscow and Bullitt went to see him to broach his idea about a pragmatic settlement, as he had explained it to Krestinskii and Rubinin. Litvinov listened politely. He then responded that if Washington was refusing long-term credit, on the basis of Soviet counterproposals, then Roosevelt was backing away from the "gentleman's agreement." Litvinov even read out to Bullitt the relevant part of the text of the agreement to underline his point. The Soviet Union could live without a debts settlement; that was a US, not a Soviet idea. The USSR was ready to maintain the best possible relations with the United States without a debts settlement. "I do not see so tragically as Bullitt the possibility of new outbreaks of anti-Soviet agitation on the basis of non-payment of old debts, when with the exception of Finland, not one European government is paying debts far more binding and more indisputable than the Kerenskii debt and when Germany has stopped payment even of Dawes and Young obligations." However, Litvinov kept the door open a little and said to Bullitt that he was disposed to ask Gosplan (the State Planning Committee), for general ideas about what products it might wish to purchase with the $200 million credit. In exchange, Litvinov asked Bullitt, in order not to waste Gosplan's time, to put his idea to Washington for approval. Bullitt agreed, but thought it would be better if the request came from Troianovskii. Litvinov nodded approval with the stipulation that "I would refer to his initiative. Blushing a little, Bullitt said that he would not be opposed to this." Litvinov followed up with a briefing note to Stalin, asking for consent for his idea, in order to "to get negotiations moving."[59]

Moving Negotiations to Washington

Troianovskii took up Bullitt's idea in Washington with Moore, but perhaps not exactly, for he wrote of Bullitt's idea to publish the Soviet procurement plan. Moore *rejected* this idea, thinking it could cause "unnecessary controversy" and hinder negotiations. This was likely because US business elements would have pressured the State Department to come to terms with the USSR. Then, Moore suggested negotiations in Washington. This suited Troianovskii who had been waiting for his chance and he recommended acceptance to Litvinov: "I think that we must focus not on what we hope for, but on what is now possible and at the same time profitable for us." This was not a line likely to please his boss. Troianovskii suggested some numbers, but accepted the State Department's notion of revolving commercial credits through the Export-Import Bank and private firms, which the Soviet government had previously opposed.[60] Moore made his own record of this conversation. Troianovskii "concurred in my opinion," Moore wrote, "that, should he and I take up the negotiations here, we ought to find no great difficulty in reaching a tentative agreement."[61]

When Litvinov read Troianovskii's telegram, he must have blown a fuse because it would signal abandonment of his negotiating position. "Troianovskii is in fact suggesting that we agree with the State Department," Litvinov explained to Stalin, "taking on himself the obligation to reimburse the Kerenskii debt without receiving a loan or long-term credit. Revolving [commercial] credits are not long-term credits." This is what Moore also appeared to believe. The USSR obtained more or less the same commercial credits in other countries, but if the US were to accept Troianovskii's proposal, other countries might demand the US precedent. Litvinov did not oppose shifting the negotiations to Washington, but only on the basis of Bullitt's previous suggestion.[62]

Having cleared the way with Stalin, Litvinov rounded on Troianovskii. Neither Bullitt nor Litvinov had proposed the *publication* of a Soviet procurement plan. If you inattentively read my instructions, Litvinov continued, you need "immediately" to inform Moore. No ambassador would like to receive such a reprimand, but Litvinov was only getting started. "Your suggestion *instantsia* [i.e., Stalin] has categorically rejected, as a complete capitulation." Litvinov authorized negotiations in Washington based on Soviet proposals and concessions and not on the State Department's terms. "Washington has not shifted from its initial position, which you now support." Troianovskii could discuss orders and commercial credits, but not linked to the reimbursement of old debts.[63]

The Clash between Litvinov and Troianovskii

You can sense from the earlier correspondence that Litvinov and Troianovskii did not get along well. Now the tensions broke out into the open. "I remember the directives that in negotiations here," Troianovskii fired back at Litvinov, "we need to obtain our conditions, but I do not remember it in such a way that without accepting our conditions, negotiations in Washington are impossible. I certainly do not intend to argue against the decision [in Moscow], I felt compelled to offer my opinion based on the substance of the position of Bullitt and the State Department, which is to avoid fixing the loan terms and any significant lengthening of them beyond Amtorg's established practice." Boom, boom. It was like an exchange of artillery fire. Troianovskii gave as good as he got in terms of sarcasm. Basically, what he was saying was that if Moscow wanted an agreement with Washington, it would be on State Department terms with adjustments here and there. What Troianovskii did not seem to understand was that if Moscow was going to pay $100 million of the Kerenskii debt, it wanted something big in return well beyond the usual commercial credits available to it without paying anything on old debts, a tax Litvinov called it, on trade in the United States. Troianovskii replied that what Moscow wanted for its money was impossible and what he proposed to try to get was better than nothing. Therein lay the difference between Litvinov and Troianovskii. Litvinov had already told Bullitt that the USSR would like good relations with the United States even without a debts-credit agreement. This statement indicated what was in Litvinov's mind. Nor would he have trouble persuading Stalin to agree to this position. The old *kulak* was never much disposed to pay on the old debts except for *very* large Soviet advantages. Troianovskii explained the situation this way:

> The president is funking out, and we can't expect much flexibility from him before the November [mid-term] elections. The danger is that the situation may worsen after the elections. The very absence of a debt agreement will be used against us by our enemies. Politically, an agreement must be reached. Commercially, on average, credits of seven to eight years are profitable for us. In the absence of agreement or delays (which we should expect) we will have to buy for cash or on short-term credits. $200 million, when billions are thrown around, is not so large a sum that it would tempt us to make big concessions. My "capitulationist" position may be completely unattainable in the future.[64]

The row with Troianovskii was far from over. It was 21 July, two weeks after Litvinov and Krestinskii had written their latest dispatches. Litvinov wrote again to Stalin to complain that Troianovskii had proposed a confusing idea about mutual renunciation of claims and still did not seem to understand his instructions. I asked for clarifications, Litvinov said, but had received a reply that "still did not introduce any clarity to the question." Troianovskii was supposed to resume negotiations with the State Department, but Bullitt had complained that no negotiations were underway and that Troianovskii had "contented himself with random conversations at lunch with Moore." What was going on? Litvinov had not had a row like this since 1924 when he clashed with the councillor in Paris, Aleksandr G. Shliapnikov.[65] "I understood this [Bullitt's complaint] as a remark from the American side about a renewal of negotiations and I immediately sent instructions to go to the State Department to clarify if it had any new instructions … Instead of carrying out the instructions, Troianovskii sends some confused new proposals." Litvinov asked for input.[66]

Troianovskii had only been in Washington since January so you might think he would let matters rest with the narkom. He did not do that, however; in fact, he wrote to Stalin, without sending a carbon copy to Litvinov, asking to be recalled. In the circumstances, that was throwing down the gauntlet. It was open war. Troianovskii complained about trifles, Litvinov's pinprick about Bullitt's suggestion for a procurement plan, but then about negotiations being conducted in both Moscow and Washington. Then, it was Litvinov's further jab that Troianovskii was simply proposing the same ideas as the State Department. In other words, he was throwing in the towel. "This is a very serious accusation," Troianovskii wrote. Yes, it was, but Troianovskii denied doing any such thing. I cannot let these accusations pass, said the polpred. There followed a barrage of counterfire. "I know that this individual [the narkom, his boss] is angry with me to the last extremity because the TsK [Central Committee] did not agree with him on the matter of appointments for the embassy and consulate in America. His malice he now takes out on me in the TsK. He has enough pettiness to go as far as making accusations like the one above. But the trouble is that in this situation, when this person is blazing with anger, my work here cannot be productive." Troianovskii did not stop there: he accused Litvinov of picking on him and looking for pretexts to criticize him. "I think that it is necessary to recall me," he added for effect, "for I am aware that it is impossible to remove Litvinov." Troianovskii was suggesting, in fact, that Stalin should sack Litvinov. That was going too far. "By the way," Troianovskii added as a last knife in the back, "the main trouble in our negotiations with the United States about debts is that Litvinov did not want to agree on them when he was here." In doing this Troianovskii made a large mistake, apparently induced by his discussions with Moore at the State Department, who also pursued Bullitt's policy of targeting the narkom.[67]

As readers will remember, when Litvinov was in Washington he kept in close touch by cable with Stalin, who approved everything that Litvinov proposed to Roosevelt. To criticize Litvinov was therefore to criticize Stalin. Nevertheless, Stalin instructed Kaganovich, the TsK secretary, to reject Troianovskii's request for recall. And then he added, "The letter, we should not show to Litvinov." Kaganovich and Molotov both agreed. One easily understands why: the narkom would have at once demanded Troianovskii's resignation, or he would have resigned himself, which would have caused a scandal in Washington, not to mention elsewhere, and would have damaged Soviet-US relations. Stalin was not ready to give up on them yet. Troianovskii stayed in Washington, but lost the argument. The Politburo approved a resolution to the effect that he should continue with his previous directives, that is, Litvinov's instructions.[68]

On the same day Troianovskii wrote his letter to Stalin, he also wrote to Litvinov, as though he had not just attempted to bring him down. "Dear Maksim Maksimovich," he began, and then continued to describe how Soviet relations with the United States had gone cold, pointing out that opposition to recognition never went away especially in the Republican Party, and Roosevelt himself had backed away from his earlier enthusiasm for diplomatic recognition. Far Eastern affairs played a big role in recognition and remained important, but large parts of the US population were thinking more about trade than about Japan. All this sounded like setting up Troianovskii's argument to let him take over negotiations. Good relations with the United States, he said, would be impossible without settling the old debts. All this prefaced Troianovskii's new proposals to the State Department, the ones which Litvinov found so confusing.[69]

In the meantime, Litvinov let his temper cool. He did not reply to Troianovskii's telegram, but instead wrote him a long, detailed dispatch on Soviet policy regarding the tsarist debts. His first point was that the USSR had been in a sixteen-year-long struggle with the outside world because of the Soviet repudiation of the tsarist debt and the nationalization of foreign-held property without compensation. In this struggle all means of pressure and threats had been used, especially by France and England, to compel the Soviet government to change its policy. And, of course, the United States withheld recognition. The USSR had successfully resisted these pressures so that France and England had to abandon them. The Soviet government had always refused, Litvinov said, to recognize in principle the old debts, but had said that it was open to "practical deals" based on the "indispensable" quid pro quo of corresponding loans. The US government had likewise refused a loan directly or through the intermediary of US banks and this voided the "gentleman's agreement." Litvinov conceded that Roosevelt had encountered difficulties in delivering the loan, but once this condition fell, so did the Soviet commitment to discharge the Kerenskii debt.

Litvinov then enumerated several concessions offered to Washington (with which readers will already be familiar) that were left unreciprocated. Next,

Litvinov offered a lesson on the differences between ordinary commercial credits and bank credit. The State Department was offering – and this is what Troianovskii proposed accepting – commercial credits of various periods of time, possibly revolving, but not a government or government-guaranteed loan. Soviet trade organizations could obtain commercial credits in Europe without having to pay on the old debts. Litvinov repeated once again that the Soviet government did not wish to create a precedent in the United States that other governments could use to reopen their claims for compensation. The focus on the Kerenskii debt was intended to avoid setting such a precedent. Litvinov went into some detail to explain these differences to Troianovskii, as though he were lecturing a first-year business student. Nor could he resist describing, once again, Troianovskii's proposals as a "capitulation" or suggesting that the polpred "inattentively" read his instructions.[70] So it was not all bygones be bygones.

Krestinskii also wrote to Troianovskii, in a more collegial way, summarizing Litvinov's main points, essentially emphasizing Soviet concessions to which the State Department had not responded, except on the edges of its own proposal. He concluded that the negotiations were going nowhere. Then, he made this interesting observation: if a more "Americanophobic" government came to power in Japan and the United States wanted to demonstrate closer relations with the USSR, it could drop the "unreasonable stubbornness, and then negotiations will be easier."[71] This was an ironic comment since Bullitt had also made it in reverse. Given the Soviet concessions and the absence of them on the US side, the weight of argument favoured Moscow, not Washington.

In fact, Bullitt went around to see Litvinov – it was 9 July – and said, when the topic came up, that Troianovskii had not taken up any discussions at the State Department. Litvinov replied that Troianovskii "had misunderstood" his instructions. Criticizing his polpred in front of an ambassador underlined Litvinov's irritation. He mentioned the long dispatch he had just finished writing, and even read parts of it to Bullitt. "Intransigence," was how Bullitt described the instructions, rendering Troianovskii's job "impossible." He warned Litvinov, but the latter replied that the USSR had relations with other states and these could not be jeopardized over debts and claims. Any agreement with the United States must be such that the precedent is impossible for other governments to contemplate.[72] When Litvinov was worried about this or that development, Bullitt said he tried "to fertilize" it, especially where US-Japanese relations were concerned. "I intimated that our relations with Japan showed improvement and asked him if there had not been a great improvement recently in the relations of the Soviet Union with Japan." Litvinov laughed: "The only improvement is that we are not yet at war."[73] Hull replied to Bullitt that he should ease off on the pessimism about future negotiations. If Troianovskii offered to negotiate, then they would "canvass [the] entire situation with him and endeavor to impress him with the importance of speedy agreement."[74] The way Bullitt saw matters:

good news was bad news. Walter Duranty, the *New York Times* bureau chief in Moscow, told him that "many American bankers and industrialists" would offer credits to the USSR whether the State Department liked it or not. Bullitt reacted negatively: the news "would further stiffen Litvinov's attitude." Ironically, Duranty's telegrams on this line were blocked by the Soviet censor. "Litvinov told Duranty that the cables looked too much as if they had been inspired by the Soviet Government."[75]

Bullitt's Change of Strategy

In Moscow, Bullitt began to play a dangerous game targeting Litvinov as the main obstacle to reaching agreement on debts and credits. "I venture to express the opinion," he wrote to Hull, "that so long as Litvinov adheres to his present attitude toward the United States we shall not be able to count on any genuinely friendly cooperation from him." Hence, Bullitt opposed the sending of a US warship to visit a Soviet port. He seemed to be getting information from a Soviet source, "private information," he claimed, that Litvinov might not have complete support inside Stalin's circle. "Stalin and the military authorities feel strongly that cooperation with the United States must be strengthened and not destroyed and I do not consider Litvinov's intransigence irreversible." In fact, *everyone* in the Soviet leadership wanted better relations with the United States, but not on *any* terms, and Litvinov was by no means "intransigent" towards Bullitt or the United States. What exasperated him was that the Soviet side had offered concessions to the State Department, but got none in return. Bullitt was looking for trouble. The US ought not to go too far "in indicating frigidity as to antagonize those leaders in the Soviet hierarchy who desire close collaboration with the United States. I propose to take the general attitude that we are most anxious to cooperate with the Soviet Union but that Litvinov is indifferent to the establishment of such collaboration."[76] The narkom was not "indifferent" to better relations with the United States. Bullitt was once again providing inaccurate information to Washington.

Litvinov still attempted to maintain good personal relations with Bullitt, inviting him to lunch at his *dacha* outside Moscow. He brought up the procurement plan – remember this was Bullitt's idea – and said the State Department had vetoed it. Litvinov indicated "that so far as the Soviet Government was concerned the matter was now at rest." Bullitt pleaded ignorance. "Litvinov went out of his way to be personally cordial yesterday," Bullitt advised, "and it is my impression that he hopes now that negotiations with regard to claims and indebtedness will lapse into a peaceful and permanent coma."[77]

Bullitt continued to target Litvinov. There were "unusual demonstrations of friendliness toward this Embassy during the past week," he cabled to Hull, "as a result of apprehension that Litvinov's intransigence … might result in a prolonged [US] disinclination … to cooperate in any field with the Soviet Government." Soviet diplomats were convinced that Japan would not launch a war in the Far East, but the soldiers were not so sure and worried about "Litvinov's stubbornness." It was thus a favourable moment to begin negotiations with Troianovskii.[78]

On 26 July, Litvinov lunched with Bullitt and the two of them went together to watch "the first polo match ever played in the Soviet Union." Bullitt had imported polo equipment to teach the sport to Red Army cavalrymen. Voroshilov was also present and returned with Bullitt to the US embassy where he stayed until the early hours. Voroshilov had a convivial personality. "In the hours of a very long and an intimate conversation … I found as I had suspected that Litvinov had not given Stalin and Voroshilov an altogether accurate version of our discussions." Bullitt also advised that Voroshilov was strong on better US-Soviet relations and that he would "use his influence with Stalin … to soften Litvinov's obduracy."[79]

As it happened, Voroshilov also made a record of his conversation with Bullitt. Voroshilov reported that for Bullitt, the big problem in US-Soviet relations was a "misunderstanding" and Litvinov's attempt to obtain US government credit "by any means." Nor did Bullitt want to hear about US government involvement in lending to the USSR by banks and industry. This was true. Bullitt sang his usual song about "public opinion," angered by the refusal of governments to pay war debts, being opposed to any kind of lending to any government whatsoever. "Bullitt several times (and almost angrily)," Voroshilov reported, "emphasized Litvinov's persistent unwillingness to move off his position 'without which it is impossible to move the negotiations from a dead end.'" He continued:

> Bullitt concluded in somewhat pathetic tones, that now in fact was being determined the direction of American foreign policy: would it go along the path of rapprochement with the Soviet Union or would it be obliged to take up an English [hostile] orientation. The latter policy is possible if we continue to be stubborn, and by doing so, irritate American public opinion, which inevitably would affect the president's position.

That sounded like a threat. Voroshilov was polite in reply. It is not true, he told Bullitt, that the problem is Litvinov's stubbornness. Since the US government wanted to hold the USSR responsible for the Kerenskii debt, it was normal to discuss credit with the US government and not with banks and business. Voroshilov added, almost innocently, that he could not understand why the irritation of public opinion with France, Britain, and other states for not paying their war debts should also wash over the USSR. The Soviet government paid its debts to the last kopek. This was true. The Soviet Union would not recognize the tsar's debt as Litvinov often said. As a last point, Voroshilov observed that the Kerenskii debt did not belong to the Soviet government, but to a "government against which we fought."

Voroshilov concluded with this comment: "It is now obvious to everyone that we traded [with the United States] much better before the restoration of diplomatic relations than we do now. This absolutely abnormal situation must be liquidated as soon as possible and it can be done with the good will of both sides. We have it in sufficient quantity, and the American side can and should show it."[80] It appears that Voroshilov said this or said it in so many words to Bullitt. Whatever he said, however, Bullitt should have drawn the conclusion that trying to scapegoat Litvinov would not work for if Voroshilov defended him, it was because Litvinov was defending Stalin's policy. Bullitt's and Voroshilov's accounts of their discussion are as different as night and day.

Bullitt did *not* get the message and he continued to blame Litvinov for his problems. "I have not been able to get anywhere with Litvinov," Bullitt wrote to Roosevelt, "and, while maintaining very cordial personal relations with him, have tried to build a back fire in the Kremlin by way of Voroshilov and Karakhan." The "backfire" did not work because Litvinov's policy was Stalin's policy, which is why Voroshilov defended it. As for Karakhan, he had once enjoyed close relations with Stalin, but no longer did. He would soon be headed to Turkey, as polpred in Ankara. "We have had dozens of indications lately," Bullitt continued, "Stalin, Voroshilov and Molotov are most anxious to develop really friendly relations with us and I think the most important thing I can do at the moment is to get my feeble Russian into shape to have conversations with them." Bullitt was right that Stalin and his colleagues wanted better relations with the United States. This had been Soviet policy since 1918, but not at any price and not at the price of compromising Soviet policy with respect to the old debts. Better relations could not be consolidated by trying to buy them with $100 million and large orders for US goods, only strong common national interests, with respect to Japan and Nazi Germany, could do that. Bullitt did not seem to get it. "In the end I think we shall be able to beat down Litvinov's resistance."[81] It was not Litvinov's resistance; it was Stalin's resistance. The tougher Litvinov bargained, the more respect he gained from the "boss."

US policy was to let the USSR make all the concessions, which is what angered Litvinov. At the end of the July, the Export-Import Bank offered to do business with all countries except the USSR. That caused Troianovskii to ask Hull for an explanation. It sounded to some US newspapers as though the bank's action "was intended as a club over the Soviet Government." Some people never learn: strong arm tactics did not work in Moscow. Hull said that the State Department had nothing to do with the bank's statement.[82]

It was a rare occurrence for Litvinov to criticize a polpred in the presence of a foreign diplomat, but he continued to complain to Bullitt about Troianovskii not understanding his instructions and sending an "unintelligible telegram" to

Moscow about US proposals. The narkom meant to warn the State Department that Troianovskii's statements or proposals should be checked with Moscow. In fact, he asked for the US proposals in writing, so he could see an actual text and not have to depend on Troianovskii's "interpretations."[83]

Litvinov considered Troianovskii to be a broken arm, but he did not see any other option but let him meet with the State Department. That was his job, after all. He warned him to be careful.[84] At the beginning of August there were meetings between Troianovskii and Hull, Moore, and Kelley. The discussions in Washington did not lead to agreement or even to any narrowing of differences. The Politburo approved instructions for Troianovskii, reiterating that the original Kelley proposals were "unacceptable" and that he should stick to his earlier instructions. A meeting in Washington on 10 August went badly. Troianovskii had to inform Hull that Moscow considered the most recent State Department proposal as "worse than the first." Rubinin made a summary of the negotiations and concluded that the most recent US terms offered no improvement "whatsoever" on the earlier positions.[85] Troianovskii's information for Hull did not go down well. "Most unsatisfactory," according to the State Department: "Our Government is greatly disappointed at Mr. Litvinoff's position, and that the negotiation appears to be getting nowhere."[86] The State Department seemed blind to its own obduracy, refusing to go beyond commercial credits and its original proposals.

Troianovskii warned Moscow that the negotiations were headed towards rupture. Roosevelt had approved the State Department position so that a worsening of relations was certain. "I have long been told," Troianovskii cabled, "that Roosevelt is very angry and curses Litvinov." This line originated with Bullitt. Troianovskii could not resist the opportunity to blackguard Litvinov and blame him for the impasse in negotiations. He still did not understand that Litvinov's policy was Stalin's policy and that of the Politburo. "At the last meeting, Moore, who most reflects Roosevelt's mood, was burning with anger and could not listen to me without indignation and hatred. To such an extent, the outrage was for me unexpected." Troianovskii did not think it would come to a rupture of relations; it was after all Roosevelt's policy. Troianovskii thought the best way to proceed would be to say to the State Department that "we have made many concessions, now it's the turn of the State Department: if it makes a really better proposal, then we in our turn will try to meet them halfway." He suggested, *inter alia*, going back to the $200-million loan and dividing it in two: $100 million as a long-term (twenty-year) credit, a loan in effect, and $100 million as shorter-term commercial credits. Troianovskii seemed confident that further concessions would lead to agreement.[87]

The idea of more concessions to the State Department did not initially go down well in Moscow. Krestinskii, who was acting narkom in the absence of Litvinov, was against them: before the mid-term US elections, Roosevelt would not make any move, nor should the USSR. Further concessions would provoke similar demands from the French and British. On the day after the conclusion of an agreement with the United States, *all* the creditor states would at once put in their bills in Moscow. Krestinskii recommended sticking to the Soviet proposal of $100 million for the debt and $200 million in long-term credits. He argued that the State Department was blackmailing the Soviet government, using as a lever any increase in tensions in the Far East. Bullitt, of course, had been using just such an approach. Krestinskii recommended holding the line.[88] Kaganovich and Molotov supported Krestinskii's position and advised Stalin, who had gone south to Sochi for his holidays. Troianovksii, they opined, was "a little prone to panic."[89]

Stalin did not agree. "It seems to me in what Troianovskii says, there is a portion of truth, and we could make some concessions to Roosevelt. Keep in mind that the agreement with Roosevelt can make easier both the implementation of the Eastern Regional Pact with all its ensuing consequences, and the fight against Japan, which is very important for us."[90] The *vozhd* had spoken. The Politburo approved the main point of Troianovskii's compromise proposal and instructed him to hand over a written proposal to Hull.[91]

Krestinskii sent Troianovskii a long dispatch explaining Soviet policy. The position was not new but a few points are worth emphasizing. The most important was this: the Soviet government was worried about dangerous precedents. The distinction between the Kerenskii debt and the tsarist debts was purely technical and the French, for example, would see through it. A debts agreement with the United States might have a negative influence on relations with France. "At the present time these relations are a more important hinge (*ser'eznyi sterzhen'*) of our foreign policy than relations with America." The Soviet position on negotiations with the State Department flowed from that calculation. "We do not want an aggravation of relations. On the contrary, we want to come to agreement with the Americans more for political than economic considerations." Relations were more about security than about old debts or trade. As always for the Soviet Union, since the beginning, economic relations were potentially a stepping stone to better political relations.

On the other hand, Krestinskii said in effect that the USSR did not like being pushed around by the State Department. "We … do not like it that the Americans continue to permit themselves to accuse us of bad faith – in violating the agreement of November 15th [the gentleman's agreement]." Finally, Krestinskii asked for feedback from Troianovskii on the Soviet proposals, or Litvinov's ideas introduced into the proposals for Hull. "My request for feedback on the M.M. [Litvinov] scheme should not be understood in any way in the sense that if you find this scheme unacceptable, you can delay the delivery of our memorandum to the State Department. No, you must, regardless of your attitude to the M.M. scheme, carry out the instructions that will be sent to you by telegraph." An interesting conclusion to Krestinskii's long dispatch, which appeared to be a warning to Troianovskii to follow instructions and not his personal inclinations on policy.[92]

The Soviet proposal was yet another compromise that Troianovskii presented to Hull on 24 August. The Secretary of State waved it off, refusing even to discuss it. Here is how he reported the meeting to Bullitt: "He [Troianovskii] was informed that his proposal was entirely unacceptable and following the conversation the press was informed that the 'Soviet Ambassador presented a counter-proposal in writing in view of which it is not possible to be optimistic that any agreement will be reached.'"[93] Hull not only rejected the Soviet proposal, as though he were dealing with Guatemala, but he informed the press that he had done so. That meant in effect an end to the negotiations and the end of the attempt to actualize the "gentleman's agreement."

Still, one had to give Bullitt credit; he did not abandon his intrigues against Litvinov. In early September, he saw Radek for "a long conversation." Radek, who had a bad habit of meddling in NKID business, as readers will remember, opined that Litvinov had not kept Stalin fully informed on the course of negotiations and that he sought "to obtain a personal triumph as a bargainer." Radek said he would check the files in Stalin's secretariat and then get back to Bullitt.[94] A week later, the two conspirators spoke again. Radek advised that he had read the entire file in Stalin's office and that he had concluded that Litvinov "reported the facts to Stalin without noteworthy distortions." Damn it all, Bullitt must have thought, but then Radek offered more hope. He had seen Voroshilov's report to Stalin about his meeting with Bullitt. Readers should remember: the discussion took place at the US embassy in Moscow after the Polo match in late July. According to Bullitt, "Voroshilov made a detailed report to Stalin on our position and had demanded that our proposals should be accepted." That is *not* what Voroshilov wrote in his record of conversation. Then Radek related the sense of Krestinskii's dispatch to Troianovskii, about the importance of relations especially with France and not creating a precedent that could cause France and Britain to make similar demands on the old debts. Stalin said that good US-Soviet relations were of "prime importance." This was true, but everyone in the NKID agreed on that point. Radek opined that the Soviet government needed to "work out a new formula" that would satisfy the United States but not France and Britain. Yes, thought Bullitt, "the formula" was the key, "although the Soviet Government will doubtless continue to haggle over interest rates."[95]

Except that the formula was *not* the problem: what the Soviet side wanted was long-term credit to buy for cash, and the US side did not want to offer it. That was the problem. The Soviet government was prepared in effect to pay $100 million, for long- term credit over twenty years. That was a win-win-win solution for the United States: $100 million in the pocket over time for the Kerenskii debt; $100 million credit, a loan in effect, to be paid back with interest over twenty years and $100 million in shorter-term commercial credits; and business, big business for US firms. What was wrong with that, even for the notorious, tight-fisted Yankee trader? Nothing. The problem was that the State Department did not see it in the same way and Roosevelt was too distracted with other problems to put his foot down. There was also a larger problem: Bullitt did not report Soviet positions accurately to Washington, which encouraged the State Department trio of Hull, Moore, and Kelley to persist in thinking that if they held to their hard position long enough, the Soviet side would come around. This was the worst possible advice to send to Washington.

Still, the negotiations did not yet die. Moore, as acting Secretary of State, held a news conference on 4 September and addressed questions about the conduct of the negotiations. He acknowledged criticism that the US government was responsible for the delay in reaching an agreement and that the State Department was "trying to drive a hard bargain." Moore denied that this was so. "Nothing can be further from the truth," he said. "When the facts are revealed, it will be found that our attitude has not only been conciliatory but extremely liberal and generous."[96] Perceptions are a relative thing, of course, but if one side, the Soviet, made important concessions, and the other side, the US, made none of a substantive nature, one might have cause to doubt Moore's perception of the negotiations. Since there seemed to be doubts among the assembled journalists and among a wider audience, it was decided to convoke another meeting with Troianovskii, which was scheduled for 5 September at 8:30 p.m., rather late in the day for such a meeting. Hull was absent; Moore, as acting Secretary of State, led off the discussion reviewing the state of negotiations. He came quickly to the point about where the negotiations had stalled, which was the Soviet demand for long-term credit. If the Soviet government insisted on "a loan" as the quid pro quo of agreeing to pay the Kerenskii debt, discussions were "hardly worth" continuing. Moore went over US proposals for commercial credits with a duration of eighteen months to five years depending on the type of goods ordered. To this, Moore noted that Roosevelt "might agree to grant special terms in exceptional cases, say for equipment for large industrial projects," and agree to terms of six or seven years. Troianovskii reverted to the Soviet position on precedents created and thus the Soviet demand for a long-term loan. He replied in so many words that he had exhausted "my powers of invention" with the last Soviet proposal, but he was open to any counteroffers "along this line," which the State Department might suggest. Troianovskii held out no hope of the Soviet government yielding on the issue of a loan.[97]

Moore issued a public statement on the following day, saying that the most recent meeting with Troianovskii had produced no results: "We have gone the limit in making concessions … to go further would be an unthinkable sacrifice of the public interest."[98] Well, that was laying it on pretty thick, obviously to quiet down the sceptics. The limit of US concessions was the extension of commercial credits for six or seven years in exceptional cases ... but no promises. That was not much of a concession. Moore advised Bullitt: "Personally I have little idea that the Soviet officials will come to any reasonable agreement. Litvinoff won his victory when he obtained recognition and regards everything else as of minor importance."[99] No, that was not true.

Troianovskii still had an itch to succeed and sent a fresh proposal to Moscow, cutting to $50 million the twenty-year credit or loan, $50 million of commercial credits up to five years, and $100 million on terms between five and ten years.[100] One can only imagine how Litvinov would have reacted to this latest proposal from Troianovskii, but he was still in Geneva and Krestinskii was acting narkom. Krestinskii was more patient than Litvinov, but no less tough, in fact, sometimes he was tougher still:

> Why do you consider that you have to take the decision about a minimum [proposal] lower than that which we would go under any circumstances, when the telegram of August 21, on behalf of *instantsiia*, informed you that our concessions set out in the memorandum of the same date are the limit (emphatically – the limit). I do not understand why you propose to change the decision of *instantsiia* and move to new concessions although four weeks have past and the Americans have not taken one step in our direction. Why must we lose our nerve and rush forward with new concessions?

Our position has improved in the Far East, Krestinskii noted, and we are discussing terms of trade in Europe that are "significantly better" than what the United States is offering.[101]

On Troianovskii's initiative, there was yet another meeting with Hull (back in Washington), Moore, and Kelley on 21 September, three days after Krestinskii dated his telegram to Washington. Troianovskii appeared to have disregarded Krestinskii's cable – the cable connection between Washington and Moscow was very good, less than twenty-four hours – and apparently the polpred had sent, or directed to be sent, to the State Department a memorandum signed by a third party regarding a settlement of the old debts. It was all rather mysterious since Troianovskii denied that the views expressed in the memorandum were his, though he was aware of it and appeared to know its author. During the meeting, Troianovskii stated that Moscow insisted on a loan or long-term credit – that was correct – but then he added that it might be less than $100 million (that was not correct). Was the polpred skating on his own? He would surely have received Krestinskii's telegram, but he told Hull that he had received no fresh instructions from Moscow. Hull indicated that a loan was "impossible," but he showed some flexibility on longer commercial credits. That sounded like a US concession. There was a further discussion about interest rates, the US proposal not having changed much.[102]

In Troianovskii's telegram to Moscow he noted that Moore had invited him to the meeting; he did not say that he had asked for it. He went through the details of the meeting, corresponding with the US version of the discussion, and then, *incredibly*, proposed that he should make the very same proposals to Hull, which Krestinskii had told him were *out of the question.*[103] Litvinov was still in Geneva, and therefore was not immediately aware of Troianovskii's latest act of insubordination. In Moscow, Krestinskii advised Bullitt a few days later that he had summoned Troianovskii home for consultations. Krestinskii made clear during a long discussion that the proposal of 24 August was the last Soviet idea on the table for debts and credits. "Impossible," said Bullitt, in his usual sort of peremptory reply whenever the Soviet side raised the idea of long-term credit. Krestinskii was irritated with Bullitt's usual accusations, but kept his temper under control. Bullitt did the same apparently. He wondered whether he should leave Moscow – he was planning to return to Washington via China and Japan – before Troianovskii's arrival to convey "the impression that I was so disgusted with the behavior of the Soviet Government that I felt that collaboration between our countries had been made almost impossible."[104] This was the statement of someone who liked to showboat, or did not and could not understand the point of view of his Soviet interlocutors. No need to wait for Troianovskii, came the reply from Hull in Washington. "You and we have done all that is possible in the way of making a most liberal proposal." Their consciences were clear, then. "Our information," Hull added, "is … that Troyanovsky believes it [the State Department proposal] should be accepted and that his trip to Moscow is on his own initiative to endeavor to persuade his Government to accept it."[105] This is an interesting statement, since Krestinskii appears to have taken the initiative to recall Troianovskii for consultations. It was the obvious move in view of an ambassador's disregard for instructions. Litvinov was expected back home in the first week in October. Would Troianovskii's conduct prompt an explosion?

Skvirskii's Conversations

Skvirskii was in Moscow on leave in September and made records of two interesting conversations. One was with the US military attaché, Major (at the time) Philip R. Faymonville. He is an interesting character in the narrative of Soviet-US relations, especially after the Nazi invasion of the USSR in June 1941. He got on well with his Soviet counterparts, which prompted suspicions from colleagues who did not get along with them or who did not like or respect Russians, or the USSR.[106] Skvirskii had known Faymonville for a long time and therefore went out to lunch with him in Moscow. They talked business, with Skvirskii trying to explain to his old acquaintance how the Soviet side saw matters regarding relations with the United States. They talked about the impasse in negotiations on debts and credits, and how this was souring relations. Skvirskii repeated the

Soviet position on unwillingness to create undesirable precedents that could cause trouble in Paris or London. US government policy was "under the influence of the State Department," which had not moved from its original proposals but seemed to have drawn back from the position it held when Litvinov was in Washington. The State Department accused Litvinov of not keeping his commitments. Skvirskii thought Roosevelt could accept the Soviet proposal without fear of opposition because US business wanted and needed the contracts in the USSR. Faymonville agreed and opined that the situation might improve after the mid-term elections that November. Faymonville added that Bullitt's influence with Roosevelt had grown over time. He thought that the ambassador might be more open to argument from Skvirskii than from others. For his part, Skvirskii reported that Faymonville had good connections to the White House, and that he would work with him to bring Bullitt around and to counteract US anti-Soviet opinion.[107] Faymonville had his own adversaries who tried to undermine him.

On the following day, Skvirskii accepted an invitation from Bullitt to talk. They finally got around to the debt-credit negotiations and Bullitt repeated his usual view that US public opinion would not accept any loan or long-term credits for the USSR. It was a long monologue, which readers have heard before. Skvirskii recognized an impasse: "It was completely clear and knowing Bullitt I have long suspected it, that he does not understand our situation, that he is also not fully understood, and that the accumulating irritation makes the possibility of such mutual understanding even more difficult."

"I therefore decided," Skvirskii wrote in his record of the conversation, "to disassemble in detail Bullitt's arguments in order to prove our case." It was not true that the USSR was "now less interested than before" in "genuinely friendly relations" with the United States. Skvirskii said that the United States had not reciprocated Soviet overtures. Then there was Bullitt's view that the Soviet government was only interested in political relations, not economic, because of the Japanese and German threats, and mainly security considerations led to recognition. This is untrue, said Skvirskii, who had been in the United States for a long time. He said that there had been and were still strong pressures from US businesses that wanted to trade with the USSR. He offered a number of examples to prove his point. Bullitt argued back that settlement balances and terms of credit were key factors. Businessmen were interested in marketing their products in Russia, Skvirskii replied, and did care about balances. And then Skvirskii turned to the question of the Soviet demand for long-term credits, going over the various arguments, which Bullitt had heard before. He was convinced that Roosevelt could win public opinion to his side in facilitating trade with the USSR. After all, that was the US interest behind offering long-term credits for the purchase of US-produced goods, which profited businesses and workers who gained employment fulfilling Soviet orders. It was a win-win outcome for the United States. Where was the problem? "That is what capitalism is for." As for the Kerenskii debt, most of that money – well, this was according to Litvinov – went to support the various White Guard armies that sought to overthrow Soviet power. By what logic could the Soviet Union be held responsible for these debts?[108]

Bullitt seemed to come around a little at the end of the long discussion. Skvirskii tried to persuade him to take up with Roosevelt the arguments in favour of accepting the last Soviet proposal. Skvirskii was not confident that this would work. Bullitt was closely tied politically to Roosevelt; he would not want to do anything to harm the president's political position. If Roosevelt refused Soviet offers, it would mean that his political situation did not allow him to accept them. We need to understand, Skvirskii concluded, that the "honeymoon" in US-Soviet relations was over. "Enemies were beginning to raise their heads, and the State Department is already beginning to remember about 'propaganda.' The sooner an agreement on debts is concluded, the better."[109]

Skvirskii's attempt to calm down Bullitt produced no results. Impatient to leave Moscow, for his long trip home across China and Japan, Bullitt seemed to bounce off the walls of his embassy to be on his way. He developed a line which he brought out with his Soviet interlocutors that there was little time left to get US-Soviet relations right and that if no deal was struck on debts and credits, those relations were headed into the dark. This message was a threat in effect: either accept State Department terms or else. Bullitt repeated his line that the USSR appeared to have lost interest in better relations. These statements were never used with France or Britain, which owed more money to the United States than the USSR and openly refused to pay. Readers may wonder why.

Bullitt's Parting Shots

On 5 October, Bullitt tried his lines on Litvinov who was back in Moscow after holidays in France and a long stint in Geneva. "Litvinov instead of replying in his usual belligerent manner sat silent looking profoundly discouraged." In a telegram to Hull, Bullitt seemed to boast of his threats. "I did my [best] to produce in him as complete a state of gloom as possible with regard to the future of Soviet-American relations if no settlement should be made and I hope that I may have prepared somewhat the ground for Troyanovsky's arrival."[110] Reading between the lines of some of the telegrams back and forth to Washington, one might get the impression that Troianovskii was in cahoots with his US counterparts.

A New US Offer

There was finally a little movement in Washington. At the beginning of October, the State Department conveyed new terms to Bullitt. The latest US proposal did finally make some concessions, although not on the key issue of credits.

The State Department was prepared to accept either $100 million as the sum of Soviet indebtedness with interest or $125 million without interest, payable over twenty to twenty-five years. Commercial credits through the Export-Import Bank would be granted up to $200 million with extra interest going to pay off the debt. Five years would be allowed on all credits – that represented an improvement – and longer time allowed, but not specified, "in exceptional cases."[111] A "most liberal proposal," said the State Department. Alright, but then why did Bullitt need to make threats to get the Soviet government to accept it? And why were the Americans counting so much on Troianovskii?

The State Department policy of threats and blackmail nevertheless continued. Moore initialled the following telegram for Bullitt: "It is highly desirable to give to [Litvinov] the impression that in case of violation of pledges he made when here and failure to agree to debts settlement on such reasonable terms as we have proposed, the relations between the two governments will inevitably be less close and friendly than anticipated and the reason for our Government doing many things contemplated may disappear."[112] The latter line was a threat to stop the construction of a new embassy building and the establishment of new consulates. It was still Litvinov reneging on commitments in Washington and refusing "reasonable terms," the implication being that the State Department was a better judge of Soviet interests than the Soviet government.

Bullitt had another meeting with Rubinin, but the conversation was not as cordial as others had been. The ambassador went through his lines again, the same as he had used on Litvinov. "You don't have a lot of friends in the United States," he said, "and none better than me and the president." The Soviet government should not throw away its chances; it did not have that many to lose. Rubinin replied in detail to Bullitt's various observations. Readers have heard most of the Soviet points before. Rubinin added the following in so many words: The Soviet government had always sought out good relations with those countries which wanted good relations with them, but it would not run after them. "On the American side, we find in both larger and smaller matters a constant unwillingness to take into account our public opinion, our domestic legislation, and our ways of doing things." As an example, Rubinin raised the issue of the functioning of the US consulate in Moscow. Why did Soviet citizens have to go to Riga or Berlin to obtain a US visa? This was a minor dispute, and not the only one, compared with the debt-credit negotiations. And finally Bullitt raised the old stand-by issue of the Comintern. When was it to meet in Moscow? Rubinin could not remember but said the newspapers had published the dates. Bullitt said he had received a long telegram from Washington about communist activities in the United States, instructing him to take up the matter with the NKID. "I decided not to do this," Bullitt remarked, giving Rubinin "a sour look."[113]

That was enough. The next day, Litvinov wrote to Molotov asking for authorization to use tough language with Bullitt. He was sick of the threats, subtle and otherwise. He reminded Molotov that he had firm instructions to recognize the Kerenskii debt only on condition of obtaining a loan in return, not commercial credits. "There is no doubt," Litvinov noted, "that America has backed away from the [gentleman's] agreement and from there all the difficulties." Remember that the Americans accused Litvinov, their scapegoat, of repudiating the Washington agreement. The narkom then opined, "We do not need a loan, and are ready to let it go, if the issue of debts is left open. We are ready to trade with America on the same conditions as those of other countries. But we can also do without this trade if America considers it necessary to remain on the ground of the Johnson Act." We want good relations with the United States, Litvinov added, but not at the expense of aggravating our relations with European countries. "With us it is not possible to negotiate in the language of threats and intimidation, for the result will be the opposite of what is expected."[114]

Bullitt met Molotov two days after his meeting with Rubinin. US-Soviet relations were a small, tender plant, Bullitt said, which required special care, "and on which one should not piss." Molotov replied that from the Soviet side there would always be "unconditional courtesy," but also remarked that such should be the case with both sides. That took the wind out of Bullitt's usual lines, and he hastened to agree with Molotov who then laid on a thick coat of honeyed words to sooth the ambassador.[115] Would these agreed-upon rules of engagement last long?

A trial run came the next day. It was 10 October. Bullitt paid a farewell call to Litvinov, and the meeting started well enough. They talked about the assassination of Barthou in Marseille and the situation in the Far East. They then turned to the harder issue. Litvinov repeated the basic Soviet position on "a loan" and reiterated what he viewed as the intention of the "gentleman's agreement." The Soviet government was not demanding the fulfillment of the agreement if the president could not do it, but at the same time, Litvinov added, "we cannot accept that one accuses us of not respecting the agreement." Such accusations, according to Skvirskii, were circulating in Washington, "seemingly from the State Department itself." And then Litvinov warned, throwing benzine on what must have been a growing fire, that if such accusations continued, the NKID would publish the text of the Washington agreement. We don't need a loan, the narkom continued, and we are ready to promise not to raise the issue, if the question of the old debts is also not raised. That was clear. Litvinov then repeated other points of the Soviet position regarding negotiations with the United States, and notably about adverse precedents, with which readers are familiar. The question of the old debts had been put to sleep in France and Britain, he said, and the Soviet government did not want the issue awakened and then to become a bone of contention in those countries. And finally Litvinov repeated that the Soviet government did not respond well to threats. Now the proverbial heat in the narkom's office must have risen.

Bullitt replied with his usual complaints, according to Litvinov's record. The Soviet government, he said, did not "want to do anything for America." The USSR equated the United States with other countries where relations were not so good and thus would not make concessions. Roosevelt was interested in developing the rapprochement with the USSR, but if the Soviet government stuck to its positions, Roosevelt would not be able to do anything. There were few people in the United States who were interested in relations with the USSR, and then there was the matter of the Comintern. Litvinov was in no mood to let anything pass and accused Bullitt of confusing issues. As for the Comintern, the Soviet government "knows that … [it] is for all countries the reserve fund from which is drawn or not drawn arguments depending on whether they want to improve or aggravate relations with us … In any case, we cannot understand that the axis of our relations with America must be uniquely the question of $100 million, in which some three or four private companies are interested, and that dependent on this small question must be other problems of peace and in general the world order." In the "interests of peace," Litvinov continued, France had managed to put aside the question of the tsarist debts to solidify a rapprochement with the USSR. This was all the easier for the United States where the government had greater power and more stability than France. "Bullitt left somewhat embarrassed," Litvinov wrote in his journal.[116]

Readers may wonder whether Bullitt made a record of this conversation, and indeed he did. There were the usual omissions, sabers drawn, and inversions of voice. Litvinov "embarked upon a series of declarations which were obviously intended to impress me with the determination of the Soviet Government *to make no concessions whatsoever* [emphasis added] to the Government of the United States." Then Bullitt reported on Litvinov's attribution to the State Department of accusations that the USSR had broken the Washington agreement. "He said … that the President had broken the agreement." The discussion became "extremely acrimonious"; Litvinov "grew purple." The discussion might have become "acrimonious" but Litvinov did not blame Roosevelt personally for the broken agreement, if anything, he blamed the State Department.

Bullitt continued, "I replied that it was obvious that he had no wish for friendly relations with the United States. I went on to say that if a negative attitude with regard to a settlement of debts and claims should be followed by activities of the Comintern directed against the United States, our relations would become so difficult as to be almost impossible." Bullitt reported Litvinov's comment on the Comintern but distorted it: "no nation ever starts talking about the activities of the Comintern unless it wishes to have as bad relations as possible with us … [they] are merely an excuse for breaking diplomatic relations." That is not how Litvinov put it in his record. Then Bullitt made a further threat that "he [Litvinov] might expect the most drastic reaction in case the Comintern Congress should take place and there should be evidence of interference in the internal affairs of the United States." What was Bullitt doing? Was he showboating for the State Department, or trying to exacerbate US relations with Moscow? Or both?

Bullitt then turned to the negotiations on debts and credits. Troianovskii's name comes up in Bullitt's account, but not in Litvinov's. Bullitt again reduced the Soviet position on undesirable precedents to this: "If the question of payment of debts and claims [note *not* debts and credits] were settled in any way whatsoever, he would have grave difficulties in his relations with England and France." Litvinov never explained unfortunate precedents in that way. It was one distortion after another. Bullitt was trying to incite the State Department and aggravate US-Soviet relations. There was more chest thumping and puffery from Bullitt. "He [Litvinov] finally said that he would make a final proposal through Troyanovsky and then would refuse to discuss the matter further." The narkom would not have spoken this way and certainly did not report having said anything remotely similar to the lines attributed to him. And again Bullitt tried to scapegoat Litvinov: "I deeply regretted that he seemed determined to kill all possibility of really close and friendly relations between our countries." Then there was this quasi-racist statement implying a reference to Litvinov's Jewish family descent: "I had the impression today that I was talking with the traditional bazaar bargainer of the Near East."[117]

There is no indication in Litvinov's report that he tried to bargain with Bullitt; there was only what seemed to be a plea to the United States through Bullitt to be reasonable and to try to see matters from a Soviet perspective. If that was Litvinov's intention, he failed. His message was not conveyed to Washington. If Litvinov had read Bullitt's record of the conversation, he would have stopped talking to him. Litvinov said no more than what Bullitt had heard many times from Skvirskii, Rubinin, Krestinskii, Voroshilov, and even Molotov. The scapegoating of Litvinov, representing him as a saboteur of relations with the United States, must have been in fact an attempt to discredit or even topple the narkom, thinking that Troianovskii could deliver a deal to the State Department with Litvinov out of the way. If that was Bullitt's idea, or the State Department's, it was wishful thinking.

Exit Bullitt, Enter Troianovskii

Bullitt left Moscow the day after his meeting with Litvinov, and headed for Vladivostok on the Trans-Siberian Railway. The contrast between Bullitt's arrival in Moscow the previous December and his departure eleven months later must have been striking. There is no record of it, which is record enough. Troianovskii arrived in Moscow a short time after, hoping to obtain support for his ideas of a settlement. On 20 October, he met Wiley for lunch. "I asked him," Wiley reported, "what progress he had made in discussing the question of the settlement of debts and claims with his Government." Troianovskii replied that he had seen Litvinov and Molotov "briefly." That should have signalled to Wiley that their bet on the Soviet ambassador was lost. Stalin, Kaganovich, Voroshilov, and others had still not returned from the south to Moscow. According to Wiley, Troianovskii had "the 'conviction' that a settlement should be accepted by his Government substantially on the basis of the last proposals of the Department." The ambassador "conveyed an impression of confidence that he would be able to bring the Soviet Government to his point of view." December would be the key month in the negotiations. "From one or two facetious remarks," Wiley reported, "it is evident that his relations with Litvinov are not good."

After lunch, Wiley met Litvinov for "an animated but amiable debate of one hour with much give and take." This was the kind of conversation that Bullitt ought to have been having with the narkom, and perhaps Litvinov wanted to get his point of view over to someone else who might convey it correctly to Washington. It was basically the explanation that he had given many times before but that had failed to register with Bullitt. Litvinov was a wily fellow and probably wanted to give the message to Wiley that it was NKID policy and not Troianovskii's that was supported by *instantsia*. Wiley came away from the meeting with a far different conclusion than Bullitt's. "I do not feel that the question of solving our differences with the Soviet Government is at all hopeless." He thought that Moscow wanted a deal in "the relatively near future and that the present stage of the negotiations is, on the part of Litvinov, in the obstreperous stage, which is characteristic of his method of approach to financial problems."[118] Wiley's telegram was forwarded to Roosevelt, who would have understood that he was not getting the whole story from Bullitt.

Troianovskii put his proposals directly to Stalin, but Litvinov headed him off with a draft resolution for the Politburo with instructions for Troianovskii to inform Roosevelt that the Soviet government would not abandon its position on debts and credits. That was that: there would be no more concessions to the United States.[119] The next time Troianovskii saw Wiley at an official Soviet lunch three weeks later, his dish was humble pie. Wiley noted, "Troyanovsky told me that the question of a settlement of debts and claims ... was encountering serious difficulties." That was putting it mildly. "It is reported," Wiley added, "that Troyanovsky's relations with Litvinov since his return have been stormy." On another occasion Wiley had said they "impacted like stags in rut." So the secret was out. Troianovskii was staying in Moscow to try to make his case to other party leaders, but he was wasting his time.[120]

Or maybe he wasn't? Three days later, on 13 November, Troianovskii told Wiley that he had seen Stalin, and, Wiley noted, he "tells me that he expects to confer with him again." Troianovskii said he told Duranty, the *New York Times* bureau chief, that the Soviet government was still sticking to $100 million in long term credits. Then Wiley had this to say: "Subsequently a high

Soviet official who is in the confidence of the Kremlin came to my apartment quite privately." He denied "categorically current rumors that Litvinov's situation was precarious (he declares the party leaders pointedly ignored Litvinov at the Kremlin reception on the 7th)." Wiley thought the high official had visited on "specific instructions from the Kremlin."[121] Was a plot being prepared to oust Litvinov? Or was it the usual sort of intrigues that took place among ambitious people in places of power? Alphand also reported the rumours, but did not make too much of them. And what about Troianovskii's claim to have met Stalin? According to the Kremlin logs, Stalin had no meetings with anyone between 9 and 14 November. On that day, the day *after* Troianovskii said he had already met Stalin, there was a long meeting with Litvinov, a little under three hours. Molotov, Kaganovich, Voroshilov, and Andre Zhdanov, someone close to Stalin, were also present. Troianovskii joined the meeting late, staying for one hour and leaving before Litvinov.[122] It was on that same day that the NKID clerk Khaim Semenovich Veinberg wrote a report stating that the Politburo "had decided that it would make no further concessions to the Americans."[123] So it appears that Troianovskii was exaggerating his importance. He had not yet met Stalin, at least formally, on the day he talked to Wiley, and when he did see Stalin on the following day, Litvinov and the *troika* were also present. According to the Kremlin log, Troianovskii did not visit Stalin again. On the following day, Litvinov left for Geneva to attend meetings with Laval, among others. Decisions had been made, and the narkom had other important business on his agenda, notably with the French. Dogs bark, but the caravan moves on.

Litvinov had been nursing Soviet relations with Laval after the death of Barthou. Wiley saw him as pro-French. This was not true. Litvinov was pro-Soviet and nothing more. Foreign diplomats always have an eye cocked on what their colleagues are up to; and Wiley was no different. It was Litvinov's policy with France or Litvinov's policy in the Far East. But Litvinov did not budge without clearing whatever he wanted to do with Stalin. His policies were not personal, they were government policy. Wiley was reading too much into the rumours he picked up in Moscow. He saw Troianovskii again at a lunch put on by the French embassy. Troianovskii was boasting about his stint in Tokyo. "I was never wrong in my diagnosis of things." This was someone, a prima donna, in above his head. In a place like Moscow, he was playing with fire, and he was still talking down Litvinov. According to Wiley, "it has been an open secret that Troyanovsky and Litvinov have long been working at cross purposes … [he] is understood to be an outspoken opponent of Litvinov's American and Far Eastern policies." He had delayed his return to Washington because the Kremlin wanted "the benefit of his views." To the Americans, Troianovskii *looked* formidable, a man who could get it done, perhaps because he also thought so. Litvinov and Molotov had little time for him and Stalin met him for one hour in Litvinov's presence. Troianovskii was puffing himself up and Wiley fell for it.[124] Apparently, the polpred was spreading the word around Moscow that he was optimistic about concluding an agreement with the State Department on his return to Washington. Troianovskii could not keep his mouth shut.[125]

He was at it again with Wiley just before he left Moscow to return to Washington via the Far East. "The question of a settlement of debts and claims … has become progressively more difficult." That was spinning the story. Troianovskii never had a chance going against Litvinov *and* Stalin. He also saw intrigues by other countries, England, Germany, but especially France, which were talking lower interest rates on commercial credits in order "to thwart negotiations" for agreement with Washington. He seemed to arrogate to himself the right to speak for Stalin, especially "friendly" to the United States. The situation was "difficult" but "a way must be found" to move forward. Troianovskii was one of a kind, not seen in the NKID since the 1920s.[126] Here is how Wiley described him:

> I think he is very pleased with himself, patting himself on the back for having been able to extract really important concessions from the American Government. He probably feels that he can obtain still further concessions and is, in consequence, jealous of opponents at home or abroad who upset his applecart and prevent him from consummating a deal which he considers not only advantageous to his country but a feather in his own cap. From having observed Troyanovsky at length, I have gained the impression that he is a very independent *Tovarish* who knows his way through the intricacies of the Party hierarchy and is a person with whom one should reckon.[127]

Troianovskii Returns to Washington

Wrong. Wiley overestimated his man. He later heard that Litvinov had "*déjoué*," thwarted, Troianovskii and that he had left Moscow "most disappointed."[128] The wind was out of his sails when he arrived back in Washington at the end of January 1935. He had two meetings at the State Department and could offer nothing new in response to the last US proposals. With that, Hull decided to pull the plug on negotiations announced in a press release on 1 February.[129] This suited Litvinov who asked Stalin for authorization to reply. He also asked for approval of the following instructions to be sent to Troianovskii: "That we are not interested in resuming negotiations and suggest that he should not encourage such negotiations, and also not impose on us the proposals that he defended in Moscow and which were already rejected by the Politburo."[130] That was a wooden stake in the heart. The Soviet government, as readers will see, was moving towards a decision to refuse any further negotiations about the tsarist debts with any country.

In Washington, Bullitt was still taking it out on Litvinov for his "snotty policy."[131] "It seems to me," he wrote to Wiley, "that Litvinov's policy is about as dangerous as any he could pursue. The good will that has been built up for the Soviet in this country in the past three or four years has been demolished … The only thing that can recreate good feeling is a settlement of debts and claims and establishment of decent trade."[132] "The only thing," Bullitt said, as though incapable of dealing with anything but zero sums. The seeming US obsession with imposing US terms on the Soviet government as a condition of better relations appeared odd to Litvinov. How could $100 million, he asked, be more important than common US and Soviet security interests? The trade issues should have been secondary. The State Department, however, did not yet recognize the great danger of Japan and Nazi Germany. What danger there was could be mitigated by negotiations. "Germany seems to have taken the place of Japan as the bogey man," Wiley opined. Hence Nazi Germany was only a "bogey man," the danger being imagined in Soviet eyes, but not real. Wiley did not much care about the debts-credits negotiations – note again the difference with the American styling of "debts and claims." Credit was absent from the formula. It could be "throwing good money after bad." Wiley told Bullitt he had a clear conscience. The last State Department proposal was "impeccably generous." There were some reprisals in Moscow because the Soviet government would not accept US proposals – the consulate general in Moscow was abolished and absorbed into the embassy, two of the military attachés were recalled and the embassy staff was reduced. That was not going to force a change in Soviet policy, as Wiley noted. So it was done for spite then … to send a signal that "we" are not pleased.[133] Litvinov would only have shrugged in response, thinking there would come another time when he would try again to improve relations. It did not come for six long years.

Chapter Ten

Koshmar: The Agonizing Turn in Relations with France, 1934–1935

Soviet Damage Assessments

While relations with the United States were going downhill, relations with France also turned sour. Litvinov was right to fear French political instability, which had intensified after the disorders in Paris in February 1934. During the spring there were frequent confrontations in the streets of various French cities between right-wing paramilitary organizations and communists and syndicalists. A change in government or a change in minister could throw a wrench into French foreign policy. It was still Litvinov's *koshmar*. Only this time, it was more than just a bad dream. Even when the trio Herriot-Boncour-Barthou were charged with the conduct of French foreign policy, there was hidden opposition to the USSR, not least among the *apparat* in the Quai d'Orsay and elsewhere in the government. In spite of *Mein Kampf*, the preference for a deal with Nazi Germany, the "Daladier option," remained strong. On 13 October 1934, President Doumergue named Laval to succeed Barthou because he thought, as improbable as that might seem, that he could be counted on to continue Barthou's policy. The Doumergue government fell a few weeks later, and Doumergue's successor, Pierre-Étienne Flandin, a centre-right politician, retained Laval as a shield against the *superpacifistes* and *anglo-saxon germanophiles*. Flandin thought he could continue the policy of building up a "barrage against German ambitions" with Laval as a concession to the *germanophiles*.[1] It was all a bit ridiculous since French governments scarcely ever lasted more than a few months. In any case, Flandin was dead wrong. Investing in two contradictory policies at the same time seldom leads to success. *Utopique*, Alphand, still French ambassador in Moscow, called the manoeuvre.[2] It had to be one or the other. German public opinion was encouraged by Laval's arrival at the Quai d'Orsay, as if to confirm Alphand's analysis.[3]

Laval would have read Alphand's warning about Soviet anxieties over the stability of French foreign policy. On 19 October, he called in Rozenberg, the Soviet chargé d'affaires, to reassure him that he would continue Barthou's policy towards the Soviet Union. "Europe is in danger of war," Laval said, "any jolt could lead to a bloody *dénouement*." Well, at least on that point he shared common ground with Litvinov. According to Rozenberg's report, Laval's nomination had raised hopes in Germany since he made no secret of his desire to improve Franco-German relations. If an agreement was possible with Germany, Laval added, only by taking a bypass through an agreement in Moscow, he would try it. This was often Soviet policy, seeking agreement in one capital in order to obtain agreement in another. But could it work with Hitlerite Germany? Laval was surrounded by people pushing him towards a German rapprochement. And he was preoccupied with local politics in Aubervilliers in the Paris suburbs where communist militants were trying to oust him. "I have confirmed from numerous sources," Rozenberg added, "that Doumergue, under the influence of Tardieu and because of other factors, has recently become more reserved toward us."[4]

Rozenberg called on Doumergue a few days later to see for himself where matters stood. Doumergue was not at all reserved. "He began by saying that he had for a long time wanted to meet me, and then he had other agreeable things to say." Doumergue came right to the point as if he wanted to dispel the rumours about which Rozenberg had advised the NKID. As Rozenberg described it:

> Doumergue spoke at great length about the German danger, declaring that one could expect anything from these lunatics (*ot etikh sumasshedshikh*). He said that memories of the alliance with Russia [during the Great War] were still strong among the French people and in spite of obvious obstacles the rapprochement was not up against great resistance. You have to be an idiot (*durak*) or ignorant (*nevezhdoi*), Doumergue exclaimed, not to understand the commonality of interests of the governments of France and the USSR.

Doumergue said that Britain had to be drawn into the cooperation between France and the USSR. He several times used the terminology of the Triple Entente, the Anglo-Franco-Russian accord prior to the Great War. As to the Poles, Doumergue was dismissive. Independence had gone to their heads, he said in so many words (*Poliakam vredna nezavisimost'*), citing the nineteenth-century polemicist Pierre-Joseph Proudhon. This was all good news for Rozenberg; he proposed that Franco-Soviet relations be made more concrete. Doumergue suggested meeting again in a fortnight after the political situation had become clearer.[5] Unfortunately, that meeting did not take place. In a fortnight the Doumergue government would fall (on 9 November). Doumergue was gone; Laval remained. What a roller coaster.

Vladimir Petrovich Potemkin

In Moscow, Litvinov went back to Stalin to gain approval for a new polpred in France to replace Dovgalevskii, who had died in Paris on Bastille Day. In Geneva, French diplomats let it be known that they were "rather offended" by the lengthy absence of a Soviet ambassador in Paris. Litvinov recommended the appointment of Vladimir Petrovich Potemkin, then polpred in Rome and before that in Athens. Potemkin was born in 1874 in the Tver, a town 180 kilometres northeast of Moscow. His father was a physician; the family thus lived comfortably as part of the provincial bourgeoisie. Vladimir Petrovich eventually enrolled at the University of Moscow and like so many others of his generation became involved in the revolutionary movement. In so doing, he ran afoul of the tsarist police and was briefly jailed. Eventually completing his university education in 1900, he began to teach history in *gimnaziia* while at the same time resuming his revolutionary activities in the Moscow committee of the Russian Social Democratic Workers' Party. After the October Revolution, he worked in the Commissariat for Education. In 1919, he joined the Bolshevik Party and fought at the front during the civil war. In 1922, he entered the diplomatic service. He was a good diplomat and functioned well with foreign interlocutors. In the existing photographs, Potemkin hardly looks like a Bolshevik *frontovik*, his face is round, his hair is receding, grey, and fluffed out over his ears and around the back of his head. He wore spectacles that made him look like the school teacher he actually had been. At his new embassy in Paris, he worked tenaciously to improve relations with the French, eventually becoming disillusioned and cynical. Potemkin had the patience of a saint and needed it in dealing with the French. His reports were for the most part unemotional, perceptive … and fascinating for present-day historians. Faced with the wobbly French, and later with *perfide Albion* after becoming NKID zamnarkom in 1937, he could be sharp-tongued and reserved with Western interlocutors. His records of meeting with them are a good indication of which way the wind was blowing in Moscow. In that role, I call him Comrade Barometer.

Rozenberg, still first secretary, had carried more and more of the load as Dovgalevskii became less able to work, but he did not have Potemkin's seniority (he was twenty-two years younger than Potemkin). Paris, wrote Litvinov, is at the present time our "most important" diplomatic post.[6] Even more important than Washington, Krestinskii had told Troianovskii.[7] The Soviet government was playing *va banque* in the Casino de France; it was a huge risk, but what better option was there?

Figure 10.1. Vladimir Petrovich Potemkin, ca. 1930s, AVPRF.

Gambling in Casino de France

Alphand recognized the risk Litvinov was taking. He had committed himself to the rapprochement with France to the extent that if the policy failed, it could cost him "his prestige and his situation." In other words, it could cost Litvinov his job. The French government could not let the rapprochement fail. There were doubts in Moscow about the French commitment to relations with the USSR, Alphand warned, it was essential – "a priomordial interest" – to dissipate them. Unless of course, Alphand suggested, France wanted to leave an opening to Germany in Moscow. He asked for authorization to give formal assurances to the Soviet government, if Laval did not want to offer them to Rozenberg.[8] In fact, Laval had already done so three days earlier, for whatever value those assurances might have had.

The day before Rozenberg met Doumergue, on 24 October, Alphand in Moscow signed an important letter to Laval. He appeared to want to get the new minister's attention before the Germanophiles cornered him. The Moscow press in various obituaries had praised Barthou's work as foreign minister:

Litvinov himself, in a very unusual gesture, had convoked the Havas representative in Mocow to the NKID and read him an official statement on the death of Barthou. This praise for the dead minister was not sentimentalism, Alphand noted, the Soviet government wanted to underline the value it attached to the "policy of entente" with France. The "international situation" was disquieting. Poland and Germany caused the most concern. Everyday there were new signs of a Polish orientation towards Germany and the other "revisionist" powers. In Moscow, they think that an ultimatum (*mise en demeure*) should be issued to Warsaw to choose "between the French alliance and German collusion." Poland would then have no option but to come around. Without French and Soviet support, Poland would be nothing more than "a power of the second order destined to become a satellite of the Reich." Moreover, there was no denying Soviet concerns about a recurrence of opposition to the rapprochement among French Germanophiles. France could not have it both ways, Alphand wrote, it would be foolish to think it could, as long as Germany did not repudiate its "dreams of expansion." It was seductive to think, like "certain English conservatives," that offering a free hand to Hitler in Poland and the Ukraine would lead Germany into a bog. Alphand remembered Napoleon's disaster. But it might not turn out that way; Germany could weaken the Russian "counterweight," and then turn back to the west having once destroyed the European balance of power.

Like Doumergue, Alphand recalled the old Franco-Russian alliance as a deterrent to German power. It was hard to forget. Republican France had supported tsarist Russia even though their "conceptions of government" had differed. Nothing had changed. There was also the danger that the Soviet government could look to another option, *une solution de moindre effort*. This would be an accord with Germany to direct its expansion towards France or towards Austria and thus away from Soviet frontiers. The rise of Hitler had caused the USSR to opt for another policy in order to contain the Nazi menace. Recent rumours of a Soviet-German détente were "quite improbable." Soviet policy, Alphand concluded, can be resumed in a formula that Litvinov had often used: "We are adversaries of anything which can increase German strength and partisans of everything which can weaken it."[9]

Here was the argument, laid out by Alphand, in favour of Franco-Soviet cooperation against Hitlerite Germany. It was the same as Herriot's evocation of the sixteenth-century alliance between Francis I and Suleiman the Magnificent. It was the Catholic king and the Muslim sultan, or in 1934, the French bourgeois and the Soviet Bolshevik. The enemy of my enemy is my ally. If one did not like that principle, Alphand identified the Soviet option, which Moscow actually pursued in 1939. Would Laval heed his ambassador's plea for Franco-Soviet cooperation, and his warning against failing to pursue it?

Litvinov's Report to Stalin

One week later, Litvinov sent a briefing note to Stalin similar to Alphand's to Laval. "The increasing rearmament of Germany outside the limits of the treaty of Versailles leaves no doubt." It is only a question of when Germany will be ready for war, say, "in a year or a year and a half." That is all it will take. No one is talking about longer time frames.

> Of course, to be ready for war does not yet mean make war. It is possible that at the outset Germany will use the strengthening of its military power for the diplomatic reinforcement of its international position, for the attraction of allies, and the guarantee at least of the neutrality of those governments which will not become its allies. Military power attracts, and this objective it will achieve. Then the question will arise about the use of this power … I think nevertheless that Germany in the near future, without special necessity, will not want to measure its strength against France … Germany will not be satisfied with the sole acquisition of Austria, which is likely to become a factor much earlier, possibly even without war. In the event of a continuation of the Franco-Polish alliance, Germany dare not needlessly attack Poland. Probably Germany will seek an outlet for its building military energy in the direction of the Baltics, the USSR, and the Ukraine across Romania, in other words, it will carry out the plan of [Nazi ideologue Alfred] Rosenberg and Hitler himself outlined in his program-book, *Mein Kampf*. For this it can count fully on the support of at least Japan, Poland, and Finland.

In these circumstances what could the Soviet government do, Litvinov asked rhetorically, what "mutual insurance" did the Eastern Pact provide us in its previously envisaged framework (when discussed with Barthou)? It required fewer obligations for the USSR in the existing circumstances because of the absence of common frontiers with Germany and limited Soviet assistance to countries that would become victims of German aggression. Such an agreement had a more immediate value to the USSR, Litvinov argued, in that it would in some measure guarantee against an anti-Soviet French agreement with Germany. This idea had been mooted by Daladier and more recently by Laval. Before his arrival in power, Laval had said openly to Rozenberg that he had discussed with the Weimar chancellor Heinrich Brüning an "agreement directed against the USSR." Moreover, Laval did not hide that the "focus of his efforts" would be an agreement with Germany. It was a fool's errand, Litvinov noted in so many words: "An agreement with Hitlerite Germany is impossible on the basis of peace and it must necessarily be directed against someone." German and Polish proposals were intended to break the earlier iteration of the Eastern Pact, which, it was noted, Germany "greatly fears" because it would interfere with its expansionist plans. Litvinov then discussed various permutations of a mutual security pact or pacts and asked for a discussion in the Politburo based on his note.[10]

On the following day, 2 November, Litvinov sent specific recommendations to the Politburo, which included the possibility of an Eastern Pact without Germany and Poland in the event of an agreement on this with France and Czechoslovakia. Nor should the USSR on its own initiative propose a "legalization of German rearmament." If France proved open to legalization, then we should propose to France that it insisted on German adhesion to the Eastern Pact. Finally, Litvinov recommended a proposal to France for an agreement on the mutual obligation of the USSR and France not to conclude any political agreement with Germany without prior mutual consultation. These recommendations were approved word for word by the Politburo.[11]

Alphand and Mendras Warn Paris

Alphand and Colonel Mendras continued to hear of Soviet disquiet over a possible change in French government policy. It did not help that Laval kept repeating to the four winds that he would seek a German rapprochement. Soviet anxiety over the continuity of French policy, Mendras warned in early November, was far from being reassured.[12] Alphand sent similar dispatches and telegrams to the Quai d'Orsay. The NKID was also sending messages through the Soviet press, written by Radek. Both Mendras and Alphand noticed. If France moved away from the USSR, Alphand warned, Moscow would not hesitate to change course, to steal a march on France, and respond to German advances. The Quai d'Orsay noticed this telegram and responded on the morrow with instructions for Alphand to reassure Litvinov.[13] Still, Alphand returned to the charge advising of rumours of a possible disgrace of Litvinov. The French ambassador had good contacts in the Soviet government who were well informed and not reluctant to talk. There was a quiet struggle inside the government being waged against Litvinov, but Alphand's informants thought he would survive them. In fact, Litvinov was too sure of himself, and demanded – well, no one demanded anything from Stalin – let's say, insisted on being consulted on foreign policy. He could rub colleagues the wrong way, like Kaganovich and Molotov, though even the latter acknowledged Litvinov's successes. The rivalries were mainly personal, therefore, and not susceptible of causing a change in direction. Stalin, Voroshilov, and Kalinin backed Litvinov's policies, though Stalin was the only one who counted as time went along in the 1930s. In fact, most of Litvinov's main recommendations to Stalin were passing through the Politburo word for word as Litvinov wrote them. Alphand's information was generally correct. Still, he could not conceal his own lingering disquiet. He noted that France had an interest, *un grand intérêt*, in Litvinov staying at his post.[14] What Alphand did not say was that the Politburo, Stalin in effect, was making a huge gamble on France, and that the odds in favour of success, by any objective evaluation, were not promising.

Even Litvinov acknowledged the difficulties. "Germany is making desperate efforts to delay our rapprochement with France," Litvinov wrote to the new polpred in Berlin, Iakov Zakharovich Surits, "and to involve it in some kind of negotiations. With this in mind it is frightening France, spreading rumours, on the one hand, about an alleged German-Japanese agreement and the possibility of an imminent joint attack against the USSR, and on the other, about serious political and economic negotiations with the USSR, which must lead to the reestablishment of previous Soviet-German relations. At the same time it [Germany] is very active in Belgrade and Bucharest trying to tear away these two countries from France, with the assistance of Polish diplomacy."[15]

The Polish Skunk

The fight for collective security was thus being fought on many fronts, and the Poles were playing the role of skunk in the woodpile on almost all of them. Zamnarkom Stomoniakov long suspected Polish motives and had clashed with the former polpred in Warsaw, Antonov-Ovseenko. In the absence of Litvinov, Stomoniakov, writing from Moscow, proposed a tougher public line in response to Polish foreign policy. Poland's "German orientation" was deepening, he advised, and the Polish press was becoming more hostile, not as bad as before the Soviet-Polish rapprochement, but bad enough. The press loyal to Marshal Piłsudski was resuming old anti-Soviet lines and "terminology." Some of the worst comments came from Jan Berson, alias Otmar, the Polish correspondent in Moscow, who wrote for the Polish news agency and for the semi-official *Gazeta Polska*. Berson was close to Łukasiewicz, the Polish minister in Moscow, and Bogusław Miedziński, the editor of *Gazeta Polska*, who had served as a go-between with Radek in 1933. Berson had written favourably of the Soviet-Polish rapprochement, but his line had turned hostile over the last year. Such articles were being employed at home to fight pro-Soviet opinion. So what to do? Stomoniakov did not think Berson's expulsion was a good idea, at least for the time being. Why make a hero of him in Warsaw? It would be better to reply to Berson in the Soviet papers. Radek could write the necessary commentary. Who better to know how to employ scorn and sarcasm? It would be Pole against Pole.[16] Stomoniakov still hoped to influence pro-Soviet elements in Warsaw, but where were they? Whereas in London, Paris, and other places such elements were frequent visitors to Soviet embassies, they did not often turn up at the Soviet embassy in Warsaw. They were nameless spectres, mostly flickering shadows in the night.

The French were also none too happy with the Poles. Mendras referred to the "latent defection" of Poland, and speculated that if Japan attacked the USSR,

Poland and Finland, supported by Germany, might also attack in the west. The Poles were on their high horse, according to Mendras, "they are playing a bold game with this congenital taste for intrigue and for combinations *à double fond* that their past as conspirators could only help to develop."[17] Mendras was being relatively kind. Others in the French establishment were less so. "If Poland does not want to follow France into a military alliance with the Soviets ... *eh bien*, we will do without [Poland]," said the chief of staff General Weygand in 1933. "We will count on Russia, and not bother any more about Poland," rejoined the late Barthou, who was at the limits of his patience in his last meeting with Beck.[18] That was the trouble with the French, the words of complaint came easily, but they could never put their foot down, translating words into action, least of all Laval. If France did not "bother" anymore with Poland, and concluded a genuine alliance with the USSR, it would mean the end of the *cordon sanitaire*. Poland could go over to Germany, and defeating Germany would mean defeating Poland. Its certain destruction would lead to the disappearance of the main barrier against penetration of Soviet influence into the heart of Europe. The memories of King Francis I and Suleiman the Magnificent captured the imagination but ran up against cold realities. Was France ready to ditch the *cordon sanitaire*?

Litvinov and Laval Meet in Geneva

Litvinov remained uneasy. He cabled Rozenberg with instructions to contact Herriot. "Tell him ... that Laval's ambiguous position and his repeated emphasis on the desirability of a Franco-German agreement are causing misgivings here; in as much as Laval has already had sufficient time to familiarize himself with affairs, we should be able to expect a clearer statement of his attitude toward Franco-Soviet collaboration." Litvinov planned to meet Laval in Geneva, and hoped to hear something more definite on the further development of relations. In order to be sure to get Laval's attention, Litvinov instructed Rozenberg to tell Herriot that Moscow was getting various economic and political suggestions from Germany. The Germans could also be making similar proposals to France. "You can tell Herriot ... that you, say, are afraid that this could give rise to mutual suspicions between France and us, which is what Germany is trying to achieve."[19] Herriot replied that Laval had abandoned (*otrepsia*) his previous views "on the possibility of a Franco-Germany agreement." Anyway, Laval had said that he "will not allow a reversal of policy."[20] This news should have been reassuring to Litvinov, but it was not.

Litvinov and Laval met in Geneva on 21 November. They spent two hours together. "He again repeated," Litvinov cabled to Moscow, his "usual" lines about continuing Barthou's policy and the effort to obtain an Eastern Pact. A discussion then ensued about Poland and Germany. Litvinov eventually asked if the French government had discussed the eventuality of Polish and German refusal – in fact, they had refused already – to agree to an Eastern Pact. There had been no discussion, replied Laval. He must have been reading Litvinov's mind, because he stated "categorically" that France would not enter into agreements with other powers without the USSR. "He did not hide his efforts to obtain agreement with Germany, but he thinks of this only with the help and participation of the USSR." These were now Laval's familiar lines.

Litvinov continued, "I told Laval about the German attempts to seduce the USSR with various tempting economic and political proposals; Germany was probably also making such proposals in Paris with the objective of sowing discord between the two countries." Having succeeded in alienating Poland and France, Germany was now attempting to do the same with France and the USSR. "I asked Laval if he did not think it necessary to prevent this process." Laval replied by asking if Litvinov had specific proposals to suggest? I If so, he said they could discuss them.

Litvinov proposed a mutual commitment not to conclude a political agreement with Germany without prior discussion and to agree to constant sharing of information. Laval at once embraced the idea, according to Litvinov. "Later on, however, he caught himself and began to step away from this agreement." His minder from the Quai d'Orsay, Bargeton, was participating, and Laval suggested mulling over an appropriate formula, stressing also the need for secrecy "to avoid giving the impression of a Franco-Soviet alliance." Here was an essential task of Quai d'Orsay senior officials to keep transient ministers from going off script or too hastily agreeing to a policy contrary to the policies of the Quai d'Orsay *apparat*. Certainly, Litvinov replied, suggesting they each think about a formula, consult their governments, and then talk again at their next meeting. They did so on the following day, 22 November. Laval proposed a unilateral French declaration; Litvinov countered with a formal bilateral agreement. He had the draft text of a formal agreement in his pocket and read it to Laval, and one supposes, to Bargeton who must have been present.[21] Laval informed his ambassador in London, Charles Corbin, about the discussions with Litvinov and the recent German offers to improve relations. Litvinov wished to be able to overcome "hesitations" which these offers had provoked in Moscow. The agreement was "purely formal and transitory."[22] In other words, Laval instructed Corbin to reassure the Foreign Office that there was little to the agreement. It was a modest concession to Litvinov.

That same evening, Litvinov invited the US diplomat Hugh Wilson for dinner, *à deux*. Litvinov did not bring up his meeting with Laval, nor did he raise the problem of the impasse over debts and credits with the State Department. He was still casting about for some way to get the United States involved in Geneva and involved in a broader coalition of states to hold potential aggressors in check, namely Germany and Japan. On this point, Wilson was discouraging; US public opinion did not want to get involved in European problems. Litvinov accepted that his idea was not going to work, Wilson noted, and he "would have to think of something else." One thing was clear in Wilson's mind. "Throughout the conversation Litvinov displayed the most complete distrust of Germany. To him, so long as there is a Hitler regime, just so long is Germany a mad dog that can't be trusted, with whom no agreements can be made, and whose ambition can only be checked by a ring of determined neighbors."[23]

On 5 December, Litvinov and Laval met again. Laval repeated his usual refrain about trying to improve relations with Germany, though this intention was not aimed against the USSR. Laval stated that his objection was not only to assure peace between Germany and France but also between Germany and the USSR. That sounded naïve, although Litvinov did not say it. He advised Moscow that agreement had been reached with Laval and Bargeton on the draft, which Litvinov had proposed on 22 November.[24] Laval and Litvinov signed the protocol that same day. The final text envisaged a continuation of efforts to obtain an Eastern Pact, stipulating that neither signatory would embark on negotiations for other multilateral or bilateral agreements which could undermine the common effort to secure an Eastern Pact. The agreement of course would not have been necessary if the two sides trusted each other, had the same objectives, and evaluated the international situation in the same way.[25] But trust was the main issue, and how could anyone trust Laval? Laval might have countered with how could anyone trust a Bolsh? On paper, the protocol seemed a step forward. That is how Litvinov saw it. He might better have concluded that the Herriot-Boncour-Barthou line was for the time being suspended. Laval had broken, or was trying to break, the policy momentum of his predecessors. For him the protocol was a cover to pursue the policy which he had always intended to pursue, and to get Litvinov off his back, at least for a little while. It would soon be the Christmas holidays; he could expect a few weeks of relief. For the Soviet Union, it was a risky policy, as Litvinov would certainly have recognized, like playing roulette in a casino where everyone knows that the odds are stacked in favour of the house. In France this meant that there were already too many forces lining up against a deepening of the Franco-Soviet rapprochement. Why could they not see, as the Soviet side could see, the menace of Hitlerite Germany?

Soviet Intelligence Reports

Soviet intelligence reports on German intentions appeared to point in two directions. The German high command would expand towards the southeast across Austria and westward against France. Or Germany would attempt to settle the issue of the Polish Corridor by an "amicable agreement" with Poland, even if at the expense of Lithuania. France, on the other hand, seemed a logical target. It had been going downhill since the time of Napoleon. The Great War had weakened France even more. It would be at least three decades before the French Army could wage war on its own. Germany would have irresistible military superiority and could impose its conditions on France either by ultimatum or by overwhelming force.[26]

According to another report from Red Army intelligence, the German Army would be ready for war in the spring of 1935. The German high command fully accepted the Nazi view on the necessity of war against the USSR. With Polish and Finnish allies, the German Army would attack through the Baltic states, the "north-eastern variant." The attack would begin only after a Japanese offensive in the east. According to the German high command, France would remain neutral in such an eventuality. There was, however, disagreement over when the German Army would be ready for war.[27] Who really knew in which direction the German Army would move?

Military intelligence was contradictory, but a few things were certain. Hitlerite Germany would one day be ready for war. The Soviet Union would eventually become a target. And France was a poor bet as an ally. It was fatally weakened, and would eventually fall to German arms. The evaluation of France proved apposite.

At the end of December a spectacular report arrived on Stalin's desk, mainly about France and about Laval's policy towards Germany. "All of Laval's tactics are now calculated on being able to place public opinion in France before the fact of necessity to come to agreement with Germany." That was the first sentence in the report from an unidentified agent known to Stalin. Piłsudski and his group considered Laval to be the "loyal man" of the "Tardieu-Weygand group acting under their orders." He was "smart, very devious, and a careful diplomat." That was the opinion of Piłsudski. The informant seemed to know a lot about Piłsudski's calculations concerning Laval and France. He had "high hopes for Laval" and reckoned that the Flandin government would fall not later than the last half of January 1935. The Flandin government would fall because of a law aimed at disarming the paramilitary league of Colonel François de La Rocque, the *Croix de feu*. It sounded like a real *complot*. Tardieu was involved, making calculations about an eventual Laval government, backed by Colonel de La Rocque's league, with the Radicals but without Herriot. There was more about French deputies visiting Germany, meeting with Hitler and other Nazi notables, with Laval's knowledge. This sounded like a good theme for a spy novel except in large part it was true, and it provoked considerable publicity in France.[28] Laval would meet with Nazi notables in Paris; he would even meet personally with Hitler. What a story! And the British were involved too. They were to put pressure on the Flandin government, if it survived presumably, for the need to come to terms with Hitlerite Germany.

The source of all this information, the unidentified agent known to Stalin, had contacts in high places, including Beck with whom he had spoken directly. The "fact of Franco-German negotiations was an extraordinarily serious business." If successful, it could lead to Piłsudski's "old idea" of the creation of a Poland-Germany-France bloc. It could happen soon, according to the agent, "and the fact of the creation of this bloc is already the beginning of intervention against the USSR." If it all worked out for Laval, based on well informed sources in the Tardieu-Weygand group, a French general would be sent to Berlin as ambassador, possibly even Weygand himself. A general would also be sent to London as ambassador replacing Corbin.

Then Stalin's agent turned to the Litvinov-Laval protocol. Beck said he had been informed on 2 December. At the same time a "trusted person" from the Tardieu-Weygand group was sent to Warsaw to explain to Beck that Laval was obliged to sign the protocol "because of tactical considerations both internal and foreign." It was a temporary arrangement, limited in scope and time, according to the report, and this explanation corresponded to that sent to Corbin on 30 November. According to Beck, "Litvinov sought this protocol from Laval in order to calm Moscow, and, perhaps, Moscow reassured, is what we also need. Time is needed for Germany and France to come to terms." The agent did not exclude the possibility of Franco-Soviet alliance but in two months, it could be too late. Then there was the Eastern Pact. Poland would not sign it "under any circumstances." Laval renewed negotiations only as a "tactical manoeuvre," yielding to pressure from the Radicals (like Herriot and Cot, though they were not mentioned) and from the USSR, Czechoslovakia, and Romania.

According to Beck, there were two points about which Litvinov was not informed by the French, the first being the primacy of the Franco-Polish alliance, and the second being that in case of the conclusion of an Eastern Pact, with or without Poland, France would guarantee "that troops of the USSR in no case will pass across its territory and also Soviet aviation will not fly across the territory of Poland." Here again was the passage issue, already frequently discussed in 1934 and every year thereafter until August 1939. There is no confirming French evidence that these points had been conveyed officially or unofficially to Beck, though it is possible that they were, given Laval's double dealing. If the agent's information was correct, then genuine "mutual assistance" was already dead in the water at the end of December 1934.

Let's allow Stalin's agent to continue his report. He had more fascinating things to say. Again according to Beck, the French had put the question to Warsaw: Are you for us or against us? Are you "with Paris or Berlin"? Apparently with British support, Beck had replied, "With Paris and with Berlin together, but Poland will not pave the way for the rebirth of the Franco-Russian alliance." This meant, the agent continued, that "Poland will not sign the Eastern Pact and will act against its organization." Laval's position was that an Eastern Pact without Germany and Poland was unthinkable:

> *Since a Franco-Soviet alliance threatens the complete alienation of Poland from France and ultimately to its passing to the side of Germany*, a Franco-Soviet alliance does not present any interest for France, that is, this alliance is not the pre-war Franco-Russian alliance, for now between Germany and Russia is Poland – an armed state, which reduces to zero the eventual aid to France from the side of the Red Army. In these circumstances, *it was necessary to abandon the idea of a Franco-Soviet alliance* [emphasis added].

And that was not all. Franco-Soviet military cooperation could also risk the alienation of Britain on which France would be most dependent in the event of war with Germany. Again, in these circumstances Franco-Soviet cooperation would be "dangerous." Thus, an agreement with Germany seemed the logical alternative since the German government had reassured France there were no disputes between them which could lead to war. France could therefore have it both ways: come to terms with Germany, retain its special relations with Britain and its alliance with Poland. The agent went on with further details of Polish views, those of Piłsudski and Beck on the Eastern Pact. Poland would never sign it. In effect, the Eastern Pact was dead, and had been for some time. France feared to risk its relations with Britain, which had no army to speak of, and with Poland, which would have no chance at war against Germany, for the sake of an alliance with the Soviet Union, whose armed forces were rapidly growing and whose government sought an anti-Germany alliance under the rubric of collective security. France was going to sacrifice everything for nothing, Stalin might have concluded. He underlined the key points in blue pencil and initialed the agent's report to be sent to his archives.[29] One wonders whether Litvinov read this report, and if he did, what he thought about it. He often doubted the credibility of intelligence sources, though in this case the source seems to have been well informed. Soviet policy, nevertheless, continued as before. There was no other choice.

Another disturbing anecdotal report arrived in Moscow from the Soviet military attaché in Warsaw, General N.A. Semenov. The report came from a TASS journalist in Warsaw relating the story of one Feldman whom he knew as the husband of a friend of his wife's. Feldman had spent some time in a Polish prison for "communist activities" and then fallen on hard economic times, eventually taking a job as a travelling salesman. During a social visit, Feldman had related an "adventure" that took place a short time before during a trip to Stanisławów in the Polish Ukraine. He often travelled there on business and was having dinner in a restaurant he liked. The only other people in the restaurant at the time were a group of senior Polish officers who were drinking heavily and talking loudly. "Unnoticed, F. took a seat at a corner table and ordered dinner and waited to be served." In the meantime the officers under the influence of alcohol became more and more "happy" and "loud" as they proposed toasts. "I raise my glass," F. remembered one officer saying, "to our alliance with Germany and Japan. War for a soldier is the same as water is for fish. I drink to future war. I raise my glass for some division (F. did not get which one) which had received the order 'Virtuti Militari' for taking Kiev to be received for the same task a second time [the first time being in May 1920 during the Soviet-Polish war]." At that moment one of the seated officers noticed Feldman. Rather drunk, he got up from his chair saying, "This civilian son of a bitch has heard everything." With that he pulled a revolver. "Thanks only to the fact that at the last moment they [his companions] grabbed his arm, the bullet did not hit F. but struck a lamp. After the shot was fired, the owner of the restaurant and the waiters ran up to F. and escorted him to another room in the hotel, and the owner said to him in a whisper: get out of the hall quickly, you know that among the officers is General [Gustaw Konstanty] Orlicz-Dreszer himself who is inspector of the army." This was one of the most senior officers in the Polish army and someone close to Piłsudski's ruling group.

The next morning the police arrested Feldman and held him for interrogation. "What did you hear?" they wanted to know. "I heard nothing and know nothing," Feldman replied. This was the right answer, apparently, for the police were satisfied and let him go unharmed. It was not, of course, Feldman's fate that interested the Soviet military attaché but the drunken toasts to a Polish alliance with Germany and Japan and to the taking of Kiev a second time in which a general, an inspector of the Polish army, would participate. This incident is "extremely valuable for describing not only Polish-German relations," Semenov wrote in a cover letter, "but also shows what is really sitting in the heads of generals. It is likewise known that Orlicz is a big lover of 'parties' surrounded by the company of officers and thus creating his own popularity. For a long time already we have considered Orlicz to be our open enemy." Semenov reckoned the report to be reliable.[30] Orlicz-Dreszer died two years later in a plane crash.

Laval's "Little Steps"

Laval was looking for security where he could find it, but he was not thinking clearly about what security he would be getting. The Soviet option was tainted, according to the French right, which was less inclined, as Kerillis had earlier written to Payart, to set the German danger higher than the Soviet danger. At the beginning of 1935, Italy, fascist though it was, had not gone over to Nazi Germany. When Austrian Nazis had attempted a coup d'état in July 1934 against the Austrian government and assassinated the chancellor Englebert Dolfuss, Mussolini ordered troops to the Brenner Pass, the Italian gateway to Austria, as a warning to Hitler to keep his hands off. Laval went to Rome to meet with Mussolini in early January 1935. On 7 January they signed the so-called Rome accords which, *inter alia*, proposed a regional non-aggression pact to protect Austrian independence. When the Italian side proposed staff talks to deal with potential German aggression, Laval hesitated. That was one of Laval's problems. It was a "little step" here and a "little step" there, as the late Academician Duroselle put it.[31]

Litvinov had no problem with France improving relations with Italy. On the contrary, he was well disposed to such a move; the Soviet Union was also attempting to do the same. What troubled Litvinov was that the regional non-aggression pacts, envisaged in the Rome accords, did not include the USSR. This could create the impression of Soviet "isolation." It was not that the Soviet government was less interested in Austrian independence, he wrote to Potemkin, the new Soviet polpred in Paris, than other states in the region. He mentioned Turkey, Greece, and Romania. If we made inquiries in Paris and Rome, Litvinov observed, we might face a possible question, "do we ourselves wish to participate eventually in the guarantee of Austrian independence, and this question remains under discussion."[32]

Herriot Intervenes

It was Laval's "little steps" that irritated almost everyone. Europe was in crisis and "little steps" were not going to protect European security. Herriot was furious with Laval and did not hesitate to say it in a conversation with Potemkin on 11 January. Readers will have noticed that Herriot was an important Soviet informant. He was someone to whom Soviet diplomats turned when they needed information or support in pursuing the rapprochement with France. Herriot was an influential politician and remained a minister without portfolio in the French cabinet and was the *président* of the powerful Radical Party. He was firmly committed to the Franco-Soviet rapprochement. "Today I visited with Herriot," Potemkin wrote in his record of the conversation. These Soviet records are important because Herriot and other French politicians rarely left corresponding notes about their conversations with Soviet diplomats. "I found him [Herriot] extremely irritated with Laval and his policies." First, there were the Rome accords. Laval had agreed to the cession of some North African territories to Italy, and Herriot was incensed. Nor did he think that Germany would agree to a guarantee of Austrian independence. And on and on he went from one topic to the next, unloading his scorn on Laval. Quite understandably, he asked Potemkin "to observe every care" in conveying his judgements to Litvinov. The report was duly marked "very secret." One can see why.

"He [Herriot] again reaffirmed that as long as he lived, France will not be in the camp of our enemies." Stick to your guns, he advised, take a hard line on the original proposals for an Eastern Pact and the Geneva protocol with Laval. Don't place too much hope in Nicolae Titulescu, the Romanian foreign minister, who is too pro-Italian, or Eduard Beneš, the Czechoslovak foreign minister, who is "too flexible … more French than a Czechoslovak minister." Herriot continued, "We will succeed in overcoming hitches and difficulties which have arisen on the road to a rapprochement of the USSR with France." Potemkin replied by stressing the "historical importance" of the rapprochement and the readiness of the USSR to devote all its efforts to reinforcing it. Herriot agreed. "He responded," wrote Potemkin, "with an animation and vehemence which I have never before observed from him."

"I am an old politician," Herriot continued, "accustomed to good weather and bad … After the clouds always comes the clear sky. Everything passes. After the Lavals, others will occupy their places." Laval wants "to make himself popular," Herriot added, "'to inflate his balloon,' but sooner or later the balloon will burst and fall to the ground."[33]

Krestinskii and Litvinov would have been justified in having their doubts about Laval, but Herriot's vehement defence of the rapprochement may have given them some hope that everything might turn out all right after all. It was a fight, and it would have to be seen through until the end because there was no other option if one wanted to protect Soviet, but really European, security against Hitlerite Germany. Laval's "balloon" already seemed to be losing altitude.

Chapter Eleven

Bridging the Gap: The Anglo-Soviet Rapprochement, 1934–1935

Before resuming the account of Soviet efforts to obtain an accord with France, it is necessary to go back in time to catch up on Soviet diplomatic activities in London. For the Soviet Union, Britain was as necessary as France in building up a system of collective security and mutual assistance against Nazi Germany. Soviet policy could not succeed without the support of France and Britain. With the Metro-Vickers affair settled in early July 1933, Maiskii could begin to work on binding up the wounds of that crisis. The first step along that path was to complete the interrupted negotiations for a new Anglo-Soviet trade agreement. Better economic relations often opened the way to better political relations. At least this was a basic principle of Soviet policy even if it often did not work. Economics were a means to an end, and readers will perhaps remember that Litvinov's efforts to settle the Metro-Vickers crisis were motivated by his increasing anxiety about Nazi Germany. In this, he had Stalin's full support. Litvinov's success in Washington in obtaining US diplomatic recognition as well as the developing rapprochement with France strengthened the narkom's credibility at home. He would need it in dealing with Britain.

Perceptions of Litvinov

During his stay in London in July 1933, Litvinov met Foreign Office official R.A. Leeper, with whom he had dealt in 1918 as the first Soviet representative in Great Britain. The meeting offered Litvinov the opportunity to vent his spleen with Leeper about Anglo-Soviet relations. Their personal meeting left a deep impression on Leeper who wrote a long record of their conversation, a part of which reads:

> In 1918 I was in almost daily contact with him for many months at a time when he was being subjected to innumerable annoyances & indignities. I had then found him, apart from occasional explosions, good-tempered & reasonable. He

> was in fact as frank & natural as the circumstances permitted. Fifteen years have passed ... I had been told by journalists ... that if I met him again I should find him very much changed with a hard crust of cynicism which he employs as a weapon of self-defence in dealing with foreigners ... I found nothing of the sort. Away from the atmosphere of Moscow he was exactly the same in his manner as formerly, affable & natural.

Leeper noted that Litvinov "spoke with regret rather than with bitterness" about the difficulties of dealing with the British government. "There were constant setbacks," Litvinov had said. And Leeper continued:

> His main desire had always been to establish satisfactory working relations with us. He had married an English wife, he had lived longer in this country than in any other outside Russia, & he had in consequence a greater regard for it. Yet in conducting official relations with the British Government he was confronted with much greater difficulties than with any other Government ... Nowhere were the press & Parliament so vindictive against Russia ... He could only conclude that there were powerful influences at work here to prevent any kind of working arrangement between the two Governments.[1]

Some of Litvinov's laments could be taken with a grain of salt; one could easily imagine him saying the same thing, *mutatis mutandis*, to a sympathetic French diplomat. Soviet relations with France were scarcely easier than with Britain. And many Foreign Office officials would have scoffed at Litvinov's complaints, blaming the Soviet government for all the difficulties.

Maiskii's Campaign

Nevertheless, the new Soviet policy towards France, confirmed by the Politburo resolution of 19 December 1933, implied of necessity an improvement of relations with Britain. At the beginning of 1934, therefore, the door seemed open for polpred Maiskii to move forward. These included the embassy's relations with the British press. Maiskii proposed an "allowance" for a British periodical, which he called "N.L." If the initials are those of a British paper, then the only one that fits is *New Leader*, edited by Henry Noel Brailsford during the 1920s. Communists would have considered it to be *faux* left. Krestinskii was not "convinced" of the need for an allowance. "There is a big difference," he wrote to Maiskii, "between subsidizing a bourgeois, obviously anti-workers' newspaper and a newspaper that claims to be socialist in nature and even to a certain socialist leftism. 'N.L.' is leading a frenzied struggle against the Comintern, the Communist Party of England, and the left circles of the Independent Labour Party, trying to influence those circles of British workers who are most ready to make the jump to the Communist ranks." "N.L." was more dangerous than Labour or bourgeois newspapers because it masqueraded as a workers' advocate. "Therefore, the issue of subsidizing this journal should be approached not so much from the point of view of the possible benefits of printing in the journal of this or that article favourable to the USSR, but from the point of view of the general harm caused by this journal." Krestinskii was "personally opposed" to subsidizing the paper, but advised that he would consult the NKID *kollegiia*. He proposed to send Maiskii a telegram that would say "my number such and such is confirmed," meaning yes; or "my number such and such wait for the letter in the next mail," meaning no.[2] Readers must think this was all very secret, with coded messages about a journal called "N.L." and who could be sure whether this was, in fact, referring to the *New Leader*? It may well have been. The NKID had been trying to buy favourable notice in the French press for many years but without notable success. Subsidies for British papers are less well known.

The NKID *kollegiia* did not make an immediate decision. Maiskii was unhappy with the delay and returned to the charge with Krestinskii, writing:

> Here I have before me the *Daily Herald*, the organ of the Labour Party – this newspaper pretends to be socialist and deftly hides its anti-worker character under the flag of the hot defence of the cause of labour. It systematically leads the fight against the Comintern and has often opposed the Soviet Union and its foreign policy. If we support this newspaper with our advertisements, are we not creating confusion in the minds of the workers? Keep in mind that the *Daily Herald* is read by 2 million people per day (such is the circulation of the newspaper) – therefore, the scale of confusion, provided it takes place, is very large. In England, workers generally read the bourgeois or Labour press, and the *Daily Worker* has a circulation of only around 20 000, i.e., about the same as "N. L."

So where was Maiskii going with his line of argument? "If one takes your point of view," he replied to Krestinskii, "it will be impossible to subsidize any press in Great Britain." This was very likely Krestinskii's idea, since it was a waste of money. But Maiskii did not agree: "My point of view, therefore, remains the same: for the time being, not to refuse a subsidy, but to monitor the situation closely and, if the newspaper again opposes the USSR or its foreign policy, or if its circulation begins to fall strongly, to reconsider our attitude towards this organ of the press." He pointed out that the file was in Moscow and insisted that they make up their minds. "A few days ago, I received an unsigned cipher from Moscow, which reported that in the *kollegiia* the question of 'N. L' is not resolved. How am I to understand this? The coded telegram also mentioned the 'relapse' of 'N.L' in part because of anti-Soviet speeches. I do not know of any relapses … I await your instructions by return mail."[3] Well, here Maiskii revealed a relatively unknown aspect of his personality. He had taken up the cause of an Anglo-Soviet rapprochement and he was prepared to fight for it in Moscow. The time was right to try.

The British elite was beginning to sense the danger of Nazi Germany. Six months ago, Maiskii noted in early January 1934, when the Soviet representative spoke of the danger of war, the British scoffed. It was seen as just the same "old Soviet propaganda." Or as "you are exaggerating." Now everything was different. "The situation has changed beyond recognition," Maiskii wrote. "When I arrived in London in early December [1933], I was immediately caught in the midst of very lively and relentless discussions about war. In government circles, among members of Parliament, City businessmen, on Fleet Street … everywhere you heard only talk about an impending war. Now, on the contrary, it has become a sign of good manners to say that war is inevitable, that war is just around the corner here, and that we need to get ready for war." Arguments were about when war would break out and if it would become a world war. "The majority of people with whom I have spoken these last months see Germany as the main source of the threat of war."[4]

Collier, head of the Northern Department in the Foreign Office, noted the change in Soviet dispositions, but was rather smug about it. "We, unlike the French," he observed, "do not feel the need of their support [i.e., Soviet]; and they are now beginning to feel the need of *our* [emphasis in the original] support in maintaining the present territorial status quo, the prospects of keeping them from action against our interests in the immediate future seem brighter than they have been hitherto, to say the least." His boss, Sir Lancelot Oliphant, was more positive: "If the Soviet were to run straight, no harm would arise from being in the same camp … If they feel menaced by Japan in the East or Germany in the West, it is quite on the cards that they will run straight with us, if only on the principle *amant deum metuunt* [They love the God they fear]."[5] What Oliphant meant was that the "Bolsh" would embrace old enemies as allies when in need.

The settlement of the Metro-Vickers dispute allowed the resumption of Anglo-Soviet trade negotiations, which led on 16 February 1934 to the conclusion of a new Anglo-Soviet trade agreement, barely a month after Soviet negotiators signed a similar accord with France. Shortly before the signature of the new agreement, Maiskii told a prominent Conservative that the USSR wanted better relations with Great Britain.[6] The Soviet government put out the same message in the press: *Izvestiia* was hopeful that relations would improve, but said that the next move was up to Great Britain. Foreign Office officials were dubious: "The usual hopes for improved relations & real cooperation," noted one clerk. Another commented: "When the Comintern ceases its pernicious propaganda against the British Empire," relations might then improve. "But it is for them to make the move."[7] And when the time came to attend a luncheon to mark the signing of the trade agreement, there was grumbling all around about who would go – and who would pay the bill. It was a corvée, said Oliphant, who was Assistant Permanent Undersecretary, and the Secretary of State should be spared the bother.[8]

Maiskii appears to have been unaware of Foreign Office boredom with the Soviet embassy, and he broached with Moscow the idea of a non-aggression pact with Britain. His idea was to let the new trade agreement gain traction and then to decide whether or not to make an official proposal to the British government.[9] According to Maiskii, the Metro-Vickers settlement and the new trade agreement represented a turning point in Anglo-Soviet relations. Even the Conservatives were beginning to come around. While US recognition and the improvement of relations with France and Italy were elements in this development, the "victory of Hitlerism in Germany" was likewise "not a little factor" that favoured Soviet interests. The enemy of our enemy should be our ally (*khudshchee – vrag khudogo*), according to Maiskii, was the principle influencing wide circles of opinion in Britain, including "moderate Conservatives of the Baldwin type." In other words, he wrote, "because Hitlerite Germany seems … a more direct danger to European peace than the USSR, they [the British] are now ready to treat more gently and kindly the country of the proletarian dictatorship." In this vein, Maiskii heard from a Tory MP Robert Boothby, who was well disposed to the USSR, that even the Die-Hard Winston Churchill was starting to come around: "The international situation has become such that perhaps we will need to take a more friendly position towards … [the USSR]."[10] Exactly, the enemy of my enemy is my ally. Even for Churchill.

In early March, Evgenii Rubinin, NKID bureau chief, had a conversation with the British chargé d'affaires in Moscow, Noel Charles, which seemed to confirm Maiskii's assessment of the British governing elite's evolving views. The conclusion of the trade agreement had made a difference, according to Rubinin. Charles complained about the negative Soviet press comment towards Britain, but Rubinin advised him not to make much of such articles. Rubinin was seeing two tendencies in British policy towards the USSR: one was positive, characterized, for example, by the trade agreement, and the other was negative. The negative policy was characterized by the "Zinoviev Letter" in 1924 and the raid on Arcos in 1927. "Unfortunately," Rubinin said, "this latter trend often prevails and this, of course, leaves a definite trace in the minds of the Soviet public."

Charles agreed about the two tendencies. "He is convinced, however, that the second tendency does not have much influence in England now … In England, the desire to live in peace with the Soviet Union prevails." But Charles then reverted back to the "fierce anti-British propaganda" in the Soviet press; there could hardly be a "genuine rapprochement with the USSR" as long as these attacks continued. The USSR had an advantage in these exchanges of fire because the British government did not have the same means to reply. Here,

Charles was being rather innocent since the News Department was quite capable of conveying a message that it wanted published in the press. Rubinin diverted the conversation back to the NKID line: "We should not get into an assessment of the internal systems that exist in our countries, the more so since it cannot have any influence on the relationship between us." The Soviet government had established better relations with France and the United States, Rubinin went on, and there was no reason not to have better relations with Britain. The "common ground" of a rapprochement was political, he proposed, that is, the "mutual interest in strengthening peace." This was Soviet code for strengthening collective security against Nazi Germany. On this point, Charles agreed: "The embassy, for its part, is ready to make every effort in this direction."[11]

Maiskii Meets J.L. Garvin

In early March, Maiskii listened to the debate in the House of Commons on the approval of the trade agreement, and reported back to Moscow that all had gone well. An "anti-adventurist, realistic frame of mind" was growing in the Conservative Party.[12] Later that month, Maiskii met for the first time with James L. Garvin, the well-known editor of the *Observer*, a London Sunday newspaper. Garvin had a lot of interesting things to say, enough to cause Maiskii to write an eight-page report that landed on Stalin's desk in Moscow. The venue of the discussion was Garvin's country home. It was a Sunday and Maiskii's wife, Agniia, accompanied him. They had lunch and "five o'clock tea" with Garvin and members of his family, making it strictly a family affair. Garvin's daughter Viola was there, as well as another unnamed daughter who resided in Florence, and a stepson, Olivier Wood, who was a student at Oxford. It was often thus that these "intimate" occasions, according to Maiskii, led to frank exchanges on politics and international relations.

On that Sunday afternoon in March 1934, Germany was an important subject of discussion. Garvin had personal reasons not to like the Germans, or even to hate them; his only son had been killed in 1916 during fighting at the Somme. He was very hostile towards "Hitlerite Germany," according to Maiskii: "He considers German national-socialism to be a wild, misanthropic and very dangerous theory" (these words were underlined by Stalin). He called *Mein Kampf* a "gospel of hatred to other races and peoples." So Litvinov was not the only one to have read "Hitler's book." Like the narkom, Garvin did not believe anything Hitler said about peace and security. "This is only a manoeuvre," Garvin said. "Hitler needs to play for time in order to rearm, and in the meantime, he is ready to assure other people of his good will and in his readiness to renounce war as a political tool. The value of all these pacts of non-aggression that Hitler has signed or will sign is not worth a farthing. They will be violated by Germany as soon as it feels strong enough to do so." There was no better proof of Hitler's double-talking than *Mein Kampf*, Garvin opined, which continued to sell in the millions of copies across Germany and was being fed to a new generation of German youth. Other proof was the "not less important fact of the rapid rearmament of Germany." These lines, too, Stalin underlined in blue pencil. And on and on Garvin went: "Hitlerite Germany is the greatest danger to peace." Again, Stalin underlined these words. "Germany dreams of world domination." Litvinov or Stalin needed no convincing.

When it came to Japan, Garvin was no less hostile: it was, like Germany, a threat to peace. Sooner or later, England would have to confront Japan. There was also the additional danger that Germany and Japan might form an alliance or at a minimum a rapprochement directed against the USSR. Garvin suspected that Poland might have "some secret agreement with Germany for bilateral action against USSR aimed at the seizure of Lithuania and the Ukraine." Again Stalin underlined key lines from Maiskii's report. The publications of Hitler and Alfred Rosenberg, according to Garvin, "left no doubt" that Germany had a fully developed plan for eastward expansion. One needed to take such things at face value. Garvin considered that the USSR had to arm to the teeth in order to parry attacks from the east and the west. It was the only way to discourage aggression and keep the peace. Again, Stalin underlined these passages. Garvin apparently wanted to pass a message to Moscow, which was duly annotated in the Kremlin.

Maiskii finally asked the inevitable question: What will England do if Hitler attacks France? Garvin at once replied that England would defend France. If England abandoned France, it would sign its own death warrant. Garvin saw an alliance of the Big Five powers – the United States, England, France, the USSR, and Italy – as the best guarantee of peace and security. Most of the small and medium powers would flock to such an alliance. This would be "a peace bloc," and Germany and Japan would think twice before challenging it. Again, Stalin applied his blue pencil. The League of Nations also came up in conversation. Garvin opined that the US and Soviet entry as members would strengthen it, and permit the "peace bloc" to operate within its bounds. And, finally, Maiskii observed that the Big Five necessarily would depend on improved Anglo-Soviet relations. Garvin agreed.[13] The Soviet strategy was clear. The Metro-Vickers crisis had caused some delay in implementing collective security. Maiskii wanted to make up for lost time.

The Sceptical Foreign Office

Maiskii must have been encouraged by what he heard at lunch that Sunday, but Garvin's views were far from being shared by everyone, least of all in the Foreign Office. Two weeks earlier, the Soviet government had sent a feeler to London through the British embassy in Ankara that it wanted better relations. Sir Percy

Loraine, the British ambassador in Ankara, was discouraging. He reminded the Turkish foreign minister "that a very large proportion of opinion in England held the view that the whole political system and creed of Soviet Russia was the work of Satan and that in my country such widespread opinion had to be taken into account."

The ambassador has made "a mistake," noted Prime Minister Ramsay Macdonald in his minutes, pointing out that Lorraine's remarks would surely get back to Moscow and into the Soviet press. But Simon, the Foreign Secretary, advised Loraine that there was no need to rush into negotiations with the Soviet government; rather, it was better to wait "until they show more willingness to stop the abuse and propaganda which the Comintern still showers on us and to meet us on the many questions of some importance ... in which their attitude is still obstructive." The Soviet government, he said, should "make the running."[14]

Collier made the point to Maiskii at a Soviet reception on 22 March, having been tapped to attend. Maiskii replied that he was "anxious to make the signature of the Trade Agreement the starting point for a general rapprochement." So much the better, responded Collier, but why "dissemble your love"? If we keep "rubbing it in," Collier advised, the Soviet government might eventually get the point. Vansittart, the Permanent Undersecretary of State, approved: "Inform [Douglas] Lord Chilston [the new British ambassador in Moscow] & tell him to rub in Mr. Collier's lesson at a convenient opportunity."[15] Charles had already done so with Rubinin. Soviet press enthusiasm for attacking England was a long-standing problem dating back to the 1920s. The NKID, both Chicherin and Litvinov, complained repeatedly to Stalin about "our orators" who were too quick to slash and burn. Sometimes they succeeded in calming their orators' élan and sometimes not. One was never quite sure what to expect from Stalin. It often depended on the stage of development of the struggle for power with his rivals.[16]

Litvinov, who readers will remember was seriously ill with the flu, finally replied to Maiskii's keenness for better Anglo-Soviet relations. It was a bucket of cold water. He was not opposed to a non-aggression pact with Britain, but he did not think the British government would agree to it. It was not a form of agreement to which the British were inclined, and least of all with the USSR. Nor did he think the moment was opportune for various reasons to broach the subject with the Foreign Office. Better to do nothing than to risk a rebuff. "I believe that one of the most urgent tasks of our policy is to improve relations with Britain and create appropriate sentiments there," Litvinov advised. "Unfortunately, we cannot get out of the zone of potential conflicts with her."[17]

As readers will recall, Soviet entry into the League of Nations was an important issue in 1934. Initially, France supported the USSR, but the Foreign Office was not so enthusiastic. The French feared Nazi Germany, but also feared a renewal of Soviet-German cooperation, broken up by Hitler's anti-communist attacks. The Soviet government was willing to enter the League – after blackguarding it from the beginning as an instrument of capitalist intrigue and aggression. Ambassador Chilston said that the Soviet leadership needed security for "internal consolidation"; war would "interfere … dangerously" with Soviet economic development. "This is not surprising," commented one Foreign Office clerk, "but it shows how terribly scared the Soviet Government must be that they are even willing to swallow all their past jibes against the League of Nations." Vansittart was caustic and mocking: "The Soviet Union is feeling frightened. Fear … is evidently a most healthy medicine in Russia. A little more will do her no harm, and she will certainly get it." Vansittart mellowed only slightly when he later qualified his position, though not his derision of the League: "For a not very exclusive, and at present rather hard-up, club, I should not dream of blackballing the candidate, though I should be very cautious in the cardroom."[18]

Sir Robert Gilbert Vansittart

As Permanent Undersecretary of State, Sir Robert Vansittart dominated the Foreign Office during the mid-1930s. He was born in 1881 into a family of the English bourgeoisie. His father was a captain of the Dragoon Guards; his mother, the daughter of a wealthy landowner. He was well-educated, as was normally the case with children of the British elite, attending Eton, and then travelling in Europe for two years, especially in France and Germany. He was trilingual, speaking both French and German. As a young man, Vansittart was certainly handsome and clean shaven; he had no walrus moustache, often a mark of masculinity and of the alpha male at the end of the nineteenth century. In one photograph, he looks cold and aloof. In later photographs, his face is deeply ridged. He married twice, his first spouse died in 1928. They had one daughter. Three years later, Vansittart remarried to Sarita Enriqueta Ward, herself a widow and mother of three sons. She was ten years his junior, a remarkably beautiful woman, so it was said, sophisticated, and sure of herself. Her first husband had also been a diplomat.

In 1902, Vansittart entered the Foreign Office and served in such places as Paris, Teheran, and Cairo, quickly moving up the ladder of responsibility. He was named Assistant Permanent Undersecretary of State in 1920, served as principle private secretary to Prime Ministers Baldwin and MacDonald, and became Permanent Undersecretary of State in the Foreign Office in 1930.

Vansittart, or "Van" as he was called by people who knew him well enough, was not simply an ambitious civil servant who rose rapidly through the ranks of power. He was also a poet, playwright, and novelist. He published his first play in 1902 at age twenty-one when he was just getting his start at the Foreign Office, and he published his first novel when he was serving in the British embassy in

Cairo. He was confident, debonair, and a model of British ruling class. In most photographs, Vansittart is dressed in sharp-looking, well-tailored suits. Outside he wore a dark, broad-brimmed fedora. He had houses and servants, was a member of the modestly posh St. James Club, and he enjoyed playing cards. Indeed, clubs and cards turn up as images in his minutes and memoranda. One can tell that he was a man of letters from his Foreign Office minutes with their sharp epigrams and turns of phrase, written in a large, flourishing hand. Vansittart was confident of his policies and world view, to the point where he irritated his ministers, for no matter how great his influence and his power, the Foreign Secretary was still his boss. In fact, one of his future bosses, Anthony Eden, who did not like such a strong and willful Permanent Undersecretary, said he was "in mentality" more a Secretary of State than a permanent official.[19] As we shall see, Eden wanted to get rid of him.

Vansittart practised realpolitik, having neither permanent friends nor permanent enemies, only the interests of Britain to his mind. He did not like the Bolsheviks, far from it, but learned to tolerate them and to advocate getting along with them after Hitler took power in Germany. He was suspicious of the Germans, and hated the Nazis, increasingly as the 1930s unfolded. He believed that power generated international respect and loyal allies, while the lack of it led to abuse of British interests and to isolation. He showed great impatience in the mid-1930s when the British government was too slow in rearming and would not take the Nazi danger seriously enough. And this impatience got him into trouble with his Tory masters.

Vansittart developed a loyal following among his subordinates in the Foreign Office – his "boys," as they were sometimes known. Among them were Ralph Wigram and Laurence Collier. Wigram, head of the Central Department, died prematurely in late 1936, and Collier became Vansittart's main foil in promoting a British rapprochement with the Soviet Union and in opposing endless concessions and capitulations to Nazi Germany.

The League of Nations

This is, however, getting a little ahead of the story in London. At the beginning of 1934, Vansittart was still sceptical and sarcastic about the Soviet Union, and this showed in his attitude towards Soviet entry into the League of Nations. In Moscow, Litvinov took a very cautious position on the League. It was March 1934. The Soviet government had become wary in view of the change of governments in France and the February disorders on the place de la Concorde. Poland had concluded a non-aggression pact with Nazi Germany and was becoming distinctly cold towards Moscow. No wonder Litvinov was guarded. "As for the League of Nations," he advised Maiskii, "we have publicly, clearly stated that we have no doctrinal-based, negative attitude towards it and we do not refuse any form of cooperation with it, if we are convinced that such cooperation will serve the cause of peace. The League or its individual members must convince us of this, but they do not take any initiative. At one time, France had taken the initiative, but even this has stalled so far thanks to the change of cabinets."[20]

Chilston did not think that Russian communists had renounced their revolutionary principles, and neither did most Tories in London. Of course, Bolsheviks did not think the British elite had renounced capitalism. It took two to tango. Maiskii, nevertheless, tried to reassure his English interlocutors. "At first we were very excited with our revolution – and so were you! We thought your system could be overthrown in a few months, and you thought we could not last beyond a few months. Now we know that we must put up with each other." Vansittart was still sceptical: "The difference in spirit between Russia and Germany and Japan is that she feels it will take her longer to get fit."[21]

Litvinov did not want to run after the British, but Maiskii was less averse to a more active approach. In a conversation with Strang, who had returned to the Foreign Office from the Moscow embassy, Maiskii probed for information, essentially following Litvinov's instructions. Maiskii mentioned press opinion suggesting that the British government was rather negative on the question of Soviet entry into the League. Strang replied sharply that these reports were untrue. "At the same time, he gave to understand that the British government is not inclined to take any initiative in this matter. I remember his phrase," Maiskii noted, "it is one thing to take the initiative on the issue of involving the USSR in the League of Nations, and then after some hesitation, but I cannot imagine a situation where England would vote against the entry of the USSR into the League of Nations.'"[22]

Maiskii Probes

Maiskii continued to probe the ground for a rapprochement. Chilston was on leave in London and visited the Soviet embassy with his wife as a courtesy call. After some chit-chat about theatre and art in Moscow, Chilton turned to business, sharing his impressions of his first months on the job. "He, in his words," Maiskii noted, "is generally pleased, although he admits that he still does not know much and [that] much in our life is a mystery to him. Until now, he has not seen anything except Moscow; however, in the near future he is going to go to Leningrad, as well as to see some other parts of the Soviet Union. Leningrad is his first priority." Chilston then turned to his impressions of London and the "big shift" in relations with the USSR. The mood was much better than when he had first left for Moscow. The conclusion of the trade agreement had been critical in changing attitudes. Even among the Die-Hards there was no overt belligerence towards the USSR.[23]

That might have been a little hard to believe in Moscow. Maiskii continued his soundings, this time with Collier and Strang. A clever conversationalist, Maiskii tried a provocation to see what kind of reply he would get. "I made the remark that, according to my observations, there are many advocates in England of a rapprochement with Japan and Germany." Strang took the bait, responding that of course there were some such people in England, but that over the last six to seven months their influence "had quickly fallen." On the contrary, in the Foreign Office, Strang continued, it was increasingly the view that over the course of the next five years, Germany and Japan would represent the main "factors of concern and danger in the international sphere." Japan was perceived increasingly as a threat to British interests. Continuing his provocations, Maiskii, "smiled and in the form of a joke," asked Strang in what order of priority he would put the "Anglo-Soviet conflict (*protivorechiia*)." According to Maiskii,

> Strang hesitated for a moment, but then replied that the Anglo-Soviet conflict seemed to him a conflict of a more theoretical nature, that neither side encroached on the territorial or financial interests of the other, and that, therefore, the Anglo-Soviet contradiction seemed to him much less acute and urgent than the contradictions of the Anglo-German and, in particular, the Anglo-Japanese. He believes that there are no serious reasons for quarrels and complications in Anglo-Soviet relations in the near future and quite admits the possibility of a much more friendly, collaborative work between the two countries for the benefit of peace, both in Europe and in Asia.

This is the line of reasoning that Maiskii adopted as the main argument in favour of improved Anglo-Soviet relations. You can see how far Strang had moved in less than a year after the eruption of the Metro-Vickers affair. The conversation continued, turning to the subject of Japan. Strang asked "rather diffidently" if the US recognition of the Soviet Union would have any effect on Soviet-Japanese relations. "I replied," Maiskii noted, "that there was no doubt, and that this act of rapprochement between two great Pacific powers had sobered up a little those militaristic heads in Tokyo." And what about an Anglo-Soviet rapprochement, Strang asked, "somewhat emboldened," would it have a favourable effect in the Far East? "I replied," Maiskii continued, "that the rapprochement of two great powers such as the USSR and Britain, if it became an accomplished fact, would have extremely large consequences for the consolidation of peace in the world, in particular in the Far East. Strang said that he also thought so, and at the same time began to complain bitterly about the extraordinary impudence and aggressiveness of Japan."

From Maiskii's record of the conversation, one might think that only Strang was involved in these discussions. Others from the Foreign Office – Collier,

Frank Ashton-Gwatkin, and E.H. Carr – were also present as the conversation turned to the question of how many more years of peace one could count on. Imagine Maiskii sitting around the table with several Foreign Office clerks discussing when peace would fail. Five years was the majority view; Carr, the future eminent historian, reckoned more optimistically on ten. A debate erupted between Carr and Collier and Strang, wherein the latter two argued that Carr was "given to completely unreasonable optimism." Everyone was "absolutely unanimous in expressing great anxiety about Japan and its intentions in the Far East … they stressed that the Japanese threat is now the most pressing and most difficult problem to resolve for Great Britain."[24] Nazi Germany hardly came up at all in the conversation.

Not all of Maiskii's reports were about life-or-death issues of diplomacy. He did once again attend social events at the Foreign Office, which must have underlined a return to normalcy for the Soviet embassy since during the Metro-Vickers affair it was partially boycotted and social events with Maiskii were *verboten*. A lot had changed in eleven months. Dinners and receptions were Maiskii's preferred venues for interactions with British interlocutors, for he had a gregarious personality and was good at getting his interlocutors to talk. People were more at ease, their discretion loosened by whisky and wine. After such a dinner at the Foreign Office in early June, diplomats were in what must have been the smoking room. Simon was making his rounds among his guests and finally came up to Maiskii for a chat. "He began, as usual, with a discussion about the weather." Simon was not complaining. There was a drought in England, which did not seem to bother the Foreign Secretary. According to Maiskii, he finally got around to politics … well, of a lighter nature. It appears as though Simon had a sense of humour that he shared even with the Soviet ambassador. Was it a sign of détente? Let Maiskii describe the scene.

> Then he [Simon] switched to politics. He remembered Geneva and suddenly, making a dramatic gesture with both hands and clutching his head, exclaimed: "Geneva! … Oh, it's so empty now, such a boring place." A moment later: "Mr. Litvinov made a big speech in Geneva. I always like to listen to his speeches. He knows how to joke. This is the only person in Geneva who knows how to give you a good joke. Here now, for example, Mr. Litvinov said: the conference is dead – so let's keep it that way! Is this not a first-class joke?"

Hmmm, readers may have their doubts, but perhaps it was a first-class joke among the diplomatic cognoscenti who knew Geneva. In any case, Simon revealed a side of Litvinov's personality not widely known, well, not in any case to historians. In this chit-chat with Simon, Maiskii of course did not leave out his reply: "I looked at Simon attentively and said, 'But you, sir John, have also made a speech or two in Geneva … perhaps without jokes, but very weighty …'

Simon spread his hands vaguely, as if to say: everyone does what they can." The conversation then turned to a more serious subject. Anthony Eden, an up-and-coming young Conservative MP, had recently been named Lord Privy Seal. According to Maiskii, Simon was none too pleased with this situation, suggesting that Eden would become a rival for power in the cabinet on matters of foreign policy.[25] This is the first time that Eden appears in the narrative, but as readers will soon learn, he becomes an important factor in relations between Britain and the Soviet Union, and someone with whom Maiskii establishes a familiar relationship.

There was definitely movement now towards better Anglo-Soviet relations, only a year after the Metro-Vickers crisis. On 21 June, Vansittart organized a lunch for Maiskii at his flat in London. Also present was Vansittart's wife, Sarita; Simon without his spouse; Conservative MP Boothby; Ishbel MacDonald, daughter of the prime minister; and Simon's principal private secretary and former head of the Northern Department, H.J. Seymour, and his wife. Maiskii was seated between Sarita, on his right, and Simon, on his left. "This is the first lunch of its kind during my stay in London," Maiskii noted, "and it seems to mark a small step forward in establishing a simpler relationship between the Soviet Mission and the Foreign Office. It will be interesting to see what happens next." Maiskii formed a high opinion of Sarita. "I had a long talk with Vansittart's wife," Maiskii noted in his report to Moscow:

> She is a very intelligent woman, educated and interested in politics. In any case, she is aware of all the major political events. The temper of Lady Vansittart is clearly anti-German and pro-French. She is also rather unfriendly to Japan and told me that she considers Japan to be the greatest threat to British economic interests. She talked a lot about how she is afraid of war and how her husband was concerned about the preservation of peace. He is now looking for ways and means to preserve it. Lady Vansittart also asked me about comrade Litvinov and our plans and intentions in the realm of foreign policy. I told her that our plans and intentions are very simple: we want peace.

Well, yes that was certainly true, but unstated Soviet policy was, as readers will know at this stage, rather more complicated than that. In any event, after the brunch, Maiskii spoke with Sir Robert and rather bluntly at that. "I noted that public opinion in the USSR has been lately watching the development of British politics with a certain concern. It is widely believed in our party and among the Soviet masses that Britain is trying to push Japan and Germany into hostile actions against the USSR, and that this explains the unfriendly attitude of the British government to the 'Eastern Locarno' project." Vansittart reacted with some irritation to these comments, stating unambiguously that Soviet suspicions were unfounded:

> The English want only one thing – peace. He, Vansittart, cannot understand how we can suspect England of wanting to start a war. It is quite clear to him that if a war began between Germany and the USSR or Japan and the USSR, it could not be localized and sooner or later it would draw in Britain as well. And Britain does not want war, the mood of the British population is extremely pacifist. However, about "Eastern Locarno" V. said nothing.[26]

On 21 June, the same day Maiskii and his spouse lunched at the Vansittarts' London flat, Litvinov met Chilston in Moscow. Among other items, Chilston raised concerns about the comments being made in the Soviet press and its "undesirable tone" towards Britain. Putting aside the disagreeable representations of Britain in political cartoons and posters, Chilston objected to the editorials in *Pravda* and *Izvestiia*, which claimed that Britain was "inciting" Germany and Japan against the USSR. These assertions "did not correspond to reality," according to Chilton. "It would be good," he added, "if we [Litvinov was reporting] would exert influence on our press with a view to ending the insinuations and anti-British tone." Chilston acknowledged the anti-Soviet tone in the British press and in statements from people like George Ambrose, Lord Lloyd, a noted Die-Hard, but added that the British government could not control the press or individuals. Well yes, that was true up to a point, but the News Department could always find willing collaborators at the *Times* or elsewhere when it wanted to convey a message "unofficially." It is surprising in fact that the narkom did not raise this point, though he was never short of an appropriate riposte when necessary. "I said," Litvinov wrote in his *dnevnik*, "that we also do not have control over the press, that we do not have prior censorship." Litvinov might have liked to have control, however, if one is to judge from his frequent comments about "our orators" during the 1920s. Chicherin likewise often complained about the Soviet press.[27]

In any case, Chicherin was retired and Litvinov passed over that particular point. He opined, however, that when influential Conservatives like Lord Lloyd spoke in favour of inciting Japan and Germany against the USSR, the Soviet press needed to fire back, whether or not the comments came directly from the British government. Litvinov was getting to the point with Chilston, stating, "Diplomatic relations exist only nominally between us, but not in fact." So how was the Soviet leadership to know what the British government thought on this or that issue of importance to the USSR, when there was no direct contact with one another? Like any other press anywhere else, the Soviet press collected information from various sources, and then made "assumptions and guesses." Litvinov must have enjoyed drafting this record of conversation. "I do not see the basis," he added, "for interfering in this file [on the Soviet press], the more so, since I myself cannot proceed from any other facts or declarations of a contrary nature." Then Litvinov added the following: "Such a situation is inadmissible when the English press is free to bark at us without any limitations, and our press must be muzzled in advance. If relations between us and the English improve to which end we are sincerely working, then the tone of the press will also itself change."[28] That was the rose amidst the thorns, and the main message that Litvinov wanted to deliver to the Foreign Office.

Chilston did so without Litvinov's lecturing and without the "what's good for goose is good for the gander" lesson. "Litvinov said he wished the Soviet Union could have more understanding and better *political* [emphasis in the original] relations with Great Britain," according to Chilston's report, "because in his mind there was no doubt that Great Britain and Russia were the most important factors for peace of the world." Chilston further indicated that his government was ready to exchange military attachés with the USSR; and Litvinov indicated that the Soviet government had definitely decided to join the League of Nations.[29]

Even so, Vansittart was riled by Chilston's sanitized account of his 21 June meeting with Litvinov. The Foreign Office clerks did not like being reminded that the pot calls the kettle black when it came to the Soviet press. "Blackmail," Collier called it. "Satan rebuking sin," Chilston would say a few months later, which was a distinctly British point of view.[30] But then who could say who had thrown the first stone? In any event, Collier and Oliphant did not think it was worth complaining about, but Vansittart disagreed:

> I shall also tell M. Maisky the next time I seem him that it is of no use whatever to speak of *improved* [emphasis in the original] relations in one breath and to blackguard us systematically with the other – despite my very friendly response to his advances … The Soviet Government cannot in fact have it both ways, and they have now got to choose. They will never reassure the public here of their friendly intentions if they go on with this nonsense. If they want better relations – for which we are quite ready – they must be reasonably polite to and reasonably truthful about us.[31]

Ivan Mikhailovich Maiskii

Ivan Mikhailovich Maiskii was born Jan Liakhovetskii in 1884, in a family of Polish-Jewish descent. His father was an army physician and his mother was a village school teacher. He was born in the small town of Kirillov, above the golden circle of medieval towns, almost due north of Moscow. As befitted the sons of the tsarist middle class, he was well educated, entering St. Petersburg University, only to be expelled for revolutionary activities. In 1903, at age nineteen, he joined the Menshevik wing of the Russian Social-Democratic Workers' Party. Like so many other students of his generation, he ran afoul of the tsarist police and was exiled to Siberia. In 1908, he left Russia and settled in Germany

Figure 11.1. Ivan Mikhailovich Maiskii, ca. 1930s, AVPRF.

where he finished his university education in economics at the University of Munich. He eventually settled in London in 1912 where he became friends with Chicherin and Litvinov and other Russian expatriates. There was a lively expat community there. He was a polyglot, speaking German, French, and English; yet another among the first generation of erudite Soviet diplomats. In stature, he was short but with a handsome, gentle-looking face; a receding hairline contrasted with a well-furnished moustache and modest chin whiskers. His smile was broad and endearing. He became a writer and novelist of considerable talent. His reports to Moscow sometimes indulged a wry sense of humour.

During the Russian Civil War, he cast in his lot, oddly enough, with an ephemeral anti-Bolshevik Socialist Revolutionary (SR) government in Samara. He fled to Mongolia after Admiral Aleksandr V. Kolchak took power in Omsk in November 1918. Remarkably, Maiskii was able to make his peace with the Bolsheviks, who accepted him into the party in 1921, though he was never quite allowed to forget the early error of his ways. In the mid-1920s, he was posted for the first time to London as first secretary. In 1929, he was named minister in Helsinki before returning to London as ambassador in the autumn of 1932.

Litvinov recommended him strongly for the post: "He lived for a long time in England, knows the country, has ties to Labour circles, and by his activities in Finland demonstrated his ability to defend our interests and to persevere in achieving the goals we set for him."[32] In some ways, Maiskii was a natural for the job, although he once admitted to a British friend that he did not like diplomacy. He was sociable, gregarious, approachable, and definitely not the traditional, snobbish diplomat who would scarcely deign to speak to anyone beneath his standing. Instead of avoiding diplomatic receptions – which could be a crashing bore of superficial encounters – he plunged into them looking for the subjects of his next reports to Moscow. In this he had help from his wife, Agniia Akeksandrovna, who was just as gregarious and sociable as he was, perhaps more so. At Maiskii's right arm, she was his best ally in London for reaching out to the British elite of whatever political inclinations.

Maiskii made friends with the former Liberal prime minister David Lloyd George and with Beatrice Webb and visited with them on the weekends. He knew everyone who counted; his address book would have been a Who's Who of the British elite from Labour notables to Conservative ministers. He moved in that society so well and with such intimacy that it often drove the Foreign Office clerks to record long and spiteful minutes.

Vansittart, for his part, had a high regard for Maiskii. "[M]any avoided him," Vansittart wrote in his memoirs. "I was sorry, since his hold at home was precarious … I thought that he might be killed if he were not a success." Vansittart and Maiskii took a liking to each other; their wives, according to Maiskii, had facilitated matters by getting along first. "Helping lame dogs over stiles is no duty," wrote Vansittart, "when theirs is to bite, but my wife and I did our best to provide him and his with connections, and had them to meals *à quatre* or in company." The "meals" were not only convivial, but useful, as readers will have already come to realize.[33]

The Maiskii-Vansittart Meetings

On 3 July, Maiskii saw Vansittart for the first of a long series of meetings that set into motion the Anglo-Soviet rapprochement. The polpred drafted a thirteen-page report of his conversation at the Foreign Office. He began by adding some interesting details to his earlier report on their lunch conversation (on 21 June at the Vansittarts' London flat) with Lady Vansittart. At the table, she was sitting on one side of Maiskii and Simon on the other, so she had to cover her voice. "Since she spoke in a low voice and turned to face me, in the midst of the general buzz at the table (all the guests were speaking at once) her words, probably did not reach Simon." This was a good thing. "Lady Vansittart expressed doubt that Simon was pursuing the right line in foreign policy, in particular at Geneva, and at the same time emphasized that the 'salt of the earth' in the Foreign Office is her husband. He essentially forms 'public opinion' in the Foreign Office and he influences to a very strong degree the position of the cabinet on this or that international question." At the end of the discussion she asked Maiskii why he did not discuss with her husband the various issues brought up around the table. Her husband wanted to maintain the peace; the USSR wanted peace. "It seems to me," she said to Maiskii, "your collaborative discussions with my husband could produce positive results."

"I replied," Maiskii wrote in his report, "that until now I had not spoken with V. about the large questions of international relations simply because here, in London, we practically did not have normal diplomatic contact between the Soviet embassy and the Foreign Office, but that I am always ready for such conversations if V. really wants to have them." Lady Vansittart – let us call her Sarita for the sake of informality – replied rather hotly to Maiskii that "of course her husband would welcome a 'quiet and frank' conversation with the Soviet ambassador on the most urgent questions of the international situation." Sarita went further, indicating that she would speak to her husband that evening and let him know "how and where" they could meet together.

Maiskii drew three conclusions from this long conversation. First, "that between Simon and Vansittart there were bad relations, political and, possibly, personal. Second … that V., obviously thinks that Simon's role, as Foreign Secretary, is coming to an end. Otherwise, it would be difficult to explain the sharp criticism of Simon's political line by Lady V. during conversation with me. Third … that at the limit the Foreign Office apparatus is beginning to feel the necessity to look for some channel of contact with the USSR." Nor did Maiskii think that the wife of the Permanent Undersecretary of the Foreign Office could possibly have such a conversation with the Soviet ambassador without the approval of her husband, although Maiskii, erring on the side of caution, acknowledged that the conversation could have arisen by chance.

"Thus," Maiskii wrote in his report, "I waited with a certain curiosity for what would happen next." He had to wait for a little while being absent from London for a few days. He returned late in the evening of 26 June. On the following morning, Agniia Akeksandrovna, Maiskii's wife, received a note from Lady Vansittart. Among other things, the letter said, "Convey to your husband that if he wishes to have a quiet and substantive conversation with my husband, it would be good if your husband telephoned my husband and agreed on a convenient day and time to meet." As Maiskii noted in his report, he was finally convinced that his table discussion with Lady Vansittart had not been without purpose, and he rang up Vansittart on the following day to set an appointment to meet. He also cabled the NKID for instructions, which he received from Litvinov on the following day, listing a number of issues to air out with Vansittart, some of which Maiskii had already raised in his report.[34] These included British relations with Japan and Nazi Germany and Soviet entry into the League.

"Say that we on our side sincerely hope for the creation of better relations with England."[35] That was a clear mandate.

The meeting took place as planned on 3 July. Maiskii started, according to his report, by expressing his appreciation of Lady Vansittart's role in getting the ball rolling for the meeting. More personal contact between the embassy and the Foreign Office could only be to the good. The absence of such contact was a serious "shortcoming" of Anglo-Soviet relations. "I completely agree with you," Vansittart responded, "it is a large shortcoming. We learn about the thoughts and moods of one another third hand and this has as its inevitable result an increase in all kinds of misunderstandings, mutual suspicions, and suspicions." Maiskii agreed, adding that personal contacts would not remove all difficulties but would make it easier to resolve them.

Then, as Maiskii put it, they moved on to business. "The basic principle of our foreign policy is peace," Maiskii began. This was not just a principle for public consumption, but the real policy of the Soviet Union. If Vansittart had any doubts on this score, he should say so directly. This was not an issue, Vansittart replied, he did not doubt the Soviet interest in maintaining the peace. This was also the objective of British foreign policy, he added, which meant the two governments were pursuing parallel objectives. These overlapping interests, Maiskii proposed, should serve as the foundation for better relations. He continued:

> I understand that the given task is not so simple. Above Anglo-Soviet relations gravitate traditions and memories of the past, recent after the revolution and more distant, relating to the nineteenth century, but this obstacle is not insurmountable. As regards present relations between both countries, then I do not see at the present moment a single serious problem which makes impossible a significant improvement of these relations and, possibly, even the transformation of them into genuinely friendly relations.

To all this, Vansittart readily agreed, apart from an important punctual issue of the Lena Goldfields concession dating back to 1925. The Soviet government had breached the concession and the Foreign Office was supporting stockholder claims for compensation.

Maiskii said he wanted to get "some difficulties" out of the way. "Soviet public opinion at the present time is concerned with a well-known suspicion of English policy on two very important questions of great concern to the USSR – questions, which in short can be characterized by two words: Japan and Germany." Maiskii began with Japan. Right-wing circles in Japan are in a very "aggressive mood." They have large ambitions under the slogan "Asia for Asians." They "dreamed" of establishing Japanese domination over the entire Asian continent. In fact, they not only dreamed, but were acting to achieve this end.

"You are entirely right," Vansittart interrupted, "we know about the phantasmagoria of Japanese right circles, especially Japanese military elements. These ideas are undoubtedly very dangerous. In general, I consider that Japan at the present time is the strongest focus of military danger." Well, that made two for the tango. Naturally, Maiskii was pleased to learn of this "concurrence" of points of view. Can we dance then? he wondered. Japanese ambitions threatened the USSR, Maiskii said. And again, Vansittart interrupted. "Yes, I know about Japanese desires in regard to Kamchatka, the maritime territories, and apparently all of eastern Siberia to Lake Baikal." Maiskii said that Soviet-Japanese tensions had relaxed somewhat. "Yes," Vansittart interjected, "thanks to your own [military] strength … A year ago it seemed to me that war between Japan and the USSR was inevitable in the very near future, but now I don't think so." The conversation continued along these lines for quite a while. Maiskii thought Japan too weak to achieve its objectives by itself and was looking for allies, in particular Germany. Vansittart agreed. And yet Maiskii was confused by what he read in the British press. He mentioned for starters the leader writer at the *Sunday Times*, "Scrutator" (Herbert Sidebotham), and Tories like Lord Lloyd, who were creating the impression in the USSR that the British government, if it were not directly pushing Japan towards war with the USSR, would have nothing against the eruption of such a conflict. Maiskii asked Vansittart to react to these Soviet misgivings. "Our Far Eastern policy is very simple," Vansittart replied, and continued:

> I consider Japan a great danger for British interests in the Pacific Ocean. We have many complications with Japan – economic, political and so on, but we are "very *vulnerable* [in English in original] in the Far East," and therefore must be careful. Least of all, would we desire a Japanese-Soviet war. People, who think otherwise, are simply crazy. In our time, war between two great powers cannot remain isolated, and we, Great Britain, quite simply do not want to go to war.

But even if, supposing hypothetically, Japan were to win such a war, what benefit would there be for Britain? Japan would be stronger and an even a greater menace in the Pacific Ocean. Scrutator and Lord Lloyd did not represent the views of the British government. Lord Lloyd was known to "roll down an inclined plane"; he had no influence. As for the press, it "far from always" represented the views of cabinet. The Soviet government gave more credibility to Scrutator's columns than they merited. And then, Vansittart turned the tables. In the USSR, he said to Maiskii, "you also have people who preach very wild ideas." He mentioned Dmitri Zakharovich Manuil'skii, soon to be number two in the Comintern, who claimed in a speech that the British government was creating "an anti-Soviet coalition from Japan and Germany." Vansittart rather heatedly, according to Maiskii, repeated that Britain did not want war in the Far East.

Maiskii expressed scepticism. If that was so, why did responsible people from the government not make public statements to this effect? Such statements would be very helpful in alleviating Soviet misgivings. "This is not a bad idea," Vansittart replied, making some notes. "I will take it up with the appropriate people."

Then the subject changed to Germany. "I pointed out to V.," Maiskii wrote, "that Hitlerite Germany, for reasons of a somewhat different order than Japan is also driven by an extraordinarily aggressive spirit." Vansittart nodded his head in agreement. Like Japan, Maiskii continued, Hitlerite Germany was motivated by "very dangerous ambitions related to aspirations to world domination … [it] very clearly threatens the interests of the USSR for, in the first place, it establishes as the order of the day the problem of expansion in the east."

"Oh yes," Vansittart interjected, "I know very well Hitler's *Mein Kampf*; I am familiar with Mr. Rozenberg's [*sic*] plans regarding the Ukraine and the Baltic region."

"The Soviet government," Maiskii continued, "cannot remain indifferent to this new danger from the West. We want peace, but we must by every means insulate our country from the possibility of attack from this direction." Maiskii identified the Eastern Locarno as a concrete means of doing so, and asked in a long monologue where the British government stood on this question. There were doubts in Moscow about the British line. Did the British government want to push Germany towards the East against the USSR?

"I fully agree," Vansittart replied, "that Hitlerite Germany represents a great danger for the entire range of countries surrounding it, and I am by no means surprised that these countries are trying to find some effective means of self-defence." And then perhaps unexpectedly for Maiskii, Vansittart mentioned Hitler's recent blood purge of his former colleague, the SA leader Ernst Röhm, which did not seem to augur well for any change in German foreign policy. In the circumstances, an Eastern Locarno could be "a useful thing" if Germany was a contracting party. It might be the only way to oblige Hitler to remain quiet. Maiskii acknowledged that the cabinet had not taken a formal position on the Eastern Locarno, but asked whether the Foreign Office had a position on it. Vansittart avoided a direct reply, but reaffirmed his belief that Germany was a "great danger to peace and quiet in Europe." Maiskii thought he saw a "strong" divergence of views between Vansittart and Simon on Eastern Locarno, the latter opposing it.

Vansittart later spoke "with evident irritation" about the *Times*. In the large majority of cases, it did not represent the point of view of the Foreign Office. Vansittart said he rarely agreed with its editorials and especially on the "German question." "I find them too pro-German and not portraying the true interests of Great Britain." A.L. Kennedy had written most of these editorials for which "he draws his inspiration largely from the German embassy." Eventually Vansittart said to Maiskii that if the ambassador had questions about Foreign Office policy that he should pose his questions to him. Maiskii suggested a public statement on the subject from someone in cabinet. Vansittart responded sympathetically.

The final subject of discussion at that meeting was disarmament and the League of Nations. The former was a pipe dream. Maiskii repeated Litvinov's view that "disarmament at the moment did not have any chance of practical implementation." Vansittart agreed that disarmament was "hopeless." Then, of course, Soviet entry into the League arose. Here, Vansittart added nothing to what the reader will already know, to wit, that Britain would support Soviet entry but not take the initiative in proposing it.[36] With that, a long meeting came to an end, and Vansittart and Maiskii both retired to their studies to make their respective records of the conversation.

In fact, Maiskii sent two records to Moscow: the first was a telegram and the second was his multi-page dispatch. The telegram is brief and provides the bare outline of the discussion.[37] The dispatch is far more detailed and reports on both what Maiskii and Vansittart said. The Foreign Office account was sent out as a numbered dispatch from Simon to Chilston in Moscow. The differences between the two accounts of the meeting are remarkable. Lady Vansittart's role in getting the ball rolling is entirely absent, of course. The long exchanges on the danger of Japan and Nazi Germany are absent. You would not know from the British account that the Soviet Union was worried about the threats to its security from the two aforementioned states except for passing references: "There were," Maiskii said, "two points at which his country men were suspicious of British policy, to wit, Japan and Germany." The Soviet preoccupation with the threat to its security in both the east and the west can only be assumed, inferred. *Mein Kampf* does not come up. There is almost no other indication that Vansittart *agreed* with Maiskii's assessment of the Japanese and German dangers to peace and security in Asia and in Europe. It is absent, hidden really, in the Foreign Office account and this can only lend credence to policy differences between Vansittart and Simon to which Maiskii drew attention in his report. Vansittart, in effect, did not feel comfortable revealing to cabinet his own views about the dangers of Japan and Nazi Germany.

Maiskii gave short shrift to Vansittart's complaint about an article in the Soviet press; Vansittart gives it rather more attention. Vansittart treats Maiskii's reports of Soviet concern over British policy as "sinister," as if they were the result of paranoia and not based on the experience of actually dealing with the British government in various parts of the world. The Foreign Office account addresses the topics of Soviet entry into the League of Nations and the British position on Eastern Locarno. The editorial policy of the *Times* also comes up. There are no striking differences in the two accounts on these issues. It is Maiskii who wants something, who takes the initiative; Vansittart is reflexive, and who agrees to "better and more frequent contacts."[38] Maiskii's account is revelatory; Vansittart's obfuscating what is most important: his own views on Japan and Nazi Germany, and *his* perception, shared with Maiskii, of common Anglo-Soviet security interests.

This meeting greatly influenced Maiskii, so much so that he wrote an additional dispatch about it to Litvinov.

> First of all, I think it is necessary to note that this conversation, as far as I can judge, is the first of its kind in the history of our relations with England. It is possible that during periods of Labour government, the same conversation has occurred (although on this point I am not quite sure), but absolutely there is no doubt that such a conversation as I have just had with Vansittart, has not occurred until now and could not have occurred under a Conservative government. There is no doubt that the atmosphere, tone, and content of the conversation itself marks a certain shift in the mood of the British government favourable to us, for I cannot believe that Vansittart would dare to have such a conversation with me at his own risks and perils. It must be assumed that he had previously consulted with members of the government, at least with Baldwin.

Maiskii also persisted in thinking that there were policy differences between Vansittart and Simon. He referred back to his conversation with Sarita, Lady Vansittart, at the June lunch, but he had also "repeatedly" heard similar opinions from other sources:

> The essence of these differences is summarized as follows: Simon is *pro-Japanese* and *pro-German*; Vansittart is *pro-French* and *anti-German*, and along with this, also *anti-Japanese* [words in italics are in English in the original], (or more cautious – with great apprehension regarding Japan). The apparatus of the Foreign Office, the head of which is Vansittart, essentially shares his point of view. The struggle has already gone on for a long time between Simon and Vansittart. The fact that Vansittart decided to have such a conversation with me, as he did, demonstrates, in my opinion, that Vansittart's line is beginning to win out in cabinet over Simon's. The behaviour of Vansittart's wife at lunch obliges one to think that, in Vansittart's opinion, Simon's days as foreign secretary are numbered.

All the same, Maiskii was not sure where cabinet directives to Vansittart ended and where his personal opinions began. It would be interesting to see if public statements from cabinet with regard to British policy would be forthcoming, as Vansittart agreed to obtain. "We will have to wait and see (*pozhivem – uvidem*)," he concluded. This was Maiskii's favourite axiom when speculating about the future of Anglo-Soviet relations. He added that he had noticed other signs of improving Anglo-Soviet relations, but he emphasized, repeating what Vansittart had said, that a solution needed to be found for the long-standing conflict over the Lena Goldfields concession.[39] Given that Vansittart in his own report of the 3 July meeting hid his expressed personal views and underemphasized by a long way the German and Japanese dangers, it may be that he was speaking largely on his own initiative and not with authorization from above.

Nevertheless, if Maiskii was pleased with the meeting of 3 July, so was Vansittart. "M. Maisky said that there was a strong and earnest desire in his country for closer and better Anglo-Soviet relations," according to Vansittart. "This desire was, of course, to a large extent created by fear of Germany. His Excellency was quite frank on that point." So was Vansittart, according to Maiskii's account.[40] Vansittart and Maiskii often put into each other's words the desire for better relations. It made the case more compelling to their sceptical superiors, especially if either felt he was going beyond his instructions or his government's policies.

A week after the Vansittart-Maiskii meeting, French foreign minister Barthou came to London to ask for British support for Soviet entry into the League of Nations and for an Eastern Pact on security. As readers will remember, Barthou's mission was successful. Vansittart briefed Maiskii. The French ambassador in London, Corbin, told Maiskii that Barthou had expected greater British opposition to French policy, and went away from the meetings "very satisfied with the results."[41] According to Maiskii, "Barthou knew how to make good use of his opportunities. I learned that he put the question to the British government very suavely: either you support the security pacts (Eastern [Locarno] and Franco-Soviet), or in the very near future you will have a Franco-Soviet alliance. This worked and forced the English cabinet to speak in favour of the pacts. And such a declaration, in turn, inevitably entailed a certain softening in Anglo–Soviet relations."[42] Here was one of the rare times in the 1930s when a French foreign minister demonstrated spine in dealing with "the English." On the day following Maiskii's discussion with Corbin, 13 July, Simon made a statement in the House of Commons to the effect that the British government would welcome the USSR into the League. Other Tory MPs made statements approving of better Anglo-Soviet relations. Was Maiskii right about the shift in Conservative government policy?

Maiskii and Vansittart met again on 18 July. They went over the ground of their meeting of 3 July, restating the desire of their respective governments for improved relations. Vansittart gave Maiskii further assurances that British relations with Germany and Japan were not directed against the USSR, and he complained about allegations to this effect in the Soviet press. Such vituperation provided opportunities to hostile journalists and MPs who wanted to make trouble over Anglo-Soviet relations. Of course, the British government did not mind "normal" Soviet press criticism, but it was going too far to accuse the British government of promoting war against the USSR.

"I understand your concerns," replied Maiskii, "but I have to say that it was only two weeks ago that I had the opportunity to hear an explanation from a responsible Foreign Office representative, of the point of view of the British government on the most important international issues." Before that, Maiskii said he had to get his information from the newspapers or from "third hand" accounts. It would take time for Soviet opinion to note the change in British policy. The history of Anglo-Soviet relations had created great mistrust: it "cannot vanish at once, overnight." People will ask, "For how long is this [shift in British policy]"? Is it just a temporary manoeuvre? "So, don't expect a miracle," said Maiskii.

Such comments about Soviet policy, of course, could have and did come from Foreign Office officials, though Vansittart did not say so. He only asked Maiskii to use his influence to encourage prudence in Moscow. Vansittart said he was convinced of Maiskii's commitment to an Anglo-Soviet rapprochement, and the Soviet ambassador in his turn recorded that he was also persuaded of Vansittart's commitment to the same end.[43] "I want to believe," said Litvinov, commenting on the results of Maiskii's first meeting, that Vansittart's statements are "sincere and without ulterior motive."[44] Apparently, Simon wanted to believe also, for he authorized a letter to Chilston restating Vansittart's main points to Maiskii; and he reinforced Vansittart's words that "we officials were quite ready" for better relations – by striking out "officials."[45] If there was originally a difference of opinion between Simon and Vansittart on British policy toward the USSR, it appears to have disappeared. On 25 July, five days after Simon wrote his minute to Vansittart, Austrian Nazis assassinated the Austrian chancellor Englebert Dollfuss. It was another warning of the Nazi danger, though Vansittart and Maiskii scarcely needed one.

The initial meetings between Vansittart and Maiskii had some effect in Moscow. On 7 August, Chilston reported "marked improvement" in the tone of the Soviet press towards Britain, even if there were occasional lapses. "There *is* 'a marked improvement,'" minuted Vansittart, "though it might well go further."[46] Vansittart and Maiskii met again on 9 August for another "very serious political discussion," to quote the latter. Their separate accounts of the meeting are remarkably similar.

Vansittart did not foresee any problems with Soviet entry into the League. "So soon," Vansittart remarked, obviously in a jolly frame of mind, "we will become members with you of the same 'club.' I am very glad." He hoped that the USSR, once in – he again likened the League to a "hard-up" club for gentlemen – would cease its vitriolic attacks on the British government. "What would be the position in any club card-room," Vansittart asked, "if members were continually accusing each other of having the fifth ace and a Thomson submachine gun under the table?" Maiskii smiled at this comment, but Vansittart, showing his talent as a writer, went on. I am "happy to hear" that there has "been a real improvement in the attitude of the Russian press." Maiskii said he had done what he could, but he noted that hostile British attacks continued on the USSR in the *Times* and other papers.

Naturally, no one could expect "complete perfection would be attained in these matters," replied Vansittart – and according to Maiskii, he added that the Soviet government should not pay much attention to such attacks. "In fact, the expression of hostile opinions and of hostile propaganda had ... become a luxury which should no longer be indulged." It was important to avoid anything that could disturb Anglo-Soviet relations. The interests of "high politics," said Vansittart, should take precedence: they should stress what unites them, not what divides them. Maiskii agreed, and emphasized that the Anglo-Soviet rapprochement was "an extraordinarily important factor for peace." "I do not see at the present time," added Maiskii – in what became the stock expression of interest in better relations – "any important international problems which could seriously divide us." *La marche des événements*, as Vansittart put it, was pushing the two countries together both in Europe and the Far East. You know "what the real world situation is," said Vansittart, better Anglo-Soviet relations are "the path of real statesmanship" and "of ordinary common sense." The discussion briefly turned to Hitler. President Hindenburg had died in June. According to Vansittart, this made Hitler the "real boss" of Germany. Who knew what he wanted? Would it be "peace or war"? The "touchstone" would be Austria. "Hitler always follows the prescription of 'Alice in Wonderland': 'They all the time promise jam tomorrow; they never give jam today.'" Vansittart asked Maiskii to tell Litvinov what he had said. Maiskii replied that he would, and he was as good as his word.[47]

Vansittart was apparently ahead of Conservative opinion on Anglo-Soviet relations, as Corbin had reported a week after Vansittart's last meeting with Maiskii. The Tories mistrusted the Soviet government, and did not like to see it moving closer to France. For most Tories, Corbin opined, the rise of Nazism had only slightly overshadowed their continuing fear of the "communist peril."[48] This evaluation was less optimistic than Maiskii's, but only a little. Who was right? Litvinov must have wondered at times. Remember that on 18 September 1934, the USSR was admitted to the League of Nations, though entry proved more difficult than Litvinov had anticipated. He told Eden, the Lord Privy Seal, who was also in Geneva, that "he was afraid that he had acted in advance of public opinion in his country and that his position in the next few months would be difficult." In the Foreign Office, Collier interpreted Litvinov's comment to mean that some Soviet officials were dubious about the new policy, preferring a return to good relations with Germany.[49] Collier was worried for nothing. There was no interest in Moscow to go back to the "old policy" towards Nazi Germany during the summer of 1934. The German embassy requested permission for a Lufthansa flight over Siberia. Kaganovich recommended a negative reply, endorsed by Stalin.[50] Remember Bullitt's telegram from Moscow: Stalin strongly favoured good Franco-Soviet and Anglo-Soviet relations and wanted on no account to disturb them.[51]

Relations Begin to Warm Up ... a Little

Beyond the discussions between Vansittart and Maiskii, Anglo-Soviet relations showed some tangible signs of improvement. In late July, Maiskii reported the recent statements (on 13 July) in the House of Commons by Austen Chamberlain, the former Foreign Secretary, who "thundered" against Germany and strongly supported Soviet entry into the League of Nations. And then Churchill also rose to speak. Maiskii was astounded: "When Churchill welcomed 'the return of Soviet Russia to the Western European system' as a truly 'historical event' and unconditionally recognized the USSR as the largest factor in the preservation of peace – I could hardly believe my ears." He continued:

> I knew before (I even wrote to you several times about this) that both Churchill and Chamberlain in recent months, due to the current world situation, were beginning to change their former sharply hostile attitude towards our country. However, I did not expect that this process had already gone so far. Most of all, I did not expect that both of these sworn enemies of the Soviet Union would speak openly in our favour. The spectacle, which I observed on 13 July from the diplomatic gallery of Parliament, was a real spectacle for the gods.

Maiskii attributed the change in attitudes to the growing political, economic, and military strength of the USSR. The Metro-Vickers crisis was a "test of strength," added Maiskii, which did not translate to British advantage. Then there was US recognition and the rapprochement with France, as well as the Japanese decision not to test the strength of Soviet frontiers in the Far East. He went on:

> English Conservatives respect strength, and when they saw and felt that the Soviet Union had become a great force, they began to scratch their heads and reexamine their tactics. Everyone knows the old English maxim: "If you cannot strangle the enemy, then embrace him." A major role was also played by numerous demonstrations of the power of the Red Army, and especially the brilliant success of our aviation. From this point of view, the rescue of the Cheliuskinites [the 104-member crew of the Soviet steamer *Cheliuskin*, which became icebound and sunk in Arctic waters in 1934 en route from Murmansk to Vladivostok] was, among other things, of great international political importance.

Maiskii went on at great length about Anglo-Japanese relations and how British Conservatives were abandoning their traditional view of Japan as an ally for that of a potential adversary. Increasing Soviet strength began to look to British Conservatives like a potential force with which to counter Japan. And then there was the problem of Nazi Germany. Many British Conservatives were "very sympathetic to Hitler," but did not like the rough edges of Nazism. Nor did they like the Nazi threat to Austria and the breakneck speed of Nazi rearmament. But these Conservatives all the same did not want to overthrow Hitler, he pointed out:

> They only wanted to comb his hair a little, to tame him, put him in a tailcoat and top hat. The British Conservatives calculated that Hitler would succeed in creating a durable and stable regime in Germany, eliminating the "communist danger," strengthening the country as a desirable counterweight to the excessive power of France, and turning the "Third Reich" into a potential crusader against the USSR. True, this regime still needs to settle down a little and get stronger, but English Conservatives were confident that this process would take place more or less on the "Italian model" without sharp zigzags and hard shocks. In particular, the British Conservatives a few months ago considered it almost certain that they would be able to limit German weapons (especially air weapons) at a more or less acceptable level for them. By the way, the Conservatives love to say that the Germans simply do not have enough money for too many tanks and airplanes.

But things were not turning out quite as the Tories expected. At the end of June and beginning of July, the Rölm purges (the murder of the SA leadership ordered by Hitler and the ruling elites) disturbed not only Liberals and Labour but also Conservative circles. Nazi Germany was not looking to turn out like the "Italian model," but rather was beginning to appear like a threat to Britain. The same elements – industrialists, Junkers, and so on, which had provoked the Great War – looked to be gaining influence. Some Tories even feared "a proletarian revolution" in Germany, a "prospect which throws the Conservatives quite simply into a state of cold chills." Tories were bitterly disappointed. They were saying to the German conservatives, "We … trusted you, and you let us down." No one could say which way events would turn. The big question had by no means been resolved in the British cabinet, and Maiskii hastened to add: "However, there is no doubt that the belief in Hitler and his regime, which was widespread among Conservatives last year, is now severely undermined by serious and deep doubts." What is certain, Maiskii concluded, is that the British turn towards the USSR is the result of growing fears of Japan and Nazi Germany. The big question was whether the shift in British policy would continue over the longer term. Could French ambassador Corbin have been exaggerating Tory Sovietphobia? Or was Maiskii getting carried away? He did not know himself. "I am inclined to treat the 'new course' in Anglo-Soviet relations with definite mistrust and scepticism." In spite of Vansittart's declarations, "I say: we will have to wait and see (*pozhivem – uvidem*). Until then, we must as before remain on alert."[52]

A Soviet military attaché soon arrived in London. Litvinov had first raised the idea "with competent comrades" in May. We are interested, Litvinov advised Maiskii, but do not want to be in a rush or "show excessive interest" in the idea.[53] In June, Chilston advised Litvinov that the British government agreed to exchange military attachés. It was only in August that matters were settled. Vitovt Kazimirovich Putna would go to London as military attaché. He made his reputation in the Red Army during the civil war and during the war with Poland, and was "a very savvy military man." He had previously served as military attaché in Japan, Finland, and Germany.[54] This was further indication that the Soviet side was getting serious about better relations with Britain. Yet another was the British embassy's attempt to get on better with its Soviet interlocutors. Rubinin noted the improvement. In the absence of Chilton, who was on leave, Rubinin reported that the chargé d'affaires Noel Charles, "at each meeting with me, emphasizes the friendly relations of the ambassador and himself to the USSR." In a *reprise* of Litvinov's conversation in June with Chilston, Rubinin noted the continuing hostility of the *Times* and *Daily Telegraph*, among other British papers. Charles replied that the British government could not "influence the newspapers" (although clearly it could), *but* he thought that if the Soviet side deemed it necessary, the Foreign Office could issue a sufficiently clear statement distinguishing government policy from statements in the press. In his report, Rubinin also mentioned a warm speech Charles had made at a reception put on by the Red Army's Main Directorate in honour of the new British military attaché in Moscow. It was the usual exchange of toasts, loosened up by spirits. Nevertheless, Charles's speech was greatly appreciated and marked in little ways, according to Rubinin, "a somewhat new tone of the local British embassy, seen over the past few months."[55]

A further sign of improvement, even more important, was the resolution of the Lena Goldfields dispute. Vansittart had raised this file with Maiskii at their first meeting on 3 July. On 4 November, the long-standing dispute was finally settled. Litvinov was as anxious as Vansittart to see the matter resolved; the Soviet government agreed to pay the modest sum of £3 million over twenty years to liquidate the dispute.[56] "Thank the Heavens," Maiskii wrote in his journal.[57] It was grist to the mill as Maiskii, returning from leave, resumed his campaign in favour of better Anglo-Soviet relations. He saw Tory MP Boothby on 6 November, repeating all the desiderata of his summertime meetings with Vansittart. Reaction in the Foreign Office was mixed, for and against Maiskii's statements to Boothby. The Deputy Permanent Undersecretary of State, Victor Wellesley, was not much impressed. He noted:

> Maisky is of course right when he says that what this country and Russia have most to fear are the ambitions of Germany and Japan and this certainly would seem to offer some sort of basis for co-operation; but unfortunately Russia has always

> proved herself to be a very unreliable partner. For what it is worth we should of course welcome these advances, but I should be more inclined to exploit them for the purpose of getting outstanding questions settled than to place much faith in being able to pursue a common policy for any length of time.[58]

Maiskii conveyed his usual messages to Simon during a reception put on by the Persian embassy. Simon was friendlier than usual and invited Maiskii to the Foreign Office for a discussion. It was 9 November. The polpred had a lot to say and a lot to record about that conversation in a twelve-page dispatch, as well as by telegram and in his journal. It must be said that Maiskii was not acting on his own initiative in speaking to Simon, but rather on instructions from Litvinov. Since the signing of the trade agreement in February 1934, "a good beginning" had been made, according to Litvinov, in improving relations. Maiskii conveyed this information to Simon, repeating the "realist" argument that differences in ideology should not obstruct better relations. Interests should determine such relations. And Maiskii went through the entire inventory of Soviet interests to demonstrate that they did not clash with British interests. It was getting to be a speech full of clichés. The Soviet preoccupation was with Nazi Germany and Japan. Everyone in the Foreign Office understood this, but, as is clear from Maiskii's dispatch, Simon was not as quick as Vansittart to embrace Maiskii's line of argument.

The Soviet government wanted and needed peace, said Maiskii, along the lines he had used with Boothby. The USSR was rebuilding and developing its economy. The last thing we needed was a war to disturb our internal development. What about British policy? Maiskii asked. "We also want peace, only peace," replied Simon, "war would be folly." Maiskii responded by asking about the possibility of "a nice little war" between Japan and the USSR in the Far East, as he had done with Vansittart. Simon gave him the same reply: it was not government policy. Then Maiskii brought into the discussion security in Europe. "Soviet interests could be explained in one overriding concern: to prevent by available means the disturbance of … peace from the direction of Germany." How did Britain see its "basic interest"? Maiskii asked, and continued, "It seems to me that it [British interest] could be formulated in about the same way." And here, unlike Vansittart, Simon had little to say. "Simon did not object," Maiskii noted in his report, to the proposition of common interests. The discussion finally got around to the Far East, in fact, to Japan. Again Maiskii proposed that Soviet and British interests coincided. Here, Simon was even more reticent. "Simon, however, remained silent, not expressing either agreement, or disagreement. He was, apparently, thinking about something." After Maiskii had finished what apparently was a long exposition of common Anglo-Soviet interests, or at least no serious conflicts, Simon took over the conversation. In general, of course, he expressed agreement with much of what Maiskii had to say. But Simon emphasized that good British relations with other governments should not be aimed against third parties. Britain wanted to have good relations with everyone.

Then, Simon brought up the subject of "propaganda," which seemed to preoccupy him more than the danger emanating from Japan or Germany. Anglo-Soviet interests, as he put it in his own record of the conversation, "would be best served if there was a definite dropping of Communist propaganda backed or inspired by Soviet Russia in countries outside it."[59] This led to a discussion of the commentary being published in their respective newspapers. Maiskii observed that the Soviet press was doing better, but that British papers did not seem to want to call off the mudslinging. Maiskii took a couple of examples out of his pocket, which he just happened to have with him, to show the Foreign Secretary. "Simon was clearly embarrassed. He quickly ran his eye over the citations … and immediately returned the papers to me, with such a gesture, as if to be afraid of being burned by them." He did not want to appear to be receiving some formal note from the Soviet ambassador.

The conversation resumed briefly that evening at the annual dinner put on by the Lord-Mayor at Guildhall. During a brief conversation Maiskii had got the impression that he and Simon were not on the same page about Japan. He therefore asked for a brief meeting at the Foreign Office to clarify that the Soviet desire for better relations did not conceal an *arrière-pensée* to "encircle" anyone or in particular Japan. Good Anglo-Soviet relations, Maiskii added, would of themselves exert a restraining effect on "aggressive forces" such as Germany and Japan. Simon agreed, adding that he had so understood Maiskii on the previous day. Simon indicated that he intended to bring the issue of future Anglo-Soviet relations to cabinet for discussion. Maiskii wrote in his journal that he still had his doubts, as well he might have had in view of Simon's reticence. Was this all just a "soap bubble" or a "serious historical event"? That would depend on the British cabinet. "I am sitting in front of the typewriter," Maiskii wrote in his journal, "and I wonder which of these two possibilities it will be. We wait and see."[60] In reading Maiskii's reports of conversation with Vansittart and Simon, Litvinov would certainly have noticed the difference between Vansittart's enthusiasm and Simon's reticience. Maybe there *was* something to Lady Vansittart's view that her husband and the Foreign Secretary did not see eye to eye.

After meeting Simon at the Foreign Office, Maiskii dropped in on Collier to keep him sweet and to have a chat. Collier was in a good mood, and happy about the settlement of the Lena Goldfields dispute. The Northern Department was quiet, Collier told Maiskii, "there is almost no business, for Anglo-Soviet relations, which used to bring me the most work, are calm and developing normally." Now, it was the Central Department, dealing with Germany, which was getting all the work. "I answered with a smile," Maiskii noted, "that, fortunately,

Collier's department being freed from 'bad files' in Anglo-Soviet relations, why not load up with 'good files' – to improve and develop these relations." The more so since – and this point Maiskii never failed to mention – there were no major issues dividing Britain and the USSR. "Collier entirely agreed with my opinion and mentioned my conversation with Simon yesterday, about which he had already heard from his boss. Collier added that, in his opinion, in the realm of international politics, the USSR and England are increasingly 'on the same side of the fence.'" This was true in Europe certainly, Maiskii observed mischievously, but what about the Far East?

"Collier choked for a moment and then replied: 'My personal opinion is that we are in the Far East also on the same side of the fence.' But not everyone thinks that way." In the end, they agreed that Soviet and British interests in the Far East were "roughly" the same. "Roughly?" What did that mean?

"Our interest in the Far East," Maiskii said, "is the peace, integrity and independence of China and the prevention of a disturbance of the peace by Japan."

"And our interest is to maintain the status quo in the Far East and preserve the doors open to trade in China," Collier replied. "It's about the same thing you want."[61]

This informal conversation intended simply to keep Collier friendly, turned a little sour and increased Maiskii's doubts about British policy in the Far East. "In English governing circles a struggle is underway between two tendencies," he advised Litvinov. "One – for a rapprochement with the USSR and, possibly, for some cooling of relations (but not a rupture) with Japan, and the other – for a strengthening of somewhat shaky relations with Japan and for a cooling of relations, or at least, for a halting of the further process of rapprochement with the USSR." Things could go either way. His conversations with Simon and Collier underscored the struggle underway between the "two tendencies." Simon still remained pro-Japanese in opposition to Vansittart, "who supports the line of a rapprochement with us." Maiskii recommended a proactive policy towards London: "It is very dangerous to leave matters to chance."[62] Maiskii was right about the two "tendencies" in British policy, and there was considerable discussion in the Foreign Office and in cabinet during the summer and autumn of 1934 about better Anglo-Japanese relations and their impact on an Anglo-Soviet rapprochement. Neville Chamberlain, then Chancellor of the Exchequer, and Simon jointly signed a memorandum for cabinet in October proposing an Anglo-Japanese rapprochement. In fact, Maiskii may have overreacted to Simon's hedging in early November for he (Simon) had written to the prime minister in early October that a rapprochement with Japan would provoke adverse reactions in the United States and the USSR. There was also strong opposition in the British embassy in Tokyo to a rapprochement; Japan would never agree to any serious concessions to British interests. Cabinet discussed the possibilities at the end of October and decided to let matters lie for the time being.[63]

Maiskii was an unflagging lobbyist for better Anglo-Soviet relations. He saw Eden, the Lord Privy Seal, a few days later. The subject of Japan did not come up, but Germany did. According to Maiskii, Eden thought events in Germany were leading towards war, whatever Hitler might say about his desire for peace. Although during the summer Eden had expressed his doubts about the advantages of an Anglo-Soviet rapprochement, he seemed to be moving towards Vansittart's position. Eden reacted favourably to Maiskii's line that there were no major conflicts of interest between Britain and the USSR.[64]

Three weeks later, it was Walter Elliot, the Scottish Minister of Agriculture on whom Maiskii set his sights. It was the usual topics of conversation. The belief that Russia was "the enemy" is an "old idea," nourished for centuries, Elliot noted: Russia as "a friend" is a new idea of only a few months. It would take time "and the right circumstances" for the idea to take root. "I think," Elliot added, "that the new idea of Russia as a friend of Great Britain will gradually conquer England." And what about Germany? Maiskii asked. Elliot shrugged: "Germany makes the danger of war an extremely urgent problem. Our rapprochement with the USSR is partly delayed by the fear that Germany would suspect us of striving for its 'encirclement.'" Already the Franco-Soviet rapprochement was arousing fears in Germany that this was the first step towards encirclement. So Britain had to move carefully, Elliot continued, an Anglo-Soviet rapprochement could strengthen such sentiments. Eastern Locarno did not mean encirclement, Maiskii responded. Germany was envisaged as a signatory. Elliot acquiesced, noting that the British government supported the idea. In Germany, encirclement was just a palaver, a good line to paralyze the British and French. Litvinov had already formulated an unspoken policy of containment of Germany and the recreation of the First World War's anti-German Entente if containment failed. Of course, he could not come right out and say so. Imagine the scandal, exploited by Nazi Germany. As usual, Maiskii also raised the problem of Japan and drew a similarly cautious reply from Elliot.[65]

Simon had promised Maiskii at their meeting in early November to inform cabinet of their discussions, but he had not done so. It is not clear why, perhaps he had second thoughts. Maiskii reacted badly: it's a "dirty trick" (*nekrasivyi triuk*), and either Simon wanted to hide their conversation from cabinet or delay informing it. Maybe not, for it appears that Simon did not misrepresent Maiskii's proposals.[66]

Maiskii and Vansittart: The Refrain

Maiskii met Vansittart in mid-December – Van had been on leave – to resume their earlier dialogue and to permit the Soviet ambassador to pass his messages by another channel other than the Foreign Secretary. Vansittart repeated the by-then familiar refrain that there were no serious political or economic conflicts between Britain and the USSR anywhere in the world. In Europe? Maiskii asked. He wanted to be sure. "Our British interests," replied Vansittart, "are completely identical to yours. Peace and the prevention by all means available to us of the disturbance of peace from the part of Germany." That was clear. And "finally, the Far East?" Maiskii asked. Maiskii laid out Soviet interests; and Vansittart replied by explaining British interests, with somewhat different wording than Maiskii but coming to the same ends more or less.

"That's good to hear," Maiskii replied, "does everyone in England think in the same way?" There are "groups in the Conservative camp which believe that 'a nice little war between the USSR and Japan' would be very useful for British interests in the Pacific Ocean."

"To want a Japanese-Soviet war can only be crazy," Vansittart said. "Such a war would inevitable become a world war. People sharing such views mentioned by you are a paltry handful, having no weight in British politics." This part of the conversation went on for a while. Finally, Maiskii asked Vansittart how he would describe British policy in the Far East. "Caution and again caution," Vansittart replied.

Although Maiskii had promised Litvinov not to raise the subject of Simon's offer to speak to cabinet about Anglo-Soviet relations, he did so in the end. "Vansittart raised his eyebrows in astonishment." No, he replied, he knew nothing about such a démarche to cabinet, but he said he would inquire. In Vansittart's account, he recorded that Maiskii must have misunderstood ("some slight misunderstanding"). "I asked V. not to be concerned," Maiskii indicated in his *dnevnik*, "but for myself I concluded that Simon, with his usual duplicity, had obviously not done what he had told me." At this point Vansittart's secretary interrupted him for an urgent matter, and the conversation came to end. Too bad, for one wonders how Vansittart would have responded to Maiskii's comment, which was audacious to say the least.[67]

Maiskii and Vansittart resumed their conversation a few days later, on 18 December. It was the usual topics, although Maiskii did not pursue the matter of Simon's failure to report to cabinet on Anglo-Soviet relations. The two records of the conversation were remarkably similar in emphasis. According to Vansittart's record:

> Sir R. Vansittart replied in all good humour that he thought M. Maisky's Government were far too full of suspicions; indeed, they seemed to be obsessed by them. He did not in the least object to the Ambassador ventilating them with him; indeed, he welcomed it, for suspicions were like a diseased tooth, and it was much better to have them out.

The two men exchanged further observations about the hostility of their respective presses, both sides being extremely sensitive to abuse. Maiskii hoped to remove these sources of friction for "what he really had in mind was a desire to accelerate the progress of Anglo-Soviet relations."

> He reminded Sir R. Vansittart that, in their last interview, he had said that, when relations were good and normal, he thought not only that they could well look after themselves, but that this was the best course. He agreed that relations were good, but good only as compared with the rather stormy period from which they had emerged. He would like, in fact, to see the stormy period succeeded by more warmth and favourable wind and sun.[68]

This meeting had a strong impact on Foreign Office officials. "The USSR was born into a world filled with suspicion," noted George Mounsey, Assistant Permanent Undersecretary. He continued:

> Its own genesis and youth were such as to necessarily foster this general atmosphere & suspicion on the part of its neighbours; and suspicion consequently within its own bosom. So it is not surprising to find this obsession still keeping a heavy hand on the Soviet and their representatives. But it *is* [emphasis in the original], I think a good sign and a step in advance that the latter will now come forward and voice their doubt and grievances …
>
> All the more reason, therefore, to reassure the Soviet in any way we usefully can. But this must take time and can be achieved better by deeds than by words.[69]

The Foreign Office clerks and undersecretaries seemed to be coming around. But what about the politicians, were they? Maiskii continued to wonder and with some justification, as it turned out. On 17 December, he had lunch in Parliament organized by Boothby. In attendance were Leslie Burgin, parliamentary secretary to the Board of Trade, and Robert Hudson, parliamentary secretary to the Ministry of Labour, among others. In a "gloves off" (in English in original) discussion, Burgin and especially Hudson defended the idea of an Anglo-Japanese alliance and the partition of China into "spheres of influence." "I challenged them," Maiskii wrote in his journal.

Obviously concerned, Boothby reported the row to Vansittart, who immediately invited Maiskii to come to see him. "Vansittart was really frightfully irritated with Burgin and Hudson. They are 'foolish people' [English in original], who understand nothing about foreign policy and do not in the least reflect the views of the British government on questions concerning the Far East." Vansittart repeated what he had said previously about British policy in the Far East, and added that there was no intention of renewing the Anglo-Japanese alliance. Vansittart also said that he had been thinking a great deal about their previous conversations and thought that perhaps it would be a good idea to send a British minister to the USSR to get the lay of the land. Maiskii was all for this idea.[70]

Collier quite naturally was informed about the loose talk in the House of Commons from unnamed MPs about Anglo-Japanese cooperation. Such "foolish language," as Vansittart put it, had come from no less than two undersecretaries of state. Foreign Office officials were ever so discreet and did not mention the names of Burgin and Hudson, but Maiskii did in his journal. Collier wrote a long minute describing various British circles in favour of better relations with Japan. He thought the Soviet embassy – "quite well informed of what goes on in London" – also knew a lot. A "pro-Japanese policy," Collier wrote, "is supported in high official circles in London, particularly in the Treasury." Treasury meant Neville Chamberlain. No wonder Maiskii was suspicious, Collier said in so many words.

In the United States and the Dominions, "which have notoriously been disquieted in recent months by the apparent willingness of certain people in this country, including some holding high official position, to contemplate 'doing a deal' with Japan at the expense of China and other countries in Asia (including the Soviet Union) and 'sharing the swag.' For my own part," minuted Collier, "I find it difficult to understand how anyone in his senses could advocate any policy which would strengthen Japan ... our most dangerous and implacable enemy." Collier also had this to say though he was going beyond the remit of the Northern Department: "We cannot convincingly preach the gospel of the *status quo* in Europe if we cannot show the other European Powers that we are also upholding it in the Far East; and though I am not saying that we are not now upholding it there to the best of our ability, I do say that in present circumstances, it is not obvious to the world at large that we are determined to continue to do so and to make no compromise with Japanese aggression."[71] Maiskii was not so paranoid after all. Collier was beginning to stake out a position in favour of an Anglo-Soviet rapprochement, which he defended with such determination that it may well have cost him being promoted to assistant undersecretary.

Vansittart was not going to let Maiskii off on Burgin and Hudson without a tit for tat. He raised – to keep the balance even and "as a friend" – the continuing British grievance. "It was really time that any interference by the Comintern in our domestic affairs should cease." I have "unimpeachable knowledge," said Vansittart, "that such interference ... [is] going on." Maiskii interrupted that he knew nothing about it. But Vansittart had no doubt, and "it was most important for the Soviet Government and/or the Comintern ... to stop it." Vansittart had said it all before: we have "more important fish to fry." Surely they did not want to offer a pretext to those who sought to block an Anglo-Soviet rapprochement. Vansittart "repeated that, from the Soviet point of view, the horizon was surely not so unclouded as to permit of these goings-on, and that this little game was emphatically not worth the candle compared with the greater and more real problems of European politics."[72] Maiskii also duly recorded these remarks in his journal and in a numbered dispatch. His version is quite candid in reporting Vansittart's words:

> He, as a "friend," had to warn me that all our efforts can go to pieces if from the Soviet side there will continue to be interference in the internal affairs of Great Britain. And just in the very last days he had learned about the existence of such facts. I expressed surprise at the words of V. and asked him to explain to me more precisely what kind of facts exactly did he mean, because, not knowing what it was about, I could not react in any way to his words. V., however, refused to go into details. He only added: I know that you, as the ambassador of the USSR, of course, must and will deny the presence of such interference. It's your responsibility.

Vansittart was not inclined to attach too much importance to Comintern meddling, but other people would also be informed, and they could provoke "a big scandal," which could stop the improvement in Anglo-Soviet relations.[73]

At the end of 1934, Anglo-Soviet relations were about as good as they had ever been during the interwar years, though the improvement was still largely at the stage of discussion between Maiskii and his British interlocutors, most notably Vansittart. At the outset, talk was important, but a real rapprochement would have to move on to action, as Maiskii and Vansittart had discussed and, indeed, as Mounsey had recognized. Relations had come some way since the beginning of the year when Foreign Office officials winced at attending a Soviet luncheon. Nazi Germany and Imperial Japan continued to provide incentive for further development of the rapprochement. However, the British government and the Conservative Party were large terrains. Vansittart was the Permanent Undersecretary, not the Foreign Secretary. He was an official, not a Conservative politician. He had a large influence in the Foreign Office and in cabinet. In the Treasury and in other departments, however, and among influential members of the Conservative party, there were other people who did not agree with Vansittart's view of Nazi Germany and Japan as sources of danger, and they certainly did not see the USSR as a potential ally. So, if Anglo-Soviet relations were improving, it was going to be a fight to consolidate and extend them.

Litvinov's Caution

This was more or less how Litvinov saw the situation, and he wrote to Maiskii in early January advising him to be careful:

> I have no objection to your meeting with Simon and Vansittart, but I cannot hide from you that a careful reading of the records of conversation left me with the impression that you were trying too hard to get something out of them. The initiative remained in your hands all the time, and your interlocutors limited themselves

> to general, insignificant courteous assent and you, nevertheless, again returned to this theme. I think that we have shown enough interest and that we need to wait for the other party to respond. I fear, however, that it will not happen.[74]

It did indeed appear from Moscow that Maiskii was pressing the case with his British interlocutors. It also appeared that he was getting more interest from Vansittart than he was from Simon. His reports did not attempt to exaggerate his progress. His confrontation with Hudson and Burgin was a case in point. Was he pressing too hard? The British had got the message that the Soviet government was genuinely concerned about Nazi Germany and Japan. Was there no such danger? The first reaction, that of Wellesley, for example, was let's see what we can get from Moscow, but Oliphant and later Mounsey were more responsive. Simon was cautious, almost non-committal; Vansittart, more frank. All of these people were Foreign Office officials; they were not politicians except for Simon. That would have been obvious to Litvinov in comparing Maiskii's records of conversation with Simon and Vansittart. In short, the narkom did not want Maiskii to fail. He wanted him to be careful in pursuing the Soviet objective of better relations with Britain.

Maiskii defended himself. The initiative had not always been his, he wrote to Litvinov, sometimes it had been Vansittart's. He especially drew attention to the meeting on 27 December. At other times, he had wanted to verify the movement in British policy through his continuing conversations. Maiskii really did not like Litvinov's reference to "insignificant, courteous assent." The polpred bristled. "I do not quite agree with you," he replied, in a definite, diplomatic understatement. He then reviewed Vansittart's various statements about the common danger of Nazi Germany and Japan, but not so much Simon's positions. Litvinov would have noticed. Maiskii insisted: "My general impression comes to this, that my conversations with Simon and Vansittart make more sense [than you think]. You know well England and English foreign policy. You know very well that the English are addicted to a slow pace and do not like sharp turns and jumps. The process of improving Anglo-Soviet relations, which has been going on since last spring, cannot and will not be a rapid process. Everything will happen here slowly, slowly, step by step, without haste." Maiskii repeated his mantra that there were no serious conflicts of interest between the USSR and Britain, and this view was spreading among the British elite. He nevertheless acknowledged Litvinov's directive to let the British take the next step.[75] To this end, developments in Europe lent a hand.

Reasons to Worry

On 13 January 1935, the Nazis won an overwhelming majority in a plebiscite in the Saar for reunification with Germany; the votes for France were derisory. This was not one of Hitler's sham electoral demonstrations; the plebiscite was organized by the League of Nations. During the autumn, Litvinov told the new German ambassador Werner von der Schulenburg that the Soviet government did not have a direct interest in "the Saar problem." He had even refused to meet in Geneva with some anti-Hitler delegates from the Saar.[76] It would have been a pointless gesture anyway, and grist for the mill of Nazi propaganda. At the time, as readers will soon learn, Litvinov was in Geneva grappling with the cagey Laval and representatives of the Little Entente. Back in Moscow, Litvinov wrote to Maiskii to advise that a visit by Elliot and Vansittart to the USSR would be welcome.[77] This was in response to Vansittart's idea, which he raised on 27 December. Events in Europe were going in the wrong direction and would not permit the Soviet government to await a further initiative from the Foreign Office.

In early February the French and British met in London. On 3 February they issued a final communiqué on their deliberations in which the Eastern Pact was barely mentioned. It is true, however, that the Eastern Pact was long dead. If readers will be patient, they will find the details of the London meeting in the following chapter. In the meantime, Vansistart was worried. "With every month that passes," he wrote, "I obtain more evidence that confirms my suspicions & convictions as to Germany's ultimate policies & intentions. I think they will soon become evident to all but the biased and the blind."[78]

The "biased and the blind" were nevertheless represented in important numbers inside and outside the British government. Among them was Philip Kerr (Lord Lothian) who visited Berlin to "hobnob" with Herr Hitler in February 1935. The *Times* let loose a campaign, featuring Lord Lothian's statements in Berlin: "Herr Hitler … has said explicitly to me, as he has also said publicly, that what Germany wants is equality, not war; that she is prepared absolutely to renounce war."[79] "Balderdash," snarled Vansittart, Lothian is "an incurably superficial Johnny-know-it-all."[80]

"This was the kind of thing we had to listen to, day in, day out," remembered anti-appeaser A.L. Rowse.[81] "MacDonald and Simon with the support of the *Times*, *Daily Mail*, and some other papers," Maiskii wrote in his journal, "are leading a systematic campaign to silence the Eastern Pact and to concentrate all attention on questions of 'western security.' In other words, they are saying, addressing Hitler: 'Leave France and Britain in peace, and, as a form of compensation, do what you want in 'Eastern Europe.'"[82] Litvinov cabled Maiskii to get clarification on the British position. Even the Germans did not believe that Britain had the slightest interest in an Eastern Pact.[83] Hitler seemed to be having the last laugh as he was often to do with the French and British. What a difference a few weeks made. Maiskii was happy with Litvinov's announced change of strategy. Laying back was not possible. "He [Litvinov] also considers it expedient to offer some 'plain words' [in English in original] on current questions. He recommends concentrating attention on the evidence that 'peace is indivisible' (there cannot be 'western security' without 'eastern security')."[84]

From Moscow, Chilston reported Soviet anxiety, and Vansittart called in Maiskii to talk.[85] "I told him," recorded Vansittart, "exactly what I think of Lord Lothian & the *Times* ... & I don't care who knows it." He advised Chilston to give the same message to Litvinov.[86] It was a "preposterous" idea, said Vansittart, to think that Great Britain could profitably untie Hitler's hands in the east. Maiskii quoted Vansittart as saying: "We need to look at things realistically ... The basic fact, in Vansittart's opinion, remains unchanged: in Europe has emerged an armed and rapidly rearming Germany, the true intentions of which no one knows precisely. This situation (similar also to that before 1914) is pushing together the countries bordering on Germany."

"Let's not dredge up old quarrels," said Vansittart, referring to nasty comments in a speech by Molotov about Ambassador Ovey. "Our task now is to work on the improvement of Anglo-Soviet relations ... The past should be left to lie in the grave; we need to think about the future." Litvinov was not fully reassured by Maiskii's report.[87]

Vansittart sensed the Soviet disquiet, and wrote to Chilston: "We are very conscious of the importance of Russia in the present situation and of not doing anything which might make her feel that we and France were going to leave her in the lurch and that therefore she had best make terms with Germany before it is too late."[88] Readers should remember Vansittart's prophetic words four years hence, when the USSR finally abandoned collective security.

At this same meeting, Maiskii informed Vansittart that he and Elliot would be welcome to visit Moscow. Vansittart reacted favourably to this news thinking aloud that Simon might go instead of Elliot and himself. Maiskii wrote sarcastically in his journal that of course he approved the choice, though without enthusiasm. It was then that Vansittart also mentioned that Eden had been mentioned as a possible candidate to make the trip. Maiskii's obvious lack of enthusiasm for Simon led Vansittart to think that Eden would be the better choice.[89]

According to Maiskii's detailed numbered dispatch, Vansittart stated unequivocally that the British government supported the conclusion of an Eastern Pact. "Without such a pact," he told Maiskii, "there could be no pacification of Europe." British diplomats in Berlin and Warsaw had pressed the case in vain; the German and Polish governments were against it. "Nothing has changed," said Vansittart. "If the Germans are spreading the rumour that the British government supposedly is not interested in the Eastern Pact, then they are only following the axiom 'the wish is father to the thought.' The theory according to which supposedly the British government has nothing against German aggression in the East is complete stupidity. Even a child understands that, if war broke out in Eastern Europe, it would inevitably spill over into Western Europe." What about Simon and the others? Maiskii wanted to know, as always. And what about the *Times* and Lord Lothian? "That's *balderdash* [original in

English]," Vansittart had replied. Here the accounts of Maiskii and Vansittart are in perfect accord, but Maiskii recorded in greater detail Vansittart's scorn for the *Times*, a newspaper which had "systematically" gone downhill. There were no strong writers. A.L. Kennedy, who often wrote on foreign affairs, was "a person of low literary and political calibre." This was a newspaper "living off its former glory." Foreign diplomats needed to understand that "it is impossible to identify the *Times* with the Foreign Office."

Vansittart tried to reassure Maiskii about the Anglo-French discussions earlier in the month. "He asked me to convey to the Soviet government that neither the Anglo-French agreement nor the upcoming discussions with Germany will exert any unwelcome influence either on the Franco-Soviet rapprochement or on the development 'greatly improving relations between Great Britain and the USSR.'" These were "Vansittart's exact words," according to Maiskii. Vansittart then added that in Moscow people were too suspicious. "In foreign affairs," Maiskii replied, "suspicion is in any case better than carelessness." With that comment Maiskii prepared to leave, but Vansittart held him back to raise one last subject.

"V. steered me over to the burning fireplace and, speaking in the most intimate tone's privately talked about Labour. He, of course, has a lot of friends among Labour circles, but he had to admit that the position of Labour in some external-political issues is absolutely ridiculous." The English, Vansittart continued, could be very sympathetic to the down and out, and for Germany in recent years there had been a great deal of sympathy not only in the Labour Party but among Liberals and Conservatives. "But that Germany, with which the English then sympathized, now no longer exists. At present there is a completely other Germany – dangerous, threatening, bristling with machine guns and airplanes." Labour did not seem to notice and, "in many cases, mechanically continued that same line of conduct which was fully correct and natural before the arrival of Hitler to power." He just wanted to draw this to Maiskii's attention, Vansittart said in so many words, so that when Maiskii was speaking with Labour people, who might listen to him, if he could see his way clear, "it would be not bad at all, if [you] could try to explain to them the harm and danger of their present position." Maiskii admitted that he had conversations with Labour people along political lines as he did with Liberals and Conservatives. "I also sometimes did not agree with those views, which Labourites developed," Maiskii replied, "in particular in relation to European problems, but Labourites are stubborn people, and like all the English, like to have their own opinions."[90] So ended another conversation with Vansittart, a plain spoken diplomat, who did not always share what he had said to Maiskii with his Foreign Office colleagues.

A week later, Vansittart put up a paper to cabinet, making similar points: "For nearly a year it has been becoming increasingly evident that Russia is suffering from the fear of Germany which now animates, or paralyses, Europe." Russian policy had changed; Comintern propaganda had diminished; the Soviet government wanted better relations with Great Britain. "These things have a significance which we, as realists, must not miss; we must not overrate the change of heart, and we must not underrate the uses to which it can be turned in the acute world-problem ahead of us."

Soviet fear of Nazi aggression had caused the formation of two schools in the Soviet government: one led by Litvinov and the other by the commissar for war, Voroshilov. Litvinov's policies "were to our profit both politically and economically"; Voroshilov advocated the traditional policy of rapprochement with Germany, a position which, Vansittart warned, should not be discounted in spite of Hitler's virulent anti-communism. "It is manifest," concluded Vansittart, "that our interest lies in the predominance of the Litvinov school." To strengthen it, the British government should accept Maiskii's often proffered suggestion of a visit to Moscow by a British minister. It would be "at little or no cost to ourselves," and Maiskii had been "pressing"; a rebuff would damage Litvinov's "precarious prestige."[91] Vansittart was right and wrong about Soviet policy. There were not two "schools" of thought in Moscow. There was only one "school," which was Stalin's. Voroshilov was Stalin's man; he would not go against his chief. If he had personal opinions or doubts, he kept them to himself. While there were always rumours going around the Western embassies in Moscow about Litvinov's imminent dismissal, they would not materialize until 1939. In 1935, Stalin supported Litvinov's policy recommendations, often word for word. If Stalin supported them, so did Voroshilov.

On Litvinov's instructions, Maiskii saw Simon about waning British support for an Eastern Pact. Eden was also present. Simon gave assurances that the British government supported the Eastern Pact, but Maiskii was not so sure. The Foreign Secretary asked if the Soviet government would be open to "changing the character of the Eastern Pact." Weakening it, he meant, turning it into a scrap of paper. It was doubtful whether even that would be acceptable in Berlin and Warsaw. Out of the question, was Maiskii's reply, according to his cable to the NKID.[92] Litvinov must have continued to wonder about the firmness of British policy in comparing the records of conversations with Simon and Vansittart. Maiskii probed, asking the same questions, getting the same answers. Consider the following exchange taken from the record of conversation by Maiskii. It was in the midst of a long discussion about the Eastern Pact.

What would happen, Simon asked hypothetically, if it was not possible to conclude the pact? British public opinion might grow impatient, "and say: 'If the agreement on Eastern Europe at the moment is unattainable, is it not better to set yourself more modest and limited tasks?' If this were indeed the case, the British government would have to reckon with public opinion."

"So," Maiskii exclaimed, "you admit that under certain conditions the Eastern Pact may fall out of the London program?" According to Maiskii, "Simon waved his hands and began to argue that he did not at all think this. He was only theoretically discussing various possibilities."

"Then Eden unexpectedly interrupted and loudly interjected: 'If there is no security in the East, there is no disarmament. Don't you think so?' – he added, turning to me."

"I confirmed that, of course, if the system of 'western security' is implemented, and Germany in the East will have a free hand, it is difficult to think that any of the Eastern states could contemplate disarmament."

"'Quite right!' Eden exclaimed. And then, turning to Simon, he noted that without a solution to the problem of 'Eastern security,' in general it would be difficult to make any significant step forward."

"Simon, not objecting to Eden's words, helplessly spread his hands and said: 'But the Germans under no circumstances want the Eastern Pact. What to do with them?'"

Maiskii replied, "German opposition to the Eastern Pact was largely the responsibility of the British government. In Berlin, there was a strong belief that the British government views the Eastern Pact indifferently if not with hostility. That's why the Germans are so stubborn about the Eastern Pact."

Simon heatedly denied that this was so. "It's not true," he said, though he hedged a little on British support. Maiskii certainly knew how to probe and provoke. "'Where did the Germans get this idea? Have you heard anything about it?' Simon asked, turning to Eden. Eden gave a vague shrug."

Maiskii's account of the exchange between Simon and Eden was beginning to sound like a Laurel and Hardy routine. Stan Laurel was British and Oliver Hardy was American. They got their start in Hollywood in 1927 and so would have been well known in England. Nevertheless, Vansittart would not have resorted to evasive shrugs. The conversation continued for a time, but inconclusively. Simon did most of the talking. "It's time to get a move on," Maiskii said. "It is necessary to act and not to cry."[93]

Following this conversation, Maiskii alternated between pessimism and optimism. His subsequent journal entry and numbered dispatch were more positive about a shift in British policy, which recognized Litvinov's axiom that "peace is indivisible" and that security in Europe could not be assured without Soviet participation. Nevertheless, powerful political forces in Britain favoured a rapprochement with Germany and opposed recognizing the USSR as "a genuine great power." The present favourable mood in Britain could change for the worse. "We must remain very much on the alert." In passing, Maiskii noted that the *Times* and *Daily Telegraph* had published what appeared to be an article inspired by the Foreign Office pointing out that the British government was contemplating sending a minister to Moscow. He took this as a good sign.[94]

An English Visit to Moscow

Just to make sure, he asked Vansittart two days later whether the stories in the papers were a canard or inspired. Vansittart answered by saying that he had polled cabinet ministers about the Moscow visit and obtained a favourable reply.[95] Litvinov was not so sure of what was going on. Maiskii was still worried that Simon "was continuing his anti-Soviet line and by any means wants to reach agreement with Germany if only on the basis of conceding it free of action in the East. Only it will not work. We will not allow it."[96]

Litvinov asked for instructions from Stalin. "I do not think Simon's visit to Moscow is particularly desirable, but at the same time we should not give him the impression that we do not want him to come." Litvinov proposed that in the event of an informal request or probing, Maiskii should respond that the arrival of Simon or other ministers in Moscow would be welcome.[97] The NKID did not, however, consider the notes in the *Times* and *Daily Telegraph* as authoritative, Maiskii would have to wait for some indication from the Foreign Office. He objected to Moscow, but was advised that the NKID was unsure that Simon even wanted to visit the USSR. Maiskii finally got his way, more or less, when Litvinov authorized him to invite Simon to Moscow, but only Simon. Eden would be better, Maiskii wrote in his journal.[98]

On instructions from Litvinov, Maiskii met Vansittart on 28 February. They were getting to be old friends. Maiskii again inquired about the cabinet position on the visit to Moscow. Only two ministers were against the idea during cabinet discussions. Vansittart would not name them, but Maiskii had heard from other sources that it was Hailsham, Secretary of State for War, and Sir Samuel Hoare, then Secretary of State for India. Press reaction was positive. If a formal Soviet invitation had been extended three or four days ago, Vansittart noted, a decision would have been taken in cabinet the day before. Simon would be welcome in Moscow, replied Maiskii, the delay was due to not knowing whether the invitation would be accepted. The discussion then turned to logistics, not an unimportant matter, but about which it is perhaps not worth belabouring readers. Maiskii finally asked if Eden would accompany Simon to Moscow. "That's not clear yet," Vansittart replied.[99]

As it happened, Simon was in Paris and met Laval to discuss the Eastern Pact. Since Poland and Germany had already rejected this proposal, the continued discussion of it in London and Paris could only be considered a sign of desperation to find some solution short of mutual assistance. Litvinov remained mistrustful of Simon, and instructed Potemkin to see Laval *before* meeting Simon to head off any attempt to weaken the Eastern Pact or replace it with non-aggression pacts.[100] As if Potemkin could have prevented Laval and his officials from double-crossing the Soviet government if that would have opened the way towards Berlin. Litvinov was watching Simon like a hawk. Inform Vansittart, he wrote to Maiskii, of an editorial in *Izvestiia* about the "servility" (*ugodlivost'*) of the English towards Hitler. The London papers were now writing that Simon might not after all visit Moscow in order to avoid irritating Hitler. Worse than that, Simon was already contemplating concessions to Hitler before even meeting him and pressuring the French to do the same. Litvinov indicated that he would be glad to see Eden and Vansittart in Moscow.[101] No wonder. The narkom worried about what could go wrong. He hoped, and so did Maiskii, that Eden and especially Vansittart could act as political "commissars" to keep Simon in line. Litvinov also had to keep a close eye on Paris, trying to prevent Laval from caving in to Simon or being duped by Hitler.

Maiskii's job was now to make sure that the visit to Moscow actually came off. He was seeing Vansittart almost every day or every other day. On 4 March there was a dinner at the embassy for Vansittart and Sarita. Readers who remember their last encounter with Lady Vansittart will not be disappointed for she again vented her spleen about Simon, not caring apparently who overheard her. "Being a senior guest," she sat right next to Maiskii, relating all the difficulties that Vansittart faced at the Foreign Office. "Vansittart and Simon look at many questions quite differently. More than that, Simon spends little time in the Foreign Office and dumps all the great mass of current worries on Vansittart. He is literally sewn up at work, being occupied from early morning to late at night while at the same time Simon is playing golf and going to his summer cottage each weekend." The last two weeks, Sarita continued, have been "a living hell" with meetings with the French and the organization of Simon's foreign trips. Simon interfered all the time: today he says yes, tomorrow no, and the day after tomorrow he will recommend that the question be postponed. It was like that.

Sarita continued her tales of woe. On 27 February, the cabinet approved a ministerial trip to Berlin, but not Moscow. Vansittart thought this was a mistake, argued for both but could not carry the cabinet in part because the Soviet position on the visit was not yet known. Vansittart wanted to get the question settled as quickly as possible, but for several days after Simon's return from Paris he did not even look in at the Foreign Office. He was at his cottage or playing golf. Vansittart tried to track him down, but Simon avoided him. Finally, on 3 March, Vansittart went to see Baldwin and then MacDonald. After long discussions with them he obtained authorization for Simon's trip to Moscow. Vansittart was at the end of his patience, still according to Sarita. Why not spend the Easter holidays in Moscow, as tourists, Maiskii suggested. "I would love to visit Moscow," Sarita responded, but Simon would probably upset their plans. Maiskii finally asked if Simon would be going to Berlin with Eden. "Fortunately, together with Eden," she replied. "Simon is very fond of flattery, and Hitler in this regard probably will not stint. This could push Simon into making some imprudent declaration in Berlin. Eden will restrain him and straighten things out."[102] Readers will no doubt draw two conclusions from this conversation: first, that Vansittart vented with his spouse, and second, that she did not like or respect Simon. A further conclusion might be that Sarita was either indiscreet or that she liked Maiskii and wanted to help him and her husband pull off the trip to Moscow. Litvinov was rightly mistrustful of Simon and did not want to be caught in a situation where the Foreign Secretary after being invited to Moscow, cancelled his trip.

After dinner, still around the table, Maiskii sat down next to Vansittart for some small talk about literature. But Vansittart interrupted to say that he wanted to discuss business, namely the British visit to Moscow. Baldwin and MacDonald fully supported it. Other cabinet members were either sympathetic or at least did not oppose the trip. Even the two ministers who were in opposition had softened their position. The next cabinet meeting was in two days and it looked like the trip would gain approval, but we need, Vansittart said, a Soviet invitation. Maiskii explained his instructions, to wit, that he could not make the formal invitation until he knew cabinet had approved the visit. Isn't that enough? Maiskii asked. Here we go again. It was a fresh act of the Alphonse and Gaston routine. Vansittart thought for a moment and then said it might be. "My impression," Maiskii noted, "was that some new combination had come to his mind."

The conversation then turned to the Simon visit to Berlin, planned for early March, and how Moscow would fit in afterward. The discussion was about logistics and tactics. The conversation turned to who exactly would go to Berlin and then to Moscow. In other circumstances, Moscow would welcome a visit by Eden alone, as he was well regarded by Litvinov and others in the government.

> However, in this case and in this situation the trip by Eden alone to Moscow after Simon and Eden went to Berlin, naturally could give a reason for all sorts of undesirable interpretations. We must try to avoid such interpretations. V. fully agreed with me, but added: "Still, as an extreme case, I think a visit by Eden is better than no visit at all." And when I asked V. what was the matter? Why Simon after a visit to Berlin could not with equal success make a visit to the Moscow? – V. smiled sourly and said with some irritation: "For any visit, besides the possibility, there must also be the desire."

Maiskii continued to worry about British concessions in Berlin. He warned Simon and Eden (on 20 February) against any caving in on the Eastern Pact. But when Simon went to Paris, he tried to persuade Laval to give up an Eastern Pact entailing mutual assistance for weaker bilateral non-aggression pacts. Without firmness, Hitler would simply harden his demands. Vansittart agreed, but he repeated what he had said before that Britain would not get directly involved in an Eastern Pact for geographical and political reasons and would not guarantee it. This limited British possibilities to encouraging agreement of the more directly interested parties. Finally, the two agreed to meet two days hence after the cabinet meeting to see where matters stood.[103]

On that same day, 4 March, the British government released a Defence White Paper calling for increased military spending. On the following day, Hitler suddenly announced that he had fallen ill and could not meet Simon and Eden; their visit being planned to begin on 7 March. The Führer was down with laryngitis; the meeting was postponed indefinitely. On 6 March, Maiskii went in to see Vansittart, as agreed, to learn what had occurred in cabinet. It was not good news. One look at Vansittart's face announced difficulties. A decision on the Moscow visit was again put off. Hitler's "illness" had upset the applecart. The Berlin trip thus hung in the air, and the Moscow trip was slowed down. But Vansittart hastened to add that the general discussion of the Moscow trip was positive. Cabinet would need, however, the formal invitation so that some ministers could not find fault with procedures. When Maiskii asked Vansittart what he thought about Hitler's "trick," he loosed some expletives.[104]

On the following day – it was 7 March – Vansittart telephoned Maiskii to tell him that the cabinet had approved visits to Moscow and Warsaw, independent of the Berlin visit. Eden would go. Simon was to announce the decision in the Commons that day. Maiskii replied that he would have to consult Moscow for instructions since he did not have authority to invite Eden alone. It was the "maximum," Vansittart replied, that he could obtain in the present circumstances. Maiskii noted:

> Then V. sought to convince me that the candidacy of Eden from all points of view is very appropriate and advantageous. Eden is a young, fresh, flexible diplomat who understands the international situation and the importance of the collective system of peace. He speaks languages, is well acquainted with Litvinov, and is interested in the USSR. Moreover, Eden is very influential in the Conservative Party, where he is seen as a rising star. He, V., therefore thinks that Eden's trip to Moscow will undoubtedly be a major step forward on the way to improving Anglo-Soviet relations.

Maiskii had no problem with the choice of Eden, but thought about appearances, Eden was less senior than Simon. Maiskii wondered aloud if Eden could not replace Simon in Berlin. "Vansittart sniggered and said that the question of the Berlin visit was now hanging in the air, and when Hitler's voice recovered, details [of the visit] would be discussed again."[105]

Eden Goes to Moscow

"So, Eden is going," Maiskii wrote in his journal. "Very good!"[106] He at once informed Moscow by telegram, and Litvinov responded that he should immediately inform Vansittart that the government was "officially inviting" Eden to Moscow. "We would consider desirable his immediate arrival," Litvinov indicated, "but if that is not possible, then immediately after the Berlin Anglo-German discussions."[107]

Maiskii recommended high-profile publicity in the Moscow press and a meeting with Stalin, even if Vansittart or Eden had not yet raised the subject. "Eden's visit, regardless of its immediate results," Maiskii opined, "will have an extremely large international political significance. This is the final 'recognition' of the USSR as a great power on the part of another great power and, moreover, [one] such as Great Britain." Maiskii was lyrical: "The moment is undoubtedly historical." British press reaction, he added, was "positive" with the exception of the *Daily Mail* and *Daily Express*.

Not all the news was good: the Labour Party remained a cause for concern. Maiskii must have followed up on Vansittart's plea to talk to his Labour contacts. "I have lately had a lot of unpleasant conversations with Labourites," he advised Litvinov. "These people are now completely at a loss in the field of international political affairs and are doing one stupid thing after another." He continued:

> Accustomed to treating pre-Hitlerite Germany with compassion and sympathy, as a victim of Versailles, they very often, even now, sing the same old song, not noticing, or not wanting to notice that now they have to deal with a completely different Germany. As a result, there have been a number of statements in the press and in Parliament, which simply pour water on Hitler's mill. Some Labour leaders are absolutely pessimistic about foreign policy. Today, for example, [George] Lansbury [former Labour Party leader] was at the embassy. His general attitude is as follows: there is a furious arms race underway, and to stop it is impossible. War in the near future is inevitable, and there is no force capable of preventing the impending catastrophe. Hence the sublime disregard for all practical measures to reduce or put off the danger of war, such as the Eastern mutual assistance pact.

So what to do? Maiskii had no intention of quitting the fight. "I have not hidden nor do I hide my assessment of such sentiments from any of my Labour acquaintances. On some of them, this approach is beginning to work. But in general … at this point of international-political development, the Labour Party appears to have been taken unaware and is drifting without a rudder and without sails."[108]

Meanwhile in Berlin, Hitler recovered from his diplomatic laryngitis. On 9 March, the Nazi government announced the existence of its air force, the *Luftwaffe*. A week later, on 16 March, in defiance of its obligations under the Treaty of Versailles, Hitler announced the reintroduction of conscription and the existence of a German Army of 500,000 men. These actions, logically, ought to have been further incentive for better Anglo-Soviet relations. Even Simon seemed to come around at least for the duration of a meeting. On 13 March, Maiskii reported seeing Simon about the upcoming visit: "Eden's visit will have, according to Simon, historic importance, as visible evidence that 'Russia has returned to Europe' and become an integral part of European politics."[109]

"An important historical date," Maiskii wrote in his journal a few days later. "A major step has been taken on the path to a new world war. Thus, let's put cards on the table. The Treaty of Versailles has been openly and triumphantly torn to pieces. Fascist Germany is turning into a menacing military power."[110] Yes, it was.

To make matters worse, the British government stumbled. On 18 March, at 4 p.m., the Foreign Office sent a note to Berlin asking Hitler if the planned meeting should still take place. No stiff note of protest … nothing. Three hours later, the Germans government agreed, and at 9 p.m., it was announced in the House of Commons. Maiskii knew it was coming. *Slabo*! No courage, he wrote in his journal. "What a disgrace. What a fall."[111] The British government failed to consult France or the USSR before announcing that the Simon visit was back on. "I had never contemplated that H.M.G. were going to rush their fences in this tragic manner," noted Vansittart. "We have forfeited confidence all round."[112] That was true, except that Vansittart had the day before taken a softer line with Corbin.[113]

The most scathing dissection of the British capitulation came from Krestinskii. He offered some ideas to Maiskii, who had been authorized to accompany Eden to Moscow. The situation was worse now than it was even a week before. The Germans had introduced the Luftwaffe, Krestinskii said, and they had reinstituted conscription repudiating the military stipulations of the Treaty of Versailles. And what had been the reaction in London? "The English government," Krestinskii explained, "not only did not react sharply to this, not only did they not demand an emergency convocation of the Council of the League of Nations, but [instead] they sent a modest note asking the Germans not to cancel the Berlin meeting." It was like a sharper in a card game, pulling the high spade from his sleeve, and instead of upending the table, the British asked the sharper to deal the next hand.

> Naturally, with such an alignment of forces, the leading role in the Berlin negotiations will belong to the Germans. The English have nothing to offer the Germans, for the Germans themselves have taken all the English trumps in the last days. The English role will now be that of petitioners, frightened by the scale of the German deployment of the army. The English will ask the Germans to reduce the number of corps and divisions. The Germans will argue that they were forced to increase the manpower of their army, and they will demand from the English political compensation, not for the reduction of the planned size of the German army, but for not increasing it further.

"Our position, naturally, remains the same," Krestinskii continued. "A one-and-a-half-day trip with Eden [to Moscow] will give you the opportunity and to find out in detail everything that the British talked about and maybe agreed to in Berlin with the Germans, and to influence Eden in the right sense. In short, you will have the opportunity to do some preparatory work for Maxim Maksimovich."[114] It is remarkable that in spite of every disappointment, whether from the French or the British, among others, the Soviet side kept picking itself to warn yet again of the danger of Hitlerite Germany. This was not, of course, the "after-mindedness" of latter day historians, but the perceptiveness of people on the spot, who did not know the future (or in the case of Krestinskii, who would never know it, having fallen victim to the Stalinist purges) but who had a clear idea of what it would be.

In London, Vansittart attempted to limit the damage from the British note to Hitler. He was the concierge cleaning up government messes. On 20 March, Vansittart invited Maiskii to a meeting at the Foreign Office. First of all, he laid on the thanks to Maiskii for his efforts to improve Anglo-Soviet relations and to pull off the planned Eden trip to Moscow. "I am expecting a great deal," Vansittart said, "from the Eden mission to Moscow … [it] is an important step on the path towards establishing [better relations]." Of course, Maiskii agreed. It was a kind of meeting of mutual admiration and comradeship in a great cause for European peace and security. The two made a good team, an odd couple, the English patrician and the Russian revolutionary.

According to Maiskii, Vansittart also wanted to talk about the events of the previous few days with regard to the off again, on again Simon visit to Berlin. "He spoke with obvious emotion, sometimes with half-hints, but in general so that I could understand." The preparations for the Moscow visit looked good; Stalin had agreed to meet Eden. The Soviet authorities were planning an elaborate welcome. Vansittart hoped that the Soviet government would not be disappointed by Simon's absence. "Maybe it is for the best," Vansittart said. Eden was coming along. In the British government, and the Foreign Office too, a fight was underway between "softs" and "hards" about Germany. As readers can now guess, Simon was for the "soft line" and Vansittart, for the "hard." "In fact, the Hitlerite bomb demanded a far sharper reaction from Great Britain," according to Vansittart. "Any weakness only encourages Hitler. He argued this, insisted on it, but unfortunately, without success. He even learned of the sending of the 18 March note after the fact. V., however, thinks that events in the end will show him to be right, as they have until now." He also thought that the Berlin visit would accomplish nothing and prove instructive for the Labour and Liberal Opposition as well as for certain Conservative cabinet ministers. "By his actions, Hitler is greatly assisting those who, like V., have already long concluded that Germany is the greatest danger to peace."

Maiskii asked for information about directives to Simon for the Berlin discussions. "I pointed out at the same time," Maiskii noted in his report, "that the conduct of the British government over the last few days had produced on me an extremely depressing impression, and that in Moscow it is being evaluated, as a complete capitulation and triumph for Hitler." So what then was Simon going to say and do in Berlin? Maiskii wanted to know. It was hard to understand where Simon stood on the big issues. He had not even crossed into Germany and already he was making public statements about concessions on the Eastern Pact. Vansittart gave assurances that Simon would take a hard line, and Eden would be there to make sure he did. The visit was purely exploratory. When Simon and Eden returned to London, they would report to cabinet and there would be consultations with France and Italy, both of which, along with other states, had protested against British conduct.[115] The intimacy of this meeting and Vansittart's sharing of such confidential information was a sign of his confidence in Maiskii and of his belief in the importance of Anglo-Soviet relations. It was a remarkable event to observe unfolding in Maiskii's reports.

On 22 March, Vansittart saw Maiskii again, this time with Eden. They went over logistics. Maiskii would meet Eden in Berlin and they would travel together by train to Moscow. There was also some brief discussion of the program for the meetings in Moscow. Vansittart repeated what he had told Maiskii at their previous meeting about the importance of Anglo-Soviet relations. Eden signalled his support for Vansittart's point of view.

"I replied," Maiskii noted in his report, "that any improvement in relations between the USSR and England will undoubtedly meet with support from the Soviet government. Vansittart, who has dealt with me during the course of two years, can easily confirm this. V. nodded his head sympathetically … It is necessary only to keep in mind, that the strengthening of friendly relations between [our] countries cannot be expressed only in pretty words; good deeds are also necessary." This was the familiar Soviet refrain with their would-be Anglo-French allies. The Soviet government was still worried about Simon's rescheduled visit to Berlin. "In all relations with Hitler," insisted Maiskii, "the British must demonstrate firmness, firmness, and still more firmness. Any weakness in Berlin, would create further difficulty in Moscow."

"You can rest easy," Eden replied, "about the outcome of the Berlin visit. The British delegation will make no binding promises and cannot make them, for the visit itself has the objective of clarifying points of view, but not of making any decisions whatsoever." In other words, Simon did not have plenipotentiary powers. Eden had no problem acknowledging the importance of the Soviet role in Europe: "To say that European peace can be constructed without the USSR is idiocy. This is clear to everyone; it is clear to the British delegation." As for "firmness" with Berlin, Eden seemed to wobble a little. "Everything will go well," he said. "British ministers are going to Berlin in order to have a tough and candid discussion with Hitler." Well, maybe; maybe not.

Eden noted half-jokingly that the Soviet press had over the last few days had some rather unflattering things to say about British policy. "And doesn't

England deserve it," Maiskii replied also half in jest. The polpred knew how to cut and thrust just as well as his British interlocutors.

"From your lips to God's ears," Maiskii wrote in his journal. "We will see how the business plays out."[116] Nazi policy, of course, was to sow discord between the French, British, and Soviet governments. Hitler fulminated against the danger of Bolshevism, and he accused the USSR and France of trying to "encircle" Germany. These lines appealed to many Tories and to certain Foreign Office officials.

Whatever Litvinov's disdain for British wobbling, Eden was coming to Moscow; it was a chance to solidify relations with Britain, however tenuous they were. A coalition of determined states was the only way to stop Hitlerite Germany, and Britain had to be brought into the circle. In his briefing paper for Stalin, Litvinov was all business, dropping the contempt he had shared with his ambassadors. Eden was coming to Moscow, according to his own statements, to exchange opinions on various issues among which were security, disarmament, and the German return to the League of Nations. "There is now no basis for thinking that Germany will agree to any Eastern Pact whatsoever, even without mutual assistance." Nor was there any reason to think, Litvinov added, that Germany would agree to any acceptable compromise solution.

"What is particularly important is the question of the Baltics." It was Litvinov's prime concern, as he continued:

> France decisively refused to extend its guarantee of the Baltics in case of an attack on them ... If we consider that the occupation of the Baltic area is the beginning of an attack the USSR, then we have to sit with arms folded in expectation of the German army crossing our frontiers. Even if we succeeded in obtaining from the Baltic states the passage of our troops to meet the German Army, we would then be deprived of the aid of France.

Readers will now be familiar with Litvinov's arguments. It is true, the narkom added, that the League might offer a solution by recognizing German aggression, but its processes were slow, providing more than enough time for Germany to occupy the entire Baltic area. Hence, it followed that we might also obtain from France, exploiting its present state of anxiety, the extension of guarantees to the Baltics:

> It is necessary to underline the extremely unstable position of Estonia and Latvia, which from the very beginning have been more than indifferent to the Eastern Pact. They understand that we can help them against Germany only after passing through their territory, and they are afraid that we would refuse to withdraw our troops from the Baltic region, adding it again to the USSR. Poland has also expressed such fears. *Obviously, we will have to agree to special guarantees for the evacuation from the Baltic region and eventually from Poland, of troops that would temporarily find*

> *themselves on this territory in order to provide military assistance* [emphasis added]. The Baltic states would most of all welcome the guarantee of their independence by the Western powers, namely France and especially England. We must, therefore, discuss whether we should, in our conversations with Eden, sound out England's attitude to its participation in the general guarantees of Baltic independence.

Was there any need to point out, Litvinov added, that after the Saar plebiscite, Germany's appetite for territorial expansion will "grow with the eating"; and that the easier it manages to expand, the more rapidly it will carry out the rest of its intended program of conquest. "So I would consider it inappropriate," Litvinov said in rather an understatement, "to encourage any handouts to Germany, and even more so in the east." Readers may rightly wonder how this Soviet statesman could see so clearly what many of his counterparts in the West so obstinately refused to see.

With regard to Britain, Litvinov continued, the Soviet Union did not have any important conflicts "if both governments will stand on the ground of the preservation of peace not only in Europe, but in the rest of the world." We would be ready to sign a non-aggression pact. The Soviet government was not making any demands on Britain concerning freedom of speech or the press with regard to the USSR; it asked only that, in the press and in Parliament, the USSR be shown the same respect (*korrektnost'*) as with other states. The Soviet government was ready to reciprocate on these points. Litvinov then spelled out what non-aggression meant in Central Asia where Russia and Britain traditionally clashed. Litvinov also drew attention to the danger of Japan, which did not hide its hegemonic intentions in Asia. He had in mind the creation of a pact of mutual assistance in the Far East against Japan, similar to the Eastern Pact as it was originally proposed by France when Barthou was foreign minister.[117] Litvinov's agenda was robust and comprehensive. He met with Stalin on five different days in the week before Eden's arrival in Moscow, mostly alone, but on one occasion with Stomoniakov who had responsibility for dealing with Poland.[118] Obviously, Stalin took Eden's visit very seriously. Would Litvinov's agenda produce results?

Vansittart did his best in London to persuade cabinet of the importance of improving relations with the USSR. It was thankless, uphill work. On the eve of Eden's visit to Moscow, two great themes characterized Anglo-Soviet relations. In December 1934, Assistant Undersecretary Mounsey had stressed the importance of *deeds* in improving relations with the USSR.[119] Maiskii also adopted this line, which he may have picked up from Vansittart. The other theme was "realism", a term often employed by Vansittart to describe the driving force behind his policies. "I am not anti-German," he explained to Sir Eric Phipps, the British ambassador in Berlin.

> I consider that the military preparations, both material and moral, being made by Germany ... far exceed in dimensions anything which could possibly or

> conceivably be necessary for ... the maintenance of [internal] order, alone. If these warlike preparations of body and spirit and steel were changed, I should be the first to change also with a great sigh of relief ... But until those facts, and they *are* [emphasis in the original] facts, are changed I am not going to have my attitude changed by words alone.

"I expect from those who work with me in the Foreign Office," Vansittart continued, "to be realists as I am."[120] Maiskii picked up on this theme in his correspondence to Moscow: for Vansittart, "'realist' is a synonym for someone who recognizes all the seriousness of the German threat."[121] In his memoirs, Maiskii observed that, in regard to Anglo-Soviet relations, there were two main British political groupings: the one that was driven by "class hatred" held the upper hand over the other, which was motivated by "state interests."[122] Eden put it a little differently. He remembered that cabinet was "unenthusiastic" about Anglo-Soviet relations, some members "regard[ing] communism as anti-Christ." If the Nazi menace caused other cabinet members "to consider supping with the devil ... [they] doubted whether he had much fare to offer."[123] In fact, for many members of the British elite, the spoon for supping with the Bolshevik devil could never be long enough.

Eden in Moscow

Eden's visit to Moscow was preceded by the stop in Berlin with Simon to meet Hitler and other German officials. That meeting produced no tangible results, as Vansittart had foreseen. Simon returned home and Eden, accompanied by Maiskii, moved on to Moscow.

The meetings there went off without difficulties. Litvinov laid it on thick, warmly welcoming the Lord Privy Seal during a formal banquet. "I raise my glass," Litvinov declared, "to the health of His Majesty, the King of England, to the prosperity and happiness of the British people, and to your good health, Sir." How extraordinary, the Bolshevik toasted the King of England.[124] At a lunch held at Litvinov's dacha, the butter on the tables was imprinted with Litvinov's well-known maxim, "peace is indivisible." Apparently, not wanting to obliterate Litvinov's message, no one touched the butter plates.[125] Most of the discussions were between Eden and Litvinov, but Stalin and Molotov also joined one of three meetings on 28–29 March. Discussions were in most respects a recapitulation of the Soviet-Western dialogue since Hitler's rise to power. Eden gave an account of Simon's meetings in Berlin, but the real topic of discussion was the Nazi threat to peace: "Mr. Eden said that the British ministers had gone to Berlin to find out whether Germany was likely to play her part in European security. If not, and it rather looked as though this was the case, a good deal of hard thinking would be necessary."

"We do not have the slightest doubt," said Litvinov, "about German aggressiveness. German foreign policy has been inspired by two basic ideas – *revanche* and

Figure 11.2. Eden's arrival in Moscow (Lord Chilston is on his right and Litvinov is on his left), 28 March 1935, AVPRF.

domination over Europe." Hitler counted on continuing Anglo-Soviet antagonism to advance his agenda, and "he obviously considered that hatred of the Soviet Union in the world at large was so great as to excuse any adventure on his part." It was too early to say in which direction Hitler would strike first, but he *would* strike somewhere. Litvinov added that he thought "Germany had not forgotten the lessons of history, demonstrating that if one could sometimes invade [Russia], it was not so easy to remain there or to withdraw without loss." Then Litvinov had this to say:

> The Soviet Government were concerned not merely for their own frontiers, but for peace in Europe. They had enough work to do at home to keep them busy for half a century and it would take them decades to catch up with the rest of the world in technical developments and the standard of life. They did not want to be disturbed and they believed that a war in Europe, even if they were not directly involved, would eventually drag them in. It was for this reason that they strongly supported the idea of collective security.

Figure 11.3. Eden meeting with Litvinov in Moscow (Lord Chilston is on the left and Maiskii is on the right), 28 March 1935, AVPRF.

Eden replied that the British government was "not so convinced" of German aggressiveness and that it "had hitherto wished not to believe badly of Germany's intentions." Germany wanted "to keep her hands free," replied Litvinov. Molotov had challenged Hitler to renounce his designs for conquest in the USSR, described in *Mein Kampf.* Hitler did not respond, though the Soviet government construed his silence to be an answer of sorts. Litvinov repeated his concerns about the vacillation of British policy: "It was perfectly true that Soviet public opinion was highly suspicious … If any government showed signs of being too indulgent towards Germany, the Soviet public jumped easily to unfavourable conclusions."[126]

Discussions about "propaganda" ensued, unfolding along the same lines as those between Vansittart and Maiskii. Eden admitted that "Anglo-Soviet relations had been a party matter in England for a long time." Litvinov eventually replied that grievances over propaganda "usually served as a cover for an anti-Soviet policy." Although Eden did not say it, this was sometimes a view held by Foreign Office clerks.[127]

Eden's meeting with Stalin and Molotov took place on 29 March. Stalin considered present circumstances to be more dangerous than in 1913 because of two potential aggressors. Eden thought the situation "anxious" though not "alarming." Stalin restated Litvinov's views, but emphasized that future European security, or the lack of it, would depend on British policies. The conversation went on for a while. Stalin talked of British power to maintain the peace, if it would. Eden was non-committal.[128] That was the problem. Litvinov's agenda for the talks was too ambitious, blocked by Eden's evasions. The Soviet side was ready to march, but the British, not so much. Alphand thought the meetings had gone well, but Chilston worried that Litvinov overestimated Eden's influence in London. Chilston noted that the commissar was playing a big role, and for big stakes, he could have added. If things were to go wrong, it "could cost him his place."[129]

Litvinov saw Eden off to the train station, wishing him well. "Your success," he said, "will now be our success."[130] Eden had his doubts; Vansittart would have had them also, as he read over the records of Eden's meetings. Vansittart's view of Nazi Germany was far closer to Litvinov's (and Maiskii's) than it was to Eden's. Their divergence of opinion would not facilitate the Anglo-Soviet rapprochement when Eden became Foreign Secretary in December 1935 and the time came to move from words to deeds. This, however, is getting ahead of the narrative.

For the moment, events seemed to be going in the right direction. In mid-April, French, British, and Italian ministers met in Stresa, Italy. Mussolini was there; so was MacDonald. They agreed to continue to support Austrian independence and to resist any further unilateral German rearmament leading to the destruction of the Treaty of Versailles. In the meantime, the Foreign Office split over the issue of Anglo-French and Franco-Soviet relations. The French and British governments were scarcely on the best of terms. They were like a married couple, who were still intimate, but cheated and bickered constantly. In 1933–4, the French pursued a more or less resolute course for security against Nazi Germany; the British thought in terms of disarmament and accommodation, and considered the French to be insensitive and belligerent. "France was 'a bad show'" in some British circles, noted Vansittart, though the French reciprocated the disaffection.[131]

Foreign Office Opposition to Soviet Collective Security

After the assassination of Barthou, the French compass began to wobble, and the Foreign Office noticed. As readers have seen, Laval obstructed the Franco-Soviet rapprochement with support from Quai d'Orsay officials. So did Sir Orme Garton Sargent, the Assistant Permanent Undersecretary. It was proxy opposition to the Anglo-Soviet rapprochement. In January 1935 Sargent wrote a long memorandum against further British support for an Eastern Pact, a Russian conception, he said, bound to fail because of German and Polish opposition. Litvinov really wanted a Franco-Soviet alliance, and the French, unable to obtain adequate British security guarantees and having "lost faith" in the

Poles, "felt compelled to accept Russia's offer of co-operation." However, the French were not entirely persuaded of "Russia's honesty" or of a Franco-Soviet community of interests, and wanted to avoid "an all-embracing alliance if they could help it, especially as they realised that such an alliance would shock and offend Great Britain."

Continued British support for the Eastern Pact, argued Sargent, would play into German hands, allowing Herr Hitler to attract sympathy from British public opinion. A Franco-Soviet alliance would be "a first step" towards "a return to the pre-war grouping of Powers." This prospect was "so horrible" that the British government should press the French government to adopt new policies. "We too have means of influencing the French Government, and British support and approval is still of great value to France."[132]

Sargent attracted opposition: polite from Vansittart, but caustic from Collier. Vansittart agreed that they ought to find an alternative to the Eastern Pact that would be acceptable to Germany. But he disagreed that the British government should attempt to pressure the French into refusing a Soviet alliance. "Silence would be best on our part. We could not, of course, approve. But I don't think we should lecture."[133]

Sargent noted that the different Foreign Office departments had "somewhat divergent" views, and he suggested a memorandum trying to reconcile them.[134] The opposite occurred: the memorandum ignited the simmering dispute. Collier, head of the Northern Department; Wigram, head of the Central Department; and C.W. Orde, head of the Far Eastern Department wrote the piece that concluded, among other things, that the British government ought to be prepared to envisage the conclusion of a Franco-Soviet mutual assistance pact.[135]

"A wise & excellent memo," Vansittart noted in his minute. "We must not for a moment imagine that it is only a French interest to 'ménager' Russia. On the contrary it is very much a British interest also; and we must have this fact constantly present to our minds, if we are to be the political realists, which the gravity of the times demands."[136] Sargent returned to the charge, but Vansittart held him off. A Franco-Soviet alliance was not desirable, Vansittart admitted: "But if it happens we shall have to make the best of it, as of many other things in an imperfect world."[137] Collier refused to sign a compromise memorandum that implied a Franco-Soviet accord should be discouraged. To resolve the impasse, Vansittart signed a modified draft that stood between the opposing positions of Sargent and Collier, though closer to the latter.[138]

Vansittart's signature did not end the dispute. While preparations unfolded for Eden's trip to Moscow, Sargent hammered away, not liking too close a relationship with the USSR: "We don't want to give them an exaggerated sense of their own importance or to suggest to them that they can dictate our German policy to us."[139] And Sargent strongly discounted the possibility of a

Soviet-German rapprochement – which often worried the French. This was a "bluff," sneered Sargent: it was the "argument which Litvinov has used all along in order to bring the French Government up to the scratch."[140] Sargent restated his abhorrence of a return to "the pre-war system of the balance of power." Was this just a pretext for Sovietphobia? Collier countered Sargent: "We are … already back in the days of the 'balance of power.'" Sargent paid no mind: "British opinion might look askance at the idea of co-operating very closely with a French Government whose foreign policy was controlled by a Franco-Russian alliance."[141] The French had "let themselves be bluffed and dazed by Russian threats and promises … If Russia is allowed to dictate to France – and ourselves – the conditions on which we are to carry on its [*sic*] affairs of Western Europe – and that is what it is rapidly coming to – we may say goodbye to any European settlement. We shall have all our time cut out in pulling the chestnuts out of the fire for M. Litvinoff!"[142]

Sargent's opposition was unrelenting: "If … we closed to Germany all means of expansion in the east, where she is less likely to come into conflict with British, or indeed any other, interests than elsewhere, we must be prepared for German pressure down the Danube to be increased proportionately." Ambassador Phipps warned against putting up too much "barbed wire" in the east or south, lest the Nazi "beast" head west. Sargent agreed: "I have never quite been able to accept the truth of M. Litvinov's dictum about the 'indivisibility of peace.'"[143] Litvinov would have been horrified, and Maiskii also. Stalin's habitual crude cynicism would have been set on fire. But apparently Sargent's secret ranting did not leak. He declared that British opinion would view a Franco-Soviet alliance "with the gravest suspicions." Vansittart allowed his irritation to show: "Well, so do I, and so, I think, do we all." But as long as Germany remained "obdurate," Britain would have to support collective security "with or without Germany." "There is no other way, and we must now face facts and Europe as they are and not as we would wish them in a more reasonable world." Central Department head, Wigram, backed this view: "We are now in the realm of stern reality. It is useless any longer to play with words."[144] Wigram was right, of course. Sargent, Sovietphobic and relentless, was wrong. Vansittart could not control him, and Simon did not try.

Maiskii and Vansittart Return to Business

For the time being, the Foreign Office put Franco-Soviet relations to the side, and turned to other matters. On 26 April, Vansittart and Maiskii resumed their meetings for the first time since Eden's visit to Moscow. Vansittart raised again his complaint about Labour foreign policy. The Labourites were stuck in the past. They had not yet understood that Hitlerite Germany was not Weimar

Germany. As a result, Labour was obstructing the government's efforts to pursue "a more energetic" foreign policy. Maiskii reported Vansittart's concerns:

> They [Labour] continue to sing the old tune. Thus, the government, in particular the Foreign Office, is put in a difficult position. Elections are coming, everyone is thinking only about votes. The cabinet is often hesitant to take a step (which he, V., would consider useful in the interests of the European peace) solely from considerations of how this step would provide additional opportunities to the Labour Party. Thus, for example, Labour raised a terrible commotion against the increase of ten million pounds in the military budget, which was recently proposed. And, all the same, this increase is a mere trifle. How can England actively participate in system of collective security if it does not have sufficient armaments at its disposal?

After this long preface, Maiskii noted, Vansittart finally came to the point. "V. in a somewhat open, but sufficiently definite form began to ask me to exercise my influence on the Labourites in the sense of changing their position in international affairs and in matters of rearmament."

Well, this was a "delicate" question, Maiskii responded prudently. Soviet ambassadors have strict directives against interfering in the domestic affairs of the countries to which they are accredited.

Of course, responded Vansittart. He would not dream of encouraging "directly or indirectly" the Soviet ambassador to interfere in British domestic affairs.

> However, he would certainly consider it useful that if, when meeting with Labourites, I would simply acquaint them with the state of international affairs and with the policy in this sphere pursued by the Soviet government. This kind of talk would be very valuable. He, for his part, will conduct the same "educational" work among those elements of the Conservative Party who still do not want to understand the need for a more firm policy towards Germany.

Maiskii remained prudent, as well he might. After all, he had, not so long before, advocated a subsidy for the British paper "N.L." Maiskii was no innocent in such matters. But he was not going to walk into a trap, however unintended. "I replied," Maiskii reported, "that the Labourites knew our point of view quite well, but that they were rather stubborn people and, besides, no less than the government are absorbed in electoral considerations. It's hard for me to do anything."

Conversation then turned to Eden's visit to Moscow. "Personally, he, V. , is particularly pleased: it was his idea to send a British minister to Moscow, some of the members of the government treated this idea with distrust and even hostility, because they did not believe that such a trip could turn out well – and now

V. has every reason to triumph. He was right, not his opponents." So what's next? Maiskii asked. "Educational work" on the right and left, Vansittart replied, then perhaps further ministers' visits to Moscow. But there was no need to hurry. It was a modest agenda for the improvement of relations.[145]

On 28 May, Maiskii met Vansittart to discuss the implications of Hitler's "peace speech" of 21 May, promising the usual good intentions and railing against Bolshevism. Vansittart had another agenda item to which he "suddenly" turned, according to Maiskii. Comintern subsidies for the communist paper the *Daily Worker*. There is no use in denying it, Vansittart said, "the matter was not open to argument." The subsidies are "a waste of money" and self-defeating on the level of "high policy which should not be occupied with or disturbed by petty considerations."[146] For the Soviet Union, however, "propaganda" was part of its identity and the rough and ready of relations with the capitalist West. Ironically, the Comintern formally went over to a "united front" strategy against fascism in 1935, which instead of reassuring Anglo-French conservatives, disquieted them even more.[147] According to Maiskii's record of the conversation, Vansittart repeated what he had said in the past, that if the subsidies became widely known, they could disturb the development of Anglo-Soviet relations.

"Pebbles"

Maiskii referred Vansittart to Litvinov's discussions with Eden and evaded a direct reply. He never let his British interlocutors, or Vansittart, escape without the tit for a tat when such subjects came up, as indeed he remarked in his report to Moscow. He reminded Vansittart of the Archbishop of Canterbury's recent prayer at a London church for Russian Christians at which many White Guard priests were present. The riposte had the desired effect. Vansittart was "immediately embarrassed" but argued that the analogy was not pertinent. In order to head off Maiskii's expected rebuttal, he nevertheless declared that he was not making an "official *démarche*," but only a friendly word to the wise from someone who supported the strengthening of Anglo-Soviet relations and feared that "a pebble" in the road could render more difficult the rapid consolidation of their rapprochement.[148]

Litvinov watched closely for the "pebbles," sharing his worries with Maiskii about possible vacillation towards Nazi Germany: inform Vansittart that the Soviet government opposes any side deals with Hitler, guaranteeing security in one part of Europe but not in another.[149] This was a timely instruction. On that very day Maiskii was present at a dinner for the "dying swans," the outgoing government ministers. A cabinet reshuffle was expected any day as MacDonald was stepping down as prime minister. On his right, Maiskii sat next to an outgoing the Conservative Minister of Health Edward Hilton Young, a most interesting historical character and a highly decorated soldier who had lost an arm when serving in the Great War. He had this to say during dinner conversation:

> The military danger from Germany? Nonsense. All these rumours are frightfully exaggerated. And even if there is such a danger, what is it to us, English, this business? We had the stupidity during the last war to send on the Continent a million strong army – this will never happen again. Enough – war. If Germany and the USSR come to blows – that is their business. For us this will even be advantageous: both sides will be weakened and we will profit.

Maiskii did not doubt that many Conservatives reasoned thus, but from a minister of the Crown, it was a bit much. "Clearly, in Hilton Young's head, some rivets were missing." Maiskii hastened to add that on his left sat Edward Lord Halifax, then Minister of Education, who held to completely different opinions, that is, to views quite similar to those of Vansittart's. Without any prompting from Maiskii, Halifax began to unburden himself "about the German danger."

"It's extremely disagreeable, that in Europe there has again appeared the German danger. I would give a lot if someone could convince me that such a danger did not exist. But facts are facts." Would Vansittart have said it any differently? "Since German intentions are not clear," Halifax continued, "then in our practical calculations we have to plan not on the best, but on the worst case probability."[150] Exactly, that is what Litvinov thought. For Maiskii, this was singing to the choir. It was, nevertheless, a welcome intervention in the polpred's calculations for and against collective security. Readers will meet Halifax again, and before too long, for in February 1938, he would become Foreign Secretary. If only he would then have continued to sing the same song.

On 6 June, Maiskii delivered Litvinov's message, reinforced perhaps by his dinner conversation with Hilton Young. Vansittart replied with his usual assurances about British policy, and he advised "privately" that Sir Samuel Hoare, Secretary of State for India, would be replacing Simon as Foreign Secretary. Vansittart was "somewhat concerned" that the appointment might be greeted, "as it were … with [fixed] bayonets" in Moscow because of Hoare's previous anti-Bolshevism. Don't worry about Hoare, said Vansittart, he is "a realist." He will soon invite you in for a talk, continued Vansittart: Then you will see that you have nothing to fear. Maiskii commented that deeds, not words would determine the Soviet view of the reshuffled cabinet.[151]

Maiskii's job, as readers by now will have come to understand, was to meet influential people whenever possible, of whatever political inclinations, to listen to what they had to say about foreign or domestic policy issues, and to report that information back to Moscow. Ultimately, his biggest job was to find or make converts to the side of collective security and mutual assistance. He did this well – his gregarious personality certainly helped – meeting people at diplomatic receptions, official or unofficial lunches and dinners, formal meetings at the Foreign Office or the Soviet embassy and more informal meetings in Parliament. After Eden's visit to Moscow, Maiskii began to extend his range of contacts and acquaintances. He was meeting people with whom he would maintain relations throughout the rest of his tenure as polpred in London.

Maiskii Dines with Lord Beaverbrook

One of these contacts was Max Aitkin, Lord Beaverbrook. A Canadian from New Brunswick who moved to Britain in 1910 and became one of the most important, if not the most important, press baron of the interwar period. He was the owner of the *Daily Express*, a paper not so friendly to the USSR, but also of the *Evening Standard*, in which David Low drew his scathing cartoons against Hitler and Mussolini and against the appeasement politics of the Conservative government. Low was said to have close relations with Maiskii, though he is rarely mentioned in Maiskii's journal or in his available reports to the NKID. Low and the thirty-eight-year-old Labour MP Aneurin Bevan acted as go-betweens to set up a meeting between Beaverbrook and Maiskii. "On 29 May the Labour MP Bevan, meeting me in Parliament, asked on behalf of Beaverbrook," so Maiskii reported to Moscow, "if I would object to seeing and talking to Beaverbrook." According to Bevan, the press baron wanted to meet the Soviet ambassador and to have "a serious discussion" of important questions of international relations. "I replied," Maiskii said, "that I had no objection." Beaverbrook followed up with a letter inviting him to lunch, which took place on 4 June.

Beaverbrook opened the serious part of their conversation by saying that he thought Maiskii and the government in Moscow had the mistaken impression of him that he was an "enemy of the USSR." "This is not true," Beaverbrook said. He related how, in 1919 in his newspaper, he waged a press campaign against the foreign intervention and, in 1927, against the rupture of diplomatic relations. If he had not spoken out as a friend of the USSR, neither had he been an enemy. He visited Moscow in 1929 and felt poorly received. Allegedly, he did not like the Moscow cuisine and this may have determined his position towards the USSR in later years. "The food was fine," Beaverbrook said. "I can testify to it with complete sincerity." There were "other reasons" which soured his visit, although he did not go into what they were. "He is a press baron," Maiskii wrote, "who in England creates and breaks governments, but in Moscow he was not shown the appropriate honours!"

"I interrupted," Maiskii continued, "and said let the dead bury the dead. Why dig into the past? It's important for us to think about the future."

Of course, Beaverbrook responded, agreeing entirely. He wanted to talk about the present saying he was less than ever an "enemy of the Soviet Union." Beaverbrook considered that Hitler's arrival in power had transformed Germany into "the highest danger for Great Britain." This is the "basic problem" not only for Europe, but for the British Empire. The best way to confront the German danger, according to Beaverbrook, was "political isolation," but he did not think this idea would be acceptable to the majority of the British people. "So what to do?" he asked rhetorically. There was only one option: "alliance between Great Britain and France and rapprochement between Great Britain and the USSR." Then Beaverbrook repeated what had become Maiskii's canticle: there are no major conflicts of interest between Britain and the USSR and one common enemy – Germany. The conclusion was obvious: we need to work together. "You, of course, do not think," Beaverbrook continued, "that I like you very much. No, I do not love you, I love Great Britain. But for the very reason that I love Great Britain, I find, that our British interests now demand a rapprochement with the Soviet Union."

"I welcome your candidness," Maiskii replied, "I am always suspicious of those foreigners who begin by assuring me that they love the Soviet Union. But when you say that calculating from a realistic consideration of British interests you think a rapprochement between England and the USSR is useful – that is a completely different affair. Such language I like very much, and on such a basis we can easily build something."

Beaverbrook agreed, "These are relations that I can understand. I cannot endure sentiment." His newspapers, he thought, should undertake a campaign to popularize Franco-Soviet and Anglo-Soviet relations. But therein lay a problem. The majority of British people are still not conscious of the "great danger" emanating from Germany. They are still in a "state of hibernation."

"And what about the government?" Maiskii asked.

"You know," Beaverbrook replied, and continued:

> That I am not used to stroking the head of the present government, but I must nevertheless say that the majority of its members are aware of the German danger. Baldwin is undoubtedly aware, so are Eden, Hailsham … Samuel Hoare, Elliot, and some others. MacDonald for a long time held to a pro-German line, but two months ago he changed his position. He considers that Hitler swindled him [and] that therefore it is necessary to prepare for a struggle with Germany. Simon does not have his own opinion; he is ready to adapt himself to anyone.

The cabinet reshuffle would lead to a better sensitivity to the German danger. But the government would have "to manoeuvre," calculating the public mood as elections approached. Hence, inevitably zigzags and wavering would occur. Beaverbrook was nevertheless convinced that "in the near future" public opinion would swing "against Germany." He, of course, would do his part "to apply pressure." He was only waiting for the "appropriate circumstances." If the Germans, for example, seized Memel from Lithuania. "Do you think they will … soon?" Beaverbrook asked. Maiskii shrugged his shoulders. Who could say? Austria came up and then conversation passed to Italy, central Europe, and the Far East, among other topics.

They then got to talking about the British press. Beaverbrook thought the pro-German line of the *Times* and *Daily Mail* was "completely scandalous." The Germans, he said, "were spending in London colossal amounts of money for propaganda, hundreds of thousands of pounds." They were sending lobbyists to work on members of the government, high-profile politicians, and "press barons." Was Beaverbrook dropping a hint? He also mentioned that Lloyd George was following a pro-German line. This derived from his hatred of the French, and Poincaré in particular. "The French," he continued, "do a lot of stupid things." Ambassador Corbin also came in for criticism for badly promoting French interests. He had been too passive, and should have tried to bring around Lloyd George.

Thus passed a conversation of two hours. The press baron and the polpred hit it off. The conversation was not quite over. As Maiskii rose to take his leave, Beaverbrook burst out, "And you must be a crafty fellow."

"I laughed," recorded Maiskii, "and said, 'Why do you think so?'"

Beaverbrook looked at Maiskii slyly and replied, "Oh, I have my sources of information. You have a good name not only among Labourites but also among Conservatives. That's not easy to combine, but it is very important. Of course, Conservatives sometimes make gaffs, but the Labourites even more, but all the same they are the two basic parties of Great Britain. From them, there is nowhere to go."

Maiskii thanked Beaverbrook for the compliment. Was he only getting ready to ask for the accreditation of his correspondents in Moscow? That was in the back of Maiskii's mind. The polpred replied that it was the circumstances that had changed. "The Soviet Union was maturing and getting stronger. On the horizon has risen the Hitlerite danger – that's the problem!"

Beaverbrook was obviously laying on the honey with a large butter knife. "If only the French would send here such an ambassador," he added, "then much could be done." Maiskii mused again about how things had changed since Metro-Vickers. Then Beaverbrook "was following me with five detectives and photographers, looking for the slightest opportunity to discredit me in the pages of his newspapers." And now, Maiskii added, Beaverbrook was full of compliments, 90 per cent of which, "if not more, is pretense and hypocrisy, but all the same … Beaverbrook does manage to turn his tongue to pronounce such words." They shook hands warmly, Maiskii reported, and Beaverbrook walked out with him to his car. "We should meet again," he said, "and keep in close contact."[152]

Maiskii Meets the New Foreign Secretary

On 12 June, Maiskii met Hoare for the first time to convey Litvinov's concerns. The new Foreign Secretary replied evasively, not wanting, as he noted, to be cornered by the ambassador's "legalistic cross-examination of our attitude."[153] According to Maiskii's report, he went over the by-then usual issues to determine if Hoare would follow the policy basically laid out by Vansittart and accepted more or less by Simon. Thus, Maiskii asserted and Hoare acquiesced that there were two serious sources of instability in the world without naming Germany and Japan, but emphasizing the danger in the Far East. Maiskii also pressed the point that there were no serious Anglo-Soviet conflicts either in Europe or in Asia. Hoare agreed. According to Hoare, he had strongly raised the propaganda question, along the usual lines.[154] According to Maiskii, Hoare did not much insist on the propaganda issue, admitting that it had lost its former "acuity."

The conversation inevitably turned to European affairs. Maiskii asked how Hoare thought peace might best be preserved. The Foreign Secretary shrugged his shoulders and commented that he had only been on the job for three days, and therefore could not say anything definite. Maiskii pressed, but Hoare pleaded that he needed time to learn his portfolio. The Foreign Secretary nevertheless opined, "English public opinion wants somehow, something, somewhere to be done." Maiskii did not like the sound of that: it could be dangerous, especially the "somewhere" part of the statement. Did that mean security in the West but not elsewhere? This was Hitler's idea, said Maiskii. He wanted to realize his plans laid out in *Mein Kampf*. He wanted to make war in the east while keeping his rear in the West quiet. Did the British government agree with such a strategy? That was rather an aggressive question for a minister only three days on the job. Hoare was "somewhat taken aback," according to Maiskii, but hastened to insist that he understood the Soviet position and that peace could not be preserved in the west while war raged in the rest of Europe. As Maiskii was getting ready to leave, Hoare said that he hoped the Soviet government and press would hold its fire on the new cabinet until it worked out its foreign policy line. "I am inclined to consider our first conversation," Maiskii replied, "like the preface to a book … Usually a book is not to be judged by its preface but by its contents." This was a variation on the polpred's usual line that deeds would determine the Soviet position. "From all points of view," Maiskii concluded, "it would be unwise to keep us waiting for good deeds for too long."[155] That sounded a little over the top. No wonder Hoare was not in a hurry to have another conversation with Maiskii, and preferred that Vansittart see him instead.[156] In a telegram, Maiskii warned Litvinov that Hoare, "as the new man [in the Foreign Office] and wanting a success," might seek a quick agreement with Germany. But they would have to wait and see.[157]

A New "Friend"

In the meantime, Maiskii continued to make new acquaintances. One week, it was Lord Beaverbrook, and the next, it was someone even more important and well known. Still a Conservative Party *bête-noire*, Winston Spencer Churchill, continued to berate the government for its miserly, short-sighted defence expenditures and policies. The British government had started to rearm, but far too slowly for Churchill. Maiskii, of course, had heard long before that Churchill was beginning to take a more positive attitude towards the USSR. As it happened, Sarita, Lady Vansittart, had written to Agniia Aleksandrovna, Maiskii's wife, to invite them to dinner at the Vansittarts' London flat. It was to be a dinner *en famille* on 14 June. In a postscript, Sarita added that Churchill and his wife, Clementine, would also be present. There would probably be the opportunity to talk about current affairs. In a second note, Sarita advised that Churchill "very much wanted to meet" with Maiskii. "He is 'a friend'!" Sarita added. They were six at dinner, Vansittart, Maiskii, and Churchill and their wives. It was an informal affair.

> After dinner, the women, by English custom, withdrew to another room, and the men remained in the dining room for conversation. Vansittart several times was called to the telephone, and once or twice he went to visit with the ladies. As a result, Churchill and I sat alone together for a long time. Churchill was very lively and drank like a horse, wine, cognac, whisky, and in huge quantities, but it had almost no effect on him. He only blushed slightly and began to speak with greater expression.

The conversation went on for almost two hours. "Churchill began with a self-justification. Eighteen years ago, said Churchill, I led the struggle against the Russian revolution because it threatened the British Empire." On this point, Churchill continued for quite a while. "I smiled," Maiskii noted, "and said that Churchill, as events had shown, really knew very little about Russia, and that those informants on which the British government had depended during the war and revolution … obviously, did a bad job for their money (*darom eli khleb*)." This comment was rather ironic for Maiskii himself had chosen the wrong side during the foreign intervention and civil war. That might have been Churchill's rejoinder but, of course, he was not there to score points with the Soviet ambassador. As Maiskii had said to Lord Beaverbrook, he finally said to Churchill: it was better not to delve too much into the past, but to focus on the present and the future. Except Maiskii could not resist a parting shot. "In any case," he quipped, "I add … my thanks on behalf of the Red Army for the arms and kit which it received via [anti-Bolshevik leader Admiral A. V.] Kolchak from you. It was of very good quality and a powerful reinforcement."

Vansittart who was present when Maiskii launched his needle, "slyly glancing at Churchill, laughed out loud. Churchill was a little embarrassed, blushed, and having downed another half glass of whisky, passed to other subjects." Obviously Maiskii was impressed by Winston's ability to hold his drink. It would keep him in good stead should he ever visit Moscow.

Churchill asked about Soviet aviation and the latest harvest, all the while, according to Maiskii, drinking his fill passing from whisky to wine. "I am very glad to hear it," Churchill said finally, "if your country will be strong and powerful, then from this we can only profit." After some musing on the successes of Soviet socialism, it was Maiskii's turn to change the subject. "What do you think about the international situation?" he asked. "The problem of all problems is Germany," Churchill replied. Eighteen years ago he would have answered otherwise, that the greatest danger to the British Empire was the Russian Revolution.

Now, times have changed. Churchill did not see the USSR as a danger at least not in the short term, say the next ten to fifteen years. Then Churchill picked up one of Maiskii's (and Litvinov's) themes that the USSR and Britain had a common interest to maintain peace and security. The USSR does not need war, Churchill agreed: it would only cause harm. The "greatest danger" now was Germany, "a huge, scientifically organized war machine, led by typical American gangsters. From it anything can be expected. No one knows exactly what they want and what they will do tomorrow."

"And then, splashing a decent glass of cognac into his mouth," Maiskii noted with apparent admiration, Churchill continued his monologue. The USSR was nothing like Hitlerite Germany. There, "half a dozen brutal gangsters … do whatever their right foot wants." Who knew where they would strike first? It would not be the USSR, which was too strong. It might be Holland or somewhere in Southeast Asia. At this point Vansittart, who had returned to the dining room and was listening, interjected that such a move would bring Germany into conflict with Japan. Or it could be Austria or Czechoslovakia, Churchill continued, or the Balkans with the object of establishing a German *Mitteleuropa*. Then the British Empire would be at the mercy of Germany. Such a situation would be intolerable. Hitler could send his bombers against London, Churchill continued. A hundred thousand, a million people could be killed or wounded, the city could be flattened, "but we, the British nation, we will not put down our arms."

"He swallowed another glass of cognac," Maiskii noted, "and then continued his reflections aloud, during which I occasionally inserted leading questions, then explanatory remarks." The German danger is so great, Churchill opined, that he was ready to forget everything else. He was against creating any "complications" with Japan, although he was greatly alarmed by Japanese aggression in the Far East. The British position in China and Southeast Asia was sustained only because of Japanese forbearance. "At any moment Japan can strike … a crushing blow … for the time being Churchill was willing to allow Japan a free hand in China."

Maiskii asked what concrete measures Churchill envisaged to check the German menace. It is, he replied, "completely clear and concrete. The logic of things is essentially creating an international situation similar to that before 1914. England, France, and the USSR must unite their forces in order to prevent a new war. Other governments, also interested in the preservation of peace, should group themselves around the three above powers. Hitler must be opposed by a coalition so powerful that any attempted aggression would be for him a great risk." Churchill's idea was to create a defensive alliance to preserve the peace. Of course, because of "tactical considerations, especially in England," one could not openly call his "alliance" by its proper name. One had to "parade" under the pseudonym of "collective security" within the framework of the League of Nations. Maiskii recorded no immediate reaction to Churchill's remarks, but he must have thought that this line was exactly the unstated policy of the USSR.

If Germany succeeded, said Churchill, "England would become a plaything of German imperialism."

Churchill then turned to the domestic situation in England. He did not attempt to hide that a "big internal struggle" was underway. There was "a strong tendency" in favour of "Western security," that is, agreement with Germany to guarantee peace in Western Europe in exchange for a freedom of action in Eastern and Southeastern Europe. These people reasoned thus, according to Churchill, it was all the same to them if Germany needed to fight somewhere. Let it be in Eastern, Southeastern, and Central Europe, but leave England and France in peace. This was no surprise to Maiskii; he had heard it all before. Churchill considered this kind of thinking to be "sheer idiocy," but "unfortunately it still enjoys considerable popularity in well-known circles of the Conservative Party." Churchill remained confident, however, that people like himself and Vansittart would eventually win out for the indivisibility of peace and that England, France, and the USSR would be the backbone for a defensive alliance to hold Germany in check. Churchill "fully approved" of the Soviet pacts with France and Czechoslovakia (about which readers will learn the details anon) and in general considered Soviet foreign policy very sensible, restrained, and without mistakes. Churchill spoke briefly about Hoare with whom, he noted, he did not get along because of differences on India policy. He took Vansittart's line that Hoare was capable and "a realist." He was not perhaps fully cognizant of the German danger to British interests, but he would come around. He needed to be given time. In Conservative circles there would be zigzags and wobbling in regard to Germany, "but we must in advance stockpile sufficient patience and endurance." Patience was necessary, for Churchill shared Vansittart's opinion about the Labour Party leadership. Tories were not the only ones to spout "idiocies" when it came to Hitlerite Germany. "Churchill's ears often just wilt when he hears the slobbering arguments of Labour leaders." They had recently been coming around, however, especially in the parliamentary smoking room where people spoke, according to Churchill, most openly, though not yet from their benches in the House of Commons. Thus ended a long conversation, sometimes a monologue. Churchill expressed his pleasure at meeting Maiskii and hoped it would not be their last encounter.[158]

A British "Zigzag"

A "zigzag" occurred four days later, on 18 June, when the British government signed a naval limitation agreement with Nazi Germany. The German Navy could build to 35 per cent of British naval forces. It was a bilateral denunciation of terms of the Treaty of Versailles. Britain thus became complicit in German naval rearmament. Anglo-German negotiations were concluded on 12 June, the same day Hoare met Maiskii for the first time. Little wonder the new Foreign Secretary was diffident about Litvinov's fretting over possible side deals with Hitler. If the new British cabinet was to be judged by its deeds, it was off to a bad start.

Litvinov did not sound all that surprised when he first heard the news. It was the usual egoism of *perfide Albion*. "The conclusion of the naval agreement," Litvinov opined to Maiskii, "is a flagrant violation not only of the Treaty of Versailles, but also of English agreements with France, both in London and at Stresa. France, of course, has every reason to protest. Nor do we feel the necessity to comment on the merits. If the agreement was already concluded with the consent of Samuel Hoare, then this rather violates the idea of him as a Francophile."[159]

On 20 June, Lord Beaverbrook came to the embassy to have lunch with Maiskii. They talked politics, obviously, and the new government. Beaverbrook was not too hard on it, thought Baldwin aware of the German danger, and desirous of close relations with France and better relations with the USSR. But Baldwin was a politician, who was too "bogged down" in party politics to take a strong, consistent policy line. "Beaverbrook was very unhappy about the Anglo-German naval agreement," according to Maiskii, "he considered it dangerous not only from a political but a military point of view." The agreement was supposed to establish "a bridge between England and Germany," but it offered no guarantee of security to Britain. And the allowed tonnage to Germany concentrated in the North Sea would represent "a constant threat to British security, especially in the case of any war." Then why did the British government sign such an obviously unprofitable agreement? Maiskii asked. "Electoral considerations," Beaverbrook responded. Labourites and Conservatives were waging "a fierce struggle" for "pacifist votes" in the coming parliamentary elections. There were many such votes to be won, and both parties were trying to outdo the other in their professed commitments to peace. Beaverbrook did not mention it, but the so-called Peace Ballot was underway. The results of the poll would be released at the end of June. They would demonstrate the strength of "pacifist" sentiment in Britain. Beaverbrook said he was only waiting for the appropriate moment to launch a campaign against the Anglo-German naval agreement. "Let the first 'raptures' on the occasion of the agreement subside a little," Maiskii wrote of Beaverbrook's position, "let a more cold-blooded attitude towards the naval agreement become possible – then he will strike."[160]

The French and Italian governments were angered by the agreement. "Great Britain had snatched at an apparent advantage," said Maiskii, "as a greedy boy will snatch at a cake on the table; the result is likely to be an attack of indigestion … Besides, what value do we really attach to Hitler's promises?" Foreign Office official Frank Ashton-Gwatkin met with Maiskii and tried to defend the British position: "Germans had told me that without armaments Germany would be regarded and treated as a second-rate country and they were tired of that, but that they do not want to fight." Go tell *that* story to your *babushka*, Maiskii retorted in so many works.[161] Why would the polpred want to underestimate a *babushka*'s wisdom? A few days later, Maiskii saw Ashton-Gwatkin again, who was then more reserved, stating that "this agreement in fact gives nothing to England and at the same time embroils it with France and Italy. In general, Ashton-Gwatkin spoke without enthusiasm about the 'successes' of the last month in … British foreign policy."[162] That sounded like an understatement.

"I remember the shock which Litvinov seemed to have received when he first spoke to me of the Naval Agreement," reported Chilston some months later. "In genuine dismay he declared that it was a complete playing into the hands of Herr Hitler's aims."[163]

One Foreign Office clerk offered the lame excuse that the French had been given ten days prior notice, even suggesting that the Anglo-German agreement was the quid pro quo for the Franco-Soviet pact (of which a great deal more will be discussed in the following chapter). Tit for tat, then? It was in effect each for himself.[164] Just the kind of attitude Herr Hitler wanted to encourage.

Albion remained, so it seemed, as perfidious as ever. First it tried to undercut Soviet negotiations with France – readers should remember Sargent's railing – and then it was the sudden conclusion of the Anglo-German naval agreement. "Can we trust these bastards?" might well have been Stalin's reaction. Bastards or not, the only way forward was collective security with Britain and France. The USSR could not pursue this policy on its own.

Chapter Twelve

Showdown: Negotiating the Franco-Soviet Pact, 1935

January 1935

While Maiskii and Vansittart worked to improve Anglo-Soviet relations, the Soviet embassy in Paris continued to pursue the will-o'-the-wisp of mutual assistance with France. We have to go back a little in time, about six months, to the beginning of 1935. Soviet diplomats kept close track of Laval and other important French politicians. They had solid ties with French journalists; indeed, some were on the embassy payroll. This should not come as a shock to readers, for most French journalists in Paris were on someone's payroll, sometimes that of the Quai d'Orsay, sometimes one or more of the embassies. Geneviève Tabouis, who wrote for the Paris daily *L'Oeuvre* during the 1930s, is a good example. She often spoke with Soviet diplomats, her name turning up in their reports to the NKID, and eventually she began to receive a monthly "allowance." She was close to Herriot, in fact, called him every evening on the telephone to brief him on the day's events, particularly in Central Europe and the Balkans.

Evgenii V. Girshfel'd, the new counsellor at the Paris embassy, chatted regularly with Tabouis, Rozenberg having been transferred to Geneva. Girshfel'd was a skilled diplomat who easily took over Rozenberg's role, establishing good relations with French politicians and journalists. Tabouis was an insider; she knew a lot about what was going on in the dog-eat-dog world of French politics. She did not like what she saw. "Tabouis painted the general situation … in quite dark hues," according to Girshfel'd. She was in particular pessimistic about the prospects for an Eastern Pact. "It is impossible in any way to trust Laval," she said. That would not have been a revelation to the Soviet embassy. The USSR, the Little Entente, and the Balkan countries were going to have to bring pressure to bear. Herriot would also, especially on Flandin, with whom he was on good terms. Remember that Pierre-Étienne Flandin was still président du Conseil. The Romanian foreign minister, Nicholae Titulescu, and his Turkish counterpart, Tevfik Rüştü Aras, were "besides themselves" with Laval, and "climbing the walls." Eduard Beneš of Czeckoslovakia was "more calm" and "manoeuvring," pushing the Eastern Pact and a Danubian agreement. Who knows, Tabouis opined, maybe Beneš's "complicated game" will produce results. The "main actor" was still Laval "who might be more reliable if he were not subjected to so many different influences." And Tabouis was particularly worried by increasing pressure from "the English."[1]

Readers will remember that the Saar referendum had just taken place with its overwhelming vote in favour of rejoining Germany. Litvinov had tried to maintain a reserved position on the Saar question, but the lopsided vote worried him. It overshadowed the modest success of the Rome accords between Laval and Mussolini. Hitler was talking sweet reason saying he had no territorial claims in Western Europe; the narkom thought that England and also France could fall for such lines. Not everyone was blinded or fooled. Some elements of French public opinion recognized the "danger being created by the gradual collapse of the Versailles structure," Litvinov pointed out that the Saar victory could go to Hitler's head, and indeed it had, making him increasingly difficult. "I am not remaining passive," Litvinov reported from Geneva, "and am taking all measures to counteract German agitation." He also mentioned having spoken to the well-informed journalist, Pertinax (André Géraud), who told him that the French general staff would demand the introduction of two years of mandatory military service in the event of the "legalization" of German rearmament. Litvinov advised that he hoped to have a "serious discussion with Laval" before he left Geneva.[2]

On the following day, 18 January, Litvinov met Laval and other potential allies over dinner to discuss all the pressing issues. Potemkin was there and took notes. Litvinov seems to have taken the high road with Laval, saying that on the generalities of European security they had no differences.

It was on tactics that disagreements arose over the Eastern Pact, the Rome accords, Poland, Germany, and Britain. The British, with exceptions like the journalist J.L. Garvin, did not seem to pay much attention to *Mein Kampf*, and as Litvinov put it, were more interested in German rearmament and Germany's return to the League of Nations. Fine, Litvinov said, let Britain act in Berlin to obtain German agreement on the Eastern Pact and the Rome accords; and if Italy wants to guarantee Austrian independence, this could only be done through an Eastern Pact. Let Italy and Britain exercise their influence to obtain agreement for it.

As for Poland, Litvinov proposed that Laval should have a serious conversation with Beck. "Is Poland going with France or is it finally passing to the side of Germany?" At first Beck was adamantly opposed to the Eastern Pact, but now he seemed to have changed position. Laval replied that he intended to intervene in all the major capitals, but he insisted that "friends," the USSR, the Little Entente, and the Balkan governments, should demonstrate the necessary confidence in him. He complained that he was being pressed too hard. His preference was for "careful, flexible tactics." For that he needed the unity of French allies … but they in turn needed a strong, decisive France. That was the key to collective security.[3]

Nicolae Titulescu

Nicolae Titulescu, also present at the dinner on 18 January, asked Laval what he intended to do if Germany and Poland refused to sign on to an Eastern Pact. It was obvious that they would refuse, or rather that they already had. Titulescu answered his own question: France had to set a deadline for answers from Warsaw and Berlin. In the event of negative replies, the Quai d'Orsay should declare that it would conclude agreements with those powers that were willing. An alliance with the USSR should be concluded "immediately" and wedded to existing agreements and pacts, including the Little Entente and the recently organized Balkan Entente (Greece, Turkey, Yugoslavia, and Romania). A firm line was necessary; it was the only way forward. According to Potemkin's notes:

> Titulescu reminded Laval that Romania could not stay out of the envisaged agreements. Romania is not strong enough to organize independently its own defence. If it were convinced that France was only looking to its own fate, Romania could be forced to come to terms with Germany out of fear for its security. Titulescu stressed that he himself will not forever hold the office of Romanian foreign minister. Others can replace him.

Romanian policy could change. The Franco-Soviet alliance was indispensable; Germany would be "helpless" against it.[4] That was a clear warning to Laval.

In the spring of 1935, Titulescu played an important role in supporting the Soviet drive for mutual assistance. Readers should become acquainted with him. He was born in 1882 and was educated in the law in France. After teaching for several years in Iaşi and Bucharest, he turned to politics and diplomacy. He was a member of the Conservative-Democratic Party, was elected to the Romanian Parliament for the first time in 1912, and was finance minister during the 1920s. Titulescu then became a diplomat as Romanian minister in London and twice as foreign minister during the 1920s and 1930s. He was widely respected and served as president of the League of Nations' General Assembly at the beginning of the 1930s. His photographs, of which many have survived, show a clean-shaven man with hair slicked back with Brillantine in the style of the day. He had an odd look about him, like a man ready for a night out. Not without his wife, however, for Titulescu was married to Ecaterina Burcă, the daughter of a wealthy landed family. They had no children. She never once comes up in correspondence about his diplomatic and political activities. The far-right in

Romania, scurrilous and dangerous, apparently accused him of homosexuality.[5] It was part of their array of accusations against him. Titulescu had the courage to stand up against the unremitting attacks made against him.

With Litvinov, Titulescu got on well most of the time. In April 1934, as Barthou was settling into his job at the Quai d'Orsay, Titulescu took the initiative to establish diplomatic relations with the USSR. In Geneva, he advised the Soviet legation that he would like to meet Litvinov. I want to talk "about everything," he told Boris Efimovich Shtein, who was holding the Soviet fort in Geneva. When Shtein asked for specifics, Titulescu responded, "about the establishment of relations and the entire system of foreign policy and relationships with other governments." Shtein replied diffidently that for establishing diplomatic relations, negotiations were not necessary.

"I can't do what others do," Titulescu replied. "The establishment of relations with the USSR is a large and deep question. We want to know if we can be friends, and for this we need beforehand to remove difficult questions." The political right in Bucharest was "cursing" him, Titulescu continued, about the likely establishment of relations with Moscow. This was not just a case of exchanging official letters, but something rather larger and more important. "I again asked 'about what,'" Shtein reported. Titulescu responded finally: about Bessarabia, propaganda, and Romanian funds (i.e., gold) held in Moscow. Shtein again pressed for clarifications in case Moscow asked about what the minister wanted to negotiate. Titulescu wanted recognition of Romanian sovereignty over Bessarabia, and on propaganda, did not want any more than Soviet assurances to other governments. On Romanian gold, "I know," he said, "that I will not receive one centime from you, but it is necessary to throw a bone to public opinion in the form of a joint committee which will find nothing and decide nothing." Shtein said he would forward the information to Litvinov. Germany and Italy, Titulescu added, "are working against the establishment of relations."[6]

After the Romanian government established diplomatic relations with the Soviet Union in June 1934, Titulescu and Litvinov often met to try to settle differences, most notably concerning the disputed territory of Bessarabia, which Romania seized in 1918, with French support, during the early months of Soviet power, the Bolsheviks being unable to defend it.

More than that, Titulescu sought to protect Romania from German domination; he thought the only way to do so was through stronger relations with the Soviet Union and by supporting the Franco-Soviet rapprochement. "I am," Titulescu said to Ostrovskii, the first Soviet polpred in Bucharest, "a supporter not only of friendship with the Soviet Union, which for [me] will always remain Great Russia, but a supporter of the most ardent friendship." His policy was based on the principle that "either Romania should be in very good relations with the Soviet Union, or it must die. And since Romania is not going to die, therefore, it must establish the friendliest relations with its eastern neighbour."

Figure 12.1 Meeting in Geneva between Litvinov and Titulescu, M.I. Rozenberg in the background, June 1934, AVPRF.

His central idea was that "the main foundations of peace in Europe" were the Little Entente, the USSR, and France. Titulescu did not think much of Polish policy despite the fact that Poland and Romania had a formal defensive alliance aimed against the USSR. He did not hold back with Ostrovskii even though it was their first meeting: "*Polish policy is the policy of suicide and its rapprochement with Germany must lead to Poland losing its political independence* [emphasis added]." Chemistry was good between the Romanian minister and the Soviet polpred. "Last year," Ostrovskii wrote in his report of their meeting, "he [Titulescu] made his first visit to Warsaw. Beck met him very politely, but very cautiously. As for Marshal Piłsudski, he made the impression on Titulescu of a madman, in the literal sense of the word, 'sick up here' – he [Titulescu] said, tapping himself on the forehead."[7]

Mikhail Semenovich Ostrovskii

Mikhail Semenovich Ostrovskii was a good choice for the Soviet embassy in Bucharest; remember he had come from Paris where he was chief representative of the *neftesindicat*, the Soviet oil syndicate. He was born in Fastov, southeast of

Kiev, in 1892. His parents were schoolteachers. Not much is known about Ostrovskii's early life. He pursued his university studies in St. Petersburg, and served during the Great War as an officer in the Russian army. He joined the Bolsheviks in 1919 and fought in the Red cavalry; served on Voroshilov's staff, and was said to be his right arm. They must have remained friends for Ostrovskii wrote to him from Paris to brief him on developments in France. Ostrovskii appeared to be on the track of a military career when he became vice-commissar of the Red Army military academy. Although there are not many photographs of Ostrovskii, he had the look and posture of a soldier. His head was shaved and one can see the bare trace of a moustache. In 1925 he became a Soviet *kupets* in the *neftesindicat*, sent abroad to Turkey, Germany, and then to France in 1930. He was in Paris at the beginning of the Franco-Soviet rapprochement and was named *torgpred* in 1933. He spoke good French and appeared to get on well with his French counterparts. In fact, he was certainly a Francophile; he liked to drop French phrases into his dispatches to Moscow. The Quai d'Orsay clerks had a high of opinion of him and told Titulescu that he played an important role in the early development of the Franco-Soviet rapprochement. Remember, he was a go-between with de Lattre de Tassigny, Weygand's *éminence grise*.

"Titulescu often groaned about our non-assignment of Davtian to Bucharest," according to Litvinov, "and it turned out that he needed an envoy who would like the women of Bucharest. Maybe he meant [Elena] Lupescu [King Carol's mistress]." Another British source reported that Titulescu had certain requirements for the new Soviet envoy: that he "a) was not a Jew; b) did not look like a Bolshevik; c) spoke French; d) could converse with Romanian ladies."[8] In fact, Ostrovskii was born into a Jewish family, but the Quai d'Orsay regard for him must have overcome any biases. As for looking like a Bolshevik, anti-communist posters almost universally portrayed Bolsheviks as dangerous looking scoundrels and anarchists, dressed like bums, unwashed, with broken teeth, ready for mayhem holding a long dagger in one hand and a smoking bomb in the other. No Soviet diplomat looked like that. Ostrovskii took up his post in Bucharest in August 1934. He got on well with Titulescu, seeing him often when the minister was in Bucharest, but he also had excellent relationships with other Romanian politicians and officials. In short, he was good at his job. Titulescu trusted Ostrovskii more than he did his own cabinet colleagues. Their relationship was quite remarkable.

Discussions in Geneva

There was a certain commonality of interests between Romania and the Soviet Union if they could get past Bessarabia and keep France on track. The basic principle of collective security and mutual assistance was to stand together or risk falling one by one to Nazi Germany. Titulescu thus worked closely with

Litvinov and pressured the dodgy Laval to conclude a mutual assistance pact with Moscow. The Romanian far right and the fascist Iron Guard did not like his foreign policy, which made his position as minister unstable, but Titulescu carried on strongly, not outwardly worrying about opposition in Bucharest.

At that dinner in Geneva on 18 January, Laval replied to Titulescu that he agreed with him, *but* he did not think serving an ultimatum to Germany and Poland would do any good. There was always a "yes but" when Laval talked about collective security and mutual assistance. He reiterated his view that more "flexible and careful tactics" were necessary, and that France and its allies must demonstrate their "solidarity" and unity of policy.[9] In fact, while Laval was in Geneva, he had two discussions with Beck, one before and one after his meeting with Litvinov, Titulescu, and the others. Laval did appear to have done what Litvinov had asked of him. He put the question to Beck, are you with us or are you with Germany? Beck replied with his usual aplomb and with the usual Polish lines about balancing between two great powers. "I added," Laval reported to Laroche in Warsaw, "*that in my opinion Poland, in persisting in its present attitude, would be committing a serious perhaps even irreparable error* [emphasis added]. In any case, it would expose itself to become one day the victim of one or the other of its great neighbours. Moreover, it was not even practising now the policy of balance which Monsieur Beck had explained to me." What had come over Laval? He was beginning to sound like Barthou or even Litvinov. The conversation unfolded "in an atmosphere of great cordiality," Laval advised. "I have the impression that Monsieur Beck will reflect on the consequences for his country which a refusal to respond to the appeal of France would have in a negotiation the success of which could be of greater interest to Poland than to France."[10]

Litvinov also had a go at the Polish minister, but without positive results. Litvinov said that he had heard from the French that Poland had accepted in principle the Eastern Pact on condition of German participation. Beck at once replied that the French had "misunderstood" the Polish position. "I only said that we were not against a continuation of negotiations."[11] Slipping and sliding, Beck dodged the hard questions. Almost all his interlocutors warned him that Poland was going down a dangerous path, to ruin in fact, but Beck never heeded the message. Not once.

Would Laval have any better luck; would he hold a firm line with Beck? Tabouis, who was looking for a story in Geneva, did not think he could, and Soviet intelligence reports indicated that Poland was pursuing an anti-Soviet policy. The discussions in Geneva led nowhere. At least, Laval and Litvinov *seemed* to be working positively together. Otherwise, it would be hard to get agreement on anything.[12]

All Laval's talk about patience and solidarity carried little weight with people who did not trust him. A week later, Potemkin, who was back in Paris, reported

Figure 12.2. Laval and Litvinov in Geneva, 1935, AVPRF.

the concerns of French "friends" who feared that Laval might surrender "our position" and do "irreparable" harm to the Franco-Soviet rapprochement.[13]

A French Visit with the "English" in London, February 1935

Still looking for a way around German opposition to the Eastern Pact, Flandin and Laval, remember président du Conseil and foreign minister respectively, went to London to talk to their British counterparts. Discussions had an odd beginning. The British proposed a debate on a final communiqué before discussing substantive issues.[14] It was a clever way to set an agenda and present the French with a *fait accompli*. The British idea seemed to be to promise "abrogation" of the Versailles restrictions on rearmament in exchange for vaguely defined negotiations with Berlin about disarmament and European security. The French did not like the word "abrogation" and said so during their meetings with the British. Laval and Flandin interpreted the British idea as giving something for getting nothing in return. The French side then proposed a binding British commitment to come to the aid of France in the event of an unprovoked air attack, which could only come from Nazi Germany. Other governments could come into the agreement later on if they so wished. The British delegation did not want to give such a commitment offering as a pretext that the British cabinet had not considered the matter. During the discussions, the USSR scarcely came up at all. Laval defended the Eastern Pact, the Rome accords on Austria, and correctly represented the observations that he had heard in Geneva from Litvinov, Titulescu, and others. He sounded at times like Litvinov himself when he talked about the indivisibility of peace in Europe.

In fact, if one reads a French note on the conference, written afterward by Roland de Margerie, a councillor in the French embassy in London, the discussions did not go well at all. Margerie gives the distinct impression that the British were trying to pull a fast one on the French, in effect proposing to abrogate the Versailles stipulations on German rearmament without any concrete quid pro quo. When the British realized that Laval and Flandin had caught on to them, a little comedy ensued with the prime minister and others, red faced, trying to avoid a commitment to French defence in case of an air attack. The French after all could not be so easily duped.

Here is an excerpt from Margerie's note, which should give readers cause to laugh at the author's wit:

> There began *une bonne scène de comédie*. At one in the same time relieved and dismayed by this formal notice for which they were waiting and feared and at the same time wished for, the English demonstrated the most amusing embarrassment. The prime minister all the time insisting on the necessity to consult the cabinet, the impossibility of meeting on a Saturday morning, watching the clock to calculate at what time he would arrive at Chequers [the prime minister's country residence], declaring that he could not even sleep at Downing Street because his servants had left for the weekend. Sir John Simon remained quiet. Mr. Baldwin [past and future prime minister] withdrew behind the barriers of his semi-deafness and his ignorance of the French language. The [British] delegates who wished to come to agreement … whispered among themselves and tried to help move things forward. Monsieur MacDonald, having said for the fourth or fifth time that it was impossible to convene the cabinet on a weekend morning, Monsieur Laval intervened to assure everyone, in the most natural and gracious way, that he understood perfectly well that there was this major impossibility, but that, for his part, he was not at all in a rush, that he would gladly wait for the outcome of cabinet deliberations until Tuesday, if they should take place on Monday and until Wednesday if they could take place any later, in short he would adopt himself entirely to the *us*, customs, and wishes of his British friends.
>
> The English side of the table at once took on a haggard look, showing by a deathly silence, which lasted several moments, a cold sweat flowing down their backs at the thought of seeing the French minister of foreign affairs, flanked by fifty journalists, passing half the week at the Hotel Savoy in conversations with the most varied sorts of people.

Such was the tone and dry humour of Margerie's note. Everyone breathed "a profound sigh of relief" when the prime minister asked for a brief adjournment and then returned to announce that there could be, after all, a cabinet meeting on Saturday morning. One supposes that the prime minister could in a pinch turn down his own bed at 10 Downing without the help of servants. There was also some difficulty with the final communiqué with first ministers and foreign ministers arguing over a draft that clerks should have drafted. "They finished by agreeing more or less on an awful text (*un texte barbare*) of which the French translation violated the ear even more than the original English." The text was polished – *si l'on peut dire* – if one could say, and released to the press.[15]

The remarkable thing – and this was *not* so amusing from certain points of view – is that the concerns of Litvinov, Titulescu, and others came up only once during the discussions in London.[16] It was as though, with the one exception of Laval's remarks on the first day of the conference, the security of Eastern Europe was not a matter of great concern. If Litvinov had had access to the minutes of the meetings, he would have been appalled. *Perfide Albion* had got his hand caught in the cupboard door, but the appeasement of Hitlerite Germany had nevertheless begun, offering big concessions for the first time at other people's expense, for nothing in return. Another skunk, the British, had joined the Polish skunk in the woodpile to thwart mutual assistance and collective security. Where was Vansittart? He and Maiskii were beginning to discuss sending a British minister to Moscow. The French appeared unaware of their activities, as did the British cabinet until the last week in February.

Litvinov's Assessment of the London Negotiations

Based on the London communiqué, Litvinov, who was back in Moscow, cabled Potemkin on 4 February, to say that he had drawn "rather pessimistic conclusions," the most important being the apparent Anglo-French loss of interest in an Eastern Pact. He instructed Potemkin to ask for a meeting with Laval to get clarification.[17] That same day, Potemkin wrote to the NKID that he did not like what he had learned of the London negotiations. He talked about "minuses," the first being the growing disinterest in the Eastern Pact, thus confirming Litvinov's impression. Another appeared to be the eventuality of agreements that excluded the USSR and the Little Entente. Potemkin did not like the communiqué at all. He read into it a desire to water down any pact into some kind of an all-European agreement attempting to solve various problems, including disarmament. Insoluble problems, he might have added, as long as Nazi Germany pursued its expansionist policies.[18]

As it was, when Litvinov made a report to Stalin on the London meetings, he only had for information the published communiqué, which "as usual …

contains many obscurities and haziness." Laval being ill, Potemkin was unable to obtain clarifications, but Alphand offered some information. The link between the "legalization" of German rearmament and the Eastern Pact remained intact. No decisions were taken in London about further negotiations. In fact, judging from the French and British press, Laval had stuck to his guns in London, taking a hard line on the Eastern Pact and obligations to the USSR and the Little Entente. "Apparently there was no shortage of trying by the British," Litvinov noted, "to knock him off this path." According to the French minutes, all this information was correct. Litvinov must have been pleasantly surprised. This did not mean, of course, that Litvinov's mistrust of Laval and the French was diminished.

In his briefing paper to Stalin, Litvinov noted that the only serious result of the London conference was the proposal for an air pact, which would control the production of war planes. The narkom pointed to pros and cons. He saw some potential use for such an agreement in strengthening European security, but he also saw potential negative outcomes. This was mainly that increased Anglo-French cooperation might create the impression that an air pact would lessen French interest in an Eastern Pact. Opponents of an Eastern Pact, and even Laval, had gained room in which to manoeuvre. Germany had also gained an advantage, opening the possibility for Anglo-German agreement on various points, excluding the USSR and the Little Entente. All this was calculated on Germany accepting the air pact and various other proposals, which was unlikely. The abandonment of the Eastern Pact was nevertheless possible. The fight would focus on dropping mutual assistance. Laval and Flandin were under pressure from us and the Little Entente not to do so, Litvinov observed, and the increase in the power of the Red Army to be announced at the forthcoming party congress might have a positive effect. The worst-case scenario, according to Litvinov, would be a Franco-German agreement, under pressure from Britain, where mutual assistance was sacrificed to obtain it. The fallback position would be to state that "without a guarantee against the evident Hitlerite danger, the USSR would not agree to any limitation of armaments." Litvinov thought that the Soviet government had strong trumps to play in order to "knock over all the English calculations."

As for tactics, Litvinov recommended opposition to any conferences without participation of the USSR and the Little Entente. Pressure should also be exerted on France not to use Britain as an intermediary in negotiations with Germany. The Soviet government should insist on the immediate resumption of negotiations for an Eastern Pact, and that a final in or out answer from Germany and Poland be demanded. In the event of a negative reply, we must put the question to France, can we conclude an eastern pact without Germany and Poland?[19] On 11 February, the day after Litvinov sent his briefing paper to Stalin, the Politburo approved the narkom's recommendations as he had written them. Stalin still supported mutual assistance and still backed Litvinov to carry out that policy, whatever rumours arose annually about his dismissal.[20]

Meanwhile in Paris, Potemkin confirmed much of what Margerie had written about the London discussions, having been briefed by Léger and by the well-informed Pertinax who wrote for the right-wing Paris daily *L'Écho de Paris.* Both confirmed that Laval had defended the Eastern Pact and the general positions of the USSR. This was true. Pertinax who met with Potemkin at the Soviet embassy, said that the British did not like Laval. They treated him like a *parvenu*, with a "doubtful personal and political past." He had made a large fortune but "not in the right way." As if British imperialists, marauding and plundering in Africa and Asia, had made *their* money in the right way. "In a word, in London they did not consider Laval to be a gentleman." He felt the lack of respect from the British, according to Pertinax, and therefore kept aloof and remained tense throughout the negotiations. No doubt reacting to British arrogance and legerdemain, Laval called out his interlocutors.[21]

Georges Mandel

Potemkin mobilized the embassy's resources and staff to launch a campaign against the British plan and to lobby politicians and journalists. "From the representatives of political circles, I have spoken with Herriot (twice) and with [Georges] Mandel (once)," so Potemkin reported to Moscow. Herriot was still a minister without portfolio and Georges Mandel was Minister of Communications (post, telegraph, and telephone). Herriot had long been a go-between, but Mandel was someone new to the array of Soviet political contacts. Readers should therefore make his acquaintance. Mandel was born in 1885, the son of a Jewish tailor. His father had left Alsace in 1871 after German annexation in the aftermath of the Franco-Prussian war in order to preserve his French citizenship. Mandel was an autodidact with little formal education. At the age of twenty-one, he became an acerbic journalist under the patronage of Georges Clemenceau and then was his *chef de cabinet* when Clemenceau again became président du Conseil in November 1917. He gained a reputation for being Clemenceau's *exécuteur de basses oeuvres*, or hatchet man, which made him many enemies.

In 1919, Mandel was first elected to the Chamber of Deputies; he was a politician of the right. Clean shaven, hair parted down the middle and slicked down with Brillantine, Mandel did not look like the part of a tough, courageous French politician, let alone a Clemenceau hatchet man. He was a strong nationalist who hated the Germans, the more so when Hitler took power in 1933, and he was like other French conservatives who supported a French alliance with the USSR against the greater menace of Hitlerite Germany. As the French journalist Kerillis had advised Payart, the French chargé d'affaires in Moscow, in the autumn of 1934, many politicians on the right abandoned support of the Soviet rapprochement after the disorders on the place de la Concorde and the mobilization of the French left. Not Mandel, who seems to have met Potemkin for the first time during the autumn of 1934. That made two cabinet ministers with whom Potemkin could speak off the record, apart from more formal contacts with Laval and Flandin.

Potemkin's Remarkable Contacts

Politicians were not the only ones on the Soviet embassy's list of contacts. Potemkin met frequently with the Turkish, Greek, and Czechoslovak ministers, and with an unnamed, secret confidant of Titulescu. It was agreed to take a common position with regard to the Eastern and Danubian Pacts, the latter intended to preserve the independence of Austria. "With the press," Potemkin advised, "I communicate through Tabouis, [Léo] Gaboriaud [*Ère Nouvelle*], [Henri] Rollin [*Le Temps*], and Pertinax." Tabouis and Rollin (since the 1920s) were on the payroll of the Soviet embassy. These journalists represented the centre and centre-right press in France. Potemkin's staff, among whom was the skillful Girshfel'd, were also involved in the "propaganda" campaign and in contacts with politicians and journalists. It was a major lobbying effort. "As regards direct inspiration of the press, in connection with the London conference," according to Potemkin, "we conveyed three articles to *Ère Nouvelle*, three to *L'Oeuvre*, two to *L'Écho de Paris*, and a whole line of notes and telegrams to *Information*" – also on the Soviet embassy's payroll. But that was not all.

Herriot continued his role as the primary Soviet go-between and advocate in the French Council of Ministers. Here are a few lines from Potemkin's report to Moscow:

> I have already informed you that Herriot, in the presence of Mandel and Souad Bey [the new Turkish ambassador in Paris], promised me to defend in the council of ministers the need to continue the negotiations on the Eastern Pact, hurrying its conclusion, independently from the draft of a general convention [the British proposal]. Today, he reported through Tabouis that he had a long conversation on this subject with President [Albert] Lebrun. Mandel, a man close to Laval and an ardent hater of Germany, also expressed his sympathy for us. Pertinax, who is assiduously pursuing our line in his articles, urged me to get acquainted with [Léon] Noël [then French minister in Prague], who is now Flandin's right-hand man on foreign policy issues. According to him, Noël is a staunch supporter of the Eastern Pact. He has promised me to arrange this meeting in the coming days.

While the lobbying campaign intensified, Potemkin went to see Léger who assured him that the Eastern Pact would not be subordinated to the arrangements made in London. These arrangements were conditional on German acceptance of the Eastern Pact. As Léger put it, the pact would be the *sine qua non* for the London proposals. If Germany did not agree, the Eastern Pact would be concluded without Germany and the proposed abrogation of Versailles or "legalization" of German rearmament would fail. Léger insisted that mutual assistance would be a part of the Eastern Pact, but Potemkin had his doubts.[22]

He finally was able to see Laval three days later. They went over all the key points. Laval essentially said that compromises were necessary. The British wanted to gut the Eastern Pact removing any obligations from it. Laval insisted on the obligations of mutual assistance, saying to the British that in the contrary case he could not continue the negotiations, but for Flandin that would mean resignation. Potemkin wanted an immediate resumption of negotiations and a yes or no reply from Germany. Laval replied that there was no advantage in rushing the Germans. It was more expedient to draw them into a multilateral air pact. Potemkin tried to hold Laval to his promise to move on without Germany in the event of its refusal to join an Eastern Pact. That is my personal view, Laval replied, but the government has not yet taken a position. Potemkin insisted that France not permit Britain to act as a French intermediary in negotiations with Germany. Laval replied that it was impossible to exclude the British, but that France would negotiate independently. Laval was willing to conduct negotiations in close consultation with the Soviet Union. Potemkin's general impression was that Laval had not taken a firm position on any of the key questions. Léger's replies were more decisive than Laval's. In order to prevent a shift in Laval's positions, a "maximum of unity" would be necessary with the Little and Balkan Ententes.[23]

Potemkin's doubts about Laval would only have been reinforced by a remarkable conversation with Paul-Boncour a few days later. Their discussion immediately turned to the Eastern Pact:

> He [Paul-Boncour] … considers himself to be the principal initiator of this business. Even more is he upset, seeing that it [the pact] has not only been delayed, but also exposed to the undoubted risk of collapse. From this perspective, the London agreements, Boncour considers as the surrender of the original positions of France … to the benefit of England, counting on an agreement with Germany.
>
> According to Boncour, we must fight all-out against such a surrender. In his eyes, it is a direct violation of the moral and political obligations assumed by France in relation to the USSR … France itself had sought the entry of the USSR into the League of Nations, stressing to the Soviet ambassador and through him Moscow that this would greatly facilitate the implementation of the Eastern Pact and would inspire public opinion with much greater confidence and sympathy for the Soviet Union. For Soviet entry into the League of Nations, the French government promised to conclude the Franco-Soviet pact of mutual assistance as soon as possible.

France, Paul-Boncour said, was not keeping its end of the bargain. What was more, the London accords appeared to tie up the Eastern Pact with other agreements and other unanticipated conditions. The situation was "completely irregular." Not being any longer a member of the government, he could only exert influence in the *Sénat*, among friends, and in the press. Potemkin replied he would try to keep in closer touch.[24]

Meanwhile in Moscow

While the lobbying and consultations in Paris went back and forth, diplomats remained active in Moscow. Laval left Alphand out of the Soviet negotiations, doing business with Potemkin in Paris or with Litvinov in Geneva. Nevertheless, the French ambassador continued a steady stream of telegrams to Paris with information he picked up from his well-informed NKID sources. Soviet officials, he advised, were suspicious of the British government fearing it might encourage France to let Germany have a free hand in the east to march with Poland against the USSR.[25] Soviet suspicions of the British were not entirely unfounded. In a discussion with Rubinin at the NKID, Alphand reported the opinion of a right-wing politician in Paris, Henri Leméry: a free hand in the east in exchange for peace in the west "would only give France the advantage that Cyclops gave to Odysseus – 'to be eaten last.'" Such an opinion on the right, Alphand noted, was worth ten such opinions on the left.[26]

Stomoniakov told Alphand that Germany would most certainly refuse to join an Eastern Pact and that this would be all for the better since it would permit other governments to get on with negotiations without Germany. Nor did Stomoniakov have much patience with Poland, which fell under his responsibility as zamnarkom. "The policy which it is pursuing can only be explained by an unhealthy, evil megalomania."[27] On this point, Stomoniakov was preaching to the converted. Alphand had earlier commented to Rubinin that no one in France had "any illusions about Poland."[28] The Poles knew very well that in Paris they had blotted their escutcheon. "The idea of the alliance," Laroche told Polish vice-minister Szembek, "is profoundly shaken." Will France sign a pact with the USSR and Czechoslovakia, Szembek asked, even without Poland and Germany? "It's possible" (*il y a des chances*), Laroche replied. Laval told Beck in Geneva, according to Szembek, "that if you do not march [with us], he was going to continue the enterprise."[29] It remained to be seen whether Laval would actually *do* what he *said* he would do.

In London, Maiskii also picked up on French anger against Poland. "I want to spit on Poland," Flandin said to the editor of the *Daily Telegraph*. Laval spoke in a similar vein in private conversations. As for the British government, "it obviously wants to play the role of intermediary between Germany and Geneva (concretely France), but the French don't seem to like it very much."[30] It began to sound as though the British cabinet wanted to step into the role of procurer for Herr Hitler.

Tempers were frayed. In Moscow, Litvinov had a go at the Polish ambassador Łukasiewicz. The ambassador gave Litvinov a convenient opening when he complained about "the unsatisfactory state of Polish-Soviet relations." Apart from the non-aggression pact, there had been no progress in cultural relations or any other issue. "I replied," Litvinov wrote in his *dnevnik*, "that we could least of all accept reproaches from Poland directed at us. One should not mix up various issues and compare large with insignificant matters." The Soviet government viewed the non-aggression pact as only the first step in an improvement of Polish-Soviet relations and especially of political cooperation. "Unfortunately, all our proposals in that direction have drawn no response from the Polish side." Litvinov mentioned as examples the Baltic guarantee and the Eastern Pact. Polish excuses were unconvincing. The Soviet government did not ask for any sacrifice from Poland; it made proposals only where the two sides had common interests and faced common dangers (Litvinov meant Nazi Germany but did not say it). "It seemed to us that the proposed Eastern Pact would shield Poland from danger more than us. Not only us, everyone is puzzled by the negative attitude of Poland." Since no one could come up with plausible explanations for Polish policy, naturally people began to look for hidden motives. In spite of everything, Litvinov continued, the NKID needed to persist in developing cultural relations with Poland. Even on the exchange of theatre groups, nothing had worked. It was the same for books, newspapers, magazines, and films.

Larger Soviet foreign policy objectives, Łukasiewicz replied, should not prevent the development of friendly relations. "We should not see danger for Poland there when Poland itself does not see it; in particular, it considers itself completely secure from the side of Germany not only by the Polish-German agreement but by the alliance with France." So what is the problem? The Soviet Union had non-aggression pacts with all its western neighbours, and it did not have a common frontier with Germany. "We don't understand your disquiet," Łukasiewicz said.

This conversation, like Litvinov's with Beck a year earlier, is yet another story of Soviet foresight and Polish blindness. "I said to L.," Litvinov recorded,

> that he was clearly being naïve when he asked us not to be alarmed about Germany. Does he seriously believe that the Lithuanian or Latvian armies can serve as a barrier against an attack on us by Germany? Does he not understand that even the present Reichswehr can overrun these armies in three days? But let's assume that the Germans remain on your frontiers seizing only the Baltic area. Is Poland ready to live with this? After all, neither the Polish-German agreement nor the alliance with France is a guarantee against a German attack on the Baltic region.

Łukasiewicz "muttered," Litvinov noted, that Germany knows how the Baltics relate to Poland. "I picked up on this," the narkom added, "observing that there was not a single word in the Polish-German agreement about the Baltic territories. Maybe Poland had other agreements with Germany about which no one else knew anything." In that case, Litvinov continued, not one rational person would believe that Poland could remain indifferent to the German seizure of the Baltic states. To Litvinov, Polish policy was incomprehensible. The initiative for the Eastern Pact came from France. To which Łukasiewicz interjected that "France denies this and attributes the initiative to us."

There was no secret about any of this, Litvinov replied. Paul-Boncour first raised the subject, although only about a Soviet-French agreement. "We replied," he continued, "with a proposal for a collective pact with the Baltic states, Poland, and Czechoslovakia." The pact had a very clear objective: guarantee peace in Eastern Europe and give equal guarantees to all participants. Thus did the conversation continue. What could Łukasiewicz say? If Litvinov's account of the conversation is accurate, the Polish ambassador was left on his back foot, "muttering" this and that. Whenever Poland made "some small step forward," Litvinov concluded, it then immediately took a longer step backward. After some further comments, Litvinov suggested to Łukasiewicz that further discussion that day would be pointless.[31]

It was 13 February, a few days after the meeting with Łukasiewicz and before Litvinov had received Potemkin's latest telegrams on his meetings with Laval and Paul-Boncour. On that day, he sent a further briefing note to Stalin. The subject was the same: the Eastern Pact and how to get negotiations on it moving again. The key question, as Litvinov explained to Stalin, was about Laval's willingness to conclude any agreement without Germany. Laval would no doubt reply that he could not answer that question before having a German reply to the Anglo-French communiqué, and before a decision of the French Council of Ministers. He therefore proposed waiting for the German reply, which was expected in the coming days and which would no doubt reject an Eastern Pact, either outright or by evasion. At that point, Litvinov proposed, we can put the question through Potemkin to Laval on an agreement without Germany, yes or no, and demand a prompt reply.[32]

Litvinov did not have long to wait for the German reply. It came on the following day, 14 February. It was a clever response making no mention of the Eastern Pact, but lauding disarmament, and declaring that in principle Germany was ready to enter negotiations for an air pact subject to preliminary bilateral discussions with Britain. Neurath informed the French ambassador that all the other current issues, including a possible German return to the League of Nations, would be dependent on future discussions. Germany preferred to start discussions with Britain.[33] That made sense as Britain was the weakest link in the chain of collective security.

This was just the reply that Litvinov expected, trying to separate the air pact from all other negotiations and trying to use the British as a dumb intermediary. "We must consider as unacceptable," he wrote to Potemkin, "any negotiations whatsoever with Germany on the basis of its response, which has the definite aim of breaking off the air pact from all other proposals and of deciding it independently." Now that Litvinov had received the expected reply from Berlin, he could go back to Laval. The question had not yet been discussed by the Politburo (*s avtoritetnymi tovarichshami*), and so, as Litvinov noted, he could not yet give Potemkin directives. However, he thought, "personally," as he put it whenever he did not yet have formal authorization, that the Politburo would approve an immediate appeal to Laval. So not wanting to delay, he sent Potemkin a draft text for Laval, which he thought the Politburo would soon approve. It said essentially that Germany would reject an Eastern Pact, and that further negotiations with Germany would be a waste of time. "It is also unacceptable for us," Litvinov continued, "that the matter of the direct interests of the USSR and the discussion which has begun between it and France is becoming more and more complicated by negotiations that are being conducted between other governments without our participation and which begin to intertwine with an increasing number of political problems." Having said this, Litvinov included a summary of the negotiations with France. For Litvinov, it mattered that France had taken the initiative in discussing mutual assistance, a point which Paul-Boncour had himself affirmed to Potemkin. It was necessary to get on with discussions of mutual assistance with those willing states. As for Laval's replies to Potemkin's questions, they were not "reassuring." Laval clearly did not like any agreement without the participation of Germany and Poland, and it was just this question that blocked any advance. "There is no doubt that France, thanks to the [possibility of an] air convention, which further raises the value of cooperation with England, will not dare to take any steps against which England would adamantly object." It remained to be seen, Litvinov concluded, how insistently England was prepared to push its agenda regarding the air pact and other issues.[34]

On that same day, 17 February, Litvinov requested Stalin's approval for the draft that he had sent to Potemkin on his own authority. He advised against a threat – which Titulescu had suggested – to abandon the December protocol with Laval. "Hints" of Soviet impatience would emphasize "our determination to put an end to the uncertainty of the situation." These hints, he added, along with rumours of a Soviet-Reichswehr flirt should be enough to focus French minds. Still, there was always the chance that a flat rejection of the Soviet démarche could call into question the December protocol. "I do not think that France will respond at the moment with a categorical refusal. Very likely, the answer will be more or less flexible, elastic, not blocking completely action on the Eastern Pact. Our statement, however, will remind

Laval of the need to reckon with us in his further negotiations with England and Germany."[35] This was a strange recommendation: it proposed a stiff note to Laval, which might risk a French rejection, but was far more likely to draw an evasive reply. In short, it seemed to propose an action with little prospect of success and some risk of harming relations with France. It was undoubtedly an indication of Litvinov's frustration at finding an effective way to get Laval moving.

Litvinov took a softer line during a meeting with Alphand, also that same day. According to Alphand's report, Litvinov had indicated his intention to approve the "general lines" of the Anglo-French communiqué on condition that France accepted the principle of indivisibility of European security. Litvinov told Alphand that he had submitted a draft for approval and expected to have a reply in a few days. If Germany rejected the Anglo-French offers, why should other interested governments not continue to organize their security, without Germany, "in order to be sheltered from the only elements at present susceptible of troubling it?"[36] Had Litvinov changed his mind about the draft that he had sent to Potemkin? Based on Alphand's report to Paris, it sounded as though the narkom, or in fact Stalin, was leaning in that direction.

Vansittart's Views

Meanwhile in London, Vansittart tried to calm obvious Soviet discontents since he was also attempting to improve Anglo-Soviet relations and a potential row or even a breakup over the Anglo-French communiqué would only serve German interests. "I don't know how to calm Litvinov's really unhealthy obsession vis-à-vis the German menace," Vansittart said in passing to Corbin. Could Vansittart's comment have been more ironic? He of all people in London was also known to be "obsessed" with the German menace. Soviet anxieties were difficult to understand, Vansittart said, since the USSR did not have a common frontier with Germany and could not possibly fear an immediate danger given the actual state of German armaments. Litvinov would, of course, have responded to Vansittart in much the same way he had to the Polish ambassador. Corbin noted that even Vansittart, though less so than some of his Foreign Office colleagues, was loath to sacrifice an improvement of relations with Germany for a mutual assistance pact with the USSR. They assumed that an improvement of relations with Berlin was possible, and that was just what worried Litvinov. Vansittart indicated to Corbin that he was going to call in Maiskii to try to convince him of "the sincerity of the British government."[37] That would be easier said than done.

Vansittart has invited me to the Foreign Office on 13 February, Maiskii cabled to the NKID. Litvinov responded at once. It was an opportunity to open a second front in the fight for mutual assistance. "Clear up the lack of clarity in the London communiqué," Litvinov directed. "Say that it is a widely held view that the English are attempting by any means to persuade the French to give up the Eastern Pact, that the English care only about security in the west and are not interested in the east or southeast where they are ready to give Hitler freedom of action. In spite of the reference to the Eastern Pact in the [February] communiqué, even the Germans do not believe that the English are in the slightest degree interested in this pact." Litvinov suggested hearing what "the English" had to say.[38]

Vansittart used all his persuasive arts on Maiskii. The situation with Germany looks like this, he said: "The negotiations will be lengthy, difficult and probably with little chance of success. In Vansittart's opinion the Germans reacted relatively well to the air pact, can perhaps live with the Rome accords, but they are against the Eastern Pact, against a return to the League of Nations, and against any limitation at all on their rearmament." Before there were any negotiations at all, the Germans would ask "a thousand and one questions" requiring detailed replies. Vansittart turned to the questions that mattered to the Soviet government. All the issues discussed in the Anglo-French communiqué were considered to represent elements of the same complex of issues. What about the Eastern Pact? Maiskii wanted to know. Maybe some changes would have to be made, Vansittart replied, but the British government remained committed to it. He asked Maiskii to convey to the Soviet government that it should have no anxieties about the Anglo-French agreement or upcoming negotiations with Germany. These negotiations should not affect the Franco-Soviet rapprochement or rapidly improving Anglo-Soviet relations. "We have to look at things realistically," Vansittart said, "the basic fact … remains unchanged, in Europe [there] has appeared an armed and rapidly rearming Germany whose true intentions no one knows precisely. Such a situation (just as before 1914) is inevitably pushing nations around Germany towards a rapprochement." Vansittart dismissed the idea that Britain could profit in any way from untying Hitler's hands in the east.[39]

Unfortunately, Vansittart was only the Permanent Undersecretary of State, a civil servant, not the Foreign Secretary and not the prime minister. He had no control over them, influence yes, but no control and he served at their pleasure. There were Tories, in fact many Tories, who saw Hitlerite Germany as a bulwark against the USSR and against the spread of communism in Europe. They had no problem with untying Hitler's hands in the east, however foolish that idea, as Vansittart noted. Vansittart himself had been ringing the alarm bells about Hitlerite Germany; he was being heard in cabinet up to a point, but even some of his Foreign Office colleagues were mulling the idea of a Nazi free hand in the east. The very fact that the British government thought that there was any point at all in negotiating with Nazi Germany raised doubts in Moscow. Litvinov had long before given up on that idea as long as Hitler dreamed his big dreams of conquest. The only thing to do, therefore, was arm to the teeth and form alliances with those European states that felt threatened, and of course with the United States. Litvinov was the able spokesperson of the NKID, but the policy he defended was that of the government, that is, the Politburo and Stalin himself. In the diplomatic corps in Moscow, it was well known that Litvinov's position depended entirely on his relations with Stalin and that these relations at the beginning of the 1935 were good.[40] It is so easy in hindsight to say, well everyone should have known, or should have seen what was happening. Some people *did* see at the time, among them Litvinov, Krestinskii, Herriot, Paul-Boncour, and indeed Vansittart and Churchill; they had no need of hindsight. In that winter of 1935, however, the Soviet government was alone in its clarity of vision about the menace of Hitlerite Germany and what to do about it.

A Remarkable Patience

In some ways, Soviet patience with the British and French was remarkable, but if you looked at the situation from a Soviet point of view, the only available allies against Nazi Germany were those powers with which it was trying to move towards a common ground. The Soviet government had no other options but patience and persistence. A good example of Soviet patience is how it dealt with the Anglo-French communiqué of 3 February. Between 17 and 20 February, Litvinov moved from an aggressive *aide-mémoire* to Laval to a conciliatory reply three days later in response to a request from the French and British ambassadors.[41] On 19 February Litvinov, along with Krestinskii and Stomoniakov, met with Stalin for more than two hours.[42] We do not know, of course, what was discussed, but it is easy to imagine that the principal topics of conversation were the Eastern Pact, the Anglo-French communiqué, the German position, and how to respond to the request from the French and British governments. There was really only one choice and that was a conciliatory reply, which was issued on 20 February. It welcomed the Anglo-French initiative and then laid out the Soviet agenda with which readers will be familiar based on Litvinov's previous comments and instructions to Potemkin. Essentially, the Soviet declaration proposed the formation of pacts of mutual assistance supported by the USSR, France, Britain, and Italy and also by the Little and Balkan Ententes "to oppose military aggression." The Soviet declaration was published in *Izvestiia* on the following day.[43]

Some people in Paris and London must have breathed a sigh of relief. The following day Alphand saw Litvinov to express his thanks for the Soviet declaration. The French and British governments, he said, were well aware of the German strategy directed at separating out the various elements of the Anglo-French communiqué and sought to "frustrate" German objectives. Litvinov's reply to Alphand was polite and conciliatory without any of the bile of his previous letter to Potemkin.[44] Laval and Simon also expressed their thanks and offered reassurances, which Potemkin and Maiskii forwarded to Moscow.[45]

The exchange of expressions of relief and appreciation did not reduce Litvinov's disquiet about the mushiness of the positions of Laval and Simon. Would they stick to the agenda of an Eastern Pact, mutual assistance, and the indivisibility of security in Western and Eastern Europe? At the end of February there were the discussions about Laval and Simon going to Moscow and Simon to Berlin. As readers will remember, Simon's visit was postponed because of Hitler's diplomatic "illness" after the publication on 4 March of a British Defence White Paper calling for increased military expenditures. On 9 March, the Nazi government announced the existence of the Luftwaffe. A week later, on 16 March, in defiance of the Treaty of Versailles stipulations, Hitler announced the reintroduction of conscription and the existence of a German army of 500,000 men. *Finis* Versailles.

Remember that Litvinov was not enthusiastic about Simon making a visit to Moscow, although the NKID could not give the impression that his visit would be undesirable. From Geneva, Litvinov heard that Simon was still trying to draw France away from mutual assistance, and that Flandin was wobbling, waiting to see which way Britain would go.[46] Simon was not alone in leaning on the French. Léger was also trying to slow matters down. Léger and other Quai d'Orsay clerks, according to Foreign Office contacts with the French, "were not in favour of a bilateral Franco-Soviet pact and were hostile to any increased intimacy in the Franco-Soviet connection."[47] In a conversation with the British ambassador, Sir George Clerk, Léger said that he "had consistently combatted this tendency [for bilateral Franco-Soviet mutual assistance] even at times against his own ministers (Boncour and Barthou) on the ground that it would not be conducive to the restoration of confidence which is the sole basis of lasting peace." How wrong could he be? Laval was also against a bilateral pact. "He [Léger] told me," Clerk reported, "that he was anxious to avoid a Franco-Russian agreement except as a part of a homogeneous regional arrangement."[48] There were many people talking out of both sides of their mouths about collective security and mutual assistance, but it was not Litvinov or Stalin.

Potemkin was seeing Laval almost every day, and in the evenings too during diplomatic social events, where of course they often discussed business. Directed by Litvinov, Potemkin tried to hold Laval on course and to advise him on how to keep Simon from pursuing a unilateral British policy of concessions to Hitler.[49] It was the former school teacher trying to get a poor "student" to pay attention to his studies. In vain. The Foreign Secretary was said to be pressuring the French to make concessions in Berlin.[50] Maiskii heard that Laval was being devious (*krutit*).[51] That would not have been a surprise in Moscow.

Litvinov still worried about the security of the Baltic states. In a briefing paper for Stalin, he brought up the subject yet again. "In the negotiations with Barthou … we also sought to extend the pact of guarantee to the Baltic countries, pointing out that the German occupation of these countries would be the beginning of an attack on the USSR, that we could not wait while the German army crossed our frontiers and that therefore France must help us immediately upon German military forces crossing their eastern border." France did not agree to this stipulation, but Litvinov insisted and Barthou took the question twice to the Council of Ministers, which twice refused to agree. "I told Barthou," Litvinov added, "that I was not happy with this decision, and that I would not abandon the demand concerning the Baltic countries, and Barthou agreed to discuss again this question at the appropriate time."

It was plain that, for Litvinov, the weak point in Soviet defences against Nazi aggression was the Baltic region. British ideas of "compromise" for a multilateral non-aggression pact and non-binding "consultations" did not address Soviet concerns. Litvinov noted:

> I must say, however, that I am by no means sure that even a compromise proposal will be acceptable to Germany. Both under the compromise and under the original form of the pacts agreed upon with Barthou, the Baltic countries remain unprotected. Even if we wanted to come to the aid of these countries, in the event of a further development of military operations and a German offensive on our borders, we would already lose French assistance, since we ourselves would be the first to start a war with Germany to protect the Baltic States. In this area, we will obviously have a big dispute with France and England.[52]

Litvinov was relentless on this issue and brought it to Potemkin's attention on lines similar to those he had sent to Stalin. In the event of a German threat, "we shall be obliged to watch impassively the occupation of the Baltics and wait for the crossing of our frontiers by the German army, in order that the guarantee of France will enter into effect."[53]

Litvinov wanted to draft the texts of an Eastern Pact in the unlikely event that Germany agreed to one, and in the event it did not, a mutual assistance pact with France.[54] In fact, Hitler was thumbing his nose at France and Britain. When the French ambassador came in to talk, Litvinov gave the impression of taking matters calmly. The Soviet government was not a signatory to the Versailles Treaty, he shrugged, in answer to a question from Alphand. That was being coy. "We will wait and see what France does. What do you think?" the narkom then asked. The ambassador did not rise to the bait, and responded evasively. Litvinov needled: British "tactics," supported by France, had encouraged German aggressiveness. According to Alphand's report of the meeting, Litvinov suggested that the British might cancel Simon's upcoming visit to Berlin.[55] That was also needling.

An Absence of Trust

Events moved quickly. The news broke that Simon would after all go to Berlin. "M.M. [Litvinov] is frightfully angry," Maiskii noted. "He considers it [the British note proposing that Simon go to Berlin after all] a complete capitulation to Germany." That is what Litvinov also said to Alphand.[56] It was no way to build confidence with would-be allies, or even old ones. To put it in Litvinov's own words, Britain was like the indulgent father scolding an offending son (Hitlerite Germany). "As for France … taken in tow by the promise of an air convention, it will not pull away from England and will not yield to it in indulging Germany. It is to be feared that Hitler's last decisive step will finally confuse Laval and prompt him to make even greater concessions." Litvinov was contemptuous of the British: "We know from various, very reliable sources that England has reconciled itself to the possibility of a Soviet-French guarantee pact. However, it will probably refuse [to support the pact], when it [England] becomes aware of Hitler's negative attitude."[57] Still, Litvinov had to tack to the wind. Maiskii and Vansittart were in the midst of finalizing Eden's trip to Moscow.

Litvinov was right, by the way, about the French, if one is to judge from Laval's exchanges with Corbin in London. He burned hot when he first learned of the German announcement of 16 March, but then turned cold and retreated. The British note, he said in a telegram to London and Rome, although not to Moscow, caused "deep disappointment" in Paris, but gave "every satisfaction" to Hitler. "Unity of action" between France, Britain, and Italy was essential, Laval wrote: "Any recrimination is pointless." Laval did not mention the Soviet Union anywhere in his telegram.[58] It must have been a Freudian slip. Did the USSR really count for Laval?

Potemkin had to handle Laval carefully, nudge him along as far as that was possible. On Laval's idea to visit Moscow (first mooted in late February), Potemkin did not think he was serious. We will have to wait him out to see what his real intentions are. One day Potemkin was not sure; the next day he thought Laval might be coming around. Then there were Laval's personal issues. "Laval unexpectedly complained to me about his relations with the Communist Party and the socialists, about which he gave to understand that he would be grateful to us, if we could help halt [their] campaign and even contribute our well-known moral support as statesmen, working in favour of the Franco-Soviet rapprochement." That sounded like Vansittart pleading with Maiskii for help with Labour. Readers will remember that Laval was up for re-election to the Senate in October 1935. If he lost, his political activities would be over at least for the time being. If he could count on the support of the communist-socialist front, his reelection would be certain, and he would keep his ministerial post. "Our friends from the *front commun* [the coalition of the French socialist and communist parties] confirm that they would have nothing against providing the aforementioned support if we recognized that it was useful for the Franco-Soviet rapprochement." Potemkin reported that Jacques Sadoul, a well-known French communist, had come to see him about this very question. "I refrained for now from giving an answer in order to put the question to you," Potemkin wrote to Krestinskii. "My opinion is that the Sadoul project could be implemented only if Laval committed himself honestly to implement the Eastern Pact or, better yet, to implement it before the Senate elections." Readers may have concluded at this point in the narrative that it would have been difficult to imagine the slippery Laval "committing himself honestly" to anything. "Of course, discussions with him [Laval] about this would have to be conducted with his former friends – the current members of the *front commun*. We ourselves would have to stay away from such an agreement. I am informing you of this plan and asking you to inform me how you feel about it."[59]

Readers may wonder how Krestinskii or Litvinov responded to Potemkin's query. Unfortunately, the NKID's reply, if there is one, remains elusive. To say the least, Potemkin did not trust Laval. He had dragged out the negotiations for an Eastern Pact, thinking of compromises for an agreement with Germany and trying to persuade Simon not to go to Moscow. He was the zigzag man who preferred weak solutions, not strong ones, in order to reach agreement with Hitlerite Germany.

In Moscow, Stalin received an NKVD report, based on "documentary material from the French foreign ministry." That meant an intercepted document. It was quite a story. "Eden arrived in Paris with the mission of obtaining from France plenipotentiary powers to negotiate with Hitler Germany's return to the League of Nations but also on the basis of a future convention on limitation of armaments." The report did not give any date for when this meeting occurred, but it was before Simon's visit to Berlin. Laval refused Eden's request. The conversation continued. Eden said an Eastern Pact should not mask a military alliance, which could push Germany into "desperate steps." Eden's line was delay, delay, delay. And not to do anything to provoke Hitler. Delay the conclusion of a mutual assistance pact with the USSR until Germany returned to the League. The British proposals reeked of weakness. Laval replied: "France could wait for a few months more, but the Little Entente and the USSR are demanding the immediate signature of a pact of mutual assistance."

It was not just Litvinov pressing, so were Titulescu and Beneš. According to Laval, he had already tried to persuade the USSR to opt for conventions on consultation and non-aggression. The Soviet side refused. Laval told Eden that France could only abandon mutual assistance with the USSR and Little Entente on the condition of the conclusion of a formal Anglo-French military alliance. Eden was going to Moscow to persuade Soviet authorities to delay the conclusion of a pact of mutual assistance. Could all of this be true? Was it the imagination run wild of an overzealous *razvedchik*? On and on the report went. There were "upcoming elections [in Britain]; a desire of the leading British politicians to go to the possible limits of concessions to avoid war, and the new tendency to indulge in a political game on the contradictions between the USSR and Germany." There was even the idea that Britain hoped to be left in peace while Nazi Germany and the USSR fought it out. There then followed a warning against banking too much on that idea. "German-Soviet hostility is by no means a permanent factor in international politics on which to base policy for the long term. It even seems that there is a certain calculation in this hostility and that Germany is trying to involve France in a bargain in which the USSR would be left to Germany." That strategy could backfire if Germany and the USSR came to terms in a way "unprofitable to France." Stalin left a note on this report: "Important. Most likely."[60] In any case, it was the scenario, which *mutatis mutandis*, played out in 1939.

On 26 March, Laval telephoned Potemkin to say that the Council of Ministers had approved his heretofore elusive trip to Moscow. This meant he could not avoid it, Potemkin opined, but he hid his intention to limit his discussions in Moscow to empty phrases. How could such an interlocutor be trusted? The Franco-Soviet rapprochement was a "trump" in his game: he did not want to play it, but he dared not lose it. There was, of course, another motive behind Laval's desire to visit Moscow, the personal motive, which was to win over the left in the electoral district of Aubervilliers. Here is what Potemkin wrote to Krestinskii. "As you know, the *front commun* occupies a very significant position in this district. Laval is going on a pilgrimage to the land of the Soviets to return to these voters from the Soviet Mecca." He continued:

> Laval believes very much in our omnipotence vis-à-vis the left front, and sometimes it seems to him that we have already given a directive – to support his candidacy as a person useful for the rapprochement of the USSR with France … "Yesterday I was at a meeting in Aubervilliers," – he [Laval] said to Sadoul: "It seems to me that there is already a directive – not to defame me. Communists and socialists have behaved very well for me in the meeting." Sadoul says that he did not attempt to contradict Laval. I should note that from our side we until now have not encouraged Laval with a single word, nor disappointed his hopes for [our] expected support.[61]

In other words, Potemkin implied, two could hold trump cards. Apparently, Litvinov was not interested. The Soviet government was about to conclude a trade agreement with Germany. Sometimes in Soviet relations with the West, economic negotiations were the doorway to political negotiations. In his frequent dudgeons about France, Litvinov thought about playing the German trump. Not this time. He cabled Potemkin to advise him of the conclusion of the trade agreement in Berlin. It was a business deal, he advised. The Germans offered better credit arrangements than could be obtained in other countries. "No political significance should be attributed to the deal."[62] That was clear.

The Minder and the Miscreant

In the meantime, in Paris, Laval saw Potemkin again, as Eden's visit to Moscow was winding down. Potemkin must have felt like Comrade Minder, hounding, nagging, imploring Monsieur Zigzag to get a move on. It finally happened, or seemed to happen at the end of March. Laval was feeling pressure on his left, and of course he had to think about Aubervilliers. Remember, mayoral elections would take place in early May. He must have thought Eden's visit to Moscow gave him some leeway from London. Hitler's announcements on the Luftwaffe and conscription were also incentives. It appeared as though Potemkin was seeing Laval almost as much as Léger and Bargeton. "He [Laval] said to me," Potemkin advised, "that he did not yet have sufficient information about the Berlin negotiations. Nevertheless, he did not consider all hope lost in drawing Germany into the Eastern Pact." This statement must have exasperated Potemkin. "I did not have much trouble leading Laval to the conclusion that his optimism was baseless and that we had arrived straight up against the question about conclusion of a Franco-Czech-Soviet pact of mutual assistance." That was not what Laval wanted to hear. Laval pointed out that there was opposition in the National Assembly and he felt "besieged" by senators and deputies warning against an agreement with the USSR. Potemkin tried to pin down Laval, but he "dodged." It was again Comrade Minder up against Monsieur Zigzag. France, Laval said, did not want to be drawn into a war. That is not what you promised us, Potemkin replied. Should he inform his government of Laval's evasive position? "Laval spun around, began even more to beg me to wait, he began to develop new plans with the participation of Italy, which allegedly will be more easily accepted by public opinion in France, most of all afraid of a military alliance with the USSR." Potemkin was losing patience. "I said, that it was not a question of a military alliance, that a pact of mutual assistance was promised to us by the French [government] in exchange for entry into the League of Nations, that Barthou had declared openly to allies his government's intention in the event of a German refusal, to conclude the pact without them."

According to Potemkin's report, Laval was "clearly upset." He replied that he would ask Léger for the files and "for the preparation of concrete proposals which he will discuss with me in the coming days." I had scarcely returned to the embassy, Potemkin noted in his telegram, when Laval telephoned to ask me to come to see him the next morning so they could get to work on written proposals.[63] In the back and forth, it seemed that Potemkin had gained a little ground with Laval, but had he? Perhaps, that day he had, but there was opposition in the Quai d'Orsay to a bilateral Franco-Soviet accord. The political director, Bargeton, was in open opposition. The pact would play into German hands and close off the possibility of a change in German policy. What change could that possibly be? Bargeton must have believed in fairy stories. Any agreement with the USSR should be temporary, he argued, or risk the conclusion of a bilateral pact "openly directed against Germany," which would become "the permanent basis of our policy."[64] No wonder Laval squirmed uncomfortably with Potemkin.

In Moscow on that same day, 29 March, Payart, who had just returned from leave, had a conversation with Marcel' Rozenberg, who was about to depart for Geneva. Payart said that he had spoken to Laval who was "absorbed" in the electoral campaign in Aubervilliers. Laval had spoken about Aubervilliers with Potemkin, as indeed readers will remember, and Alphand had also raised the subject at the NKID.[65] Potemkin's refusal to intervene and Sadoul's game of trumps were having their effects on Laval's nerves.

On the following morning, 30 March, Potemkin met Laval again at the Quai d'Orsay, this time in the presence of Léger. Monsieur Zigzag repeated that he had not lost hope about the conclusion of a non-aggression pact with Germany, but that naturally negotiations could drag out. Potemkin noted, "In order not to lose time, and not to allow the demoralization among the friends of France and to sow doubts about [French] loyalty in relation to the USSR, Laval has decided to act." His idea was to reinforce security in central and Eastern Europe. So far, so good, Potemkin would have thought, but where was the hitch? Laval proposed the conclusion of bilateral agreements for mutual assistance with France and Czechoslovakia, and in the future possibly with Italy. A Franco-Soviet agreement could be concluded "in the near future" independently from any agreements with Germany. That was a step forward, and satisfied a Soviet requirement for negotiations. Then Laval handed to Potemkin the draft of an agreement in two basic paragraphs tying up mutual assistance in the clauses of the League of Nations.[66] Ah, there was the hitch. In his comments on the French proposal, Potemkin pointed to the problem of linking mutual assistance to the League of Nations. Its processes were slow, complicated, and required unanimity. There were other problems with the text: what would happen if there was no unanimity in the League council? Nor was there provision for immediate assistance. Potemkin talked over the situation with Titulescu, who was in Paris. According to Titulescu, Laval's proposal could be well received by public opinion, in spite of its shortcomings. The Turkish, Greek, and Yugoslav ministers thought it was "a step forward." Potemkin noted that he had been unsuccessful in cooling down the Turkish minister's favourable impression of the draft.[67]

Sir George Clerk, British ambassador in Paris, saw Laval that same day, to "find out what was going on" and to deliver a message from Simon to slow down. Titulescu was in town, Clerk noted, and of course the British were well informed about his ideas on mutual assistance. Titulescu was not Laval's only pestering interlocutor. Herriot was another. Laval even complained to Clerk about Herriot who was "violently anti-German."[68] When Clerk finally saw Laval in the late afternoon, he noted: "I got the impression of catching a schoolboy who had just banged the door of the store cupboard but had not yet got hold of the jam."[69] No wonder, for Laval had earlier in the day given Potemkin the French draft for a bilateral pact of mutual assistance. It was too late to wait, but there were many ways to delay.

New Proposals in Moscow

On 2 April Litvinov sent fresh proposals to Stalin in response to Laval's draft. He explained all the problems of linking a mutual assistance pact to the League of Nations. It was too problematical and too impractical. What Litvinov proposed was "immediate" mutual assistance in the case of "overt aggression." Such a clause was intended for the air pact, and Eden had said to Litvinov that the Locarno accords were not an obstacle to France lending assistance to the USSR in the event of an attack against it. Hence, a clause on immediate intervention should be added to the proposed pact of mutual assistance as part of a counterproposal. Titulescu had asked for such a clause and it was refused, Litvinov noted, thus the NKID needed to ask for it again.

Litvinov then returned for the umpteenth time to the problem of the Baltics: Laval's proposals had left the Baltic countries without defence against Germany. He was convinced that France would never agree to cover the Baltics in a bilateral pact. Litvinov therefore recommended that the question of a regional pact composed of the USSR, France, Czechoslovakia, and the Baltic countries be considered before accepting Laval's suggestions. Even a Franco-Soviet-Czechoslovak pact would be preferable to a bilateral agreement. These ideas Litvinov formalized in a three-point proposal for Stalin.[70] Between 2 and 9 April, on the four days that Stalin held formal meetings at the Kremlin, he received Litvinov. Mutual assistance and Litvinov's briefing paper would have been obvious subjects of discussion.

Litvinov replied to Potemkin by telegram on 2 April with directives approved by Stalin. There could be an Eastern Pact, without Germany and without Poland, but it had to include France, Czechoslovakia, and the Baltic countries. If Germany refused the Eastern Pact, there should be no Western air pact. "On this position," wrote Litvinov, "we stand and will continue to stand." As for Laval's proposals, Litvinov was not happy. "Say clearly to Laval that his prevarications are widely known and are having a negative influence not only on the position of England, but also on Germany and Poland, and on the Little and Balkan Ententes, and are producing an unfavourable impression on our public."[71] Litvinov also signalled to Potemkin that he was still thinking about Poland. "If there is the least chance of bringing Poland into a pact of mutual assistance, we should not miss it." The Soviet government would exclude from the definition of mutual assistance, Litvinov added, Red Army passage across Polish territory. That was a *major* concession to address a major Polish preoccupation.[72]

Unfortunately, but in no sense a surprise, the still open door in Moscow for Poland did not attract Beck. Eden passed through Warsaw on his way home from Moscow. He saw Beck and asked him if Poland would participate in a multilateral pact of mutual assistance. Beck responded in the affirmative on two occasions. Davtian, who met Eden and heard from him what Beck had said, was sceptical. Just because Beck said yes, Davtian noted, did not necessarily mean yes. Beck could say yes, so as not to offend France, knowing full well that Hitler would issue a categorical no. Poland would not enter any arrangement, according to Beck, which might run up against Germany.[73] Litvinov heard a little different version of Beck's yes. It meant that Poland would not under any circumstances participate in an Eastern Pact without Germany. A new attempt to torpedo regional pacts was some kind of pan-European agreement. It was dust in the eyes; nothing would come of such an idea. Litvinov wrote to Aleksandrovskii in Prague to warn Beneš. He also forwarded the statements of an unidentified Polish diplomat to a Soviet polpred, to the effect that Poland would not object to the German seizure of Austria or even Memel. Soviet intelligence agencies had also received similar information. Poland did not agree with the formula "peace is indivisible." They reckoned in Warsaw that if Germany was to annex Austria, then any war would be local, or there would be no military resistance, or the Italians would only rattle their swords. The source confirmed Polish opposition to the Eastern Pact especially because it had a grudge against Czechoslovakia dating back to the 1920 Polish-Soviet war when the Czechoslovaks seized territory where a plebiscite should have been organized.[74] According to what Beneš heard from Eden who had also visited Prague, Beck categorically rejected the principle of mutual assistance. This should not have been a surprise to anyone; it had been the Polish position since the Eastern Pact was first proposed. Beneš told Eden that any modification of the original proposal for the Eastern Pact would be a "capitulation."[75]

Incredible as it may seem, the Politburo, which was Stalin in effect, still hoped to draw Poland and Germany into a pact of collective security. As Litvinov explained to Potemkin, "From the very beginning we considered the Eastern Pact to be valuable only in the case of the participation of it of Germany and especially Poland. In order to obtain this objective we undertook an offensive, declaring, that in the case of a refusal of Germany and Poland to join the pact, we would conclude it without them. This was done with the idea of influencing Germany and Poland, to incline them to participate in the pact." So, the Soviet side was bluffing, up to a point, but the bluff did not work. Germany and Poland refused to join the pact. Now the circumstances had changed, according to

Litvinov. Germany was putting out rumours to the effect that "supposedly their refusal responded to our wishes, for we allegedly were looking for a pact without Germany and against it." To counter the rumours, the Soviet government considered it necessary to insist on having Germany and Poland in the pact. Then Litvinov added this key point: "To this it is necessary to add that some comrades here still have not quite lost hope in a change of position not only by Poland, but even also by Germany." This was why the Soviet government agreed with the idea that Laval should stop in Warsaw before arriving in Moscow. Perhaps Laval could use his powers of persuasion on Beck. This decision, Litvinov added, was taken on 3 April, before it became known that Eden had not persuaded Beck to change his position. If one reads between the lines of what Litvinov was saying to Potemkin, it was that Stalin had reined in a little of Litvinov's impatience and aggressiveness towards Nazi Germany. This conclusion is supported by Mendras's observation from the previous year. From time to time, Stalin pulled on Litvinov's bridle.

Let us permit Litvinov to continue his explanations to Potemkin. The Soviet position, he wrote, was getting a little complicated for Moscow would not refuse a pact at the worst without Poland and Germany. The preference was still for a multilateral approach, the more so, because public opinion in France preferred it even if only with Czechoslovakia. Litvinov also returned to the question of the Baltics. Litvinov still sought to obtain French agreement for an extension of guarantees to the Baltic countries. Barthou had tried and failed to get agreement from the Council of Ministers, but the government had changed and so therefore the government position could also change. Litvinov argued that a Baltic guarantee was in French interests because in case of a German attack on France, the USSR would be able to offer "more effective" assistance; in other words, the Red Army could pass through the Baltic countries to attack Germany. Litvinov was also looking for "immediate" assistance in the event of aggression. In all these matters, the Soviet could afford to wait a little. "There is no inclination here to force too much the discussion with France," Litvinov noted, "hence, the postponement of negotiations before my meeting with Laval in Geneva." The situation, according to Litvinov, was the following:

> The arming of Germany in every domain exceeds all expectations. There is not the least doubt that already now or in the near future Germany will have ground forces with a numerical superiority over France. It is also catching up with and overtaking France very quickly in military aviation. France is therefore losing its position as the most powerful military state in Europe. The [German] war potential not only in human resources but also in arms production exceeds that of France by many times. *Given the complete solidarity of Poland with Germany, France cannot therefore count on an effective alliance with Poland* [emphasis added]. The Little Entente does not generally represent a strong force; moreover, there may not be

> confidence in France that it can retain Yugoslavia and Romania in its orbit, for which a stronger Germany could become an attracting force.

Who could argue with Litvinov's analysis of French weakness and vulnerabilities? He called it France's "dilemma": "Either it enters an alliance with Germany and in the role of weakest partner plays a secondary role, and thus recognizes German hegemony in Europe, losing all its friends and allies; or, it looks for support in the strengthening of its ties with the Little Entente and it seeks agreement with us." Litvinov omitted to mention France's dependence on Britain, of which he was well aware. "I have no doubt," he concluded, "that in France there are many supporters of the first exit out of the dilemma, but common sense is likely to lead France to another way out. I therefore believe that interest [in the latter option] has now increased more for France than for us."[76]

Remember, it was April 1935. In Moscow, the German ambassador Friedrich Werner von der Schulenburg visited Litvinov at the NKID to complain. That was nothing unusual, the Germans in Moscow were always complaining. This time it was an article by Tukhachevskii about German armaments. It is "unacceptable," Schulenburg said, that such a senior official was speaking publicly about the details of German armaments. Anyone could see that Tukhachevskii counted everything three times. If the German government did not like the figures, Litvinov replied facetiously, it could certainly reply in the press. The NKID preferred a more open approach in discussing such matters. "We know that Hitler holds to another method and prefers to speak behind our backs with the English about the danger which, allegedly, the Red Army represents for Germany and for all of Europe, about our aggressive intentions, and so on." Litvinov did not pull his punches. "It's a question of taste," he continued. "We prefer not to hide what we think about German policy."[77]

In Paris, people were worried, angry, and uncertain about the future. On 6 April there was a meeting of the Council of Ministers. According to Herriot, Laval said he would deal with "the Soviets" if only to support the Little Entente and to prevent a "German-Russian accord." This was always the bare minimum French position in favour of relations with the USSR. It was ironic too since a Franco-German accord was Laval's preferred option. "But, basically – and he admits it," according to Herriot, "he fears the possible action of a Bolshevik army on the French army."[78] Laval's anti-communism was his fatal obsession.

Shifting Sands

The Soviet embassy in Paris kept the NKID well informed of the shifting sands of French public opinion. Vladimir A. Sokolin was the Soviet liaison with the French press. "In recent days," he wrote, "the press close to the government has increasingly reflected Laval's reluctance to commit to the Eastern Pact, until the complete exhaustion of other possibilities. From the above-mentioned press and from statements made by people close to Laval, the following sentiments of Laval emerge: he, of course, prefers a broad pact, with the participation of Germany." Laval was counting on the "initiative" of the English to convene a big conference, with the participation of the Germans, which could lead to the conclusion of a general pact for consultation, non-aggression and non-assistance to the aggressor. This was just the outcome that Litvinov wanted to prevent. Sokolin added the observation, almost as an afterthought, that Laval became bad tempered "at the mention of the Eastern Pact, of the position of the USSR, of the need to make a decision, Laval's irritation is becoming very intense." Readers should not be surprised since Potemkin or Litvinov were always close by to remind him that further stalling was unacceptable. Laval's policy of "little steps" and delay had worked for a while. Litvinov now wanted to end it.

Sometimes the oddest information turned up in reports to Moscow, mixing information and disinformation. Sokolin reported hearing:

> From a Masonic source, under the "big secret," it is reported that the representatives of the General Staff in the "Grand Orient" [lodge] talk about a preventive war in June 1935 as a decision taken. Difficulties and objections to the Eastern Pact are exaggerated for camouflage. France, secretly from us and from its allies, will suddenly open hostilities, in the belief that the Allies will willingly help her, after the outbreak of the war.

Could this information have represented the views of certain French officers? It certainly did not represent the formal views of the high command. Then there was this further information from Sokolin's Freemason: The general staff allegedly believed that if a Franco-Soviet pact was concluded, it would not be able to count on effective assistance, but in case of further procrastination in negotiations with the Soviet side, it might come to terms with the Germans. This was the recurring French *cauchemar* and dilemma. The most favourable moment to count on Soviet help, according to the Freemason, was now.

Sokolin was not gullible. He challenged his Masonic source, apparently a French military officer. It sounded like "fantasies," Sokolin replied.

The information was true, the Freemason insisted, for the sake of friendship, he was giving Sokolin a great state secret. He should not treat it so lightly.

Sokolin asked for clarifications, but the Freemason would only say "that the General Staff could not be responsible for the integrity of France if the war was delayed for even another year."

Pierre Laval

Sokolin concluded his journal entry with an interesting portrait of Laval:

> A typical French peasant. Cheerful, inclined to frankness, of which he himself is afraid: in the midst of a conversation, he may suddenly become withdrawn. Extremely scornful regarding the external attributes of power, he takes offence if people do not show a proper minimum of respect for him. He does not like the military of any country. He is convinced that the Red Army, as an offensive force, "does not exist." He repeats it to those around him. "I'm only interested in their aviation," he says, "and they [the Soviet] claim that they emphasize machines more than in other armies."
>
> He really does not like the English and cannot stand Americans. He loves "cosy" people, simple, "intimate" to some degree. He is extremely attentive to his daughter from whom he does not part (there is gossip about her connection with [Jacques] Doriot and her own father).
>
> He considers that he is more able than any other French minister to understand us, because he was a poor peasant, he was a poor man, he passed through a socialist school. He is demagogically cynical, but also softens when remembering the struggle of French workers for the republic. He is very stingy and greedy. Can be charming, especially with workers.[79]

Sokolin's portrait of Laval was more generous than others might have written about him. He was born in Chatêldon, almost due west of Lyon and south of Vichy, in 1883. His father was, among other occupations, a café and hotel proprietor. The young Laval worked to support his studies, sometimes as a *garçon* in his father's café, sometimes as a tutor in *lycées* around Lyon. He went to Paris for his *bacc*, then to Lyon for a *licence* in zoology before returning to Paris to study law. In 1909, he married and the couple soon had a daughter, Josée. He became a lawyer for various union men who got into trouble with the law. In a photograph taken in 1913, he looks like an attractive, innocent fellow with a thick main of hair combed to the side, clean shaven save for an unflamboyant moustache. In 1914, he won election to the Chambre des députés as a member of the Socialist Party. He was never much of a socialist, however, as he himself admitted, and he did not renew his party card in 1922. In the following year he became mayor of Aubervilliers. He made money as a lawyer, but he also got into business acquiring a reputation for shady dealings and even shadier contacts with French financiers and businessmen. Eventually, he bought a newspaper in the Puy-de-Dôme and there too he made money.

No doubt Laval was a shady individual, but perhaps not more than so than many others of his generation who enriched themselves in the "Republic of Pals." This was where, as readers will remember, "rigorously honest men were on good terms with fairly honest men, who were on good terms with shady men, who were on good terms with despicable crooks." In this pantheon of dubious people, Laval moved ever further into the shadows. In politics as in business one could say he was an operator with no fixed principles except perhaps for making money and for his hatred of French communists who were a constant thorn in his side in Aubervilliers. His political compass was set towards Berlin and his dealings with the Soviet Union were forced by people on the centre-left ranging from Herriot to communists and by the Little Entente. He often said one thing, as readers will have already seen, and then *did* another. In short, for the Soviet Union, he was unreliable, though Litvinov and Potemkin tried to work with him.

Titulescu's Démarche

On the same day that Sokolin was sketching his portrait of Laval, Titulescu paid a call at the Soviet embassy. He saw Potemkin and gave him a letter in French for Litvinov. Potemkin considered it urgent and had the letter sent on to Moscow by diplomatic courier. The NKID translated it into Russian and forwarded it to Stalin. "I consider the need for the conclusion of an accord of mutual assistance between France and the USSR to be more urgent than ever," Titulescu wrote. "The non-conclusion of this accord would at once signal a new triumph for Hitler's policy. He introduced conscription and no serious measure was taken by the three great powers against this repudiation of the treaty of Versailles. German audacity had found there [in the failure to react] an encouragement, the consequences of which cannot yet be foreseen." Hitler has openly opposed an Eastern Pact, Titulescu continued, if he succeeded in obstructing a Franco-Soviet accord, German audacity "would know no bounds." Not only could peace be suddenly threatened, but Nazi influence in Central and Eastern Europe could grow rapidly. The "most dangerous instability" could take the place of the relative stability within the Little and Balkan Entente states. Whatever the legitimate reticence of the Soviet government, it could not continue an inflexible line without undermining common interests.

The situation among French ruling circles was such, Titulescu warned, that any false move could aid the cause of those elements working against a Franco-Soviet accord. "Great interests" were at stake and these interests meant accepting the present situation as it was and not as one might like it to be. The French government had made a proposal; the Soviet government should reply to it promptly, suggesting the necessary modifications. It would be best not to give Laval a pretext for changing his mind. An urgent reply was necessary, proposing modifications, in preparation for the meeting in Geneva between Laval and Litvinov on 15 April. No delays should be risked.

In the meantime, Titulescu proposed two modifications to the French draft proposal: a waiving of the League of Nation's unanimity rule and a stipulation for the automatic entry into effect of treaty obligations in the event of "flagrant aggression." The signature of the Franco-Soviet accord should take place before any other security agreements. Discussion of larger agreements before the conclusion of the Franco-Soviet agreement would be a means of delay or sabotage. At the end of his letter, Titulescu offered to meet Litvinov in Geneva in mid-April.[80] Titulescu was preaching to the converted, but the urgency with which the Soviet embassy in Paris and then the NKID in Moscow treated Titulescu's note indicates how important they considered it to be.

On the day before Titulescu dropped off his note at the Soviet embassy, Potemkin had seen Laval to convey Litvinov's instructions from his cable of 2 April. Potemkin delivered the message "with particular firmness." Laval responded with his usual objections and concerns. He did not close off, however, modifications of the original French proposal and suggested that Potemkin work with Léger on revisions. Potemkin replied that in as much as the Eastern Pact had not yet been declared dead, he had no instructions to discuss anything beyond it. Potemkin warned Laval, who was preparing to go to Stresa to meet with his British and Italian counterparts, that the "least inattention" could lead to the collapse of the "front of governments," which sought to protect the peace of Europe. Laval nodded his agreement.[81]

Litvinov's Recommendations

Events were moving fast now. Litvinov sent another briefing paper to Stalin on 7 April. "Opponents of the Eastern Pact have intensified their activity in recent days, making the primary point of their new offensive against the pact the final refusal of Germany and Poland to agree to mutual assistance. It seems to me that the pact is already, at least 75 per cent wrecked." Litvinov had received the impression from the Italian ambassador Bernardo Attolico that Mussolini had thrown in with Poland against the Eastern Pact. After his visit to Berlin, Simon started to promote the idea of a more universal security agreement with the sole objective of "torpedoing" any further discussion of the Eastern Pact. Mussolini thought that by promoting Simon's ideas he could separate Poland from Germany. In fact, the new proposals had little chance of success, but in as much as they would require long months of discussion, the Eastern Pact would thus be sidetracked and the original goal thus achieved. Litvinov speculated that Mussolini would try to kill off the Eastern Pact at Stresa without actually appearing to have done so.

So what to do? "If we continue to attach importance to the agreement with France on mutual assistance," Litvinov wrote, "we must act immediately by pressuring the French government." The pressure could take the form of a kind of a *mise en demeure*, similar to the one Litvinov had proposed in mid-February when it was decided to take a softer line. Basically, Litvinov proposed to ask the French government if it still held to the line of approach of Paul-Boncour and Barthou, that is, to the conclusion of an agreement for mutual assistance with the USSR, Czechoslovakia, and the Baltic states. At the least, an agreement without the Baltics, would remain open to Poland and Germany, along with corresponding collective pacts of non-aggression. He also proposed to inform the British and Italian ambassadors of Soviet opposition to the abandonment of concrete proposals for collective security for the sake of pointless discussions about vague, ineffectual combinations. "Since we have nothing more to lose," Litvinov added, "we must discuss separately whether we should now, in conversations with Laval, express a willingness to return to him and ourselves the freedom of action by abolition of the Geneva Protocol [of December 1934]." These positions should also be published in the press.[82] The NKID prepared a draft statement for Laval in line with what Litvinov proposed to Stalin. Litvinov's recommendations to Stalin were deleted from the text, which Potemkin handed to Laval on 9 April.[83] It is not hard to understand why. Essentially, what Litvinov wrote to Stalin is that the USSR could not trust anyone, not Simon, not Mussolini, certainly not Laval, and least of all Poland and Germany. It was a no-win situation, but accepting that it was no-win meant abandoning collective security and mutual assistance, and this, Stalin was not *yet* willing to do.

On average during the 1930s, Litvinov met Stalin every two weeks or so. During this period, he saw Stalin sometimes three or four times a week. From 7 to 9 April, it was every day. On 9 April, the Politburo issued new directives, again taking a softer line than proposed by Litvinov. It approved revisions to the Quai d'Orsay's *projet* given to Potemkin on 30 March. The key revisions were the provision of immediate mutual assistance before League of Nations action in the case of "undeniable aggression" and acceptance of Titulescu's suggestions for revisions to the French draft, using technical arguments about the interpretation of League statutes.[84]

Dénouement

On 10 April Litvinov left for Geneva after forwarding the new Politburo directives to Potemkin.[85] The stage was set for the meeting with Laval five days later. It was again Litvinov's turn to face Monsieur Zigzag. In the meantime, Potemkin kept up the minding in Paris. On 9 April Laval agreed to a joint communiqué stating that France and the USSR had agreed to conclude a bilateral pact of mutual assistance not later than 1 May. The following day Potemkin cabled Litvinov that his meeting with Laval had not gone well. Although Laval said he was committed to the Boncour-Barthou policy line, he dragged his feet on a "gentleman's agreement" to move forward on Litvinov's 2 April last-chance proposals for an Eastern Pact. Laval replied that he did want to risk "irritating" his British and Italian colleagues before meeting them at Stresa. That response did not sit well with Potemkin.[86]

At an official breakfast at the Quai d'Orsay where Titulescu and ministers from the Little and Balkan Ententes were present, Laval gave a speech underlining French loyalty to its allies and promising to defend their interests. Mandel was also present. Was he there to keep an eye on Laval on behalf of like-minded ministers? He might have been. Laval expatiated on the "elegance of French policy." In order "to introduce some clarity" into the proceedings, Potemkin reported sarcastically, "I queried him [Laval] on all points." As always, it was to try to pin him down. Some people in France, Potemkin said before all present, had dared to state that the USSR was trying to force the negotiations, claiming that France was less interested in a pact of mutual assistance than the USSR and casting doubt on Soviet power and claiming that France had "sacrificed itself" in entering into cooperation with Moscow. Potemkin thought it necessary to correct the record. "The French themselves had proposed the pact to us," he said, "and persuaded us to enter the League of Nations in order to speed up its conclusion." This was all true. Then Potemkin sunk in his knife. He mentioned the Geneva protocol, effectively an agreement not to double-cross one another, and noted that the French "had repeatedly violated their obligations." Was that what Laval meant by the "elegance of French policy"? An "elegant" stab in the back? The ministers present must have collectively sucked in their breath. Mandel would have been concerned. Potemkin drove in his last knife by noting that Laval had rejected his "gentleman's agreement" of the previous day. According to Potemkin, his colleagues in the room agreed with him. Laval responded "solemnly" that the Franco-Soviet pact would be concluded by 1 May and that nothing "shameful" would occur at Stresa. "Either I resign from the government, declared Laval in so many words, or I will bring the negotiations for a pact to a successful conclusion." Titulescu intervened at this point to stress the importance of the Franco-Soviet pact. Here was a diplomatic reply to relieve the tensions in the room. "The scene ended in toasts and outpourings," Potemkin noted, "very much like a village wedding proceeding." No one can say that Potemkin lacked an acidic sense of humour. "Laval was all in a sweat, his wife asking me to believe in 'this man' who is finally linking his fate with us."[87]

According to Sokolin's sources, Laval wanted "to neutralize" Titulescu who was "raging" in favour of an Eastern Pact. "It is not necessary to report to Moscow about the notorious manoeuvres of Laval" – this line was apparently Laval's to Tabouis – "it is necessary to portray the problem, so that if there is a little more give and take, then *voilà*, the problem will fade away (*vygorit*)."

Laval's indiscrete remarks leaked quickly. In Paris where scandals made excellent newspaper copy, discretion was not an asset among journalists. Again, according to Sokolin, "Laval's insolent manner of representing the matter of the

Eastern Pact, as a concession to us, as a favour, spreads through journalists close to him, then to wider circles of the public and 'friends,' they [want to] persuade us not to insist on the impossible, but to reconcile ourselves to what France 'gives.'" Sokolin also heard about Laval's breakfast at the Quai d'Orsay:

> In connection with Laval's "promise," given to them at breakfast on 9 April, in the presence of the polpred and representatives of the Little and Balkan Ententes, "to sign" before 1 May, journalists, Havas types, and friendly figures put two questions. Is Laval's April promise to be taken more seriously than his January statement in Geneva [on pursuing an Eastern Pact]; and does he personally undertake to sign before 1 May? Such tactics suggest the possibility that he will offer a completely unsatisfactory text, we will reject it and he will say that he is not guilty, and that we are guilty if by 1 May nothing has come out.[88]

Laval was cunning, and that might well have been his intention. It was a risky strategy, however, for there was still important support for the pact in the Council of Ministers and among French allies in Central and Danubian Europe.

There was then a lull of sorts in negotiations while Laval went to Stresa and Litvinov to Geneva. In the meantime, while Litvinov waited for Laval in Geneva, he reported on the buzz of rumours about the 2 April proposals for a Franco-Soviet agreement. "I am being warned," he cabled to Moscow, "against new intrigues set in motion by Poland to disrupt the agreement. It [Poland] pushed all the buttons in Paris to influence the French, but Laval still claims that he is now bound by a gentleman's agreement." That would not have been a surprise. The British were apparently likewise at work in Stresa trying to disrupt Franco-Soviet negotiations. "This is also the opinion of Beneš, who has just visited me," Litvinov added.[89] The Eden visit to Moscow was thus already showing signs of being a show.

The British and Poles were not the only ones working against a Franco-Soviet pact. The Quai d'Orsay clerks were planning to reject Litvinov's revised draft of the pact, which he gave to the French in Geneva on the morning of 15 April in preparation for the meeting with Laval on the following day. "It will be blackballed tomorrow," noted René Massigli, deputy head of the French mission in Geneva.[90]

On the morning of 16 April, there remained only fourteen days to the 1 May deadline. That day and the next Litvinov and Laval tried to come to agreement. Laval rejected the Soviet demand for automatic, immediate assistance. Everything was tied up in League statutes and procedures. On 18 April Litvinov reported to Moscow that he and Laval had agreed on a text. Litvinov was not very happy about it:

> He [Laval] was hard on concessions, referring to his earlier proposal to Potemkin; it was the limit, beyond which the Council of Ministers did not authorize him to

> go. In his behaviour and conversations he underlined his complete indifference to the pact which became more noticeable after Stresa, having strengthened French relations not only with England but also with Italy. He said to friends that, with regard to our pact, he felt like a hounded dog.

Laval made some concessions on mutual assistance even without League unanimity and on some changes of formula. He refused immediate assistance before a League decision and the definition of an aggressor. The French were afraid that Germany would see the pact as contrary to the Locarno accords and then denounce them. Laval was also against a guarantee of the Baltic countries. Mutual assistance would come into play only in the event of a direct German attack on France or the USSR. Litvinov opined that the pact as written was "problematic," because of French commitments under the Locarno accords and because of League involvement, and on the Soviet side because of the absence of common frontiers with Germany. It had great political importance, however, in that it would lessen the "temptations" of aggression by Germany, Poland, and Japan. According to Litvinov, it would likewise prevent – and this was highly ironic given the mirror French position – the establishment of close ties between France and Germany. "It is also necessary to take into consideration," Litvinov added, "the adverse effect of a rejection of the pact after all the months of negotiations." This point reflected Titulescu's view. After some further details on procedures, Litvinov said that it was up to the Politburo to decide whether or not to sign the pact.[91] The Politburo responded to Litvinov's request for instructions, by directing him to return to Moscow. "We can approve the text of the treaty … after personal conversations with you, as it is not possible to agree by telegraph on such an important document."[92]

On the following day, 19 April, there was a meeting of the Council of Ministers in Paris. According to Herriot, the war minister, Louis Maurin, did not much believe in the value of the Red Army and feared the influence of Bolshevism on French troops. Louis Marin, a conservative minister without portfolio, approved the pact and even asked for military agreements.[93] There were in effect no provisions in the draft pact for staff talks. Inside the war ministry, opinions were divided in spite of War Minister Maurin's reticence. In one report, covered by a note signed by Maurin on 8 April, the view was positive about different forms of Red Army assistance in the event of war. The passage of Red Army forces through various Eastern European countries was also examined and various scenarios discussed. In short, the study was objective and positive about potential Soviet assistance in the event of war.[94] In another report, only two weeks later, dated 24 April, a rather negative view was taken of the Red Army and a "Russian alliance." A Franco-Soviet pact would, for example, tie France "to a government which betrayed us in the midst of a war, ruined our small investors, whose doctrine is to undermine our institutions and in particular our military institution."[95] What business was it of the war ministry to worry about small holding investors?

Treachery in the Quai d'Orsay

While Litvinov waited for instructions in Geneva, Potemkin returned to Paris on 19 April. "I saw Herriot to whom I said that we were not pleased with the results of the negotiations concerning our pact and that is why we asked for authorization from the Soviet government to sign the draft developed in Geneva, because we did not want the collapse of the agreement knowing that there would be adverse international repercussions." In reply, Herriot promised to push for early approval of the draft. Potemkin had agreed with Laval to see Léger about the final draft to which Laval and Litvinov had agreed in Geneva. Then there was a problem. Potemkin almost immediately noticed that there had been a "significant change" in the draft, which Léger and Jules Basdevant, the Quai d'Orsay solicitor, had made in Paris to the text. The revised language subjected mutual assistance even in the case of sudden attack to League approval. Potemkin considered the revision to a text already approved by Laval and Litvinov in Geneva to be unacceptable. Obviously. This he said to Léger who then tried to haggle for the removal of the word "immediate" from the draft, as in immediate mutual assistance. In other words, Léger was trying to weaken still further mutual assistance in the wording of the pact. Potemkin telephoned Litvinov in Geneva who insisted on the agreed-upon language. Then Laval called to say that the Council of Ministers had approved the text revised by Léger and Basdevant and authorized him to sign. Not before sorting out the disagreement over the unilateral French revisions, Potemkin replied. The draft had already been approved, Laval retorted, it could not be changed now.

In any case, the disagreement was over wording. Potemkin again telephoned Litvinov, who authorized him to say to Laval that the narkom was "astonished" by French methods of negotiation and that it was inadmissible to introduce revisions into an already agreed-upon text. In Moscow there was already dissatisfaction with the draft; there could be no question of aggravating the situation. "Under these conditions Litvinov will return to Moscow and he suggests to Laval that if he wants to respect his obligations … he should also go there with the shortest possible delay to sign the agreement." Potemkin passed on the message to Laval, who, "becoming alarmed," asked him to come at once to the Quai d'Orsay.[96] Readers can certainly see why Laval would be alarmed. This narrative is beginning to resemble a farce only it was getting no laughs. The late Dovgalevskii had once said you could never trust the French to respect an agreement even in the presence of stenographers. Here was a case in point. But there is still more to tell in this *rocambolesque* narrative because Potemkin had yet to describe what happened when he arrived at the Quai d'Orsay.

Laval received Potemkin with Léger present. "He [Laval] was clearly bewildered," Potemkin wrote. "He tried to convince me that there was nothing unacceptable for us in the drafting of the changed protocol, as he looked helplessly at Léger, who was also depressed." Would Litvinov come to Paris from Geneva, Laval asked, obviously hoping that matters could be ironed out with him. In fact, Litvinov had already left for Moscow, and this meant a change of plans in Paris. It was embarrassing because an official lunch planned for Litvinov had to be cancelled. Of course, Laval thought about what they would say to the press that was expecting to have news of the conclusion of the pact. They agreed to say there would be a delay of a few days, and that the pact would be initialled in Paris and signed in Moscow. "From Laval, I went to Herriot," Potemkin wrote in his telegram to Moscow. "It's a catastrophe," Herriot exclaimed after hearing Potemkin's story. Readers can see why Léger and Basdevant had revised an already agreed-upon vitally important treaty text and then tried to present a *fait accompli* to Potemkin. "He [Herriot] said that the Council of Ministers had not been informed by Laval of the details of the negotiations. The pact was presented in general terms and approved unanimously." While Potemkin and Herriot were talking, Herriot received a telephone call from Léger asking him to come at once to the Quai d'Orsay. Herriot then left Potemkin, "promising to straighten matters out before the evening and to berate Laval for committing an 'indiscretion' and causing the greatest harm to France with his 'vulgar policy.'"

About an hour later, Potemkin said, Herriot returned to see him at the embassy. He said that he had just come from Laval having told him that he had "to correct what had been done" before the press got hold of it to make a huge scandal. Herriot brought with him a new version of the text that he himself had suggested and committed to take to the government. He read the text to Potemkin who copied it into his telegram for Moscow. It did not seem like much of an improvement, but Potemkin offered no comment (until he wrote a longer dispatch to Krestinskii). Herriot asked Potemkin to telephone Litvinov at once to assure him of the French government's sincerity and its desire to conclude the negotiations as soon as possible. He even wanted to talk directly to the narkom. In the end, Herriot calmed down and left Potemkin once he had ordered the call to Moscow. Potemkin talked briefly to Krestinskii who said that the file was going to the government, that is, to the Politburo for discussion as soon as Litvinov returned to Moscow. Potemkin also indicated that the French press, including on the right, was expressing concern about Litvinov's failure to come to Paris. Government circles were saying that nothing unusual was going on. The embassy was being careful not to say anything specific except that the Soviet government was studying the Geneva text and would make a decision after having heard Litvinov's report.[97]

Through his contacts in the NKID, Alphand heard about the row in Paris. Laval claimed it was only a disagreement over the language of the treaty, but

Alphand worried that it might be more than that. He noticed Soviet anger, and warned Paris that Stalin could break off negotiations.[98] Potemkin confirmed Alphand's observations in a more detailed dispatch. When Laval first saw Potemkin on 19 April, he did not initially believe that Litvinov had left Geneva for Moscow. After Potemkin finally persuaded him that this was true, Laval tried vainly to convince him that the disagreement was only over wording. As the potential consequences of Litvinov's departure sunk in, Laval's discomfort grew. Potemkin replied that the disagreement was not over words but over the conduct of Léger and Basdevant. Laval stuck to his line, but Potemkin only shrugged and replied that, in any case, Litvinov would make a report to the government and then new instructions would be prepared.

The initial restraint of the French press, which Potemkin reported in his telegram, did not last. Some newspapers reported that Litvinov's refusal to come to Paris was a fit of caprice and due to fault-finding and excessive demands. This sounded like an inspired comment, which could not be left without reply, and Pertinax, Tabouis, and even the socialist leader, Léon Blum, weighed in. What really worried Potemkin, however, were attacks against Laval in the communist daily *L'Humanité*, accusing him of being the "first accomplice of Hitler" and "Laval-*la guerre*." Of course, after 1940-41, these accusations became true, but in 1935, not yet. Laval reacted "painfully" to the assault and was preparing to return fire with an election poster in Aubervilliers attacking the Comintern. In the past, these exchanges had led to anti-communist press campaigns, as Potemkin well knew, one of which contributed in 1927 to the recall of the Soviet polpred. "On the eve of the resumption of our negotiations on the pact," Potemkin observed, "it is hardly possible to observe all these appalling polemics tied to the question of the Franco-Soviet pact, especially when it becomes the property of the street and at the same time raises speculation about the active involvement of the Soviet embassy in it." Matters could easily get out of hand, spreading from Aubervilliers to Paris and to all of France.[99]

If readers are wondering if the Quai d'Orsay made records of Potemkin's conversations with Laval, it appears not. Even if there were such records, they would not have been as revealing as the Soviet accounts given the Quai d'Orsay's duplicity. Nor did Herriot make written records of his meetings with Potemkin. He had virtually taken into his own hands the responsibility for saving the mutual assistance pact, if only in its mutilated form. No wonder Laval was annoyed with him.

Potemkin's telegrams made a very bad impression in Moscow. The behaviour of Laval and his "clerks," Léger and Basdevant, appeared to resemble, at least in Potemkin's telling, a slap-stick American comedy routine, but in Moscow, Stalin and his close colleagues were not laughing. On 20 April the Politburo met again and issued a new directive to Potemkin: "We advise not to commit yourself too much on account of the agreement with the French, and not to rush forward, in order then to be embarrassed if the draft treaty is not approved in Moscow.

This is the second time that we caution you not to rush forward and not to create thereby the illusion that we need the pact more than the French. We are not as weak as some suggest." On the following day, TASS published a brief communiqué, proposed by Stalin and approved by the Politburo: "The negotiations between Comrade Litvinov and Laval have been temporarily suspended. Comrade Litvinov has been recalled to report to the Council of People's Commissars."[100] No wonder Laval backtracked a little, for he might have been forced to resign if the negotiations had collapsed. And there were also the elections in Aubervilliers never far from Laval's mind.

Litvinov was back in Moscow on 22 April, and back in Stalin's office that day and the next, in the company of Krestinskii, all told for about three hours. On two previous occasions, it had been Stalin who reined in Litvinov's anger with the French, now it was Litvinov's turn to calm Stalin's anger. On 23 April he sent a briefing note to Stalin and the Politburo's inner circle on how to fix the wording of the draft agreement with which Léger and Basdevant had tampered. These were revisions agreed to at a meeting the previous day.[101] Litvinov also submitted a discussion paper arguing for approval of the draft text. Readers should forebear if I go into some detail, for Litvinov's observations are of considerable interest. "I think the recall to Moscow was correct and it corresponded to my own wishes," Litvinov began: "This may be explained rather by my personal feelings: I did not want to go to Paris, and, in addition, I was furious at the attempts by the French to change seemingly agreed-upon texts."

The French were acting in bad faith. Readers may remember that Quai d'Orsay officials, especially Léger and Bargeton, had always opposed bilateral mutual assistance. They sabotaged Paul-Boncour's movement in that direction and could get away with it because the French cabinet was about to fall. Now they worked for Laval, who led their activities. To tamper with an agreed-upon text was to show disrespect to Soviet diplomats, to treat them in effect, like amateurs who could be "swindled" – a word which Stalin liked to use – at the very last minute. In times of danger, allies have to trust one another. How could Soviet diplomats trust the French? The answer is obvious, but in 1935, the Soviet side did not have other options.

Litvinov's Logic

Let us therefore return to Litvinov's arguments in favour of agreement with the French. We are not going to obtain further concessions from the French, he said first of all. "There is also a danger that many opponents of the Soviet-French pact will try to use the hitch and press all the springs to break the pact. Among its external enemies, in order of importance, are Poland, Germany, England, and Italy. The Turks, our 'friends,' also seem to be unhappy." Then there were the opponents of the pact inside France. Litvinov gained the impression in Geneva that France had little interest in the pact: "Until now Laval's eyes have been turned towards Berlin, and in fact he would be happy if the pact was derailed without it being possible to reproach him personally." According to Laval, Flandin himself was behind the tampering with the draft text (although this might have been Laval's attempt to throw responsibility to higher authority (Flandin then being président du Conseil). In any case, Flandin, as Litvinov saw it, would only agree to terms that did not arouse British objections.

Herriot, of course, strongly supported the pact, but he was not very influential in the cabinet, and more or less defended Laval's position with respect to the text. So, apparently, did Mandel. As for other ministers, nothing leaked out. Among former ministers, "defenders" of the USSR, there was little support. "In the opinion of our Paris comrades," Litvinov continued, "the pact is not very popular among the intelligentsia, or among the petty bourgeoisie, or even among workers (non-communist)." Apart from communists, and even not some of them, no one loved the Franco-Soviet pact. Litvinov wrote that Il'ia G. Ehrenburg, a Soviet journalist, "told me that he recently visited the northern departments of France, most affected by the World War, and there workers expressed fears that the pact would hasten war with Germany. It was even said, 'Let Germany fight against the Soviets, it will in the worst case weaken Germany.' Most of the supporters of the pact are on the right."

This must have been sobering reading for Stalin and the troika (Molotov, Voroshilov, and Kaganovich). But Litvinov was not finished yet with his discouraging analysis. "Generally, the [French] government considers itself morally committed, and even would not want to forsake the pact, so as at least to make our agreement with Germany impossible, but the pact should not impose too many obligations on France. The characteristic expression of Laval and Léger, often used by them, is 'we have to sign something.'" In the back of Laval's mind was always Germany. He would do nothing to provoke them, or especially to give them a pretext to denounce the Locarno accords. Laval would sacrifice the pact, if there were any danger of that. However, that option was not in his plan while he did not see the outlines of some agreement with Germany. "The best thing for Laval," Litvinov wrote, "would be to drag out the negotiations in the hope that with the help of England, Germany will make France some tempting offers. That's why my departure to Moscow rather disturbed Laval." Although Litvinov did not say it, he did not need to; if Franco-Soviet negotiations collapsed, Laval would lose his main trump with Germany.

Litvinov explained his strategy for negotiating with Laval. Essentially, the text developed in Geneva resembled what Léger had earlier proposed to Barthou and then during Litvinov's last trip to Geneva (in February):

> We considered it desirable to make some amendments to [the French] proposals. In offering these amendments, I knew in advance that not all of them would be

> acceptable for France, and some of them I considered only chips for bargaining. For example, the French strongly rejected automatic immediate assistance and our definition of aggression. Both contradict the Locarno agreements. However, we have achieved agreement on the optionality of unanimity decisions for the [League] Council, and this is extremely important. Laval had to agree with me that the requirement of unanimity of the Council would make our assistance highly problematic.

Litvinov did not make too much of the French textual changes, which were intended to underline no automatic assistance. But he also raised other issues with Laval, and, not surprisingly, returned again to the question of security in the Baltics. Litvinov proposed that in the event of Soviet action in the Baltics to counter a German threat, it should be considered a trigger for French obligations to the USSR under the pact. Laval categorically refused this proposal. Litvinov then said that in a similar case in the west if France were to go to the aid, say, of Belgium, or was to enter the demilitarized Rhineland, the Soviet Union would not be obliged to intervene against Germany. Laval immediately agreed to this interpretation. "Next, I proposed," Litvinov continued, "a protocol on most favoured nation, that is, in the event that France concluded a pact with a third state and interpreted the charter of the League in the direction of automaticity, this interpretation would pass to our pact. In Geneva, Laval and Léger accepted this offer, but, having arrived in Paris, they took their consent back."

It was an extraordinary thing that Laval should refuse Litvinov's offer of Soviet security guarantees, in effect, along France's eastern borders with Belgium, the demilitarized Rhineland and even with Switzerland. How could the Baltics be a larger stake for France than Belgium? The British objected for one thing, and incidentally the Foreign Office heard via its Moscow embassy, from Alphand, that when the French refused the Baltic guarantee, the Soviet side "refused to guarantee Belgium."[102] When it came down to fundamentals, the French like the British were afraid of losing the Baltic and Polish barriers to Soviet expansion towards the west. If a Franco-Soviet pact pushed Poland into the arms of Germany, as one French report noted, the USSR would not need to request Polish authorization for passage of the Red Army.[103] Nor, in fact, would France need to be further concerned. The French government could never bring itself to go that far.

Litvinov concluded his report to the Politburo with the observation that the hollow shell of the pact was better than nothing:

> I can only repeat my earlier expressed point of view. We should not place serious hopes on the pact in the sense of actual military assistance in case of war. Our security remains in the first place in the hands of the Red Army. The pact for us has a predominantly political value, reducing the chances of war not only from

> Germany, but also from Poland and Japan. In addition, the pact may prove to be an obstacle to the implementation of Poland's ambition to create an anti-Soviet bloc of Poland, Germany, and France, plus some other countries. If you take this point of view, then this or that formulation of articles and protocols significantly loses its importance.[104]

The Politburo accepted Litvinov's arguments to take the empty shell of a pact as opposed to no pact at all. On 23 April Litvinov sent instructions to Potemkin with maximum and minimum positions for agreement. The Soviet side still sought a French guarantee for the Baltics in exchange for a reciprocal Soviet guarantee for Belgium, but if the French refused the Baltics, then the Soviet side would refuse Belgium. Litvinov still wanted a most favoured nation clause, but refused any wording that would require a reference to the "Locarno powers" for mutual assistance. He proposed alternative wording in some places to remove what amounted to French escape clauses. He instructed Potemkin to push for the maximum Soviet desideratum and accept the minimum, which was closer to what the French demanded.[105]

The negotiations resumed in Paris to settle the remaining differences. Laval did not inform Alphand of the detailed exchanges with Potemkin and still insisted that remaining differences were over drafting of the final text of agreement.[106] On 24 April, Litvinov met Alphand and there the ambassador received a version of the negotiations that did not fit in with Laval's explanations. The narkom said he had the impression that the French government was no longer bringing to negotiations an "indispensable, sincere collaboration." French negotiators had pulled out of the agreement what was advantageous to the Soviet side. "We want a serious, loyal agreement capable of keeping the peace," Litvinov said. "We do not need simple appearances of satisfaction. It is necessary for the two sides to obtain concrete advantages." According to Alphand, Litvinov suggested a Soviet concern about the western signatories of the Locarno accords turning a blind eye to German expansion in the east. What could Alphand say? He knew nothing about Sargent's position as head of the Central Department in the Foreign Office. The Quai d'Orsay had not kept him informed about the negotiations, but he insisted on the French government's desire to reach agreement.[107]

English Sabotage

Litvinov would not have accepted such assurances without Potemkin's confirmation, and that he did not get. On 27 April, Potemkin sent an urgent telegram, saying that the British chargé d'affaires Ronald Campbell had called at the Quai d'Orsay on instructions from Simon to express concerns about the absence of references to the League of Nations in the wording of the pact agreement. On this point, the Foreign Office was misinformed. Apparently, Campbell had proposed that the pact be framed not only within League statutes but also within the terms of the Locarno accords to which the USSR was not a signatory. Campbell spoke to Laval on 19 April based on the Foreign Office instructions. It was in the midst of Potemkin's clashes with Laval and Léger. In fact, Laval hid from Campbell, or rather deceived him about the "hitch" in negotiations. "The Russians were making difficulties as they were not satisfied with what they were getting," Laval claimed. As readers will understand, the "hitch" was caused by French tampering with the already agreed-upon draft.[108]

The Soviet embassy's information was correct about the attempted British sabotage. Sargent inspired the instructions to the Paris embassy, approved by Simon, to remind the French government not to go beyond its Locarno obligations in any pact with the Soviet authorities. Vansittart appears to have been backed into a corner. The split between Vansittart and Sargent was creating problems in Foreign Office messaging. There were zigs and zags. Maiskii heard about Campbell's démarche, and saw Vansittart on 26 April to ask if the British government would oppose the Franco-Soviet and Czech-Soviet mutual assistance pacts, then nearing conclusion. "I asked the question twice," reported Maiskii, but both times Vansittart repeated that the British government would not oppose the pacts, and that this was "not only his personal opinion, but also the opinion of the government." Vansittart cautioned that it was "very important" to keep the pacts "'within the bounds of the League of Nations, for this mystical phrase, as he put it, will greatly facilitate favourable or at least tolerant opinion towards the pacts in British political and press circles." He did not say one word about Sargent.[109]

"About this [British] démarche," Potemkin advised, "it was clearly prepared with the French themselves, Léger triumphantly said today to Laval in my presence. In our present negotiations, Laval has all the time hidden behind the English and their warnings. I communicate this [information] to give you a clearer idea of the atmosphere of the negotiations."[110] Léger behaved "triumphantly," said Potemkin, as if the British should have the last word. The negotiations took on the appearance of a contest where the Soviet side was trying to trick France into accepting a genuine alliance against a mortal enemy and the French had to outsmart their Soviet counterparts, as if the pact was of little use to France, and as if the French were doing the USSR a favour. According to Clerk, the British ambassador in Paris, the French might make some "slight" concessions to allow the Soviet side to "save face." They had "the worst of the bargain," according to Laval, as if boasting. "If it came to the point, French assistance would be of immeasurably greater advantage to Russia than Russian assistance would be to France."[111] In the spring of 1940, when it did "come to the point," France might have saved itself with a strong Soviet ally. When readers think about the markers on the French road to collapse in 1940, start here in the spring of 1935, when Laval and Léger argued with aplomb that *they* were doing the USSR a favour by signing the Franco-Soviet pact. Remember, the USSR stood the test of war; France did not.

It appears that no one on the French side told the British that Léger and Basdevant had tampered with an agreed-upon text, and that it was this crude legerdemain and not Litvinov's "huff" that had caused the "eleventh-hour hitch" and the "stiffening" of the Soviet position. When Ambassador Clerk asked about this puzzling situation, Léger replied that it could be attributed in part to "oriental methods of bargaining" and a Soviet-German "flirtation" over a trade agreement.[112] As Léger knew very well, the hitch was of his making, and the flirt was no flirt at all, as Litvinov had earlier instructed Potemkin to say to the French. Léger was not just avoiding the truth, which is considered acceptable diplomatic practice; he was lying, which is not.

The Franco-Soviet Pact

Laval and Potemkin finally came to terms on 30 April. They signed the pact officially in Paris on 2 May. The late Jean-Baptiste Duroselle called it "a *chef d'oeuvre* of rigmarole."[113]

That was about right. Litvinov did not feel like it was a triumph. "In view of Laval's intransigence during the negotiations and the methods he used," Litvinov wrote to Potemkin, "I could not bring myself to write the superfluous 'cordial' telegram to him. In order not to irritate him too much, I found it necessary to refrain from sending a telegram to Herriot. I am glad that you remembered about him. During Laval's stay here I will find an occasion to mention Herriot publicly."[114] That would be just to rub it in, knowing how much Laval resented Herriot's involvement.

In the meantime, Litvinov reacted electrically to the news of British meddling, sending a telegram to Maiskii to ask what was going on. "We also have information from other sources about English pressure with the objective of wrecking the pact." Go see Vansittart, he instructed.[115]

In the Foreign Office

Vansittart once again reassured Maiskii, adding that the Soviet side was overreacting. You are "too suspicious," he said. "Of course, in England," he added, "there are people who want and consider possible an agreement with Germany. Important educational work is still necessary for the appropriate restructuring of British public opinion."[116] On 2 May, Simon reinforced Vansittart's position by declaring in the House of Commons that the Franco-Soviet pact was acceptable to the British government.[117] Mark up a win for Vansittart and a loss for Sargent.

Figure 12.3. Potemkin and Laval in Paris sign the Franco-Soviet pact with officials looking on, 2 May 1935, AVPRF.

Litvinov followed up with Maiskii after the dust had settled:

> There can be no doubt that the démarche of the English chargé d'affaires in Paris was intended to hamper negotiations on the pact, and this goal was indeed achieved. The French trumpeted this démarche in reinforcing their position against our amendments. For clarification, I must say that we did not seek automatic assistance, but only objected to attempts by the French to underline too sharply the lack of obligations for automatic assistance. But this is already a matter of the past.

As for the pact itself, Litvinov said to Maiskii what he had said in his briefing paper to Stalin: "One should judge the pact not from the point of view of possible military actions, but from the political effect that it will produce, and on the role that it can play in the matter of discouraging the aggressors from adventures." As if looking for the bright side of things, Litvinov observed that there was never any formal alliance between the tsarist government and France, only an exchange of notes and agreements between the general staffs. Moreover, since the USSR has no common frontier with Germany, it "puts us in a more advantageous position in comparison with France."[118]

Vansittart's assurances to Maiskii irritated Sargent. As far as he was concerned, Simon's statement in the House – Vansittart's win – did not change his view that Litvinov had "browbeat the French, in a moment of panic," into concluding "a one-sided bargain."[119] This was not what had happened. Sargent's minutes were one of many he left in the files in his campaign against Franco-Soviet cooperation. He did not share Litvinov's view of Hitler, bent on war, nor did he agree with the concept of the indivisibility of peace. He thought an Eastern Pact, or even worse, a bilateral Franco-Soviet pact would be a provocation to Germany and lead to a pre-1914 polarization of Europe into two opposing coalitions of states. The French were coming around to see the dangers, as Sargent saw them, and it was about time. They wanted to avoid "an all-embracing alliance if they could help it, especially as they realized that such an alliance would shock and offend Great Britain." The prospects were "so horrible" that the British government should press the French to adopt new policies. "We too have means of influencing the French Government, and British support and approval is still of great value to France."[120] This assessment was certainly correct. It was about the only element of his analysis that Sargent got right.

Eduard Beneš and the Pact with Czechoslovakia

Once the Franco-Soviet pact was concluded, the question of mutual assistance with Czechoslovakia immediately arose. Czechoslovak interest in better relations with the USSR began after Hitler took power in Germany. Czechoslovakia had a long frontier with Germany and a sizeable, disloyal German population in the Sudeten territories. In April 1934, Titulescu was not the only one who wanted to talk to Shtein in Geneva. Eduard Beneš, the Czechoslovak foreign minister, also did, and wanted to discuss the establishment of diplomatic relations. He was a man in a hurry: "Time does not wait, circumstances are becoming complicated and the danger from the direction of Germany is growing." In Czechoslovakia everyone understands, Beneš continued, "what a mistake they had made in not renewing relations with the USSR several years ago." The Czechoslovaks, even more than the French, should have sensed the danger. Germany was rapidly rearming. "Time does not wait," Beneš repeated. "All German tactics are based on the *fait accompli*."[121] This was true.

In June 1934 the Czechoslovak government extended diplomatic recognition to the USSR. A Czechoslovak-Soviet rapprochement developed for the same reason that other European states began to look to the USSR as a potential ally. The main Czechoslovak interlocutor with the Soviet side was Beneš. Litvinov thought he was an impossible dreamer, who sinned too much on the side of optimism, which led him into errors of judgment and policy.[122] Beneš was born in 1884, the son of a Bohemian peasant in the Austro-Hungarian Empire. He was highly educated, having studied philosophy, sociology, and law. During his studies, he spent a number of years in Paris. He was a lecturer in sociology at Charles

University in Prague before the First World War changed everything for him. He became an organizer of the Czecho-Slovak independence movement and ended up in exile in Paris in 1915. There he participated in the organization of the Czechoslovak National Council and a Czechoslovak Legion organized in Russia to fight against Austria-Hungary. In the spring of 1918, the Legion, then spread out along the Trans-Siberian Railway, en route for France via Vladivostok, was co-opted and suborned into fighting against the new Soviet government, with help from French diplomats who passed at least 15 million roubles to young Czechoslovak officers eager to prove their value to France and its allies. Czechoslovak soldiers were effective when they fought undisciplined and poorly trained Red Guards, but not so valiant when they faced War Commissar Trotskii's better disciplined Red Army. The Czechoslovak legionnaires fled eastward and eventually bought their way out of Siberia with gold captured from Soviet authorities in Kazan and with the White Guard commander Kolchak. It was not a glorious chapter in the history of the Czechoslovak independence movement.[123] The Siberian fiasco left a legacy of Soviet-Czechoslovak hostility that lasted until the rise of Hitler encouraged a re-evaluation of Czechoslovak security interests.

In 1935, Beneš spent a lot of time with the Soviet polpred in Prague, Sergei Sergeievich Aleksandrovskii. If you want to know what Beneš thought about any particular issue, Aleksandrovskii's frequent reports of conversation are a valuable source. Beneš was a talker and Aleksandrovskii wrote down in detail what he had to say. On Poland, Beneš was unsympathetic. One had to be on guard, to expect "any sort of tricks." Poland was making the same mistake it had made in the eighteenth century: pursuing "a policy of permanent enemies and permanent quarrels with all its neighbours." Towards the Czechslovaks it bore a "deeply engrained, poorly hidden hostility." During the Versailles conference in 1919, the French elite, as Beneš saw it, believed that Poland could replace Russia as a European counterweight. This idea was based on two premises: that Russia for fifty years was "dead" as an international factor and that Germany likewise would not renew itself for thirty years. There was time for Poland to grow into its role as a Russian "surrogate." In fact, according to Beneš, Poland could not be an effective counterweight against Germany or a barrier against the USSR. It could only justify its further existence as a German *place d'armes* for an attack against the USSR.

As for the Soviet Union, Beneš believed that it was resuming its place as a European power. No problem in Europe could be resolved without its "active participation" or against its will. No one should have any doubts about the role of the USSR in maintaining the peace in Europe.[124] The Rome and London accords were not going to protect the security of Eastern Europe. Beneš shared Litvinov's view that to secure European peace would be a "difficult task," requiring a policy of *Durchhalten*, of sticking it out. Beneš was quick to say that he harboured no "scepticism" about France, but that did not relieve him of the necessity to follow closely the evolution of the European political situation. As for Britain, "public opinion" would not support "direct and public engagement in European affairs." It was a considerable achievement that the British government had agreed to the London communiqué (in February 1935). Beneš defended Laval, saying to Aleksandrovskii that he had just spoken to him on the telephone. It was 6 February. Laval gave the same assurances to Beneš that he had given to Potemkin, essentially that he would do nothing "behind the backs" of the USSR and Czechoslovakia. On this point, Aleksandrovskii interjected "that such statements have to be believed, but that faith is not ruled out by doubt and especially the desire to know with certainty." Beneš, of course agreed, repeating his belief in the need for vigilance and a close monitoring of events. He distinguished between the "subjective sincerity" of France, Laval in effect, and "objective circumstances" that might lead to a change in the former "sincerity."[125]

Aleksandrovskii continued his discussions with Beneš after conveying to him Litvinov's doubts about the London communiqué and British attempts to push the French away from the Eastern Pact, Vansittart's views notwithstanding. Beneš agreed with Litvinov's concerns. He seemed to believe that the British did not oppose the French position on the Eastern Pact, which might actually have been true if one considered Léger's opposition to it, about which neither Beneš nor Aleksandrovskii were informed. Beneš acknowledged that "we would all be naïve politicians" if we did not believe that the British *might* in fact be opposed to the Eastern Pact. Here, Beneš seemed to be equivocating. Nevertheless, the Czechoslovak minister in London had been talking to Vansittart who had tried to be reassuring. That was, of course, Vansittart's job, but remember, he was not the minister; he was a civil servant, and what he said might or might not be representative of cabinet policies.

Concerning Laval, Beneš had this to say, according to Aleksandrovskii: "As for the fact that Laval should not trust the British or conduct further negotiations with Germany through them, Beneš counts on the continuous jealousy of the French towards the English in everything that concerns Germany. According to Beneš, Laval in any case will not leave the matter in the hands of the British, if he believes that France will have to make even the slightest concessions." This estimate soon proved to be wrong for Laval did, in fact, leave the initiative to the British to conduct negotiations with Germany. Beneš was often wrong about French policy, and that would become a large European tragedy. Aleksandrovskii did not comment on French policy, but then reported this bit of wisdom from his interlocutor: "It is always more advantageous, and even more so for France in its position, to make a concession directly to an adversary and to use this for the praise of its [i.e., French] policy rather than to leave the laurels for some intermediary to reap … Beneš thinks Laval will not let the initiative fall from his hands." In fact, who could say what Laval would do? Benéš, in any case, insisted on the need for clarity in all the current negotiations. This was preaching to the converted. "It is necessary first of all to convey to France, so to speak, the need for clarity and in this Beneš sees his task and the task of the USSR." He had even warned Laval in Geneva that if France did not conclude an agreement with the USSR, Romania would necessarily go with Germany. This was also Titulescu's view.

This particular conversation was not quite over, for Beneš, speaking of Romania, took a run at Titulescu who he saw as a rival interlocutor with France. This is amusing for Titulescu reciprocated the feelings. Beneš saw Titulescu as too "temperamental," too direct, and too noisy. You cannot threaten the French, or try to tempt them with "brash promises," or throw tantrums to get their attention. "They say that the French know Beneš well and really value his quiet and peaceful manner to discuss this or the other vital interests of Czechoslovakia." Beneš did not like to speak ill of "his personal friend Titulescu," but he did all the same, commenting that Titulescu did not know how to conduct himself with the French. Titulescu, on the other hand, complained to Litvinov about Beneš, which prompted the narkom to opine that relations between the two ministers "left much to be desired." In Geneva Titulescu complained of Beneš's "pliability and inclination to compromise."[126] In other words, he was too quick to fold his position.

In fact, Litvinov was delighted with Titulescu's activities. "In Geneva, he had come straight away to see me at my hotel," Litvinov advised. This was on 21 February. Titulescu had just come from a conference of the Little Entente in Ljubljana where it had supported Soviet policy. This was just what was needed in dealing with Laval. According to Litvinov, Titulescu pursued the "strongest and most friendly policy" towards the USSR of the Little Entente ministers. Titulescu pursued this policy with little support at home. Indeed, for his own security he felt safer abroad than he did in Bucharest.[127] Titulescu was like the little Dutch boy who put his finger in the dyke to keep it from crumbling before the deluge. Alphand was sceptical that he could hold back the tide. "It would be sufficient," he told Rubinin, "for Titulescu to go, and Romanian policy could change drastically."[128] That was also Titulescu's view.

The quarrel between Beneš and Titutlescu had more to do with pride of place than it did about policy. They both held to the same course, or at least that is what they said. Titulescu was clear on policy towards the Soviet Union. Here is what Beneš had to say in a further conversation with Aleksandrovskii. It was after Eden had passed through Prague on his way back to London from Moscow and Warsaw. Beneš said, "England could not isolate itself from direct participation in European affairs." One could not "dream" of peace and security in Eastern Europe without lending a hand to protect it. "Peace is absolutely indivisible," he said to Eden, borrowing a line from Litvinov: there cannot be peace in the west of Europe if there is no peace in the east of Europe. It was a good line and true too, as events would demonstrate. According to Beneš, Eden "fully understood" him.[129] Maybe, but that did not mean Eden invested in the idea, or that the cabinet in London did either. Beneš certainly knew what to say about peace and security in Europe, but he did not always know what to *do* to protect it.

Aleksandrovskii had a certain sympathy for Beneš, though he did not believe he was someone to count on. Titulescu was right about him. "To clarify the atmosphere in which my conversations with Beneš take place," Aleksandrovskii reported to Litvinov,

> I must say that Beneš is all the time obviously impersonating our lines. He is always and invariably excited about your considerations and immediately expresses his full agreement with them. He immediately "understands and recognizes" everything, however, as soon as he begins to develop his own course of thought, he at once falls into either official, sometimes very naive optimism, or begins to engage in politics more like political intrigues, in which too much happens because of personalities, their qualities, connections, sympathies, etc.

Beneš had placed all his chips on France, according to Aleksandrovskii, and now he was not so sure. He "feels that his elementary, basic line of conduct, a one hundred percent bet on the role of French vassal, is now heavily blotted."

> I feel at times from him the direct confusion of a man lost between three pines. Of course, I do not want to say that Beneš has lost in some measure his bearings, or that he does not understand the international situation. Such an assertion would only be to say that on Beneš reflects strongly the difficult international situation of Czechoslovakia, in the face of which he has largely lost his former aplomb and is far from being so definite in his judgements about the alignment of forces on his chessboard.[130]

Aleksandrovskii's comment about the Czechoslovak minister's attachment to France was apposite. In mid-April, Beneš was in Geneva. He repeated to René Massigli what he had already said to Laval and Léger, that is, "that he does not want to commit himself in regard to the USSR more than France itself does. He has therefore decided to sign a text identical to that which France will sign."[131] In Massigli's record of conversation with Beneš, one gains the impression of someone trying to curry favour. Aleksandrovskii's characterization of Beneš as a French vassal thus appears about right.

Beneš also advised Litvinov that he would only sign a text identical to the French. Czechoslovakia would render assistance to the USSR only together with France, but not alone. Beneš feared that if Czechoslovakia had to go to war with Germany without France, and in the absence of a common Soviet frontier with Germany, it could suffer the same fate (or defeat) as Serbia during the Great War. This danger, Litvinov noted, was without basis because Germany could "deal" with Czechoslovakia in short order. With regard to Poland, Beneš was willing to discuss the possibility of mutual assistance in the case of a Polish attack but he did not think this would be accepted in Prague. Litvinov asked for instructions, but opined that it was unnecessary to insist on mutual assistance against Poland. On this telegram, Stalin scrawled that the question of an agreement with Czechoslovakia should be put off until Litvinov returned to Moscow for consultations.[132]

It was on 3 May, having learned of the signing of the Franco-Soviet pact in Paris, that Beneš called in Aleksandrovskii to discuss an agreement mirroring the Franco-Soviet pact.[133] He had already thought out his position, *mutatis mutandis*, with Massigli and Litvinov in Geneva. Beneš asked for two amendments to the French-based text: (1) that Czechoslovakia should not have an obligation to come to Soviet assistance in the event of a Soviet–Polish war; and (2) that the operation of the pact be placed within the framework of the 1925 Locarno accords. Once again, Litvinov advised Stalin to agree: the French had approved and it would thus be hard to refuse to proceed. According to Litvinov, he had already informed Beneš that the two pacts could not be identical since Czechoslovakia was not a signatory of the Locarno accords. Repeating what he said to Litvinov in Geneva, Beneš told Aleksandrovskii that "Czechoslovakia could offer help only in those cases where such help is also offered by France." The Soviet Union had no common border with Germany, and, in the case of war, Czechoslovakia would quickly be defeated unless France entered the fighting against Germany. Beneš had another motive, as he told Massigli in April: he did not wish to go further than France in his commitments to the Soviet Union, and inclusion of the reference to Locarno would have added a further limitation on Czechoslovak obligations. Like Laval, Beneš wanted the treaty to be directed only against Germany and not against Poland. This might be dangerous, Litvinov observed, since Czechoslovakia could find itself without allies in the case of Polish aggression and thus be "crushed." Beneš admitted that the Soviet observation had merit and he promised to think it over, but Litvinov did not believe that the Czechoslovak government would change its position. As Litvinov put it to Potemkin, the Czechoslovaks want the same "narrow" terms as the French, and these circumstances "compel us to be cautious."[134]

On 4 May, the Politburo approved the text of the pact but with the inclusion of a stipulation that Soviet aid to the victim of aggression was conditional on France also rendering such aid.[135] The French did not want a pact with firm commitments; Beneš did not want one without France, and under the circumstances neither did the Politburo. The position of France was therefore critical: if it did not render assistance, Czechoslovakia could face an aggressor alone. In fact, the Soviet Union could never play an effective role in mutual assistance without full French *and* British approval. Without it, the Little and Balkan

Ententes would not commit themselves to a Soviet alliance. Even Czechoslovakia, which needed that alliance most of all, shied away. All this was not the doing of the Soviet side, which pressed as hard as it could to get a French commitment to a real alliance. It was the four-flushers, Laval, Léger, Bargeton, and Basdevant, among others, who rejected the Soviet offered alliance, encouraged and pressured by the Foreign Office, Vansittart's position notwithstanding.

Laval Visits Moscow

Laval stopped off in Warsaw on his way to Moscow where he met Beck and others but not Piłsudski, who was on his deathbed and died on 12 May. Laval boasted about having reduced the language of the Franco-Soviet pact to wobbles. He did not wish to give to French policy "an allure Russophile." France "absolutely did not have pro-Soviet tendencies."[136] This was music to Beck's ears – *finis* Barthou's policy – but really, how could anyone trust Laval?

On 13 May, Laval arrived in Moscow where he was well received with flags, bands, a drive through Moscow crowds, and banquets. Laval's visit was more ceremony than business. He had two formal meetings, one at the NKID with Litvinov, Krestinskii, and Potemkin and the other at the Kremlin with Stalin and Molotov. At the Kremlin everyone was smiling. Looking at the official photograph, you would never know the pact turned out to be a junk agreement.

No records were kept of either meeting. Krestinskii wrote to Maiskii that Laval brought up the issue of the tsarist debts, but that discussion did not go very far. Stalin waved it off, saying in effect that it was a dead issue, and that in any case the French themselves did not pay their debts. "When Laval said that the French payments to the Americans are linked to receiving payments from the Germans, Comrade Stalin jokingly said," according to Krestinskii, "that we too are ready to discuss questions about debts, linking them to losses from [the foreign] intervention. If the French are willing to cover these losses, we, perhaps, could talk about debts." Laval then beat a hasty retreat. Krestinskii had the impression that Laval himself did not take the issue seriously, but raised it to say back in Paris that he had done so.[137] According to Potemkin, Laval himself raised the question of staff talks to strengthen the Franco-Soviet military cooperation. The French high command had not been informed of Laval's discussions in Moscow, but was open to the idea, waiting only for Laval's authorization to begin them. As was typical of Laval, after returning to Paris, he delayed the start of military conversations.[138] Stalin agreed to a joint communiqué that included a paragraph supporting French national defence.[139] The exiled Trotskii was appalled, but why not support French national defence, since it was a question of organizing an anti-Nazi alliance? Well, for Stalin, that was the objective, but who could say about Laval? As for Trotskii, what he thought was irrelevant, except to reinforce Stalin's determination to eliminate him.

Figure 12.4. Stalin and Laval meeting in Moscow with (from left to right) Alphand, Léger, Litvinov, Potemkin, and Molotov, May 1935, AVPRF.

Maiskii later heard, third hand, that Stalin had been blunt with Laval. The latter, immediately after the opening exchange of compliments and *politesse*, expressed his satisfaction that the Franco-Soviet pact was not directed against any particular country.

"What do you mean, not directed?" Stalin replied: "On the contrary, it is directed and very much directed against one specific country – Germany."

"Laval was rather taken aback, but immediately tried to regroup and with that same charming politeness began to express pleasure about the frankness of Stalin. So, they say, only true friends may speak like that."

Stalin interjected: "You were just now in Poland. What is happening there?"

Laval: "While a pro-German mood in Poland is still strong, there are signs of improvement, which will gradually lead to a change in Polish policy ..."

Stalin interrupted: "In my opinion, there are no such signs. You are a friend of the Poles, *try to convince them that they are playing a ruinous game. The Germans will deceive them and lead them on. They will draw Poland into an adventure, and when Poland weakens, they will then take it or will share it with some other power* [emphasis added]. Why do the Poles need this?"

Laval was again taken aback by Stalin's candor, and changed the subject, turning to the Catholic Church. He wondered whether Stalin could not find a "bridge" to the Pope to conclude some kind of a pact.

Stalin smiling: "A pact? A pact with the Pope? No, not a chance. We conclude pacts only with those who have armies, and the Roman Pope, in so far as I know, does not have an army."[140]

On his way back through Poland for Piłsudski's funeral, Laval said that he was in no way opposed to a "Franco-German entente." If war broke out, Laval commented, "we will be invaded by Bolshevism."[141] As for Stalin's advice to Laval to warn the Poles against their folly, he did nothing of the kind. That was Laval for you, showing his true colours – impossible to trust.

Chapter Thirteen

No Bridging the Gap: Erosion of the Anglo-Soviet Rapprochement, 1935

The Anglo-German naval agreement did not shatter the Anglo-Soviet rapprochement, though it aggravated Soviet mistrust of the British government. Vansittart, still pressing the case for good relations with the USSR, was frustrated by his inability to make the government see the urgency of rearmament against Nazi Germany. We need to keep the Soviet "friendly," he said, and "we should not be led astray in pursuit of the 'jack-o-lantern' of placating Hitler." The pro-Germans at the *Times* and in the House of Lords were "living in a fool's paradise." Only "timely realism" could lead the way out of "that dangerous realm." "There is not a week to lose," Vansittart later noted in his minutes, "in rearming against Germany."[1]

Maiskii's Discussions in London

Vansittart appeared to hold the government on course – if only barely. He also had to steady Maiskii, discouraged by the Anglo-German naval agreement. This was the purpose of a meeting on 9 July, a little more than a year after their first discussion about improving relations. First, Vansittart dismissed rumours – he assumed Maiskii had heard of them – that he was going to be named British ambassador in Paris. "Well wishers … dreaming," according to Vansittart. He was not leaving London. At the apogee of his influence in the Office, who were the "well wishers" trying to push him out the door only three months after Eden's visit to Moscow? Was a sour Sargent involved? "Out of the question," Vansittart said about Paris, but readers should note that his position was not as strong as it seemed. Vansittart also wanted to reassure Maiskii about Hoare. He is a "realist" and that meant "anti-German and pro-French." There was not going to be any change in British foreign policy. That was Vansittart's opinion, but how long could he hold the government on a course that was already wobbling?

Maiskii wanted to talk about the Anglo-German naval agreement: "The events of the past weeks had caused me great embarrassment. The naval agreement was undoubtedly a rupture of the Stresa Front ... Involuntarily, every outside observer had the impression that since the arrival of the new boss in the Foreign Office, British foreign policy has undergone major changes. Just two months ago, England, together with France and Italy, categorically denounced the unilateral violation of the Treaty of Versailles by Germany, and on 18 June, it [England] itself authorized such a unilateral violation." In so doing, the British government had undone much of the goodwill it had earned over the last year or so in Moscow, and strengthened the prestige of Nazi Germany.[2] Vansittart defended the naval agreement – even a mangy sheep gives a tuft of wool (*s parshivoi ovtsy khot' sherst klok*) – it was better than nothing. One had to give Herr Hitler the benefit of the doubt, which sounded like a hollow excuse coming from Vansittart. Maiskii reckoned there were electoral considerations, according to Beaverbrook's view, of winning the pacifist vote. There was also a loss of belief in collective security, though Maiskii might have added that the Foreign Office had never invested in it. He would have been even more disillusioned had he known of Sargent's vociferous memoranda and minutes. Maiskii reckoned that anti-Soviet politics still held sway. Why not let Germany strengthen its position in the Baltic? That would be a Soviet problem.[3]

In July, Hoare and Prime Minister Baldwin met Maiskii one after the other. The meeting with Hoare was discouraging. In the early summer of 1935 the prospects of an Italian invasion of Abyssinia (the Ethiopian Empire) began to turn up in Maiskii's correspondence. Hoare raised the subject during their conversation. War in Africa was inevitable, he thought, which could only serve German interests and destabilize European security. The conversation eventually turned to security in Western and Eastern Europe. The Eastern Pact looked dead – in fact, it was long dead – and Hoare admitted that the British government might contemplate an air pact in the West. He insisted that a separate Anglo-German pact was "unthinkable," but Maiskii was doubtful and warned Litvinov that Hoare appeared ready to contemplate some kind of "compromise" agreement with Germany based on Western security. Only the French or British "Francophiles" could discourage such a development.[4]

A meeting with Prime Minister Baldwin seemed to go better a few days later. Maiskii stressed the danger of Germany and Japan, along the lines of discussions with Vansittart. He added Italy to the list, given the impending "Abyssinian problem." On the latter issue, Baldwin expressed his agreement. Maiskii stressed the importance of the formation of a large coalition of small and large states to preserve peace and security. When Maiskii did not mention Britain on his list, Baldwin interjected that he should include it. The discussion ranged widely – Maiskii's dispatch was seven pages long. The usual point about common interests and the absence of conflicts of interest also came up. As if not quite certain on the latter point, Baldwin slyly raised the question of India, recalling tsarist designs. Maiskii laughed at that remark, noting that the USSR had absolutely no interest in India. "In my youth," Baldwin replied, also laughing, "I remember that the Russian campaign against India was a recurring nightmare in England." Then, the conversation passed to other subjects, better trade relations, for example, which Baldwin favoured. At one point there was a philosophical turn in the discussion, about the advantages and disadvantages of revolution, before Maiskii returned to brass tacks, that is, to European security. Baldwin must have anticipated the question for he quickly reassured Maiskii that there had been no change in British policy and no abandonment of the principle of indivisibility of peace in Europe. But in politics, Baldwin added, one had to be realistic, and elastic, he might have added. "It is difficult beforehand to fix those ways and methods by which it is easiest to achieve the desired results." These were matters best left to discussion with the Foreign Secretary.[5]

The Abyssinian Crisis

The Abyssinian question began to preoccupy Litvinov in the late spring and early summer. The Italians were preparing to invade Abyssinia, and the matter was bound to go to the League of Nations. The Italian ambassador, Bernardo Attolico, went to see Litvinov to discuss current affairs, but the Abyssinia issue quickly arose. The European powers did not understand Italian interests. Because of outbound immigration, Italy had suffered a large loss of population and was looking for other lands to colonize. This was, of course, a strange conversation to have with a Soviet narkom whose country opposed European imperialism and colonization. Nevertheless, Litvinov was not unsympathetic. In that case, Litvinov opined, Italy made a mistake in voting for the admission of Abyssinia to the League of Nations when it could have opposed membership based, *inter alia*, on the existence of slavery and its "low cultural level." Nonetheless, Abyssinia was a League member and Italy could not demand that the League refuse to defend one of its members. England in its own interests would oppose Italy in Abyssinia, a point that Rome would have to take into account even more than any League decision. Attolico agreed and confessed that he was not fully sympathetic to his government's policy on the Abyssinian question. "I told Attolico," Litvinov wrote in his *dnevnik*, "that we in no way want to harm Italian interests. We share the French fear about the weakening of Italian influence in European matters because of the Abyssinian affair … Unfortunately, Italy takes into account, apparently, to a lesser degree our interests if one is to believe burgeoning information about the basis of Italian discussions with Germany and Poland." Litvinov mentioned Italian intrigues intended to draw the Ukraine out of the USSR. Attolico ridiculed this idea, but promised to write to Rome about it.[6] Litvinov envisaged Italy as a member of an anti-Nazi Entente, and worried that he might be losing it because of Italian ambitions in Abyssinia.

Before Maiskii left on annual leave, he asked Litvinov for information on Soviet policy. The Soviet government found itself in a difficult position, and Litvinov did not want to air out his difficulties. Essentially, it was going to be damned if you do and damned if you don't. Support Britain's position and quarrel with Italy; lay low and cross the British. So Litvinov wrote a complicated sort of dispatch venting his irritation with the British whom he characterized as hypocrites:

> We can fully understand the interest of British political, and especially government circles, in our position on the Abyssinian question. Interested in restraining Italian aggression in Abyssinia, England is not averse to using our general policy on peace and our especially negative attitude to colonial invaders. This is our position and it has not changed, but I do not see the need now to inform all and sundry about our possible position in Geneva, in case the issue comes up. We will undoubtedly take into account not only our general ideological position, but also the specific situation, as well as the possible attitude of other members of the League Council. We will likewise take into account England's position in Japan's attack on Manchuria and China. For some reason England then forgot about its duties as a League member [in 1931]. We will also take into account England's separate naval agreement with Germany outside the League and beyond any cooperation even with the most interested states.

Litvinov instructed Maiskii not to go beyond generalities in answering even the most persistent queries about Soviet policy and to indicate that he had no information about Soviet intentions in Geneva. "You must not give any answers," Litvinov added, "that could be used against us in Italy to support English theses." This meant that *perfide Albion* was pursuing an egoist's policy and he, Litvinov, was damned if he was going to walk down a one-way street for "the English," at least not without compelling reasons.

Litvinov took out his irritation on Maiskii:

> I consider it necessary to challenge the thesis, expressed by you and other polpreds, of the need for them to be aware of all the intentions and plans of the Soviet government on any issues, including those that do not even concern their country of residence. I can assure you that no diplomatic representative in Moscow is in a position to provide information on future or possible decisions of his government, even on issues directly related to the USSR. I am sure that Lord Chilston could not give me an answer on the English position at the next session of the League Council. Moreover, I can assure you that the question of our attitude in Geneva to the Abyssinian conflict was not raised and not discussed here in any session of the Politburo, because so far this has not been necessary.[7]

Maiskii defended himself against this blast from Moscow: "You must also take into account my situation." Adding:

> The information at the disposal of the polpred on the most important events of our foreign policy is extremely unsatisfactory. I, for example, feed mainly on newspaper information (from the Soviet and foreign press), but you, of course, will understand that this is not an entirely dependable source, especially on any complex and emerging issues. Meanwhile, in such busy hubs as London and Paris, where the Soviet polpred every day has to meet and talk on current political topics with dozens of different people from government and the political and journalistic world, based only on newspaper material plus his own – sometimes successful and sometimes unsuccessful – interpretation of it is quite risky. Naturally, therefore, I sometimes send you a telegraphic request concerning at least the general line of conduct on this or that current question.[8]

Maiskii thanked Litvinov for a recent diplomatic pouch containing correspondence from Moscow and from various ambassadors – it was an olive branch – but he had a point. In the Foreign Office, the clerks respected those ambassadors who were well-informed and well-connected to power at home, and regarded those who were not as unreliable and not particularly useful interlocutors.

In early August when Maiskii was on leave, Litvinov was in Geneva grappling with the Abyssinian problem. There was little time left for keeping mum. On 3 August he wrote to Stalin: "For the Abyssinian question, it has so far been possible to find not a solution, but a 'formula' that allows it to be postponed until the next session of the Council, scheduled for September 4th." He continued:

> As with the English, so with the French, there are those who, pinning their hopes on the increasing Italian financial and economic difficulties, expect that the longer a solution is delayed, the less eager Mussolini will be to fight. Laval and others, on the other hand, are convinced that war is inevitable. In any case, Geneva will have to deal with the Italian-Abyssinian issue in its entirety in early September, and Council members will have to take definite positions. It will be about the possible application to Italy, as an aggressor, of measures envisaged by the League Covenant, perhaps including economic sanctions. England, Turkey, and most small Nations will be advocates of sanctions. I do not think that France, which is still serving as Italy's solicitor, will vote to derail these measures. As much as we would not like to spoil relations with Italy, we can only stand against the violation of peace and an Italian imperialist war.

Litvinov hoped to shame the British into action by reminding them of their abdication of responsibilities at the time of the Japanese invasion of Manchuria, and obtaining from them a commitment to rigorous application of the

Covenant in the event of future acts of aggression. The trouble with that idea was that no one could shame "the English" when it came to practical matters. Even Churchill was ready, as Litvinov knew from Maiskii's report, to buy time against Japan at the expense of China. What Litvinov had in mind was a tripartite Anglo-Franco-Soviet declaration committing to firm League action against any future aggression. France would not go for it, Litvinov reasoned, but Britain might, if it stiffened its back, and in that case, Turkey, the Little Entente, and other states could sign on. "Of course, we cannot make such a statement a *sine qua non* for our vote against Italy," Litvinov concluded, "but we can try to obtain the above-mentioned compensation. I propose to act in that spirit here, unless you object."[9]

There is no available record of Stalin's response to Litvinov's request for approval of his approach, and the crisis intensified in August as Italy completed mobilization and the British built up their naval and air forces in the Mediterranean and in Egypt. Even for Litvinov, Abyssinian interests were not paramount.

The Crisis Intensifies

With the meeting of the League of Nations in early September, the crisis became acute. In Sochi where Stalin was taking his annual holidays, the *vozhd* appeared to make a joke of it all. The NKID doubted the admissibility of exports to Italy in the event of League sanctions. Stalin wrote:

> "I think the doubts of the Narkomindel," Stalin opined, "derive from a misunderstanding of the international situation. The conflict is not only between Italy and Abyssinia, but also between Italy and France on one side and England on the other. The old entente is no longer. Instead of it, two ententes have evolved: the entente of Italy and France on one side, and the entente of England and Germany on the other. The more intense the fight between them, the better for the USSR. We can sell bread to one and the other so they can fight. In general, for us it is disadvantageous that one of them will now beat the other. For us it is better, that the fight between them is as lengthy as possible but without a quick victory for one or the other."[10]

One could always count on cynicism between Stalin and his two chief deputies, Molotov and Kaganovich. Obviously, Stalin was referring to the Anglo-German naval agreement when he wrote of an Anglo-German "entente." This agreement, concluded only two and a half months after Eden's visit to Moscow, ignited Stalin's ever-smouldering cynicism. For him, *Albion* would always be *perfide*. He was not entirely wrong in this regard, but Litvinov was trying to rebuild the First World War Entente, not cheer over its collapse.

In early September, Litvinov, again in Geneva, lost election as a League vice-president by a single vote. The French had to pull a string to obtain an additional place for the Soviet Union. Litvinov did not take the reverse very well. He sent a telegram to Moscow asking for authorization to walk out of the assembly. Molotov, Kaganovich, and Voroshilov recommended accepting an additional vice-president's place. Stalin did not agree: "I think that it will be more correct to accept Litvinov's suggestion and demonstratively walk out of the assembly, and for Litvinov to leave immediately for Moscow to report to the government. Let the assembly itself deal with the Abyssinian mess."[11]

There followed another telegram to Sochi indicating that the wrangle in Geneva had been settled with a vice-presidency for the Soviet representative. Litvinov recommended "considering the incident closed" and not walking out of the assembly. To this, Stalin replied with a longer comment:

> Obviously, Litvinov was himself frightened by the results of his suggestion and hastened to smother the incident. As you can see, he did not think out his suggestion and did not understand that his suggestion would lead to the departure of our delegation and the threat of leaving the League of Nations, if the League swindler-directors would not treat the USSR with the necessary respect and courtesy. He does not understand that if we entered the League, this did not mean that we must be obedient members. He does not understand that if we will not from time to time stir up the League shit, we do not know how to use the League in the interests of the USSR. All Litvinov's conduct is dictated, in my opinion, not only by the interests of the policies of the USSR, but also by a personal, ulcerating vanity. This is sad, but this is a fact.

Stalin criticized Litvinov for not pointing out the hypocrisy of France and Britain, which also had their colonial interests in Abyssinia whose independence was only a mere "shadow." Of course, Litvinov had vented his spleen to Maiskii on this very point. But Litvinov was still thinking of an anti-German entente and therefore obviously could not insult his would-be allies. The narkom hated the position in which he found himself, but he was obliged to swallow his offended principles. Hence, Stalin took a cheap shot and not for the first time. It was easy to do on holiday in Sochi where he did not have to handle the mess in Geneva. "In other words," Stalin noted, "he [Litvinov] did not note the difference between our position and the position of England and France. This is, of course, bad. Litvinov wants to sail in England's waterway, whereas we have our own waterway, superior in quality to any other … in which he is obliged to sail. By the way, it would be good to develop this point in our press from our point of view, blurred by Litvinov in Geneva." As for Litvinov's original proposal, Stalin conceded that it would "unfortunately" be necessary "to consider the incident closed." In ending, Stalin joked that "even with a broom, Litvinov would now not leave the presidium of the assembly."[12]

Stalin did not mind contradicting himself. He was still in Sochi when Kaganovich and Molotov sent him the text of a Comintern declaration condemning German and Italian fascism and favouring cooperation with the Socialist International in Brussels *and* the League in Geneva. They thought the draft text was "inexpedient" but asked for Stalin's opinion. "I am not against," he replied.[13] So Litvinov's handling of the Abyssinian crisis was not so bad after all. There had to be some kind of coordination between the policies of collective security (NKID) and the Popular Front (the Comintern). In fact, trying to deal with the crisis, as Litvinov pointed out in his telegrams from Geneva, was a rat's nest of conflicting interests. Kaganovich and Molotov asked Stalin if he had instructions for Litvinov. "I do not have any instructions," Stalin replied.[14] In other words, let Litvinov handle it.

War in Abyssinia

On 3 October 1935, the Italian army invaded Abyssinia. Four days later, the League of Nations declared Italy to be an aggressor and approved some economic sanctions but none on important commodities, such as oil or steel, the denial of which could have hurt the Italian economy and its war effort. On the same day that Italian forces crossed Abyssinian frontiers, Litvinov sent a long briefing note to Stalin. The Italians had not acted without taking into account the positions of France and Britain. According to Litvinov, improved Franco-Italian relations had given a green light to the Italian government. Mussolini had informed Laval in January 1935 of Italian plans and obtained from him "not only agreement, but also a declaration to the effect that France would not interfere with them." It was less clear, Litvinov noted, whether the Italians had informed the British government of their plans. "Possibly, according to Mussolini, England had long been aware of Italy's preparations for the seizure of Abyssinia, but, acting as usual cautiously, and not confident in the support of public opinion, it [the Foreign Office] decided against any binding warning to Mussolini. This circumstance misled Mussolini, who decided that he would not meet serious opposition from England."

Litvinov heard that several Italian ambassadors, including Attolico, opposed the invasion. It was also reported that there was opposition in the fascist party and among the general population, especially in those families with sons conscripted into the army. "Under such circumstances, the war with Abyssinia has become, as it were, Mussolini's private affair, and this makes it particularly difficult for him to retreat, for which he must be personally and solely responsible. He seemed to admit in a conversation with the French ambassador that he was putting the fascist regime and even his own head on the line, adding, however, that for him the ways of retreat were … cut off."

Mussolini appeared to count on Laval to prevent harsh League action and to avert an armed conflict with England, the latter eventuality feared by Mussolini and by Italian public opinion. According to Litvinov, Mussolini thought he could get around sanctions by a quick military victory or with help from Germany and Japan. He was also open to negotiations outside the League, either alone with England or with the mediation of France. Such ideas are illusory, Litvinov opined, given the British position. "England is not so much interested in turning Abyssinia into its own colony, but in preventing the possession of this country by Italy. It cannot allow the domination of Abyssinia by a strong European state that would threaten English possessions in Africa and its communications with India." The British government was using the League as a cover to pursue its colonial or imperialist interests in Northeast Africa. Public opinion appeared ready to support the government under the League flag, an important consideration in view of forthcoming parliamentary elections. The British government looked to want to give Mussolini a bloody nose and damage his prestige. On the other hand, there were elements in the Conservative Party and even the Labour Party who favoured large concessions to Italy and opposed sanctions. This situation caused the British government to contemplate a softer line on the crisis.

As for France, Laval had defended Italian interests more effectively than the Italians themselves. "In so far as it was up to him [Laval]," Litvinov noted, "he would have conceded to Italy all along the line. He does not stop even before the prospect of damaging the prestige of the League." This was a personal policy, however, not the policy of the French Council of Ministers, where there was considerable opposition, led by Herriot, to Laval's conduct. To understand Laval, one had to remember his irritation with the British over the Anglo-German naval agreement and his view of the Franco-Soviet rapprochement as more a "sin" than an advantage. *Albion* would always be *perfide*, and the *Bolchos*, always a menace. That left only Italy as a potential success for Laval's foreign policy, and it was not much on which to build. If he lost it, he would be obliged to accept greater dependence on Britain, a prospect he regarded with distaste, even more so, because he did not want to move closer to the USSR. "Even before the assembly opened," according to Litvinov, "Laval admitted to me that he did not believe in the possibility of preventing war in Ethiopia." And he continued:

> Thus, he had already given up on mediation between England and Italy. He only sought to ensure that the League Council did not take too harsh a position against Italy, did not force her to withdraw from the League and left open the possibility of French mediation after Italy's first military victories. According to Laval, he told me that Mussolini allegedly cares about redeeming the military defeat of Italy in the last war with Abyssinia [in the nineteenth century], and therefore after several victorious battles Mussolini will be more amenable (an assumption which

> is clearly ridiculous). For all that, Laval must realize that he cannot long defend his position in the Council. France cannot prefer Italian friendship to English, but he [Laval] has decided, as a last resort, to make a demonstration of resistance to England in the Council to squeeze out some compensation in the form of an English commitment in the event of aggression, in particular in the Danube basin. The policy of Laval in Geneva may have the effect of impairing the prestige of the League and promoting the aggression of Mussolini. However, there is no doubt that regardless of any compensation from England, France will follow it [i.e., that policy] to the end.

Essentially, public opinion was polarized along political lines between fascists and quasi-fascists who were friendly to Germany and who backed Italy, and working-class organizations, radical parties, and the intelligentsia who did not. They opposed Nazi Germany, supported the League and the necessity to punish Italian aggression in order to send a message to Hitler. Litvinov knew his boss well and decided to return to Moscow, leaving Potemkin in Geneva, in order to report to the government. When Litvinov spoke in Geneva in mid-September, he had no "specific instructions," only an exchange of views with Stalin.[15]

After the circulation of Litvinov's briefing note, instructions came quickly from the Politburo. The Soviet government, Stalin in effect, declared its willingness to fulfill League obligations along with other states. The Politburo approved instructions for Litvinov to follow an independent Soviet line and under no circumstances to give the impression of subordinating Soviet policy to that of the British. "Do not manifest greater enthusiasm for sanctions than other countries, maintain contact, as possible, with France."[16] Stalin had criticized Litvinov's conduct in Geneva in September, but he was following Litvinov's policy of avoiding damage to relations with France and Britain, and in so far as possible with Italy.

On 5 October, the new Italian ambassador in Moscow, Baron Arone di Valentino, paid a call on Litvinov seeking clarification of Soviet policy. The ambassador criticized the League as a tool of a few powers, or perhaps only one of them. He complained about Britain, which did not understand the Italian psychology and combined negotiations with threats. "Our line of conduct," Litvinov replied, "is impossible to confuse with the English although these lines of policy at particular moments overlapped." Furthermore:

> The English objective is not to allow the political and especially military domination of Italy in Abyssinia and it is ready to bring to bear all means, diplomatic and other, in order to achieve its goals. We have no objectives whatsoever in Africa. To whom Abyssinia belongs – England or Italy, is a matter of indifference to us, although from the point of view of equality one might have to give preference to Italy having in the past been deprived of colonies. However, we cannot take this

> point of view because we are against any system of colonies. This does not mean that we, as a government, must actively interfere in colonial conflicts of third governments, and as long as the conflicts occur outside the League, we do not interfere in them. Our interest develops only from the moment of the posing of the question in the League. We want and we strive to make the League an instrument of peace and with this objective in mind we also entered the League. We feel that League passivity in the event of war between two of its members – a passivity having once already occurred – will a second time ruin the League, and that it would encourage aggressor countries. We therefore at a minimum want to fulfill loyally our obligations as a League member.

That was Litvinov's explanation of Soviet policy and it left the door open to the re-establishment of good Italian-Soviet relations. Unfortunately, a part of the Italian press did not appreciate the subtleties of the Soviet position. "In Rome they should understand," Litvinov added, "that if we were not interested in preserving the best relations with Italy, or if before us in place of Italy would be another, belligerent country, I would speak in Geneva, in a completely different language and I would manifest a completely different activity. It seems to me, that we have done in Geneva, the minimum which we were obliged to do." Litvinov added that in spite of unidentified pressures, the USSR would continue economic relations with Italy, "which unfortunately in Rome are not appreciated." Valentino went away from the meeting in a better mood.[17]

Shortly thereafter, Litvinov returned to Geneva to steer Soviet policy through the thicket of conflicting interests and clashes, especially between France and Britain. Everyone's temper was on edge. Litvinov reported that the Anglo-French row appeared to have been resolved at least temporarily. Laval was still looking for "reconciliation" with Italy; the British would not "hear of it."[18] Although Litvinov did not say so out loud, it seemed like the only one who would profit from the Abyssinian mess was Hitler. When Kaganovich and Molotov proposed a revision to Litvinov's "incorrect" policy ideas, Stalin replied that Litvinov's original "theses" were too general and could be misinterpreted. Litvinov should stick to the lines of his last speech in Geneva and avoid any impression that Soviet policy was subordinated to that of Britain.[19] Litvinov had said as much to the Italian ambassador Valentino before leaving for Geneva. There was no sarcasm in Stalin's instructions for Kaganovich and Molotov, and he removed the word "incorrect" from their proposed telegram to Litvinov. There was no need to criticize; Litvinov was handling a difficult file.

On the question of sanctions, some countries did not want to go all in, France, for example, and others did not want to cooperate at all. Litvinov cautioned Potemkin in Geneva not to be too enthusiastic about tough measures against Italy. Laval was still trying to support Rome if only by stalling the implementation of sanctions. There was a serious row between France and Britain outside of Geneva concerning French support for the Royal Navy in the event of an attack on it by Italy. The British had put the question to the French government, but Laval had "wriggled out" of a reply. In order to reinforce his position, Laval mobilized the "right and fascist press," which "probably received for that purpose stimulation of a material character" from Italy. The Quai d'Orsay also had a special budget line for such purposes. There began a furious press campaign against Britain to which the British press returned fire. The Foreign Office also protested. Herriot and his supporters joined the fray: "all the left press" attacked Laval for undermining Anglo-French relations. According to Litvinov, "Laval himself was frightened by the results of the campaign, which crossed his own objectives and he barely managed to stop it." The row might even hasten the fall of Laval's government and see him replaced by Herriot, a prospect that frightened the right-wing papers.

The French Army high command also put pressure on Laval through a meeting with Weygand and Mandel. They reproached him for leading France into isolation and warned him that if he was counting on an agreement with Germany, he should think twice because the British would "outrun him." According to what Litvinov had heard, "Laval allegedly burst out laughing, giving to understand that he had already outrun England." Litvinov had not quite finished his account, however. Laval, concerned by the warning from Weygand and Mandel, hastened to send a friend, journalist Fernand de Brinon, to Berlin to sound out the Germans. The latest papers from Paris reported the failure of his mission. Laval was finally obliged to give a positive reply to the British request for support for the Royal Navy. The Anglo-French row had nevertheless "weakened the meaning of possible military sanctions against an aggressor."[20] Litvinov's report was no doubt grist to the mill of Stalin's cynicism, although still in the south on holidays, there appears to have been no more correspondence about the Abyssinian crisis.

On 2 November, Litvinov submitted to Stalin a list of "theses" on the impact of the Abyssinian crisis on Soviet interests. The Italian war in Abyssinia and the intensifying Anglo-Italian conflict did not cut across Soviet interests. Italian defeat or a forced ending of the war would be "a death blow" not only to Mussolini, but also to fascism in general and to Germany in particular. The withdrawal of Italy from the "so-called concert of great powers" created an opportunity (*predposylko*) for closer collaboration between Britain, France, and the USSR. Successful League action against Italy would "weaken the chances of aggression on the part of Hitler." The USSR would not be against further League or other sanctions against Italy if imposed by England alone. Some deterioration of Soviet-Italian relations was inevitable because of Soviet fulfillment of League obligations. Further deterioration of those relations was undesirable. "Therefore, it is not necessary to take the point openly (*zastrel'shchik*) for radical measures against Italy."[21] These ideas show that Litvinov was not overly discouraged by the chaos created in relations between France, Britain, and Italy, or even by the disruption of relations between the USSR and Italy. Litvinov's objectives remained the same: organize an Anglo-Franco-Soviet entente against Nazi Germany and attempt to keep Italy in play despite the Abyssinian crisis. His assumption that an Italian check in Abyssinia would have adversely affected Nazi Germany seems naïve. Nevertheless, Litvinov continued to see the League as a potential arm against German aggression, if sanctions could be made to work. None of these eventualities proved out.

Litvinov still tried to avert a collapse of Soviet relations with Italy in spite of the risk of irritating the Foreign Office. He made records of two further meetings with Valentino. Litvinov once again said that the Soviet government was not interested in any broadening of sanctions, nor would it participate in sanctions other than those respected by all. He added that Italy had not reciprocated Soviet attempts to avoid aggravating relations. In Rome, there were attacks on Soviet officials. Valentino responded that there had been demonstrations outside the Italian embassy in Moscow. Peaceful demonstrations, Litvinov replied, are not the same as attacks on Soviet citizens. Relations were deteriorating.[22] Valentino returned a week later, in early December, to raise again the question of sanctions. "We do not seek to harm Italian interests," Litvinov repeated, "but at the same time we do not speak against this or that swing in the Geneva establishment." He continued:

> We assume that we will have to turn to Geneva in the future, in particular, in the case of a German attack on the Baltic countries, and we do not want that we could then be reminded of speaking against sanctions in other cases. If Mussolini considers that our position finally compromises Soviet-Italian relations in the future, then we also of course will have to draw from that the necessary conclusions.

The Soviet position, however, had not changed, Litvinov stressed, in spite of various unfriendly acts in Italy including a systematic anti-Soviet press campaign. Valentino responded with his own complaints, which solved nothing. Soviet-Italian relations were headed in the wrong direction.[23]

Back in London

On the other hand, Litvinov did not know what to make of British policy. The USSR and Britain had overlapping interests concerning the Abyssinian crisis, and yet in Geneva the British had not only not sought Soviet support, but even avoided those contacts which Eden had previously maintained with Litvinov. What was going on? Litvinov wrote to Maiskii:

> I do not think that this can only be explained by articles and comments in our press, which are disagreeable to England. Possibly England is disappointed with

> us. It may have believed that by joining the League, we were abandoning all our principles and we were ready to make any compromises. From the principled position we have taken on imperialism and the colonies, the English could have concluded that an agreement with us on the issues of interest to it would be impossible and that we were not at all a suitable partner. However, it is possible that there is another – the worst assumption, namely, that hostile to us, Hoare has already decided to opt for the creation of a new European combination, with or without France, but including Germany and excluding the USSR.

Litvinov's speculations led him to think that Hoare might be contemplating some kind of deal with Germany at Soviet expense. The looniest idea, it seems, although reported in the *Times*, was to obtain German cooperation on sanctions against Italy in exchange for France abandoning the ratification of the Franco-Soviet pact. Hoare would certainly have found a suitable partner in Laval, if that is what the British were contemplating. Litvinov instructed Maiskii, who had returned to London from leave, to probe for answers when next he met with Vansittart and Hoare.[24] He had reason to worry. Based on a conversation with Charles, the British chargé d'affaires, Rubinin had warned earlier that Eden and Vansittart were meeting with opposition in attempting to pursue their line of cooperation with the USSR.[25]

Maiskii returned to London in early November and began to re-establish contact with his usual interlocutors. On 6 November, he met Hoare who greeted him with such courtesy, doused with so much sugar, that it put Maiskii on his guard. On instructions from Litvinov, he asked about rumours to the effect that the British would make concessions to Germany to support sanctions against Italy. Hoare denied them. This evoked Maiskii's approval. "In fact," he added, "to pay Germany a bonus for participation in sanctions against Italy would be equivalent to treating influenza with an injection of typhus." Hoare laughed and added that Soviet suspicions were without foundation.[26] If you read the reports of these two, one the Johnny-come-lately Bolsh, and the other an English Tory, they seemed to get on alright. Hoare laughed at Maiskii's suspicions, but Maiskii persisted in probing for information. The Soviet government wanted to make sanctions work against Italy, Maiskii said, as a "warning" to other more powerful aggressors, unnamed but obviously Germany and Japan. Italy was not a very dangerous aggressor, Hoare replied.[27]

The Hoare-Maiskii exchange settled nothing. Sargent had not changed his mind; he was all for trying for "a settlement with Germany" when or if the time was right.[28] Come to think of it, when did the Soviet ambassador ever talk to Sargent? Never is the answer, which could not have been accidental. Maiskii saw Vansittart two days after talking with Hoare; they had the usual sort of conversation. Still following Litvinov's instructions, Maiskii asked many questions. "The one on which he was most pertinacious," according to Vansittart, was if there were any truth to rumours of an Anglo-Franco-German agreement "at the expense of Russia." Vansittart replied, that there was no truth whatsoever to such rumours, though of course he did not mention Sargent's views. "M. Maisky was evidently very suspicious, although I think he departed tranquillized." As the ambassador was rising to leave, Vansittart raised the usual question about propaganda and in particular about interfering in the British parliamentary elections. Maiskii dodged the question in the usual Soviet way with the usual Soviet aplomb, though of course Vansittart was not convinced. He laughed. Of course, he would. "I cannot understand you Soviet people at all. I would understand you if communists had chances to elect to Parliament 150 MPs. Now at a maximum they can only count on one or two seats. How can this have any practical value? Is it worth spoiling relations? In my opinion the game is not worth the candle." Maiskii stuck to his usual lines.[29] Remember, Vansittart was alright with Maiskii having a word with Labour and Liberal interlocutors.

Litvinov was unconvinced by Maiskii's report: "I got the impression that Vansittart was not telling you something and did not behave in the same way as in previous conversations." Maybe that was when Vansittart started talking about propaganda. It usually signalled a defensive manoeuvre and a desire to change the subject.[30]

Ten days later, Maiskii and Vansittart resumed their discussion at greater length. Vansittart asked Maiskii about his impressions on being home on leave. In response, Maiskii was remarkably blunt, or so he reported to Moscow. The Soviet government favoured the further development of Anglo-Soviet relations, he said, but in the last few months doubts had arisen about the direction of British policy. "The fact of the conclusion of the Anglo-German naval agreement produced an especially strong impression on our public opinion. During my stay in the USSR, I heard from all sides worried questions: What does this agreement mean? Is this not the beginning of an Anglo-German Entente, the point of which is directed against the Soviet Union?"

Vansittart denied that there was any basis to rumours about an Anglo-German or Anglo-Franco-German entente, nor was there any deal for security in the west in exchange for clearing the way for Hitler in the east. On the Abyssinian crisis, Vansittart claimed that the British government was committed to supporting the League of Nations in Africa and in Europe. British policy, he said, was League policy, and this position had strong public support. Britain stood resolutely against Italian aggression. Vansittart also repeated his usual lines about the indivisibility of security in Europe. Was he whistling in the dark? A few weeks later these remarks were going to sound ridiculous.

Maiskii was like a Crown attorney pursuing a relentless interrogation. "What would be the British reaction if, for example, Germany attacked Czechoslovakia?"

"Vansittart replied that in this case, Great Britain's stand against the aggressor would be even more violent and decisive than against Italy. Czechoslovakia is very popular in England. It is a peaceful, democratic, cultural country, about which no one can say anything bad … Hitler's attack on Czechoslovakia would undoubtedly cause a great wave of indignation in England, and the government would have been very firm in pursuit of League policy towards Germany." Maiskii did not react to this statement, and he could not know in advance that Britain would sacrifice Czechoslovakia to the Nazi Mordor less than three years later. However, it would only be three weeks before he and his colleagues in Moscow would know what meant the British commitment to the League Covenant.

What about Memel or Lithuania? Maiskii broke in to ask. The British government "would stand against the aggressor," replied Vansittart, but he could not hide the fact that public reaction to an attack on Lithuania would be weaker than in the case of Czechoslovakia. Then Vansittart brought up the case of Austria, much to Maiskii's surprise. "Hitler surely wants to swallow Austria," he said, "but he almost certainly will do so not from outside but from within, through the organization of a national socialist uprising in Vienna. If this happens, it will create a very difficult situation. How to convince the broad masses of the British population of the need to consider the national socialist putsch in Austria as a form of German aggression? And without such broad public support, the British government will not be able to decisively oppose the aggressor in the case of Austria." Would Litvinov in Moscow reading Maiskii's report be convinced of British resolution to stand against Hitlerite aggression?

Maiskii offered no comment about Austria. He reported that the conversation turned to France and more particularly to Laval:

> [Vansittart] suggested that our concerns about the creation of the Anglo-Franco-German Entente are fed mainly by French sources (Brinon's trip to Berlin, the expected arrival in Paris of [Joachim von] Ribbentrop, etc.). Vansittart knew about Laval's flirt with Germany, but he does not know its current stage. For Laval does not consider it necessary to inform the British government about his conversations with Germany, and all the FO information on this issue is drawn mainly from other sources.

"If you think that this flirt is taking place with the consent and support of the British government, then you are very wrong," Vansittart said. "British policies should not be confused with French or, rather, with Laval's policies, for Laval and France are not the same." Vansittart continued:

> The British government has its own policy. As for Laval, he makes one mistake after another … take for example Laval's position in the Italian-Abyssinian conflict. The British government at the beginning of this year warned Mussolini that if Italy's policy put England before the need to choose between the League or Italy,

> England would choose the League. Mussolini got a timely warning. If the French government, for its part, had done the same, there would probably have been no current war in Africa.

Instead, Laval tied himself to Mussolini through his January accords. Later, Laval was forced to defend the League position and to agree to sanctions. So what was the result? Vansittart asked rhetorically. France aroused suspicions everywhere, in England, with the Little Entente and worst of all reinforced Mussolini's determination to pursue the war.

"Now Laval begins his flirtation with Germany and immediately gives rise to – well, to put it mildly – bewilderment in the USSR and grumbling in … the Little Entente." Vansittart did not see any grounds for France to come to terms with Germany except on the basis of ceding the territories of its allies to Hitler. Readers may appreciate the irony of this statement, for it is exactly what France and Britain would do at Munich in September 1938. Of course, that is getting ahead of the narrative. In November 1935, Vansittart could not conceive of such an eventuality. Laval was trying to ride two or three horses at the same time. He was bound to fall and hit his head.

Maiskii asked finally how Vansittart saw the future of Anglo-Soviet relations. It was the usual sort of answer. "Vansittart replied that the course to improve and strengthen these relations, which a year and a half ago was started by our political talks with him, should continue. The British government considers it right and in the interests of England." This was Vansittart's opinion, but what about the Conservative Party? Maiskii did not ask. The parallelism in British and Soviet policy had increased in recent months especially since the beginning of the Abyssinian crisis. "There are therefore no obstacles," Vansittart continued, "to strengthening political cooperation between the two governments."

The interrogation was not quite finished. Maiskii wanted to test for Litvinov's perceptions of British coldness in Geneva. He therefore asked if the British had objected to any Litvinov's recent speeches in Geneva. Vansittart was surprised by this question since he knew of no British objections to them. What about Eden? Maiskii asked. "How do you explain the underlined restraint, almost coldness, which the British delegation, in particular Eden, exhibited in relation to the Soviet delegation over the past weeks in Geneva?" Vansittart was bewildered. He could not venture a guess; perhaps Eden had been too busy trying to hold wavering delegations in line on sanctions. In any case, if there were any difficulties in Geneva, Vansittart said he would know about them.[31]

Vansittart made his own less-detailed record of the conversation, which continued for an hour and a half. It underlines Maiskii's concerns about the Anglo-German naval agreement and in general about the British commitment to collective security. Vansittart expressed irritation at the continued "harping" over the Anglo-German naval pact. His irritation, however, would not change Soviet views of it. Vansittart's record skips over the discussion of German aggression against various states with the exception of Lithuania where Vansittart put off the blame on the Lithuanians. Maiskii's account confirms Vansittart's record. "I think I was able by the end of [the discussion]," Vansittart reported, "to dissipate some of the ambassador's doubts."[32]

Maiskii continued his fact-checking for he had a meeting with Eden three days later. That conversation briefly resumed the discussion with Vansittart. Eden himself launched the discussion by asking about the mood in Moscow to relations with Britain, and he assured Maiskii that there had been no cooling of British relations with the USSR either in London or in Geneva. Eden praised Litvinov's work and noted the "parallelism" in British and Soviet policy on the Abyssinian crisis. Maiskii raised the Anglo-German naval agreement as he had with Vansittart. Eden replied that it did not have a broad significance and did not conceal dangers for the USSR. Eden then repeated Vansittart's assurances about future Anglo-Soviet relations. There were, of course, some difficulties. Eden had heard expressions of mistrust in the USSR and complaints about Soviet money spent in Britain to subsidize communist propaganda. Maiskii vehemently denied Eden's accusation, offering the usual distinction between the Comintern and the Soviet government. Of course, Eden did not buy that argument, but he said in the end that this was a "small issue" and that the prospects for Anglo-Soviet relations were good.[33]

Litvinov remained unconvinced by Maiskii's reports, and if the narkom was not convinced, then neither was Stalin. In fact, Litvinov had his doubts about Vansittart's *démenti*: "French official circles are stubbornly spreading rumours that France is conducting negotiations with Germany at the insistence of England." Litvinov authorized Maiskii to take up these rumours with the Foreign Office. He also asked him to convey verbally or by personal letter to Eden that Maiskii had heard no observations from the narkom about Eden.[34] Litvinov considered Eden someone to count on to improve Anglo-Soviet relations. That was a mistake.

If Eden told Maiskii that the "propaganda" was a small matter, this is not what he said to his colleagues in the Foreign Office. Having read Vansittart's record of meeting with Maiskii on 18 November, Eden left this note in his minutes before his own meeting with the Soviet ambassador: "I have no sympathy to spare for M. Maisky. I hope the next time M. Maisky comes with complaints he will be told that our goodwill depends on his Govt's good behaviour; i.e. keep their noses & fingers out of our domestic politics. I have had some taste of the consequences of this lately & M. Maisky will get no sympathy from me. I am through with the Muscovites of this hue."[35] Apparently, British communists criticized Eden during the parliamentary election campaign, though the attacks could only have been a minor irritant. Eden won his constituency by a large majority.[36] He held a grudge, nevertheless, and remembered it often when proposals came up for better Anglo-Soviet relations. In fact, in his record of conversation, he made a lot more of his complaint about Soviet propaganda than Maiskii did and certainly did not say that it was a "small" matter.[37]

Based on what Maiskii had learned since his return from leave, he wrote to Litvinov on 25 November that he did not detect any deterioration in Anglo-Soviet relations:

> Everything that I see, hear, and observe here leads me to the following conclusion: the British government for the time being would like to maintain and develop good relations with the USSR, however, without excessive intimacy. When the British in this regard speak about "intimacy," they mean, first of all, France. For some reason they believe that Franco-Soviet relations have become very intimate, and that as a result of this the Soviet government intervenes in internal French affairs, in particular through the "Popular Front." The English do not want this and are afraid. Hence their attitude "without intimacy."

Maiskii felt certain that the government was not interested in an Anglo-German or Anglo-Franco-German entente, although some individuals might have been entertaining such ideas. Anglo-German relations were cool. The Foreign Office was focused on the Abyssinia crisis. But who knew how things would develop? "What will the balance of forces and influences be in a few months? At the moment it is difficult to predict."[38]

Maiskii appears to have missed Eden's growing impatience, if not anger over the issue of "propaganda" and support for the British Communist Party. Vansittart had more than once warned Maiskii about the potential repercussions of such Soviet activity, and, in Moscow, Litvinov for many years had tried to restrain the worst excesses of Bolshevik propaganda about which he sometimes wrote to Stalin. Maiskii was quite right to note that there remained some British interest in a settlement with Germany, even in the Foreign Office. Sargent appears to have been the leading proponent, but he was not alone. Even as Maiskii was interrogating Vansittart about a possible British interest in a German entente, Vansittart's subordinates were discussing this very question not only in relation to France where Laval might completely upend European security, but also in relation to the USSR, which out of fear, might also seek a rapprochement with Germany. "I'm not at all sure that in a few years' time," Wigram noted in his minutes on the same day that Maiskii wrote to Litvinov, "we shan't find Russia with Germany. And that is one of the reasons why – as soon as the time is ripe, I would like to see us at any rate make the attempt to get our own settlement with Germany." Sargent noted, "I agree." Vansittart added his own comment: "There is always the danger of a Russo-German rapprochement. But it is surely not very serious at present – unless M. Laval double-crosses the Russians as well as us."[39]

Maiskii could not penetrate deep enough into the Foreign Office to hear of Sargent, but he sensed the potential danger of a British turn toward Germany. There was a *sauve qui peut* mentality exhibited in the discussions in the Foreign Office, but this mentality also existed in Laval's mind, and in Stalin's. Maiskii, Vansittart, Litvinov, among others, were against it, but could they succeed in rallying sufficient support in favour of collective security and mutual assistance? Time would tell, as Maiskii often wrote in his *dnevnik*.

Maiskii and Beaverbrook

Maiskii saw Lord Beaverbrook again at the beginning of December, always checking the Tory pulse. The press baron had been to Berlin to meet Hitler and he related the conversation to Maiskii. Beaverbrook did not have much to add to what he had already said in the past. "The best policy for England would be the policy of isolation, but if that does not work, then it will have to be an alliance with France and a rapprochement with the USSR. The policy of isolation from my point of view, is healthy; a combination with France and the USSR – a cold, and rapprochement with Germany – typhus." Beaverbrook was more convinced than ever that Germany was preparing for war. Maiskii asked his habitual questions about Anglo-Soviet relations. Beaverbrook was optimistic, and he seemed to be well informed. He was ready to do his part to facilitate improved relations, but Maiskii responded cautiously, noting that time would tell how Beaverbrook would conduct himself.[40]

Maiskii Talks Again with Churchill

A week later, Churchill invited Maiskii to dinner, maybe to buck him up, but also to send a message to Moscow. This time it was in Churchill's London flat, though without spouses. "The dinner was quite intimate," Maiskii reported, besides Churchill the only other person present was the Leader of the Liberal Party, Archibald Sinclair. He was a personal friend of Churchill. During the conversation, Churchill and Maiskii did most of the talking.

"Churchill began the discussion with a question: 'Well, how are things going? What do you think? In my opinion, things are going badly, very badly.'"

What do you mean by "badly"? Maiskii asked.

The world needs peace, Churchill replied, a new war, with modern weaponry, would be the greatest sort of catastrophe. "It would leave no stone unturned. Meanwhile, Germany is frantically rearming … is spending colossal sums on war *matériel*." In the spring or summer of 1937 the critical moment will come when Hitler could "throw a torch in the powder keg. The danger of a new world war will reach its apogee. Given these circumstances, we need to create a program for action."

Maiskii finally broke into Churchill's monologue to ask him how he saw the movement of British public opinion since last they met during the spring. Was there a growing awareness, especially in right-wing circles, of the approaching German danger? Maiskii spoke again about the Soviet reaction to the conclusion of the Anglo-German naval agreement and the distrust it had aroused. Vansittart had tried to break Maiskii's habit of raising this subject, but obviously without success. Many people in the USSR, Maiskii continued, saw the naval agreement as a first step towards an Anglo-German entente.

Did you speak to Vansittart about this? Churchill asked. Yes, Maiskii replied. Churchill, nodding his head in approval, commented that the naval agreement was a huge (*krupneishei*) political mistake. It gives Britain nothing because the Germans will build to the maximum of their financial-technical capabilities and have aroused suspicions, and "rightly so," in a number of other countries similar to those in the USSR. However, Churchill did not think too much should be made of the naval agreement. It had limited meaning. The government was constrained by pacifist opinion, and the Admiralty could not obtain the funds to build up the British fleet. People were asking against whom there would be a naval build-up. They could not see any country becoming a "serious enemy." The Admiralty reasoned that in agreeing to the German proposal to build to 35 per cent of the British fleet, they would be creating a phantom on the horizon with which to frighten public opinion. According to Churchill, this calculation had worked.

Maiskii was doubtful and countered that there was a strong current of "Germanophile" opinion in Britain in favour of obtaining Western security in exchange for a Hitlerite free hand in the east. Both Churchill and Sinclair hotly denied that this was a real danger. There were people who believed in such ideas but they were a minority and they did not direct British foreign policy. Awareness of the German danger was growing in Britain and among right-wing circles, and would continue to grow. Unfortunately, the British government had not lost all hope that some "acceptable compromise" with Hitler could be obtained. Churchill did not see it, however. Time and events would teach the ill-informed. In the meantime, the government did not want to irritate Hitler because obviously they feared him, especially given the present unsatisfactory state of British armaments.

Maiskii asked how Churchill saw the future of British foreign policy. If Britain could work through a strong League of Nations, events might turn out alright. The League was popular in Britain, as demonstrated by the results of the Peace Ballot, a nation-wide poll of opinion on the League and collective security (announced at the end of June 1935). Hence, if the League were not "bankrupted" by the Abyssinian crisis, British policy would have a strong foundation upon which to build. If the League failed, then "chaos" would erupt in Europe. In that case, there would be a "convulsive" reaction in Britain and the conclusion of an alliance with France. Either way, Churchill continued, there needed to be a "huge increase in rearmament," even if the League remained credible, and not only in Britain.

Churchill then turned the conversation to the Far East. He saw the danger of war increasing as Japan began to exploit European instability to its advantage. Churchill's views had not changed since the June meeting. Britain was in no position to stand alone against Japan. If the Japanese wanted to take it, Hong Kong would fall in twenty-four hours. Britain needed US cooperation to stop Japanese aggression, but even Anglo-American power might not be enough. Churchill foresaw a maritime blockade against Japan reinforced by Anglo-American-Soviet cooperation.

The subject of discussion eventually turned to Anglo-Soviet relations. Churchill asked many questions about Soviet internal developments. The country had been through difficult times, Maiskii replied, but those difficulties had been overcome. They agreed quickly, as they had before, about the absence of conflicts of interest and the common overlapping objectives in Europe and the Far East. A strong Soviet Union would be a "powerful counterbalance" to Japan and Germany, said Churchill, and a "direct British interest." According to Maiskii, "Churchill welcomed the strengthening of the military might of the USSR." It should be promoted in Conservative circles. "And then, almost inspired," Maiskii noted, "eyes burning, Churchill said, 'I would like to say to the USSR only one thing: arm yourselves, arm yourselves, and again arm yourselves! For our common enemy – Germany – is at the gates.'"[41] One could always count on Winston for rousing words, which he hoped would reach the right people in Moscow, although it is not clear whether a copy of Maiskii's record was sent to Stalin. Voroshilov received a copy and his was marked up in blue pencil.[42]

The Abyssinian Tar Baby

Meanwhile, the Abyssinian crisis continued to unfold. It was like the tar baby in the *Uncle Remus Tales*: the more one tried to get unstuck from the tar baby, the more one got covered in tar. Ironically, Litvinov's lack of enthusiasm for defending Abyssinia was similar to that of Laval and Hoare. Litvinov was constrained by a certain respect for principles, notably anti-colonialism, and by Stalin who kept an eye on his narkom's wobbly Bolshevik values. This was not a constraint for the two greatest colonial empires. How could they object in principle to the Italians taking the only available piece of African territory that was not gobbled up in the vicinity by France and Britain? It is true that Britain did not like to see Italy making itself comfortable so close to Suez, but colonial powers could cut deals, while Litvinov could not. It is also true that there were parliamentary elections in Britain in mid-November where support for the League of

Nations was a popular campaign line even among the Conservatives who were returned to power albeit with a smaller majority than before. Nonetheless, the British government did not feel constrained either before or after the elections from negotiating a settlement of the Abyssinian crisis trading Abyssinian territories in exchange for Italy's continued membership in a potential anti-Nazi coalition.[43] Supported by the realist Vansittart, Laval and Hoare agreed during meetings in Paris to a secret proposal: Mussolini would stop his colonial war in exchange for two-thirds of Abyssinian territory, leaving what remained to the Abyssinian government sweetened slightly with a port on the Gulf of Aden. They had no concern for the Abyssinian people per se, but Litvinov did not have much either. That Vansittart accompanied Hoare to Paris is interesting. Normally, when the Foreign Secretary was abroad, the Permanent Undersecretary remained in the Foreign Office.

Laval and Hoare came to terms on the weekend of 7 December. Two days later, the plan was leaked to the press in Paris and in London. The two journalists who spilled the story in Paris were Tabouis (*L'Oeuvre*) and Pertinax (*L'Écho de Paris*), both of whom had close ties to the Soviet embassy in Paris while Tabouis was on the Soviet payroll. They attacked the agreement as a large price to pay to buy off an aggressor. It was that, but it was not appeasement in the sense of future Anglo-French concessions to Hitler. The idea was to keep Italy on side as a potential anti-German ally. Tabouis wrote in her memoirs that the Hoare-Laval plan was an open secret being talked about freely among the Paris cognoscenti. Tabouis bumped into Vansittart in Paris at the house of a friend of hers. Vansittart was willing to talk about the negotiations, and she noted: "I got the impression from him that in London the attitude had become, 'Well, it's too bad for Ethiopia, but it can't be helped.'" That was also Litvinov's attitude. According to Tabouis, the Quai d'Orsay and the Foreign Office forbade the press corps from even alluding to the new proposal to settle the Abyssinian crisis. Yet with all the loose talk going around Paris, it is not surprising that the story leaked.[44]

According to French historian Renaud Meltz, Léger passed the agreement to François Quilici at Havas, who must have passed it on to Pertinax and perhaps Tabouis.[45] Quilici was likewise on the Soviet embassy payroll. Was that just a coincidence? In January 1934 Léger sought to sabotage Paul-Boncour's plan for mutual assistance with the USSR; there was no reason why he would not sabotage another minister whose policies he disliked. What about Potemkin? Was he involved in the leakage? Advised by one of the French "*habitués*" of the Soviet embassy, would he have given his endorsement to the leak? Litvinov wanted to see Laval gone, but he also wanted to prevent the Abyssinian crisis from ruining his plans to rebuild the anti-German Entente cordiale of the First World War. Tabouis and Pertinax did not topple Laval right away, but Hoare resigned on 18 December, nine days after the leak.

Litvinov later explained the position to Boris Efimovich Shtein, then polpred in Rome: "No matter how we explain to the Italians our position in Geneva, reduced solely to the consistent implementation of the Covenant of the League of Nations, they still continue to attribute to us statements and actions with which we have absolutely nothing to do." These accusations originated with Laval and the Poles, and the anti-Soviet newspaper *Journal de Genève*. In spite of Mussolini's hostility, Litvinov instructed Shtein "to make every effort to explain clearly to him once again, our position":

> The fate of Abyssinia does not interest us and we will not oppose any resolution of the conflict, in so far as it will originate outside the League and will not offend the latter. We sincerely wish for the swift liquidation of the conflict and we sincerely wish that Italy comes out of the conflict strong, and capable of fulfilling its role in the guarantee of peace in Europe. At the same time, we are convinced that the slightest compromise of the League in this affair in the event of the rejection of sanctions and all the more of a formal agreement on the partition of Abyssinia, would mean the end of the League of Nations and the end of the system of collective security. Hence, in every case we will stand up in defence of the authority and the Covenant of the League – not more and not less.

What Litvinov had said to Ambassador Valentino, he repeated in his instructions to Shtein: "If we were not attempting to maintain our previous relations with Italy or if we had come to the conclusion that these relations had finally been compromised, we would speak in Geneva in an entirely different language and we would really take upon ourselves the leading role."[46] In short, Litvinov wanted it both ways. Could the USSR protect the League, keep Mussolini on side, and support League sanctions against Italy however unenthusiastically?

Maybe the Hoare-Laval plan could have worked out, all things being equal. The late British historian A.J.P. Taylor opined that their proposal was a "perfectly sensible plan" that would have ended the war in Abyssinia and satisfied Mussolini, if not so much the Abyssinians. "It was a beautiful example," Taylor wrote, "… of using the machinery of peace against the victim of aggression." Instead, the plan put paid to the League's credibility. "One day it was a powerful body imposing sanctions … the next day, it was an empty sham."[47] Tabouis and Pertinax, or rather their scoop, killed the League. Taylor had a gift for recognizing the ironic, especially in his *Origins of the Second World War* in which he took evident pleasure in irritating his more conventional colleagues. The interests of Abyssinia were not paramount in any one's mind except perhaps among literate, progressive Abyssinians and there were not too many of them. Here is what Litvinov advised Stalin:

> It seems to me that we should take the following position. The proposal of Laval-Hoare means the partition of Abyssinia and the violation of its integrity. This is

> contrary to the League Covenant, which guarantees to all members of the League the inviolability and integrity of their territory, in the name of which the League of Nations intervened in the conflict and began to apply sanctions. The League of Nations cannot therefore endorse such proposals. Of course, if Abyssinia, for whatever reason, considered it possible to accept the proposal, the League of Nations should not encourage it to continue the war, but rather should register the agreement between the warring parties. As long as Abyssinia will not declare quite voluntarily its acceptance of the Laval-Hoare proposal, the League of Nations may not in any way approve it.[48]

This position was consistent with what Litvinov had proposed since the beginning of the crisis, and differentiated the Soviet position from that of the colonial powers. Stalin and his troika approved Litvinov's policy line, annotating his recommendation with their familiar "*za*" to indicate "for." The Politburo formally approved it on the following day, 14 December.[49]

On the day after Hoare resigned, 19 December, Litvinov drew pessimistic conclusions in a dispatch to Maiskii: "My prediction of the behaviour of the Conservative government after the elections seems to have been correct. You report today that the new zigzag, carried out by Hoare in Paris, was conceived before the elections." As readers will remember, this was true. Litvinov also recounted various rumours about a putative British deal with Germany. Memel, Danzig, Austria, and colonies were all on offer as a quid pro quo. The only items on that particular list that Hitler did not eventually obtain were the colonies. Litvinov was not sure what to make of the rumours, but his trust even in Vansittart was shaken, and he so advised Maiskii. "The 'Paris plan' [i.e., Hoare-Laval plan]," Litvinov concluded, "after the Anglo-German naval agreement finally undermines the remnants of any confidence in British policy."[50] Remember, if Hoare and Laval had been able to pull off their plan, outside the League and with the consent of Abyssinia, Litvinov would have taken a different line.

Maiskii wrote a remarkably detailed, insider report on the development and fate of the so-called Paris Plan. The British cabinet was divided on the question of sanctions, the older group of ministers being opposed and the younger ones, like Eden, in favour of them. Vansittart opposed them based on the principle that "the main enemy is Germany, for the struggle with Germany it is necessary to support the Stresa Front, plus the USSR, and for this it is necessary to liquidate the Abyssinian-Italian conflict." Sanctions could only aggravate Anglo-Italian relations, throw Italy into the arms of Nazi Germany, and make more difficult the formation of an anti-German coalition. That position was similar to Litvinov's.

Already at the beginning of November, but in fact earlier, Vansittart, "with the blessing of ministers," was preparing a plan to settle the Abyssinian crisis. Before the parliamentary elections, this planning was undertaken in the strictest secret. Maiskii remembered sitting beside Hoare at the Lord Mayor's annual banquet on 9 November where he (Hoare) had said – and it must have been with a smile – that British "policy after the elections will be the same as before the elections." This was true from a sophist's point of view: the planning to partition Abyssinia had been underway before the election call. The leak of the plan on 9 December caused an uproar in Britain. In fact, the younger gang of ministers, led by Eden, called for repudiation of the plan and, of necessity, the resignation of Hoare. The older ministers resisted. Baldwin tried to finesse. He reckoned that he had the electorate in his pocket and that the country would eventually "swallow" the plan. Backing the position of the older generation of ministers, Baldwin obtained cabinet approval to the intense displeasure of the "young" ministers. As Maiskii noted succinctly, Baldwin's calculations did not work out. Public opposition was intense and Baldwin faced a party revolt. Churchill, the Conservative outcast, who was on holiday in Majorca, even sent a telegram protesting that the "British lion had folded before Mussolini." Eden and several other "young" ministers threatened to resign if the "Paris Plan" was not ditched. Baldwin recognized that he would have to choose between saving Hoare and saving his government. On 18 December, Hoare resigned.

Eden was appointed to replace Hoare, much to the displeasure of the "old" ministers. Maiskii speculated that Eden would offer stronger support to the League and to the principles of collective security. The "old" ministers would lie in wait "to take down a not very agreeable for them 'young fellow.'" Maiskii concluded that Litvinov had been right to assume that the British government could turn its back on the League of Nations. However, Maiskii claimed that he had also been right to say that because of the recent elections, the new government would have greater difficulties betraying League principles than in the previous Parliament.[51] As readers will see, Maiskii was wrong. The British government had no problem at all betraying League principles.

A British Loan to Moscow?

The Abyssinia crisis was not the only front in the battle for the Anglo-Soviet rapprochement. Better trade relations, and in particular a British loan to the USSR, would test whether Anglo-Soviet relations could move from talk to deeds. The idea of a loan was not new: it had arisen periodically almost from the beginning of Anglo-Soviet relations. The Soviet government needed a loan or long-term credits; in exchange, the British wanted Soviet orders and a settlement of tsarist debts to British nationals. The US position was similar. Maiskii had again broached the idea in June 1934; and Foreign Office and Treasury officials began to consider it seriously at the beginning of 1935.[52] This was just at the time the US State Department abandoned debt-credit negotiations with the Soviet government. From the outset, the loan had political implications.

According to Vansittart, it would "get rid of a troublesome dispute in our relations with Russia, which we both wish to improve in view of the clearly growing German menace." A settlement would also satisfy British claimants, who had "votes and friends." Simon concurred on both points.[53] The Foreign Office idea was to combine a long-term loan to the USSR at over-market interest rates, with the so-called Baring balances, former tsarist cash deposits in Barings and other London banks, to settle British claims against the Soviet government. The difference between the higher and market interest rates and the Baring balances would be used to pay off the claimants. It was not much, but it was better than nothing. In April 1935 Victor Cazalet, a Conservative MP and advocate of the claimants, broached the idea, as did Marshall of Becos Traders, who promoted it with Maiskii and the City. According to one Treasury official, improving Anglo-Soviet relations might make such an arrangement "feasible." Collier was of a similar opinion.[54]

Maiskii was incredulous "that the present government should ask Parliament to guarantee a loan to Russia." Moreover, he discouraged any connection between a loan and a debts settlement: "Anglo-Soviet cooperation was a new-born infant … It might sicken at any disagreeable references to the past." Soviet officials complained about high interest rates; Anglo-Soviet trade, they said, was like "love without joy." British officials rejoined that if the USSR wanted cheaper, longer credit, it must settle British claims. Naturally, the Soviet government preferred cheaper, longer credit *without* settling the claims, but Maiskii said it "might be prepared to discuss" such an arrangement if convinced that the British were serious.[55] On the tsarist debts, Maiskii was exceeding his brief. In 1933 Krestinskii had advised him to keep the debts issue out of trade negotiations. The Politburo was not interested in starting debt negotiations again.[56]

Opposition arose among officials in the Treasury, but especially at the Board of Trade, where antagonism to a Soviet loan was unstinting, reaching from its lowest clerks to its president, Walter Runciman. Board of Trade resistance was ostensibly based on the risk of default being greater than if existing commercial credits were extended and increased, and if premiums were reduced. Runciman also opposed the loan for "political reasons." Treasury official S.D. Waley noted that the guaranteed loans were "usually unpopular." The British press, Waley noted, "would no doubt feel that if we wanted to develop any country with guaranteed loans we had better choose our Colonial Empire rather than Communist Russia, and a good many people would sympathise with … [this] view." The economic difficulties were not "insuperable … the decision must really turn on the question whether a proposal to guarantee a loan for Russia is politically practicable."[57] Neville Chamberlain, the chancellor, "wasn't going to have any serious party difficulties over it. He thought Hailsham [Douglas Hogg, Lord Chancellor, and a Tory Die-Hard] & his sort would be very hostile."[58] And one Treasury official thought that "Litvinoff is likely to claim a great diplomatic victory: he will not of course admit any obligation on Russia's part to compensate the claimants but will assert that he has persuaded the British Govt. to find the compensation themselves."[59]

Vansittart, supported by Hoare, promoted the loan proposal: "From the FO point of view the loan is better business."[60] At the same time, Ambassador Chilston observed that the loan would "have a marked political effect on the European situation. The Soviet Government would certainly make use of such an event to prove that Great Britain really means more than what she says about the Eastern Pact and it would thus serve as a further weapon in the Soviet campaign against Germany."[61] Similarly, Ashton-Gwatkin, head of the Economic Relations department, had "gained the impression that a loan from H.M.G. would restore in Soviet eyes the balance upset by the [Anglo-German naval] agreement, as it would show the world that we trusted the Soviet Government."[62] The proposal dragged during the summer of 1935 because of the Abyssinian crisis and then because of the parliamentary elections in November. Collier was impatient with the delays and tried unsuccessfully to "get a move on."[63]

Board of Trade opposition blocked Collier's efforts, but there was also opposition in the Foreign Office. Sargent, who disliked the Anglo-Soviet rapprochement as much as the Franco-Soviet one, opposed the loan. Of course, he would. In this narrative, one can count on Sargent to be on the wrong side if one supported an Anglo-Soviet rapprochement. It is astonishing that he was not sacked in May 1940 when Churchill became prime minister after being wrong on almost every major question in the lead-up to war. His ire was aroused by a meeting in September between a British go-between and Litvinov in Geneva to discuss the loan and quid pro quo of a debts settlement. Litvinov ruled out a formal settlement, but the USSR would consider a long-term loan at over-market interest rates. The margin and the Baring balances would go to pay off claimants, though the Soviet government would not acknowledge that it was doing so. Litvinov said he would support such an arrangement and thought that his government might accept it.[64]

A month later, Maiskii confirmed the position: what the British government did with the proceeds of a long-term loan was not a Soviet affair.[65] This was not, in fact, confirming Litvinov's comments in Geneva. It was an evasive reply. Maiskii had put the idea to Moscow in late September for partial compensation of the "old debts" in exchange for a British government loan. This was the same idea tried out in Washington. Krestinskii was against it and the Politburo supported him.[66] Troianovskii, still polpred in Washington, rather incredibly continued to try for a debts settlement, writing dispatches directly to Stalin, despite contrary directives from the NKID. What was he thinking? In late November 1935, Stalin finally put his foot down. The Soviet government was no longer prepared to discuss any reimbursement of the tsarist debts.[67]

Sargent would have been greatly relieved to know the true Soviet position, but based on what he read in his document boxes, it sounded too much like movement forward on an agreement. What, he asked, would Germany, Poland, and France have to say? The loan "will have a very real political effect however much we may protest that it represents a purely financial arrangement. In fact, the matter ought to be considered as part of the whole of the European complex." Vansittart disagreed. "I don't think we should hesitate on account of what any of these three countries may say. France will be jealous, Poland will perhaps be annoyed – but what expensive altruism has Poland ever displayed for us? As for Germany, why, they have tried to do practically the same thing. We should only be succeeding where they failed."

Hoare was in favour, but Eden was not so sure. "What will the Russians do with the proceeds of a loan, spend some part of it in communist propaganda, here & elsewhere? This is an aspect of Russian policy that remains most unsatisfactory from our point of view." Collier intervened to reassure Eden. He was only reluctantly converted "in view of happenings in his constituency."[68] Eden sounded prickly on the subject of Soviet "propaganda," and this proved a sign of things to come.

"Cat Burglary"

The issue of Soviet or British Communist Party criticism remained an issue inside the British government. The Foreign Office intervened with the British Broadcasting Corporation (B.B.C.) to stop a broadcast by British communist Harry Pollitt. Vansittart put the case plainly: "So long as we are expected to make representations to the Soviet Government against Soviet propaganda in this country, it is clearly an embarrassment to have the B.B.C. lending themselves to that propaganda."

The parliamentary undersecretary Lord Stanhope noted:

> It seems to me that the B.B.C. & its Board have not appreciated the point, which is that the spreading of Communism in this country is an offence and if undertaken by an individual in government service entails his dismissal … Why did they not give talks on cat burglary. Both were illegal but at any rate cat-burglary was more exciting and, to the individual, sometimes more lucrative. I suggest that the illegality of preaching communism should be impressed on the B.B.C.[69]

The question dragged on until February 1936 when cabinet finally intervened to cancel the broadcasts: "Communist propaganda," said a cabinet paper, "though probably ineffective in this country, remains a considerable danger in other parts of the Empire, particularly India." The hitch was that the HM Government did not want to be seen to be intervening with B.B.C. The cabinet was well satisfied when Pollitt was dropped without disclosure.[70]

What about the Loan?

If "propaganda" hindered Anglo-Soviet relations, other circumstances still favoured rapprochement. Collier saw the loan as a means of guaranteeing Soviet orders and "scooping" the Russian market for British manufacturers.[71] Competitors for Russian business – at that moment France and Nazi Germany were both negotiating with the USSR – roused those in the Foreign Office, who favoured a British loan.[72] Hoare pressed the case, and he obtained Chamberlain's consent, but not Runciman's.[73] Even Treasury officials had their doubts. Waley noted that the "Chambers of Commerce oppose a loan to Russia." Sir Frederick Phillips, a Treasury undersecretary, thought "the F.O. proposal … a rather tactless line of approach which might easily get us into trouble." And Chamberlain changed his mind: "The more I think of the loan proposal the less I like it."[74]

Impatience in the Foreign Office was palpable. "I am becoming most alarmed at these long delays," Vansittart noted. "We shall – as in other matters – miss a very large boat if we cannot make up our minds even now." Frustration was equally palpable. "We are up against a determined effort by the Board of Trade," noted Collier, "to obstruct the loan proposal at all costs." The Board of Trade had "constantly shifted the ground of their objection to the loan." Whenever the Foreign Office knocked down one argument, the Board of Trade advanced another.[75] Maiskii "is beginning to wonder," said Vansittart, "whether we really intend to do anything at all to improve Anglo-Soviet trade, or Anglo-Soviet relations generally."[76]

On the other hand, Chilston signalled from Moscow that Anglo-Soviet relations had never been better, though it would "take a long time" before Soviet suspicions entirely disappeared. It was December 1935. Chilston took for granted that Soviet suspicions were unfounded, but on this point he was mistaken. Nor were Anglo-Soviet relations on the rise, even though on 18 December Baldwin confirmed Chilston's assessment in the House of Commons.[77] This was the same day that Hoare resigned as Foreign Secretary.

Watching the unfolding events, Churchill offered the same advice as he had to Stalin via Maiskii, but he could not persuade his colleagues to act with sufficient urgency and resources. Without ministerial office, there was little he could do. The Hoare-Laval affair was bad news for Churchill and other advocates of collective security. Nor was Churchill pleased by Eden's appointment as Foreign Secretary to succeed Hoare. "The greatness of his office," he wrote to his wife, Clemmie, "will find him out."[78] Maiskii had higher hopes. He wrote a letter of congratulations to Eden, recalling his visit to Moscow and stressing the importance of Anglo-Soviet relations. Eden acknowledged Maiskii's letter with a perfunctory single paragraph.[79] The cursory reply was the first whiff of ill wind that would cool the Anglo-Soviet rapprochement. Despite his acutely sensitive antenna for trouble ahead, Maiskii missed the signs. He thought Eden was a "friend," and never saw that he was mistaken.

Chapter Fourteen

The Weak Hinge: France and Its East European Allies, 1935–1936

Paris was "the hinge" of Soviet efforts to organize an anti-Nazi entente, but the hinge was made of poor metal and incapable of bearing the weight assigned to it. We last left Laval on his way back to Paris after stopping off in Warsaw for Piłsudski's funeral where he reassured Polish officials not to worry about the Franco-Soviet Pact. Monsieur Zigzag was telling the Russians one thing and the Poles another. It turned out that in Moscow he had raised the question of general staff talks, necessary to actualize mutual assistance in the event of German aggression. This idea coming from Laval must have surprised Litvinov, and appeared too good to be true. According to Potemkin, the French general staff knew nothing about staff talks. Laval also promised speedy ratification of the pact, but already it looked like this would only happen in the autumn at the earliest. Like the late Dovgalevskii, Potemkin maintained a certain reserve towards the French for fear that too much Soviet interest in building closer ties would have the opposite effect. Moreover, the embassy reported increasing anti-communist agitation. The bourgeois press feared the growing strength of the Communist-Socialist Front commune. *Le Temps* was still a large problem. "Don't forget," Alphand said, "that of all the French papers, it is the most corrupt (*prodazhnyi*) … and the most bourgeois of all the bourgeois papers in France." In the political salons there were laments about too much Soviet influence in French internal affairs. The Soviet government needed to sweeten the pot, Alphand advised, and not think that the rapprochement could be based "solely … on mutual assistance," Moscow needed to settle the debts issue. It's a question of French "psychology." It would create more "enthusiasm" for Franco-Soviet relations.[1] Alphand obviously had not heard that the Soviet government had finally rejected the idea of reimbursing the tsarist debts. Did Alphand really think the Soviet government would trust an ally it had to buy?

A political cartoon in a Norwegian newspaper summed up the French attitude towards the Soviet Union: a burly-looking Bolshevik, wearing a *budenovka* (a civil war campaign cap) had the fair and innocent Marianne (symbol of the French Republic) on his arm with an apprehensive child carrying her wedding train.

"Are you content?" the Bolshevik spouse asked.

"Yes," Marianne replied, "but I would be more so, if I did not detest you so."[2]

British reaction to the "marriage" was also unenthusiastic. At the Foreign Office, Sargent thought the French had been had: "In this particular mutual guarantee treaty, it is Russia that obtains the benefits and France that assumes the practical obligations. If so, we must take off our hats to M. Litvinov for his very astute and successful diplomacy whereby he has been able to bluff and browbeat the French, in a moment of panic, into concluding this advantageous and one-sided bargain."[3] Sargent was wrong again. The bargain was one-sided, but not in the way he imagined. In fact, Litvinov was "furious" with Laval for weakening the pact and only declined to send him a "cordial" telegram about it, to avoid making matters worse.[4] Readers will remember Quai d'Orsay official René Massigli boasting of "blackballing" Soviet proposals. France thought only of a temporary agreement with the USSR to leave the door open to Berlin. The French general staff was against a deepening of the pact: France had a number of accords with its allies: there was "no particular reason" for another with the Soviet Union. This was a peculiar statement for a country in desperate need of powerful allies, but the general staff did not want to give Germany a "pretext" for reoccupying the demilitarized Rhineland, or Poland a reason for allying with Hitler against "the Russian danger."[5]

Litvinov was not having a good year. The pact with France proved to be a *pis-aller*, a last expedient, and not a "hinge" at all. *Perfide Albion* had signed a naval accord with Nazi Germany thus collaborating with a potential enemy to violate stipulations of the Treaty of Versailles. Then there was the impending Abyssinian crisis about which Litvinov could do little on his own. During the summer, Soviet diplomats liked to take their holidays, not least Potemkin, who reminded Litvinov that the "off season" was beginning. "I do not believe," Litvinov commented, "that this year there will be any off season." But the narkom was not going to stop Potemkin's holiday. He assured him of that. At the same time he worried about Laval who had become président du Conseil on 7 June while remaining Minister of Foreign Affairs. These combined functions would not lead to better relations with Moscow. In fact, Litvinov agreed with Potemkin that the British "betrayal" (i.e., the naval agreement with Germany) could lead to a similar "betrayal" by Laval. "I consider it a great misfortune," Litvinov continued, "that we were not able to force Laval to expedite the ratification of the pact." Laval was having us on about delays in ratification, Litvinov continued: "He wants to keep this trump in his hands for negotiations with Germany." A French "betrayal" might thus follow that of the English.[6] In August, Litvinov complained about the delay in ratification when he met Laval in Geneva, but it did no good. Laval countered with a protest about communist activities in Indochina and agents being trained either through the Comintern or through the Soviet government at a school in Moscow carrying Stalin's name. This was Laval's old trick that he used whenever Litvinov complained about French

Figure 14.1. Litvinov and Beneš exchange ratification documents in Moscow (Krestinskii is on Litvinov's left), 8 June 1935, AVPRF.

policy. Litvinov replied that Laval's information was bogus and his documents, counterfeit. The time had long since past when the Lord Curzons or others like him could propose, as the narkom put it, "that if there were no Soviet government, there would be no discontent and no anti-government movements in India and other colonies."[7] This was not a cordial meeting between would-be allies against Nazi Germany, and the ratification of the mutual assistance pact was put off until the new year.

Did the Soviet Union have any close allies in mid-1935? It is true there was Czechoslovakia. Beneš and Aleksandrovskii signed the mutual assistance pact on 16 May 1935, and Beneš visited Moscow a few weeks later to sign ratification documents.

This development was all to the good in appearance. However, Soviet-Czechoslovak relations depended on Soviet relations with France and in particular with Laval. He was not a close ally. Neither was Britain, which signed the Anglo-German naval accord just after Beneš returned to Prague. In all of Litvinov's files, things looked uncertain. Even the cunning Titulescu was proving difficult. This time he was "blackmailing" France to obtain support for a Romanian mutual assistance pact with the USSR, a desirable objective according to Litvinov, by threatening to refuse passage to the Red Army across Romanian territory, if France did not support the pact.[8] One can see why Titulescu might contemplate blackmail against Laval, but would it work? Litvinov was in principle not against such tactics, but only if they offered a solid chance of success.

The Problem with Poland

If Litvinov could at least hold out hopes of drawing Britain, France, and Romania into his plans, he had no such expectations regarding Poland. Litvinov's meetings with Beck in February 1934 had led the NKID to conclude that Poland could not be counted on and that he, Beck, could not be trusted. In May 1934, the subject of Poland came up in a discussion between Litvinov and Alphand. The ambassador was going on leave and he asked if Litvinov had messages for him to take back to Paris. Alphand said he did not share the narkom's "pessimism in regard to Poland." There was mistrust on both sides, and Poland did not believe in the stability of Soviet policy. Apparently, that line was circulating in Warsaw. Litvinov did not like Alphand's diplomatic attempt to see both sides of the Soviet-Polish relationship. "I replied," Litvinov wrote to his *dnevnik*, that "if we talk about our distrust, it is based on facts. We had very serious conversations with Poland about cooperation and these conversations were stopped at the initiative of the Poles." Litvinov then went into some detail about which readers are already informed. He added that there was gossip circulating "about secret Polish-German agreements." Information from French sources appeared to confirm the rumours. He urged the French not to blame the Soviet government for the trouble with Poland. It was not their doing. "I therefore expressed astonishment," Litvinov continued, "that Alphand could speak to us about mistrust." Obviously, the French ambassador had touched a raw nerve.[9]

Alphand wrote his own record of this meeting in which he failed to convey Litvinov's angry message about Polish deceit. The ambassador reduced the narkom's indignation to the mention of "certain reserves" about "Polish misgivings (*réticences*) with regard to the USSR." That was a fine way of putting matters. Alphand added that since his arrival in Moscow, he had not noticed any change in Soviet policy; the USSR still sought closer relations with France and its allies and an ever-growing *détachement* from Nazi Germany. Then Alphand added an unsubtle warning: "If a modification of this policy occurs, it could only be in the event where, not having encountered with its new friends reciprocal fellow feelings, the USSR could return to a policy from which it drew important advantages during twelve years." Readers will recognize the reference to Rapallo.[10] There would be other warnings of a return to Rapallo from the French embassy in Moscow, Alphand's, and those of his successors and of the chargé d'affaires, Payart,

Map 14.1. Eastern Europe, 1930s.

right up to the summer of 1939. Nor did Litvinov and his colleagues hold their fire against Poland. The trouble was that the French government could not bring itself to break with Warsaw and so clerks in Paris filed the warnings from Moscow.

Even while Litvinov recommended to Stalin a continuation of Soviet efforts to improve relations with Warsaw, he made sure that his Western interlocutors knew exactly what he thought about Polish policy in general and about Colonel Beck in particular. Several months after unburdening himself with Alphand, he had a similar conversation with the US minister in Warsaw, John Cudahy. "I briefly exchanged opinions with him about Beck personally and about Polish policy. We both agreed that Beck had learned the old method of diplomacy – to hide his thoughts behind words, and that Polish politics were most mysterious and, I added, treacherous. I think I told him how Beck, while negotiating the Baltic declaration with us, was at the same time negotiating with the Germans in the opposite direction."[11] Litvinov was referring to a quip by the French diplomat Charles-Maurice de Talleyrand, who once observed that human beings had obtained the power of speech in order to conceal their thoughts (*La parole a été donnée à l'homme pour déguiser sa pensée*). The narkom's indirect reference to Talleyrand is interesting since some Western observers saw Litvinov as the Soviet reincarnation of that French diplomat.

The NKID still hoped for the "will-o'-the-wisp" of an Eastern Pact. Litvinov was not naïve about an eventual Polish epiphany; it was simply that he saw no other options. Nor did he give up on Beck. Litvinov still prodded him but without any result. Litvinov did not get any further with the Polish ambassador Łukasiewicz. In their recent conversations the narkom "had got the impression that Łukasiewicz had come with the definite intention to pursue a policy of nagging, protesting." Since the Germans were using similar tactics, it begged the question of whether the stalling was merely a coincidence or "the result of some German-Polish agreement."[12]

As 1935 unfolded, the Soviet assessment of Polish intentions worsened. The NKID wondered which way Polish policy would go after the death of Piłsudski. The Soviet embassy in Warsaw closely monitored the Polish press and noted a tilt on the right and even in "semi-official" circles towards greater cooperation with Nazi Germany. "From completely reliable sources," which meant, in NKID parlance, intelligence sources, Stomoniakov had heard that even Laval was convinced that Polish intimacy (*blizost'*) with Germany had gone further than previously believed in Paris. Moreover, the NKID continued to be irritated with "swindling" (*sharlatanskie*) Polish attempts to blame Moscow for the failure of improved relations.[13]

There was some speculation in Moscow and at the Soviet embassy in Warsaw whether Beck had inspired or even written articles in the press advocating closer relations with Germany. Davtian, the Soviet polpred, did not think so. "Beck is too flexible a player to place an irrevocable bet on this card now. So the chatter [in the press] did not much suit him. Beck will continue to manoeuvre for a while yet ... maintaining a certain balance between Germany, France, and us until the international situation becomes clear … and while his personal internal situation remains uncertain. In essence, his foreign policy is pro-German." Davtian did not expect any big changes in Polish policy unless there were Soviet setbacks such as a deterioration of relations with Japan or with France. For Davtian, this suited Soviet interests. "I again believe that the most profitable thing for us is to wait calmly on events and maintain correct relations. A further strengthening of our international positions will also help to strengthen our positions in Poland."

Davtian's relations with the government and foreign ministry were "very passive"; in fact, they had been at the freezing point for some time. That meant no political contact with Beck, except at diplomatic receptions. Essentially, the Poles were doing nothing to improve relations, and neither was the Soviet side. Davtian supported tolerable, "correct" relations with his Polish counterparts, especially on a personal level. He even noted that Beck had been "very kind and helpful" with him in their personal interactions. Relations were also good with foreign ministry officials. Davtian invited them to embassy dinners, "some of them two or three times." That seemed to work well. "I believe," he added, "that we should continue to maintain a correct, 'collegial' relationship here and in Moscow." Davtian approved of Stomoniakov's reciprocity in "feeding" Polish embassy staff.[14] The missing people on Davtian's visitors' list were Polish oppositionists.

So Litvinov, it would seem, was not such a cad after all. Keep the doors open if the Poles want to walk through them; if only they would. In early July 1935, Stomoniakov had a meeting with Łukasiewicz – not always a pleasant conversationalist with Soviet interlocutors. They discussed various subjects without any problems. "The entire conversation had a very peaceful character," Stomoniakov noted, "confirming Comrade Litvinov's impression, that L. and the Poles for the time being had decided to avoid conflicts and aggravations."[15]

As Stomoniakov wrote these lines, Beck was setting out for Berlin to pay a call on Hitler and other Nazi officials. The reaction in Moscow was immediate. From Stomoniakov's point of view, the visit after Piłsudski's death signalled that Polish-German cooperation had not weakened but on the contrary had deepened. Clearly, it did not take much to provoke Soviet mistrust. Stomoniakov instructed Davtian to find out as much as he could about the talks in Berlin.[16] It was a happy coincidence when the French ambassador, Léon Noël, paid a call at the Soviet embassy and Davtian could query him about Beck's intentions. There was not much to know. Prior to his departure, Beck had advised Noël, but not Davtian, that no new agreements were signed. The visit returned a German visit to Warsaw by Herman Goering. Beck hoped to lift his public profile at home, but the Germans had not obliged him with any special gestures.[17]

Noël could only speculate, and so did Davtian when two days later he reported to Stomoniakov. "Beck's position, after the death of Piłsudski (who was his only support), became very uncertain. It will depend on the good will of the ruling elite, with many members of which he has bad relations. He needs something to strengthen his position and convince everyone that he is indispensable as Foreign Minister." Davtian continued:

> In my opinion, one of the main political reasons for Beck's trip was the Poles' fear of a possible German-French rapprochement and their desire to mediate in this matter. The Piłsudskiists, of course, want this rapprochement, calculating, not without reason, that it will weaken Franco-Soviet cooperation and even completely bring it to naught. But they do not want this rapprochement to bypass Poland and so would like to play the role of mediator. This effort of the Poles follows logically from their entire position, to break up the Franco-Soviet-Little Entente bloc in Europe and to oppose to it a German-Polish one, with the participation of France. Whether Beck was able to do anything in this direction, is difficult to say.[18]

Davtian may have felt that Stomoniakov was too hostile towards Beck, and so he wrote a dispatch for Litvinov, marked personal and very secret, making a fresh attempt to persuade Moscow to keep options open for the Poles to change policy. "I want ... to raise with you," Davtian wrote, "the question of the fate of our future relations with Poland." Over the last six months or so, they have reached the point where we have "neither political nor cultural contacts." Outwardly, our official relations continue to be "correct." Beck says to foreign diplomats, and in particular to Noël, that Soviet-Polish relations are "normal and good."

"But this, of course, is the purely external side of things," Davtian continued. "The truth is that our actual relationship is full of all kinds of annoyance, anger, and distrust. The Polish press does not miss an opportunity to speak out against us more or less openly ... A significant part of the attacks against us are directed at Russia's foreign policy." On any subject, positive articles about the USSR had almost completely disappeared from the Polish press. It was the same for Soviet films and books, which were not available anywhere.

Davtian then returned to the question of Polish "irritation" over Soviet foreign policy and to the "hostile activities which the Poles were pursuing against us on all diplomatic questions and in all European and other countries." Now the Soviet press was beginning to return fire, sometimes overdoing it. This, the Poles had noticed. "What will happen next?" Davtian asked rhetorically. "We know very well about Polish aggressive intentions, their 'feelings' towards us, we know that they are stubbornly preparing for war with us, putting together a bloc against us, everywhere shitting on us, and so on. And yet even now we are not preparing for war with Poland and in general we want normal and peaceful relations." For the time being the Polish press was more or less holding fire, except, Davtian noted, when it wants to exploit Soviet difficulties in particular in the Far East. "Having established closer relations with Germany, the Poles do not want to break off with France and spoil relations with us ... Beck is always looking back at France and the USSR, avoiding anything that could strengthen our mistrust. The Germans have also noticed this." Let's work up "some kind of plan of action" and "some kind of 'gesture'" to kick it off, Davtian proposed, knowing that Litvinov or Stomoniakov might be touchy about such a suggestion. So he added that he was only "thinking out loud."[19]

Davtian soon returned to Moscow on leave. He would have met Litvinov and Stomoniakov to discuss his ideas, but there is unlikely to be any written record of their conversations. In fact, Stomoniakov readily acknowledged that the "Piłsudskiists" were putting out feelers to indicate interest in calming relations and to quiet down criticism in the Soviet press. He attributed this interest to "pressure from all sides" on the "Germanophile" policy of the Polish government and especially on Beck. Poland is isolated, Stomoniakov noted, "and in the pages of the world press it is more and more identified among those governments seeking war, alongside Japan and Germany." Even in Poland pressure was growing on the Piłsudskiists' foreign policy and "Beck's adventurism." Given the circumstances, it was not surprising that the "Piłsudskiists" and "especially Beck and his friends" would want to turn down the volume of external and internal criticism of Polish policy. Let the Poles twist a little in the wind, was the NKID's position. "We are not interested," Stomoniakov wrote to the Soviet chargé d'affaires in Warsaw, Podol'skii, "in easing the situation of Beck and the 'Piłsudskiists.' In response to any attempts to obtain such an alleviation [of relations], you should indicate that our attitude towards Poland and the attitude of our press are only a weak reflex to the anti-Soviet policy of Poland." Even so, Stomoniakov added as a further instruction, probably tongue in cheek, that the chargé d'affaires could say, if asked, that the Soviet press was "relatively moderate" when it came to Poland, which was more than one could say about the "vicious articles against the USSR" in the Polish press, especially from semi-official sources.[20] If the Polish press was trying to quiet down its nastiness towards the USSR, it was not taken seriously in Moscow.

Apart from the mutual slagging in the daily papers, there were other problems which made it difficult to go ahead with Davtian's proposed overture in Warsaw. There was a Soviet overflight of Polish territory – this led to difficulties – and a reciprocal expulsion of Soviet and Polish journalists. In early September, Polish "elections" led to an unexpected setback for the ruling "Piłsudskiists." Stomoniakov hoped it might lead to a change of government in Warsaw, though he did not expect a change in foreign policy or foreign minister. The NKID closely followed Beck's activities and standing in the Polish government and hoped against hope that the foreign minister might be forced to resign. Apart from Beck, there were other minor incidents which, taken together, added to the general impression in Moscow of Polish anti-Soviet hostility. Davtian's idea of a fresh initiative in Warsaw was thus dead in the water.[21] He apparently returned to the need at a minimum of avoiding a further irritation of Polish-Soviet relations. Stomoniakov had no problem with that notion, but saw no way forward with it either. There was another incident in Moscow when a chauffeur at the Polish embassy, driving recklessly, killed one or some pedestrians. Łukasiewicz claimed diplomatic immunity for the chauffeur, which the NKID refused to accept.[22]

Poland and Romania

It was one thing after another. According to NKVD foreign intelligence, "Poland and Germany were undertaking all measures to break up negotiations between the USSR and Romania on mutual assistance." The Poles even threatened to rupture the Polish-Romanian alliance unless the Romanian government abandoned Titulescu's policies and opted for a rapprochement with Germany. King Carol II even said he intended to pursue an "active rapprochement with Germany" and if the government did not like it, he would change the government. On his copy of this report, Stalin marked all the above sections in red pencil.[23]

The NKID received reports that the Polish minister in Bucharest, Mirosław Arciszewski, had met with King Carol warning him against "an alliance with the USSR," a country which sought to promote world revolution. In fact, the Soviet embassy in Bucharest was well informed about this meeting and sent a lengthy report to Moscow. According to Soviet informants, Arciszewski reproached Titulescu for dragging Romania into the Franco-Soviet-Czechoslovak "orbit." Even Yugoslavia was being pulled in, or so it seemed. These developments, according to Arciszewski, could prove to be a problem between Poland and Romania.[24] There appear to have been several versions of how the king replied to the Polish minister, which were both favourable to collective security and not. King Carol did not wish to alienate Germany, and court officials apparently encouraged the Polish mission in Warsaw to pursue an anti-Soviet line. The polpred Ostrovskii characterized the struggle as a head-to-head clash between the Polish minister and Titulescu, which the latter seemed to be losing, especially because of his long absence from Bucharest. Arciszewski was allowed to run amok, "deftly wav[ing] the spectre of communism and Sovietization of Romania" so that Titulescu's most loyal supporters were left in doubt. Titulescu's only reaction, again, if rumours were to be believed, was to contemplate resignation. He hoped for sympathy and a stronger hand, but obtained neither.[25] Of course, if one could not count on France, in view of Laval's zigzags, what could the king of a small Balkan power do but play it safe? That meant keeping all options open.

At the same time, Arciszewski met with the interior minister to issue a similar warning. Apparently, the minister replied that "in as much as the Poles were tied to the Germans, they would be obliged to concede to Germany the [Polish] corridor and to look for compensation in the east and southeast … Polish expansion would be directed not only towards the Ukraine, but also to Bukovina and Bessarabia."[26] It was hard to trust the Poles, even in Bucharest. The Poles were worried that Romania might agree to passage rights for the Red Army to go to the aid of Czechoslovakia in the event of Nazi aggression. Because of the

Polish-Romanian alliance, Poland considered that it had the right to intervene in Bucharest to block a Soviet mutual assistance pact. Romania does not need it, said the Poles, and it "could bring incalculable damage to Poland and Germany."[27]

Polish relations with Czechoslovakia were also worsening, and Polish officials did not attempt to hide why: it was because of "Beneš's pro-Soviet policy." Davtian reported this news to Moscow from the Czechoslovak chargé d'affaires in Warsaw. "I am not at all surprised," he replied to his Czechoslovak colleague, "[that] the Poles were also conducting discussions with the Romanians and French … to abandon their rapprochement with the USSR." Davtian laughed for he did not think Polish intrigues would succeed. It was "common interests" that were uniting France, the Little Entente, and the USSR, and no one could do anything about it.[28] Davtian was dead wrong; the Poles had every chance of success. Their activities begged the question: on whose side was Poland?

In part, thanks to the Poles, Titulescu was in trouble in Bucharest. In November, he finally resigned as foreign minister because of opposition to his pro-Soviet policy, but the prime minister, Gheorghe I. Tătărescu, along with the king, urged Titulescu to reconsider. He agreed, and lived to fight another day, but he was isolated and politically wounded.[29]

Davtian and Anatole de Monzie

In Paris, Laval was still in power. The French capital was thus a fertile field for Polish sabotage. In late November 1935, Davtian met Anatole de Monzie twice in Warsaw; he brought some good news and some bad from France. He had arrived from Bucharest where he had seen Ostrovskii. Monzie was then optimistic about the ratification of the Franco-Soviet Pact, but less so when he arrived in Warsaw.[30] Perhaps he had received news from Paris. Davtian and Monzie were old acquaintances, having met in Paris during the negotiations in 1926–7 for financial and trade agreements. Their meeting in Warsaw was cordial, and Monzie spoke freely. Seven out of ten French politicians at least were in favour of the rapprochement, according to Monzie: ratification of the mutual assistance pact was not in doubt. *But* the delay in ratification had created the impression that something was wrong. What is the situation now? Davtian asked. Shrugging his shoulders, Monzie implied that he did not like Laval's conduct, but he avoided openly attacking it. What Monzie did say directly was that Laval was intentionally delaying ratification, and that he disliked Laval's policy towards Germany. It had produced no results, and could never do so. This sounded like what Vansittart had said to Maiskii in London. German policy was obvious and directed at the seizure of all of Central Europe. This meant Anschluss, the dismemberment of Czechoslovakia, imposition of indirect control over Hungary, and then an attack on Poland. Davtian agreed. Monzie was singing to the choir.

Discussion then turned to Franco-Polish relations. Monzie asked for a frank comment from Davtian and got it: relations between Poland and Germany were close; between Poland and France, not so much. "The keystone of European politics now is German belligerence and the struggle against it." Poland remained the spoiler. Davtian continued: "Whether Beck goes or not, in my opinion, nothing will change in the foreign policy of Poland, for so long as the Piłsudskiists remain in power. It is very possible that the Poles for tactical reasons will replace Beck in order to create additional illusions in Paris. But this will change nothing in substance." About Franco-Soviet relations, Monzie thought they were "very good," but the rapprochement had not yet become a deep conviction (*sblizhenie eshche ne doshlo do glubiny dushi*). That was one way of putting it.[31]

Monzie went back to see Davtian three days later, and they had a long conversation over lunch at the embassy. Monzie reported on his conversations with Polish officials and politicians, including Beck and Arciszewski, who happened to be in town. Not surprisingly, the Poles were very solicitous of Monzie and organized meetings for him. According to Davtian, Monzie stated quite categorically that the Poles were "strongly anti-Soviet" – this would not have been a surprise – and he had heard old complaints about the Eastern Pact and the "danger of communism," among other issues. In reply, Monzie had made clear his own position in favour of a Franco-Soviet "alliance." That could not have gone down well with his Polish interlocutors, though they would have brushed it off. According to Monzie, the Poles harped on the "danger for Europe" of Soviet policy, "in particular for France and Romania." The discussion eventually turned to Franco-Polish relations and there Monzie was sceptical. There had been an improvement in the "tone" of relations, but this was just a show because Poland still needed the Franco-Polish alliance as leverage in Berlin and also in Paris to obtain "money." Monzie talked again about Romania, and noted in particular that Arciszewski was waging an all-out campaign against Titulescu. According to his information, Monzie warned that local fascists "had planned or were planning an assassination attempt against not only Titulescu but also Ostrovskii." He did not have any detailed information, but asked that Ostrovskii be warned.[32]

Good News, (Mostly) Bad News

The news flowing into the NKID was dismal. Laval was conniving against pact ratification. The Poles were trying to wreck Soviet collective security. Britain had "betrayed" the anti-Nazi bloc and the Stresa Front with its naval accord with Hitler, and the Italians had provoked a crisis over Abyssinia and jeopardized the League's credibility. Still, Litvinov, with Stalin behind him, was a long way from giving up the fight. At the end of June 1935, the narkom met with the Bulgarian minister who asked about Soviet policy in the Balkans. "Our attitude to Bulgaria has not changed," Litvinov replied. "We have no special interests either in Bulgaria or in other Balkan countries, we do not seek anything from them, and our attitude towards other countries *is determined solely by the question of the attitude of these countries to the question of peace or war, and therefore in particular the attitude of these countries towards Germany* [emphasis added]."[33] That was a clear, accurate statement of Soviet policy, but in view of all the setbacks, could the Soviet government continue to defend it?

Not all the news was bad. A French military mission attended Red Army manoeuvres in the Ukraine in September 1935. General Lucien Loizeau, head of the mission, wrote a favourable report, which countered the negativity beginning to develop inside the French general staff.[34] Alphand made mention of the report as good news in a meeting with Krestinskii in October. He also advised that trade negotiations in Paris appeared to be going well. Two pieces of good news, said Alphand, to counter the general flow of bad news.[35] Litvinov was quick to push the economic negotiations and at once took up the matter with Stalin through the Politburo. It was traditional Soviet foreign policy: improve economic relations to improve or to consolidate political relations. Molotov recommended approval of Litvinov's proposal and instructions were issued to pursue the discussions in Paris.[36]

Unfortunately, the stream of information flowing into the NKID was mostly adverse. Laval was the main problem, and he was Litvinov's main concern, as he advised Potemkin in Paris:

> Although I treat carefully the reports of intermediaries and journalists, especially the gloomy Tabouis, about Laval's position, I still have the impression that Laval has decided, insofar as it depends on him, to wreck [*sorvat'*] at any cost Franco-Soviet cooperation and to join the German anti-Soviet bloc, and that he actually wants to adopt Beck's foreign policy, which it appears, to this point, he himself has not been able to carry out. I consider it possible that if Laval survives the immediate [political] crisis and, having intimidated the Radicals, not only remains in the government, but also strengthens his position, he will even refuse to ratify the [Franco-Soviet] Pact. But in the case where he is forced to submit the pact for ratification, he will take care to create such a strong opposition, both in the Chamber [of Deputies] and outside it, as to devalue the fact of ratification and thus turn the pact into a scrap of paper.

Litvinov was pessimistic about seeing the end of Laval. "If he falls now," he advised Potemkin,

> he will continue to play a large role in French politics and will rise to the surface in every government crisis. From the point of view of our interests, we could welcome at least his temporary departure from the cabinet, which would allow us not only to carry through ratification [of the mutual assistance pact], to arrange it properly, but also to destroy the harmful effects of Laval's influence on the Little Entente and in part even on England. However, this requires the departure of Laval not only as head of government, but also as foreign minister. He will still be able to do harm if he remains in the cabinet as minister without portfolio. Herriot shows great naiveté if he thinks that it will be possible to maintain Soviet-French cooperation under Laval.[37]

Litvinov, Ostrovskii, and Titulescu

Laval's conduct created ripples of trouble across Europe. His wriggling to get out of the Franco-Soviet Pact encouraged Polish wrecking and discouraged Titulescu who was waging a lonely fight for a Romanian-Soviet rapprochement. Litvinov met Titulescu in Geneva to talk things over. "I have never seen him in such a depressed mood," Litvinov wrote to Ostrovskii. Titulescu was frustrated by a long list of problems. The most important was "Laval's exit from the policy of rapprochement with the USSR threating even ratification of the Franco-Soviet Pact." Litvinov also reproached his own colleagues, presumably Stalin, Molotov, and Kaganovich, for "our negative and evasive attitude to his proposal for a general mutual assistance pact." It is not clear what Litvinov meant by this language, perhaps the actual terms of an agreement or the Bessarabia stumbling block.

There were other problems with Laval, notably his attempt to reconcile Italy with Yugoslavia while ignoring Czechoslovakia and Romania. There were also attacks on Titulescu at home. Remember, Monzie had heard of a planned attempt to assassinate the minister as well as Ostrovskii. Bucharest could be a rough place and Titulescu felt safer spending long periods abroad. The problem was that when the cat is away, the mice will play. Titulescu's absenteeism, his most recent absence from Bucharest being four months, left the door open to the Polish legation.

There were Soviet gestures of friendship towards the Romanian government: one was Stalin's agreement for a Titulescu visit to Moscow. Stalin rarely agreed to meet foreign visitors. This was thus an important gesture.[38] Titulescu did not hide the fact that he hoped to sign a mutual assistance pact with the USSR, similar to those with France and Czechoslovakia. He openly talked about it and about an autumn visit to Moscow during a dinner in June at the Soviet embassy in Bucharest.[39] A further gesture was agreement to rebuild a bridge across the Dniestr River between Soviet Tiraspol and Bender on the Romanian side. Titulescu wanted to name the bridge "Eternal Peace on the Dniestr." Litvinov must have thought that was overdoing it and that "Peace Bridge" would do.[40]

There was also the issue of Titulescu's *démenti*, a denial that he had discussed Red Army passage across Romania to reinforce Czechoslovakia. Litvinov had agreed to the *démenti* even though it was untrue in order to help Titulescu get enemies off his back. Some of the narkom's colleagues objected, but Litvinov replied in effect that it was a *pis-aller*, making the best of a bad situation. The problem was not simply a denial to throw predators off Titulescu's trail. "I believe that the discussion in the press, and questions in [the Romanian] Parliament," Litvinov explained to Ostrovskii, "damaged not only Titulescu personally, but also our prestige, as well as our relations in general with Romania.

Figure 14.2. Ostrovskii (front row second from left) and embassy staff in Bucharest, ca. 1936, AVPRF.

In addition, they [Titulescu's enemies] have mobilized all those forces that are hostile to us. One could tolerate the attacks if Titulescu was in Bucharest and in one way or another responded to them. With Titulescu constantly sitting in Cap Martin [in southern France] and his complete passivity, one-sided discussion was extremely harmful and had to be opposed."[41] Titulescu had taken a bold step in proposing the Romanian-Soviet rapprochement, but once started, he could not let the rapprochement take care of itself while he enjoyed a comfortable existence on the French Riviera.

The Romanian *démenti* surprised the French minister in Bucharest who had heard of Titulescu's earlier comments during the dinner at the Soviet embassy in June. Titulescu then visited the French embassy a few days later to discuss details of the draft pact. Red Army passage was a subject of conversation. "It is better to agree to it," Titulescu had said, "than to have it imposed." The French minister thus concluded that the *démenti* was untrue and a cover for retreat. The Germans did not believe it either.[42]

Litvinov could not do more in Bucharest until Soviet relations with France had been sorted out. Again, he explained to Ostrovskii what he had said to Titulescu in Geneva:

> I summarized my position as follows: until the Franco-Soviet Pact is ratified and relations with France are clarified, we cannot enter into any further agreements with the Little Entente countries. The question of the pact has not been raised by me or discussed by our government. In general, we have been referring to regional pacts against a certain possible aggressor, not general pacts against any aggressors. I personally believe that our government will never accept a pact that would oblige us to defend Romania against any state, and Romania would be exempt from helping us against one of our most likely enemies, Poland. If Titulescu is ready to give up the idea of excluding Poland, then the issue can be discussed during Titulescu's visit to Moscow, and I will try to prepare our government for this discussion in advance.

Basically, it came down to who is your enemy and against whom are you ready to go to war? On these questions, Litvinov had this to say:

> Titulescu declared that, since Poland would not attack us without Germany, Romania, having pledged to help us against Germany, would also act against Poland. In any case, Romania is ready to help us against Germany and other European neighbours, except Poland. I pointed out the possibility of an attack against us, under certain conditions, by Poland alone, with the informal material support of Germany. I laughed at the idea of [Romania] helping us against Latvia, Estonia, or Finland. I emphasized finally that I was not making any offers, but only seeking to clarify Titulescu's position, and I asked him what he thought of a pact that would oblige each side to come forward in the event of an attack on the other by any two states. Titulescu rejected this idea as well.

Litvinov and Titulescu then discussed the legal problems raised by the Polish-Romanian defence pact, which would raise obstacles for Soviet-Romanian mutual assistance. Litvinov drew the conclusion that Titulescu's "legal references" were only a pretext and had nothing to do with his position. "He simply proceeds from the feeling that the alliance with Poland is so popular in Romania that neither the king nor the country will agree to any pact, even theoretically directed against an aggressive Poland."

Titulescu also had Laval in the back of his mind. "I got the impression," Litvinov wrote, "that Titulescu was beginning to doubt the possibility of continuing the present line of foreign policy, especially if Laval carries out his anti-Soviet plans, and that he, Titulescu, was already thinking, if not of changing his policy, then of softening it." Litvinov continued:

> It was not for nothing that he asked [Turkish foreign minister] Aras in Geneva how Turkey managed to establish and maintain very decent relations with Germany

> while being friendly with the USSR. I therefore expect Titulescu to make a few bows to Germany in Bucharest. Moreover, I assume that he will refuse to go to Moscow under one pretext or another. True, he assured me that he would definitely visit us on 25 November, but he would probably finally resolve the issue in Bucharest by measuring the strength of anti-Soviet sentiment, but also depending on Laval's behaviour. A planned or rather predicted turn in Poland's foreign policy should ease Titulescu's position, but this turn, unfortunately, is still directed only towards France, and not the USSR.

Finally, Litvinov returned to the Poles. "I would consider it very useful to make public the content of the conversation between Arciszewski and the king. Is it possible?" Litvinov wanted to know from Ostrovskii. If so, ask Vinogradov "to write something like a correspondence from Bucharest about the anti-Soviet intrigues of the Polish envoy and the content of his conversation with the king." It could be published in Moscow in the *Journal de Moscou*.[43] Boris Dmitrievich Vinogradov had served in Berlin as first secretary and also as an NKVD agent, but was then first secretary in Bucharest.

Honourable comes to mind when one thinks about Litvinov's relations with Titulescu. Not only did he help cover for him on the question of Red Army passage, he also let him off the hook on the visit to Moscow, which means he had spoken to Stalin to explain the situation in Bucharest. "Titulescu informed me," Ostrovskii reported to Litvinov, "that in the last conversation with him, you did not insist on his trip, leaving the decision to him depending on the internal situation and on the possible impact of this trip on the firmness of his ministerial portfolio. Titulescu added that he was deeply moved by this display of sincerity and cordiality." Ostrovskii opined that the trip to Moscow was more than ever "absolutely necessary."[44] In principle, Litvinov agreed. Was Titulescu coming to Moscow or not? He needed to make up his mind. If he was coming, who would accompany him, how many days would he stay, and what did he want to see in Moscow? There were options: the theatre or opera, ballet, museums, art galleries, factories. Ostrovskii was to find out and cable Litvinov.[45]

A few days later Litvinov took up the question again, reminding Ostrovskii that the initiative for the trip to Moscow came from Titulescu, not from the Soviet side. Unfortunately, he (Titulescu) had talked to the press about the prospective visit, which provoked problems in Bucharest. The idea was to go to Moscow to sign a mutual assistance pact, or to acknowledge Soviet recognition of Romanian sovereignty over Bessarabia. "He obviously does not want to go for nothing," Litvinov noted. "The trip will not do us any good either, if it is followed by some turn of events in Romanian politics." Everything depended on the situation in Bucharest: would the king and the government continue to back a Soviet rapprochement? If not, Titulescu would cancel out. So he was not to be pushed, Litvinov instructed, since he could say to the press that we were pressuring him. But he was to be asked for a final answer, since it would be necessary to make preparations for the visit.[46]

Three days later on 19 November, Titulescu advised Ostrovskii that the trip was off. His political situation was uncertain. He never trusted anyone a day beyond a promise made, so Ostrovskii reported, the only one he "firmly counts on is the king." The king of course, Titulescu said, would never be an *ami des Soviets* (in the original, "a friend of the Soviets"), "but he is afraid of you, both as a moral force and, especially, as a material force … so the king is quite convinced that it is better to have the Soviets as friends than as enemies." Carol, however, was getting pressure from all sides, and the Franco-Soviet Pact was not yet ratified.[47] Even the French weighed in. German sources had it on good authority that the French deputy chief of staff, General Victor-Henri Schweisguth, who was in Romania to observe manoeuvres, had suggested "slow[ing] down the rapprochement with Russia."[48] It is doubtful whether Schweisguth would have offered this advice on his own initiative.

Ostrovskii met frequently with Titulescu trying to find ways forward. On 23 November, they met to go over the deteriorating situation. Titulescu was worried and said so. The Turks and Yugoslavs, particularly the new Yugoslav prime minister Milan Stojadinović, were flirting with Poland and Germany, and looking to improve relations. The solidity of the Little Entente was threatened. Then there were Laval's policies – it was Laval who worried Titulescu, and the "impudence" of Poland. "*I have always said,*" Titulescu quipped, "*that it is not my king who will break my neck; my neck will be broken by my allies: Poland, first, then Turkey, Yugoslavia and now Laval* [original in French; emphasis added]. I have hitherto been able to convince the king that a pro-German policy would isolate Romania from her allies in the Balkans and Central Europe, and would isolate her from France and England. Now the king will be able to tell me that Romania, insisting on her policy, may find herself isolated."[49]

In a dispatch to Aleksandrovskii in Prague, Litvinov repeated a little of the news about Titulescu that he had shared with Ostrovskii, and then he went further. "From some quarters we heard in Geneva that pro-German sentiment had increased in the Little Entente. Titulescu himself told me that he was now for the first time concerned about the position of Yugoslavia, calling Stojadinović [the new Yugoslav prime minister] a Germanophile. Titulescu was worried, mainly by the attacks on him in Romania for ostensibly negotiating with us about the eventual passage of the Red Army through Romania and about the mutual assistance pact." That meant two of three members of the Little Entente were either giving ground to Nazi Germany or thinking about it. As for Czechoslovakia, it remained a question mark, according to Litvinov, but he admitted he had no immediate cause for alarm. Or so he said. "I was told before leaving Geneva that Beneš had again pointed out to Laval the need for the speedy ratification of the Franco-Soviet Pact, and that he seemed to have obtained a corresponding promise from Laval."[50]

Litvinov considered Beneš to be an incurable optimist, for after all, what was Laval's promise worth? Beneš was beginning to have his own doubts. Laval had told Potemkin, Titulescu, and others that he would proceed with ratification of the pact. He could do that, or he could conduct negotiations with the Germans, concluding agreements with them and thus depriving the pact of any political significance. There were unofficial discussions going on in Berlin, and Laval was said to be seeking guarantees for Czechoslovakia. Even if he obtains formal guarantees, "Hitler will never give up his plans for Austria, and the possession of the latter makes any guarantees for Czechoslovakia completely illusory." Still, if ratification went ahead, this would allow Beneš to continue the policy of rapprochement with the USSR. Litvinov felt that the NKID would have to keep a close eye on Czechoslovak foreign policy. Beneš was looking to become Czechoslovak president, and Litvinov appeared to worry that the new prime minister and foreign minister, Milan Hodža, might not be so committed to collective security.[51] Anything could go wrong. Czechoslovak policy was dependent on French policy, that is, Laval, and therefore fragile and dependent on domestic political developments.[52]

More Problems

On the French negotiations with Germany, Potemkin reported information from well-informed sources, including Mandel that Laval was seeking guarantees on French, Belgian, and Czechoslovak borders, as well as some kind of five-year German "obligation" not to attack the USSR. What Laval would offer Hitler in exchange, no one seemed to know. One German minister, Hjalmar Schacht, had suggested that a German free hand in the east was the desired quid pro quo. Potemkin speculated that such a deal was too risky even for Laval. Then there was the habitual question about the ratification of the mutual assistance pact. Would it happen? Potemkin thought that, barring the unexpected, it would eventually be approved in the Assemblée nationale though not without resistance on the right. However, even a ratified Franco-Soviet Pact could remain a scrap of paper. "It seems that the Laval government is neither willing nor able to implement this agreement in its original conception of the organization of collective security."[53]

From the NKID, it looked like Laval had indeed transformed the pact into a junk agreement and a tool to be used *against* proponents of collective security. France, went the argument, did not *really* want to go too far with the USSR, and therefore, other states should not either. The Polish minister in Bucharest was not the only one making trouble for Titulescu. So was the Yugoslav prime minister who also went behind the back of the Romanian ministry of foreign affairs to tell King Carol, *inter alia*, that Laval had allegedly told Stojadinović that the Franco-Soviet Pact was "dead."[54] There were wheels turning within wheels of treachery in Europe. This was just what suited Nazi Germany.

Necessity Makes Strange Bedfellows

Paradoxically, even some Poles worried about Laval. The Polish military attaché in Bucharest, Lt. Colonel Jan Kowalewski, paid a call to the Soviet first secretary and *razvedchik* (intelligence agent), Vinogradov, who wrote:

> He bombarded me with questions about our point of view on Laval's policy. Is it true that Laval is seeking an agreement with Hitler? I replied to Kowalewski that I could refer in this case to well-known facts, and in particular, to Laval's repeated statements at the League that he was in favour of an agreement with Germany under certain conditions. It is another matter whether he will be able to achieve this agreement and what its content will be. Kowalewski openly told me that Poland is worried … You understand, said Kowalewski, we are not against France and Germany living together in peace. However, this rapprochement may cross certain borders and become dangerous for Poland. We are afraid of this …
>
> Further, Kowalewski asked me why Laval did not ratify the Franco-Soviet Pact and whether he intended to exchange this pact for an agreement with Hitler. Kowalewski's anxiety was so great that it seemed that he was interested in the early ratification of the Franco-Soviet Pact. I replied to Kowalewski that I did not know how Laval would manoeuvre … when negotiating with the Germans, but as for the pact itself, according to my private information, it would be ratified. Kowalewski told me that Beck will stay, but his policy will undergo some adjustments. It was decided to improve relations with France, the cooling of which has gone too far.

This was a strange sort of conversation between a relatively senior Polish officer and the Soviet chargé d'affaires, in fact between two *razvedchiki*, intelligence agents. Even the devious Poles did not trust the devious Laval. That is the thing about diplomacy; necessity makes strange bedfellows. Kowalewski is an interesting figure, involved in intelligence work and cryptography. His prior posting was in Moscow until he was expelled in 1933. Kowalewski did not hold a grudge for his conversation with Vinogradov was remarkably frank. Everyone who counted in Bucharest knew that the Polish minister Arciszewski had threatened to kill Titulescu, and so Vinogradov turned the conversation to that topic, and Kowalewski had no objection talking about it:

> Kowalewski told me what I had already partly heard from my other interlocutors. Two months ago, Arciszewski met with a prominent Romanian journalist, for [the Bucharest mass circulation newspaper] *Universul*, [Iosif] Fermo. In conversation with Fermo, Arciszewski expressed his outrage at Titulescu's pro-Soviet policy and Titulescu's spreading rumours of a Polish-German-Hungarian alliance. Arciszewski further told Fermo that he had received letters from many Polish officers who had written to him that, in their private lives, conduct similar to that of Titulescu's would have led to a duel or to punching him in the face. After this conversation, rumours spread in Bucharest that 200 Polish officers were looking forward to the moment when Titulescu left the government and became a private person again. Then they would come to Bucharest and would, apparently, either challenge Titulescu to a duel or simply beat him up. According to Kowalewski, Fermo was silent for a long time, and only after that, as with a part of the Romanian press, led a campaign against Titulescu's trip to Moscow. Fermo told the editor of *Universul*, Stelian Popescu, and other journalists about his conversation with Arciszewski. Popescu with one of his colleagues then talked to Arciszewski. They told him that the Romanian press and political circles would boycott the Polish Legation in response to such attacks against Titulescu.

Kowalewski added that Arciszewski had been involved in conflicts with the foreign ministers of the three countries where he had been posted. Use this information if you like seemed to be the message. "I got the impression," Vinogradov added, "that he, as a colonel in active military service, wanted to distance himself from the retired colonels [who led the Polish government], to which group ideologically Arciszewski belongs." As a postscript, Vinogradov reported that King Carol was up in arms about Titulescu and had snubbed the Soviet and Czechoslovak ministers at a recent reception. It was the delay in ratification of the mutual assistance pact and a right-wing press in Paris, which was feeding opposition in Bucharest. Although Titulescu still had some support, you can see why he was becoming wobbly about closer cooperation with the USSR. What could he do but look for cover? The main trouble always led back to Laval. One Romanian journalist commented that as soon as the pact was ratified, everything would quiet down. "Romania cannot but be an ally of France and this determines its foreign policy, in particular, new financial agreements with France and orders for the supply of war *matériel* for the Romanian army determine Romania's foreign policy."[55]

Vinogradov was fascinated by his conversation with Kowalewski. It was a rare event when Soviet and Polish officials sat down for a candid discussion. They met again three weeks later, and Vinogradov wrote another entry in his *dnevnik*. He also added an addendum to his previous record. Kowalewski had observed that the electoral campaign of the Front populaire was an additional cause of Laval's delay of ratification. This was the expanded centre-left coalition that the Radical-Socialist Party had joined in the summer of 1935. Laval knew very well, Kowalewski added, that the Comintern existed and that no one was going to shut it down. However, the Comintern was only a pretext. The main reason for the delay was Laval's wish to negotiate with the Germans and to use the mutual assistance pact and ratification as a trump in his game in Berlin. "Kowalewski stated unambiguously that Warsaw was afraid of a Franco-German agreement at the expense of Poland."

> In fact, he says where and at whose expense the Germans – who are very "dynamic" – will seek compensation. Would it be colonies? – impossible. The only hope of the Poles is that the Germans will go first along the line of least resistance, that is, they will seize Austria and the Sudeten territories. In this case, the Poles will not only not try to block German expansion, but they will even encourage it, in so far as it would move away from Poland. However, Kowalewski immediately recognized that the line of least resistance is conditional. Resistance could come from both Italy and France. But who knows, maybe Italy will be so weakened by war [in Abyssinia] and provoked against France that Mussolini will withdraw his troops from the Brenner. The Germans are "dynamic," he repeated. As for Poland's foreign policy, relations with France, Czechoslovakia, Romania and the USSR will improve and are already improving.[56]

Unfortunately, that did not happen. One can see, however, that there were views in Warsaw other than Beck's. One sees also just how ruinous Laval's activities had become in wrecking collective security and mutual assistance against Nazi Germany.

In the meantime, Vinogradov's anonymous article in the *Journal de Moscou* had the desired effect in Bucharest, even though there were some official notions about banning that particular issue of the paper. Everyone who was anyone in Bucharest had read the article, though the censor allowed no reprints or commentaries about it. That prevented the "fascist press" from launching a campaign against the Soviet embassy. The Poles were "furious," according to Vinogradov, and accused the USSR of interference in Romanian affairs. That took a brass neck given Arciszewski's activities and his alleged threat against Titulescu's life. Romanian journalists saw the positive effect of the article and thought that Titulescu had inspired it. "Due to the circumstances," Vinogradov noted, "the sole outlet which could openly tell Romanian political circles about Polish intrigues against us and against Titulescu is the 'Journal de Moscou.'"[57] Litvinov knew a thing or two about how to answer the Poles. It says something, however, that Arciszewski was not expelled; in fact, he remained in Bucharest until 1938. Romania was an important battleground in the war against collective security. The war was going badly for Titulescu and the Soviet Union. It was late autumn 1935.

Laval and the Germans

The Soviet embassies in Bucharest, Warsaw, and Prague kept the NKID well informed of the negative impacts of Laval's manoeuvring. So did the embassy in Paris. Laval himself took up the question of a Franco-German entente directly with Roland Köster, the German ambassador in Paris. It was mid-November 1935. Köster did not take Laval seriously; it was all for show to impress either the British or the Russians, or to calm his critics at home.[58] However, the Italian ambassador in Paris, Vittorio Cerruti, thought Laval's ideas were worth considering. The Italian government forwarded them to Berlin. The general idea was that the Franco-Soviet Pact would be "absorbed" into a security agreement for Eastern Europe and would thus become "obsolete."[59]

You have to say one thing about Laval; he did not hide his intentions, even from Potemkin. In a meeting in late November, Laval told him about recent discussions between François-Poncet, the French ambassador in Berlin, and Hitler. Laval made two points about their discussions. First, both France and Germany wanted to establish good relations in order to guarantee European peace. Unfortunately, the greatest obstacle to a Franco-German rapprochement was the "pact of 2 May." The existence of Franco-Soviet collaboration within the context of the treaty of mutual assistance, Laval said, did not only not guarantee security in Europe, but also threatened to break up "his policy of peace." This was a clear signal that the Soviet Union was losing the fight for collective security in Paris. "At the moment when the [French] Parliament must consider the question of ratification of the Franco-Soviet Pact," Potemkin observed in a colossal understatement, "these signals from the head of the government naturally must compel us to be cautious." That was not all: "Laval is trying to prepare us psychologically for the rejection of the pact of mutual assistance and the substitution for it of an agreement on, or even a derisory German declaration of non-aggression … Obviously, we have before us a plan, already ripening in the head of our unreliable partner." Laval talked about going as far as "a crime" for the sake of peace, which Potemkin took to mean in reference to the mutual assistance pact.

As if this was not enough, Laval also tried to incriminate the Soviet government in rumoured activities against "the governmental order" and "in the campaign [in France] being conducted against himself." This was Laval's tried-and-true strategy when he wanted to push away the Soviet Union. Potemkin protested and Laval "retreated" to the argument that the Comintern was "an instrument of our Communist Party and comrade Stalin." That was not a bad argument, but he went further. "Laval significantly gave to understand that on him depended the fate of our pact. If he remains in power, if the campaign against him being conducted by the left press abates, the pact could be ratified, although opposition will be strong against it." Potemkin took these last comments to mean that either Laval was openly proposing a deal "close to blackmail" or that he was warning that the pact would be so discredited in the Assemblée nationale that even if it passed, it would have no "moral authority."[60]

Potemkin's record of conversation mirrored what Laval or his ambassador in Berlin had been saying for months to German interlocutors. Laval shared the Führer's concern about Bolshevism. "In France … the danger was not underestimated." The Franco-Soviet Pact was an attempt to lead Russia away from "Bolshevizing Europe"; it was not directed against Germany. According to François-Poncet, Laval had gone to Moscow "to take the wind out of the sails of the powerful parliamentary group in Paris … of communists, Marxists, Freemasons, and Jews." If Germany and France can come to terms, Laval told Köster, "France would hand her paper back to Russia … After all," he joked, "you do mean to play the Bolsheviks a trick or two one of these days." Laval was incorrigible. His lines to Potemkin about the incompatibility of "the pact" with a rapprochement with Germany appear to have been taken directly from the German ambassador in Paris.[61] In 1945, there were many words and deeds, which Laval would have liked to take back. He recognized that he had made mistakes, but his epiphany was too late to save him from execution for treason and collaboration with the enemy.

For Laval, there was more to it than achieving agreement with Germany and abandoning the rapprochement with the USSR. The Front populaire would collapse if France could sign "a non-aggression undertaking" with Germany. The Socialist and Radical-Socialist Parties would pull away from the Communist Party. "Once the foundation had been laid [between France and Germany]," as Laval explained it to the German ambassador, "one end of the tangle would have been found and one could hope to unravel it." Neurath left a handwritten note on Köster's telegram: "Is it M. Laval or Köster who is being too optimistic?"[62]

Exactly, it was not going to be as easy as that. Laval's November meeting with Potemkin took place in the midst of a pitiless political struggle in which Laval's authority was crumbling in Parliament. His leaked secret negotiations with Hoare to cede a large part of Abyssinia to Mussolini weakened him. Also in the news were French journalist's Fernand de Brinon's trip to Berlin and François-Poncet's conversation with Hitler. Nothing came of these meetings. Litvinov was not surprised. He told Alphand that the talks with Hitler little troubled him because he could not see the basis for a "serious" Franco-German agreement. The only result would be to spread mistrust and disquiet. As Litvinov saw matters, the main element of mistrust in the political situation was due to the French government. "This mistrust," the narkom emphasized, "can be noticed not only in Moscow, but also in other capitals, like Prague, Bucharest, and especially in London." Alphand tried to defend his boss: he was unhappy about the raucous parliamentary election campaign. There were articles in the press about communist propaganda and targeting the Front populaire.[63] It was December 1935. "The anti-Soviet role of Laval has become more and more obvious," Litvinov said. "There is a chance of Laval leaving the cabinet, but I consider it possible, given the absolute flabbiness of the French Radicals and Herriot, that Laval will not only remain in the cabinet but will strengthen his position, in which case there will not be Franco-Soviet collaboration in the near future."[64] Treachery in France was turning Litvinov into a deep pessimist. It is not surprising that the narkom was subject to bouts of cynicism. "I do not give up easily," he sometimes said to his ambassadors, and that was true. Neither did Stalin who continued to support him.

Litvinov's Calculations

In Moscow, Litvinov was still trying to figure out how to kick off ratification in Paris. Could they get Paul-Boncour named *rapporteur* in the Senate? he asked Potemkin.[65] This was just the question that Potemkin had taken up with various people in Paris, among whom were Herriot, Paul-Boncour, and Henri Torrès. How could they get the ratification moving, how could they get it through the Sénat once it cleared the Chambre des députés? There were strategy sessions at the Soviet embassy between supporters of the pact and Potemkin. If there were diplomatic battlefields in Central and Eastern Europe, there was another in Paris. Potemkin even tried to operate through Magdeleine Decori, widow of a well-known Paris lawyer (Félix) and an early mistress of the late Raymond Poincaré. She also presided over of one of the political salons in Paris. Mme Decori became Potemkin's intermediary to an old Soviet nemesis, Joseph Caillaux, an influential *sénateur* known to oppose the pact.[66] How paradoxical, the old Bolsh and the elegant bourgeoise working together for ratification and collective security. Great causes often made strange bedfellows.

Caillaux and others were trying to link approval of the pact, a matter of national defence, to the old issue of the defaulted tsarist debts. Stalin had made clear to Laval in Moscow that there was nothing doing on resurrecting the old debts. Was it simply an attempt to leverage the pact or to sink it? Paul-Boncour thought Caillaux was grandstanding, but Potemkin was not so sure. Caillaux had help in the Chambre des députés, from no less than a socialist cabinet minister. The only rose among the thorns was that the negotiations for a big trade deal seemed to move ahead with two French banks, Louis Dreyfus and Seligmann.[67] An additional headache was the Hoare-Laval plan, which had just been leaked to the press. Laval was furious, but had few friends. Potemkin was well informed.[68]

While Hoare resigned as Foreign Secretary, Laval still clung to power. Litvinov was discouraged, although he himself, as readers will remember, would have embraced a deal on Abyssinia if it could be done quietly, quickly, and outside of the League. "The 'Paris plan' to eliminate the Abyssinian conflict proves once again," Litvinov advised Potemkin, "that in the person of Laval we have a consistent, persistent enemy of the collective security system, including the League of Nations, who has decided to create a completely new system of international relations." That was giving Laval far too much credit. Litvinov's dispatch is dated 19 December. It is possible, therefore, that he had not yet heard of Hoare's resignation the day before. Not having the latest news, Litvinov thought Laval might hold on to power until the spring 1936 elections. If he did, all traces would disappear of the previous French foreign policy. "First, he will do everything in his power to, if not to disrupt, then to slow down for a long time the Soviet-French Pact. If now the League Council meets his wishes [on Abyssinia] even a little, then the League of Nations will soon be nothing but a memory."[69]

Chit-Chat

Alphand went home on leave for the Christmas holidays and met Potemkin in Paris several times over the New Year's holidays. It was evident from their wide-ranging discussions that, again, domestic politics were adversely affecting Franco-Soviet relations, especially, the strength of the Front populaire, which was campaigning for the parliamentary elections in the spring. According to Alphand, the political situation was worsening. Laval was alarmed by the growth of the French Communist Party and the consolidation of the Front populaire. The communists did not trouble him while they remained a small "extremist" group; they counterbalanced similar groups, like the Action française on the right. But when the Communist Party changed its position to support national defence, it gained legitimacy. Now Laval thought that his government might soon fall. The activities of the Comintern did not help, Alphand noted, could not Moscow do something about them.[70] Paradoxically, the Comintern was pursuing a policy of a united front against fascism and it was just this policy that troubled Laval and others on the right. The left was becoming too strong, and in the campaign against it, the right treated the Front populaire as a Stalinist marionette. While Alphand was in Paris, the French chargé d'affaires in Moscow had an interesting conversation with the NKID bureau chief, Aleksei Feodorovich Neiman. When Payart was in charge of the embassy, he liked to drop in at NKID to chat with whoever happened to be around. On that particular day, Payart wanted to know how the Soviet government was getting on with Britain. "Relations are improving," Neiman replied. The British Empire, being threatened with aggression in various parts of the world, was beginning to understand the "validity of the principle of the indivisibility of peace." This was a good thing, Neiman continued, and helped to improve relations. "However, the movement of British policy in the direction of collective security could be more consistent and less zigzagging, but in this respect French policy bears a share of the responsibility." Payart nodded in agreement, raising the subject of French and Italian policy: "France made a great mistake when it saw fit to pay Italy for participation in the Stresa Front by encouraging its colonial designs. After six months, Italy would have joined the Stresa Front without compensation. French policy had thus created dangerous illusions in Italy."[71] Yet Litvinov might have done something similar if it could have been done without a scandal and outside the League.

At the beginning of 1936, Potemkin was seeing a good deal of Georges Mandel, who had joined the cabinet in November 1934 under the président du Conseil Flandin. In late December they chatted after lunch at Tabouis's flat, which had become an informal political salon. Potemkin asked if he would be willing to accept an invitation to form a government. He would not shy away from it, Mandel replied in so many words, then "the line of the cabinet in both domestic and foreign policy would become quite definite." According Potemkin, "Mandel … condemned Laval for playing with the two centres of fascism, Rome and Berlin, which could lead to the final isolation of France on the European continent." He had apparently been talking to Eden who contemplated a potential alliance of the United States, Britain, and the USSR, where France might be left to its own fate if it a pursued a tête-à-tête with Germany. Eden must have been talking through his hat, or trying to frighten the French. "Laval has no sense of international relations," said Mandel. "He sees foreign policy from the angle of his own personal domestic political interests and from the point of view of a short-sighted provincial pacifism."[72]

Bad News

It was January 1936. There seemed no immediate solution to the deadlock in France. Laval still clung to power and the Franco-Soviet Pact remained a document in a box at the Quai d'Orsay, unratified. Litvinov asked Potemkin to update him on the prospects for ratification and on "Laval's future." He wanted to make another push to get the pact through the Assemblée nationale and worried that if Laval remained in power, he could cause "irreparable harm."[73]

Potemkin offered a situation report a week later. It was bad news. "The status of ratification of the pact cannot be considered satisfactory," he wrote, and continued:

> Laval is undoubtedly dragging things out. Although he tells people that he intends to fulfill his moral and political obligations to us and to the allies interested in the

> organization of collective security in Eastern Europe, we are aware of his other statements. He continues to say that we are "not worth" the ratification of the pact, that for external political reasons, it is better not to rush it, and that, in any case, it should be obvious to everyone how much influential political groups are against us and the rapprochement with Moscow, which is conducting subversive work in France and its colonies.

Everything depended on Laval. There was not much Potemkin could do. "Our friends," he said, Herriot, Blum, Mandel, amongt others, were still out of Paris because of the New Year's holidays. Potemkin did have a conversation with Torrès, who said "the 'atmosphere' is not entirely favourable for us." Apparently, the pact was still not on the agenda paper of the Chambre des députés. Torrès and others were going to try to get ratification started, but who knew if they could overcome Laval's stalling.[74]

There was other bad news. The one-billion franc credit for Franco-Soviet trade, which had been under discussion for months with the Louis Dreyfus and Seligmann banks, collapsed. The French right-wing press – including *L'Action française*, *Le Matin*, *La Victoire*, and *Je Suis Partout*, and other papers – had launched a campaign against the credit plan and the campaign was intensifying. "We know for certain," Potemkin advised, "that all this agitation is inspired by circles close to the Comité des forges and the Banque de France."[75] This was true. The Banque de France and the Comité des forges were leaders of the opposition against better trade relations with "the Bolsheviks." Months before, Alphand had underlined the importance of a Soviet trade deal and warned that the French banks were "the great obstacle" to success.[76] In fact, the Banque de France refused to endorse the one-billion franc credit obliging the government to approach the Caisse des dépôts et consignations, the state savings bank, for financial backing. The Caisse announced its unwillingness to back the deal in early January, saying in so many words that it feared a hostile press campaign.[77] Potemkin continued, an agent from the Banque, Seligmann, "told me that the representatives of the press who are fighting against the loan to us, have frankly raised the question of the price that can buy their silence, if not support for this plan. Even those papers which take a more or less decent position towards us clearly do not dare to oppose the violent campaign raised by our enemies." Potemkin thought the deal was sunk. "Laval has the final say in this matter. Formally, in the Council of Ministers, he did not object … But, in fact, he is constantly consulting with [Jean] Tannery [governor of the Banque de France] and, of course, as always, listening to the voice of the street [that is, the press]." [78]

There were still more wheels turning within the wheels of treachery. The killing of the trade deal was another battle lost in the struggle to solidify Franco-Soviet relations. Everywhere a blow was struck, Laval's hidden fist appeared to be behind it.

As for how much longer Laval might hang on to power, no one could say. Everyone had an opinion. "My impression is that Laval will hold on at least until the new elections," Potemkin opined, and continued:

> There is no unanimity among ministers and members of the Radical-Socialist Party on the issue of leaving the government. Herriot is inactive or utters pious formulas. Mandel is intriguing, trying to incite the more impulsive oppositionists, but he does not seem to be counting too much on the fall of Laval in the near future. The majority of the left-wing opposition prefers to wait until Laval runs out of steam and is completely bankrupt. In any case, until [the League meetings in] Geneva [at the beginning of February], I almost certainly rule out the possibility of the fall of the Laval cabinet.[79]

Potemkin's dispatch prompted Litvinov to action in Moscow. First, he instructed Potemkin to see Léger in order to get some straight answers. A meeting with Laval, he said, would immediately leak to the press; a meeting with Léger might pass unnoticed. He instructed Potemkin to tell Léger that it had been almost nine months since the mutual assistance pact was signed and still it had not been ratified. "Say that we do not intend to sit quietly while the pact serves endlessly as the subject of domestic or foreign intrigues for France, and that we want, finally, some clarity and to know why the pact until now has not been put on the agenda of the Chamber and when it will be put on the agenda." He instructed that his message be forwarded to Laval and that Potemkin should visit the Quai d'Orsay in a few days to obtain an answer.[80] On the following day, Litvinov passed his message to Alphand, who warned of the increasing tempo of the press campaign in France against the Soviet-French rapprochement. According to Litvinov's record, Alphand "was shocked by the force of this campaign in Paris, which had not only engulfed the press but also the political salons." He thought Laval would remain in power until the spring elections. Litvinov replied in the sense of the message he had cabled to Potemkin the previous day. Enough was enough. Alphand agreed, but could promise nothing.[81]

The French ambassador also made a record of the conversation with Litvinov. It skipped over most of the details of Litvinov's statement but emphasized a point absent from Litvinov's record. This was that impatience was growing in Moscow over the delays in Paris. There was a feeling that the USSR should build up its defences and go it alone, dropping the mutual assistance pact with France. Litvinov advised that he was fighting against such ideas, which explains why he did not mention it in his own record.[82]

Litvinov also alerted Stalin to the problems in France. He recommended increasing the NKID annual budget for the French press to 2.9 million francs. This was necessary, Litvinov advised Stalin, because of Laval's hostile policies and "the obvious instability demonstrated by friends in French circles including even Herriot ... We need to do more to cultivate French public opinion by means of further penetration in the French press." Litvinov followed this up in February with a detailed budget request, including nearly 500,000 francs per annum for *Le Temps*. On the Soviet payroll there remained Rollin and also the anti-fascist journalist Tabouis (5,000 francs per month). The Soviet embassy could not sound out the most influential journalists, Litvinov said, without "confidence that their requests [for allowances] will be satisfied." Litvinov had in mind such journalists on the right as Pertinax, Jules Sauerwein, and André Pironneau.[83] Likewise, for "orders for separate articles by high-profile journalists, for the publication of brochures, for the organization of public reports, conferences, and the like, we need to allocate at least 35,000 francs."[84] Litvinov had come a long way from the early days when Chicherin considered him stingy on budget issues. Who would have believed that Soviet patience with *Le Temps* would be so enduring or how committed the Soviet government remained to the rapprochement with France? Half a million francs to *Le Temps*? How long could the NKID go on paying for nothing?

Potemkin saw Laval after all on 15 January, to pass on Litvinov's message. The delay in the ratification of the Franco-Soviet Pact had created "an extremely unfavourable impression" in Moscow, said Potemkin. "What do you want?" Laval retorted. The pact had aroused opposition that had increased "many times" since May. "Public opinion in France," he said, "sees that in the last half year there has been extraordinary growth of the revolutionary movement ... This is the work of the Comintern." It was Laval's usual lines. He acknowledged "the difference between the government of the USSR and the Comintern, but the centre of the latter is in Moscow, and the bosses of the Russian Communist Party direct the activities of the Third International." *L'Humanité*, the communist daily in Paris, outdid itself in heaping filth (*grubost'*) upon the "head of the government." One can imagine, said Laval, the reaction of "the moderate elements of French society" that were now less favourable to the Franco-Soviet Pact.[85] It was not just *L'Humanité* that irritated Laval; Herriot, Cot, and other Radicals and Socialists did also, the more so because they were advocates of a Franco-Soviet rapprochement. In fact, Laval seemed to lump together the Front populaire and the Comintern. Not coincidentally, this was the main line of the right's electoral propaganda.

Potemkin warned Litvinov that Laval could try to confront him in Geneva with his famous "dossier" of evidence of Soviet or Comintern interference in French affairs. It is not the first time, Potemkin observed, that Laval had threatened us with his notorious dirty dossier, and who knew if it even existed. Then there was the perennial question of ratification. Potemkin remained in touch with his parliamentary contacts, Torrès, Delbos, Paul Bastid, Mandel, and Herriot, the latter being "more passive than the others" and "in a state close to confusion." What had happened to Herriot? Potemkin seemed to depend more on Mandel who provided tactical advice on how to get the pact ratified. We appeared to have "entered the decisive phase," Potemkin advised, there were estimates of approximately 150 députés in the Chambre, who would vote no. That was not enough to block ratification, but it was enough to raise concerns. In addition, who knew what would happen in the Senate? Mandel was sure it would all turn out alright; the sénateurs would not dare to vote against ratification once it had passed the Chambre des députés on a question that the majority of the French population saw as a matter of French and European security.[86]

The government crisis finally came to a head and Laval rushed back to Paris from Geneva. According to Potemkin, it remained a guessing game as to what would happen next. Some Radicals still wanted to support Laval. Herriot resigned as president of the Radical Party to be replaced by Daladier. Herriot "cursed" the Front populaire and refused to support its program. He said it would push the country to the right. Léo Gaboriaud, a Herriot confident and editor of *L'Ère nouvelle*, went to see Potemkin to "spit fire at Daladier, the like-minded Laval, Daladier-the-Germanophile." He opined that potential candidates to replace Laval were not optimal to say the least, though on the list was Laval's eventual successor, Albert Sarraut. In France in the 1930s there was always a successor in the wings, waiting to replace the actual président du Conseil. "I think," Potemkin warned, "that among them only Laval knows what to do. It is not for nothing that one of the papers today calls him 'a Phoenix who can be reborn from its ashes.'"[87]

Chapter Fifteen

Collapse in London: The Failure of the Anglo-Soviet Rapprochement, 1936

When Eden accepted his seals of office in December 1935, he was only thirty-eight years old. Many of his colleagues considered him still to be inexperienced. He had a reputation for being precious and thin-skinned, as indeed was demonstrated by his over-reaction to criticism during the election campaign in November 1935. On the other hand, Vansittart was a generation older, single-minded, and not one to suffer fools gladly. He was used to having his way with Simon and Hoare, and he thought any idiot should see the clear and present Nazi danger to British security. In his memoirs, Eden characterized Vansittart as "a sincere, almost fanatical, crusader … more a Secretary of State in mentality than a permanent official." The overly susceptible Eden had to prove who was boss – a task made easier because the Abyssinian fiasco had damaged Vansittart's reputation. He never recovered, and Eden would never let him.[1] Four months before, Leeper had remarked to Bruce Lockhart that "foreign affairs" in Britain were "run by Baldwin, Neville Chamberlain, Hoare, and Vansittart, and the greatest of these is Van[sittart]."[2] Not anymore.

These circumstances would affect Anglo-Soviet relations in a year, which Churchill predicted, would bring "measureless perils" to Europe.[3] The Hoare-Laval affair and the resulting damage to the League of Nations' credibility weakened the possibilities of resistance to Nazi aggression. That was one front in the battle for better Anglo-Soviet relations; the other was the British loan. If the British cabinet had been of one mind, it would have been logical to strengthen ties with the USSR to counterbalance the fiasco in Abyssinia. The first order of business, therefore, should have been to proceed with the loan to the USSR, but this did not happen.

The simmering dispute between Sargent and Collier blew up again in December 1935 in the midst of the Abyssinian crisis. War Office and Foreign Office intelligence had picked up evidence of a possible improvement in German-Soviet relations. Collier used this intelligence to press the case for greater collaboration with the USSR and for the loan. Sargent strongly objected and tried to brake Collier's enthusiasm for better Anglo-Soviet relations. The best way to combat a Soviet-German rapprochement, Sargent believed, was through a British policy of collaboration "with *both* [emphasis in the original] Germany and Russia, and more particularly with Germany ... We ought ... to test Hitler's intentions & sincerity, before putting all our eggs in the Russian basket." "Collaboration" with Germany and Hitler's "sincerity," Sargent said. Could he get anything right? Although Vansittart declined to enter the debate, he noted that a Soviet-German rapprochement was not an "immediate possibility" – unless "we mismanage the situation."[4] As readers will see, this was the right call.

Anthony Eden: "Friend" or Foe?

Maiskii saw Eden on 6 January 1936 to urge a deepening of the Anglo-Soviet rapprochement and the conclusion of the loan. Eden was polite, but according to Maiskii's report, it sounded as though the new Foreign Secretary was going through the motions, politely asking what the ambassador thought and then repeating the usual litany about common interests and no conflicts of interest. Maiskii asked about Anglo-German relations which seemed to catch Eden off guard. If Maiskii was hoping for a Vansittart-type reply, he did not get it. Eden's record of the meeting was only a few paragraphs. "In the course of his conversation, Maisky several times indicated his desire to bring about a closer understanding between HMG and the Soviet Government," Eden recorded. "I was convinced that the only solid basis upon which to proceed was ... that each Government should rigorously abstain from interference in the internal affairs of the other." Maiskii noted this remark in his record, but did not make much of it. He should have. It appeared as though Eden thought Britain would be doing the USSR a favour by continuing tolerable relations.[5]

Vansittart understood what was in the back of Maiskii's mind. He warned that the ambassador was getting impatient: "He is *most* [emphasis in the original] anxious that no further time should be lost, and professes himself unable to understand the delay." The loan would "counter all the premature talk of an agreement with Germany, to which M. Laval has given so much currency." And Vansittart added, as if to confirm Churchill's statements to Maiskii in December 1935, "There is also a lot of loose talk and looser thinking on the subject *here* [emphasis in the original], of which he [Maiskii] is well aware."[6]

As readers might now expect, Sargent did not let Maiskii's advocacy of the loan pass unchallenged. "May I put in a plea that ... due consideration should be given to the political effects abroad of such action," Sargent noted. The loan would "appear to public opinion throughout Europe as a highly significant act implying an unusual and close political co-operation between the two Governments." And Hitler would claim that the loan was part of "the French encirclement policy." Such developments would make it more difficult for the British government "to come to terms with Germany."[7] Collier never accepted this line of argument. "The Germans would not hate the [Franco-Soviet] pact so much," Collier commented months later, "if it were not a real obstacle in their way."[8]

Eden, who liked Sargent's argument better, still worried about Comintern propaganda, and was reluctant to take the loan to cabinet. "I could do so," he noted, "with more conviction were I not troubled with the suspicion that some at least of this money will find its way into communist propaganda in the Empire." He had noted earlier, "I don't trust [the Soviet] & am sure there is hatred in his heart for all we stand for."[9]

The parliamentary undersecretaries, Lords Stanhope and Cranborne, also weighed in. "I ask myself," said Stanhope, "what is our policy? Is it to improve our relations with Russia *or* [emphasis in the original] with Germany & Japan?" Stanhope continued:

> I cannot say that I look with much enthusiasm on being friends with Russia or Germany or Japan – I mistrust them all, but I mistrust Russia most of the three. Apart from the fact that the "Russian steam-roller" was of little benefit to us after 1916 … I share with S. of S. the suspicion that a good deal of this money is likely to be used for the break-up of the greatest bulwark against Bolshevism viz. the British Empire.

And Stanhope concluded: "I think we must first decide as to our future policy – is it to be anti-German & pro-Russian or the reverse, or can we ride both horses simultaneously." Cranborne came to similar conclusions: The Soviet government "will remain unalterably malignant to the British Empire, & will intrigue against us whenever and wherever they can."[10]

Vansittart replied that the British government should look after its own interests in trade matters and that we should "not allow ourselves to be intimidated by rivals." On the issue of European security, Vansittart doubted whether Germany could be "brought back into the comity of nations" at a price which Great Britain could afford to pay. If the British government was unprepared to pay the price, said Vansittart, it should not negotiate: "Until we know the answer to the possibilities of bringing Germany back, we ought to be careful to discourage no one who is in the same boat. There are many of them, and one happens *for the present* [emphasis in the original] to be Russia."[11]

Collier also replied in a long memorandum, recapitulating the arguments in favour of close Anglo-Soviet relations. If the Soviet government wanted a British "political gesture" in the form of a loan, "they are actuated, not by a desire to attack Germany, but by fear of aggression from her." If the British government yielded to German pressure against a loan, the Nazis "would deduce that we were too much afraid of them to hamper their ambitions in Eastern Europe." Collier put heavy emphasis on the commercial advantages of a loan.

As for Comintern activity, it "is not likely to be much affected either way, but if anything, is more likely to be directed against other Governments if the Soviet Government enter into an arrangement which will give them as much interest in our stability as we shall have in theirs."[12]

"Very good special pleading," Stanhope replied, who also complained that the loan proposal had gone "straight up to the Permanent Under-Secretary & the S. of S." without wider vetting – where he and others could have blocked it.[13] Of course, Stanhope did not put it that way, but everyone would have understood his words. The issue was temporarily put aside until the return to London of Ambassador Phipps from Berlin.

Maiskii and Vansittart

In the meantime, Maiskii and his first secretary, Samuil Bentsianovich Kagan, made the rounds to check on the temperature of Anglo-Soviet relations. They were getting good feedback to the affect that the rapprochement continued as before. On 9 January 1936, Maiskii saw Vansittart for the first time since early December. Agniia Akeksandrovna had invited Sarita Vansittart and her son to the embassy on a social call. Maiskii dropped in to say hello. Sarita scolded him. "My husband is astonished,' she said, "that you have not been to see him for so long a time. He is always glad to see you." Maiskii noted in his report that he had no business to take up with Vansittart, but for part of that period Vansittart was in Paris and after he returned to London, it was not such a good time to drop into the Foreign Office. Anyway, Sarita's scolding prompted Maiskii to go see Vansittart. They talked about the Hoare-Laval plan. "I approved of it," Vansittart said. The reason of course was his "growing fear of German aggression" and the desire to hold together and strengthen the Stresa Front. According to Maiskii, Vansittart tried to make the best of a bad situation:

> During the crisis and as a result of the crisis, members of the government and British public opinion saw more clearly the 'reality' of the international situation as it is. The lesson is hard but useful. For the most important thing now is political realism. And all that serves to strengthen realism, to clarify the minds of the masses of Great Britain – all this is for the good. He, Vansittart, had to survive a few difficult moments. Some elements who knew about his attitude towards Germany tried to use the situation to remove him from this place (V. pointing to his chair) but the attempt failed.

Vansittart said he would remain in the Office and carry on the fight. Maiskii noted that Sarita had told him that during the crisis, Vansittart had been offered the Paris embassy, and not for the first time.

Maiskii said he was very glad that Vansittart would remain in his chair, and he asked if he could pose some questions. What are the prospects, he wondered, for the Italian-Abyssinian war? Vansittart could not say, except that the British government would have to be careful in any attempts to liquidate the crisis. Then, Maiskii asked about relations with Nazi Germany. The British ambassador Phipps had met with Hitler in mid-December. Did Hitler ask the British to intervene to block ratification of the Franco-Soviet pact? Vansittart replied in the negative. Anglo-German relations were nowhere good enough for Hitler to risk such a démarche. Vansittart added that the cabinet had to determine German intentions and then make decisions concerning national defence.[14] Maiskii was relieved to hear that Vansittart would keep his job, but his comments on British foreign policy could not have been too reassuring. Vansittart had dodged a bullet in the aftermath of the leak of the Hoare-Laval plan, and his position had been weakened. This was obvious from the boldness of Sargent and the parliamentary undersecretaries in attacking the loan proposal for the USSR. It was attack the loan; attack Vansittart. With Maiskii, Vansittart was careful not to mention of any of this, nor did information appear to leak by other conduits to the Soviet embassy.

Maiskii and Austen Chamberlain

In the meantime, Maiskii had an interesting conversation with Austen Chamberlain, Neville's half-brother and former Foreign Secretary after the Tory electoral victory in 1924. They talked about the usual subjects. Chamberlain thought Europe could still count on five years of peace: Maiskii countered with eighteen to twenty-four months. Remember, it was January 1936. "In the Far East, according to Ch[amberlain], war, in fact, is already underway, but it has a kind of chronic, creeping character. He does not see forces, which could prevent further advance of Japanese aggression in China. Practical politicians have to reckon with the fact that in the coming years, Japan is likely to tear off from China one province after another, without meeting any effective resistance." Chamberlain thought the prospects in Europe were better. If the great powers could agree among themselves, the other powers would follow. Maiskii asked Chamberlain to elaborate on what he meant.

> Ch[amberlain] replied that now the situation is quite clear. The League of Nations has four great powers – England, France, the USSR and Italy. Italy, he had always considered, as an unreliable member of the League, and now even more so. But the other three great powers – England, France and the USSR – can and should work together for peace. They have every reason to do so. If Italy wants to join these three powers – very well. If not, the three powers are so great and powerful that, with a united front, they can easily lead the rest.

Chamberlain thought the three powers operating in a League framework was the only way forward, and ironically this is also what Litvinov had proposed before the Hoare-Laval fiasco. Chamberlain did not seem to think that the Abyssinian crisis had ruined the credibility of the League. Was a united front really possible? Maiskii asked. Chamberlain answered in the affirmative, saying tripartite cooperation was not only possible but desirable, although he cautioned about Comintern activities. It was the one "dark spot" standing across Anglo-Soviet cooperation. Of course, Chamberlain knew that the Soviet government claimed to have no responsibility for the Comintern, but he did not accept that assertion. Maiskii countered with his usual arguments to the contrary, and Chamberlain did not wish, as he put it, to return to past grievances. The Comintern seemed to have become less of an issue in recent years, but he warned that if it returned as an important problem for the British government, "all the current favourable prospects for their rapprochement would be reduced to nothing." This was Vansittart's view as well.

Maiskii asked his habitual question about the prospects for a "so-called 'Western front' of England, France, Germany, and Italy," which appealed to large sectors of Conservative opinion. Chamberlain responded that he did not think a Western entente was a serious policy option:

> After all, what exactly would such an entente mean? It would mean the creation under Hitler's domination of that "Mitteleuropa," which was the goal of pre-war Germany. Such a "Mitteleuropa" would pose the greatest threat to the British Empire, and England would inevitably have to go to war with Germany even before the outlines of "Mitteleuropa" would be specifically looming on the horizon. The idea of the Western entente is devoid of any reality. The League of Nations is the only way. But there is one necessary caveat. Much will depend on which League of Nations emerges from the Italian-Abyssinian conflict. If it gets out alive, strengthened as an organisation – Ch[amberlain] does not doubt that the League of Nations will indeed become a cornerstone of British foreign policy. If the League of Nations fails, then it is likely that isolationist tendencies will increase enormously in Britain. Britain will set itself foreign policy limited tasks – the protection of France, Holland, Belgium from German aggression, and the rest of Europe, it will give up.[15]

This was in effect conceding "Mitteleuropa," and much more, to Nazi Germany, which, according to Austen, would mean "suicide" for Britain. You can see how people looking for a way to confront Nazi Germany – Churchill, Austen Chamberlain, Herriot, Litvinov, among others – were coming to the same conclusions. The only question was, could they pull it off?

For a "Will-o'-the-Wisp"

On 20 January 1936, King George V died. On 26 January, Litvinov arrived in England from Geneva, along with Marshall Tukhachevskii, for the king's funeral. Afterward, he met Vansittart and Eden, the narkom pressing the case for collective security and advocating for the development of concrete actions to make it a reality. Litvinov had a successful meeting with the new King Edward VIII, and this apparently was the talk of the town. With Vansittart, along with Maiskii, Litvinov promoted a new Triple Entente of Britain, France, and the USSR, leading the way in the League. Exactly. This was Austen Chamberlain's idea too, but Vansittart did not respond enthusiastically to it, disappointing Litvinov and Maiskii.[16] At a meeting at the Foreign Office, Litvinov said to Eden that Nazi Germany "understood no other language than that of force." Only a determined coalition of the European powers could discourage Nazi aggression. Litvinov warned that some of his colleagues were beginning to doubt the wisdom of collective security. He blamed these doubts on Laval who was stalling ratification of the Franco-Soviet pact and who been caught flirting with Hitler. Nevertheless, Litvinov stressed his continuing support for collective security – it was the only way forward. Like Maiskii, Litvinov said he wanted to "do everything in his power" to improve Anglo-Soviet relations.

"Was there not any further step that could be taken?" Litvinov asked.

"I could think of nothing new," Eden replied.[17]

Sargent dissed the Soviet position: "M. Litvinov advocates the policy of encirclement pure and simple." Collier rejoined, "'Encirclement' is a tendencious [*sic*] word!"[18] Vansittart, who must have known the battle for the loan was lost, did not give up the fight, even though he was wounded by the Hoare-Laval fiasco:

> I have been willing to wait for Sir E. Phipps by way of fair play to those who think that our moves in this game should be governed by the fear of offending Germany & compromising our chances of a distant and hitherto undefined agreement – undefined even in our own minds ... In anticipation of that I would again urge that our guiding star should be our own interests and not a will- o'-the-wisp. They are the only safe guide.[19]

Phipps, who came to London in early February, discouraged the loan because it would offer Hitler a pretext to reoccupy the Rhineland demilitarized zone. At the same time, possible French and German loans fell through, removing the threat of competition. The German embassy in London also applied pressure. Phipps was the last straw, Eden refused to take the loan to cabinet.[20] Vansittart and Collier, unpersuaded by Phipps, reckoned that Hitler would do whatever he could get away with. When Collier mentioned Phipps's objection to Board of Trade officials, they responded "with incredulous laughter." Sargent and Collier were both annoyed, but for different reasons.[21]

Unaware of the rejection of the loan, Maiskii saw the Secretary of State for War, Duff Cooper, on 5 February, and Eden a few days later. Maiskii had no trouble with Duff Cooper, who shared Churchill's view of Germany, but he made no headway with Eden.[22] Collier lunched with Maiskii on 13 February to give him the bad news. The loan was "off," Collier advised, it did not have sufficient support in cabinet. Longer credits were approved, and this was "better than nothing."

"A pity," said Maiskii, "a loan would have been worth ... while for political reasons," but credits were less interesting. Maiskii, who knew of the Board of Trade's opposition, asked why the Foreign Office recommendation had been turned down. Collier could not say that Eden had blocked the loan, so he explained that cabinet anticipated strong opposition in the House of Commons – though Collier himself did not believe this to be so. The Foreign Office in general and he in particular favoured the loan, Collier said disingenuously, but not the cabinet. The majority in cabinet wanted to trade with the USSR and were ready to lend money, "but they wanted to do it with the least possible commotion." A long-term loan "would undoubtedly provoke a great hubbub and would have a large political effect." Credits would reduce commotion to the minimum.[23] Obviously, Collier could not say that Eden, the two parliamentary undersecretaries, and especially the vociferous Sargent disliked Comintern "propaganda," distrusted Soviet motives, and did not want to irritate Herr Hitler. Nor could he have wanted to say that he and Vansittart were isolated. It is surprising that Sargent's permanent hostility did not leak to the Soviet embassy.

The second front in the battle to actualize the Anglo-Soviet rapprochement was lost. Maiskii's meetings with Vansittart thinned out. Sargent's policy held sway. He argued against a visit by Duff Cooper to the USSR and, more importantly, against French ratification of the Franco-Soviet pact, which Laval had delayed for nearly nine months before his resignation at the end of January 1936. It is a "fatal policy," said Sargent, "which can ... only lead to one ultimate result, namely a European war in which the Soviet Government, in their capacity of agents of the Third International, would probably be the only beneficiaries."[24] This was a cogent argument for Eden: he declined to intervene with the French, but Duff Cooper's visit was dropped. Eden even blocked a low-level War Office mission to study the Red Army. Sargent was contemptuous – in spite of favourable estimates of growing Soviet military strength.[25] It was always Sargent putting a spoke in the wheel. Eden was on his side. It was he and not Vansittart writing memoranda to the "Secretary of State."

Vansittart stopped reacting to minutes advocating distance from Moscow and more proximity to Berlin. Sargent almost gloated in his minutes, sarcastically mocking the value of an "Anglo-Soviet Pact."[26] How wrong could he have been? The idea was to send Vansittart to Paris to get him out of the way; such an idea was never mooted for Sargent, who would help lead Britain to disaster in September 1939. In the autumn of that year Britain would have been glad to have an "Anglo-Soviet Pact." A suitable British consulate in some far distant corner of the world, where the roads were unpaved and the sewers were open, should have been found for Sargent to get *him* out of the way. Unfortunately, he was far from finished in doing harm to Anglo-Soviet relations.

"The Possibility of a General Understanding with Germany"

The derailing of the Anglo-Soviet rapprochement took place as the cabinet struck a committee "to investigate the possibility of a general understanding with Germany." Sargent advised that the government should not do anything "which might cause unnecessary irritation or suspicion in Germany." His ideas are worth quoting at length:

> We should in the first stage act alone and not discuss proceedings with third parties, so as to avoid leakage and obstruction; and … we should not, while this policy of an understanding with Germany is being tested, commit ourselves to any other policy which might be held to conflict with this "German" policy.
>
> In accordance with these principles we have argued against the … grant to Russia of a guaranteed loan; we have dissociated ourselves from the action of the French Government in ratifying the Franco-Russian Pact; and we have been careful not to take the French Government into our confidence, since we propose to start our German soundings without consulting them beforehand …
>
> It is fairly obvious that the Soviet Government should view with dislike any rapprochement between Great Britain, France and Germany. Their fear of Germany drives them to seek an ally among the mammon of capitalism, and they naturally realise that their own value in the eyes of the bourgeois States of Western Europe depends largely on the extent to which the latter are themselves equally afraid of Germany.
>
> In these circumstances I suggest that during this stage considerable caution should be used in discussing our German policy with M. Maisky or other Russians. It would be particularly regrettable if more were said to M. Maisky than is said to M. Corbin, and we must, I submit, avoid at all costs getting into the position where we are expected to discuss with M. Maisky a *common* [emphasis in the original] Anglo-Franco-Russian policy.[27]

Oliphant described Sargent's main question, as a matter of "Germany v Russia." Eden agreed with Sargent: "Let us beware of M. Maisky. He is an indefatigable propagandist."[28] It was as though Britain was doing the USSR a favour by being polite in listening to Soviet fairy stories of a Hitlerite aggressor threatening European peace and security. In fact, Maiskii was an indefatigable advocate of an Anglo-Soviet entente, and he was becoming an irritant in the Foreign Office where Eden and Sargent held sway. It would of course have provided better dividends if the British government had paid closer mind to Maiskii's arguments. As for Sargent, he was advocating a go-alone policy keeping both France and the USSR in the dark. Everything he advocated in this shift towards Berlin was the wrong advice. It's all there in the files; there can be no doubt. When Churchill did house cleaning in May 1940, Sargent should also have been dismissed with one word: Out!

Eden riled easily over Soviet "propaganda," as he did when he read a Chilston report of hostile Soviet press coverage *in Russian* of working-class living conditions in England. Collier did not make much of it, but Eden bristled: "This article convinces me that we should hold M. Maisky & his Govt. severely at arm's length. We wish for correct relations, but any cordiality towards a Govt. that behaves like this is strongly to be deprecated."[29] Eden reiterated his position to Phipps. It was Sargent's policy: "I am really anxious to avoid giving the Germans any pretext as far as I can for believing that we are willing to join in a policy of encirclement. As for the USSR, I want the footing to be friendly … but … I have no illusions as to the real feelings of the Soviet Government towards the capitalist State."[30]

Chilston spelled out some of the "unspoken assumptions" that determined the British position. "The immense difference in the system and institutions of the government, in mentality, and in the conception of liberties of the subject, the fact that no expression of public opinion and sentiment can have any outlet in this country … all these aspects make a broad gulf which for the present has no bridge, however good may be political relations." Chilston also echoed Eden's objections to communist propaganda:

> Such is the hypocrisy of the Janus-headed Communist State which, facing both ways, stands for peace for itself, peace in its own time, while simultaneously wishing to disturb the internal security of those with whom it claims to collaborate for the "peace indivisible" and collective security … Well might the stern rebuke of the prophet – "What hast thou to do with peace?" be applied to that State which protects, nurtures and uses the Comintern.[31]

In fact, the Comintern was mobilized not to irritate the Foreign Office undersecretaries and clerks but to support popular fronts or centre-left political coalitions, to fight fascism in Europe. As readers will have noticed in France, this strategy only made the right more disposed to embrace or at least to tolerate Nazi Germany.

Maiskii failed to pick up the signals of a change in Foreign Office policy. Neither Collier nor Vansittart leaked any warning to him about Eden and Sargent. In fact, Maiskii's evaluation of Litvinov's trip was positive. "Over the past 10 days, I have had the opportunity to test the mood created by your visit to the Foreign Office, in diplomatic, political and journalistic circles. Everyone agrees that the reception given to you here has exceeded all expectations in terms of attention and 'cordiality.'" But Maiskii, all the same, was not sure of what the future would look like. Positive impressions might be misleading and "much ahead of the true facts." All the same, he opined, "we have no reason to dispel the created impression. It benefits us."[32]

"The Logic of Things"

The hard facts did *not*, however, "benefit" Soviet policy. At the end of a long dispatch, Maiskii brought up the subject of Anglo-German relations. He thought quite rightly that the British government had not abandoned the idea of a rapprochement with Nazi Germany, and he even speculated that the "cordiality" shown to Litvinov might have been to impress Hitler. Fear of Germany and Japan was growing, and "the logic of things" had to lead to closer relations with France and the USSR. Yes, in "the logic of things" this should have been so. Maiskii did not want to go too far in his prognostications, however, and, as readers will have noticed, he often back-tracked a little as he did in this particular dispatch. Britain's growing fears about Germany and Japan did not mean "that the British government has firmly and definitively decided to make common cause with the Soviet Union … No, as before, it will vacillate, manoeuvre, tack from side to side."[33] Unbeknownst to Maiskii, as he wrote the above lines, the Foreign Office, thanks to Sargent and Eden, had already begun "tacking" towards Berlin. Oliphant inadvertently noted what might have been his reaction to Maiskii's dispatch, had he seen it: "The Soviet remain the Soviet & an audience [with] the King on the part of M. Litvinoff or other civilities to individual authorities will never affect their fundamental aims – though at times they may wish to walk in step with us. But 'When the Devil was ill …' is still true."[34] The pertinent part of the adage that Oliphant left out is: "When the Devil was ill, the devil a monk would be." In other words, promises made in adversity are often not kept in times of prosperity. Observing quietly what was happening on his watch, Vansittart must have been discouraged.

Maiskii might usefully have had a chat with Sarita Vansittart, but he was never anything if not committed to an Anglo-Soviet entente. A week later he sent a long dispatch to Litvinov with a list of projects – including parliamentary trips to Moscow, especially of Conservatives, and junkets for union leaders and journalists, and various cultural and sporting events – to further the rapprochement that Eden and Sargent had just killed.[35]

Looking Foolish

While the Foreign Office contemplated a tack towards Berlin, Sargent's will-o'-the-wisp looked foolish only a few weeks later, when on 7 March 1936 German troops marched into the demilitarized Rhineland. Hitler dressed up his coup de force by condemning the Treaty of Versailles, the Franco-Soviet Pact, and offering various bits of utopianism about demilitarized zones, the return of Germany to the League of Nations, and a clutch of non-aggression pacts. It was Hitler's so-called Peace Plan and it worked like a charm. The British and French were paralyzed, and did nothing. Not everyone took it sitting down, not by a long shot, especially in France, as we shall see anon. In the Foreign Office, Vansittart, Wigram, Collier, and Leeper objected to doing nothing, but they were pushed aside by Sargent who was backed by Eden whose position was especially craven. Vansittart even authorized Wigram to leak key material to the press. Sadly, within nine months, Wigram would be dead.

There was a good deal of talk between the French and British about what to do before they decided to do nothing. Readers can follow these discussions in greater detail when the focus of the narrative shifts to France. We are in for a rough time, Maiskii reported, because British "Germanophiles" were riding high, ready to be beguiled by Herr Hitler's protestations of peaceful intent. Maiskii gave Cranborne assurances of Soviet support at the League, though not without warning once again that "Germany had become, to use an American phrase, 'Aggressor no. 1.'"[36]

How could they have got it so wrong in the Foreign Office? Churchill grumbled in the House of Commons' corridors "about funk versus national honour." The general mood "was one of fear," noted National Labour MP Harold Nicolson: "The country will not stand for anything that makes for war. On all sides one hears sympathy for Germany." For Nicolson, "pro-German" meant "afraid of war."[37] The Rhineland crisis thus passed in Britain with a great wringing of hands and no action to stop Hitler. It was the beginning of the epoch of "measureless perils."

Maiskii continued his polling of opinion. On 2 April, he saw Runciman; they discussed Anglo-Soviet trade, but they also talked about Hitler. After the stress of the Rhineland crisis, Runciman wanted to take the Easter holiday to get away. Maiskii chided that Hitler might spring another surprise and disturb his holiday. "I asked Runciman," Maiskii reported, "what should now be done?" Runciman shrugged his shoulders: "In such moments, as now, it is better *to go slow, perhaps something turns up* [original in English]."

A "typical" reply of the "old generation of British ministers," remarked Maiskii. "Why not take Hitler at his word," Runciman went on. "If only one knew what he wanted." Maiskii smiled, "I can tell you … what Hitler wants." And Maiskii proceeded to do so, stressing the importance of close Anglo-Franco-Soviet cooperation and a "powerful League of Nations" to stop him. "But this will mean the 'encirclement' of Germany," Runciman replied. "I explained … the difference between 'encirclement' and self-defence based on collective security," Maiskii reported. Runciman countered that Hitler would still trumpet "encirclement," and anyway, the strategy had not worked. It has not been tried, said Maiskii. There were many people in Britain who were afraid of Hitler, but this is no reason to turn a blind eye to the aggressor. Maiskii warned of the early outbreak of a new war, unless a powerful system of collective security was created.

"Is it possible so soon?" asked Runciman. Maiskii reiterated his position, and Runciman conceded that these were "dangerous … difficult times." So they were. Maiskii concluded facetiously that he might have spoiled Runciman's mood on the eve of his holidays.[38] How could a minister of the Crown living in such perilous times have been so fatuous? Readers may be assured that Maiskii did not get through Runiciman's wooden outer walls to disturb his Easter holidays.

Churchill: What a Contrast in Moods!

On the following day, Maiskii and Churchill lunched together; according to one source, the two had become "bosom friends,"[39] Maiskii reported finding Churchill in a combative frame of mind: sooner or later Hitlerite Germany would have to be stopped. "If by the end of this year," he said, "it is not possible to create a defensive alliance of states that may suffer from German aggression, war is inevitable." This conclusion would not have surprised anyone in Moscow, but Churchill's more important message to Maiskii was one of encouragement and prudence. "There are fools who attempt to draw a distinction between [security] in Western and Eastern Europe. Litvinov is right, peace in Europe is indivisible." To calm the doubters, one had to work within the bounds of the League, because words like "union" and "alliance" would frighten British public opinion. Direct Soviet participation in an anti-German alliance would be premature; it would frighten some Conservatives. They are coming around, but their "previous enmity is still far from eliminated." Churchill related, "with a laugh," that he had recently given a speech at an old Tory club, where he had promoted "with his thick-headed friends" the need for Anglo-Franco-Soviet cooperation against Germany. They had "swallowed" the idea regarding France, but had objected to cooperation with the USSR. "I became angry," Churchill said, "and replied, 'Be politicians and realists.'" Churchill continued:

> We would be the most complete idiots, if because of the hypothetical danger of socialism, threatening our children or grandchildren, we refused help from the USSR against Germany in the present. My arguments produced a very powerful impression on my dull-witted listeners, and they wavered somewhat in their implacability to your country. But such opinion has nevertheless to be taken into

> account ... In another year our Conservatives will be so frightened by the growth of German rearmament that they will even be able to swallow the Bolsheviks.[40]

Litvinov was interested in this conversation. Churchill's views, he wrote to Maiskii, corresponded with "our concept" of what should now be done. This amounted to agreement among "friends of peace" who would then form a united front to enter into negotiations with Germany. He did not share, however, Churchill's confidence in the League. "I don't know about Churchill, but we know that for the opponents of Hitler, like Austin Chamberlain ... the indivisibility of peace is limited to talking and worrying about guarantees for France and Belgium and for Austria and Czechoslovakia, but that they are willing to leave to the mercy of Hitler Eastern Europe, or at least the Soviet Union."[41]

A few days after the meeting with Churchill, Maiskii attempted to sum up his impressions of the British reaction to Hitler's sending of the Wehrmacht into the Rhineland. It seemed few people cared, if one was to judge by MPs' mail from constituents where there was more concern about changes in football rules than in what had happened in the Rhineland. Do not think, Maiskii remarked, that these letters only came from a few "cranks"; there were many such "cranks" in Britain:

> Along with the passivity of the masses and the chaotic state of their brains, it is necessary, however, to note one extremely acute feeling that possesses these masses: acute, instinctive, animal-like fear of war, especially before the prospect of aerial bombing. Anything, but not war! – such is the main note of local mass sentiment. Hence the deep pacifism of the masses, hence the fear of everything that in any way may resemble war, or threaten (even remotely) the outbreak of war.

In government circles there existed the same conflict between "Germanophiles" and those who wanted to organize a large coalition to counter the threat of Hitlerite aggression. In right-wing circles anti-Soviet feeling seemed to be on the rise due to the perceived increase in the power of the USSR and its more active role in Europe. They did not like to see the USSR entrenched, or so it seemed, in France and the Little Entente. There had also been an eruption of anti-French feeling. The British liked to blame the French for the "ridiculous" Treaty of Versailles and their "inflexibility" towards Weimar Germany after the war. Of course, the British were no less responsible for the Treaty of Versailles than the French. Moreover, British Conservatives did not want to be dragged into a war because of the Franco-Soviet Pact. Then, there was "the significant spread of isolationist sentiment in governing circles, fueled partly by the press campaign of the Beaverbrook papers. The policy of isolation, or at least semi-isolation, naturally dictates the elimination of close ties with France and the League of Nations, and is thus grist to the German mill." Military weakness,

Maiskii added, also influenced the British attitude towards Germany, causing it to pursue a wobbly policy in order to play for time to rearm.

Ever the optimist, Maiskii thought the Rhineland crisis had at last, during the past few weeks, given collective security a boost against the "Germanophiles," although the struggle with them was far from over. Maiskii continued to see Eden as a proponent of the Anglo-Soviet rapprochement and the strengthening of the "peace front," although the newly minted Foreign Secretary had only recently sabotaged the rapprochement with Moscow. Vansittart had thus not revealed to Maiskii the shift of opinion in the Foreign Office. Maiskii also spoke of the support of Churchill and Austen Chamberlain for "the Eden group." There was no "Eden group" in favour of a Soviet rapprochement. Churchill remained a Tory *bête noire* with limited influence and Austen would be dead in eleven months. As for Eden, he was anything but a strong advocate of holding the line on Nazi Germany. Reading Maiskii's long report in Moscow, one could only assume that the future of British policy was far from certain.[42]

The Lingering Abyssinian Crisis

As for the Abyssinian crisis, Litvinov was hard on the British. "I am very concerned about what is happening in Geneva in connection with the Italian-Abyssinian war," he wrote to Maiskii, and continued:

> I gave a directive to Comrade Potemkin to take a passive position there to show demonstratively to the English our cooling to the question of sanctions. The British should know that the most loyal supporters of the idea of collective security and collective sanctions are outraged by their behaviour towards Germany. It is not a question of England assuming obligations in other parts of Europe similar to those regarding France and Belgium. It is important to have a general position towards Germany's belligerence, its violation of treaties and its obvious preparation for war or a series of wars. All the behaviour of England only excites and encourages Germany. Members of the League of Nations should behave not only in Geneva, but also outside of it, even individually, in a spirit of intransigence toward aggression.

Litvinov's position on sanctions was complicated. "If we endorse French opposition to the strengthening of sanctions against Italy while England does not take a stronger stand against Germany, we fear that the too favourable French attitude towards Italy and a complete cessation or easing of sanctions, may cause an unwanted reaction in British public opinion and weaken the English connection with a system of collective security." Litvinov's position on a settlement of the crisis remained the same: agreement should be pursued through bilateral negotiations between Italy and Abyssinia outside the League.

Litvinov had his eyes squarely focused on the danger of Nazi Germany. Everything else was negotiable.[43]

Maiskii continued searching for a way out of the European crisis. But there was no way out, or rather the only way out, an Anglo-Franco-Soviet entente on which so much hope had been placed in 1935, was falling apart in 1936. In his correspondence with Litvinov, Maiskii cast about for solutions. Much impressed with Hitler's post-Rhineland "Peace Plan," Maiskii wondered aloud about how to respond to it. Could the Soviet government continue to pursue a policy of defending the political and territorial status quo in Europe? In February, Eden asked Maiskii how the "German problem" could finally be resolved. "I hear the same question every day, from Labourites, Liberals, and Conservatives, who in one form or another are interested in supporting a system of collective security," he responded. What to do? "The reasoning of these people goes, roughly, along these lines: German aggression is evil – we agree; to combat German aggression it is necessary to create a 'peace front' – we agree, though let's say a 'peace front' is created – then what? What will be the objectives of the 'peace front'? With bayonets maintain the status quo?" How could the status quo, Maiskii asked rhetorically, be preserved in Austria, Czechoslovakia, Memel, or Danzig?

Where was Maiskii going with these lines? "Needless to say," he added, "I can't take responsibility for all these arguments. I am just passing on for you information that I have to hear every day." Well, not entirely "just passing on," for Maiskii questioned whether advocating for a policy of status quo was still viable. Should we not propose our own "peace plan?" he asked Litvinov. Did Maiskii have some ideas in mind? We ought to respond to Hitler's plan with proposals for disarmament, for example, or a conference of League states. And on and on, Maiskii went, he was beginning to sound a little goofy. What had Maiskii been smoking? He sought to be practical, but could only come up with pipedreams. That was because the only practical solution, an Anglo-Franco-Soviet entente against Nazi Germany, was then impossible. In 1936 there was no practical solution for dealing with Hitler as long as Britain and France declined Soviet offers of collective security and mutual assistance. "One thing is clear to me," Maiskii concluded, "without any positive program to resolve European affairs, it will be very difficult for us to maintain and strengthen our influence in the Labour-Liberal society of England, and not just England alone."[44]

Litvinov replied to Maiskii. He admitted that he had contemplated a competitive plan to Hitler's. There was the French plan, which was utopian of course, but it could be improved although not now. The time was not right, he wrote.

> To come forward with a third competing plan would mean to split up forces and, following the example of a triangular vote during elections, to give indirect support to the Hitlerite plan. It seems to me more correct at this stage for all the friends of peace to stand together and act in a united front, and not on their own.

> More important, however, I consider it inappropriate to propose a plan based on slogans acceptable to the current English pacifists. To make an ideological criticism of the current status quo, to justify, at least theoretically, the association of German, Austrian, Czech, Memel and Danzig Germans, and German ambitions to obtain sources of raw materials, means grist to the mill of Hitler. Your pacifists will undoubtedly seize on this and this will justify their goodwill for Hitler. Since Hitler has legitimate aspirations and rights, it is only natural to talk to him and to come to agreement.

It was the way in which Hitler went about his business that raised objections and danger. "Anything that strengthens such a state and therefore increases the risk of a breach of the peace should be rejected. It is more useful to drive this into the heads of pacifists than to indulge their ranting about absolute justice."[45]

While Maiskii tried to resolve the dilemmas of Soviet policy, he continued his rounds, seeing Eden at the end of April and Vansittart a fortnight later. Eden had been busy looking for a possible "tack" towards Berlin. He proposed to cabinet the draft of a questionnaire for Hitler asking if he would respect the European status quo and if he was willing to sign "genuine treaties" to keep the peace in Europe. Why not ask a wolf to look after a flock of sheep? Maiskii was not the only one with goofy ideas. It is hard to see what Eden hoped to achieve with his questionnaire, which Phipps presented to Hitler in May. Naturally, the German government never responded to it. During his conversation with Eden, Maiskii reproached him for the wavering of British policy. He recited his usual ideas about European security, and he asked what was to go into the questionnaire for Hitler. Eden responded evasively. On instructions from Litvinov, Maiskii suggested a question on the Eastern Locarno – which in fact was dead as a doornail – but Eden flatly refused. Then the Abyssinian crisis and the Wehrmacht's entry into the Rhineland came up for discussion.

The conversation became heated. "I must say with all frankness," Maiskii wrote in his report,

> We have ample reason to be critical of recent British policy. Eden was just waiting for this comment and heatedly exclaimed: "You mean our attitude to Germany? Please, please, continue. Speak frankly!" I did not hold back and explained to Eden our point of view: we are not directly interested in the Italian-Abyssinian conflict, we supported sanctions against the aggressor, because we considered this case as a substantive lesson for other, more dangerous aggressors. For us, the League of Nations action against Italy was valuable, mainly as a rehearsal for similar action against Germany, if and when it comes. And what do we see now? Germany has committed a clear act of aggression with the greatest consequences. So what now? England, instead of resolutely opposing Germany, actually supports it. Naturally, the question arises, what value have tough measures against Italy? Such discrimi-

> nation between Italy and Germany in favour of Germany deserves, in our view, strong condemnation.

The Foreign Secretary put everything off on public opinion, which was hostile to France. "Eden began to argue that British public opinion draws a distinction between the open attack of Italy on foreign territory and the entry of German troops into the German region. Of course, Germany's violation of the Versailles and Locarno treaties merits condemnation, but still both acts cannot be put on the same board. And public opinion in England is a decisive force. With it, the government has to align." It almost sounded as though Eden was going to Germany's defence. Maiskii was not convinced in the least. The British government should lead, and not be led by, public opinion. After all, that is what the News Department was supposed to do. Maiskii did not like to criticize, but Eden had asked for frank speaking. The Hoare-Laval plan was at least a policy, not an admirable policy but a policy nonetheless. It might have been a solution to the war, if a poor one. Then the British government said it would hold to a League policy, but that did not happen. Instead, there has been uncertainty and hesitation. "The result is this," Maiskii said, "England has fallen between two stools, and the League of Nations is at risk. I apologize, but I have no idea what your country wants."

Eden defended British policy. We have done our best, he said, we acted in the interests of collective security. Eden put a large share of the blame on France and, in particular, on Laval, so that now anti-French feeling in Britain was intense. He was fighting against these sentiments, Eden said in so many words, trying to prevent a gap opening up between French and British policy. Maiskii was not convinced and thought Eden was making a poor case. "It often seemed to me that in essence he agrees with me and only objects mainly in an official capacity."

Maiskii went to the defence of France, though it was not his duty to do so. "France is afraid of Germany, it is looking for help – from the League of Nations, from individual great and small powers. Throughout the post-war period, France has sought a firm commitment of assistance from Great Britain in the event of German aggression, and could not get it. Every time Paris asks London whether it can count on unconditional support, London invariably answers 'Yes, but ...' And then various reservations and reserves begin. Is it any wonder, under these circumstances, that France began to look for friends in other parts of Europe?"

Eden tried to defend British policy, but Maiskii knocked down his arguments, one after the other. The conversation returned to the Abyssinian crisis. The situation looked hopeless for Abyssinia. The League had suffered a "heavy blow." If Italy in the coming weeks achieved final victory, would sanctions continue? This was unlikely, according to Eden. Maiskii responded that the only way forward was collective security and a reinforcement of the League. Eden threw up his hands.

"We have invested so much energy," Eden replied, "so much will, so much money in support of the principle of collective security in the Italian-Abyssinian conflict – with what result? How can I now, after the experience I have just had, turn to my country with a proposal to reinvest energy, will, and money in the maintenance of collective security in any other part of Europe? This country will not go there." Maiskii retorted, "Then there is only one alternative – war." To this comment Eden "helplessly shrugged his shoulders."[46]

Vansittart thought the prospects were "very dangerous," and that Austria or Czechoslovakia would likely be Germany's next targets. If nothing was done soon, Germany would establish its hegemony in central Europe, the "Mitteleuropa," against which Austen Chamberlain had warned. The British political situation was in complete disorder, according to Vansittart, but he hoped it would soon change for the better. Vansittart was bucking himself up as much as he was Maiskii. He was in a black humour: it is "uphill work" steadying "foolish & ill-instructed" British opinion. "Germany is certainly going to try to assimilate her neighbours in Central and Eastern Europe," and Vansittart did not see how to stop it, "unless our own people is prepared to be at least three or four times as virile as it is now."[47] Collier was in better spirits: "Luckily for Anglo-Russian relations, the prospect of an Anglo-German agreement is rapidly receding!" This was no doubt a shot at Sargent. But two months later he was as worried as Vansittart about a "disastrous" British *volte-face*: "I have naturally proceeded hitherto on the assumption that there was some continuity in [British] policy and that it would not be dictated by the 'Times' and Lord Rothermere [a press baron and rival of Beaverbrook] – otherwise the Northern Department might as well shut up shop."[48] As events would prove, it might just as well have.

Last Gasps

In May 1936, Collier and Vansittart tried to revive the loan to the USSR. Vansittart recommended that the question be put before cabinet, but Eden disagreed: "I do not myself feel any enthusiasm for proceeding with this loan project at present. However plausible our reasons, it will be resented in Germany & consequently diminish whatever chances may remain of a western European settlement. Nor do I want exceptionally intimate relations with the Soviets. 'Correct' is all that they should be."[49]

Maiskii knew nothing about Vansittart's last attempt to push forward the Soviet loan. But he was none too confident of future developments as he wrote to Litvinov in response to Litvinov's dispatch of 4 May. This was of course before Eden's final veto on the loan.

> I also look rather gloomily at the prospects opening up before us. Only one thing can prevent the outbreak of a big war for a relatively long period of time – the

> quick (over the next six to eight months) creation of that "peace front" about which I spoke in my speech to the Fabians on 19 March. Specifically, this means that Anglo-Franco-Soviet cooperation is so close that it could be considered, regardless of its legal form, a tripartite pact of mutual assistance. Such cooperation of the three great powers would be warmly supported by the Little Entente, the Balkan Entente, the Scandinavians, and a number of other countries of medium and small size. However, I do not see any reason to count on the possibility of creating such a "front" in the near future.

British political forces were divided into isolationists, semi-isolationists, and advocates of collective security. Maiskii saw the semi-isolationists emerging as the strongest political force in Britain and that meant ultimately a German free hand in the East and the establishment of "Mitteleuropa." The next step would then be for Hitler to move against the USSR. This was a grim, even dangerous prognostication, and Maiskii waffled around it, not wanting to close off all possibility of a tripartite alliance against Hitlerite Germany. He thought, he hoped that the French and British governments would intervene before "Mitteleuropa" was fully organized. Maiskii wrote:

> For us, however, that would be a poor consolation, for war would have already begun, and our main goal is to prevent, or at least delay war for a considerable period. Thus, if you begin to analyse the current trends in the development of European policy more coldly, you come to the inevitable conclusion that in the very near future you should expect war. And from here it is necessary to draw practical conclusions.

Where was Maiskii going with these ideas? His first thought was to warn Litvinov that he would ask for credits to build a bomb shelter on the embassy grounds. As he wrote, trying perhaps a little gallows humour, he was thinking ahead on a "small, local scale." And, of course, Maiskii would not just give up.[50] This was just as well for the approval of funds for the bomb shelter dragged on until 1939. One could not, of course, reproach Maiskii for his foresight.

By the end of 1936, Anglo-Soviet relations were returning to their usual dismal state. The question of a German-Soviet rapprochement came up again at this time, but Chilston did not think it likely. The Foreign Office was relieved, and Chilston's report, much praised. Although no one listened, Collier had earlier warned – prophetically as it turned out – that the USSR would only turn to Germany, if the British government "fail[ed] them … but not otherwise."[51]

Litvinov criticized British policy for "falling in meekly with the wishes of the … aggressors." The USSR, as he would so often say, could afford to stand back and wait to see how the Anglo-French would decide their policies. "The aggressors," he warned, "are attempting to isolate the West from the Soviet

Union; it is not a matter of isolating the Union itself, for it is the West that would find itself defenceless were the manoeuvre to succeed." There is something to be said for "Litvinov's prophecy," noted one Foreign Office clerk. And Collier noted that British "complaisance" towards Hitler had "done grave disservice to French and British interests." "People who do not wish to be complaisant must be armed," added Vansittart, "as I have pointed out for many years."[52]

British "complaisance" towards Germany was the verso side of its reluctance to move closer to the USSR. "Germany v Russia," as Oliphant had observed, was the essential question, and the British government opted for coming to terms with Germany. War was undesirable, really a "silly ... business," said Maurice Hankey, secretary to the cabinet, especially because a long war would leave Europe in ruins and "prey to Bolshevism."[53] It was the West's traditional *koshmar*. "Let gallant little Germany glut her fill of the reds in the East and keep decadent France quiet while she does so," said one Tory MP. "Otherwise," he continued, "we shall have not only reds in the West but bombs in London." Prime Minister Baldwin expressed similar opinions.[54] More's the reason, observed Sargent in another context, for the British government to exercise "a *droit de regard* over French policy."[55] *Finis* the independence of France. Here were the other not so "unspoken assumptions" behind British policy, which lingered on right into the Second World War.[56] As one Foreign Office clerk observed in March 1936, if Nazi Germany was really bent on war, "there is nothing left for the ex-allies to do but to cut out Hitlerism with a knife."[57] The hitch was that only Russia could assure victory against Germany, but Russia for many Tories was one ally too many.

Chapter Sixteen

Good News, Bad News: The Fall of Laval and the Abdication of France, 1936

On 22 January 1936, Laval's government fell. Potemkin's guess that he might endure yet a while longer proved wrong. Laval, the Phoenix, would not be reborn from ashes, until the collapse of the Third Republic in May–June 1940, at which point he completed his transformation into a Nazi collaborator. A new French government was formed two days later, under Albert Sarraut, no friend in the past of the Soviet Union, but on French journalist Léo Gaboriaud's list of non-entities. Laval was out and had no place in the cabinet, as Litvinov feared he might. The *koshmar* was over; a fresh start seemed possible. Flandin, the former président du Conseil, took over the Quai d'Orsay. Paul-Boncour was back in the cabinet as a minister of state responsible for League of Nations affairs; Mandel remained as Minister of Communications, his ambition to form a government not being realized. Herriot was out. That was a loss, more or less, balanced by Paul-Boncour's return, though he did not hold an influential portfolio.

In Moscow, Alphand jumped at the opportunity to write to Flandin. Alphand was a rare Russophile in the Quai d'Orsay; he promoted the Franco-Soviet rapprochement for reasons of French security in the tradition of Herriot. He was not in a crowd at the Quai d'Orsay. There was Eirik Labonne, although in January 1936 he was far from Russian business as sous-directeur d'Amérique, and Robert Coulondre, who favoured the rapprochement. Basically, they had all been part of Anatole de Monzie's "kindergarten" in 1926–7. The saboteurs who helped Laval gut the Franco-Soviet Pact were still comfortably installed in their big chairs at the Quai d'Orsay. Léger, Bargeton, Basdevant, and others could carry on their efforts to keep France and the USSR from too close an embrace. The right-wing press in Paris campaigning against ratification offered strident encouragement to justify efforts at sabotage inside the Quai d'Orsay. Collective security had become a policy of the left, the Front populaire, when a policy of Union sacrée, from left to centre-right, was the only policy of collective security which would work. From time to time Litvinov recognized this truism, but he could only speak reason in a media storm where few could hear him.

Alphand tried to kick off a new start with Flandin hoping to circumvent Léger and his collaborators. For three years, he noted, relations with the USSR had been improving steadily, though in recent months they had gone cold. Part of the problem was Laval, and his taking on the responsibilities of président du Conseil at the same time as he was Minister of Foreign Affairs. It made him more sensitive to domestic affairs, as Litvinov himself had noted. The Comintern Congress in July-August 1935 had stirred up the right with its calls for unity against fascism. This meant the formation of centre-left coalitions or popular fronts, which was like waving a red flag in front of the right. According to Alphand, domestic politics became mixed up with foreign policy in a situation of great danger for France where the only considerations that mattered were French "national interests." This was essentially Herriot's line. Alphand, therefore, called upon Flandin to resume the "policy of collaboration" with the Soviet Union. The Soviet side had noticed the recent cold shoulder. French commitments given by Laval in Moscow – although Alphand did not identify him directly – on speedy ratification of the mutual assistance pact and the approval of bank credits for trade had not been respected. Alphand referred to recent public statements in Moscow, but he knew from his recent conversations with Potemkin in Paris and with Litvinov and Krestinskii in Moscow that Soviet confidence in collective security and the League had been shaken. These public statements were a warning of "a tendency towards Russian isolation," which meant counting only on itself and on its national defences. If such a policy materialized, France would be the first to pay the price. We can easily restore the situation, Alphand said, by prompt ratification of the mutual assistance pact and by a clear commitment in a ministerial declaration to pursue "a policy of peaceful collaboration with the USSR."[1] Alphand's telegram does not appear to have left the Bureau du chiffre, a sign perhaps of continuing sabotage by Sovietphobes in the Quai d'Orsay.

For a few weeks, the Soviet government took heart from the disappearance of Laval. Readers will remember that Litvinov was in London for the funeral of George V, which took place on 28 January. He met afterward with Eden, who had replaced Hoare as Foreign Secretary in December 1935. In a telegram to Moscow, Litvinov sounded relatively positive about the meeting with Eden. The Foreign Office record, however, was more reserved.[2] No commitments were made, and Sargent continued to rail against Litvinov and against cooperation with the USSR. Litvinov did not appear to be aware of Sargent's animosity, which means no one was talking about it or Soviet intelligence had not heard of it. The Quai d'Orsay thought that Litvinov's visit in London, along with Marshal Tukhachevskii's visit, had gone well, which made it easier for the French government to show a little more warmth towards Litvinov when he arrived in Paris at the end of the month.

Potemkin moved quickly to take advantage of the new opening, so it seemed, in French policy. On 29 January, he met with Léger at the Quai d'Orsay. It was only a week after the fall of Laval. Potemkin wanted to organize a get-together between Litvinov and Flandin, the more so since the two had not been able to meet in London. Léger agreed. The two foreign ministers needed to talk over and come to agreement on a number of common interests. "It is desirable," Léger added, "to dispel some of the misunderstandings that have arisen on both sides in recent months." That was certainly true, but the comment was ironic coming from Léger who had been Laval's right arm in contributing to the "misunderstandings."[3]

French Ratification of the Franco-Soviet Pact

Potemkin quickly came to the point. He wanted to know what the new ministry proposed to do about ratification of the mutual assistance pact. "Léger replied that he considered the delay in ratifying the pact to be Laval's biggest mistake." It had sowed ill will between the USSR and France, but also raised doubts among "the friends of France" in Eastern and Southeastern Europe who favoured collective security. That was true. "In Laval's hesitation," Léger said, "Germany found support for its tactics of intimidation and blackmail, which it still uses today, on the eve of the ratification of the Franco-Soviet pact. The German press screams that ratification will be considered by the German government as a violation of the terms of the Locarno Pact, and that Germany will draw appropriate practical conclusions from this." According to Potemkin's record, Léger did not attach great importance to German threats. The best reply was to ratify the pact. Léger spoke to Paul-Boncour who promised to speed up preparations in the Chambre des députés. The debate should take place "in the very next few days."[4]

On 1 February, Léger met Litvinov to pass on the same upbeat message. "The new [French] government," Litvinov cabled to Moscow, "was very satisfied with the reception shown to me in London, thus making possible cooperation between Paris, London, and Moscow." One can only imagine Léger's false smile outlined by his well-trimmed moustache, when he said these words, but it was nevertheless true that if London was better disposed to Moscow then it was less risky for Paris to take Franco-Soviet relations out of cold storage. Léger went even further: "The necessity of active participation of the USSR in the organization of collective security in Europe remains for France an irrefutable truth." Flandin was committed to this position, according to Léger, and considered pact ratification to be an "urgent matter."[5] What had come over Léger? Was it an epiphany? Did he want to cover up his collaboration with Laval; was he trimming his sails for the moment because of a new minister in the Quai d'Orsay? After all, Sarraut's government was a caretaker until the spring elections.

In a telegram during peacetime, one keeps it short and sweet, but Potemkin, who was present at the meeting with Léger, made a detailed record of the conversation. Even with the new minister at the Quai d'Orsay, Potemkin captured Léger trying to weasel. The line about cooperation of Paris with London and Moscow as "the fundamental condition for ensuring peace on the European continent" was deleted from the government's opening statement in Parliament. "For reasons of an editorial and, in part, tactical nature," Léger explained. There was of course only one potential ally who could even the score with Nazi Germany. Could the new cabinet say this openly while the right-wing press waged a campaign against the mutual assistance pact? Apparently not. Léger nevertheless repeated that the government would proceed with ratification "in the very next few days." Potemkin asked about news of a week's delay. Léger claimed not to be informed. Was this more weaseling, or just a government trying to get organized and past a first vote of confidence?

The conversation moved on to other topics. Was France negotiating with Germany? Litvinov asked. No, Léger replied, except that there was the question of the air pact which had come up during the talks in London in February 1935. France had left it to the British to approach the German government, but Hitler had replied evasively. Litvinov rejoined with his usual lines:

> Hitler would not come to any agreements concluded in the interests of common peace until he was convinced of the firm determination of France, England, the USSR, and other European states to oppose organised resistance to any attempts to violate this peace. Unfortunately, some vacillations observed among the participants of the well-known plan for the organisation of collective security – in particular, on the part of Monsieur Laval, contributed to the strengthening of obstruction on the part of Hitlerite Germany.

Léger agreed with Litvinov's comments, although it was Léger who sabotaged Paul-Boncour's first steps towards mutual assistance, diverted Barthou from mutual assistance to Eastern Locarno, and supported Laval's gutting and subsequent attempts to sabotage ratification of the mutual assistance pact. How reliable could Léger be, even stating the obvious? According to Potemkin's record, "Leger said that the tactics being used by Germany … [are] a probe. An end to it can only be accomplished by a resolute implementation of the plan for the organization of collective security." Of course, of course, Léger could speak the right words, but could he direct the necessary action?

Léger had his eye on wavering elements among France's allies. Coincidently, King Carol was then in Paris. He was noticeably susceptible to Germanophile currents, Léger said: he needed bucking up. In fact, the king was looking for signs of French resolution and not just empty words. Litvinov made the obvious reply "that the obstacle hitherto standing in the way was the delay in ratification of the Franco-Soviet Pact."[6]

In fact, Titulescu was in Paris with King Carol, and he told the French – there is a French record of what he said – that he had persuaded the king to pursue the Soviet line. The king had confirmed this himself saying confidentially to Léger that negotiations for a Soviet-Romanian pact should continue. Titulescu appears to have recovered his élan, indicating that Soviet "intervention" would be "indispensable" in discouraging an Anschluss. He nonetheless admitted that Yugoslavia remained hostile to better relations with the USSR. Flandin concluded that at a minimum Titulescu and the king had reconciled their differences ... at least for the time being.[7]

The following day, 2 February, Litvinov and Potemkin met with Flandin without Léger. Flandin's first question was about Litvinov's impressions of the mood in London. The narkom responded that the British were concerned about German rearmament. "They see it as the most serious threat to the common peace. It is only possible to neutralize this danger by concerted and resolute actions of those states that are real supporters of peace." This was certainly Litvinov's view, but it was not that of the British government. Hitler was only interested in bilateral guarantee pacts, Flandin said, but multilateral agreements for collective security would be a more effective guarantee of peace. Bilateral pacts with Nazi Germany were no guarantee at all, Litvinov replied, and were only a pathway to war. "This is clearly understood by Hitler, and this is what he consciously strives for."

The conversation continued on various related topics, without disagreement, moving from Europe to Asia and back again. Based on Potemkin's record, a consensus of views emerged. Flandin was not happy about the Anglo-German naval agreement, which he saw as a step towards the destruction of the terms of the Treaty of Versailles. Litvinov repeated that Germany would only agree to multilateral security agreements "if it was convinced of the firm determination of the powers interested in preserving peace to resist her expansion." Flandin agreed:

> Germany is currently trying to shake off the obligations imposed on it by the Locarno treaty in relation to the [Rhineland] demilitarized zone. Taking advantage of the Franco-Soviet pact, which allegedly contradicts the Locarno treaty, Hitler covers up his true plan, which is to erect an indestructible wall of military fortifications in the demilitarized zone, 'lock' France and Belgium behind it, and then freely proceed with the planned expansion towards Bohemia and beyond. The only way to prevent the success of these plans is ... the determination of all states interested in preserving peace, not by word but by deed, if necessary, to show Germany that they will not allow it to continue violating its international obligations.

Litvinov could himself have offered these comments, but in Potemkin's record, they came from Flandin. Was it possible: a genuine French epiphany? Litvinov added that the best way to protect European peace and security was "close cooperation" between France, the USSR, and Britain. This was not just Litvinov's view, of course, but it was the key to holding Nazi Germany in check. Flandin made the interesting reply that trilateral cooperation should be expanded to include Italy. Litvinov's reply is also interesting: "The narkom explained that he was only thinking about the present situation, where Italy, unfortunately, had in fact withdrawn from the ranks of those European states able to provide real assistance in protecting peace in Europe. It goes without saying that under normal conditions, Italy's participation in the organization of collective security in Europe is absolutely necessary."

Litvinov then turned the conversation to Franco-Soviet relations. Here he asked for clarifications:

> Because of certain oscillations observed in Laval's foreign policy, "isolationist" moods had begun to arise and crystallize in the USSR. Since the entry of the USSR into the League of Nations was linked to the intention – with the assistance of France and its friends – of organizing a system of collective security and ensuring peace, the zigzags of French foreign policy during the past eight to nine months, have created the most serious disillusionment and fears in Soviet public opinion. If this policy had continued, the USSR would have been compelled to draw the most disappointing conclusions from its experience of cooperation with the European states.

Coming from Litvinov, that was a stark warning. "Flandin replied," according to Potemkin's record, "that the new government was beginning its work with a firm determination to implement the 'national' policy of France, closely linked with its friends in Europe and aimed at preserving peace. The ratification of the Franco-Soviet pact, which is due to take place in the near future, will be a major step of the new cabinet in that direction." The ratification debate was scheduled to begin on 11 February. Flandin commented on Laval "that he was striving hard, if not for a treaty, then for some final agreement with Germany." You mean a "final" agreement with Hitler? Litvinov joked in reply. Flandin smiled and "responded that he himself doubted such a possibility."

The last topic of conversation, briefly touched upon, was Poland. Flandin acknowledged that Polish policy had been "extremely disappointing"; but he hoped that Ambassador Noël in Warsaw, who was a close friend, could make the Poles see reason. Potemkin did not record any comment by Litvinov on this point.[8] The French version of this important conversation amounts to only a few paragraphs in a larger report of various conversations in the Quai d'Orsay taking place at the beginning of February.[9] Flandin had a lot to say that did not go into the French record. He and Litvinov appeared to see eye to eye on all the big issues. As first meetings go, it was a good start.

There were many good starts in Franco-Soviet relations. Could this one be sustained? Think of a powerful sedan. The driver presses the starter; the engine ignites. It starts, but then dies when the driver engages the clutch. Ambassador Noël sent a cable the very day of Flandin's meeting with Litvinov, which was not encouraging. Although Beck tried to hide his views, Noël reported, "each of his contacts with the men of the Hitlerite state leaves M. Beck even better disposed vis-à-vis Germany, more convinced of its power and its future, more admiring than ever of the regime which it supports. In a word, it is on Germany which M. Beck believes he can place his bet, at the very moment when the army and Polish opinion, disquieted by the rearmament and political action of the Reich, wish for a rapprochement with France."[10] Readers may recall Colonel Kowalewski's comments to Vinogradov in Bucharest only a few months before which supported Noël's analysis.

Alphand saw Litvinov after his return from Paris. He was, according to Alphand, very pleased with his reception by Flandin, understandably so based on Potemkin's record of conversation. The prompt ratification of the Franco-Soviet pact, Litvinov said, would lead to the conclusion of the Romanian-Soviet Pact, and *then* would "profoundly modify the present diplomatic situation for the greater good of peace."[11] The engine ignited and then died. Litvinov's optimism was soon dashed.

The Campaign for Ratification

In Paris, Potemkin worked around the clock to lobby for ratification. At a lunch gathering at the embassy, he talked with various supporters of the pact. Even Titulescu was present. Delbos asked Paul Bastid, a Radical-Socialist député and chair of the Foreign Affairs Committee in the Chambre, how he thought things would play out in the debate. Discussions could become stormy, Bastid replied, but the vote for should be "at least 400," thus a strong majority. It would be essential for Herriot to participate in the debate, according to Bastid. Everyone present agreed.[12]

On 8 February, Potemkin saw Flandin to discuss the ratification vote. Flandin advised that the debate would probably start on 13 February, not 11 February as planned, and that the list of speakers was long. The opposition intended to make a stand against the pact. Flandin went over their arguments. The right's principal objective was to stop a deepening of the rapprochement with the USSR. Their preference was for an entente with Nazi Germany, and their argument went as follows: "Without an agreement with Germany, it is impossible to ensure peace in Europe. Meanwhile, the ratification of the Franco-Soviet Pact repels Germany away from France and condemns it to isolation, which would have dangerous consequences." In the question of preferences, most of the French right was for Nazi Germany. Ratification of the pact would lead to a Franco-Soviet military alliance, which in turn would lead to opposing alliances and to war. It would certainly prepare the ground in France for the growth of a "revolutionary movement" and for the "strengthening of the Front populaire." As Potemkin had already warned, the right was going to try to tie ratification to a settlement of the old tsarist debts. It was now or never to obtain a settlement. The final argument went along the lines that if Germany attacked France, Soviet aid would only be a fond wish "because, first, the USSR is separated from Germany by the territories of neighboring states, and, second , the Red Army, sufficiently prepared for defensive operations, can hardly be used for an offensive on foreign territory."

All these arguments were fallacious for one reason or another, but the right agenda aimed not to win academic debates but to work for a German entente and to oppose the Front populaire. Flandin assured Potemkin that he did not agree with any of the right opposition line, though he pleaded the case for a debts settlement. It was *way* too late for that. As readers may remember, the French government had a chance for a settlement in 1926–7, but the Poincaré government opposed it for reasons of electoral politics. For Poincaré, winning the 1928 parliamentary elections trumped the interests of French investors holding tsarist bonds. In other words, if there was no settlement in the 1920s, the responsibility lay with France. The USSR was *always* being pulled into French electoral politics as a weapon of the right against the left, and sometimes of the left against the right. Potemkin said the issue was "delicate," and so it was. But Stalin had not been "delicate" when Laval raised the issue in Moscow, as Potemkin noted. He was blunt: the USSR would not recognize the old tsarist debts.

Flandin replied in effect that a high tide raises all boats and that ratification would have a beneficial effect on all areas of Franco-Soviet relations. He was confident of a large majority in the Chambre, but was hesitant about the Sénat. It will not dare to oppose openly the ratification of the pact, Flandin said, "but it is not excluded that some senators will try to put the Franco-Soviet treaty on the back burner."[13] As soon as Laval was out of the way – and it seemed like a long time since his departure although it was only a fortnight – ratification returned to the government agenda. Could the damage done by Laval be undone? Flandin seemed confident, at least for the moment, that it could. His confidence was reinforced by reports from the French embassy in London. Corbin advised that Litvinov and Tukhachevskii had been well received in London. Even the normally hostile *Times* seemed to change its tune.[14] If the British remained positive about a Soviet rapprochement, Flandin could take a more confident position in the ratification debate. Unfortunately, apparently unbeknownst to Corbin, Sargent was fulminating against Litvinov, and Eden was about to put the brakes on better relations with Moscow.

Two days later Potemkin met Paul-Boncour at a reception in the Sorbonne. Sitting together and talking discreetly, they went over the ground covered by Flandin. The Chambre should approve ratification with a strong majority. "It will be good if Herriot speaks there," Paul-Boncour said. "It is best if this speech occurs on the last day of the debate, just before the vote. The country listens to Herriot's voice, believes in his unselfishness, and knows that for some fifteen years he has remained steadfastly loyal to the idea of Franco-Soviet cooperation." As for the Sénat, Paul-Boncour confirmed Flandin's view that if things went well in the Chambre, the upper house would not dare to vote against ratification.[15] Potemkin led a strong lobby campaign with French partisans to prepare for the ratification debate. It was up to the government to get the job done.

The debate finally opened on 12 February. At once Charles Lasteyrie, finance minister under Poincaré's first government in the 1920s, demanded suspension of the debate on ratification until the Soviet government had made "fair arrangements" with their French creditors. In effect, Lasteyrie demanded suspension *sine die* of the debate on ratification. The implication was that the USSR needed mutual assistance more than France and that therefore Moscow would have to pay for French ratification. Not a good start to the debate, although Lasteyrie's line of attack was expected. Flandin intervened to separate the tsarist debts from the question of French national security. It was the obvious reply. As *rapporteur* of the bill, Torrès made the first sustained defence of ratification drawing attention to German "revisionism" – without saying the words Germany or Hitler. Revisionism risked provoking a "future world war" and that the USSR and France had a common interest in guarding against the establishment of a new order of things based on the law of the strongest. Lasteyrie intervened again to demand suspension of the debate. Others on the right were doubtful about Soviet aid for France, and feared possible Soviet "imperialist" ambitions. It was a state outside the *loi commune*, in other words, outside the capitalist order. In fact, the assault against ratification followed along the lines anticipated by Flandin. One right-wing député even brought up the Treaty of Brest-Litovsk as a betrayal of France when, at the time (March-April 1918), the Quai d'Orsay opposed the policy of cooperation with the Bolsheviks against the common enemy, Wilhelmine Germany. This was very secret information, so that the larger public would not have known of the debate within the French government about whether to be a friend or foe of Soviet Russia. Brest-Litovsk was always a good argument for the French right to throw at the USSR.

The debate dragged on into a second week. Herriot's reference to Francis I and Suleiman the Magnificent came up before Herriot himself could repeat it. The right-wing député Xavier Vallat, a despicable future Nazi collaborator and anti-Semite who worked for the Vichy government after the fall of France, brought up the subject himself in order to pre-empt "realism." "Someone will not miss the opportunity," Vallat declared, "to throw in my face Francis I and the Great Turk even though, at the time of Francis I, the Great Turk did not maintain a Muslim political party in France, the intentions of which were to overthrow the monarchy and to substitute the Koran for the gospel. All the same it is a minor difference." Vallat got some applause on the right and even in the centre of the Chambre. His quip would have been funny if the question of French security had merely been a joke. He was jailed at the end of the war and, unlike Laval, was lucky not be shot.

Pierre Taittinger, député on the far right, followed up on Vallat's shelling. He was also arrested at the end of the war for collaboration and he too was lucky not to be shot. "We will be told that we are a country of ideals, a country which built cathedrals, which went on crusades," Taittinger declared. "But to go on a crusade against fascism and for Bolshevism? I cannot bring myself to it. This will be one of the main reasons why I will not vote for the ratification of the Franco-Soviet mutual assistance pact, since it appears in the intentions of the Soviets to transform a pact, which should be limited to the defence of peace, into an instrument first of war, then of civil war." These arguments had been used since 1918 to oppose cooperation against the common German foe. "Civil war," of course, meant communist revolution. Taittinger fired one last salvo: "Messieurs, I have said enough to make it clear that, for our part, we cannot trust a pact which would be signed with a country which is organizing world revolution and which has decided to draw French money and soldiers into the service of the revolution." It sounded as though the right was preparing itself for collaboration with Nazi Germany.

While the right fired bullets at the pact, defenders of ratification appeared to shoot back with blanks. They said the pact was not directed against Nazi Germany, when of course it was, as Stalin had pointed out to Laval. They said it would not lead to a military alliance with the USSR when that was certainly the intention of the Soviet side and in the minds of some French advocates. They affirmed that it was consistent with the League Covenant and with the Locarno treaty. They said that it was a pact for peace, but of course to keep the peace against Nazi Germany, it was necessary to prepare for war. An old principle, by the way – *Si vis pacem, para bellum* – it dated back to Ancient Rome.

Communist députés mostly kept out the debate, with the exception of the formidable communist journalist and orator Gabriel Péri, a French patriot executed by Nazi occupation forces in 1941. He spoke plainly. "The organization of peace rests on this premise: the aggressor will not dare to attempt an adventure if he is certain to be opposed by a coalition of massive forces (applause from the far left). The more explicit the mutual assistance, the greater the certainty of its effectiveness, the fewer the risks of conflict, the more people can live in a regime of peace and tranquility." We reject any agreement with Germany, Péri added in so many words, that would give it freedom of action in any part of Europe, and we are waiting for Germany to renounce the plans for aggression spelled out in *Mein Kampf*, "still the Bible of the Third Reich." Then Péri went after Vallat, Taittinger, and their like. He expressed his astonishment that those "patriots," as he derisively called them, could forget Sedan where, in 1870, Prussian forces crushed the French Army. How could they with such equanimity, Péri went on, give Hitler a "blank cheque" to impose Nazi control of the Ukraine, of Austria, of the Little Entente, so that Germany would then be ready for "a redoubtable tête-à-tête with France"? Taking up Litvinov's law on the indivisibility of peace, Péri said plainly, "War in the east means war everywhere."[16]

Péri was the only député to speak about Hitler's blueprint for German domination of Europe. He named the enemy of France. Did *Mein Kampf* mean what it said, or not? His interpolation drew applause, according to the *Journal official de la République française*, mostly on the "left and far left." Were these the only sectors of the Chambre capable of endorsing Péri's frank speaking and "realism"? Who was correct in the end, Péri or the future Vichy collaborators Vallat and Taittinger? Péri died a patriot at the hands of the Nazis; Vallat and Taittinger were eventually pardoned as collaborators, and lived out their lives after the war.

In Moscow, Litvinov reported to Stalin on the opening of the debates on ratification and suggested a column in *Izvestiia* or *Pravda* to reply to the arguments of the right. His briefing note is worth quoting at length:

> The right-wing deputies and the right-wing newspapers oppose the ratification of the Franco-Soviet Pact with arguments borrowed from the Hitlerite press. They have the right to take a position on the pact, but they must not portray it as if it is a question of fulfilling a request from the Soviet Union or of doing it a favour.
>
> The mutual assistance pact was proposed to the Soviet Union by the French foreign minister [that is, Paul-Boncour] on his own initiative. It naturally proceeded from the interests and needs of France, not the USSR. When negotiations were conducted with M. Barthou and then Laval, until the signing of the pact, almost the entire French press, without distinction of party, supported the pact, not excluding those journalists and press organs which now oppose it. At that time, they did not yet know the arguments that Hitler later deployed. We can therefore assume that it was Hitler who convinced them that the pact was not in the interests of France, the same Hitler who in his book *Mein Kampf* declared France to be the hereditary enemy of Germany and who set himself the task of the diplomatic isolation of France, which he pursues methodically.
>
> The USSR has no foreign policy objectives beyond the protection of its borders. It can rely entirely on the growing power of the Red Army to carry out this task. It will protect its borders without outside help. Believing, however, that by organizing a system of collective security it would be possible to reduce the chances of war, it agreed to join this system and therefore accepted the French proposal for an Eastern Pact. For the same reasons, it, at the insistent request of M. Barthou,

> joined the League of Nations, and then signed mutual assistance pacts with France and Czechoslovakia.
>
> Aggressive Hitlerite Germany is an undoubted danger to all its neighbours, including France and especially Czechoslovakia. If right-wing French patriots believe that this danger to France and its ally Czechoslovakia will be lessened by the fact that the pact will not be ratified, then let them vote their own way.
>
> In any pact with the capitalist countries, the Soviet Union can give more than it will receive. The USSR has the most solid government, closely connected with the peoples of the Union, with the Red Army, which will go everywhere at the call of its leaders. This cannot be said with certainty about all capitalist countries with their changing governments, changing moods, and internal contradictions.
>
> The USSR serenely without any fear or nervousness observes the debate in the French Chambre des députés and the upcoming vote.[17]

These points were an effective reply to right-wing deputies, and Stalin left in blue pencil his familiar "*za*" on his copy of Litvinov's briefing note. Molotov also signed off on it. Stalin forwarded Litvinov's points to *Pravda*, which duly repeated the message two days later.[18] Along with the vinegar, however, there was also some sugar. Soviet president Kalinin gave a speech in the city of Gorki citing Stalin to the effect that the USSR was "ready to exploit any movement on the ground that could obstruct war or be used for peacekeeping. The Franco-Soviet Pact is one of these movements on the ground, which meets both the interests of the USSR and France."[19]

Maybe Litvinov was trying to help Soviet "friends" in Paris since their arguments during the first days of debate had been so flaccid, excepting Péri's. It was of course not true that Litvinov looked upon the debates with complete equanimity. He had to say this to remind the French that the USSR was not running after them and that the pact was not a one-way street. He also wanted to emphasize that *Mein Kampf* targeted not only Slavs, Roma, and Jews but also the French. What Litvinov said was that France needed a genuine defensive alliance with the USSR more than the USSR did; what he meant was that France should think more about its own contribution to the pact of mutual assistance rather than solely about what the USSR would contribute, or not, to French security. The French governing elite, with some exceptions, never "got" that message.

Potemkin continued his lobbying even as the debate in the Chambre unfolded. On 17 February, he saw Torrès. There were intrigues afoot against the government, behind which was Laval. Of course, Laval yet again. The right-wing press was putting out feelers about a government headed by Marshal Pétain. Laval was helping Pierre Guimier, boss of Havas, the influential French news agency. That's how politics worked in Paris: first in the shadows with hands extended to give or receive packets of banknotes. Daladier, the Germanophile, and even Herriot were also said to be involved with Laval's intrigues. Daladier made sense, but why Herriot? He cannot reconcile himself, Torrès said, to being outside the cabinet. "The 'head of the Turk' [i.e., the severed head of a formidable enemy] turns out to be Mandel. They do not forgive him for molding the current government, and for being a supporter of the strongest possible measures to counter Hitler's action." The right was starting to target "two-three Jews" who were pushing France to war. Even supporters of Mandel were backing away from him. Torrès went on and on about the paralysis of the French governing elite. Potemkin had heard it all before. Torrès also mentioned the recent conduct of the Romanian minister in Paris, Konstantin Cesianu. A few days before he had met him at a lunch given by the navy minister, François Piétri. There were four or five right-wing députés present as well as the Polish minister. Cesianu "reviled" the USSR and reproached the French government for concluding the mutual assistance pact. This outburst must have been just as the debate was beginning in the Chambre, thus all the more inappropriate. "If I had to choose between the barbarism of Stalin and the Hitlerite regime," Cesianu boasted, "I, without hesitation, would prefer the German."

This was again the perennial question of who was enemy No. 1? The answer given by the Romanian minister, as with so many others on the European right, was wrong. One did not need "aftermindedness" to see it. According to Potemkin, "these attacks were so inappropriate that Torrès felt obliged to intervene dramatically to cut off Cesianu." I shall take this matter up with Titulescu when next I see him, Torrès warned the minister, for his activities compromised Romania and played into the hands of the wrong side.[20] Would Titulescu be in a position to rebuke his minister?

On 20 February, Herriot finally spoke, as was planned at the luncheon in the Soviet embassy. Herriot's speech followed somewhat along the lines of Péri's, though without his directness, without mentioning *Mein Kampf* (except once in passing), and without the attack on the right. "I intend to speak without polemics," Herriot said to his colleagues, "if you will permit me." He spoke first about the size and power of the Red Army, to make the point that the Soviet Union was an ally worth having. Without such an ally, France could not pursue a policy of collective security. It was as simple as that. In the assessment of French security and French interests, we have to leave domestic politics out of the equation. Otherwise, Herriot said in so many words, we are lost. "I have heard certain députés speak here about the Franco-Soviet treaty," Herriot said, "as if we could really lock ourselves into a kind of *égoïsme sacré* behind our borders, as if we could say: '*Advienne que pourra*!' We will keep guard as best we can; but we will confine ourselves to our territory, sheltered behind our fortifications." Herriot did not evoke the memory of Francis I and Suleiman the Magnificent. Vallat had preempted him. When Herriot finished, the *Journal officiel* noted, he received strong applause "on the left and far left" of the *hémicycle*, and when he returned to his place, the congratulations of his friends. Bastid's calculation about Herriot's power to influence his colleagues appeared apposite. All the same, Péri's speech was more to the point, more powerful, and better for the historical record.[21]

There was also the other problem, that of the tsarist debts. It was like a long-dead skunk still giving off a bad odour. Flandin was looking for a helping hand on this issue, which the Soviet government could not give since it had finally decided in 1935 not to conduct further debt negotiations. The United States had the last chance for a modest settlement, but the State Department, motivated by its habitual Sovietphobia and working on the principle that two birds in the bush were worth more than one in the hand, refused Soviet proposals and demanded the full measure of its own. That strategy never worked with the Soviet government even at moments of great weakness. As for the French, they had had their chance in 1927. Litvinov therefore proposed to Stalin a negative reply to Flandin. "We have never demanded recognition of a cancellation of claims or the renouncing 'hopes' for a settlement of this issue. Flandin's speech expressing such hopes does not oblige us to anything, if we do not agree … I propose therefore to advise Comrade Potemkin to say tomorrow, on the day of Flandin's speech, that he had not received a response from Moscow, but that silence did not mean in any sense consent."[22] If France wanted defence cooperation with the USSR, the requirements of French security against Nazi Germany should be enough to justify it without demanding that the Soviet government should also pay for the privilege of being a French ally.

Would Stalin take a softer line than Litvinov? Apparently not. On 23 February, Litvinov wrote again to Stalin. The debate still dragged on in Paris. Litvinov was exasperated. He had cabled Potemkin to find out how much longer the debate would continue. Another session was planned for 25 February. "If Comrade Potemkin responds with news of further delays, then I would consider it useful to express in some way our displeasure to the French government. If our declaration does not result in the acceleration of the ratification procedure, in view of the helplessness of the government, the latter should know that we are not indifferent to the debate, which has become completely obscene." Litvinov then asked for authorization to send strongly worded instructions to Potemkin. His draft may be summarized as follows: See Flandin. Tell him, that the dallying over ratification had been going on for too long. Already two weeks in the Chambre, in a debate, moreover, which was unnecessary, according to the French constitution. Laval succeeded in delaying ratification for nine months. Now some députés were abusing and insulting the USSR. "Without making any demands, my government deems it necessary to inform you that public opinion in the USSR is greatly affected by the debates and speeches of certain deputies. The nature of the debate is completely unprecedented in the history of relations between two states that are striving for rapprochement and mutual assistance in the interests of peace." *Za!* Stalin approved the draft word for word and the cable was sent.[23]

Potemkin saw Flandin on 24 February, the day before the resumption of the debate in the Chambre. The vote would take place on the 27th and the bill for ratification in the Sénat would be introduced on the 28th. There would not be a confidence vote unless there was a renewal of attacks against ratification and against government policy.[24] Could the French get anything right? Potemkin met with the président du Conseil, Sarraut, two days later to find out. Sarraut admitted that the delays had produced an adverse effect on the international situation. "He agreed that Germany, Japan, Poland, and more recently Italy were attempting to use every day of delay for their intrigues against the pact." So *that* was the rightwing strategy in the Chambre, delay in order to let ratification die on the order paper with the help of potential enemies of France. The French right's collaboration with Nazi Germany started early on. Potemkin repeated his complaints about the delays and "inadmissible anti-Soviet attacks" to which Sarraut tried to parry with fears of communist activities in France and its colonies, whipped up by the right. Potemkin responded that the communist movement had "independent roots" and that the government had not been able to prove any Soviet government interference in French domestic politics. Soviet government, of course, did not mean Comintern. Sarraut was an old hand at whipping up anti-communist opinion in France, but he did not insist on countering Potemkin's comments. The common goal was ratification.[25]

The debate continued on 25 February. Bastid and Flandin spoke for the government. Bastid addressed the right. Drop the domestic politics, he said. "You represent the Soviet Union as a sort of bloody monster, whose subversive agitation would never end." After a brief détente, they would hear once again the call for world revolution. "Messieurs, do we not experience some embarrassment in seeing grievances of this sort reappear, which one might have thought to be out of date. We are no longer – at least I hope so – at the epoch of the man with the knife between his teeth." Bastid was referring to the iconic 1919 electoral poster portraying a vile-looking "Bolsh" clenching a knife between broken teeth, dripping with the blood of innocents who had fallen during the Bolshevik Revolution.

Flandin also spoke that day reminding the Chambre that the present government had inherited the treaty from its predecessor. The pact was "neither dangerous nor without advantage." It enhances the security of France and contributes to European collective security. French policy is consistent with that of Britain, Flandin added to assure the waverers. It was, in effect, safe to vote for ratification.

The debate dragged on for another day. The same arguments were evoked for and against the pact, and readers would only tire of hearing them all again.

When the vote was finally called, the result was 353 for, 164 against.[26] The absolute majority was 259, so that the vote represented a relatively strong endorsement, though not the minimum of 400 votes anticipated by Bastid. Potemkin's estimate of 150 votes against was closer to the mark. Moreover, the ratification bill still had to pass through the Sénat, always the more conservative of the two houses. There was relief in Moscow that the ratification bill had survived the debates in the Chambre, but also worries about what would happen in the Sénat. Alphand reported that the Soviet government feared attempts in Paris to postpone the vote until after the elections. That would be a disaster.[27]

Potemkin sent a summary to Moscow of events leading up to ratification. It is a rather extraordinary document for it underlines just how closely the Soviet embassy, both Potemkin and his staff, worked with French proponents of ratification. "We set ourselves several tasks," Potemkin wrote in a dispatch to Krestinskii:

> First, we had to prepare appropriately the speeches of such defenders of the pact as Herriot, Bastid, and Flandin. Secondly, it was necessary to prevent the possibility of official interpretations of the [League] Covenant that would weaken its international political significance. Third, our concern was to expedite, as far as possible, the ratification of the pact by the Chambre and its submission to the Sénat for debate. Finally, and fourthly, we considered it necessary to work effectively in the circles of the Sénat and the government to ensure the safe passage of the pact through the Sénat.

Then there was this extraordinary and "very secret" passage on cooperation with Herriot in the preparation of his intervention in the Chambre:

> Herriot's speech was prepared through my several personal conversations with our friend from Lyon and with the active assistance of the *polpredstvo* – Comrade Sokolin, the Press Bureau and the military staff … On the eve of his speech in the Chambre, Herriot sat with us [at the embassy] for about two hours, carefully studying the materials presented to him, listening to explanations on them and making the necessary extracts for himself. After his intervention, Herriot complained to me that his speech was, in the opinion of some, too "professorial" and too overloaded with material. There is no doubt, however, that it was the central point of the debate about the pact, and that on certain issues, such as the peaceful policy of the USSR, our armed forces, old debts, and new loans to the USSR, it put forward provisions of great political value to us. Bastid was also quite attentive to our explanations, and his speech – not only thoughtful, but also quite bold – made a very strong impression in the Chambre and in political circles … Finally, as for Flandin, you are aware of the content of our conversations with him in preparing his speech. We must admit that in his speech, the current foreign minister took into account our point of view.

Potemkin also reported on a luncheon at the embassy where Herriot met with Titulescu; Štefan Osuský, the Czechoslovak minister in Paris; Henri Guernut, a member of Sarraut's cabinet; and the Turkish minister Aras. This was just one of many meetings organized by Potemkin to prepare for the ratification debates. Readers will understand that the Soviet network of influential people in Paris was large. At this particular meeting, there was a heated discussion about how the mutual assistance pact fit in with the Locarno agreements. Let Potemkin describe the discussion:

> Herriot argued that, in the absence of unanimity in the League Council on the question of recognizing Germany as an aggressor against the USSR, France must be guided by the opinion of the guarantors of Locarno – England and Italy. Titulescu hotly objected, reminding Herriot that the League of Nations, in connection with the Italo-Abyssinian conflict, embarked on the path of sanctions against the aggressor … bypassing a formal vote taking into account the presence or absence of unanimity. For my part, I proposed a formula which emphasized the sovereign right of France to decide at its discretion the question of the existence of aggression and the resulting obligations of assistance – only taking into account the conclusions of the Locarno guarantors on this issue, but by no means submitting itself in advance and mechanically to their decision.

Laval, Léger, and others wanted to tie up treaty obligations in as many potential obstacles as possible, and Potemkin was trying to guide them out of the thicket. Readers will also note that Titulescu was still firmly in the camp of collective security. His argument won the day with all present, and Herriot promised to take it up directly with Flandin.

Discussion then turned to ratification in the Sénat. Delbos, Herriot, Flandin, and Sarraut were "optimists." The Sénat would not oppose ratification once approved in the Chambre. Paul-Boncour was not so sure. "Maybe Boncour is trying to frighten us a little," Potemkin opined, "and give himself, as the defender of the pact and the organizer of its support, a special significance in our eyes; he looks concerned when talking to us about the upcoming debates in the Sénat, and warns that the matter will not be without a fight." Potemkin added that he was going to meet for dinner with Yves LeTrocquer, the president of the Sénat, with Herriot, industrialist Ernest Mercier, who favoured ratification, among others, "to create the atmosphere we need."[28] Potemkin's network of contacts was remarkable, a Who's Who of the French political elite.

It is hard to know what to think of Flandin. On 1 March, he sent a cable to François-Poncet in Berlin directing him to seek an audience with Hitler to discuss a Franco-German entente. Flandin also proposed referring the Franco-Soviet Pact to The Hague tribunal for arbitration. Did Flandin suddenly lose his nerve? France was becoming a "dangerous place" and not the "hinge" of Soviet policy. Litvinov had heard about the reference to The Hague. Readers can easily imagine his reaction. "Flandin's and Sarraut's assurances that the pact will pass quickly through the Sénat do not reassure me very much," the narkom advised Potemkin:

> The numerous opponents of the pact are now bringing all their heavy artillery into the theater of war, the first weapon of which I consider to be [François-Poncet's] interview with Hitler. Paul-Boncour's warning deserves serious attention, especially since I read somewhere that Flandin himself spoke of his intention to appeal to The Hague Tribunal. I suggest that you monitor the situation and signal us any strengthening of the enemy's position. I am now considering whether we should appeal to Flandin and Sarraut with a stronger warning against further delay. I am not sure whether we would rather prefer to break the pact ourselves than agree to The Hague procrastination, which will enable France again to make the pact an object of trade with Germany.

Litvinov was cynical although who could blame him? He thought Bastid's speech, not Herriot's, was the most effective.[29] Would he have thought it possible to praise the communist Péri?

The Rhineland Crisis

Soviet optimism aroused by Laval's fall from power was short-lived, killed first by the ratification battle in the Chambre des députés, and then by a veritable catastrophe a fortnight later. On 7 March, Hitler denounced the Locarno accords, and the Wehrmacht marched into the demilitarized Rhineland, thus cutting down the last leg standing of the Treaty of Versailles.

French military intelligence foresaw Hitler's intention, but would do nothing without British support and the British, led by Eden, would do nothing. The Soviet reaction was immediate. Litvinov was furious and lost his temper in a meeting with US ambassador William Bullitt. "Litvinov displayed almost violent rage in his comments," according to Bullitt, "… the promise of a dog, liar, and blackguard like Hitler was worthless." Litvinov hoped League sanctions would be imposed against Germany, but that was oddly naïve for him. It was not going to happen, although the narkom had always envisaged the League as a potential arm against Hitler. The Abyssinian fiasco sank that idea and still dragged on. Litvinov was "disgusted" by Hitler's offer to re-enter the League and other flimflam to bewitch opinion in Britain and France. He was "even more disgusted," Bullitt reported, by the British who would welcome Germany's return to Geneva.[30]

Alphand also reported: France must take a firm stance, Soviet sources said, and a first step in that direction would be a prompt ratification vote in the Sénat.

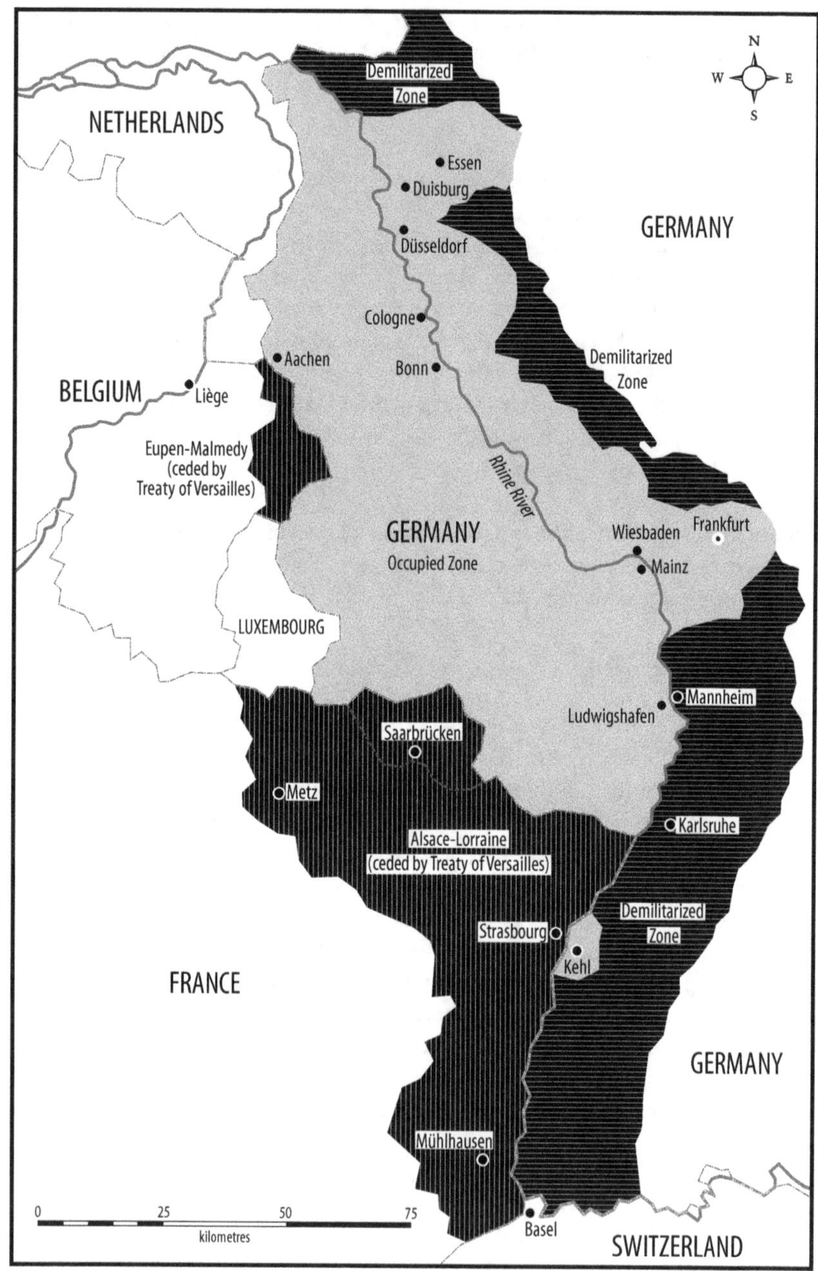

Map 16.1. France and the Rhineland frontiers, 1930s.

If France holds firm, Britain will also be forced to hold firm. "We can entirely count … on the Soviet delegation in Geneva," Alphand cabled. "Litvinov is leaving Moscow tomorrow."[31] As readers will remember, Eden, following Sargent's lead, took a weak position on the Rhineland and paralyzed any possibility of joint Anglo-French action, except for capitulation.

Maiskii reported on the slack positions of most of the British press. The *Sunday Times* was a notable exception. Corbin had advised Maiskii that Eden was talking "composure and self-control." That was not good news. The British government was contemplating talks with Hitler.[32] Reading these telegrams must have enraged Litvinov even more. "If the position taken by the English press reflects government policy," Litvinov cabled to Maiskii, "then this means a return to the policy of the prize to the aggressor, the rupture of the system of collective security and the end of the League of Nations." He continued: "Negotiations with Hitler on the second day after the violation of Locarno will have even more dire consequences than the Laval-Hoare plan. It will finally break trust in England. The League of Nations, opening wide the doors to the aggressor, will lose any value from the point of view of peace. We condemn decisively such a position and we are ready to support any actions taken collectively in Geneva against Germany." Litvinov still thought strong action could stop "German aggression and lessen its danger." He left for Geneva that same day, 9 March.[33]

Potemkin passed on the Soviet message to Flandin on the following day. The Soviet delegation was ready to support the French position at the League. It would help, Potemkin added, if ratification in the Sénat proceeded immediately, even without debate, to efface the "painful impressions" in Moscow caused by the continued attacks of the right opposition and press against the USSR and against ratification. Flandin thanked Potemkin for Soviet support and said that plans were moving ahead for ratification in the Sénat in three days, on 12 March. The debate and vote would take place on the same day in time to make an impression in Geneva. A vote without debate would only make a bad impression and was unnecessary since a strong majority would vote for ratification. Some who intended to vote no will now vote yes. "It doesn't matter if one or two of the most 'exalted' sénateurs speak out against the pact," Flandin said. "The weakness of the opposition will only be highlighted, as would the message that all the serious representatives of the nation in the Sénat are aware of the need for a Franco-Soviet pact as a guarantee of peace and security in Europe."

Potemkin then asked about the likely British position. Flandin's reply is interesting. "Flandin said that the mood in London was somewhat wavering yesterday. Today, as Corbin reports, the situation seems to be improving. Apparently, Eden is inclined to support the French point of view. In any case, we must wait for his speech in the House of Commons today. It is even more important to show the necessary firmness and solidarity in Geneva. England will hardly dare to object to the sanctions that should be applied to the violator of the treaties, if France, the USSR, the Little Entente and other states express their support for such a decision."[34] In fact, Eden was preparing to capitulate in hopes of future negotiations with Hitler. His speech that day in the House of Commons disappointed Flandin. It was mealy-mouthed and evasive. Flandin's hopes thus represented the dying gasps of an independent French foreign policy.

A series of meetings began, the first in Paris between the Locarno powers without Germany. The meeting venue then moved to London where the Locarno powers continued to meet, until a meeting of the League Council began. Litvinov met Flandin in London for the first time on 13 March. Flandin had nothing but bad news. Britain would not agree to sanctions for they would inevitably lead to war and Britain would not be ready for war before three years. Moreover, Flandin had learned that the British government without French knowledge had appealed to Germany to act with restraint in the Rhineland zone.[35] This report must have discouraged the government in Moscow.

At least there was one bit of good news: on 12 March the Sénat ratified the mutual assistance pact, 231 votes for, 52 against. The debate was short and sweet, and the vote, an anti-climax. Paul-Boncour and Flandin must have passed the word that there should be no repeat of the polemics in the Chambre. It was hard to vote against the pact after Hitler's *coup de force*, but 52 did.

Opéra bouffe

On 14 March, Litvinov reported that negotiations between the Locarno powers had produced no tangible results. It was one piece of bad news after the other. Laval and Herriot, of all people, were said to be in favour of negotiations with Hitler.[36] Four days later, Litvinov reported that there was still no agreement between the Locarno powers. Eden called for negotiations with Nazi Germany for the establishment of a demilitarized frontier zone on both sides of the Franco-German border. Flandin and Paul-Boncour blew hot and cold, Litvinov reported, but, in the end, they would be entangled by the British. Fear of war and lack of political unity explained French weakness, according to Paul-Boncour. That was it, the common denominator of all explanations for French inaction: fear and lack of unity. Only Titulescu backed a strong French position. He had more guts than most of his contemporaries in spite of his phobia for Bucharest. Of course, he knew that if the French caved in, it was the end of collective security in Romania and the end of his tenure as foreign minister. Litvinov reckoned that the isolated French would be forced to make concessions.[37]

Flandin understood that the French position in Central and Eastern Europe was unsustainable as a result of the Wehrmacht's entry into the Rhineland and said as much to Vansittart, who became the British shoulder to cry on. Vansittart noted:

> M. Flandin was today in a very depressed mood, and in a private conversation he spoke in frank and gloomy terms. He said that his mission to London had been a failure. From the first there had been a tendency to class France and Belgium, the injured party, with Germany, the guilty part[y]. It was natural that we should seek to act as mediators, but we had gone too far. The very proposals that HMG was now discussing with him were impregnated with this unjust assimilation of guilt and innocence ... Flandin further said, without any heat or ill-feeling, that the present meeting was a misfortune not only for the League but for Anglo-French relations.[38]

The British did not seem to mind. It would be easier to negotiate with Herr Hitler. Massigli, still directeur politique adjoint at the Quai d'Orsay, thought the situation was absurd: "To begin immediate negotiations with a power that had just torn up a perfectly good and valid treaty would, in French opinion, savour of *opéra bouffe*, particularly as Germany had already committed this international offence several times before."[39]

Tell that to Sargent. In a meeting with Ambassador Clerk in Paris, Léger opined that, while military action was out, *something* had to be done. He had in mind financial sanctions. Otherwise, "such countries as Italy, Poland and Turkey, which were now hesitating, would throw in their lot with Germany, convinced that her hegemony in Europe was inevitable, and the Western powers would eventually have to face a reckoning with a vastly strengthened Reich in circumstances much less favourable than the present." *C'est l'heure de Joffre, où on ne peut plus reculer.*[40] "It's the time for a Joffre ..." This sounded good, but the British had nothing like that in mind. Anyway, General Joseph Joffre who had served in the First World War was dead of old age, and there was no great commander to replace him. Léger was right, though, that the French position in Central and Eastern Europe was shattered. That was also Paul-Boncour's position.[41] The idea about sanctions did not get past Wigram, the head of the Central Department: the UK would suffer more from them than Germany.[42] There was a lot of talk, and casting about for solutions, but no action. This suited the British, and it broke the French.

Sargent thought a solid security guarantee to France might have a calming effect and would induce the French not to try to force the Wehrmacht out of the Rhineland. In exchange, "we must have a *droit de regard* over French foreign policy in Europe," he wrote. Sargent had little respect for France and thought its eastern obligations were an impediment to obtaining a settlement with Hitler. Of course "conditions change," Sargent opined, but France might cut and run out on the USSR to avoid war with Germany.[43] It is interesting that

Sargent's Sovietphobia never appeared to leak to Moscow. If so, it was a failure of Soviet intelligence. There was much hostility towards France in London, not least from Sargent who heaped scorn on Herriot and others on the "extreme Left," whatever that meant, who were "in the pockets of the Bolsheviks and are playing the Russian game, no doubt with the help of Russian money." "Pro-Bolsheviks," he noted, like Titulescu, were teamed up with Litvinov.[44] This was becoming a zero-sum game, not a good way for British to treat an ally. Sargent gets off way too easily with English-speaking historians.[45]

Corbin went in to see Vansittart to plead. That was pointless, although Vansittart tried to be sympathetic. "The supreme disaster," according to Corbin, "would be if they [the London meetings] resulted in any Franco-British estrangement, for that would mean the destruction of Europe and the domination by Germany of all the smaller states." Corbin was dead right, but who was listening and who would remember? When Corbin worried that Britain might not "stand by its obligations," Eden sneered. "It is not for France to lecture us," he snapped.[46] Sargent would have approved.

In Paris, General Maurice Gamelin thought the Germans were bluffing. Only a strong "united front" of Britain, France, Italy, and Poland would discourage Hitler. Hold on! Did Gamelin say anything about the USSR? Not a peep. And it was only eight days after the mutual assistance pact had been ratified in the Sénat. "The Germans had not changed," Gamelin opined. "If we were not firm now it would mean in a few years that we should see the 'Anschluss,' followed by the subjugation of Czechoslovakia followed in turn by that of Poland." That was a good call, though practically anyone in the know would have made it. Gamelin liked to talk, but he discouraged mobilization. Vansittart concluded that in the case of war, Britain would have to defend Belgium with ground troops. Anything else would be "fatal."[47] What ground troops? Britain had scarcely any. Two divisions for France … or the parade ground.

In Paris, Potemkin made the rounds. A ghost from the seemingly distant past reappeared briefly. Laval invited Potemkin to see him at his office in the Sénat. It was like two old adversaries reminiscing, for otherwise it was hard to understand why they met. They got to talking about the French political situation. Maybe Laval saw the chance for a comeback. "Not without some malice," Potemkin recorded in his journal. "Laval stated that the Sarraut government was at a critical moment. Laval does not believe, however, that Hitler's action was directly caused by the ratification of the Franco-Soviet Pact. The pact is only a pretext … Hitler had long intended to violate the regime of the Rhineland." It was a good time to make a move, Laval observed. France and Britain did not see eye to eye, and Italy was brooding, isolated, and angry about League sanctions. France was also locked in a divisive electoral campaign that prevented national unity. Germany was clearly winning another diplomatic battle. For Laval, "national unity" meant busting up the Front populaire: isolating the communists, neutering the socialists, and drawing the Radical-Socialists to the right. Flandin and Paul-Boncour overplayed their hand in London. Laval went on about how the situation was disastrous and how *he* might have handled it better … of course … of course. "Laval remains unfailingly true to his idea – namely, that European peace is impossible without the agreement of France and the Little Entente with Germany." There was an obvious reply to Laval, but Potemkin chose not to make it. Laval then returned to the Franco-Soviet Pact, boasting about how he had gutted it, in effect, to avoid giving Hitler further pretexts to justify his Rhineland policy. The debates would have gone better in the Assemblée nationale, Laval added, if the Soviet government were not interfering in French domestic affairs. Again, Potemkin offered no rebuttal. What would have been the point? They had been over this ground many times before and Laval was out of power.[48]

On 18 March, Potemkin saw Mandel for a very different kind of discussion. Mandel described briefly what had occurred in the French cabinet meetings after the Wehrmacht's entry into the Rhineland. The idea of sending the Franco-Soviet Pact to The Hague tribunal came up again. On 13 March, Herriot went to see Sarraut and spoke "pathetically" about the necessity to avoid war and to persuade Hitler to accept The Hague arbitration. Potemkin's report of the conversation is painful reading even now. Mandel considered such ideas unacceptable and "in practical terms dangerous." Potemkin agreed, but also pointed out that The Hague arbitration would go down badly in Moscow, as Sarraut and Flandin knew very well. It would be considered disloyalty towards the USSR. Taken together with the delays in ratification and the "unheard of tone of the debates" in the Chambre des députés, the level of exasperation in Moscow could lead to "radical conclusions" about the mutual assistance pact. On these points, Potemkin and Mandel saw eye to eye. Mandel at once picked up the phone and called Sarraut to tell him that he was meeting with Potemkin. He should come to me to discuss, Sarraut replied.

That being settled, the conversation continued. It had been decided to mobilize, Mandel said, in anticipation of the German move into the Rhineland and that the British government had been so informed on 3 March. He was referring to a note that Flandin gave to Eden in Geneva on that day. Nevertheless, when the time came to act, the cabinet folded. The French high command opposed a resort to arms. As a result, the moment to act was missed, and "Hitler shook loose all the fruit from the tree because of such hesitations." Mandel added that he "had learned that the Germans feared French mobilization in reaction and were ready to withdraw at the first signs of it. They entered into the zone, as if into enemy territory looking around and afraid of every shadow." According to

Potemkin's report, Mandel "stigmatized the cowardice of the government and high command at this critical moment." He wrote:

> In spite of the stern condemnation to which Mandel subjected the French government and high command, he did not consider the situation as completely lost. According to Mandel, public opinion in France is growing more and more indignant over the betrayal of the English and exasperated against the Germans. There is no doubt that France does not want war. But seeing that it is being attacked and that force can only be answered by force, the country may eventually lose patience, and then Germany will see before it the real France. Mandel is sure that the USSR will stand with this France.[49]

These were strong, moving words. Potemkin saw Mandel's emotions erupt and wanted to report them to Moscow so that his colleagues would understand that there were strong, determined leaders in France. The French government would need more Mandels, however, to persuade the sceptics in Moscow that France could be a reliable ally. The irony is, of course, that the French high command did not consider the USSR to be an ally, and counted every German foeman twice in order to frighten the politicians into doing nothing about Hitler's advance into the Rhineland.

Potemkin saw Sarraut on the following day, 19 March. Most of the discussion concerned The Hague initiative. Potemkin was greatly bothered by this idea for obvious reasons, but Sarraut tried to reassure him that Hitler would not agree to it. Even the British were not keen on the idea, not wanting to put pressure on Hitler. Of course, that was now a familiar refrain: "Oh my, we mustn't irritate Herr Hitler." The conversation then moved on to other topics. Sarraut reassured Potemkin of the French commitment to the mutual assistance pact, given the essential role of the USSR in guaranteeing collective security in Europe and the Far East.[50] In view of the Anglo-French failure to react decisively against Hitler's advance into the Rhineland, the value in Moscow of Sarraut's declarations was limited.

French Collapse

That same day in London, 19 March, France and Britain came to an agreement of sorts. It was the "decisive day," according to the late Academician Duroselle.[51] The British took a limp position on all French ideas, so that nothing was left in the end but a British guarantee to France and Belgium and staff talks. The latter were not worth a plugged shilling, only the promise of two British divisions without any specification as to how they might be employed. The British were adamant on that point. Two divisions; that was it. Take it or leave it. Hence, the British line was obduracy with allies; flaccidity with enemies. Even Vansittart felt obliged to alert the Foreign Secretary that two divisions would not do. "No Frenchman or Belgian would ever accept the proposition that they could do the land fighting and we would, for our own convenience, limit ourselves to air and sea."[52] Exactly, this was a point to which Vansittart would return without any result since it was still two divisions in 1939. The Conservative government resisted breaking a balanced budget to increase defence spending, a decision that would lead Britain near to the precipice of defeat in 1940. That is another story about which we will speak a little further hence.

Still in London, Litvinov cabled Moscow that an agreement had been reached. Flandin and others filled him in on the details. Not much had been achieved and the French "were sinning on the side of optimism."[53] Two days later, Litvinov cabled for instructions from Stalin. The reference to The Hague tribunal was still in the agreement. "This unfortunate idea originated with the French, [and] Herriot as well as French and English pacifists hotly supported it. Therefore it was difficult to fight against it here." There were other problems, Litvinov noted. There was no reference to security in Eastern Europe. "I will try to correct this," he reported to Stalin. "However, they will ask what concretely we want from Hitler. We can again advance the idea of mutual guarantees by us and Germany of the Baltic States, but on this Hitler will not agree. The British and French would rather support the idea of a Soviet-German non-aggression pact."[54] This is the first time readers will see the mention of a Soviet-German non-aggression pact, and the irony is that the idea originated with the British and French. To be sure, the circumstances were different in 1936 from what they would be three years later. Still, this line from Litvinov's cable jumps out at the reader.

A reply came quickly from Moscow. Krestinskii, writing on instructions from Stalin, suggested an attempt to resurrect the Eastern Locarno. Litvinov was authorized to say that "if now the question about Eastern Europe cannot be resolved, the authority of the League of Nations and the question of armaments limitation in the future will come under serious threat and that the USSR will have to take the path of a further increase in the strength of its army and air force for the USSR will consider that it has been left to its own devices." It could be that the idea of a Soviet-German non-aggression pact emerged as a compromise solution. "In this case, you could agree on this pact, having in mind that a non-aggression pact is at the same time a pact of refusal to support an aggressor in any way and that the pact loses force, if one signatory attacks a third party."[55] Stalin dropped that idea in 1939.

Problems kept turning up one after the other. On the same day that Krestinskii forwarded Stalin's instructions to Litvinov, he also wrote to Potemkin to warn him that the French were thinking of delaying the exchange of formal documents on ratification of the mutual assistance pact. In London, Flandin had promised Litvinov to see to this exchange of documents "immediately."[56] Did a French commitment ever count for anything? "The conduct of the French," Krestinskii wrote, "simply astonishes me. Even for them it must be clear, that if Hitler were only trying to break the Franco-Soviet Pact, he would not have needed to send troops into the Rhineland, it would have sufficed for him to declare in the Reichstag that he would do this, if the French Sénat ratified the pact. I have almost no doubt that if Hitler had acted thus, the pact in the Sénat would not have passed." To be sure, the pact was only a pretext to send troops into the Rhineland, Krestinskii opined, just as Laval himself had pointed out to Potemkin. The French had no choice now but to hold on to the Franco-Soviet Pact as insurance against German aggression. Delaying the exchange of ratification documents would do the French no good in relations with Germany, but would "risk doing serious harm to Franco-Soviet relations."[57] Krestinskii mocked the cravenness of French conduct after Hitler's *coup de force*; and if he was doing so, then others in Moscow, more cynical than he, were also making jokes about the French, or worse, wondering whether France could ever be a reliable ally.

On 24 March, Hitler helped temporarily to resolve Franco-Soviet difficulties. He rejected all the proposals coming out of London, including the reference to The Hague. The remilitarization of the Rhineland was thus a fait accompli, which did not seem to bother the British all that much since they favoured negotiations with Hitler. The reaction in Paris, however, was anger, in large measure because of the realization that France had been had, first by Hitler and then by the English.

Litvinov stopped off in Paris and met with Sarraut, Flandin, and Léger. They were angry about Hitler's *fin de non-recevoir*, the more so since they recognized that there was little they could do about it. Everyone recognized that a revival of Eastern Locarno was not feasible, but according to Litvinov, they declared their opposition to any agreement that did not guarantee security in Eastern Europe.[58] That was a step in the right direction, but what value did these assurances have in Moscow, given the Rhineland fiasco?

Potemkin sent a résumé of events in Paris since 7 March, including a well-informed explanation of the cravenness of French policy. The conversation with Mandel had strongly impressed Potemkin and he referred to it often in his report, beginning with the account of Flandin's note handed to Eden in Geneva on 3 March. Readers will remember that the note informed Eden that, in the event of a German violation of the Rhineland demilitarized zone, France would mobilize. "You will see that this minister unequivocally accuses the British of betrayal, manifested in the fact that Hitler was informed from London of the need to prevent England and France from agreeing to joint resistance in the event of a German violation of the regime of the Rhine zone."

Potemkin's report recapitulates a good deal from his previous records of conversation. He has some interesting things to say about how the British finessed the French out of a tough line of policy. Eden, the surrenderer, came to Paris to preside over the meeting of the Locarno signatories. It was then decided to move the meetings to London where eventually discussions passed to the League Council, also convened in London. Potemkin asked Flandin why he agreed to these arrangements.

> He told me that the English delegates had come to the Paris conference either insufficiently informed of the position of the French government, or disposed not to take it very seriously. When they found that the French were not inclined to compromise, they became concerned. Eden said that he needed to discuss the situation again with his government; that it was impossible for him to communicate with it every minute on the telephone, etc. Following this, a request came from London to move the meeting of the League Council there, and Flandin conceded.

Eden had only been Foreign Secretary for a few months, but he was already a cunning operator at least facing weak opposition. First, he had halted a deepening of the Anglo-Soviet rapprochement and, a month later, he outmanoeuvred the French, finessing them out of a vigorous defence of their most vital interests. Moving the meetings to London and bringing the League Council there was all part of an obvious strategy to swamp the French with fear of war, though there was plenty of that in Paris, along with right-wing sympathy for Nazi Germany. What little the British offered, the security guarantee and the staff talks, were worthless when the Rhineland buffer was gone and the Wehrmacht sat perched on French eastern frontiers. Eden and many of his Conservative colleagues were for negotiations with Hitler and against Franco-Soviet mutual assistance. That was a formula for catastrophe, but in the Foreign Office, Sargent was riding high and Vansittart, often disregarded.

"There is no way to describe," Potemkin remarked, "the disappointments which awaited Flandin in London." Sarraut gave an account of them, saying that Flandin was "overwhelmed with difficulties," which is just what *perfide Albion* intended should happen. Flandin and the Sarraut government were also taking fire in Paris. A campaign against the cabinet was inspired by Laval. The right-wing opposition was in full flight and Daladier was said to be active behind the scenes. According to Torrès, even Herriot was involved, of all people, condemning the tough line of Flandin and Sarraut. Herriot, "panicky" and fearing war, sought to exploit the "pacifist mood in the country" to attract votes in the spring elections. Frightened by the conflict between Flandin and the English, Herriot had gone to Sarraut, still in a panic, almost inclined to admit that the Franco-Soviet Pact was the cause of the conflict with Germany. He persuaded Sarraut to send instructions to Flandin that he could again propose a reference to The Hague tribunal. Mandel told Potemkin that Léger opposed this démarche, but his voice had been smothered by "Herriot's outcry." Sarraut had to give way in view of Herriot's position in the Radical Party and in the country. Potemkin's report read like a tragedy. The French feared a split with Britain, which it dared not risk. There was fear of war and reticence everywhere among French allies and the neutral countries. France was hemmed in on all sides.

Léger described the situation to Potemkin. "I have to say," Potemkin noted, "that I have never seen Léger, in a state of such dark and hopeless pessimism as in these last days." Hopes placed on Soviet support in the event of war were not high. "This had to be recognized with complete objectivity," Léger said. "Here everyone says that the USSR is too far away. It does not have common borders with Germany. The Red Army is insufficiently ready for offensive war." And on and on went Léger's list of laments. Then he mentioned the "insinuations" that the USSR was pushing Europe towards war and preparing for world revolution and that it would hold back on support for France at the decisive moment, and that finally it might have to fight off Japan. Given all this, one can easily recognize "the atmosphere of doubt, fear, distrust, and hesitation in which the French government had to operate, at the given critical moment."

Mandel had clearly spelled out the internal situation, according to Potemkin. "In his opinion, no one would stand before the electors as an advocate of war and a defender of a policy of firmness in regard to Germany, England, and all the reticent states. The elections must pass under the banner of pacifism. In such conditions, the government must willy-nilly avoid aggravating the conflict, play for time, wait for the election result, and on the other hand, wait for the gradual maturation of international public opinion under the influence of further blows of Hitler's fist."[59] That was the opinion of one of the toughest Frenchmen on the block. Stalin would have understood him, which is undoubtedly why Potemkin so assiduously recorded his views for Moscow. Could Mandel impose his will on his colleagues as a Jew and an outsider? Would the spring elections produce a strong government? Answers would soon come.

The late Duroselle called the Rhineland crisis a *désolante affaire* for France. "A distressing affair" in English does not begin to describe how ruinous this crisis proved to be. French prestige in Europe collapsed. The British began to treat the French without respect, as minions expected to toe a British line. No one counted on France as a strong ally against Nazi Germany. It was a message to the small European states like Romania to make the best terms they could with Hitler. In Moscow the crisis produced anger and cynicism. Was the Franco-Soviet Pact worth defending? For the time being, the answer was in the affirmative, but only because it was the only alternative. Litvinov would continue to pursue mutual assistance and collective security, though Soviet policy had been subjected to hard, in fact, mortal blows. Worse was to come.

Chapter Seventeen

Epilogue

In the spring of 1936, although it was not clear at the time, Soviet attempts to organize mutual assistance against Nazi Germany had failed. It was *not* Stalin's plan that collective security should fail. When Hitler came to power in January 1933, he upset the basic calculations of Soviet foreign policy in Europe. As 1933 unfolded, it became evident, first to Litvinov and Krestinskii in the NKID then to Stalin and his troika in the Politburo, that Rapallo was dead. There was regret that the "old policy" could not be saved, which may have surprised some readers, but then came a resolve to shift the gears of Soviet foreign policy. France and Poland were the first targets of Moscow's attention. France was an obvious choice, as Russia's First World War ally, and Poland also, as a French ally by treaty obligations. To win over France, one had to win over Poland. As it turned out, Poland was a disappointment, about which more anon. In France there were perceptions of Germany, similar to those in Moscow, as a threat to European peace and security. A French policy shift began in 1932 even before Hitler became chancellor. It was under Herriot's direction that a non-aggression pact was concluded, then Paul-Boncour and Barthou, consolidated the French turn in policy, in spite of opposition at the Quai d'Orsay.

In 1933, as the Franco-Soviet rapprochement strengthened, so also did possibilities in the United States. Roosevelt was elected president and he directed a shift in US policy. Litvinov went to Washington and concluded an agreement for recognition, on the one hand, and a "gentleman's agreement," on the other, to settle old debts in exchange for long-term credit. It seemed a great achievement for Soviet diplomacy. Two months earlier in September 1933, the Soviet Union signed a pact of friendship and non-aggression with Rome. You can see why Soviet policy formally shifted towards collective security in December 1933. It was *the* moment when the elements of a new policy of collective security seemed to be falling into place.

No sooner was the apogee achieved than Soviet policy began to come undone. In spring and summer 1934, the attempt to settle relations with the

United States collapsed. Later that year, after the death of Barthou, French policy also went awry. The new foreign minister, Laval, broke with the policy of Herriot, Paul-Boncour, and Barthou, halted the momentum of the Franco-Soviet rapprochement, and gutted the eventual Franco-Soviet Pact, reduced to an empty shell. Under pressure not only from the Soviet side, but also from Czechoslovakia and Romania, notably Beneš and Titulescu and some of his own French colleagues, Laval could not break openly with Moscow. He zigged and zagged to finesse his opposition, though he told Potemkin with surprising candor that a deal with Nazi Germany was better for France than an alliance with the Soviet Union. Laval went to Moscow to meet Stalin in May 1935, where he proposed staff conversations to solidify the pact that he had gutted. Before seeing Stalin, he stopped in Warsaw to assure Beck that he did not wish to give "an allure Russophile" to French policy. Laval thus spoke out of both sides of his mouth. Having promised in Moscow a prompt ratification of the Franco-Soviet Pact, he delayed it, hoping to conclude some kind of agreement with Germany or to make progress towards such an agreement. The pact was still unratified when Laval fell from power in January 1936. The subsequent Sarraut cabinet obtained ratification in the Assemblée nationale, although in damaged condition. Franco-Soviet relations stumbled on for yet awhile, but Laval had succeeded in breaking the *élan* of the Franco-Soviet rapprochement.

That left Italy and Britain on Litvinov's list of great powers to gather into an anti-German entente. Italy was not a solid bet under the erratic Mussolini, and Italian ambitions in East Africa and war against Abyssinia irretrievably spoiled relations with the Soviet Union. Italy moved away from mutual assistance against Nazi Germany. The last great hope was Britain. The Metro-Vickers affair temporarily set back Anglo-Soviet relations, but already in the summer of 1933, Litvinov recognized the need to draw Britain into Soviet plans for collective security. A year later, during the summer of 1934, Maiskii and Vansittart kicked off a fragile rapprochement, as US-Soviet relations stumbled, and a few months before Soviet relations with France were set back by the death of Barthou and Laval's arrival at the Quai d'Orsay. The Soviet ambassador in London and the patrician in the Foreign Office organized Eden's trip to Moscow, the high point of Anglo-Soviet relations during the 1930s. The trip was a shooting star, a bright light in the sky that burned out quickly. Eden was never fully engaged in an Anglo-Soviet rapprochement, and less than three months later, the British government signed an Anglo-German naval agreement that kicked a leg out from underneath the Treaty of Versailles. Britain concluded this agreement without consulting France, Italy, or the USSR, and became in effect an accomplice in German rearmament. The British government did not see it that way and did not make much of the agreement. Even Vansittart tried to defend it. What else could he do? In France and Italy, however, there were bitter feelings and recollections of *perfide Albion*. In Moscow, Litvinov was shocked.

Should he have been? Can a tiger shed its stripes? Litvinov and Stalin gambled that it could.

There was worse to come. In December 1935, Laval and the new Foreign Secretary, Hoare, got caught doing a dirty deal over Abyssinia. It was dirty, but even Litvinov would have accepted the arrangement if it could have been brought off quietly with Abyssinian consent. The goal was to keep Italy on side against Nazi Germany. The opposite occurred. Mussolini moved towards the Führer's waiting embrace, and the French and British traded recriminations. In the Foreign Office, Vansittart's position was weakened at the worst possible moment. Hoare had to resign, which was not a great loss, and was succeeded by none other than Eden, not a great gain. He was nevertheless Maiskii's hope and Litvinov's also. Maiskii thought Eden was on side. The polpred was wrong. In February 1936, the young, prickly rising star of the Conservative Party put the brakes on the Anglo-Soviet rapprochement. Relations between London and Moscow never recovered during the 1930s.

As for Poland, what is there to say? It signed a non-aggression pact with Nazi Germany in January 1934, rejecting thus Soviet overtures for a rapprochement. Foreign minister Beck thought Poland had outsmarted everyone and bought ten years of security. You couldn't tell Beck anything. Litvinov tried, warned him that Polish policy was folly, but Beck brushed him off. Other observers saw more clearly: diplomats everywhere in Europe said that Poland was running in dangerous company. Romanians, Czechoslovaks, the French came to the same conclusion. Beneš, Titulescu, Mendras, Litvinov, Stomoniakov, Potemkin, and Stalin saw the Poles risking ruin. Poland was in bed with Nazi Germany; Beck was Hitler's "valet." It would do no good to curry favour in Berlin, for when Hitler decided to settle his territorial claims against the Polish government, a "fourth partition" of Poland would be the inevitable result. You did not need to be a fortune-teller to prophesy Poland's doom. It was on the cards years before 1939. When Beck heard such comments, he smiled his wry smile. Poles knew best what their interests were. No, they didn't. In the meantime, the Polish government sabotaged Soviet collective security and mutual assistance especially in Bucharest – hunting Titulescu – but also in Berlin, London, and Paris, anywhere they could stick a spoke in the Soviet wheel.

The one bright spot at the beginning of 1936 was the resignation of Laval. It was another shooting star, an orphan in the sky, which quickly burned out in the tumult of the ratification debates in the Chambre des députés. Ratification of the Franco-Soviet pact proved to be a Pyrrhic victory. Approval of the empty shell attracted more and more internal opposition as if France could do without its most powerful European ally. What a tragedy. Soviet collective security and mutual assistance had fallen apart. The United States was out; Italy was out; and Britain was out. France still appeared to be in the game, but was looking for a respectable exit or even one that was not so respectable in the case of Laval.

Then came the worst shock of all, not three months into 1936. The Wehrmacht marched into the demilitarized Rhineland, making itself at home; and France and Britain did nothing to throw the Germans out. Oh, there were lots of reasons for inaction. Britain was not ready for war. The French were afraid and the chief of staff, General Gamelin, counted every German soldier twice or thrice to justify doing nothing. France might have moved if Britain had moved, but the English, with Eden in the van, preferred "the will-o'-the-wisp" of an agreement with Hitler rather than war with the Wehrmacht. So the German high command was free to fortify the Rhineland frontier with France, removing a pressure point for the French Army to assist its allies in Central and Eastern Europe. Do not imagine that this abdication went unnoticed in Prague, Bucharest, Belgrade, and Warsaw, but the British and French governing elites – with exceptions like Mandel – did not seem to understand the frightful images they had made of themselves in those places. France could no longer be counted on as a strong, reliable ally. It had capitulated, and thrown itself at the feet of the English, surrendering French foreign policy to English tutelage. There were strong leaders in France like Péri on the left and Mandel on the right; not all the French were surrenderers. But they could not swing the governing elite, least of all those two, the communist and the Jew, confronted by the "pacifism" of French public opinion. It was a spectacle relished in Berlin, but deplored in other capitals. Litvinov was dismayed, but then tried to put the best possible interpretation on events that had gone against the USSR. What choice did he or Stalin have given their perception of the Nazi danger to European peace and security?

How could all of this be? The Soviet side, almost like a naïve suitor, pressed the Western powers for a revival of the First World War Entente against Wilhelmine Germany. Had Soviet leaders abandoned their Marxism? Not at all, but they argued that Hitler threatened European peace and security. In *Mein Kampf*, Hitler telegraphed his intentions to dominate all of Europe. We need to unite against this menace – so went the Soviet argument – or accept a German "Mitteleuropa." Soviet calls for unity went unheeded. European elites would not believe what they saw before their eyes or could read in *Mein Kampf*. One by one, the potential members of an anti-Nazi coalition fell away.

Many Western historians have long held, and now more than ever, that Stalin, whatever he might say, was still the ruthless, lying, unscrupulous Bolshevik bent on world revolution. The Soviet offers of cooperation against Nazi Germany were bogus, a *ruse de guerre*, and so on. You have heard the arguments. Can we simply assume that the West had honest scruples, and the Soviet side did not? Of course, the West was not a monolith: not everyone rejected Soviet proposals. Churchill, Vansittart, Mandel, Paul-Boncour, Cot, Titulescu, among others, were ready to ally with the USSR. We have no choice but to put aside our differences, they said: it is the only way forward to security against Nazi

Germany. Without the USSR, they could not hope to prevail. Some historians would argue that Western governing elites simply could not accept at face value Soviet, that is to say communist, motives, but some did. It is not "aftermindedness" to propose that there were alternatives to surrender to Hitlerism. If you believe the evidence arrayed before you, there is only one conclusion to be drawn: the Western line on Soviet foreign policy from Adam Ulam to Sean McMeekin does not accurately characterize a more complex narrative – based on a huge Russian archival record – to which Ulam and his contemporaries did not have access and which McMeekin skimmed and abused.

There was an anticlimax to all the dismal events in Europe ending with the Rhineland crisis. Well, they were dismal events, if one sought to build collective security with the USSR against Nazi Germany. French parliamentary elections took place in the spring. Remember that the French left and centre-left had united against what they saw as a domestic fascist threat, precipitated by violent demonstrations on the place de la Concorde in February 1934. Some said the mayhem was an abortive fascist coup d'état. First, the communists and socialists formed an alliance, and then a year later, the Radical-Socialists joined to form an electoral coalition, the Front populaire, to contest the spring 1936 elections. The right and centre-right took fright. Politics polarized. The ricocheting of political forces, as readers have seen, had adverse effects on Franco-Soviet relations.

In the meantime, after prolonged negotiations in London on what to do about the Wehrmacht advance into the Rhineland, Litvinov returned to Moscow. He put on a brave face with French ambassador Alphand. The Franco-Soviet Pact had been ratified. It was better than no pact at all. Negotiations in London had gone alright, though Litvinov was gilding the lily.[1] Collective security was still Soviet policy, and therefore, come what may, France had to be kept on side. The French "hinge" had to be replaced with one made of better steel.

Litvinov was more candid with Maiskii. Concessions to Hitler would only embolden him to demand more. But what could be done to discourage him? There were some crazy ideas going around Paris about "partial sanctions" against Germany, which only underlined the despair of those who wanted to contain the Nazi threat to peace but did not see how to do it. It was hard to face up to the fact that the only realistic policy was the clenched fist if one wanted to stop Hitler.[2] What some could see clearly, others refused to see. There was great confusion about who enemy No. 1 was. Many British Conservatives were not sure, or were only too sure it was the USSR. French ambassador François-Poncet wrote a dismal report of British reaction in Berlin to the Wehrmacht's march into the Rhineland. One of Ambassador Phipps's "secretaries" had opined, so François-Poncet heard from a reliable source, "that the English should celebrate the rearmament of Germany 'because one day it would need German soldiers against Russia.'"[3] The clerk was after all only a clerk, but the clerk was far from being the only British official or politician to express such views, as François-Poncet emphasized and French reports from London confirmed. There were, of course, variations of British Germanophilia. The prime minister, Stanley Baldwin, did not see the point of "crushing" Germany in a new war since, as he said in cabinet, "it would probably only result in Germany going Bolshevik."[4] In the Foreign Office, Vansittart was subdued. He told Maiskii that his view of Germany remained the same, but that his situation was now more "difficult." He hoped for "a change for the better," although this would take time.[5] It did not happen.

In France, Potemkin made his rounds trying to assess French elite opinion. He saw Herriot in Lyon who had recovered from his uninspiring conduct in Paris during the Rhineland crisis. Herriot thought the only axis of defence against Nazi Germany was London-Paris-Moscow. Any other formula would fail.

Discussion then turned to French politics and the upcoming elections. The communists, Herriot said, stood to make important gains, with some gains also for the socialists. The Radical-Socialists, he thought, would hold their own. The right too might increase their seats. Herriot did not speculate on which parties would lose seats; someone would have to lose seats. He thought the new array of political forces could produce a Daladier government. President Lebrun had consulted Herriot about a future cabinet and said in passing that Daladier was committed to excluding communists as ministers. Herriot noted Daladier's "deep although hidden dislike of the communists, but also his closeness to Laval with whom he shares a similar Germanophilia." The far-right journalist de Brinon also appeared to exercise a strong influence on Daladier in favour of a Franco-German arrangement. Daladier needed to be watched closely; it was not to be excluded that he might bring Laval into his cabinet. Potemkin may have thought they were done with Laval, but apparently not. Herriot conceded that he might be invited to join a new government, and he would not foreswear the possibility but not with Laval in an important portfolio, certainly not Foreign Affairs. I could not work with a person who had signed the Franco-Soviet Pact "and then done everything possible in order to thwart its ratification or to transform it into a simple scrap of paper." Laval's pro-German and pro-Italian policy had "dissolved France's foreign relationships and facilitated the victories of the two fascist dictatorships."[6] That was true, but the divisions, indecisiveness, and weakness of various French governments and ministers, including Herriot himself, facilitated fascist victories.

The first round of the legislative elections took place on 26 April. The results indicated that on the second round of voting in early May, the Front populaire would win. By how much and how many seats in the Chambre des députés was not clear. In general, however, Herriot's predictions proved to be correct. Potemkin was anxious, of course, because the election results would determine the future of collective security and mutual assistance, or so he believed. Before the second round of voting, he met Flandin, who was willing to talk politics.

The victory of the Front populaire, he said, was certain. The Communist Party was likely to win between 60 and 65 seats, maybe more. According to Potemkin, Flandin was not bothered by this result. "The communists of France," he said, "display a political maturity and patriotism that attract the sympathies not only of the working masses, but also of bourgeois elements." Flandin was more worried about the socialists. In the new Chambre, their faction would occupy a prominent place. "Meanwhile, the policies and tactics of the socialists seemed to Flandin dubious and even dangerous. In particular, this applies to the position of the socialists in the realm of foreign policy." They were hostile to Italy, Flandin noted, and constantly agitating for more sanctions against the Italian government. With regard to Germany, however, their position was different. "The pacifism of the socialists leads them to a conciliatory position towards Germany." Flandin advised Potemkin confidentially that during the London meeting of the Locarno powers, the general secretary of the Socialist Party, Paul Faure, had gone to Sarraut and insisted that Flandin be given instructions to soften his position towards Germany. "The leading role that the socialists are likely to play in the new Chamber, according to Flandin, makes it much more difficult for the government to take a firm line against Hitlerite Germany." That was not good news. In fact, Faure was a determined "pacifist" and defeatist in regard to Germany and would constantly hamper Blum with whom he co-chaired the Socialist Party. His advocacy of concessions to Nazi Germany played into the hands of Hitler. After the fall of France, Faure backed Pétain's Vichy regime for which he was kicked out of the Socialist Party in 1944. Faure was lucky not to have been shot. There were many collaborators in France who turned their coats just in time and escaped justice at the end of the war.

It was for this reason that Flandin offered a surprising comment to Potemkin.

> According to Flandin, in some districts, the communists intend to abandon their candidacies in favour of socialists when they run during the second round. Flandin believes that this tactic is wrong. The communists must know that they are giving way to "Germanophiles" and other sorts of unsuitable candidates. In particular, special care should be taken with regard to socialists in electoral districts in the north and in the Pas de Calais area. The socialists there are particularly inclined to make agreements with Germany. In Flandin's opinion in these areas, the communists should, at all costs, support their candidates in the elections. [7]

Was Flandin discreetly asking Potemkin to pass on this information? It appears as though he was. If communist candidates stayed in the second round, would that not mean the election of the candidate of centre-right or right? Potemkin offered no comment on this point.

Flandin had something else on his mind. A Popular Front government had come to power in Madrid after elections in February 1936. It was a centre-left coalition similar to the Front populaire in France. As Potemkin was leaving, Flandin held him back to pass another message. It was that "excesses" in Spain, being tolerated by the new government, were having an adverse effect on French public opinion, read the French right-wing press. The excesses were clashes between left- and right-wing militants. According to Potemkin, "Flandin himself fears that the victory of democratic ideas is far from assured in Spain He does not rule out that this country [Spain] will descend to a fascist dictatorship. If this were to happen, fascism in Europe, which has already triumphed in Germany and Italy, would receive the strongest reinforcement, and democratic France would find itself in a very dangerous neighbourhood with three countries embodying the most extreme form of social and political reaction."[8] Flandin apparently did not ask Potemkin directly to intervene in Moscow, although Potemkin's dispatch came nearly to the same thing. The warning about Spain proved apposite. Civil war broke out there in mid-July.

The second round of voting in France took place on 3 May 1936, and the results turned out more or less as Herriot and Flandin expected. The Communist Party won 72 seats, up from 10, a few more seats than Flandin had anticipated. It was a big win for them. The socialists also picked up seats rising from 97 to 146 seats. Herriot had not wanted to speculate with Potemkin from where the communists and socialists would obtain their new seats. They came from his party, the Radical-Socialists. They went from 158 to 115 seats. Worse than that, their percentage of the vote dropped below that of the Communist Party. The communists had pulled votes from the socialists and the socialists from the Radicals who also lost votes to the right. They, the Radicals, were none too happy and quick to hold a grudge against the communists. Smaller parties on the left also joined the coalition. On paper, the Front populaire scored a solid win taking a total of 378 seats, equalling 57 per cent of the votes cast against the right with 236 seats. But, in fact, the coalition was fragile because of the split among the socialists to which Flandin had drawn Potemkin's attention and because of the Radicals' dislike and resentment of the communists.

From Moscow, Litvinov advised Potemkin that he did not like the look of the election results. "However pleasing these results may seem at first glance, and especially the victory of the Communist Party, I foresee that the result of the elections will strengthen the agitation of the right-wing parties and a further slant towards the fascisization of France." Litvinov continued to worry that Laval might return to the Quai d'Orsay, or that Daladier might form a government. How could this happen? Litvinov wondered aloud. "Is it possible that the Communist and Socialist Parties, which have become so strong, cannot block the road to power of the fascist Laval and his like-minded foreign policy partner, Daladier? Retaining the current Sarraut-Flandin cabinet is a rather desirable combination if a better one is not possible."[9] Today, historian Jonathan Haslam, as opposed to Haslam in 1984, says "Bolshevism was back" in the guise of the Front populaire.[10] In fact, the Front populaire arose out of fear of the spread of fascism. It was a coalition of three parties and required tolerance of differences to succeed. Ironically, Litvinov worried that the Front populaire might provoke a strengthening of fascism in France instead of its destruction.

Litvinov offered similar comments to Maiskii. On Germany he said: "Anything that strengthens such a state and therefore increases the risk of a breach of the peace should be rejected." Confidential meetings between France, Britain, and the USSR would be the best way to move forward. This was taking up Herriot's line. The initiative should, however, be left to the French and the British. A Soviet initiative would only be self-defeating. Then Litvinov concluded with these lines for Maiskii: "We must navigate and determine which way the wind is blowing. I can tell you that I am very pessimistic and, paradoxical as it may seem to you, the outcome of the French elections in this has strongly reinforced my pessimism. We will, however, fight on. For me, my own pessimism has never weakened into fatalism, but rather the contrary. I strive, as it were, to prove to myself the groundlessness (the lack of good reason) for my own pessimism."[11]

During the 1920s, Litvinov had seen the NKID, but really himself, as Sisyphus, rolling his boulder up the hill and striving to reach the mountaintop in spite of the will of the gods who sought to punish him. He had not changed much over the years. He was committed to protecting the security of the Soviet Union. He seemed sure of himself most of the time, and yet he could admit to Maiskii that for once he had doubts about the future, about his ability, in face of all the obstacles, to organize Europe against the menace of Nazi Germany. There was in the last sentences of his dispatch a nobility of spirit, that spirit of Sisyphus never to give up, even before the gods.

In Paris, the Sarraut cabinet had to give way to the Front populaire. Léon Blum, the socialist, and not Daladier, formed the government. In his cabinet were twelve socialists and nine Radical-Socialists. Herriot and Paul-Boncour were not in the cabinet, nor obviously were Mandel and Flandin on the centre-right. Blum offered the Quai d'Orsay to Herriot, who refused it, not much liking the Front populaire. He preferred, so he said, to remain président of the Chambre des députés. Litvinov probably would not have been too disappointed with Herriot's absence from the cabinet given his flaccidity during the Rhineland crisis. Paul-Boncour could not be chosen because of his erratic loyalty to the Socialist Party. That was a loss. The "fascist" Laval was out, but Faure, who did not hold a seat in the Chambre, was named ministre d'État. This posed a problem because Faure was a *pacifiste*, who would accuse Blum and his supporters of *bellicisme*, a pejorative which meant wanting to take a firm line against Nazi Germany. He would have been hard to leave out of the cabinet, however, because of his place in the Socialist Party. Another Germanophile, Daladier, was Minister of Defence and vice-président du Conseil. Pierre Cot was back as air minister. That helped to balance Faure in the cabinet, but could do nothing to counter the split among the socialists.

The Radical-Socialist Delbos became Minister for Foreign Affairs; he had been justice minister in the Sarraut cabinet. He had also been among that group of cabinet ministers and politicians who visited the Soviet embassy. Still, he would have been an unknown quantity for Potemkin. He turned out to be a weak minister, putty in the hands of Léger. A new minister was Jean Zay, a young Turk in the Radical Party, born in 1904, and thus only thirty-two when he became Minister of Education. When the chips were down, he proved to have a spine, a rare quality among cabinet-level Radical-Socialists. He was a patriot, arrested by the Vichy authorities in 1940, and murdered by the fascist Milice in 1944, a fortnight after the landings in Normandy. They say he died defiantly, crying *Vive la France*, before being gunned down. France did not collapse in 1940 because of leaders like Mandel, Péri, and Zay. It was the responsibility of others, "gravediggers," journalist Pertinax called them.

There were no communist ministers in the new government, though their seats and votes in the election would have entitled them to cabinet posts. Whether this was Daladier's doing or that of the Comintern in Moscow is not clear. The communists agreed to support the government. The Radical-Socialists held the upper hand in the cabinet in spite of their loss of votes and seats because they could form a government on the centre-right if they chose to leave the coalition. The new Blum cabinet took office on 4 June 1936. Litvinov was doubtful of how things would work out. This is understandable because collective security could not work as a policy solely of the left, however ably defended by communists like Péri.

The Front populaire was therefore a shambolic coalition in spite of its seemingly impressive majority. Like the previous Cartel des gauches, it did well in the elections but then failed to remain united afterward. Laval thought the coalition of socialists and communists would not hold together. The Front populaire was also unlucky. A wave of strikes hit France even before the new government took power. It had no time to try out the levers of power; it had to settle the strikes. At the beginning, there was a certain *bonhomie* and exhilaration on the left, but it wore off quickly as the summer unfolded. On 8 June, the new government presided over the "Matignon accords" between the *patronat* and the trade unions. The agreement provided for a forty-hour work week, paid holidays, and collective bargaining. It was not exactly a blueprint for Bolshevism. The Assemblée nationale approved the agreement a few days later, but it did not end the government's many economic difficulties.[12]

The Front populaire government took power under fire. On 14 July, Bastille Day, there was the traditional military parade in Paris. All the Front populaire leaders were on the viewing stand and all, save one, seemed happy to be there, fists raised in victory. The exception was the socialist Roger Salengro, Minister of the Interior, who had become the target of a right-wing smear campaign. In November of that year, he committed suicide, unable to deal with bogus press attacks accusing him of desertion during the Great War. His death was an allegory for the fate of the Front populaire, too fragile to govern and to make hard decisions.

Four days after the French national holiday, civil war erupted in Spain, as Flandin had foreseen. Salengro and his colleagues could not have imagined all the troubles about to befall them. It was a catastrophe, a bloody settling of accounts between right and left with reverberations spreading across Europe. Cross-party cooperation, a *union sacrée*, to support collective security and mutual assistance against Nazi Germany could not work in such an environment. The Spanish Civil War was a hard blow to Soviet collective security policy, although its chances, as we have seen, had already been narrowed by earlier failures. One could argue that setbacks might have been overcome, but not by the Soviet Union on its own. France and Britain had to buy in to collective security to make it work, but they never did even at the most critical moments. The formula is uncomplicated: the smaller European states like Romania and Czechoslovakia looked to France to stand against Nazi Germany. France looked to Britain to march, but Britain never did. An astonishing conclusion, you might think. Even when war in Europe seemed inevitable to all but the willfully blind, the Soviet side stood out for mutual assistance against the common Nazi foe. Or, maybe Hitler was not the common foe, and that was the problem. If no one else wanted to stop Nazi Germany, why should the USSR try to do so alone? But that was not so, you may be thinking. The following three years that began in the summer of 1936 would tell the tragic story, but in another narrative to come.

Notes

Acknowledgments

1. *Silent Conflict: A Hidden History of Early Soviet-Western Relations* (Lanham, MD: Rowman & Littlefield, 2014).
2. "Antibol'shevizm vo vneshnei politike Frantsii: Pol'skii krizis, 1920 g.," *Zhurnal rossiiskikh i vostochnoevropeiskikh istoricheskikh issledovanii* (Moscow, RF), no. 3 (26) 2021: 226–49; "Istoriia provala: Anglo-Franko-Sovetskii al'ians, kotorogo ne bylo, i neopublikovannaia belaia kniga Britanskogo pravitel'stva, 1939–1940 gg," ibid., no. 3 (14), 2018: 6–49; "Otdeliaia zerna ot plevel: istoki Vtoroi Mirovoi voiny," ibid., 4 (19), 2019: 64–98; " 'Komediia, obernutaia ironiei vnutri tragedii': Franko-Sovetskie popytki konsul'tatsii mezhu genshtabami (1936-1937)," ibid., no. 1 (24) 2021: 45–91; and " 'Novaia istoriia Vtoroi mirovoi,' indoktrinirovannaia i nenadezhnaia," ibid., no. 3 (26) 2021: 226–49.
3. *Tainaia voina: Zapad protiv Sovetskoi Rossii, 1917–1930* (Moscow: Izd. IstLit, 2019).

1 Introduction: Prologue to Crisis

1. "Meeting with [Peter] Schou [Danish minister in Moscow]," Litvinov, 26 Jan. 1927, *Arkhiv vneshnei politiki Rossiiskoi Federatsii*, Moscow, *fond* 05, *opis'* 7a, *papka* 32, *delo* 27, *list* 17 (hereinafter AVPRF, f., op. , p. , d. , l[l].); and Anna Di Biagio, "Moscow: The Comintern and the War Scare, 1926–28," in Silvio Pons and Andrea Romano, *Russia in the Age of Wars, 1914–1945* (Milan: Feltrinelli Editore, 2000), 83–102.
2. Litvinov (Germany) to Boris Spiridonovich Stomoniakov, secret, 4 July 1929, *Moskva-Berlin: Politika i diplomatiia Kremlia, 1920–1941* (hereinafter *Moskva-Berlin*), 3 vols. (Moscow: Nauka, 2011), II, 341–4.
3. For example, Alexander Dallin and F. I. Firsov, eds., *Dimitrov & Stalin, 1934–1943* (New Haven, CT: Yale University Press, 2000), 76; Adam B. Ulam, *Expansion and*

Coexistence: The History of Soviet Foreign Policy, 1917–1967 (New York: Frederick A. Praeger, 1968), 131, 142; Jonathan Haslam, *The Spectre of War* (Princeton: Princeton University Press, 2021), 13, 156, 181, 381 passim; and M. J. Carley, "Soviet Foreign Policy in the West: 1936–1941: A Review Article," *Europe-Asia Studies* 56, no. 7 (2004): 1080–92.

4 26 April 1939 and 25 February 1940 (Dallin and Firsov, *Dimitrov & Stalin*, 39, 122; and Haslam, *Spectre of War*, 188).

5 Robert C. Tucker, *Stalin in Power: The Revolution from Above, 1928*–1941 (New York: Norton, 1990); Silvio Pons, *Stalin and the Inevitable War, 1936–1941* (London: Frank Cass, 2002); Sabine Dullin, *Des hommes d'influences : Les ambassadeurs de Staline en Europe, 1930–1939* (Paris: Payot, 2001); Teddy J. Uldricks, "War, Politics and Memory: Russian Historians Re-evaluate the Origins of World War II," *History & Memory* 21, no. 2 (2009): 60–82; and citing Sergei Z. Sluch in Sergei V. Kudryashov, ed., *SSSR-Germaniia, 1933–1941* (Moscow, 2009), 17.

6 For example, Haslam, *Spectre of War*, 270. See also Jonathan Haslam, *The Soviet Union and the Struggle for Collective Security in Europe, 1933–39* (New York: St. Martin's Press, 1984).

7 Uldricks, "War, Politics and Memory," 66–7.

8 A.J.P. Taylor, *1939 Revisited* (London: German Historical Institute, 1981), 11.

9 George Fujii, "H-Diplo Roundtable XXII-18 on Snyder, *The Road to Unfreedom: Russia, Europe, America*," Review by Joseph Kellner, H-Diplo, 21 December 2020, https://networks.h-net.org/node/28443/discussions/6990543/h-diplo-roundtable-xxii-18-snyder-road-unfreedom-russia-europe#_Toc59206493.

10 For example, Sean McMeekin, *Stalin's War: A New History of World War II* (New York: Basic Books, 2021); see also the following reviews of McMeekin's book: Richard Overy, "Wicked Uncle Joe," *Literary Review* (April 1921), 1–3; Mark Edele, "Better to Lose Australia," *Inside Story* (25 May 2021) (https://insidestory.org.au/better-to-lose-australia/); Geoffrey Roberts, "Stalin's War: Distorted History of a Complex Second World War," *Irish Times* (29 June 2021); Omer Bartov, "Through a Glass Darkly: Barbarossa, and the Divergent Conclusions to be Drawn from One Body of Knowledge," *TLS* (30 July 2021), 3–4; and Michael J. Carley, "'Novaia istoriia Vtoroi mirovoi,' indoktrinirpovannaia i nenadezhnaia," *Zhurnal rossiiskikh i vostochnoeeropeiskikh istoricheskikh issledovanii* 26, no. 3 (2021): 226–49.

11 It was David Abraham. See Colin Campbell, "A Quarrel over Weimar Book," *New York Times*, 23 December 1984, sec. 1, 1.

12 Michael J. Carley, "The Canadian Prime Minister Needs a History Lesson," *Strategic Culture Foundation* (Moscow), 1 September 2019, https://www.strategic-culture.org/news/2019/09/01/the-canadian-prime-minister-needs-a-history-lesson/.

13 Litvinov to Stalin, no. 3064, secret, 21 Jan. 1927, AVPRF, f. 082, op. 10, p. 27, d. 2, l. 2 (published in *Moskva-Berlin*, II, 9–11).

14 Isaac Deutscher, *Russia after Stalin* (London: Hamish Hamilton, 1953), chap. 4; Lynn Viola, *Peasant Rebels under Stalin: Collectivization and the Culture of Peasant Resistance* (New York: Oxford University Press, 1996), 69–71; Stephen Kotkin, *Stalin: Waiting for Hitler, 1928–1941* (New York: Allen Lane, 2017), chap. 2.

2 A Dimly Lit Night Lamp: Early Attempts at Détente in Paris and Warsaw, 1929–1932

1 Litvinov to V.S. Dovgalevskii, Soviet *polpred* in Paris, no. L/3140, secret, 24 Nov. 1928, AVPRF, f. 0136, op. 12, p. 124, d. 406, ll. 58–54. Please note that in some AVPRF files, pagination is in reverse, that is, last number, first.

2 Litvinov to G.Z. Besedovskii, Soviet counsellor in Paris, no. L/2865, secret, 25 Aug. 1928, AVPRF, f. 0136, op. 12, p. 124, d. 406, ll. 32–31.

3 Litvinov's *dnevnik*, "Meeting with Herbette, 5 January 1929," secret, AVPRF, f. 05, op. 9, p. 43, d. 3, ll. 5–6; and Litvinov's *dnevnik*, "Record of conversation with Herbette," secret, 22 May 1929, ibid., ll. 99–100.

4 *Directeur de la police judiciaire* to the *Préfet de police*, 3 Oct. 1929, Paris, Ministère des Affaires étrangères, Europe, 1918–1940 (hereinafter MAÉ), Russie/1116, 302–6.

5 Herbette, no. 609, 10 Oct. 1929, & enclosure, MAÉ Russie/1116, 312–13; and Herbette, no. 646bis, confidential, 20 Oct. 1929, ibid., 324–7.

6 Aristide Briand to Herbette, no. 704, 23 Oct. 1929, MAÉ Russie/1116, 318; Briand to Herbette, no. 714, 29 Oct. 1929, ibid., 328.

7 Nigel West, *The A to Z of British Intelligence* (Langham, MD: Rowman & Littlefield, 2009), 46–7.

8 *Préfecture de police*, Paris, 26 Nov. 1929, MAÉ Russie/1110, 267; and Carley, *Silent Conflict*, 376–9.

9 Dovgalevskii to Litvinov, no. 210/s, secret, 14 April 1930, AVPRF, f. 0136, op. 14, p. 140, d. 586, ll. 40–37; and Record of conversation with Briand on 25 March 1930, Dovgalevskii, very secret, 1 April 1930, & enclosure in French on the Hertzfeld case, AVPRF, f. 0136, op. 14, p. 139, d. 585, ll. 30–7.

10 Dovgalevskii to Litvinov, no. 71/s, secret, 5 Feb. 1930, AVPRF, f. 0136, op. 14, p. 140, d. 586, ll. 4–3.

11 Dovgalevskii to Litvinov, no. 132/s, very secret, 6 March 1930, AVPRF, f. 0136, op. 14, p. 140, d. 586, ll. 23–20.

12 Excerpt from Litvinov's *dnevnik*, "Meeting with Herbette," secret, 26 Feb. 1930, AVPRF, f. 0136, op. 14, p. 139, d. 585, l. 17.

13 Dovgalevskii to Litvinov, no. 274/s, secret, 24 May 1930, AVPRF, f. 0136, op. 14, p. 140, d. 586, ll. 47–46.

14 Litvinov to L. M. Kaganovich, secretary of TsIK, no. L/3730, secret, 28 Sept. 1930, AVPRF, f. 05, op. 10, p. 56, d. 2, l. 90.

15 Excerpt from Litvinov's *dnevnik*, "Meeting with Herbette, 10 March 1931," secret, AVPRF, f. 0136, op. 15, p. 148, d. 659, ll. 20–18.
16 Dovgalevskii to N.N. Krestinskii, *zamnarkom* or deputy Commissar for Foreign Affairs, no. 289/s, secret, 23 May 1931, AVPRF, f. 0136, op. 15, p. 148, d. 661, ll. 52–51.
17 Carley, *Silent Conflict*.
18 Ronald H. Campbell, British chargé d'affaires in Paris, no. 964, 5 Sept. 1931, N6077/431/38, Kew, Richmond, Great Britain, National Archives (hereinafter TNA), Foreign Office (hereinafter FO) 371 15613.
19 Dovgalevskii to Litvinov, 3 May 1931, *Dokumenty vneshnei politiki* (hereinafter *DVP*), 26 vols. (Moscow: Politizdat, 1958–), XIV, 306–9; and Dovgalevskii to Krestinskii, 1 June 1931, ibid., 358–61.
20 "Note pour Monsieur le secrétaire général," Europe, ns, 20 April 1931, MAÉ URSS/1006, 16–21.
21 Ovey, no. 343, 30 June 1931, N4721/393/38; and Ovey, no. 126, very confidential, 27 July 1931, N5256/393/38, TNA FO 371 15612.
22 "Réunion chez M. Flandin," 30 May 1931, Paris, Ministère des Finances (hereinafter MF), B32015; and Flandin to Briand, no. 705–50, 2 June 1931, ibid.
23 Untitled note, J.-J. Bizot, senior Finance official, 3 June 1931, MF B32015.
24 Dovgalevskii to Krestinskii, 21 April 1931, *DVP*, XIV, 254–8; and record of a meeting with Briand, by Litvinov, 26 May 1931, ibid., 350–2.
25 Report of conversation with Briand, Litvinov, 26 May 1931, *DVP*, XIV, 350–2.
26 "Comité franco-soviétique d'experts, séance du 5 juin 1931," MAÉ Relations commerciales (hereinafter RC), Russie/2052, dos. 1. (Note: This is the original archival classification system, which has been changed since I read the files in the early 1990s.)
27 See several notes on this point in *DVP*, XIV, 367, 370, 386–7; and Ovey, no. 95, 8 May 1931, N3256/2200/38, TNA FO 371 15619.
28 Stalin to Kaganovich, 30 Aug. 1931, *Stalin i Kaganovich, Perepiska, 1931–1936 gg.* (Moscow: Rosspen, 2001), 71–3.
29 Kaganovich to Stalin, 3 Sept. 1931, *Stalin i Kaganovich, Perepiska*, 77.
30 Ibid., 77–9.
31 Stalin, Molotov to Kaganovich and Ia. E. Rudzutak, Politburo member, 5 Sept. 1931, *Stalin i Kaganovich, Perepiska*, 82.
32 Carley, *Silent Conflict*, 275–9.
33 Stephen Kotkin, *Stalin: Waiting for Hitler, 1929–1941* (London: Allen Lane, 2017), 1.
34 Stalin to Kaganovich, after 16 Aug. 1934, *Stalin i Kaganovich, Perepiska*, 439–40.
35 Boris Souvarine, *Stalin* (New York: Longmans, Green & Co., 1939); Isaac Deutscher, *Stalin: A Political Biography* (New York: Vintage, 1949); Isaac Deutscher, *Trotsky*, 3 vols. (New York: Vintage, 1965); Robert C. Tucker, *Stalin as Revolutionary, 1879–1929* (New York: W.W. Norton, 1973), 173–80, 211; Robert Service, *Stalin: A Biography* (Cambridge, MA: Belknap Press, 2004), 129–49, 284–5; Lev Davidovich Trotskii, *My Life* (New York: Pathfinder Press, 1970), 553.

36 Excerpt from Litvinov to Dovgalevskii, no. L/21663, 26 July 1931, AVPRF, f. 0136, op. 15, p. 149, d. 668, l. 79.
37 Stalin to Kaganovich, 7 Sept. 1931, *Stalin i Kaganovich, Perepiska,* 89.
38 Kaganovich to Stalin, 11 Sept. 1931, *Stalin i Kaganovich, Perepiska,* 90–7.
39 Kaganovich to Stalin, 16 Sept. 1931, *Stalin i Kaganovich, Perepiska,* 105–8.
40 Kaganovich to Stalin, 21 Sept. 1931, *Stalin i Kaganovich, Perepiska,* 113–15; and Politburo resolution, no. 63, 20 Sept. 1931, Oleg N. Ken and A.I. Rupasov, *Politbiuro Tsk VKP (b) i otnosheniia SSSR s zapadnymi sosednimi gosudarstvami, 1928–1934* (St. Petersburg: Evropeiskii Dom, 2000), 258–66.
41 Politburo resolution, no. 68, 10 Oct. 1931 & no. 76, 20 Nov. 1931, Ken and Rupasov, *Politbiuro*, 268–72, 274–6.
42 "Record of conversation ... with ... [Robert] Coulondre," V. I. Mezhlauk, Soviet trade representative, 16 Oct. 1931, *DVP*, XIV, 573–81; Dovgalevskii to Litvinov, no. 568/s, secret, 12 Oct. 1931, AVPRF, f. 0136, op. 15, p. 149, d. 668, ll. 127–26; and Dovgalevskii to Narkomindel, 25 Jan. 1932, *DVP*, XV, 55–7.
43 "Record of a conversation with Laval, Dovgalevskii, 28 January 1932," secret, AVPRF, f. 0136, op. 16, p. 154, d. 730, ll. 15–13; and Litvinov to Dovgalevskii, no. L/3338, secret, 7 Feb. 1930, AVPRF, f. 0136, op. 14, p. 139, d. 584, ll. 3–2.
44 Krestinskii to Dovgalevskii, no. f13–5006, 9 Feb. 1932, AVPRF, f. 0136, op. 16, p. 154, d. 720, ll. 5–4; and Litvinov (Geneva) to Dovgalevskii, secret, 17 March 1932, ibid., ll. 13–18.
45 Dovgalevskii to Narkomindel, 26 July 1932, *DVP*, XV, 440–1.
46 Krestinskii to Dovgalevskii, no. F13-5373, secret, 10 June 1932, AVPRF, f. 0136, op. 16, p. 154, d. 720, l. 23.
47 Excerpt from Litvinov's *dnevnik*, "Meeting with Dirksen," secret, 9 Nov. 1932, AVPRF, f. 05, op. 12, p. 81, d. 3, ll. 42–5; and Litvinov's *dnevnik*, "Meeting with [Bernardo] Attolico [Italian ambassador in Moscow]," secret, 9 Dec. 1932, ibid., ll. 10–14.
48 Kaganovich and Molotov to Stalin, nos. 54–5, very secret, 21 July 1932, *Stalin i Kaganovich, Perepiska*, 236–7n2.
49 Dovgalevskii to Krestinskii, no. 311/s, secret, 1 June 1931, AVPRF, f. 0136, op. 15, p. 148, d. 661, ll. 55–53.
50 Marcel' Israilevich Rozenberg, Soviet chargé d'affaires in Paris, to Narkomindel, 4 Sept. 1932, *DVP*, XV, 505.
51 Dovgalevskii to Krestinskii, no. 28, secret, 27 Jan. 1933, AVPRF, f. 010, op. 8, p. 32, d. 89, ll. 22–3; and Krestinskii to Dovgalevskii, no. 1069, very secret, 4 Feb. 1933, ibid., l. 28.
52 Litvinov to Dovgalevskii, no. 14/L, secret, 14 Jan. 1933, AVPRF, f. 05, op. 13, p. 90, d. 11, ll. 5–7.
53 Litvinov's *dnevnik*, "Meeting with Dejean," secret, 10 Apr. 1933, AVPRF, f. 05, op. 13, p. 89, d. 4, ll. 72–3.
54 Jean-Baptiste Duroselle, *La Décadence, 1932–1939*, 3rd ed. (Paris: Imprimerie nationale, 1985), 75.

55 Litvinov to Rozenberg, no. 81/L, secret, 19 May 1933, AVPRF, f. 05, op. 13, p. 94, d. 64, l. 5.
56 Oleg N. Ken, *Collective Security or Isolation? Soviet Foreign Policy and Poland, 1930–1935* (St. Petersburg: Evropeiskiy Dom, 1996), 53–82.
57 Stomoniakov to Antonov-Ovseenko, no. 4108, secret, 4 April 1933, AVPRF, f. 05, op. 13, p. 93, d. 48, ll. 4–6.
58 Ken, *Collective Security*, 64.
59 Stomoniakov to Antonov-Ovseenko, no. 4133, secret, 19 April 1933, AVPRF, f. 05, op. 13, p. 93, d. 48, ll. 7–11.
60 "Record of conversation with the editor of *Gazeta Polska* Miedziński, 4 May 1933," secret, *Rossiiskii gosudarstvennyi arkhiv sotsial'no-politicheskoi istorii*, Moscow, (hereinafter RGASPI), f. 558, op. 11, d. 790, ll. 20–1, Office of the President of the Russian Federation, "World War II in archival documents (collection of digitized archival documents, film and photo materials)," https://www.prlib.ru/en/collections/1298142 (hereinafter, RF, World War II), 1933.
61 Stomoniakov to Antonov-Ovseenko, no. 4149, secret, 4 May 1933, AVPRF, f. 05, op. 13, p. 93, d. 48, ll. 12–15.
62 Ken, *Collective Security*, 65.
63 Stomoniakov to Antonov-Ovseenko, no. 4163, secret, 19 May 1933, AVPRF, f. 05, op. 13, p. 93, d. 48, ll. 16–20.

3 A Steep Hill: The Soviet Quest for US Recognition, 1930–1933

1 P.A. Bogdanov, head of Amtorg, New York, to A.I. Mikoian, Commissar for External Trade, nos. 6782, 6786–7, rigorously secret, 2 May 1930, *Moskva-Vashington: Politika i diplomatiia Kremlia, 1921–1941* (hereinafter *Moskva-Vashington*), 3 vols. (Moscow: Nauka, 2009), II, 227–8; and Litvinov to Stalin, secret, 18 May 1930 & enclosures, *Sovetsko-amerikanskie otnosheniia* (hereinafter SAO) *Gody nepriznaniia, 1927–1933* (Moscow: Izd. "Materik," 2002), 282–8.
2 Skvirskii to Litvinov, 29 May 1930, *SAO, 1927–1933*, 288–92.
3 Skvirskii to Litvinov, 10 July 1930, *SAO, 1927–1933*, 303–9.
4 Politburo resolution, no P2/5-s, rigorously secret, special file, 25 July 1930; and Mikoian to Bogdanov, no. 11739, very secret, 25 July 1930, *Moskva-Vashington*, II, 261.
5 Bogdanov to Mikoian, nos. 10401, 10410–11, 10413–14, rigorously secret, 25 July 1930, *Moskva-Vashington*, II, 262.
6 Litvinov to Skvirskii, by encrypted cable, very secret, 26 July 1930; Skvirskii to NKID, no. 4723, very secret, 27 July 1930; Mikoian to Bogdanov, no. 608/ss, very secret, 28 July 1930; and Politburo resolution, no. P3/38-rs, rigorously secret, special file, 30 July 1930, *Moskva-Vashington*, II, 263–5.
7 Krestinskii to Molotov, very secret, 30 July 1930; I. V. Kosior, M.I. Kalmanovich, Soviet officials in United States, to Mikoian, nos. 10758, 10761–2, 10764–5, rigorously secret, 1 Aug. 1930; and Bogdanov to Mikoian, nos. 10993–4, rigorously secret, immediate, 7 Aug. 1930, *Moskva-Vashington*, II, 276–81, 284–5.

8 Skvirskii to Litvinov, 4 Aug. 1930, *SAO, 1927–1933*, 314–25.

9 Bogdanov to E.A. Eshba, Amtorg, Moscow, nos. 10864–6, rigorously secret, high priority, 4 Aug. 1930, *Moskva-Vashington*, II, 281–2.

10 Bogdanov et al. to NKVT, nos. 11697–702, rigorously secret, 28 Aug. 1930; and L.M. Khinchuk, deputy commissar for external trade, to V.M. Molotov, president of Sovnarkom, no. M-380-s, secret, 30 Aug. 1930, *Moskva-Vashington*, II, 294–7.

11 Bogdanov to Mikoian et al., nos. 12380–1, 12883, rigorously secret, 13 Sept. 1930; and Politburo resolution, no. P10/opr-51, rigorously secret, special file, 25 Sept. 1930, *Moskva-Vashington*, II, 301–2, 305–6.

12 Skvirskii to NKID, no. 7733, very secret, immediate, 26 Nov. 1930; Skvriskii to NKID, no. 7762, very secret, 27 Nov. 1930; and Krestinskii to Skvirskii, no. 8194, very secret, 28 Nov. 1930, *Moskva-Vashington*, II, 312–13.

13 Skvirskii to Litvinov, 29 Dec. 1930, *SAO, 1927–1933*, 387–93.

14 Bogdanov to Rozengol'ts, commissar for external trade, no. 303, secret, 16 Dec. 1930, *Moskva-Vashington*, II, 314–19.

15 Bogdanov to Rozengol'ts, Eshba, nos. 836–7, rigorously secret, 20 Jan. 1931, *Moskva-Vashington*, II, 333–4.

16 Skvirskii to Litvinov, 31 Jan. 1931; and excerpt from S.B. Kagan's *dnevnik*, very secret, 16 March 1931, *SAO, 1927–1933*, 411–17, 431.

17 Bogdanov (Moscow) to Stalin et al., secret, 28 June 1931 & enclosures, *SAO, 1927–1933*, 460–8.

18 Skvirskii to Litvinov, 29 June & 1 July 1931, *SAO, 1927–1933*, 468–84.

19 Stalin to Kaganovich, no. Nr 21/sh, 25 Aug. 1931, *Stalin i Kaganovich, Perepiska*, 64.

20 Rozengol'ts to Politburo, no. 432, secret, 19 Sept. 1931; and Bogdanov to Rozengol'ts, no. 222, secret, 26 Oct. 1931 & enclosures, *Moskva-Vashington*, II, 406–10, 412–20.

21 B.I. Veinshtein, Comintern member, to I.A. Piatnitskii, member of IKKI, very secret, 12 July 1931, & enclosures, *Moskva-Vashington*, II, 381–90.

22 Skvirskii to Litvinov, 18 Dec. 1931, *SAO, 1927–1933*, 515–17.

23 Maiskii to A.A. Nesterov, 17 Sept. 1930, Ivan Mikhailovich Maiskii, *Izbrannaia perepiska s Rossiiskimi korrespondentami*, 2 vols. (Moscow: Nauka, 2005), I, 370–1.

24 Stalin & Molotov to Kaganovich, no. 90, 16 Aug. 1932, *Stalin i Kaganovich, Perepiska*, 281.

25 Carley, *Silent Conflict*.

26 Stalin to Kaganovich & Molotov, no. 26, 21 June 1932; Stalin to Kaganovich, after 21 June 1932; Stalin to Kaganovich & Molotov, no. 40, 1 July 1932, *Stalin i Kaganovich, Perepiska*, 186–7, 205.

27 Kaganovich, Molotov, et al. to Stalin, no. 66/s, 1369/sh, 29 July 1932, and Stalin to Kaganovich, et al., no. 72, 30 July 1932, *Stalin i Kaganovich, Perepiska*, 251–2.

28 Kaganovich, Voroshilov, et al., to Stalin, Molotov, et al., no. 99/1544/sh, 22 Aug. 1932, *Stalin i Kaganovich, Perepiska*, 295–6.

29 Stalin, Molotov, et al. to Kaganovich, et al., no. 106, 23 Aug. 1932, *Stalin i Kaganovich, Perepiska,* 296.

30 Stalin to Kaganovich, earlier than 19 June 1932; and Stalin to Voroshilov, Kaganovich, et al., 7 Aug. 1932, *Stalin i Kaganovich, Perepiska,* 269–70.

31 Bogdanov to M.A. Loganovskii, deputy Commissar for Foreign Trade, secret, 30 Sept. 1932, *SAO, 1927–1933*, 611.

32 Stalin to Kaganovich, earlier than 12 June 1932, *Stalin i Kaganovich, Perepiska,* 158–9.

33 Record of conversation with Ivy Lee, Krestinskii, secret, copied to Stalin, Molotov, Kaganovich, 31 July 1932, *SAO, 1927–1933*, 597–9.

34 Record of conversation with Cooper, I.A. Livshits, deputy Amtorg agent, cc. to Krestinskii and III Western bureau, NKID, 1 Aug. 1932, *SAO, 1927–1933*, 600–1.

35 Ibid.

36 Ibid.

37 G.I. Andreichin, chief agent, Amtorg, to Politburo, 9 June 1932; and Politburo resolution, no. P106/12-rs, rigorously secret, special file, 28 June 1932, *Moskva-Vashington*, II, 486–9, 499.

38 Andreichin to Litvinov, secret, 22 Oct. 1932, *SAO, 1927–1933*, 624–7.

39 Ibid.

40 Litvinov to Andreichin, secret, 25 Oct. 1932, *SAO, 1927–1933*, 627.

41 V.I. Mezhlauk, deputy director, Gosplan, to Stalin, very secret, 7 Oct. 1932; and Bogdanov to Mezhlauk, no. 2/523 lit « B », secret, 2 Nov. 1932, *Moskva-Vashington*, II, 540–1, 550–3. See also Meredith L. Roman, *Opposing Jim Crow: African Americans and the Soviet Indictment of U.S. Racism, 1928–1937* (Lincoln, NE: University of Nebraska Press, 2012), chap. 4.

42 Excerpt from the *dnevnik* of Ia. B. Podol'skii, Soviet counsellor in Warsaw, reporting opinions of Edgar A. Mowrer, *Chicago Daily News*, secret, 2 Dec. 1932; and record of conversation with Frederick Kuh, United Press, Maiskii (London), secret, 15 Dec. 1932, *SAO, 1927–1933*, 650–1, 656–8.

43 Skvirskii to Litvinov, 22 Feb. 1933, *SAO, 1927–1933*, 670–2.

44 Iu. D. Mikhal'skii, NKID agent in New York, to Litvinov, nos. 2888, 2898, 2900, very secret, highest priority, 24 March 1933; and Litvinov to Mikhal'skii, no. 2180, very secret, 26 March 1933, *Moskva-Vashington*, II, 621–4.

45 Bogdanov to Rozengol'ts, Litvinov, no. 3659, very secret, immediate, 15 April 1933; and Litvinov to Skvirskii, no. 2811, very secret, 17 April 1933, *Moskva-Vashington*, II, 634–5.

46 Mezhlauk to Stalin, secret, 27 May 1933, & enclosures, *SAO, 1927–1933*, 692–4.

47 Skvirskii to Litvinov, 7 Oct. 1933, *SAO, 1927–1933*, 702–3.

48 Skvirskii to NKID, no. 11297, very secret, immediate, confidential, 11 Oct. 1933, *Moskva-Vashington*, III, 7.

49 Skvirskii to NKID, no. 11325, very secret, immediate, 11 Oct. 1933, *Moskva-Vashington*, III, 8.

50 Kaganovich, Molotov to Stalin, no. 66, 13 Oct. 1933, *Stalin i Kaganovich, Perepiska,* 385; and Carley, *Silent Conflict*, 352–70.
51 Stalin, Ia. E. Rudzutak, deputy premier, among other posts, to Kaganovich, Molotov, no. 74, 13 Oct. 1933, *Stalin i Kaganovich, Perepiska,* 386.
52 Litvinov to Kaganovich, secret, 16 Oct. 1933, *SAO, 1927–1933*, 706–7; Kaganovich, Molotov to Stalin, no. 86/7/2229/sh, 16 Oct. 1933; and Stalin, Kalinin to Molotov, Kaganovich, no. 78, 17 Oct. 1933, *Stalin i Kaganovich, Perepiska,* 391–3.
53 Politburo resolution no. P147/121-opr., rigorously secret, special file, 14 Oct. 1933; Skvirskii to Litvinov, no. 11488, very secret, 15 Oct. 1933, *Moskva-Vashington*, III, 9; and Stalin to Kaganovich, Molotov, no. 77, 16 Oct. 1933, *Stalin i Kaganovich, Perepiska,* 390.
54 Politburo resolution no. P148/4-opr., rigorously secret, special file, 17 Oct. 1933, *Moskva-Vashington*, III, 13.
55 Skvirskii to Litvinov, no. 11615, very secret, immediate, 19 Oct. 1933; and Litvinov to Skvirskii, no. 8481, very secret, immediate, 21 Oct. 1933, *Moskva-Vashington*, III, 13–14.
56 Litvinov to Kaganovich, secret, 20 Oct. 1933, *SAO, 1927–1933*, 707–9; Stalin to Molotov, Kaganovich, no. 88, 24 Oct. 1933; Kaganovich, Molotov to Stalin, no. 88, 24 Oct. 1933; Stalin to Kaganovich, Molotov, no. 89, 24 Oct. 1933, *Stalin i Kaganovich, Perepiska,* 402–3; and Politburo resolution, no. P148/81-opr., rigorously secret, special file, 25 Oct. 1933, *Moskva-Vashington*, III, 20.
57 Litvinov to NKID, no. 12378, very secret, 7 Nov. 1933, *Moskva-Vashington*, III, 25–6.
58 Carley, *Silent Conflict*, 401–2, and passim.
59 Litvinov to NKID, nos. 12401–3, very secret, 8 Nov. 1933, *Moskva-Vashington*, III, 28–30.
60 Livinov to NKID, nos. 12404–5, very secret, 8 Nov. 1933, *Moskva-Vashington*, III, 30–1.
61 Litvinov to NKID, nos. 12410–11, very secret, 9 Nov. 1933, *Moskva-Vashington*, III, 31–2.
62 Litvinov to NKID, nos. 12436–7, very secret, 9 Nov. 1933; and Stalin, Molotov to Litvinov, no. 9109, very secret, highest priority, 10 Nov. 1933, *Moskva-Vashington*, III, 33–5.
63 Litvinov to NKID, nos. 12464–5, 12469, very secret, 11 Nov. 1933, Litvinov to NKID, nos. 12464–5, 12469, very secret, 11 Nov. 1933, *Moskva-Vashington*, III, 37–9.
64 Stalin, Molotov to Litvinov, no. 9152, very secret, highest priority, 11 Nov. 1933; and Litvinov to NKID, nos. 12522, 12534, 12538–41, very secret, 11 Nov. 1933, *Moskva-Vashington*, III, 41–6.
65 Litvinov to NKID, nos. 12558–9, very secret, 11 Nov. 1933, *Moskva-Vashington*, III, 48–9.

66 Stalin, Molotov to Litvinov, no. 9181, very secret, highest priority, 12 Nov. 1933, *Moskva-Vashington*, III, 51.

67 Litvinov to Stalin, Molotov, no. 12580, very secret, 12 Nov. 1933; and Litvinov to NKID, no. 12589, very secret, high priority, 12 Nov. 1933, *Moskva-Vashington*, III, 52–3.

68 Litvinov to NKID, nos. 12592–3, 12597–8, very secret, 12 Nov. 1933, *Moskva-Vashington*, III, 54–6.

69 Excerpt from Politburo protocol, no. P149/64-opr., rigourously secret, special file, *Moskva-Vashington*, III, 56; and Stalin, Molotov to Litvinov, not numbered, very secret, highest priority, 13 Nov. 1933, ibid., 58.

70 Litvinov to NKID, no. 12643, very secret, 13 Nov. 1933, *Moskva-Vashington*, III, 59–60.

71 Stalin, Molotov to Litvinov, no. 9246, very secret, high priority, 14 Nov. 1933, *Moskva-Vashington*, III, 60.

72 Bullitt to Roosevelt, 15 Nov. 1933, Hyde Park, New York, Franklin D. Roosevelt (hereinafter FDR) Library, President's Secretary's File (hereinafter PSF), box 50, Russia: Bullitt, 1933–6.

73 Litvinov to NKID, no. 12688, very secret, high priority, 14 Nov. 1933, *Moskva-Vashington*, III, 61.

74 Litvinov to Stalin, nos. 12732–3, very secret, high priority, 15 Nov. 1933, *Moskva-Vashington*, III, 62–3.

75 Bullitt to Roosevelt, 15 Nov. 1933, Hyde Park, New York, FDR Library, PSF, box 50, Russia: Bullitt, 1933–6.

76 Litvinov to Stalin, nos. 12732–3, very secret, high priority, 15 Nov. 1933, *Moskva-Vashington*, III, 62–3.

77 Stalin, Molotov to Litvinov, no. 9267, very secret, highest priority, 15 Nov. 1933; and Litvinov to Stalin, nos. 12734–5, very secret, high priority, 15 Nov. 1933, *Moskva-Vashington*, III, 64–6.

78 Litvinov to Stalin, nos. 12739, 12741, very secret, immediate, 15 Nov. 1933, *Moskva-Vashington*, III, 67–8.

79 Litvinov to NKID, no. 12788, very secret, 16 Nov. 1933, *Moskva-Vashington*, III, 69–70.

80 Litvinov to NKID, no. 1282, very secret, 17 Nov. 1933, *Moskva-Vashington*, III, 72.

81 Stalin, Molotov to Litvinov, no. 9327, very secret, high priority, 17 Nov. 1933, *Moskva-Vashington*, III, 71.

82 Litvinov to NKID, no. 12862, very secret, high priority, 18 Nov. 1933, *Moskva-Vashington*, III, 73–4.

83 Litvinov to NKID, no. 12927, very secret, 20 Nov. 1933, *Moskva-Vashington*, III, 77.

84 Litvinov to NKID, 17 Nov. 1933, *SAO, 1927–1933*, 719–21.

85 "Memorandum of conversation with Mr. Litvinov, November 20th," William Phillips, National Archives, Bethesda, MD (hereinafter NA) RG 59, 701.6111/742, box 3663.

4 Setback: The Metro-Vickers Affair, 1933

1 Carley, *Silent Conflict*, chaps. 4, 5, 9.
2 R. Atherton, U.S. chargé d'affaires, London, no. 3340, 4 Feb. 1929, 741.61/210, NA, RG59, Microfilm (hereinafter M)-582/6; and Atherton, no. 382, 8 Nov. 1929, 741.61/259, ibid.
3 Minute by C.H. Bateman, Northern Department, 28 Jan. 1930, N499/77/38, TNA FO 371 14866.
4 "Notes on Anglo-Soviet Relations (1929–31)," Bateman, 25 Nov.1931, N7818/225/38, TNA FO 371 15609.
5 Politburo resolution, no. 14, p. 18, 8 March 1928, *Lubianka: Stalin i VChK-GPU-OGPU-NKVD, ianvar' 1922–dekabr' 1936* (Moscow: Izd. "Materik", 2003), 147–8.
6 "Record of conversation … with Strang, 12 March," Gel'fand, no. 18156/s, very secret, 13 March 1933, AVPRF, f. 05, op. 13, p. 91, d. 24, ll. 1–2.
7 Carley, *Silent Conflict*, 391-6, 400.
8 Excerpt from Krestinskii's *dnevnik*, "Meeting with Ambassador Ovey," secret, 13 March 1933, AVPRF, f. 05, op. 13, p. 91, d. 24, ll. 36–8.
9 Vansittart to Ovey, no. 19, 13 March 1933, N1610/1610/38, TNA FO 371 17265.
10 "Record of conversation … with Strang and Ovey," Gel'fand, no. 18158/s, secret, 14 March 1933, AVPRF, f. 05, op. 13, p. 91, d. 24, ll. 3–8.
11 Ovey, no. 39, 14 March 1933, *Documents on British Foreign Policy* (hereinafter *DBFP*), 2nd series, VII, 306–7.
12 Fitzmaurice's minute, 15 March 1933, N1658/1610/38, TNA FO 371 17265.
13 "Conversation with the British ambassador," Rubinin, no. 18161/s, secret, 15 March 1933, AVPRF, f. 05, op. 13, p. 89, d. 24, ll. 9–12.
14 Vansittart to Ovey, no. 20, 14 March 1933, N1649/1610/38, TNA FO 371 17265.
15 "Record of conversation with the English ambassador Ovey (by telephone) on 15 March 1933," Gel'fand, no. 18160/s, very secret, AVPRF, f. 05, op. 13, p. 91, d. 24, ll. 13–15.
16 "Discussion with Ovey," Rubinin, no. 18163/s, secret, 16 March 1933, AVPRF, f. 05, op. 13, p. 91, d. 24, ll. 18–20.
17 Ovey to Vansittart, nos. 47–8, 15 March 1933, *DBFP*, 2nd series, VII, 312–13.
18 Excerpt from Litvinov's *dnevnik*, "Meeting with the English ambassador Ovey, 16.III.33," secret, AVPRF, f. 05, op. 13, p. 89, d. 4, ll. 30–7.
19 Ovey to Vansittart, nos. 68–9, 17 March 1933, N1772 & N1778/1610/38, TNA FO 371 17265.
20 Litvinov to Stalin, no. 39/L, secret, 17 March 1933, AVPRF, f. 05, op. 13, p. 91, d. 24, l. 26–8.
21 "Discussion with Ovey, 17 March 1933," Rubinin, no. 18168/s, AVPRF, f. 05, op. 13, p. 91, d. 24, ll. 24–5.
22 Vansittart to Ovey, no. 27, 17 March 1933, *DBFP*, 2nd series, VII, 329–30.
23 "Discussion with Ovey," Rubinin, no. 18172/s, secret, 18 March 1933, AVPRF, f. 05, op. 13, p. 91, d. 24, ll. 29–32.

24 Excerpt from Litvinov's *dnevnik*, secret, cc. to Stalin and Molotov, not titled or dated but certainly 19 March 1933, AVPRF, f. 05, op. 13, p. 89, d. 4, ll. 40–1.
25 Ovey to Vansittart, no. 79, 19 March 1933, N1814/1610/38, TNA FO 371 17265.
26 Excerpt from Litvinov's *dnevnik*, "Meeting with Ovey, 19 March 1933," AVPRF, f. 05, op. 13, p. 89, d. 4, ll. 42–5.
27 Ovey to Vansittart, nos. 82–3, 19 March 1933, N1816 & N1817/1610/38, TNA FO 371 17265.
28 Krestinskii to Maiskii, no. B53–1136, very secret, 19 March 1933, AVPRF, f. 05, op. 13, p. 91, d. 24, ll. 34–5.
29 Collier's minute, 20 March, Oliphant and Vansittart, 21 March1933, N1850/1610/38, TNA FO 371 17265; and "Memorandum by Sir R. Vansittart for the Cabinet," 21 March 1933, N1951G/1610/38, ibid.
30 Ovey to Vansittart, no. 87, 20 March 1933, N1844/1610/38, TNA FO 371 17265.
31 Fitsmaurice's minute, 24 March 1933, N2028/1610/38, TNA FO 371 17266, and memorandum by S.W.E. Beckett, legal advisor, N2082/1610/38, ibid.
32 Vansittart to Ovey, no. 35, 27 March 1933, N2101/1610/38, TNA FO 371 17266.
33 Excerpt from Litvinov's *dnevnik*, "Meeting with Ovey, 28 March 1933," cc. to Stalin, Molotov, Voroshilov, secret, AVPRF, f. 05, op. 13, p. 89, d. 4, ll. 51–2.
34 Ovey to Simon, nos. 129–30, 28 March 1933, N2140 & 2141/1610/38, TNA FO 371 17266.
35 Ovey to Simon, no. 137 (by telephone), 29 March 1933, N2188/1610/38, TNA FO 371 17266.
36 Simon to Ovey, no. 40, immediate, 29 March 1933, N2204/1610/38, TNA FO 371 17266.
37 Litvinov to Stalin, no. 44/L, secret, 29 March 1933, AVPRF, f. 05, op. 13, p. 94, d. 78, l. 43.
38 Karakhan to Litvinov, cc. to Stalin and Molotov, no. 2732, very secret, 30 March 1933, AVPRF, f. 05, op. 13, p. 91, d. 24, l. 81.
39 Krestinskii to Maiskii, no. 1163, secret, 4 April 1933, AVPRF, f. 05, op. 13, p. 91, d. 24, ll. 94–7.
40 Gareth Jones, "The Arrest of the British Engineers," Margaret Siriol Colley, accessed 28 September 2002, https://www.garethjones.org/margaret_siriol_colley/metrovik_trial.htm#_ednref12.
41 Litvinov to Maiskii, no. L/51, secret, 4 April 1933, AVPRF, f. 05, op. 13, p. 91, d. 22, ll. 100–2.
42 Vansittart's minute, 8 April 1933, N2412/1610/38, TNA FO 371 17277.
43 "Record of conversations between the People's Commissar for Foreign Affairs and the British Ambassador, Sir Esmond Ovey," *Izvestiia*, 16 April 1933, N3091/1610/38, TNA FO 371 17270.
44 Maiskii to Krestinskii, no. 139/s, secret, 24 March 1933, AVPRF, f. 05, op. 13, p. 91, d. 24, II. 52–9.
45 Vansittart to Ovey, no. 25, 16 March 1933, *DBFP*, 2nd series, VII, 321–2.

46 "Discussion with Vansittart," Maiskii, no. 142/s, secret, 16 March 1933, AVPRF, f. 05, op. 13, p. 91, d. 24, ll. 64–7.
47 Maiskii to Krestinskii, no. 139/s, secret, 24 March 1933, AVPRF, f. 05, op. 13, p. 91, d. 24, 52–9.
48 Maiskii to Litvinov, personal, very secret, 24 March 1933, AVPRF, f. 05, op. 13, p. 91, d. 24, ll. 85–8.
49 Litvinov to Stalin, no. 45/L, secret, 31 March 1933, AVPRF, f. 05, op. 13, p. 91, d. 24, l. 146.
50 Litvinov to Stalin, no. 49/L, secret, 2 April 1933, AVPRF, f. 05, op. 13, p. 94, d. 78, l. 50.
51 Vansittart's minute, 29 March 1933, N2309/1610/38, TNA FO 371 17267.
52 Litvinov to Maiskii, no. 70/L, secret, 4 May 1933, AVPRF, f. 05, op. 13, p. 91, d. 24, ll. 248–52.
53 "Discussions, 28 March–3 April 1933," Maiskii, no. 177/s, secret, AVPRF, f.05, op. 13, p. 91, d. 24, ll. 156–63.
54 Collier's minute, 30 March 1933, and Oliphant, Vansittart, and Simon, 30 March 1933, N2183/1610/38, TNA FO 371 17266.
55 Collier's minute, 31 March 1933, N2183/1610/38, TNA FO 371 17266.
56 Untitled note, Collier, 29 March 1933, N2309/1610/38, TNA FO 371 17267.
57 Simon's note, 30 March 1933, *DBFP*, 2nd series, VII, 383–4.
58 Maiskii to Krestinskii, no. 197/s, secret, 9 May 1933, AVPRF, f. 05, op. 13, p. 91, d. 24, ll. 267–72.
59 Strang, no. 164, 2 April 1933, N2296/1610/38, TNA FO 371 17267; and Foreign Office memorandum, 2 April 1933, *DBFP*, 2nd series, VII, 400–2.
60 "Discussions, 28 March–3 April 1933," Maiskii, no. 177/s, secret, AVPRF, f.05, op. 13, p. 91, d. 24, ll. 156–63.
61 Maiskii to Krestinskii, no. 158/s, secret, 9 April 1933, AVPRF, f. 05, op. 13, p. 91, d. 24, ll. 189–96.
62 "Discussion with Simon and Runciman – 13 April 1933," Maiskii, no. 190/s, secret, 25 April 1933, AVPRF, f. 05, op. 13, p. 91, d. 24, ll. 234–40.
63 Simon to Strang, nos. 75–6, 13 April 1933, N2760/1610/38, TNA FO 371 17268.
64 Strang to Simon, no. 266, 14 April 1933, N2761/1610/38, TNA FO 371 17268.
65 Strang to Simon, no. 281, confidential, 15 April 1933, N2773/1610/38, TNA FO 371 17268.
66 Strang, no. 256, immediate, 13 April 1933, N2744/1610/38, TNA FO 371 17268.
67 "Indictment," 6 April 1933, AVPRF, f. 05, op. 13, p. 91, d. 24, ll. 104–45.
68 Jones, "The Arrest of the British Engineers."
69 "Extract from private letter from Mr. Strang to Mr. Collier," 24 April 1933, N3250G/1610/38, TNA FO 371 17270.
70 Krestinskii to Maiskii, no. 1175, very secret, 19 April 1933, AVPRF, f. 05, op. 13, p. 91, d. 24, ll. 197–8.

71 Litvinov to Maiskii, no. L/64, secret, 19 April 1933, AVPRF, f. 05, op. 13, p. 91, d. 24, ll. 199–200.
72 Litvinov to Stalin, no. 65/L, secret, 21 April 1933, AVPRF, f. 05, op. 13, p. 91, d. 24, l. 201.
73 Maiskii to Litvinov, no. 193/s, secret, 25 April 1933, AVPRF, f. 05, op. 13, p. 91, d. 24, ll. 218–19.
74 Collier to Strang, no. 92, 22 April 1933, N2990/1610/38, TNA FO 371 17270.
75 Litvinov to Maiskii, no. 70/L, secret, 4 May 1933, AVPRF, f. 05, op. 13, p, 91, d. 24, ll. 248–52.
76 Strang, no. 345, 24 April 1933; and Collier's minute, 27 April 1933, N3084/5/38, TNA FO 371 17239.
77 "Discussion with Strang, 29 April 1933," no. 18273/s, Rubinin, secret, AVPRF, f. 05, op. 13, p. 91, d. 24, l. 255; and Strang, no. 364, 30 April 1933, N3246/1610/38, TNA FO 371 17270.
78 Strang, no. 393, 11 May 1933; and Simon to Strang, no. 113, 17 May 1933, N3565/5/38, TNA FO 371 17240.
79 Litvinov to Maiskii, no. 80/L, secret, 19 May 1933, AVPRF, f. 05, op. 13, p. 91, d. 24, ll. 273–5.
80 Litvinov to Stalin, no. L/59, secret, 14 April 1933, AVPRF, f. 05, op. 13, p. 94, d. 78, ll. 60–3.
81 Strang, no. 389, 8 May 1933, N3480/1610/38, TNA FO 371 17272; and Strang, no. 417, 4 June 1933, *DBFP*, 1st series, VII, 556.
82 Litvinov to Stalin, cc. Krestinskii, no. 274, very secret, 15 June 1933, AVPRF, f. 05, op. 13, p. 91, d. 20, ll. 1–5; and "Notes of interview with Mr. Litvinoff," Sir F. Pole, 15 June, N4591/1610/38, TNA FO 371 17273.
83 Untitled, handwritten note by Leeper, 17 June 1933, N4812/5/38, TNA FO 371 17241.
84 Vansittart's minute, 19 June 1933, N4812/5/38, TNA FO 371 17241.
85 Vansittart's minute, 20 June 1933, N4611/5/38, TNA FO 371 17241.
86 Collier's minute, 21 June 1933, N4607/5/38, TNA FO 371 17241.
87 Litvinov to Krestinskii, no. 283, 24 June 1933, AVPRF, f. 05, op. 13, p. 91, d. 20, ll. 6–8.
88 Ibid.
89 Litvinov to Stalin, cc. for Molotov and Krestinskii, no. 286, secret, 24 June 1933, AVPRF, f. 05, op. 13, p. 91, d. 20, ll. 9–13.
90 Simon to Strang, no. 381, 26 June 1933, N4842/5/38, TNA FO 371 17241; Litvinov to NKID, for Stalin and Molotov, immediate, 26 June 1933, *DVP*, XVI, 366–8; and Krestinskii to Litvinov, immediate, 27 June 1933, ibid., 372–3.
91 Simon to Strang, nos. 382, 387, 388, 28, 30 June & 1 July 1933, N4842/4930/4931/5/38, TNA 371 17241.
92 Maiskii to Krestinskii, no. 130, secret, 24 March 1934, AVPRF, f. 05, op. 14, p. 97, d. 18, ll. 105–9.

93 Litvinov to Krestinskii, no. 283, 24 June 1933, AVPRF, f. 05, op. 13, p. 91, d. 20, ll. 6–8; and Litvinov to Stalin, cc. Molotov and Krestinskii, no. 286, secret, 24 June 1933, AVPRF, f. 05, op. 13, p. 91, d. 20, ll. 6–13.
94 Strang, no. 287, 23 May 1933; and Collier's minute, 31 May 1933, N4046/748/38, TNA FO 371 17261.
95 Strang to Simon, no. 410, confidential, 25 July 1933; and Collier's minute, 26 July 1933, N5526/1610/38, TNA FO 371 17273.
96 Vansittart's minute, 8 July 1933, N5356/1610/38, TNA FO 371 17273.

5 Rapallo or Not? Soviet Relations with Germany and Poland, 1933

1 "Conversation with the German ambassador [Ulrich] von Hassell, 14 February 1933," Potemkin (Rome), no. 90/s, secret, 3 March 1933, AVPRF, f. 05, op. 13, p. 90, d. 11, ll. 143–5.
2 Excerpt from Krestinskii's *dnevnik*, "Meeting with the German ambassador von Dirksen, 27 February 1933," secret, AVPRF, f. 082, op. 16, p. 71, d. l, ll. 45–41.
3 Excerpt from Litvinov's *dnevnik*, "Conversations with Neurath," secret, 1 March 1933, AVPRF, f. 082, op. 16, p. 71, d. 1, ll. 57–53.
4 Litvinov to Potemkin, no. L/35, secret, 15 March 1933, AVPRF, f. 05, op. 13, p. 90, d. 15, ll. 1-5.
5 Carley, *Silent Conflict*, 253–4, 277.
6 Litvinov to Stalin, no. 50/L, secret, 3 April 1933, AVPRF, f. 05, op. 13, p. 94, d. 78, l. 51.
7 "On the Foreign Policy of the National-Socialists," Boris Dmitrievich Vinogradov (Berlin), no. 439, secret, 13 April 1933, AVPRF, f. 05, op. 13, p. 91, d. 28, ll. 219–28.
8 Excerpt from Krestinskii's *dnevnik*, "Meeting with the German ambassador … 3 April 1933," secret, AVPRF, f. 05, op. 13, p. 91, d. 28, ll. 127–30.
9 Litvinov to Stalin, no. 58/L, secret, 13 April 1933, AVPRF, f. 05, op. 13, p. 94, d. 78, ll. 55–9.
10 Excerpt from Litvinov's *dnevnik*, "Conversation with Dirksen 3.IV.33," secret, AVPRF, f. 05, op. 13, p. 89, d. 4, ll. 55–9.
11 Dirksen, no. 60, most urgent, secret, 3 April 1933, *Documents on German Foreign Policy* (hereinafter *DGFP*), C, I, 241–2.
12 Krestinskii to Lev Mikhailovich Khinchuk, Soviet polpred in Berlin, no. G001-1214, secret, 7 May 1933, AVPRF, f. 05, op. 13, p. 91, d. 27, ll. 16–17.
13 Litvinov to Dovgalevskii, no. 78/L, secret, 17 May 1933, AVPRF, f. 010, op. 8, p. 32, d. 89, ll. 78–83.
14 Ibid.
15 Krestinskii to Khinchuk, no. G001-1232, very secret, 17 May 1933, AVPRF, f. 05, op. 13, p. 91, d. 27, ll. 37–42.
16 Excerpt from Litvinov's *dnevnik*, "Conversation with Dirksen, 16.V.1933," secret, AVPRF, f. 082, op. 16, p. 71, d. 1, ll. 195–191.

17 Excerpt from Litvinov's *dnevnik*, "Conversation with von Neurath, 29.V.33," in Kudryashov, ed., *SSSR-Germaniia, 1933–1941*, 63–4.
18 Krestinskii to Khinchuk, no. G001-1232, very secret, 17 May 1933, AVPRF, f. 05, op. 13, p. 91, d. 27, ll. 37–42.
19 Litvinov (Geneva) to Krestinskii, nos. 283 & 286, secret, 24 June 1933; and Litvinov to Stalin, no. 274, very secret, 15 June 1933, AVPRF, f. 05, op. 13, p. 91, d. 20, ll. 6–8, 9–13, 1–5.
20 Record of conversation with German state secretary Berhard Wilhelm von Bülow, Khinchuk, 22 June 1933, *DVP*, XVI, 360–1.
21 Litvinov to Krestinskii, no. 286, secret, 24 June 1933, AVPRF, f. 05, op. 13, p. 91, d. 20, ll. 9–13.
22 Litvinov to Stalin, no. 58/L, secret, 13 April 1933, AVPRF, f. 05, op. 13, p. 94, d. 78, ll. 55–9.
23 Stomoniakov to Antonov-Ovseenko, no. 4242, secret, 19 July 1933, AVPRF, f. 05, op. 13, p. 93, d. 48, ll. 23–9.
24 Ken, *Collective Security*, 67–9.
25 Radek to Stalin, handwritten notes, then typed, 12 July 1933, RGASPI, f. 558, op. 11, d. 790, ll. 23–32, RF, World War II, 1933.
26 Laroche, nos. 427–30, 17 July 1933, *Documents diplomatiques français* (hereinafter *DDF*), 1re série, 13 vols. (Paris: Imprimerie nationale, 1964–84), IV, 4–5.
27 Radek to Stalin, n.d. (not later than 21 July 1933), RGASPI, f. 558, op. 11, d. 790, ll. 59–63, RF, World War II, 1933.
28 Antonov-Ovseenko to Stomoniakov, no. 268, very secret, 20 July 1933, RGASPI, f. 558, op. 11, d. 790, ll. 52–6, RF, World War II, 1933.
29 Krestinskii to Antonov-Ovseenko, cc. Stalin, no. 1382, very secret, personal, 26 July 1933, Mikhail M. Narinskii, N.E. Kleimenova, and S.A. Skliarov, *Sovetsko-Pol'skie otnosheniia v 1918–1945 gg.* (hereinafter *SPO*), 4 vols. (Moscow: Aspent Press, 2017), III, 118–21.
30 Stomoniakov to Antonov-Ovseenko, no. 4272, secret, 4 Oct. 1933, AVPRF, f. 05, op. 13, p. 93, d. 48, ll. 33–7.
31 Laroche, nos. 691–700, 16 Nov. 1933, *DDF*, 1[re], V, 27–9.
32 Ken, *Collective Security*, 95–6.
33 Stomoniakov to Antonov-Ovseenko, no. 4326, secret, 19 Nov. 1933, *SPO*, III, 168–70.
34 Record of conversation with Beck and, among others, journalists of *Gazeta Polska*, Boguslaw Miedziński and Ignacy Matuszewski …, 20 & 23 Nov. 1933, *DVP*, XVI, 667–73; and Antonov-Ovseenko to Stonomiakov, 1 Dec. 1933, ibid., 697–9.
35 Antonov-Ovseenko to Stomoniakov, no. 449, very secret, 27 Nov. 1933, *SPO*, III, 176–80.
36 I.A. Koval'skii (Warsaw) to Radek, 28 Nov. 1933, RGASPI, f. 558, op. 11, d. 790, ll. 105 (r/v), RF, World War II, 1933.
37 Radek to Stalin, personal letter, 3 Dec. 1933, RGASPI, f. 558, op. 11, d. 790, ll. 106–7, RF, World War II, 1933.

38 Krestinskii to Vinogradov (Berlin), no. 1524, very secret, 27 Nov. 1933, AVPRF, f. 05, op. 13, p. 91, d. 27, ll. 78–9.
39 Mendras, compte-rendu mensuel, no. 9, 27 Feb. 1934, Château de Vincennes, Service historique de l'armée de terre (hereinafter SHAT), 7N 3121.
40 Antonov-Ovseenko to Stalin, not numbered, very secret, 13 Dec. 1933, RGASPI, f. 558, p. 11, d. 359, ll. 19–20, RF, World War II, 1933.
41 Record of conversation with the Polish ambassador, 14 Dec. 1933, *DVP*, XVI, 746–7.
42 Record of conversation with the Polish ambassador, 19 Dec. 1933, *DVP*, XVI, 755–6.
43 Stomoniakov to Antonov-Ovseenko, no. 4460, secret, 19 Dec. 1933, AVPRF, f. 05, op. 13, p. 93, d. 48, ll. 38–9.
44 Record of conversation with Beck, Antonov-Ovseenko, 22 Dec. 1933, *DVP*, XVI, 763–5.
45 V.V. Davydov, deputy chief, 4th *upravlenie*, RKKA (*Raboche Krestianskaia Krasnaia Armiia*), to A.I. Egorov, chief of staff, cc. Voroshilov, Litvinov, et al., no. 058246/ss, very secret, not later than 27 Dec. 1933, *Rossiiskii gosudarstvennyi voennyi arkhiv*, Moscow (hereinafter RGVA), f. 37977, op. 5, d. 335, ll. 10–14, RF, World War II, 1933.
46 "Conversation with Matuszewski and Miedziński, 21 December," very secret, RGASPI, f. 558, op. 11, d. 790, ll. 119–23, RF, World War II, 1933.
47 Antonov-Ovseenko to Radek, handwritten letter, 30 Dec. 1933, RGASPI, f. 558, op. 11, d. 790, ll.116 (r/v), RF, World War II, 1933.
48 Excerpt from Krestinskii's *dnevnik*, "Meeting with the German ambassador Dirksen, 3 June 1933," secret, AVPRF, f. 082, op. 16, p. 71, d. 1, ll. 233–226.
49 Excerpt from Krestinskii's *dnevnik*, "Meeting with the German ambassador von Dirksen, 19.VI,1933," secret, RGVA, f. 33987, op. 3a, d. 497, ll. 163–5, RF, World War II, 1933.
50 Excerpt from Krestinskii's *dnevnik*, "Meeting with the German ambassador von Dirksen, 23 June 1933," secret, AVPRF, f. 082, op. 16, p. 71, d. 1, ll. 264–261.
51 Excerpt from Krestinskii's *dnevnik*, "Meeting with the German ambassador von Dirksen, 2 July 1933," AVPRF, f. 082, op. 16, p. 71, d. 1, ll. 271–268.
52 Excerpt from Krestinskii's *dnevnik*, "Meeting with the German ambassador von Dirksen, 25 July 1933," secret, AVPRF, f. 05, op. 13, p. 90, d. 11, ll. 178–82.
53 Excerpt from Krestinskii's *dnevnik*, "Meeting with the counsellor of the German embassy Twardowski, 27 July 1933," AVPRF, f. 082, op. 17, p. 77, d. 1, ll. 271–268.
54 "Record of conversation of comrade Molotov with German ambassador von Dirksen, 4.VIII.1933," very secret, Kudryashov, ed., *SSSR-Germaniia, 1933–1941*, 66–8; and Krestinskii to Sergei Alekseev Bessonov, chargé d'affaires, Berlin, no. G001-1388, very secret, 4 Aug. 1933, AVPRF, f. 082, op. 17, p. 77, d. 1, ll. 298–297.
55 Litvinov to Bessonov, no. 95/L, secret, 4 Sept. 1933, AVPRF, f. 082, op. 17, p. 77, d. 1, l. 310; and excerpt from Litvinov's *dnevnik*, "Meeting with von Twardowski, 14.IX.1933," secret, ibid., l. 313.

56 Excerpt from Litvinov's *dnevnik*, "Meeting with Twardowski, 26.IX.1933," AVPRF, f. 05, op. 13, p. 89, d. 4, ll. 134–7.
57 Litvinov to Khinchuk, no. 128/L, secret, 4 Oct. 1934, AVPRF, f. 05, op. 13, p. 91, d. 27, 62–4; and Litvinov to Khinchuk, no. 150/L, secret, 17 Oct. 1933, ibid., ll. 67–8.
58 Stalin/Kalinin to Molotov, Kaganovich, 16 Oct. 1933, *Stalin i Kaganovich, Perepiska*, 388–9; and excerpt from Politburo protocol, no. P148/82-opr., rigorously secret, 25 Oct. 1933, Kudryashov, ed., *SSSR-Germaniia, 1933–1941*, 77.
59 Excerpt from Litvinov's *dnevnik*, "Conversation with von Neurath," secret, 28 Oct. 1933, Kudryashov, ed., *SSSR-Germaniia, 1933–1941*, 78–80.
60 Excerpt from Krestinskii's *dnevnik*, "Meeting with the German ambassador von Dirksen, 28.X. and 1.XI.1933," secret, AVPRF, f. 082, op. 17, p. 77, d. 1, ll. 347–43.

6 "Strike while the Iron Is Hot": Strengthening Relations with France

1 Rozenberg to Krestinskii, no. 519, secret, 1 Jan. 1933, AVPRF, f. 010, op. 8, p. 32, d. 89, ll. 2–4.
2 Dovgalevskii to Krestinskii, no. 2/s, secret, 9 Jan. 1933, AVPRF, f. 010, op. 8, p. 32, d. 89, ll. 8–10.
3 Léger to Dejean, no. 33, 15 Feb. 1933, MAÉ, Bureau du chiffre, télégrammes au départ de Moscou, 1933–1934; and Dejean, no. 20, 21 Feb. 1933, MAÉ, Bureau du chiffre, télégrammes à l'arrivée de Moscou, 1933–1934.
4 Rozenberg to Krestinskii, no. 76/s, secret, 11 Feb. 1933, AVPRF, f. 010, op. 8, p. 32, d. 89, ll. 30–2.
5 Krestinskii to Dovgalevskii, no. 1090, very secret, 19 Feb. 1933, AVPRF, f. 010, op. 8, p. 32, d. 89, ll. 38–9.
6 Rozenberg to Litvinov, no. 681/s, only in person, very secret, 25 Feb. 1933, AVPRF, f. 010, op. 8, p. 32, d. 89, ll. 40–1.
7 Rozenberg to Krestinskii, no. 93, very secret, 25 Feb. 1933, AVPRF, f. 010, op. 8, p. 32, d. 89, ll. 43–5.
8 Ostrovskii (Paris) to Voroshilov, unnumbered letter, 23 Feb. 1933, RGASPI, f. 558, op. 11, d. 432, ll. 61–4, RF, World War II, 1933.
9 See also Aleksandr Vershinin, "'My Task Is to Get into the French Army': Soviet Strategy and the Origins of Soviet-French Military Cooperation in the 1930s," *Journal of Strategic Studies* 44, no. 5 (2020): 685–714; and Frédéric Guelton, "Les relations militaires franco-soviétiques dans les années Trente," in Mikhail Narinskii, et al., *La France et l'URSS dans l'Europe des années 30* (Paris: Presses de l'Université de Paris-Sorbonne, 2005), 61–72.
10 Vladimir A. Sokolin to Rubinin, no. 175, very secret, 26 Apr. 1933, AVPRF, f. 010, op. 8, p. 32, d. 89, l. 56.
11 Dovgalevskii to Litvinov, no. 160, secret, 10 April 1933, AVPRF, f. 05, op. 13, p. 90, d. 11, ll. 146–8.

12 Rozenberg to Litvinov, no. 199, very secret, 10 May 1933, AVPRF, f. 010, op. 8, p. 32, d. 89, ll. 71–3.
13 Krestinskii to Rozenberg, no. 1237, very secret, personal, 19 May 1933, AVPRF, f. 05, op. 13, p. 94, d. 64, ll. 6–8.
14 Litvinov to Dovgalevskii, no. 78/L, secret, 17 May 1933, AVPRF, f. 010, op. 8, p. 32, d. 89, ll. 78–83.
15 Excerpt from Stomoniakov's *dnevnik*, "Meeting with the French ambassador," secret, 5 July 1933, AVPRF, f. 010, op. 8, p. 32, d. 90, ll. 10–16 (published in *DVP*, XVI, 411–16).
16 Litvinov (Paris) to NKID, 6 July 1933, *DVP*, XVI, 416–17.
17 Litvinov (Paris) to NKID, cc. Stalin, Molotov, Voroshilov, et al., no. 7482, very secret, 8 July 1933, RGASPI, f. 558, op. 11, d. 213, l. 23, RF, World War II, 1933.
18 Dovgalevskii to NKID, 18 July 1933, *DVP*, XVI, 847–8.
19 Note, Directeur politique (Paul Bargeton), not signed, 19 July 1933, MAÉ, URSS/1002, 86–8.
20 Dovgalevskii to Krestinskii, 26 July 1933, *DVP*, XVI, 848.
21 Léger to Alphand, no. 258, 7 Aug. 1933, MAÉ, Bureau du chiffre, télégrammes au depart de Moscou, 1933–4.
22 Kotkin, *Stalin*, II, 122–30.
23 Duroselle, *Décadence*, 27.
24 Litvinov to Rozenberg, no. 106/L, secret, 19 Sept. 1933, AVPRF, f. 05, op. 13, p. 94, d. 64, ll. 23–6 (published in *DVP*, XVI, 521–3).
25 Excerpt from Litvinov's *dnevnik*, "Conversation with Cot," secret, 20 Sept. 1933, AVPRF, f. 05, op. 13, p. 89, d. 4, ll. 126–7 (published in *DVP*, XVI, 523).
26 Excerpt from Litvinov's *dnevnik*, "Meeting with Alphand," secret, 22 Sept. 1933, AVPRF, f. 010, op. 8, p. 32, d. 90, ll. 28–30 (published in *DVP*, XVI, 527–9).
27 On Cot's mission, see Sabine Jansen, *Pierre Cot: Un antifasciste radical* (Paris: Fayard, 2002), 178–89.
28 Léger to Alphand, no. 325, confidential, 27 Sept. 1933, MAÉ, Bureau du chiffre, télégrammes au départ de Moscou, 1933–4.
29 Alphand, nos. 378–82, 28 Sept. 1933, MAÉ, URSS/1002, 133–7.
30 Mendras, no. 82, 7 Sept. 1933, "compte-rendu de conversation avec Radek," SHAT 7N 3121.
31 Carley, *Silent Conflict*, 76.
32 Mendras, compte-rendu mensuel, no. 4, 25 Sept. 1933, SHAT 7N 3121.
33 Rozenberg to Litvinov, no. 359, very secret, 26 Sept. 1933, AVPRF, f. 010, op. 8, p. 32, d. 89, ll. 162–5.
34 Dovgalevskii to NKID, 20 Oct. 1933, *DVP*, XVI, 576–78; and Litvinov (from Paris) to NKID, 31 Oct. 1933, ibid., 595–6.
35 Carley, *Silent Conflict*, 311–5.
36 See Carley, *Silent Conflict*, chaps. 4, 5, 10, and 11; and Michael Jabara Carley, "Five Kopecks for Five Kopecks: Franco-Soviet Trade Relations, 1928–1939," *Cahiers du monde russe et soviétique* 33, no. 1 (1992): 23–58.

37 Litvinov (from Paris) to NKID, 31 Oct. 1933, *DVP*, XVI, 595–6.
38 Bargeton to Alphand, no. 412–15, 25 Nov. 1933, MAÉ, Bureau du chiffre, télégrammes au départ de Moscou, 1933–34.
39 Stalin (Sochi) to Kaganovich, no. 1684/sh, immediate, 20 Sept. 1933, RGASPI, f. 558, op. 11, d. 21, ll. 21, 22–3, RF, World War II, 1933 (published in *Stalin i Kaganovich, Perepiski*, 352).
40 Krestinskii to Dovgalevskii, no. 1509, personal, very secret, 19 Nov. 1933, AVPRF, f. 05, op. 13, p. 94, d. 64, l. 35.
41 Dovgalevskii to Krestinskii, no. 139/s, secret, 9 April 1933, AVPRF, f. 010, op. 8, p. 32, d. 89, ll. 54–5.
42 Alphand, no. 311, 5 Nov. 1933, *DDF*, 1re, IV, 701–4.
43 Paul-Boncour to Alphand, no. 403, 17 Nov. 1933, MAÉ, Bureau du chiffre, télégrammes au départ de Moscou, 1933–4; and Rozenberg to Krestinskii, no. 403, very secret, 28 Oct. 1933, AVPRF, f. 010, op. 8, p. 32, d. 89, ll. 173–6.
44 Ostrovskii to Voroshilov, cc. Stalin, personal letter, very secret, 24 Oct. 1933, RGVA, f. 33987, op. 3a, d. 500, ll. 138–41, RF, World War II, 1933.
45 Rozenberg to Krestinskii, no. 424, very secret, 25 Nov. 1933, AVPRF, f. 010, op. 8, p. 32, d.89, ll. 190–4.
46 Rozenberg to Krestinskii, 25 Nov. 1933, *DVP*, XVI, 682–5.
47 Rozenberg to Krestinskii, no. 424, very secret, 25 Nov. 1933, AVPRF, f. 010, op. 8, p. 32, d.89, ll. 190–4.
48 Krestinskii to Dovgalevskii, immediate, 29 Nov. 1933, *DVP*, XVI, 695.
49 Dovgalevskii to Krestinskii, highest priority, 1 Dec. 1933, *DVP*, XVI, 696–7; and Krestinskii to Dovgalevskii, 2 Dec. 1933, ibid., 700.
50 Excerpt from Politburo protocol no. 149, 10 Nov. 1933, *Politbiuro TsK RKP(b) – VKP(b) i Evropa*, 296.
51 Krestinskii to Stalin, cc. Molotov, no. 1499, 9 Nov. 1933, RGASPI, f. 17, op. 166, d. 508, l. 15 (r/v), RF, World War II, 1933.
52 Mendras, compte-rendu mensuel, no. 5, 25 Oct. 1933, SHAT 7N 3121.
53 Litvinov (from Rome) to NKID, 4 Dec. 1933, *DVP*, XVI, 712–4.
54 Krestinskii to Dogalevskii, no. 1536, very secret, 4 Dec. 1933, AVPRF, f. 05, op. 13, p. 94, d. 64, ll. 39–40.
55 Krestinskii to Dovgalevskii, no. 1537, personal, very secret, 4 Dec. 1933, AVPRF, f. 05, op. 13, p. 94, d. 64, ll. 41–3.
56 Ibid.
57 Rozenberg to Krestinskii, no. 443, very secret, 10 Dec. 1933, AVPRF, f. 010, op. 8, p. 32, d. 89, ll. 205–8.
58 Alphand, nos. 528–31, 11 Dec. 1933, MAÉ, URSS/1003, 23–6.
59 Litvinov to Stalin, no. 166/L, secret, 15 Dec. 1933, AVPRF, f. 05, op. 13, p. 94, d. 78, ll. 169–71.
60 Litvinov to Stalin, no. 170/L, secret, 19 Dec. 1933, AVPRF f. 05, op. 13, p. 94, d. 78, ll. 191–5; and Politburo resolution, no. 151, 19 Dec. 1933, *Politbiuro TsK*

RKP(b) – VKP(b) i Evropa, 305–7. Stalin's copy of Litvinov's no. 170/L is found in RGASPI, f. 17, op. 166, d. 510, ll. 26–30, RF, World War II, 1933.

61 Paul-Boncour to Alphand, nos. 452–5, very confidential, *réservé*, 6 Dec. 1933, *DDF*, 1re, V, 173–4; and Alphand, nos. 528–31, 11 Dec. 1933, MAÉ, URSS/1003, 23–6.

62 Mendras, compte-rendu mensuel, no. 7, 31 Dec. 1933, SHAT 7N 3121.

63 Dovgalevskii to NKID, immediate, 29 Dec. 1933, *DVP*, XVI, 772–4.

64 "Note du département. Conversations politiques franco-russes," confidential, 4 Jan. 1934, *DDF*, 1re, V, 402–5.

65 Litvinov to Stalin, no. 4013/L secret, 16 Jan. 1934, AVPRF, f. 05, op. 14, p. 96, d. 11, ll. 52–3.

7 Shadows of Doubt over Moscow: Consolidating Collective Security, 1933–1934

1 Excerpt from Krestinskii's *dnevnik*, "Meeting with the German ambassador Nadolny 17 November 1933," secret, AVPRF, f. 082, op. 16, p. 71, d. 1, ll. 356–354.

2 Excerpt from Krestinskii's *dnevnik*, "Meeting with the German ambassador Nadolny 25 November 1933," secret, AVPRF, f. 082, op. 16, p. 71, d. 1, ll. 373–365; and Krestinskii to Bessonov, chargé d'affaires in Berlin, no. 1535, secret, 4 Dec. 1933, ibid., ll. 378–377.

3 Except from Litvinov's *dnevnik*, "Meetings with Nadolny, 11.XII. & 13.XII.33," secret, AVPRF, f. 082, op. 17, p. 77, d. 1, ll. 6–2.

4 Nadolny, no. 281, 13 Dec. 1933, *DGFP*, C, II, 226–8.

5 Khinchuk to Litvinov, no. 1111/s, secret, 30 Dec. 1933, AVPRF, f. 05, op. 14, p. 97, d. 29, ll. 1–3.

6 Excerpt from Litvinov's *dnevnik*, "Meeting with Alphand, 4 January 1934," secret, AVPRF, f. 05, op. 14, p. 95, d. 4, l. 10; and Alphand to Paul-Boncour, nos. 8–10, *réservé*, 4 Jan. 1934, *DDF*, 1re, V, 400–1.

7 Mendras, compte-rendu mensuel, no. 8, 30 Jan 1934, SHAT 7N 3121.

8 Twardowski's memorandum, no. A. 2848, secret, 26 Dec. 1933, *DGFP*, C, II, 274–6.

9 Twardowski, no. 291, urgent, secret, 27 Dec. 1933, *DGFP*, C, II, 278–80.

10 Unsigned note, presumably by Twardowski, 1 Jan. 1934, *DGFP*, C, II, 296–8.

11 Excerpt from Litvinov's *dnevnik*, "Meeting with Nadolny, 3 January 1934," secret, AVPRF, f. 05, op. 14, p. 95, d. 4, ll. 1–7 (published in *DVP*, XVII, 17–22).

12 Alphand, nos. 11–13, 4 Jan. 1934, MAÉ, Bureau du chiffre, télégrammes à l'arrivée de Moscou, 1933–4.

13 Nadolny, no. 3, top secret, 4 Jan. 1934, *DGFP*, C, 2, 301–4.

14 Excerpt from Karakhan's *dnevnik*, "Conversation with the German ambassador Nadolny, 5 January 1934," no. 6505, secret, AVPRF, f. 082, op. 17, p. 77, d. 1, ll. 22–19.

15 Nadolny, no. A. 90, secret, 9 Jan. 1934, and enclosure, *DGFP*, C, II, 318–32.

16 Nadolny, no. 5, 11 Jan. 1934, *DGFP*, C, II, 338–9.
17 Nadolny, no. 7, secret, 13 Jan. 1934, *DGFP*, C, II, 352–3.
18 Carley, "Five Kopecks for Five Kopecks," 39–42.
19 Alphand, no. 551, 20 Dec. 1933, MAÉ, RC, Russie, carton 2053, dossier 3.
20 Litvinov to Stalin, no. 167/L, secret, 15 Dec. 1933, AVPRF, f.05, op. 13, p. 94, d. 78, ll. 166–8; and "Note pour Monsieur le président du Conseil," not signed, 17 Jan. 1934, MAÉ, RC, Russie, carton 2054, dossier 1.
21 Alphand, nos. 21–3, 12 Jan. 1934, MAÉ, RC, Russie, carton 2054, dossier 1; and Alphand, no. 27, 14 Jan. 1934, ibid.
22 Carley, *Silent Conflict*, chap. 10.
23 Excerpt from Litvinov's *dnevnik*, "Meeting with Nadolny, 15.I.1934," secret, AVPRF, f. 082, op. 17, p. 77, d. 1, ll. 26–23.
24 Neurath to Nadolny, urgent, 17 Jan. 1934, *DGFP*, C, II, 373–5.
25 Dovgalevskii to NKID, 29 Jan. 1934, *DVP*, XVII, 101–3.
26 Geoffrey Roberts, *The Soviet Union and the Origins of the Second World War: Russo-German Relations and the Road to War, 1933–1941* (London: Macmillan, 1995), 15–16, quoting I.V. Stalin, *Works*, 13 vols. (Moscow, 1953–4), XIII, 308–9.
27 Nadolny, no. 21, 28 Jan. 1934, *DGFP*, C, II, 435–6.
28 "Conversation with Beck, 5.I.1934," Antonov-Ovseenko, no. 12/s, very secret, AVPRF, f. 05, op. 14, p. 99, d. 62, 41–2.
29 Record of conversation with Łukasiewicz, Litvinov, 11 Jan. 1934, *DVP*, XVII, 37–41.
30 Excerpt from Antonov Ovseenko's *dnevnik*, no. 48, very secret, 30 Jan. 1934, AVPRF, f. 05, op. 14, p. 99, d. 62, ll. 75–81.
31 Antonov-Ovseenko to NKID, cc. Stalin, Molotov, Voroshilov, et al., no. 1101, very secret, 27 Jan. 1934, AVPRF, f. 059, op. 1, p. 165, d. 1259, l. 10, RF, World War II, 1934.
32 Litvinov to Stalin, no. 4019/L, secret, 28 Jan. 1934, AVPRF, f. 05, op. 14, p. 103, d. 117, ll. 16–17 (published in *Moskva-Berlin*, III, 30–1).
33 Antonov-Ovseenko to NKID, cc. Stalin, Molotov, Voroshilov, et al., no. 1380, very secret, 1 Feb. 1934, AVPRF, f. 059, op. 1, p. 165, d. 1259, l. 15, RF, World War II, 1934.
34 Excerpt from Litvinov's *dnevnik*, "Meeting with Łukasiewicz, 1.II.1934," secret, AVPRF, f. 05, op. 14, p. 99, d. 61, ll. 15–20.
35 Excerpt from Stomoniakov's *dnevnik*, "Meeting with the Polish envoy," no. B-102, secret, 9 Feb. 1934, AVPRF, f. 05, op. 14, p. 99, d. 61, ll. 31–6.
36 Litvinov to Stalin, no. 4010/L, secret, 11 Jan. 1934, AVPRF, f. 05, op. 14, p. 103, d. 117, ll. 1–3; and excerpt from Politburo protocol, no. 152, 17 Jan. 1934, *Politbiuro TsK RKP(b) – VKP(b) i Evropa*, 308–10.
37 Litvinov to Stalin, cc. Molotov, Voroshilov, et al., no. 4012/L, secret, 15 Jan. 1934, RGVA, f. 33987, op. 3a, d. 635, ll. 8–10, RF, World War II, 1934.

38 Excerpt from Litvinov's *dnevnik*, "Record of conversation with the Polish foreign minister Beck, 13, 14, 15 February 1934," secret, AVPRF, f. 05, op. 14, p. 95, d. 4, ll. 53–62 (published in *DVP*, XVII, 131–40).
39 Alphand, nos. 87–90, 25 Feb. 1934, MAÉ, Bureau du chiffre, télégrammes à l'arrivée de Moscou, 1933–4.
40 Stomoniakov to Boris Grigor'evich Podol'skii, chargé d'affaires in Warsaw, no. 9570, secret, 19 Feb. 1934, AVPRF, f. 05, op. 14, p. 99, d. 61, ll. 27–30.
41 Excerpt from Stomoniakov's *dnevnik*, "Meeting with the Polish envoy," nos. 9585–6, secret, 26 Feb. 1934, AVPRF, f. 05, op. 14, p. 99, d. 61, ll. 37–44.
42 Stomoniakov to Antonov-Ovseenko, no. 9620, secret, 19 March 1934, AVPRF, f. 05, op. 14, p. 99, d. 61, ll. 47–50.
43 Litvinov to Stalin, no. 4056/L, secret, 17 March 1934, AVPRF, f. 05, op. 14, p. 103, d. 117, ll. 43–5.
44 Litvinov to Stalin, no. 4066/L, secret, 26 March 1934, *SPO*, III, 225–26; and Politburo protocol, no. 4, special session, 29 March 1934, Ken and Rupasov, *Politbiuro*, 432.
45 "Meeting with the Polish envoy Łukasiewicz," Krestinskii, 27 March 1934, AVPRF, f. 05, op. 14, p. 99, d. 61, ll. 51–2.
46 Stomoniakov to Davtian, no. 9692, secret 5 May 1934, AVPRF, f. 05, op. 14, p. 99, d. 61, ll. 65–8.
47 Litvinov to addressee cut out, but to Stalin, no. 4124/L, secret, 13 May 1934, AVPRF, f. 05, op. 14, p. 99, d. 61, ll. 69–72.
48 Dovgalevskii to Litvinov, 25 Jan. 1934, *DVP*, XVII, 70–1.
49 William L. Shirer, *Berlin Diary: The Journal of a Foreign Correspondent, 1934–1941* (New York: Knopf, 1941), 6–9, entry of 7 Feb. 1934.
50 Carley, *Silent Conflict*, 55–65.
51 Litvinov to Troianovskii, secret, 10 Feb. 1934, *SAO, 1934–1939*, 27–8.
52 Rozenberg to Krestinskii, no. 126, secret, 10 March 1934, RGASPI, f. 558, op. 11, d. 390, ll. 7–9, RF, World War II, 1934.

8 "One Step Back, Two Steps Forward": Ups and Downs in Soviet Relations in the West, 1934

1 Record of conversation with Alphand, Stomoniakov, 13 Feb. 1934, *DVP*, XVII, 140–2.
2 "Note de la Direction politique, Observations sur la communication de l'ambassadeur de l'U.R.S.S.," confidential, 26 Jan. 1934, *DDF*, 1re, V, 535–42.
3 Mendras, compte-rendu mensuel, no. 9, 27 Feb. 1934, SHAT 7N 3121.
4 Dovgalevskii to Litvinov, immediate, 24 Feb. 1934, *DVP*, XVII, 165–6.
5 Litvinov's *dnevnik*, "Meeting with Alphand, 26.II.1934," secret, AVPRF, f. 010, op. 9, p. 45, d. 154, l. 6.
6 Édouard Herriot, *Jadis: D'une guerre à l'autre, 1914–1936* (Paris: Flammarion, 1952), 389, entry of 20 Feb. 1934.

7 Rozenberg to Litvinov, 27 March 1934, *DVP*, XVII, 213.
8 Herriot, *Jadis*, 401, entry of 29 March 1934.
9 Rozenberg to Litvinov, immediate, 28 March 1934, *DVP*, XVII, 220–1.
10 Rozenberg to NKID, 30 March 1934, *DVP*, XVII, 787.
11 Herriot, *Jadis*, 403–4, entry of 10 April 1934.
12 "Négociations franco-soviétiques," not signed (annotation: "Note pour le Conseil des ministres du 17 avril"), 16 April 1934, MAÉ, URSS/1003, 112–19.
13 Rozenberg to NKID, immediate, 20 April 1934, *DVP*, XVII, 279–80.
14 Record of conversation with Léger, Rozenberg, 24 April 1934, *DVP*, XVII, 295–8.
15 Rozenberg to Litvinov, 25 April 1934, *DVP*, XVII, 299–301.
16 Litvinov to Rozenberg, 28 April 1934, *DVP*, XVII, 306.
17 Rozenberg to Litvinov, immediate, 28 April 1934, *DVP*, XVII, 309–11; and "Note de la Direction politique, Assistance mutuelle franco-soviétique," not signed [annotation: *Pour M. Léger. N'a pas été remis par lui et (sic) Rosenberg, mais seulement exposé verbalement (sauf la fin).*], 28 April 1934, *DDF*, 1re, VI, 376–8.
18 Robert J. Young, *Power and Pleasure: Louis Barthou and the Third Republic* (Montreal: McGill-Queen's University Press, 1991), 214–15.
19 Renaud Meltz, *Alexis Léger dit Saint-John Perse* (Paris: Flammarion, 2008), 428–30.
20 Rozenberg to Litvinov, immediate, 1 May 1934, *DVP*, XVII, 312–14; and Davtian to NKID, cc. Stalin, Molotov, Voroshilov, et al., nos. 5291, 5293, very secret, immediate, 27 April 1934, AVPRF, f. 059, op. 1, p. 165, d. 1259, ll. 68–9, RF, World War II, 1934.
21 Litvinov to Rozenberg, 3 May 1934, *DVP*, XVII, 795.
22 Dovgalevskii (from Litvinov, Menton) to NKID, cc. Stalin, Voroshilov, et al., no. 6324, very secret, 18 May 1934, AVPRF, f. 059, op. 1, p. 168, d. 1273, l. 9, RF, World War II, 1934; and Dovgalevskii (from Litvinov, Menton) to NKID, cc. Stalin, Voroshilov, et al., nos. 6366–7, 6371–2, very secret, 19 May 1934, AVPRF, f. 059, op. 1, p. 168, d. 1273, ll. 10–11, RF, World War II, 1934.
23 "Conversation entre M. Barthou et M. Litvinov à Genève le 18 mai 1934, Projet de pacte oriental," *DDF*, 1re, VI, 496–502.
24 Litvinov (Geneva) to NKID, 4 June 1934, *DVP*, XVII, 371.
25 Litvinov (Geneva) to NKID, 5 June 1934, *DVP*, XVII, 372.
26 Herriot, *Jadis*, 437–8, entry of 5 June 1934.
27 Litvinov (Geneva) via Dovgalevskii to NKID, cc. Stalin, Voroshilov, et al., no. 7262, rigorously secret, 6 June 1934, AVPRF, f. 059, op. 1, p. 168, d. 1273, l. 43, RF, World War II, 1934.
28 Litvinov (Geneva) to NKID, 8 June 1934, *DVP*, XVII, 378–9.
29 Mendras, compte-rendu, no. 12, 1 June 1934, SHAT 7N 3121.
30 Payart, no. 223, 28 May 1934, MAÉ, URSS/1003, 165.
31 Excerpt from Litvinov's *dnevnik*, "Meeting with Alphand, 23.VI.1934," AVPRF, f. 010, op. 9, p. 45, d. 154, ll. 12–13.

32 Alphand, no. 283, 20 July 1934, including Mendras, "Réception chez Vorochilov," n.d., MAÉ, URSS/967, 168–70 (r/v).
33 Excerpt from Stomoniakov's *dnevnik*, "Conversation with the German ambassador," no. 9678, secret, 17 March 1934, AVPRF, f. 082, op. 17, p. 77, d. 1, 110–108.
34 Litvinov to Stalin, no. 4056/L, secret, 17 March 1934, AVPRF, f. 05, op. 14, p. 103, d. 117, ll. 43–5.
35 Excerpt from Litvinov's *dnevnik*, Meeting with Nadolny, 28.III.1934," secret, AVPRF, f. 05, op. 14, p. 95, d. 4, ll. 87–89; Nadolny, no. 63, secret, 28 March 1934, *DGFP*, C, II, 683–5.
36 Excerpt from Krestinskii's *dnevnik*, "Record of conversation at dinner held by the German ambassador Nadolny, 28 March 1934," secret, AVPRF, f. 082, op. 17, p. 77, d. 1, ll. 97–92.
37 Record of conversation with Nadolny, Litvinov, 14 April 1934, *DVP*, XVII, 260–1.
38 Krestinskii to Khinchuk, 17 April 1934, *DVP*, XVII, 263.
39 Litvinov to Stefan I. Brodovskii, polpred in Riga, no. 4095/L, secret, 17 April 1934, AVPRF, f. 082, op. 17, p. 77, d. 1, ll. 104–102.
40 Excerpt from Litvinov's *dnevnik*, "Meeting with Nadolny, 21.IV.1934," secret, AVPRF, f. 05, op. 14, p. 95, d. 4, ll. 122–3; and Nadolny, no. 92, 21 April 1934, *DGFP*, C, II, 763–4.
41 Khinchuk, "Analysis of the Recent Foreign Policy of Germany," no. 193/s, secret, AVPRF, f. 05, op. 14, p. 97, d. 29, ll. 37–40.
42 Mendras, compte-rendu mensuel, no. 13, 25 June 1934, SHAT 7N 3121.
43 Excerpt from Litvinov's *dnevnik*, "Record of conversation with Neurath, 13.VI.34," secret, AVPRF, f. 05, op. 14, p. 95, d. 4, ll. 159–63; and Neurath's memorandum, 13 June 1934, *DGFP*, C, II, 902–4.
44 "Soviet-German relations," Vinogradov, no. 338/s, secret, 18 June 1934, AVPRF, f. 05, op. 14, p. 97, d. 29, ll. 1–3.
45 François-Poncet, nos. 1068–9, confidential, 13 June 1934, MAÉ, URSS/965, 108.
46 Laroche, nos. 526–38, 14 June 1934, MAÉ, URSS/965, 120–32.
47 Barthou (revisions by Léger) to Charles Corbin, ambassador in London, nos. 1080–1, 20 June 1934, MAÉ, URSS/965, 147.
48 Litvinov to Rozenberg, 11 July 1934, *DVP*, XVII, 466; and Litvinov to Rozenberg, 16 July 1934, ibid., 479.
49 Laroche, nos. 650–61, *réservé*, 14 July 1934, *DDF*, 1re, VI, 967–70; Davtian to Stomoniakov, no. 321/s, secret, 12 July 1934, AVPRF, f. 05, op. 14, p. 100, d. 63, ll. 90–94; and record of conversation with Laroche, Davtian, 17 July 1934, *DVP*, XVII, 482–3.
50 Excerpt from Litvinov's *dnevnik*, "Meeting with Alphand, 13.VII.1934," secret, AVPRF, f. 010, op. 9, p. 45, d. 154, ll. 14–16.
51 Litvinov to Stalin, no. 4167/L, secret, 14 July 1934, AVPRF, f. 05, op. 14, p. 103, d. 117, ll. 178–9.

52 Cambon, no. 881, 16 Aug. 1934, MAÉ, Grande-Bretagne/294, 53–7.

53 Laroche, nos. 503–6, 9 June 1934, MAÉ, URSS/965, 96–9.

54 Laroche, nos. 483–6, 5 June 1934, MAÉ, URSS/965, 63–5bis.

55 Untitled note (Geneva), secret, not signed, July 1934, MAÉ, URSS/967, 128–30; and Laroche, no. 514, very confidential, 16 July 1934, *DDF*, 1re, VI, 975–9.

56 M.I. Gai, Soviet military intelligence, to Stalin, 13 Nov. 1934, in Mattias Ul', Vladimir Khaustov, and Vladimir Zakharov, eds., *Glazami razvedki. SSSR i Evropa, 1919–1938* (Moscow: IstLit, 2015), 405–9.

57 OGPU report received from an agent in Paris, not later than 14 May 1934, annotated by Stalin, RGASPI, f. 558, op. 11, d. 187, ll. 9–23, RF, World War II, 1934.

58 OGPU report from "serious Polish source," very secret, not later than 29 June 1934, RGASPI, f. 558, op. 11, d. 187, ll. 28–44, RF, World War II, 1934.

59 Barthou's marginal note, 24 July 1934, on "Note de Monsieur Laroche, ambassadeur à Varsovie," 22 July 1934, MAÉ, URSS/967, 182–7.

60 Frédéric Dessberg, *Le triangle impossible : Les relations franco-soviétiques et le facteur polonais dans les questions de sécurité en Europe (1924–1935)* (Brussels: Peter Lang, 2009), 342–4.

61 Untitled note (Geneva), secret, not signed, July 1934, MAÉ, URSS/967, 128–30; and Litvinov to Stalin, no. 5150/L, secret, 2 July 1934, AVPRF, f. 05, op. 14, p. 103, d. 117, ll. 152–6.

62 Litvinov to Stalin, no. 4178/L, secret, 21 July 1934, AVPRF, f. 05, op. 15, p. 103, d. 117, ll. 182–3.

63 Excerpt from Politburo protocol no. 11, 25 July 1934, *Politbiuro TsK RKP(b) – VKP(b) i Evropa*, 314–15.

64 Litvinov to Rozenberg, 1 Aug. 1934, *DVP*, XVII, 527.

65 Litvinov (Évian-les-Bains) to NKID, cc. Stalin, Voroshilov, et al., no. 12732, rigorously secret, 14 Sept. 1934, AVPRF, f. 059, op. 1, p. 168, d. 1273, ll. 55–6, RF, World War II, 1934.

66 Dessberg, *Le triangle impossible*, 344–7; and I.A. Khormach, *Vozvrashchenie v mirovoe soobshchestvo: bor'ba i sotrunichestvo Sovetskogo gosudarstva s Ligoi natsii v 1919–1934 gg* (Moscow: Kuchkovo pole, 2011), 556–60.

67 Bullitt, no. 304, strictly confidential and secret, 15 Sept. 1934, 800.51W89USSR/124, NA, RG59, box 4610.

68 Bullitt, no. 340, strictly confidential, 5 Oct. 1934, 500.A15A4/2588, NA, RG59, box 2396.

69 Hugh R. Wilson (Geneva), US representative, no. 936, strictly confidential, 4 Oct. 1934, 500.A15A4/2589, NA, RG59, box 2396.

70 Barthou (Geneva) to Paris, Quai d'Orsay, no. 177, very confidential, *réservé*, 7 Sept. 1934, *DDF*, 1re, VII, 389–92; and Litvinov to Rozenberg, 26 July 1934, *DVP*, XVII, 501–2.

71 Pierre Bressy, French chargé d'affaires in Warsaw, no. 656, 3 Oct. 1934, *DDF*, 1re, VII, 651–7.

72 Wiley to Bullitt, personal & confidential, 1 Dec. 1934, FDR Library, Wiley Papers, Russia 1934–1935, Ambassador Bullitt, box 2.
73 Alphand, no. 361, 26 Sept. 1934, *DDF*, 1re, VII, 580–2; and Alphand, no. 365, 8 Oct. 1934, ibid., 680–1.
74 R. Young, *Power and Pleasure*, 224–5.
75 Stalin (Sochi) to Molotov, Zhdanov, no. 2448/Sh, rigorously secret, 12 Oct. 1934, RGASPI, f. 558, p. 11, d. 86, l. 89, RF, World War II, 1934.
76 Alphand, nos. 444–6, 12 Oct. 1934, *DDF*, 1re, VII, 718–19.
77 Excerpt from Litvinov's *dnevnik*, "Meeting with Alphand, 13.X.1934," secret, AVPRF, f. 05, op. 14, p. 95, d. 4, ll. 222–4.
78 Surits to NKID, cc. Stalin, Molotov, Voroshilov, et al., nos. 16277–8, rigorously secret, 19 Nov. 1934, RGASPI, no. 558, op. 11, d. 210, ll. 65–6, RF, World War II, 1934.

9 Nobody Wants "the Bolo Baby": The Failure of US-Soviet Relations, 1933–1935

1 Litvinov (Washington) to Stalin, nos. 12734–5, highest priority, very secret, 15 Nov. 1933, *Moskva-Vashington* III, 65–6.
2 Patrick Shura, "O'Neill's Strange Interlude and the 'Strange Marriage' of Louise Bryant," *The Eugene O'Neill Review* 30 (2008): 7–20; Christine Stansell, "Louise Bryant Grows Old," *History Workshop Journal* 50, no. 1 (2000): 156–80; and Robert S. Pinals, "Louise Bryant: An Adventurous Life and Painful Death from Dercum's Disease," *The Pharos* (Winter 2019): 21–3.
3 G.N. Sevost'ianov is the Soviet/Russian pioneer on US-Soviet relations. See, for example, *Moskva-Vashington: Diplomaticheskie otnosheniia, 1933–1936* (Moscow: Nauka, 2002).
4 Il'inskii to Litvinov, secret, urgent, 11 Dec. 1933, *SAO, Gody nepriznaniia*, 728–30.
5 V. Rover, TASS, to Ia. G. Doletskii, TASS chief in Moscow, secret, 11 Dec. 1933, *SAO, Gody nepriznaniia*, 730–2.
6 Bullitt to Roosevelt, personal and confidential, on board Steamship *Washington*, 1 Jan. 1934, Hyde Park, New York, Franklin D. Roosevelt (hereinafter FDR) Library, President's Secretary's File (hereinafter PSF), box 49, Russia, 1934.
7 Record of conversation with Bullitt, Karakhan, cc. Stalin, Molotov, Voroshilov, Kaganovich, et al., very secret, 13 Dec. 1933, *SAO, Gody nepriznaniia*, 732–3.
8 Record of conversation with Bullitt, Sokolnikov, cc. Stalin, Molotov, Voroshilov, et al., secret, 13 Dec. 1933, *SAO, Gody nepriznaniia*, 734–5.
9 Record of conversation with Bullitt, Stomoniakov, secret, not circulated outside the NKID, 13 Dec. 1933, *SAO, Gody nepriznaniia*, 735–8.
10 Bullitt to Roosevelt, personal and confidential, on board Steamship *Washington*, 1 Jan. 1934, FDR Library, PSF, box 49, Russia, 1934.
11 Phillips to Roosevelt, 26 Dec. 1933, covering Bullitt (Paris) to Roosevelt, et al., no. 576, strictly confidential, triple priority, 24 Dec. 1933, FDR Library, PSF, Russia, 1932–3, box 48.

12 Bullitt to Roosevelt, personal and confidential, on board Steamship *Washington*, 1 Jan. 1934, FDR Library, PSF, box 49, Russia, 1934.
13 Record of conversation with Bullitt, Litvinov, cc. Stalin, Molotov, et al., secret, 21 Dec. 1933, *SAO, Gody nepriznaniia*, 737–9.
14 Litvinov to Stalin, no. 172/L, secret, 21 Dec. 1933, AVPRF, f. 05, op. 13, p. 94, d. 78, l. 197.
15 Litvinov to Stalin, no. 174/L, secret, 22 Dec. 1933, AVPRF, f. 05, op. 13, p. 94, d. 78, ll. 198–9.
16 Litvinov to Stalin, no. 176/L, secret, 25 Dec. 1933, AVPRF, f. 05, op. 13, p. 94, d. 78, ll. 203–4; and Politburo resolution, no. P152/37-opr., rigorously secret, special file, 25 Dec. 1933, *Moskva-Vashington*, III, 85.
17 Theodore Marriner (Paris) to Hull, no. 584, 30 Dec. 1933, NA RG 59, 701.6111/743.
18 Wiley to Bullitt (care of Paris embassy), 14 Dec. 1933, FDR Library, John C. Wiley Papers, box 6.
19 Litvinov to Troianovskii, secret, 10 Feb. 1934, *SAO, 1934–1939*, 27–8.
20 Troianovskii to NKID, cc. Stalin, Molotov, Voroshilov, et al., nos. 2280–1, immediate, very secret, 21 Feb. 1934, *Moskva-Vashington* III, 101–2; and Troianovskii to Stalin, Molotov, 23 Feb. 1934, *SAO, 1934–1939*, 37–8.
21 Record of conversation with Bullitt, Divil'kovskii, secret, 7 March 1934, *SAO, 1934–1939*, 47–9.
22 Record of conversation with Bullitt, Divil'kovskii, secret, 12 March 1934, *SAO, 1934–1939*, 49–52.
23 Record of conversation with Bullitt, Krestinskii, secret, 13 March 1934, *SAO, 1934–1939*, 53–7.
24 Litvinov to Troianovskii, 14 March 1934, *SAO, 1934–1939*, 57–61.
25 Excerpt from Litvinov's *dnevnik*, "Record of conversations with Bullitt, 18.III.34 and 21.III.34," cc. Stalin, Molotov, Voroshilov, et al., secret, AVPRF, f. 05, op. 14, 95, d. 4, ll. 83–6.
26 Bullitt to Hull, no. 24, strictly confidential, 21 March 1934, FDR Library, PSF, Russia, box 49.
27 Litvinov to Politburo, 23 March 1934, *SAO, 1934–1939*, 75–6; and Politburo resolution, no. P5/26-opr., rigorously secret, special file, 1 April 1934, *Moskva-Vashington*, III, 123.
28 Bullitt to Moore, 3 April 1934, FDR Library, PSF, Russia, box 49.
29 Bullitt to Hull, no. 51, strictly confidential, 13 April 1934, FDR Library, PSF, Russia, box 49.
30 Excerpt from Litvinov's *dnevnik*, "Meeting with Bullitt, 8 April 1934," cc. Stalin, Molotov, Voroshilov, Rozengol'ts, et al., secret, AVPRF, f. 05, op. 14, p. 95, d. 4, ll. 101–3.
31 Bullitt to Hull, no. 43, urgent, 8 April 1934, FDR Library, PSF, Russia, box 49.
32 Litvinov to Troianovskii, 10 April 1934, *SAO, 1934–1939*, 109–11.
33 Krestinskii to Troianovskii, 10 April 1934, *SAO, 1934–1939*, 105–9.

34 Bullitt to Roosevelt, personal and confidential, 14 April 1934, FDR Library, PSF, Russia - Bullitt, box 50.
35 Roosevelt to Bullitt, 9 May 1934, FDR Library, PSF, Russia - Bullitt, box 50.
36 Hull to Bullitt, no. 36, 9 April 1934, FDR Library, PSF, Russia, box 49.
37 Troianovskii to NKID, 16 April 1934, *SAO, 1934–1939*, 119–20.
38 Record of conversation with Bullitt, Litvinov, 22 April 1934, *SAO, 1934–1939*, 122–3.
39 Bullitt to Hull, no. 60, 22 April 1934, FDR Library, PSF, Russia, box 49.
40 Record of conversation with John Cudahy, Davtian, secret, 24 April 1934, *SAO, 1934–1939*, 124–5.
41 Troianovskii to Litvinov, secret, 27 April 1934, *SAO, 1934–1939*, 125–7.
42 Moore to Bullitt, no. 50, strictly confidential, 23 April 1934, FDR Library, PSF, Russia, box 49.
43 Troianovskii to NKID, cc. Stalin, Molotov, Voroshilov, *et al*, nos. 5455, 5458, immediate, very secret, 30 April 1934, *Moskva-Vashington* III, 131–3.
44 "Draft of Despatch to Bullitt," Hull, n.d. (but perhaps 1 May 1934), FDR Library, PSF, Russia, box 49.
45 Litvinov to Troianovskii, cc. Stalin, Molotov, Voroshilov, et al., no. 4047, immediate, very secret, 4 May 1934, *Moskva-Vashington* III, 133–4.
46 Excerpt from Litvinov's *dnevnik*, "Meeting with Bullitt, 9.V.1934," secret, AVPRF, f. 05, op. 14, p. 95, d. 4, ll. 146–50.
47 Excerpt from Litvinov's *dnevnik*, "Meeting with Bullitt," cc. Stalin, Molotov, et al., secret, 12 May 1934, AVPRF, f. 05, op. 14, p. 95, d. 4, ll. 154–6; and Bullitt to Hull, no. 81, 13 May 1934, FDR Library, PSF, Russia, box 49.
48 Bullitt to Hull, no. 82, 13 May 1934, FDR Library, PSF, Russia, box 49.
49 Record of conversation with Bullitt, Krestinskii, cc. Stalin, Voroshilov, et al., secret, 16 May 1934, *SAO, 1934–1939*, 139–41.
50 Bullitt to Hull, no. 85, 16 May 1934, FDR Library, PSF, Russia, box 49.
51 Record of conversation with Bullitt, Rubinin, secret, 16 May 1934, *SAO, 1934–1939*, 141–5.
52 "Proposed Reply to Bullitt," n.d., FDR Library, PSF, Russia, box 49.
53 Hull to Bullitt, no. 108, 6 June 1934, FDR Library, PSF, Russia, box 49.
54 Bullitt to Hull, no. 124, 8 June 1934, FDR Library, PSF, Russia, box 49.
55 Record of conversation with Bullitt, Krestinskii, secret, 9 June 1934, *SAO, 1934–1939*, 154–8.
56 Record of conversation with Bullitt, Rubinin, secret, 14 June 1934, *SAO, 1934–1939*, 159–60.
57 Bullitt to Hull, no. 125, 8 June 1934, FDR Library, PSF, Russia, box 49.
58 Hull to Bullitt, not numbered, 8 June 1934, FDR Library, PSF, Russia, box 49.
59 Excerpt from Litvinov's *dnevnik*, "Meeting with the American ambassador Bullitt, 16.VI.34," cc. Stalin, Voroshilov, et al., secret, AVPRF, f. 05, op. 14, p. 95, d. 4, ll. 167–9; and Litvinov to Stalin, cc. Krestinskii, secret, 17 June 1934, *SAO, 1934–1939*, 160.

60 Troianovskii to NKID, cc. Stalin, Voroshilov, et al., no. 7992, rigorous secret, 20 June 1934, *Moskva-Vashington*, III, 142–3.

61 "Memorandum of conversation between the Russian Ambassador and Assistant Secretary of State Moore, June 20, 1934," 800.51W89 U.S.S.R./74, NA RG59, box 4609.

62 Litvinov to Stalin, secret, 22 June 1934, *SAO, 1934–1939*, 161.

63 Litvinov to Troianovskii, cc. Stalin, et al., no. 6020, very secret, 25 June 1934, *Moskva-Vashington*, III, 143–4.

64 Troianovskii to Litvinov, cc. Stalin, Voroshilov, et al., no. 8341, very secret, 26 June 1934, *Moskva-Vashington*, III, 144–5.

65 M.J. Carley, "Episodes from the Early Cold War: Franco-Soviet Relations, 1917–1927," *Europe-Asia Studies* 52, no. 7 (2000): 1275–1305.

66 Litvinov to Stalin, secret, 21 July 1934, *SAO, 1934–1939*, 186.

67 Moore to Francis Sayre, Assistant Secretary of State, 19 July 1934, 800.51W89-U.S.S.R./85-1/2, NA RG59, box 4609.

68 Troianovskii to Stalin, personal letter, very secret, 24 July 1934; and Politburo resolution, no. P11/73-opr., rigorously secret, special file, 25 July 1934, *Moskva-Vashington*, III, 159–61.

69 Troianovskii to Litvinov, secret, 24 July 1934, *SAO, 1934–1939*, 187–9.

70 Litvinov to Troianovskii, secret, 7 July 1934, *SAO, 1934–1939*, 168–72.

71 Krestinskii to Troianovskii, secret, 7 July 1934, *SAO, 1934–1939*, 173–5.

72 Bullitt to Hull, no. 177, strictly confidential, 9 July 1934, 800.51W89-U.S.S.R./78, NA RG59, box 4609.

73 Bullitt to Hull, no. 178, strictly confidential, 9 July 1934, 800.51W89-U.S.S.R./79, NA RG59, box 4609.

74 Hull to Bullitt, not numbered, 10 July 1934, 800.51W89-U.S.S.R.79, NA RG59, box 4609.

75 Bullitt to Hull, no. 180, 11 July 1934, 800.51W89-U.S.S.R./80, NA RG59, box 4609; and Bullitt to Hull, no. 191, 17 July 1934, 800.51W89-U.S.S.R./82, NA RG59, box 4609.

76 Bullitt to Hull, no. 167, strictly confidential, 30 June 1934, 800.51W89-U.S.S.R./76, NA RG59, box 4609.

77 Bullitt to Hull, no. 173, 7 July 1934, 800.51W89-U.S.S.R./77, NA RG59, box 4609.

78 Bullitt to Hull, no. 207, 21 July 1934, 800.51W89-U.S.S.R./86, NA RG59, box 4609.

79 Bullitt to Hull, no. 221, 27 July 1934, 800.51W89-U.S.S.R./89, NA RG59, box 4609.

80 Voroshilov's record of conversation with Bullitt on 26 July 1934, no. 12758, 27 July 1934, *Moskva-Vashington*, III, 162–3.

81 Bullitt to Roosevelt, 5 Aug. 1934, FDR Library, PSF, Russia, box 49.

82 "Memorandum of conversation between Secretary of State Hull and the Soviet ambassador Mr. Alexander Troyanovsky," 30 July 1934, 800.51W89U.S.S.R./90, NA RG59, box 4609.

83 Bullitt to Hull, no. 231, 30 July 1934, 800.51W89U.S.S.R./91, NA RG59, box 4609.
84 Litvinov to Troianovskii, no. 7528, very secret, 28 July 1934, *Moskva-Vashington*, III, 164.
85 Rubinin's report on the status of US-Soviet negotiations, very secret, 9 Aug. 1934, *Moskva-Vashington*, III, 166–71.
86 "Memorandum of Conversation," State Department, Division Eastern European Affairs, 10 Aug. 1934, 800.51W89U.S.S.R./103, NA, RG59, box 4609.
87 Troianovskii to NKID, cc. Stalin, Molotov, Voroshilov, et al., nos. 10931–2, very secret, immediate, 13 Aug. 1934, *Moskva-Vashington*, III, 173–4.
88 Krestinskii to Kaganovich, secret, 13 Aug. 1934, and enclosed draft cable for Troianovskii, *SAO, 1934–1939*, 193–6.
89 Kaganovich, Molotov to Stalin, rigorously secret, 14 Aug. 1934, *Stalin i Kaganovich, Perepiska*, 433–4.
90 Stalin to Kaganovich, no. 21, 15 Aug. 1934, *Stalin i Kaganovich, Perepiska*, 437–8.
91 Politburo resolution, no. P12/152-opr., rigorously secret, special file, and enclosed draft telegram for Troianovskii, 21 Aug. 1934, *Moskva-Vashington*, III, 176.
92 Krestinskii to Troianovskii, personal, very secret, 21 Aug. 1934, *SAO, 1934–1939*, 200–4.
93 Hull to Bullitt, no. 214, 24 Aug. 1934, 800.51W89U.S.S.R./108A; and "Conversation" between Troianovskii, Hull, Moore, and Kelley, State Department, Division of Eastern European Affairs, 24 Aug. 1934, 800.51W89U.S.S.R./112 ½, NA RG59, box 4609.
94 Bullitt to Hull, no. 292, strictly confidential and secret, 9 Sept. 1934, 800.51W89-U.S.S.R./116, NA RG59, box 4610.
95 Bullitt to Hull, no. 304, strictly confidential and secret, 15 Sept. 1934, 800.51W89-U.S.S.R./124, NA RG59, box 4610.
96 "Memorandum of the press conference, Tuesday, September 4, 1934," 800.51W89-U.S.S.R./119, NA RG59, box 4610.
97 "Conversation," with Troianovskii and Moore and Kelley, 5 Sept. 1934, 800.51W89 U.S.S.R./116 ½, NA RG59, box 4610.
98 "Statement by the acting secret of state R. Walton Moore," 6 Sept. 1934, 800.51W89-U.S.S.R./120, NA RG59, box 4610.
99 Moore to Bullitt, no. 246. Strictly confidential, 15 Sept. 1934, 800.51W89 U.S.S.R./121, NA RG59, box 4610.
100 Troianovskii to NKID, cc. Stalin, Kaganovich, Voroshilov, et al., nos. 12841–2, rigorously secret, immediate, 17 Sept. 1934, *Moskva-Vashington*, III, 181–2.
101 Krestinskii to Troianovskii, cc. Stalin, Kaganovich, Voroshilov, et al., no. 9711, rigorously secret, 18 Sept. 1934, *Moskva-Vashington*, III, 182–3.
102 "Conversation" with Troianovskii, Hull, Moore, and Kelley, 21 Sept. 1934, 800.51W89 U.S.S.R./150, NA RG59, box 4610.
103 Troianovskii to NKID, cc. Stalin, Molotov, Kaganovich, Voroshilov, et al., nos. 13056, 13062, 13069, rigorously secret, 22 Sept. 1934, *Moskva-Vashington*, III, 184–6.

104 Record of conversation with Bullitt, Krestinskii, 26 Sept. 1934, *DVP*, XVII, 612–15; and Bullitt to Hull, no. 330, 27 Sept. 1934, 800.51W89 U.S.S.R./132, NA RG59, box 4610.

105 Hull to Bullitt, no. 264, 1 Oct. 1934, 800.51W89 U.S.S.R./137A, NA RG59, box 4610.

106 James S. Herndon and Joseph O. Baylen, "Col. Philip R. Faymonville and the Red Army, 1934–43," *Slavic Review* 34, no. 3 (1975): 483–505.

107 Record of conversation with Faymonville, Skvirskii, secret, 10 Sept. 1934, *SAO, 1934–1939*, 218–19.

108 David S. Foglesong, *America's Secret War against Bolshevism: U.S. Intervention in the Russian Civil War, 1917–1920* (Chapel Hill, NC: University of North Carolina Press, 1995), 70–1.

109 Record of conversation with Bullitt, Skvirskii, secret, 11 Sept. 1934, *SAO, 1934–1939*, 219–23.

110 Bullitt to Hull, no. 342, 5 Oct. 1934, 800.51W89 U.S.S.R./140, NA RG59, box 4610.

111 Hull to Bullitt, no. 266, 2 Oct. 1934, 800.51W89 U.S.S.R./138, NA RG59, box 4610.

112 Hull to Bullitt, no. 273, 8 Oct. 1934, 800.51W89 U.S.S.R./140, NA RG59, box 4610.

113 Record of conversation with Bullitt, Rubinin, 7 Oct. 1934, *SAO, 1934–1939*, 238–40.

114 Litvinov to Molotov, 8 Oct. 1934, *SAO, 1934–1939*, 241.

115 Record of a conversation between Bullitt and Molotov, Rubinin, secret, 9 Oct. 1934, *SAO, 1934–1939*, 242–3.

116 Excerpt from Litvinov's *dnevnik*, "Meeting with the American ambassador Bullitt, 10.X.1934," secret, AVPRF, f. 05, op. 14, p. 95, d. 4, ll. 219–21.

117 Bullitt to Hull, no. 354, 10 Oct. 1934, 800.51W89-U.S.S.R./143, NA RG59, box 4610.

118 Wiley to Hull, no. 368, 20 Oct. 1934, 800.51W89 U.S.S.R./146, NA RG59, box 4610.

119 Excerpt from Litvinov to Stalin, very secret, 2 Nov. 1934; and Troianovskii to Stalin, secret, 2 Nov. 1934, *SAO, 1934–1939*, 262–4.

120 Wiley to Hull, no. 380, 10 Nov. 1934, 800.51 W89 U.S.S.R./148, NA RG59, box 4610; the last lines of Veinberg's report on the negotiations, very secret, 14 Nov. 1934, *SAO, 1934–1939*, 269–74; and Wiley to Bullitt, 26 Nov. 1934, FDR Library, Wiley Papers, diplomatic files, box 2.

121 Wiley to Hull, no. 382, 13 Nov. 1934, 800.51W89-U.S.S.R./149, NA RG59, box 4610.

122 A.V. Korotkov et al., eds., *Na prieme u Stalina: Tetradi (zhurnaly) zapisei lits, priniatykh I. V. Stalinym (1924–1953gg)* (Moscow: Novyi khronograf, 2008), 140.

123 Veinberg's report on the negotiations, very secret, 14 Nov. 1934, *SAO, 1934–1939*, 269–74.
124 Wiley to Hull, no. 389, 18 Nov. 1934, 800.51W89 U.S.S.R./151, NA RG59, box 4610.
125 Wiley to Hull, no. 396, 22 Nov. 1934, 800.51W89 U.S.S.R./152, NA RG59, box 4610.
126 Wiley to Hull, no. 397, 28 Nov. 1934, 800.51W89 U.S.S.R./153, NA RG59, box 4610.
127 Wiley to Bullitt 26 Nov. 1934, FDR Library, Wiley Papers, diplomatic files, box 2.
128 Wiley to Bullitt, 31 Jan. 1935, FDR Library, Wiley Papers, diplomatic files, box 2.
129 "For the press," State Department, 31 Jan. 1935, 800.51W89 U.S.S.R./167C, NA RG59, box 4610.
130 Litvinov to Stalin, no. 18/L, 2 Feb. 1935, AVPRF, f. 05, op. 15, p. 113, d. 122, l. 23.
131 Bullitt (Washington) to Wiley, strictly private, personal and confidential, 7 Jan. 1935, FDR Library, Wiley Papers, diplomatic files, box 2.
132 Bullitt (Washington) to Wiley, personal, 21 Jan. 1935, FDR Library, Wiley Papers, diplomatic files, box 2.
133 Wiley to Bullitt, 31 Jan. 1935, FDR Library, Wiley Papers, diplomatic files, box 2; and Wiley to Bullitt, 6 Feb. 1935, FDR Library, Wiley Papers, diplomatic files, box 2.

10 *Koshmar*: The Agonizing Turn in Relations with France, 1934–1935

1 Duroselle, *Décadence*, 123.
2 Alphand, no. 383, 23 Oct. 1934, MAÉ, URSS/1004, 22–4 (r/v).
3 Meltz, *Léger*, 438.
4 Rozenberg to NKID, immediate, 19 Oct. 1934, *DVP*, XVII, 647–9.
5 Rozenberg to NKID, immediate, 24 Oct. 1934, *DVP*, XVII, 649–51.
6 Litvinov to Stalin, no. 4238/L, secret, 31 Oct. 1934, AVPRF, f. 05, op. 14, p. 100, d. 117, l. 221.
7 Krestinskii to Troianovskii, personal, very secret, 21 Aug. 1934, *SAO, 1934–1939*, 200–4.
8 Alphand, nos. 461–6, 22 Oct. 1934, MAÉ, URSS/1004, 15–20.
9 Alphand, no. 383, 23 Oct. 1934, MAÉ, URSS/1004, 22–4 (r/v).
10 Litvinov to Stalin, no. 4240/L, very secret, 1 Nov. 1934, AVPRF, f. 05, op. 14, p. 103, d. 113, ll. 227–30.
11 Litvinov to A.N. Poskrebyshev, Stalin's personal secretary, no. 4243/L, very secret, 2 Nov. 1934, AVPRF, f. 05, op. 14, p. 103, d. 113, ll. 233–5; and excerpt from Politburo protocol no. 16, 2 Nov. 1934, *Politbiuro TsK RKP(b) – VKP(b) i Evropa*, 318–19.
12 Mendras, compte-rendu mensuel, no. 16, 3 Nov. 1934, SHAT 7N3121.
13 Alphand, nos. 505–11, 9 Nov. 1934, MAÉ, URSS/1004, 61–7; and Laval (revisions by Léger) to Alphand, nos. 493–7, 10 Nov. 1934, ibid., 68–70.
14 Alphand, nos. 518–20, very confidential, 13 Nov. 1934, MAÉ, URSS/1004, 74–6.
15 Litvinov to Surits, no. 4248/L, secret, 4 Nov. 1934, AVPRF, f. 082, op. 17, p. 77, d. 1, ll. 193–191.

16 Stomoniakov to Stalin, cc. Molotov, no. 10144, secret, 23 Nov. 1934, RGVA, f. 33987, op. 3a, d. 635, ll. 279–81, RF, World War II, 1934.
17 Mendras, compte-rendu no. 15, 5 Oct. 1934, SHAT 7N 3121.
18 André Géraud (Pertinax), *Les Fossoyeurs*, vol. 2 (New York: Éditions de la Maison Française 1943), 43; Geneviève Tabouis, *They Called Me Cassandra* (New York: Charles Scribner's Sons, 1942), 207.
19 Litvinov to Rozenberg, 6 Nov. 1934, *DVP*, XVII, 666–7.
20 Rozenberg to NKID, 10 Nov. 1934, *DVP*, XVII, 828.
21 Litvinov (Geneva) to NKID, cc. Stalin, Molotov, Voroshilov, et al., nos. 16251, 16258, rigorously secret, 21 Nov. 1934, AVPRF, f. 059, op. 1, p. 168, d. 1273, ll. 103–4, RF, World War II, 1934; and Litvinov (Geneva) to NKID, for Stalin, cc. Molotov, Voroshilov, et al., no. 16280, rigorously secret, immediate, 22 Nov. 1934, AVPRF, f. 059, op. 1, p. 168, d. 1273, ll. 105–6, ibid.
22 Laval to Corbin, no. 2042, 30 Nov. 1934, MAÉ, URSS/970, 235–7.
23 "Memorandum of Conversation with Litvinov," strictly confidential, Wilson, 21 Nov. 1934, 500.A15A4/2618, NA, RG59, box 2396.
24 Litvinov (Geneva) to NKID, cc. Stalin, Molotov, Voroshilov, et al., no. 16989, rigorously secret, immediate, 5 Dec. 1934, AVPRF, f. 059, op. 1, p. 168, d. 1273, l. 122, RF, World War II, 1934.
25 Dessberg, *Triangle impossible*, 351–2.
26 M.N. Riabinin, Red Army military intelligence, to zamnarkom for war, M.N. Tukhachevskii, 26 Nov. 1934, *Glazami razvedki*, 411–12.
27 O.O. Shteinbriuk, Red Army intelligence, to Voroshilov, 23 Dec. 1934, *Glazami razvedki*, 413.
28 See Annie Lacroix-Riz, *Choix de la défaite: les élites françaises dans les années 1930* (Paris: Armand Colin, 2006), 159–60.
29 A. Kh. Artuzov, Red Army intelligence, to Stalin, very secret, not later than 28 Dec. 1934, RGASPI, f. 558, op. 11, d. 188, ll. 31–52, RF, World War II, 1934 (published in *Glazami razvedki*, 414–20).
30 N.A. Semenov to A.A. Langovoi, with attachment, 13 Dec. 1934, RGVA, f. 33987, op. 3a, d. 635, ll. 290–1, RF, World War II, 1934.
31 Duroselle, *Décadence*, 132–3.
32 Litvinov to Potemkin, no. 10/L, secret, 4 Jan. 1935, AVPRF, f. 05, op. 15, p. 104, d. 3, ll. 40–1.
33 Potemkin to Krestinskii, no. 35, very secret, 11 Jan. 1935, AVPRF, f. 010, op. 10, p. 60, d. 148, ll. 13–20.

11 Bridging the Gap: The Anglo-Soviet Rapprochement, 1934–1935

1 Untitled, handwritten minute by Leeper, 17 June 1933, N4812/5/38, TNA FO 371 17241.
2 Krestinskii to Maiskii, no. 5039, very secret, personal, 19 Jan. 1934, AVPRF, f. 05, op. 14, p. 96, d. 11, l. 41.

3 Maiskii to Krestinskii, unnumbered dispatch, very secret, personal, AVPRF, f. 05, op. 14, p. 96, d. 11, l. 51.
4 Maiskii to Krestinskii, no. 26, secret, 9 Jan. 1934, AVPRF, f. 010, op. 9, p. 35, d. 7, ll. 4–8.
5 Minutes by Collier, 1 Jan. 1934 and Oliphant, 2 Jan. 1934, N1/1/38, TNA FO 371 18297.
6 "Record of a conversation … Lord Cecil," Maiskii, 5 Feb. 1934, *DVP*, XVII, 110–13.
7 Minutes by T.A. Shone and R.G. Howe, 19 Feb. 1934, N1069/16/38, TNA FO 371 18303.
8 Oliphant's minute, 14 Feb. 1934, N1116/16/38, TNA FO 371 18303.
9 Maiskii, no. 77/s, secret, 24 Feb. 1934, AVPRF, f. 010, op. 9, p. 35, d. 7, ll. 10–13.
10 Maiskii to Litvinov, no. 78/s, secret, 24 Feb. 1934, AVPRF, f. 010, op. 9, p. 35, d. 7, ll. 19–41.
11 "Discussion with the counselor of the British embassy, Charles," Rubinin, no. 19666/s, secret, 9 March 1934, AVPRF, f. 05, op. 14, p. 97, d. 18, ll. 67–9.
12 Maiskii to NKID, 2 March 1934, *DVP*, XVII, 167–8.
13 "Discussion with Garvin, editor of the 'Observer', 18 March 1934," no. 120/s, Maiskii, secret, 24 March 1934, RGASPI, f. 558, op. 11, d. 291, ll. 11–18, RF, World War II, 1934.
14 Loraine, no. 12 saving, 22 Feb. 1934, N1316/16/38; and Simon to Loraine, 29 March 1934, N1617/16/38, TNA FO 371 18303.
15 Minutes by Collier, 23 March 1934, N1082/120/38, and 26 March 1934, N1699/120/38, TNA FO 371 18316; and Vansittart, 28 March 1934, N1082/120/38, ibid.
16 Carley, *Silent Conflict*.
17 Litvinov to Maiskii, no. 4055/L, secret, 17 March 1934, AVPRF, f. 010, op. 9, p. 35, d. 7, ll. 56–8.
18 Chilston, no. 46, 5 Feb.1934, N755/2/38, TNA FO 371 18298; and minutes by R.G. Howe, 21 March 1934, ibid.; Vansittart, 13 Jan. 1934, N140/2/38, TNA FO 371 18297, and 22 March 1934, N1741/2/38, TNA FO 371 18398.
19 See Anthony Eden, *Facing the Dictators* (Boston: Houghton Mifflin, 1962), 271; Norman Rose, *Vansittart: Study of a Diplomat* (London: Heinemann, 1978); and B.J.C. McKercher, ed., "Robert Vansittart and an Unbrave World, 1930–37," Special issue, *Diplomacy & Statecraft* 6, no. 1 (1995), articles by McKercher, Charles Morrisey, M.A. Ramsay, M.L. Roi, Simon Bourette-Knowles, and John R. Ferris.
20 Litvinov to Maiskii, no. 4055/L, secret,17 March 1934, AVPRF, f. 010, op. 9, p. 35, d. 7, ll. 56–8.
21 Gilbert Murray, chair, League of Nations Union, to Simon, 15 March 1934; and Vansittart's minute, 27 March 1934, N1754/2/38, TNA FO 371 18298.
22 "Discussion with Strang, 5 May 1934," no. 198, Maiskii, secret, 11 May 1934, AVPRF, f. 05, op. 14, p. 97, d. 18, l. 209.
23 "Discussion with Chilston, 18 April 1934," no. 178/s, Maiskii, secret, AVPRF, f. 05, op. 14, p. 97, d. 18, ll. 149–50.

24 "Discussion with Collier and Strang, 5 May 1934," Maiskii, no. 187/s, secret, AVPRF, f. 05, op. 14, p. 97, d. 18, ll. 187–9.
25 "Discussions at the Foreign Office dinner, 4 June 1934," Masikii, no. 261, secret, AVPRF, f. 05, op. 14, p. 97, d. 18, ll. 218–22.
26 "*Dnevnik* of meetings," no. 271, Maiskii, secret, 25 June 1934, AVPRF, f. 05, op. 14, p. 97, d. 19, ll. 8–16.
27 Carley, *Silent Conflict*, 159–60, 273–4, 368, 412.
28 Litvinov's *dnevnik*, "Meeting with the English ambassador Chilston, 21.VI.34," AVPRF, f. 05, op. 14, p. 95, d. 4, ll. 172–5.
29 Chilston, no. 81, 22 June 1934, N3682/2/38, TNA FO 371 18298; and Chilston to Collier, 22 June 1934, N4027/16/38, TNA FO 371 18305.
30 Collier's minute, 12 July 1934, N4027/16/38, TNA FO 371 18305; and Chilston to Collier, 28 Jan. 1935, N559/17/38, TNA FO 371 19450.
31 Minutes by Collier, 12 July 1934; Oliphant, 13 July 1934; and Vansittart, 17 July 1934, N4027/16/38, TNA FO 371 18305.
32 Litvinov to Stalin, no. 4070/L, secret, 28 Aug. 1932, AVPRF, f. 05, op. 12, p. 88, d. 96, l. 69.
33 R. Vansittart, *The Mist Procession: The Autobiography of Lord Vansittart* (London: Hutchinson, 1958), 454–5; and I.M. Maiskii, *Vospominaniia sovetskogo diplomata, 1925–1945 gg*. (Moscow: Nauka, 1971), 222, 290–1, 300.
34 "Discussion with Vansittart, 3 July 1934," no. 304, Maiskii, secret, AVPRF, f. 05, op. 14, p. 97, d. 19, ll. 17–29.
35 Litvinov to Maiskii, 29 June 1934, *DVP*, XVII, 432–3.
36 "Discussion with Vansittart, 3 July 1934," no. 304, Maiskii, secret, AVPRF, f. 05, op. 14, p. 97, d. 19, ll. 17–29.
37 Maiskii to NKID, 3 July 1934, *DVP*, XVII, 436–7.
38 Simon to Chilston, no. 352, confidential, 18 July 1934, N4029/16/38, TNA FO 371 18305.
39 Maiskii to Litvinov, no. 300, 10 July 1934, AVPRF, f. 05, op. 14, p. 97, d. 19, ll. 42–4.
40 Simon to Chilston, no. 352, confidential, 18 July 1934, N4029/16/38, TNA FO 371 18305.
41 "Record of a conversation … with … Vansittart," Maiskii, 12 July 1934, *DVP*, XVII, 466–8; and Maiskii to Narkomindel, immediate, 12 July 1934, ibid., 468–9.
42 Maiskii to Krestinskii, no. 329, secret, 24 July 1934, AVPRF, f. 010, op. 9, p. 35, d. 7, ll. 111–19.
43 "Discussion with Vansittart, 18 July 1934," no. 322, Maiskii, secret, AVPRF, f. 05, op. 14, p. 97, d. 19, ll. 52–7 (published in *DVP*, XVII, 484–8); and I.M. Maiskii, *Dnevnik diplomata, London, 1934–1943*, 3 vols. (Moscow: Nauka, 2006–9), I, 12–13, entry of 18 July 1934. For non-Russian readers, there is Gabriel Gorodetsky, ed., *The Complete Maisky Diaries*, 3 vols. (New Haven, CT: Yale University Press, 2017). In this work all references to Maiskii's *dnevnik* are to the Russian edition.

44 Litvinov to Maiskii, no. 4174/L, secret, 19 July 1934, AVPRF, f. 05, op. 14, p. 97, d. 17, ll. 22–4 (published in *DVP*, XVII, 489–90).

45 Simon's minute, 20 July 1934, and Vansittart to Chilston, 24 July 1934, N4027/16/38, TNA FO 371 18305.

46 Chilston, no. 368, 7 Aug. 1934, and Vansittart's minute, 8 Aug. 1934, N4622/16/38, TNA FO 371 18305; and Chilston, no. 396, 18 Aug. 1934, N4840/16/38, ibid.

47 "Note by Sir R. Vansittart," 9 Aug. 1934, N4718/2/38, TNA FO 371 18299; "Discussion with Vansittart, 9 Aug. 1934," no. 350, Maiskii, secret, AVPRF, f. 05, op. 14, p. 97, d. 19, ll. 74–80 (published in *DVP*, XVII, 552–7); and Maiskii, *Dnevnik*, I, 13–15, entry of 9 Aug. 1934.

48 Corbin, no. 881, 16 Aug. 1934, MAÉ, Z-Grande-Bretagne/294, 53–7.

49 Harold Patteson, British consul, Geneva, from Eden, no. 59 saving, 19 Sept. 1934, N5455/2/38, TNA FO 371 18300; and Patteson, from Eden, no. 60 saving, 27 Sept. 1934, N5602/2/38, TNA FO 371 18301.

50 Kaganovich to Stalin, 12 Aug. 1934, and Stalin to Kaganovich, 12 Aug. 1934, *Stalin i Kaganovich, Perepiska*, 430.

51 Bullitt, U.S. ambassador in Moscow, no. 304, strictly confidential and secret, 15 Sept. 1934, 800.51W89USSR/124, NA RG 59 (1930–39), box 4610.

52 Maiskii to Krestinskii, no. 329, secret, 24 July 1934, AVPRF, f. 010, op. 9, p. 35, d. 7, ll. 111–19.

53 Litvinov to Maiskii, no. 4126/L, secret, 13 May 1934, AVPRF, f. 05, op. 14, p. 97, d. 17, l. 16.

54 Krestinskii to Maiskii, no. 5371, secret. 4 Aug. 1934, AVPRF, f. 010, op. 9, p. 35, d. 7, l. 120.

55 Rubinin to Kagan, no. 20304/s, secret, 4 Oct. 1934, AVPRF, f. 05, op. 14, p. 97, d. 17, ll. 27–8.

56 Litvinov to Maiskii, 26 Oct. 1934, *DVP*, XVII, 651; and Litvinov to Maiskii, 4 Nov. 1934, ibid., 664. See also V.V. Veeder, "The Lena Goldfields Arbitration: The Historical Roots of Three Ideas," *International and Comparative Law Quarterly* 47, no. 4 (1998): 747–92.

57 Maiskii, *Dnevnik*, I, 18–19, entry of 5 Nov. 1934.

58 Boothby to Eden, 6 Nov. 1934, N6328/16/38, TNA FO 371 18305; and Wellesley's minute, 14 Nov. 1934, ibid.

59 Simon's note on the interview with Maiskii, 9 Nov. 1934, N6462/16/38, TNA FO 371 18305.

60 "Discussions with Simon, 9/10 November 1934," no. 456, Maiskii, secret, AVPRF, f. 05, op. 14, p. 97, d. 19, ll. 96–107; Maiskii to Litvinov, 9 Nov. 1934, *DVP*, XVII, 667–8; and Maiskii, *Dnevnik*, I, 22–4, entry of 9 Nov. 1934.

61 "Discussion with Collier, 10 November 1934," no. 457, Maiskii, secret, AVPRF, f. 05, op. 14, p. 97, d. 19, ll. 108–9.

62 Maiskii to Litvinov, no. 458, secret, 10 Nov, 1934, AVPRF, f. 010, op. 9, p. 35, d. 7, ll. 124–7.

63 Keith Nielson, *Britain, Soviet Russia and the Collapse of the Versailles Order, 1919–1939* (Cambridge: Cambridge University Press, 2006), 111–14.
64 "Discussion with Eden, 16 November 1934," no. 468, Maiskii, secret, AVPRF, f. 05, op. 14, p. 97, d. 19, ll. 151–3 (published in *DVP*, XVII, 678–80).
65 "Discussion with the Minister of Agriculture Elliot, 7 December 1934," no. 513, Maiskii, AVPRF, f. 05, op. 14, p. 97, d. 19, ll. 164–7.
66 Maiskii to Litvinov, no. 507, secret, 10 Dec. 1934, AVPRF, f. 010, op. 9, p. 35, d. 7, ll. 133–5.
67 Maiskii, *Dnevnik*, I, 45–7, entry of 13 Dec. 1934; and Memorandum by Vansittart, 13 Dec. 1934, N6953/16/38, TNA FO 371 18306.
68 Maiskii, *Dnevnik*, I, 49–51, entry of 18 Dec. 1934; and Simon to Chilston, no. 612, 27 Dec. 1934, N7104/16/38, TNA FO 371 18306.
69 Mounsey's minute, 31 Dec. 1934, N7104/16/38, TNA FO 371 18306.
70 Maiskii, *Dnevnik*, I, 54–5, entry of 27 Dec. 1934.
71 Collier's minute, 28 Dec. 1934, N7104/16/38, TNA FO 371 18306; and Vansittart to Collier, 31 Dec. 1934, ibid.
72 Simon to Chilston, no. 613, confidential, 27 Dec. 1934, N7155/16/38, TNA FO 371 18306.
73 "Discussion with Vansittart, 27 December 1934," no. 1, Maiskii, secret, 10 Jan. 1935, AVPRF, f. 05, op. 15, p. 106, d. 17, ll. 1–6.
74 Litvinov to Maiskii, no. 11/L, secret, 4 Jan. 1935, AVPRF, f. 05, op. 15, p. 106, d. 16, l. 1.
75 Maiskii to Litvinov, no. 41, secret, 24 Jan. 1935, AVPRF, f. 010, op. 10, p. 48, d. 7, ll. 27–33.
76 Litvinov to Surits, no. 4258/L, secret, 9 Nov. 1934, AVPRF, f. 05, op. 14, p. 98, d. 33, ll. 44–5.
77 Litvinov to Maiskii, no. 1055, secret, 4 Feb. 1935, AVPRF, f. 05, op. 15, p. 106, d. 18, l. 4.
78 Vansittart's minute, 9 Feb. 1935, C1076/55/18, TNA FO 371 18825.
79 A.L. Rowse, *Appeasement: A Study in Political Decline, 1933–39* (New York: Norton, 1963), 32–3.
80 Vansittart's minute, 4 Feb. 1935, C785/55/18, TNA FO 371 18824.
81 Rowse, *Appeasement*, 33.
82 Maiskii, *Dnevnik*, I, 75, entry of 10 Feb. 1935.
83 Litvinov to Maiskii, 13 Feb. 1935, *DVP*, XVIII, 99.
84 Maiskii, *Dnevnik*, I, 75, entry of 12 Feb. 1935.
85 Chilston, no. 72, 8 Feb. 1935, C1278/55/18, TNA FO 371 18826; and Maiskii to Narkomindel, 11 Feb. 1935, *DVP*, XVIII, 618.
86 Vansittart's minute, 20 Feb. 1935, C1339/55/38, TNA FO 371 18826; and Vansittart to Chilston, private, 21 Feb. 1935, ibid.
87 Maiskii to Litvinov, 13 Feb. 1935, *DVP*, XVIII, 99–101; and Litvinov to Maiskii, 17 Feb. 1935, ibid., 112.

88 Vansittart to Chilston, 21 Feb. 1935, C1339/55/38, TNA FO 371 18826.
89 Maiskii, *Dnevnik*, I, 76, entry of 14 Feb. 1935.
90 "Discussion with Vansittart, 13 February 1935," no. 108, Maiskii, secret, copies to Stalin, Molotov, Voroshilov, etc., AVPRF, f. 05, op. 15, p. 104, d. 3, ll. 175–83.
91 Memorandum by Vansittart, C.P. 41 (35), 21 Feb. 1935, N912/17/38, TNA FO 371 19450.
92 Maiskii to Narkomindel, immediate, 21 Feb. 1935, *DVP*, XVIII, 122–4; and Simon to Chilston, no. 98, 20 Feb. 1935, *DBFP*, 2nd, XII, 542–3.
93 "Discussion with Simon and Eden, 20 February 1935," no. 107, Maiskii, secret, AVPRF, f. 05, op. 15, p. 104, d. 3, ll. 184–92.
94 Maiskii to Litvinov, no. 109, secret, 22 Feb. 1935, AVPRF, f. 05, op. 15, p. 106, d. 17, ll. 49–50; and Maiskii, *Dnevnik*, I, 77–8, entry of 21 Feb. 1935.
95 "Discussion with Vansittart, 21 February 1935," no. 106, Maiskii, secret, 22 Feb. 1935, AVPRF, f. 05, op. 15, p. 106, d. 18, l. 6.
96 Maiskii, *Dnevnik*, I, 79, entry of 22 Feb. 1935.
97 Litvinov to Stalin, no. 56/L, secret, 25 Feb. 1935, AVPRF, f. 05, op. 15, p. 113, d. 122, l. 53–4.
98 Maiskii, *Dnevnik*, I, 79–80, entry of 28 Feb. 1935.
99 "Discussion with Vansittart, 28 February 1935," no. 114, Maiskii, secret, 9 March 1935, AVPRF, f. 05, op. 15, p. 106, d. 18, ll. 11–14.
100 Litvinov to Potemkin, 27 Feb. 1935, *DVP*, XVIII, 144–5.
101 Litvinov to Maiskii, 3 March 1935, *DVP*, XVIII, 157; and Litvinov to Maiskii, no. 75/L, secret, 4 March 1935, AVPRF, f. 05, op. 15, p. 106, d. 18, ll. 7–8.
102 Maiskii, *Dnevnik*, I, 82–3, "Discussion with Lady Vansittart," 4 March 1935.
103 "Discussion with Vansittart, 4 March 1935," no. 112, Maiskii, secret, 9 March 1935, AVPRF, f. 05, op. 15, p. 106, d. 18, ll. 15–20.
104 "Discussion with Vansittart, 6 March 1935," no. 113, Maiskii, secret, 9 March 1935, AVPRF, f. 05, op. 15, p. 106, d. 18, ll. 21–2.
105 "Discussion with Vansittart (by telephone), 7 March 1935," no. 116, Maiskii, secret, 9 March 1935, AVPRF, f. 05, op. 15, p. 106, d. 18, ll. 23–4.
106 Maiskii, *Dnevnik*, I, 85, entry of 7 March 1935.
107 Litvinov to Maiskii, 8 March 1935, *DVP*, XVIII, 165–6.
108 Maiskii to Litvinov, no. 134, secret, 9 March 1935, AVPRF, f. 05, op. 15, p. 106, d. 18, ll. 25–7.
109 Maiskii to NKID, 13 March 1935 (two cables), *DVP*, XVIII, 172–3, 625.
110 Maiskii, *Dnevnik*, I, 92–3, entry of 17 March 1935.
111 Ibid.
112 Vansittart's minute, 19 March 1935, N524/17/38, TNA FO 371 19450.
113 Corbin, nos. 321–6, 18 March 1935, *DDF*, 1[re], IX, 603–5.
114 Krestinskii to Maiskii, no. 1170, secret, 19 March 1935, AVPRF, f. 010, op. 10, p. 48, d. 7, ll. 46–7.

115 "Conversations in connection with Eden's trip," no. 137, Maiskii, secret, 25 March 1935, AVPRF, f.05, op. 15, p. 106, d. 18, ll. 29–43; and also Maiskii, *Dnevnik*, I, 95, entry of 20 March 1935.
116 Ibid.; Maiskii, *Dnevnik*, I, 96–7, entry of 22 March 1935; and Maiskii to NKID, 22 March 1935, *DVP*, XVIII, 199–200.
117 Litvinov to Stalin, cc. Molotov Voroshilov, Kaganovich, Ordzhonikidze, no. 107/L, secret, 22 March 1935, AVPRF, f. 05, op. 15, p. 113, d. 122, ll. 117–30.
118 Between 20 and 27 March 1935, see Korotkov et al., *Na prieme u Stalina*, 157–8.
119 Mounsey's minute, 31 Dec. 1934, N7104/16/38, TNA FO 371 18306.
120 Vansittart to Phipps, 5 March 1935, *DBFP*, 2nd, XII, 605–6.
121 Record of conversation with Vansittart, Maiskii, 6 June 1935, *DVP*, XVIII, 385–7.
122 Maiskii, *Vospominaniia*, 142–3, 289.
123 Eden, *Facing the Dictators*, 181.
124 Litvinov's speech, English version, without title or date, AVPRF, f. 05, op. 15, p. 106, d. 18, ll. 57–60.
125 Eden, *Facing the Dictators*, 160–82.
126 "Record of Anglo-Soviet Conversation … on March 29 at 11.30 a.m.," *DBFP*, 2nd, XII, 784–91; and "Record of a conversation …," 29 March 1935, *DVP*, XVIII, 240–5.
127 "Record of Anglo-Soviet Conversation … on March 29 at 11.30 a.m.," *DBFP*, 2nd, XII, 784–91; "Record of a conversation …," 29 March 1935, *DVP*, XVIII, 240–5; and Bateman's interesting minutes and draft answer to a Parliamentary Question, 19 April 1932, N2418/22/38, PRO FO 371 16319.
128 "Record of a conversation of I.V. Stalin and V.M. Molotov with the Lord Privy Seal of Great Britain Eden," 29 March 1935, *DVP*, XVIII, 246–51; and Chilston, nos. 48–9, 30 March 1935, *DBFP*, 2nd, XII, 766–9.
129 Alphand, nos. 202–7, 227–9, 30 March & 3 April 1935, MAÉ, Bureau du chiffre, télégrammes, à l'arrivée de Moscou, 16 octobre 1934–31 décembre 1935.
130 Eden, *Facing the Dictators*, 180.
131 Vansittart, *Mist Procession*, 474.
132 "The Proposed Eastern Pact," Sargent, 28 Jan. 1935, C962/55/18, TNA FO 371 18825.
133 Vansittart's minute, 28 Jan. 1935, C962/55/18, TNA FO 371 18825.
134 Sargent's minute, 6 Feb. 1935, C869/55/18, TNA FO 371 18824.
135 Memorandum signed by Collier, Wigram, and Orde, 12 Feb. 1935, N927/135/38, TNA FO 371 19460.
136 Vansittart's minute, 13 Feb. 1935, N927/135/38, TNA FO 371 19460.
137 "Sir R. Vansittart," Sargent, 20 Feb. 1935; Vansittart's various marginal notes; and Collier to Sargent, 20 Feb. 1935, N927/135/38, TNA FO 371 19460.
138 "International Position of the Soviet Union in relation to France, Germany, and Japan," 21 Feb. 1935, *DBFP*, 2nd, XII, 559–63, or N880/135/38, TNA FO 371 19460.

139 Sargent's minute, 19 Feb. 1935, C1339/55/18, TNA FO 371 18826.

140 "Memorandum by Mr. Sargent …," 7 Feb. 1935, *DBFP*, 2nd, XII, 501–2; and Sargent's minute, 1 April 1935, C2656/55/18, TNA FO 371 18833.

141 Minutes by Sargent, 27 Feb. 1935, and Collier, 28 Feb. 1935, C1558/55/18, TNA FO 371 18827.

142 Sargent's minute, 22 March 1935, N1313/53/38, TNA FO 371 19456.

143 Phipps to Sargent, 4 April 1935; and Sargent's minute, 12 April 1935, C2892/55/18, TNA FO 371 18834.

144 Minutes by Sargent, 1 April 1935; Vansittart, 1 April 1935, C2656/55/18, TNA FO 371 18833; and Wigram, 3 April 1935, C2794/55/18, ibid.

145 "Discussion with Vansittart, 26 April 1935," no. 234, Maiskii, secret, 9 May 1935, AVPRF, f. 5, op. 15, p. 106, d. 17, ll. 82–5.

146 Memorandum by Vansittart, 28 May 1935, N2761/998/38, TNA FO 371 19467.

147 E.H. Carr, *The Twilight of the Comintern, 1930–1935* (London: Pantheon, 1982), 147–55.

148 "Discussion with Vansittart, 28 May 1935," no. 277/s, Maiskii, secret, 8 June 1935, AVPRF, f. 05, op. 15, p. 106, d. 17, ll. 104–8.

149 Litvinov to Maiskii, 3 June 1935, *DVP*, XVIII, 371–2.

150 Maiskii, *Dnevnik*, I, 101–2, entry of 3 June 1935.

151 "Discussion with Vansittart, 6 June 1935," no. 278/s, Maiskii, secret, 8 June 1935, AVPRF, f. 05, op. 15, p. 106. d. 17, ll. 109–11 (published in *DVP*, XVII, 385–7); and "Note communicated by Soviet Ambassador, June 5, 1935," C4564/55/18, TNA FO 371 18845.

152 "Discussion with Lord Beaverbrook, 4 June 1935," no. 281/s, Maiskii, secret, 8 June 1935, AVPRF, f. 05, op. 15, p. 106, d. 17, ll. 93–9.

153 Hoare's minute, 14 June 1935, C4564/55/18, TNA FO 371 18845.

154 Hoare's memorandum, 12 June 1935, N3187/17/38, TNA FO 371 19451.

155 "Discussion with Samuel Hoare, 12 June 1935," no. 293/s, Maiskii, secret, 13 June 1935, AVPRF, f. 05, op. 15, p. 106, d. 17, ll. 114–19.

156 Hoare's minute, 14 June 1935, C4564/55/18, TNA FO 371 18845.

157 Maiskii to NKID, cc. Stalin, Molotov, Voroshilov, Kaganovich, et al., nos. 9645–6, rigorously secret, immediate, 13 June 1935, AVPRF, f. 059, op. 1, p. 193, d. 1425, ll. 229–30; RF, World War II, 1935; and also Maiskii, *Dnevnik*, I, 106–8, entry of 12 June 1935.

158 "Discussion with Winston Churchill, 14 June 1935," no. 315/s, Maiskii, secret, 25 June 1935, AVPRF, f. 05, op. 15, p. 106, d. 17, ll. 135–43; and Maiskii's telegram, immediate, 15 June 1935, *DVP*, XVIII, 397–8. Cf., Maiskii, *Vospominaniia*, 300–2.

159 Litvinov to Maiskii, no. 196/L, secret, 17 June 1935, AVPRF, f. 05, op. 15, p. 106, d. 16, ll. 12–13.

160 "Discussion with Beaverbrook, 20 June 1935," no. 311/s, Maiskii, secret, 25 June 1935, AVPRF, f. 05, op. 15, p. 106, d. 17, ll. 133–4.

161 Report of meeting between Maiskii and Ashton-Gwatkin, 3 July 1935, N3423/135/38, TNA FO 371 19460.
162 "Discussion with Ashton-Gwatkin, 9 July 1935," no. 347/s, Maiskii, secret, AVPRF, f. 05, op. 15, p. 106, d. 17, ll. 146–8.
163 Chilston, no. 533, 6 Dec. 1935, N6304/135/38, TNA FO 371 19460.
164 J.L. Dodds to Chilston, 16 Aug. 1935, N3888/17/38, TNA FO 371 19451.

12 Showdown: Negotiating the Franco-Soviet Pact, 1935

1 Excerpt from Girshfel'd's *dnevnik*, no. 54, very secret, 25 Jan. 1935, AVPRF, f. 010, op. 10, p. 60, d. 152, ll. 10–16.
2 Litvinov (Geneva) to NKID, cc. Stalin, Molotov, Voroshilov, et al., no. 993, rigorously secret, immediate, 17 Jan. 1935, AVPRF, f. 059, op. 1, p. 190, d. 1408, l. 29, RF, World War II, 1935.
3 "Record of an Exchange of Opinions taking place at dinner with Laval, 18 January 1935," Potemkin, AVPRF, f. 05, op. 15, p. 104, d. 3, ll. 75–82.
4 Ibid.
5 Cristina A. Bejan, *Intellectuals and Fascism in Interwar Romania: The Criterion Association* (London: Palgrave, 2019), 197–8.
6 Shtein (Geneva) to NKID, cc. Stalin, Molotov, Voroshilov, et al., no. 4475, very secret, highest priority, 11 April 1934, RGASPI, f. 558, op. 11, d. 213, ll. 77–8, RF, World War II, 1934.
7 "Conversation with Titulescu," Mikhail S. Ostrovskii, no. 53, secret, 11 Sept. 1934, AVPRF, f. 010, op. 9, p. 43, d. 128, ll. 4–12.
8 Excerpt from Litvinov's *dnevnik*, report of meetings with Titulescu, secret, 16 June 1934, AVPRF, f. 010, op. 9, p. 43, d. 128, ll. 1–2; and O.N. Ken, "M.S. Ostrovskii i sovetsko-rumynskie otnosheniia (1934–1938gg.)," in *Rossiia v XX veke: Sbornik statei k 70-letiiu rozhdeniia chl.-kopp. RAN prof. V. A. Shishkina* (St. Petersburg: n.p., 2005), 336–50.
9 "Record of an Exchange of Opinions taking place at dinner with Laval, 18 January 1935," Potemkin, AVPRF, f. 05, op. 15, p. 104, d. 3, ll. 75–82.
10 Laval (revisions by Léger) to Laroche, nos. 26–33, 21 Jan. 1935, MAÉ URSS/971, 202–05; and Litvinov (Geneva) to NKID, cc. Stalin, Molotov, Voroshilov, et al., no. 1142, rigorously secret, immediate, 18 Jan. 1935, AVPRF, f. 059, op. 1, p. 190, d. 1408, ll. 32–3, RF, World War II, 1935.
11 Litvinov (Geneva) to NKID, cc. Stalin, Molotov, Voroshilov, et al., nos. 974, 976, rigorously secret, immediate, 17 Jan. 1935, AVPRF, f. 059, op. 1, p. 190, d. 1408, ll. 25–7, RF, World War II, 1935.
12 Litvinov (Geneva) to NKID, cc. Stalin, Molotov, Voroshilov, et al., no. 1205, rigorously secret, immediate, 19 Jan. 1935, AVPRF, f. 059, op. 1, p. 190, d. 1408, l. 36, RF, World War II, 1935.
13 Potemkin to Krestinskii, no. 58, very secret, 25 Jan. 1935, AVPRF, f. 0136, op. 19, p. 164, d. 814, ll. 166–70.

14 Duroselle, *Décadence*, 144.
15 "Note de Roland de Margerie, Impressions de séances, Conférence franco-anglaise de Londres," secret, 7 Feb. 1935, *DDF*, 1re, IX, 286–90.
16 "Conversations franco-britanniques de Londres (Downing Street)," morning session on 1 Feb. 1935, *DDF*, 1re, IX, 205–17.
17 Litvinov to Potemkin, 4 Feb. 1935, *DVP*, XVIII, 62–3.
18 Potemkin to NKID, 4 Feb. 1935, *DVP*, XVIII, 616.
19 Litvinov to Stalin, cc. Molotov, Voroshilov, Ordzhonikidze, no. 32/L, secret, 10 Feb. 1935, AVPRF, f. 05, op. 15, p. 113, d. 122, ll. 43–7.
20 Excerpt from Politburo protocol no. 21, 11 Feb. 1935, *Politbiuro TsK RKP(b) – VKP(b) i Evropa*, 319–21.
21 Potemkin to Krestinskii, no. 94, very secret, 10 Feb. 1935, AVPRF, f. 010, op. 10, p. 60, d. 148, ll. 43–54.
22 Ibid.
23 Potemkin to NKID, immediate, 13 & 14 Feb. 1935, *DVP*, XVIII, 103–6.
24 "The ambassador's conversation with Paul-Boncour, 14 February 1935," Potemkin, no. 100, secret, AVPRF, f. 05, op. 15, p. 104, d. 3, ll. 212–13.
25 Alphand, nos. 103–7, 10 Feb. 1935, MAÉ, Bureau du chiffre, télégrammes, à l'arrivée de Moscou, 16 octobre 1934–31 décembre 1935.
26 "Conversation with Alphand," Rubinin, no. 16081/s, secret, 5 Feb. 1935, AVPRF, f. 016, op. 19, p. 164, d. 814, ll. 74–7.
27 Alphand, nos.115–16, 14 Feb. 1935, MAÉ, Bureau du chiffre, télégrammes, à l'arrivée de Moscou, 16 octobre 1934–31 décembre 1935.
28 "Conversation with Alphand," Rubinin, no. 16081/s, secret, 5 Feb. 1935, AVPRF, f. 016, op. 19, p. 164, d. 814, ll. 74–7.
29 "Meeting with Laroche," 2 Feb. 1935, Jean Szembek, *Journal, 1933–1939* (Paris: Plon, 1952), 35–8.
30 Maiskii, *Dnevnik*, I, 73–4, entry of 4 Feb. 1935; and Maiskii to NKID, cc. Stalin, Molotov, Voroshilov, et al., nos. 2103, 2109, rigorously secret, immediate, 4 Feb. 1935, AVPRF, f. 059, op. 1, p. 193, d. 1425, ll. 31–3, RF, World War II, 1934.
31 Excerpt from Litvinov's *dnevnik*, "Meeting with Łukasiewicz, 10.II.1935," secret, AVPRF, f. 05, op. 15, p. 103, d. 1, ll. 3–9.
32 Litvinov to Stalin, no. 36/L, secret, 13 Feb. 1935, AVPRF, f. 05, op. 15, p. 113, d. 122, ll. 53–4.
33 François-Poncet, no. 389, urgent, *réservé*, 14 Feb. 1935, *DDF*, 1re, IX, 333–5.
34 Litvinov to Potemkin, no. 40/L, secret, 17 Feb. 1935, AVPRF, f. 05, op. 15, p. 104, d. 3, ll. 125–30.
35 Litvinov to Stalin, cc. Molotov Kaganovich, Voroshilov, Ordzhonikidze, no, 42/L, secret, 17 Feb. 1935, AVPRF, f. 05, op. 15, p. 113, d. 122, l. 59.
36 Alphand, nos. 117–20, 17 Feb. 1935, MAÉ, Bureau du chiffre, télégrammes, à l'arrivée de Moscou, 16 octobre 1934–31 décembre 1935.
37 Corbin, no. 110, 8 Feb. 1935, MAÉ, URSS/972, 116–19.
38 Litvinov to Maiskii, 13 Feb. 1935, *DVP*, XVIII, 99.

39 Maiskii to NKID, 13 Feb. 1935, *DVP*, XVIII, 99–101; and "Conversation with Vansittart …, 13 February 1935," Maiskii, no. 108, secret, cc. Stalin, Molotov, Voroshilov, and various ambassadors, 22 Feb. 1935, AVPRF, f. 05, op. 15, p. 104, d. 3, ll. 175–83.
40 Meeting with [Friedrich Werner] von der Schulenburg [German ambassador in Moscow], 18 Jan. 1935, Szembek, *Journal*, 20.
41 Litvinov to Maiskii and Potemkin, 20 Feb. 1935, *DVP*, XVIII, 619.
42 Korotkov et al., eds., *Na prieme u Stalina*, 152.
43 Soviet declaration made to the French and British governments, 20 Feb. 1935, *DVP*, XVIII, 117–19.
44 Litvinov's *dnevnik*, "Meeting with Alphand, 21.II.1935," secret, AVPRF, f. 05, op. 15, p. 103, d. 1, ll. 14–15.
45 Potemkin to NKID, immediate, 21 Feb. 1935 and Maiskii to NKID, immediate, 21 Feb. 1935, *DVP*, XVIII, 121–4.
46 Litvinov to Potemkin, 26 Feb. 1935, *DVP*, XVIII, 138.
47 Strang (Geneva) to Ralph Wigram, head of the Central Department, confidential, 14 Feb. 1935, C1372/55/18, TNA FO 371 18826.
48 Sir George R. Clerk, British ambassador in Paris, no. 31 saving, 26 Feb. 1935, C1558/55/18, TNA FO 371 18827.
49 Potemkin to Litvinov, immediate, 28 Feb. 1935, *DVP*, XVIII, 151–2.
50 Litvinov to Maiskii, 3 March 1935, *DVP*, XVIII, 157.
51 Maiskii, *Dnevnik*, I, 83–4, entry of 5 March 1935.
52 Litvinov to Stalin, cc. Molotov, Voroshilov, Orzhonikidze, no. 69/L, secret, 3 March 1935, AVPRF, f. 05, op. 15, p. 113, d. 122, ll. 92–3.
53 Litvinov to Potemkin, no. 72/L, secret, 4 March 1935, AVPRF, f. 010, op. 10, p. 60, d. 148, ll. 71–4.
54 Litvinov to Potemkin, no. 82/L, secret, 9 March 1935, AVPRF, f. 05, op. 15, p. 104, d. 3, ll. 223–4.
55 Record of conversation with Alphand, 17 March 1935, *DVP*, XVIII, 184–5; and Alphand, nos. 174–6, 17 March 1935, *DDF*, 1re, IX, 597–8.
56 Maiskii, *Dnevnik*, I, 94–5, entry of 19 March 1935; Alphand, no. 187, 20 March 1935, MAÉ, Bureau du chiffre, télégrammes, à l'arrivée de Moscou, 16 octobre 1934–31 décembre 1935.
57 Litvinov to Potemkin, no. 99/L, secret, 19 March 1935, AVPRF, f. 010, op. 10, p. 60, d. 148, ll. 83–5.
58 Laval to Corbin, nos. 384–9 (and Rome), 16 March 1935; and Laval to Corbin, nos. 415–17 (and Rome), *priorité absolue*, 19 March 1935, *DDF*, 1re, IX, 584–5, 631–2.
59 Potemkin to Krestinskii, no. 145, secret, 10 March 1935, AVPRF, f. 010, op. 10, p. 60, d. 148, ll. 78–82.
60 "Foreign department, GUGB (*Glavnoe upravlenie gosudarstvennoi bezopasnosti*), NKVD, received from Paris, on the basis of documentary materials from the

French Ministry of Foreign Affairs, following cable communications on 25–26 March 1935," very secret, RGASPI, f. 558, op. 11, d. 188, ll. 74–8, RF, World War II, 1935.

61 Potemkin to Krestinskii, no. 177, secret, 26 March 1935, AVPRF, f. 0136, op. 19, p. 164, d. 814, ll. 143–50.

62 Litvinov to Potemkin, 23 March 1935, *DVP*, XVIII, 202–3.

63 Potemkin to NKID, highest priority, 29 March 1935, *DVP*, XVIII, 251–2.

64 Note, Directeur politique, 19 March 1935, MAÉ, URSS/973, 107–10.

65 Rozenberg (Moscow) to Litvinov, no. 3001, secret, 29 March 1935, AVPRF, f. 010, op. 10, p. 60, d. 148, l. 95.

66 Potemkin to NKID, highest priority, 30 March 1935, *DVP*, XVIII, 253–4.

67 Potemkin to NKID, highest priority, 31 March 1935, *DVP*, XVIII, 255–6.

68 Clerk, no. 62, confidential, 23 March 1935, C2458/55/18, TNA FO 371 18832.

69 Clerk, no. 70, 31 March 1935, C2692/55/18, TNA FO 371 18833.

70 Litvinov to Stalin, cc. Molotov, Voroshilov, Kaganovich, Ordzhonikidze, et al., no. 122/L, secret, 2 April 1935, AVPRF, f. 05, op. 15, p. 113, d. 122, ll. 150–2.

71 Litvinov to Potemkin, urgent, 2 April 1935, *DVP*, XVIII, 259.

72 Litvinov to Potemkin, 3 & 7 April 1935, *DVP*, XVIII, 260, 266.

73 Davtian's *dnevnik*, "Conversation with Eden, 3 April 1935," secret, AVPRF, f. 05, op. 15, p. 104, d. 3, ll. 324–5.

74 Litvinov to Aleksandrovskii, no. 127/L, secret, 5 April 1935, AVPRF, f. 05, op. 15, p. 104, d. 3, ll. 298–9.

75 Aleksandrovskii to NKID, 5 April 1935, *DVP*, XVIII, 630–1.

76 Litvinov to Potemkin, no. 124/L, secret, 4 April 1935, AVPRF, f. 010, op. 10, p. 60, d. 148, ll. 96–9.

77 Excerpt from Litvinov's *dnevnik*, "Meeting with Schulenburg, 4 April 1935," secret, AVPRF, f. 05, op. 15, p. 103, d. 1, ll. 40–1.

78 Herriot, *Jadis*, 523, entry of 6 April 1935.

79 Excerpt from Sokolin's *dnevnik*, no. 193, very secret, 6 April 1935, AVPRF, f. 05, op. 15, p. 104, d. 3, ll. 326–8.

80 Ivan A. Divil'kovskii (Paris embassy) to Litvinov, very secret, 23h.00, 6 April 1935, enclosing the untitled, undated, unsigned document in French to which Titulescu's business card is attached, AVPRF, f. 05, op. 15, p. 104, d. 3, ll. 329–33. Divil'kovskii indicated that a summary had been sent by cable. The Russian translation is attached to E. E. Gershel'man (for Litvinov) to Stalin, cc. Molotov, Kaganovich, Voroshilov, Ordzhonikidze, no. 138/L, secret, 10 April 1935, AVPRF, f. 05, op. 15, p. 113, d. 122, ll. 163–6.

81 Potemkin to NKID, highest priority, 7 April 1935, *DVP*, XVIII, 266–7.

82 Litvinov to Stalin, no. 129/L, cc. Molotov, Voroshilov, Kaganovich, Ordzhonikidze, et al., secret, 7 April 1935, AVPRF, f. 05, op. 15, p. 113, d. 122, ll. 158–60.

83 "Declaration for Laval," not signed, 8 April 1935, AVPRF, f. 05, op. 15, p. 104, d. 3, ll. 163–6; and memorandum handed to Laval by Potemkin, 9 April 1935, *DVP*, XVIII, 274–7.

84 Excerpt from Politburo protocol no. 24, 9 April 1935, *Politbiuro TsK RKP(b) – VKP(b) i Evropa*, 322–3.
85 Litvinov to Potemkin, 10 April 1935, *DVP*, XVIII, 281.
86 Potemkin to NKID, highest priority, 10 April 1935, *DVP*, XVIII, 282–3.
87 Ibid.
88 Excerpt from Sokolin's *dnevnik*, no. 227, very secret, 10 April 1935, AVPRF, f. 05, op. 15, p. 104, d. 3, ll. 334–41.
89 Litvinov to NKID, cc. Stalin, Molotov, Voroshilov, *et al*, no. 6360, rigorously secret, highest priority, 13 April 1935, AVPRF, f. 059, op. 1, p. 190, d. 1408, ll. 52–3, RF, World War II, 1935.
90 Massigli to unknown addressee (*cher ami*), 15 April 1935, MAÉ, URSS/974, 26.
91 Litvinov to NKID, cc. Stalin, Molotov, Voroshilov, et al., no. 6570, rigorously secret, highest priority, 18 April 1935, AVPRF, f. 059, op. 1, p. 190, d. 1408, ll. 65–8, RF, World War II, 1935.
92 Excerpt from Politburo protocol no. 24, 19 April 1935, *Politbiuro TsK RKP(b) – VKP(b) i Evropa*, 323–4.
93 Herriot, *Jadis*, 530, entry of 19 April 1935.
94 Maurin to Laval, no. 485/2/SAE/ÉMA [Section des Armées étrangères, État-major de l'armée], 8 April 1935, and enclosure "Note sur l'appui qui pourrait éventuellement être demandé à L'URSS," SHAT 7N 3143.
95 "Note sur les avantages et les inconvénients de l'alliance russe," ÉMA, 2e Bureau, 24 April 1935, SHAT 7N 3143.
96 Potemkin to NKID, immediate, 20 April 1935, *DVP*, XVIII, 295–6.
97 Potemkin to NKID, highest priority, 20 April 1935, *DVP*, XVIII, 296–7.
98 Alphand, nos. 261–3, *réservé*, 22 April 1935, *DDF*, 1re, X, 384–5.
99 Potemkin to Krestinskii, no. 267, secret, 25 April 1935, AVPRF, f. 010, op. 10, p. 60, d. 148, ll. 122–8.
100 Excerpt from Politburo protocol no. 24, 20 April 1935, *Politbiuro TsK RKP(b) – VKP(b) i Evropa*, 325–6n1.
101 Litvinov to Stalin, cc. Molotov, Kaganovich, Voroshilov, Ordzhonokidze, no. 141/L, secret, urgent, 23 April 1935, AVPRF, f. 05, op. 15, p. 113, d. 122, ll. 168–70.
102 Noel Charles, British chargé d'affaires in Moscow, no. 60, 1 May 1935, C3579/55/18, TNA FO 371 18838.
103 Maurin to Laval, no. 485/2/SAE/ÉMA, [Section des Armées étrangères, État-major de l'armée], 8 April 1935, and enclosure "Note sur l'appui qui pourrait éventuellement être demandé à L'URSS," SHAT 7N 3143.
104 "For the negotiations with France," secret, 23 April 1935, AVPRF, f. 010, op. 10, p. 60, d. 148, ll. 106–9; and Litvinov to Surits, no. 147/L, secret, 4 May 1935, AVPRF, f. 082, op. 18, p. 80, d. 1, ll. 52–49.
105 Litvinov to Potemkin, no. 142/L, very secret, 23 April 1935, AVPRF, f. 05, op. 15, p. 104, d. 3, ll. 346–50.
106 Laval to Alphand, nos. 171–4, very urgent, *réservé*, 22 April 1935, *DDF*, 1re, X, 385–6.

107 Alphand, nos. 271–2, *réservé*, 24 April 1935, *DDF*, 1re, X, 394–5.
108 Clerk, no. 78 saving, 19 April 1935, C3328/55/18, TNA FO 371 18837.
109 "Eastern Pact," Sargent, 18 April 1935, C3333/55/18, TNA FO 371 18837; Simon to Clerk, no. 108, 18 April 1935, ibid.; Clerk, no. 78 saving, 19 April 1935, *DBFP*, 2nd, XIII, 191–2; Litvinov to Maiskii, 25 April 1935, *DVP*, XVIII, 299; Maiskii to NKID, 26 April 1935, ibid., 301–2; and Simon to Charles, British chargé d'affaires in Moscow, no. 227, 2 May 1935, C3251/55/18, TNA FO 371 18838.
110 Potemkin to NKID, highest priority, 27 April 1935, *DVP*, XVIII, 305.
111 Clerk, no. 80 saving, 25 April 1935, C3429/55/18, TNA FO 371 18837; and Clerk, no. 78 saving, 19 April 1935, *DBFP*, 2nd, XIII, 191–2.
112 Clerk, no. 80 Telegraphic, 27 April 1935, *DBFP*, 2nd, XIII, 212–14.
113 Duroselle, *Décadence*, 142.
114 Litvinov to Potemkin, no. 148/L, secret, 4 May 1935, AVPRF, f. 0136, op. 19, p. 164, d. 814, l. 106.
115 Litvinov to Maiskii, 29 April 1935, *DVP*, XVIII, 305–6.
116 Record of conversation with Vansittart, Maiskii, 1 May 1935, *DVP*, XVIII, 307–8; and Corbin, nos. 549–51, 2 May 1935, *DDF*, 1re, X, 452–3.
117 Corbin, nos. 573–7, 4 May 1935, *DDF*, 1re, X, 475–6.
118 Litvinov to Maiskii, no. 146/L, secret, 3 May 1935, AVPRF, f. 05, op. 15, p. 106, d. 16, ll. 5–6.
119 Sargent's minute, 4 May 1935, C3613/55/18, TNA FO 371 18838.
120 "The Proposed Eastern Pact," Sargent, 28 Jan. 1935, C962/55/18, TNA FO 371 18825.
121 Shtein (Geneva) to NKID, cc. Stalin, Molotov, Voroshilov, et al., no. 4497, very secret, highest priority, 12 April 1934, AVPRF, f. 059, op. 1, p. 168, d. 1273, ll. 7–8, RF, World War II, 1934.
122 Litvinov to Aleksandrovskii, no. 61/L, secret, 26 Feb. 1935, AVPRF, f. 05, op. 15, p. 104, d. 3, ll. 166–9.
123 M.J. Carley, *Revolution and Intervention: The French Government and the Russian Civil War, 1917–1919* (Montreal: McGill-Queen's University Press, 1983), chaps. 4, 11.
124 "Record of conversation with minister Beneš, 4.2.1935," Aleksandrovskii, no. 67/s, secret, AVPRF, f. 05, op. 15, p. 104, d. 3, ll. 140–4.
125 "Record of conversation with minister of foreign affairs Beneš, 6 February 1935," Aleksandrovskii, no. 65/s, secret, AVPRF, f. 05, op. 15, p. 104, d. 3, ll. 150–4.
126 "Record of conversation with minister of foreign affairs Beneš, 11 February 1935," Aleksandrovskii, no. 63/s, secret, AVPRF, f. 05, op. 15, p. 104, d. 3, ll. 156–62; and Litvinov to Aleksandrovskii, no. 93/L, secret, 17 March 1935, AVPRF, f. 05, op. 15, p. 111, d. 100, ll. 3–4.
127 Litvinov to Ostrovskii, no. 50/L, secret, 21 Feb. 1935, AVPRF, f. 05, op. 15, p. 109, d. 71, ll. 6–7.
128 "Conversation with Alphand," Rubinin, no. 16081/s, secret, 5 Feb. 1935, AVPRF, f. 016, op. 19, p. 164, d. 814, ll. 74–7.

129 "Record of conversation with Beneš," Aleksandrovskii, no. 151/s, 4 April 1935, AVPRF, f. 05, op. 15, p. 111, d. 101, ll. 32–8.
130 Aleksandrovskii to Litvinov, no. 114/s, secret, 8 March 1935, AVPRF, f. 05, op. 15, p. 111, d. 101, ll. 1–3.
131 "*Note du Directeur politique adjoint, Conversation avec M. Benès*," Massigli, Geneva, 18 April 1935, *DDF*, 1re, X, 361–2.
132 Litvinov (Geneva) to NKID, cc. Stalin, Molotov, Voroshilov, Kaganovich, et al., no. 6620, rigorously secret, highest priority, 19 April 1935, RGASPI, f. 17, op. 166, d. 543, ll. 39–40, RF, World War II, 1935.
133 "Record of conversation with Beneš, 2 & 3 May 1935," Aleksandrovskii, no. 191/s, secret, AVPRF, f. 05, op. 15, p. 111, d. 101, ll. 46–8.
134 Litvinov to Stalin, no. 144/L, secret, 3 May 1935, AVPRF, f. 05, op. 15, p. 113, d. 122, l. 184; and Litvinov to Potemkin, no. 148/L, secret, 4 May 1935, AVPRF, f. 0136, op. 19, p. 164, d. 814, l. 106.
135 Excerpt from Politburo protocol no. 25, 4 May 1935, *Politburo TsK RKP(b)-VKP(b) i Evropa*, 326. The draft resolution was in Litvinov's hand (RGASPI, f. 17, p. 166, d. 544, l. 77, RF, World War II, 1935).
136 Szembek, *Journal*, 70–2, entry of 10 May 1935.
137 Krestinskii to Maiskii, no. 1305, secret, 19 May 1935, AVPRF, f. 010, op. 10, p. 48, d. 7, ll. 66–7.
138 Potemkin to Litvinov, no. 355, secret, 26 June 1935, AVPRF, f. 010, op. 10, p. 60, d. 148, ll. 161–70.
139 TASS communiqué of 16 May 1935, *DVP*, XVIII, 336–8.
140 Maiskii, *Dnevnik*, I, 110–11, entry of 19 June 1935.
141 Szembek, *Journal*, 82–6, entries of 18 and 19 May 1935.

13 No Bridging the Gap: Erosion of the Anglo-Soviet Rapprochement, 1935

1 Vansittart's minutes, 17 May 1935, C3943/55/18, TNA FO 371 18840; 15 June 1935, C4564/55/18, TNA FO 371 18845; 5 July 1935, C5178/55/18, TNA FO 371 18847; and 9 Nov. 1935, C7647/55/18, TNA FO 371 18851.
2 "Discussion with Vansittart, 9 July 1935," no. 345/s, Maiskii, secret, AVPRF, f. 05, op. 15, p. 106, d. 17, ll. 157–61.
3 Maiskii, *Dnevnik*, I, 114–15, entry of 9 July 1935.
4 Maiskii to NKID, 17 July 1935, *DVP*, XVIII, 457–8.
5 "Discussion with Baldwin, 19 July 1935," no. 377/s, Maiskii, secret, 25 July 1935, AVPRF, f. 05, op. 15, p. 106, d. 17, ll. 162–9; and Maiskii's telegram, immediate, 20 July 1935, *DVP*, XVIII, 461–2.
6 Litvinov's *dnevnik*, "Meeting with Attolico, 5.VI.35g.," secret, AVPRF, f. 05, op. 15, p. 103, d. 1, ll. 68–70.
7 Litvinov to Maiskii, no. 232/L, secret, 4 July 1935, AVPRF, f. 05, op. 15, p. 106, d. 16, ll. 14–16.

8 Maiskii to Litvinov, no. 346/s, secret, 9 July 1935, AVPRF, f. 05, op. 15, p. 106, d. 17, ll. 155–6.

9 Litvinov (Geneva) to Stalin, no. 1417, secret, 3 Aug. 1935, AVPRF, f. 05, op. 15, p. 113, d. 123, ll. 59–60.

10 Stalin to Kaganovich and Molotov, no. 1642/sh, rigorously secret, 2 Sept. 1935, RGASPI, f. 558, op. 11, d. 98, ll. 1–2 (r/v), RF, World War II, 1935.

11 Kaganovich, Molotov, Voroshilov to Stalin, no. 46, 11 Sept. 1935; and Stalin to Kaganovich, Molotov, 11 Sept. 1935, *Stalin i Kaganovich, Perepiska*, 561–3.

12 Stalin to Kaganovich, Molotov, 12 Sept. 1935, *Stalin i Kaganovich, Perepiska*, 563–4.

13 Kaganovich, Molotov to Stalin, no. 71, 23 Sept. 1935, and Stalin's handwritten reply, 24 Sept. 1935, RGASPI, f. 558, op. 11, d. 90, ll. 59–60, RF, World War II, 1935.

14 Kaganovich, Molotov to Stalin, no. 80, 26 Sept. 1935, and Stalin's handwritten reply, 26 Sept. 1935, RGASPI, f. 558, op. 11, d. 90, ll. 81–3, RF, World War II, 1935.

15 Litvinov to Stalin, cc. Molotov, Kaganovich, no. 259, secret, 3 Oct. 1935, AVPRF, f. 05, op. 15, p. 113, d. 123, ll. 61–9.

16 Excerpts from Politburo protocols, nos. 34/31, 34, 84 & 142, rigorously secret, 4, 8 & 15 Oct. 1935, *Moskva-Rim: Politika i diplomatiia Kremlia, 1920–1939* (Moscow: Nauka, 2002), 373–4, 378.

17 Excerpt from Litvinov's *dnevnik*, "Record of conversation with the Italian ambassador Valentino, 5.X.35g.," secret, AVPRF, f. 05, op. 15, p. 103, d. 1, ll. 95–6.

18 Litvinov (Geneva) to NKID, cc. Stalin, Molotov, Voroshilov, Kaganovich, et al., no. 17900, rigorously secret, 15 Oct. 1935, AVPRF, f. 059, op. 1, p. 190, d. 1408, ll. 189–90, RF, World War II, 1935.

19 Kaganovich, Molotov to Stalin, no. 133, 15 Oct. 1935, RGASPI, f. 558, op. 11, d. 91, ll. 89–90, RF, World War II, 1935; and Stalin to Kaganovich, Molotov, no. 1928/sh, rigorously secret, 15 Oct. 1935, RGASPI, f. 558, op. 11, d. 91, l. 88, ibid.

20 Litvinov to Stalin cc. Molotov, Kaganovich, no. 274/L, secret, 26 Oct. 1935, AVPRF, f. 05, op. 15, p. 113, d. 123, ll. 84–8 (published in *Moskva-Rim*, 381–5).

21 "Theses from comrade Litvinov," 2 Nov. 1935, *Moskva-Rim*, 394.

22 Excerpt from Litvinov's *dnevnik*, "Meeting with the Italian ambassador Valentino, 28 November 1935," secret, AVPRF, f. 05, op. 15, p. 103, d. 1, ll. 102–3.

23 Excerpt from Litvinov's *dnevnik*, "Meeting with Valentino, 5.XII, 35g.," AVPRF, f. 05, op. 15, p. 103, d. 1, ll. 108–11.

24 Litvinov to Maiskii, no 289/L, secret, 4 Nov. 1935, AVPRF, f. 05, op. 15, p. 106, d. 16, ll. 35–7.

25 Rubinin to Krestinskii, no. 16560/s, secret, 23 Oct, 1935, AVPRF, f. 05, p. 106, d. 16, l. 34.

26 Maiskii, *Dnevnik*, I, 122–3, entry of 6 Nov. 1935; and "Discussion with Samuel Hoare, 6 November 1935," no. 508/s, Maiskii, secret, 10 Nov. 1935, AVPRF, f. 05, op. 15, p. 106, d. 17, ll. 177–82.

27 Maiskii to NKID, cc. Stalin, Molotov, Voroshilov, Kaganovich, et al., nos. 19236, 19243, rigorously secret, immediate, 6 Nov. 1935, AVPRF, f. 059, op. 1, p. 193, d. 1426, ll. 149–52, RF, World War II, 1935.

28 Sargent's minute, 30 Dec.1935, C8373/55/18, TNA FO 371 18852.

29 "Discussion with Vansittart, 8 November 1935," no. 514/s, Maiskii, secret, 10 Nov. 1935, AVPRF, f. 05, op. 15, p. 106, d. 17, ll. 173–5; Maiskii, *Dnevnik*, I, 125, entry of 14 Nov. 1935; and Vansittart's short, untitled note, 9 Nov. 1935, C7596/55/18, TNA FO 371 18851.

30 Maiskii to NKID, cc. Stalin, Molotov, Voroshilov, Kaganovich, et al., no. 19312, rigorously secret, immediate, 9 Nov. 1935, AVPRF, f. 059, op. 1, p. 193, d. 1426, ll. 154–5, RF, World War II, 1935; and Litvinov to Maiskii, no. 13959, rigorously secret, 11 Nov. 1935, AVPRF, f. 059, op. 1 p. 193, d. 1428, l. 128, ibid.

31 "Discussion with Vansittart, 18 November 1935," no. 529/s, Maiskii, secret, 25 Nov. 1935, AVPRF, f. 05, op. 15, p. 106, d. 17, ll. 198–204.

32 Memorandum by Vansittart, 18 Nov. 1935, N5966/17/38, TNA FO 371 19452.

33 "Discussion with Eden, 21 November 1935," no. 530/s, Maiskii, secret, 25 Nov. 1935, AVPRF, f. 05, op. 15, p. 106, d. 17, ll. 205–6.

34 Litvinov to Maiskii, no. 14431, rigorously secret, 23 Nov. 1935, AVPRF, f. 059, op. 1, p. 193, d. 1428, l. 146, RF, World War II, 1935.

35 Eden's note, 20 Nov. 1935, N5966/17/38, TNA FO 371 19452.

36 Minute by R.M.A. Hankey, Eden's private secretary, 26 Nov. 1935, N5566/1/38, TNA FO 371 19448.

37 Eden's note, 21 Nov. 1935, N6030/17/38, TNA FO 371 19452.

38 Maiskii to Litvinov, no. 539/s, secret, 25 Nov. 1935, AVPRF, f. 05, op. 15, p. 106, d. 17, ll. 190–7.

39 Minutes by Wigram, Sargent, and Vansittart, 25 Nov. 1935, C7823/55/18, TNA FO 371 18851.

40 "Discussion with Lord Beaverbrook, 1 December 1935," no. 553/s, Maiskii, secret, AVPRF, f. 05, op. 15, p. 106, d. 17, ll. 225–30; and Maiskii's telegram, immediate, 3 Dec. 1935, *DVP*, XVIII, 578–9.

41 "Discussion with Churchill, 6 December 1935," no. 554/s, Maiskii, secret, AVPRF, f. 05, op. 15, p. 106, d. 17, ll, 250–7; and Maiskii's telegram, 9 Dec. 1935, *DVP*, XVIII, 585–6.

42 RGVA, f. 33987, op. 3a, d. 630, ll. 192–9, RF, World War II, 1935.

43 James C. Robertson, "The Hoare-Laval Plan," *Journal of Contemporary History* 10, no. 3 (1975): 433–64.

44 Tabouis, *Cassandra*, 267–70.

45 Renaud Meltz, *Pierre Laval: Un mystère français* (Paris: Perrin, 2018), 470. See also Dullin, *Hommes d'influences*, 190–1; and Duroselle, *Décadence*, 150–2.

46 Litvinov to Shtein, no. 375/L, secret, 27 Dec. 1935, AVPRF, f.05, op. 15, p. 108, d. 47, ll. 32–3.

47 A.J.P. Taylor, *The Origins of the Second World War* (Middlesex: Penguin, 1964), 126, 128.

48 Litvinov to Stalin, cc. Molotov, Voroshilov, Kaganovich, Ordzhonikidze, no. 343/L, very secret, 11 Dec. 1935, AVPRF, f. 05, op. 15, p. 113, d. 123, l. 181.

49 Litvinov to Stalin, cc. Molotov, Voroshilov, Kaganovich, et al., no. 356/L, secret, 13 Dec. 1935, RGASPI, f. 17, op. 166, d. 554, l. 95, RF, World War II, 1935.

50 Litvinov to Maiskii, no. 367/L, secret, 19 Dec. 1935, AVPRF, f. 05, op. 15, p. 106, d. 16, ll. 48–50.

51 Maiskii to Litvinov, no. 577/s, secret, 24 Dec. 1935, AVPRF, f. 05, op. 15, p. 106, d. 17, ll. 236–47.

52 Record of conversation between Marshall, Becos Traders, and Leonard Browett, Board of Trade, by R. Kelf-Cohen, Board of Trade, 1 June 1934, N3506/16/38, TNA FO 371 18304; and Sir Frederick Leith-Ross, Treasury, to F. H. Nixon, Export Credit Guarantee Department, 1 Feb. 1935, TNA Treasury (hereinafter T) 160 791/F7438/10.

53 Vansittart's minute, 21 January 1935, N281/1/38, TNA FO 371 19447; and Simon to Neville Chamberlain, Chancellor of the Exchequer, 18 May 1935, ibid.

54 See various papers in N1883/1/38, 12 April 1935, & N2711/1/38, 28 May 1935, TNA FO 371 19447; Leith-Ross to Sir Horace Wilson, Treasury, and to Runciman, 9 May 1935, TNA T160 749/F14202/1; and Collier's minute, 27 June 1935, N3253/1/38, TNA FO 371 19448.

55 Memorandum by Ashton-Gwatkin, 4 July 1935, N3422/17/38, TNA FO 371 19451; Collier's minute, 29 July 1935, N3844/17/38, ibid.; "Note of Conversation on 29th July, 1935," Leith-Ross, N3870/17/38, ibid.; "Russia," Leith-Ross, 30 July 1935, ibid.; "Interview with Mr. Rosengolz, People's Commissar for Foreign Trade, on August 5th, 1935," Ashton-Gwatkin, N4113/17/38, ibid.; and "Russia," by Waley [?], n.d. [but early August 1935], TNA T160 749/F14202/1.

56 Krestinskii to Maiskii, no. 1089, very secret, 19 Feb. 1933, AVPRF, f. 05, op. 13, p. 91, d. 22, ll. 45–51.

57 Minute by Dodds, 31 July 1935, N3844/17/38, TNA FO 371 19451; and "Sir Frederick Phillips," by Waley, 30 July 1935, TNA T160 749/F14202/1.

58 Donald Fergusson, private secretary to the Chancellor of the Exchequer, to Waley, personal, 8 July 1935, TNA T160 749/F14202/1.

59 Minute by Sir Frederick Phillips, Treasury, 26 Nov. 1935 on "Russia," by Waley, 26 Nov. 1935, TNA T160 749/F14202/2.

60 Minutes by Vansittart, 31 July 1935; and Hoare, 4 Aug. 1935, N3844/17/38, TNA FO 371 19451.

61 Chilston, no. 352.E., 13 Aug. 1935, N4113/17/38, TNA FO 371 19451.

62 Dobbs's minutes, 3 Sept. 1935 and 21 Aug. 1935, C6091/55/18, TNA FO 371 18850; and Hoare's minute, 4 Sept. 1935, N3844/17/38, TNA FO 371 19451.

63 Collier's minutes, 10 & 25 Sept. 1935, N3870/17/38, TNA FO 371 19451; and 15 Oct. 1935, N5273/17/38, TNA FO 371 19452.

64 "Note of interview with Mr. Litvinoff at Geneva, September 1935," Ernest Remnant, 24 Oct. 1935, N5566/1/38, TNA FO 371 19448.
65 Record of conversation between Ashton-Gwatkin and Maiskii, 8 Nov. 1935, N5808/17/38, TNA FO 371 19452.
66 Krestinskii to Kaganovich, no. 1518, secret, 29 Sept. 1935, and enclosure from Maiskii, AVPRF, f. 010, op. 10, p. 48, d. 7, ll. 95–100; and Krestinskii to Maiskii, no. 1557, very secret, strictly personal, 19 Oct. 1935, ibid., l. 105.
67 Krestinskii to Litvinov (Geneva), very secret, 29 Nov. 1935, *SAO, 1934–1939*, 386–7.
68 Minutes by Sargent, 16 Nov. 1935; Vansittart, 18 Nov. 1935; Hoare, 20 Nov. 1935; and Eden, 21 Nov. 1935, N5566/1/38, TNA FO 371 19448.
69 "Secretary of State," Vansittart, 16 Oct. 1935; minutes by Stanhope, 18 Oct. 1935, and Hoare, 17 Oct. 1935, N5491/998/38, TNA FO 371 19467, and Hoare's minute, 18 Sept. 1935, and correspondence and other minutes, N4463/998/38, ibid.
70 "Proposed Broadcasts by the British Broadcasting Corporation …," C.P. 29 (36), secret, Eden, 7 Feb. 1936; Cabinet conclusions no. 6 (36), 12 Feb. 1936, and Cabinet conclusions no. 8 (36), 19 Feb. 1936, TNA FO 371 20344.
71 Collier to Hankey, 23 Nov. 1935, N5566/1/38, TNA FO 371 19448; and memorandum by Collier, 21 Oct. 1935, N5542/17/38, TNA FO 371 19452.
72 Memorandum by Collier, 7 Nov. 1935, N5743/17/38, TNA FO 371 19452; Collier to Waley & Leonard Browett, Board of Trade, very secret, 17 Dec. 1935, N6340/76/38 green, TNA FO 371 19460; cf. Carley, "Five Kopecks"; and Geoffrey Roberts, "A Soviet Bid for Coexistence with Nazi Germany, 1935–1937: The Kandelaki Affair," *International History Review* 16, no. 3 (1994): 466–90.
73 Nixon to Waley, enclosing untitled memorandum, 17 Oct. 1935, TNA T160 791/F7438/10; "Russia," Waley, 10 Oct. 1935, ibid.; memorandum by Hoare, 28 Nov. 1935, N6160/17/38, TNA FO 371 19452; and Hoare to Runciman, 4 Dec. 1935, ibid.
74 "Sir R. Hopkins [second secretary, Treasury]," Waley, 5 Dec. 1935, including Phillips's minute, n.d., TNA T160 749/F14202/2; and Chamberlain's minute, 25 Dec. 1935, on "Mr. Rowan, Russia," Waley, 25 Dec. 1935, ibid.
75 Minutes by Vansittart, 21 Dec. 1935, N6484/17/38; and Collier, 28 Dec. 1935, N6698/17/38, TNA FO 371 19452.
76 Vansittart to W.B. Brown, Board of Trade, 4 Jan. 1936, N6698/17/38, TNA FO 371 19452; and Collier to Waley, 23 Dec. 1935, N6484/17/38, ibid.
77 Chilston, no. 533, 6 Dec. 1935, N6304/135/38, TNA FO 371 19460; and parliamentary question, 18 Dec. 1935, N6601/17/38, TNA FO 371 19452.
78 William Manchester, *The Caged Lion: Winston Spencer Churchill, 1932–1940* (London: Cardinal, 1989), 164.
79 Maiskii to Eden, 23 Dec. 1935; and Eden to Maiskii, 24 Dec. 1935, N6698/17/38, TNA FO 371 19452.

14 The Weak Hinge: France and Its East European Allies, 1935–1936

1 Potemkin to Litvinov, no. 355, secret, 26 June 1935, AVPRF, f. 0136, op. 19, p. 164, d. 814, ll. 133–41; and "Conversation with Alphand," Rubinin, no. 16296/s, secret, 23 May 1935, ibid., ll. 54–6.
2 François Amé-Leroy, French minister in Oslo, no. 101, 21 May 1935, MAÉ URSS/977, 175–6.
3 Sargent's minute, 4 May 1935, C3613/55/18, TNA FO 371 18838.
4 Litvinov to Potemkin, no. 148/L, secret, 4 May 1935, AVPRF, f. 0136, op. 19, p. 164, d. 814, l. 106.
5 Note, *directeur politique*, Paul Bargeton, 19 March 1935, MAÉ URSS/973, 107–10; Note, *directeur politique*, 24 June 1935, MAÉ URSS/1004, 172–4.
6 Litvinov to Potemkin, no. 227/L, secret, 4 July 1935, AVPRF, f. 0136, op. 19, p. 164, d. 814, ll. 96–100.
7 Excerpt from Litvinov's journal, "Record of conversation with Laval on 2 August 1935," secret, AVPRF, f. 0136, op. 19, p. 164, d. 814, ll. 7–13.
8 Litvinov to Potemkin, no. 227/L, secret, 4 July 1935, AVPRF, f. 0136, op. 19, p. 164, d. 814, ll. 96–100.
9 Excerpt from Litvinov's *dnevnik*, "Meeting with Alphand, 7 May 1934," AVPRF, f. 0136, op. 19, p. 164, d. 814, ll. 27–8. This record of conversation is obviously misfiled; a published version can be found in *DVP*, XVII, 317–18.
10 Alphand, no. 174, 8 May 1934, *DDF*, 1re, VI, pp. 435–7.
11 Litvinov to Davtian, no. 52/L, secret, 21 Feb. 1935, AVPRF, f. 05, op. 15, p. 109, d. 67, ll. 9–10.
12 Ibid.
13 Stomoniakov to Davtian, no. 2186, secret, 3 June 1935, AVPRF, f. 05, op. 15, p. 109, d. 67, ll. 15–17.
14 Davtian to Stomoniakov, no. 296/s, very secret, 11 June 1935, AVPRF, f. 05, op. 15, p. 109, d. 68, ll. 106–11.
15 Excerpt from Stomoniakov's *dnevnik*, "Meeting with the Polish ambassador, 2 July 1935," no. 2272, secret, AVPRF, f. 05, op. 15, p. 109, d. 67, ll. 25–7.
16 Stomoniakov to Davtian, no. 2276, secret, 4 July 1935, AVPRF, f. 05, op. 15, p. 109, d. 67, ll. 28–30.
17 Excerpt from Davtian's *dnevnik*, "Conversation with the French ambassador Noël, 6 July 1935," no. 346/s, secret, *SPO*, III, 341–2.
18 Davtian to Stomoniakov, no. 344/s, very secret, 8 July 1935, AVPRF, f. 05, op. 15, p. 109, d. 68, ll. 131–3.
19 Davtian to Litvinov, no. 348, very secret, personal, 12 July 1935, *SPO*, III, 343–6.
20 Stomoniakov to Podol'skii (Warsaw), no. 2369, secret, 4 Aug. 1935, *SPO*, III, 348–9.
21 Stomoniakov to Davtian, no. 2500, secret, 19 Sept. 1935, *SPO*, III, 355–7.
22 Stomoniakov to Davtian, no. 2553, secret, 7 Oct. 1935, *SPO*, III, 360–2.

23 INO GUGB NKVD, agent's report from Bucharest, "closely tied to the Polish ministry of foreign affairs, not later than 3 May 1935," RGASPI, f. 558, op. 11, d. 188, ll. 93–4, RF, World War II, 1935.
24 Excerpt from Boris D. Vinogradov (Soviet first secretary in Bucharest), "Conversation of the King with the Polish envoy Arciszewski," no. 222, very secret, 18 Oct. 1935, AVPRF, f. 0125, op. 17, p. 111, d. 1, ll. 221–15.
25 Ostrovskii to Krestinskii, no. 224, very secret, 26 Oct. 1935, AVPRF, f. 05, op. 15, p. 109, d. 72, ll. 106–15.
26 G.N. Shmidt, NKID clerk, to Davtian, no. 2562, very secret, 10 Oct. 1935, *SPO*, III, 363.
27 Shmidt to Davtian, no. 2672, very secret, 19 Nov. 1935, *SPO*, III, 376–8.
28 Excerpt from Davtian's *dnevnik*, "Conversation with the Czechoslovak chargé d'affaires [Jaromir] Smutný, 5 November 1935," no. 543/s, secret, *SPO*, III, 370–1.
29 Litvinov to Surits, no. 303/L, secret, 17 Nov. 1935, *SPO*, III, 374–5.
30 Ostrovskii to Litvinov, no. 240, secret, 20 Nov. 1935, AVPRF, f. 05, op. 15, p. 109, d. 72, ll. 141–3.
31 Excerpt from Davtian's *dnevnik*, "Conversation with de Monzie, 25 November 1935," no. 572, secret, *SPO*, III, 379–81.
32 Excerpt from Davtian's *dnevnik*, "Conversation with de Monzie, 28 November 1935," no. 595, secret, AVPRF, f. 05, op. 15, p. 109, d. 68, ll. 231–4 (published in *SPO*, III, 382–4).
33 Excerpt from Litvinov's *dnevnik*, Meeting with [Dimiter] Mikhal'chev," 28 June 1935, AVPRF, f. 05, op. 15, p. 103, d. 1, ll. 78–9.
34 "Compte rendu du général Loizeau, Impressions retirées du séjour aux manœuvres de l'URSS," secret, 6 Oct. 1935, *DDF*, 1re, XII, 510–25.
35 Excerpt from Krestinskii's *dnevnik*, "Meeting with Alphand, 22 Oct. 1935," AVPRF, f. 0136, op. 19, p. 164, d. 814, ll. 4–6.
36 Kaganovich, Molotov to Stalin, 21 Oct. 1935, *Stalin i Kaganovich, Perepiska*, 607–8.
37 Litvinov to Potemkin, no. 288/L, secret, 4 Nov. 1935, AVPRF, f. 010, op. 10, p. 60, d. 148, ll. 210–11.
38 Stalin to Kaganovich, Molotov, no. 71, 26 Sept. 1935, *Stalin i Kaganovich, Perepiska*, 587.
39 Jean de Hautecloque, French chargé d'affaires in Bucharest, no. 161, 10 June 1935, *DDF*, 1re, XI, 55–6.
40 Kaganovich, Molotov to Stalin, 22 Sept. 1935, *Stalin i Kaganovich, Perepiska*, 579.
41 Litvinov to Ostrovskii, no. 290/L, secret, 10 Nov. 1935, AVPRF, f. 05, op. 17, p. 134, d. 86, ll. 1–4 (published in *SRO*, II, 30–3).
42 *Mieux valait permettre que subir* (André Lefèvre d'Ormesson, no. 407, 24 Oct. 1935, *DDF* 1re, XIII, 129–31); and Foreign Ministry circular, Köpke, Berlin, 30 Oct. 1935, *DGFP*, C, IV, 780–2.

43 Litvinov to Ostrovskii, no. 290/L, secret, 10 Nov. 1935, AVPRF, f. 05, op. 17, p. 134, d. 86, ll. 1–4 (published in *SRO*, II, 30–3).
44 Ostrovskii, no. 230, secret, 10 Nov. 1935, AVPRF, f. 05, op. 15, p. 109, d. 72, ll. 127–32 (published in *SRO*, II, 26–30).
45 Litvinov to Ostrovskii, no. 290/L, secret, 10 Nov. 1935, AVPRF, f. 05, op. 17, p. 134, d. 86, ll. 1–4 (published in *SRO*, II, 30–3).
46 Litvinov to Ostrovskii, 16 Nov. 1935, *DVP*, XVIII, 557.
47 Ostrovskii to Litvinov, no. 233, very secret, 19 Nov. 1935, AVPRF, f. 0125, op. 17, p. 111, d. 1, 262–257 (published in *SRO*, II, 34–8).
48 Circular of the Foreign Ministry, Berlin, Köpke, 7 Nov. 1935, *DGFP*, C, IV, 801–3.
49 Excerpt from Ostrovskii's *dnevnik*, "Record of conversation with Titulescu, 23 November 1935," no. 254, very secret, 1 Dec. 1935, AVPRF, f. 05, op. 15, p. 109, d. 72, ll. 161–6 (published *SRO*, II, 39–44).
50 Litvinov to Aleksandrovskii, no. 272/L, secret, 16 Oct. 1935, AVPRF, f. 05, op. 15, p. 111, d. 100, ll. 8–10.
51 Litvinov to Aleksandrovskii, no. 291/L, secret, 11 Nov. 1935, AVPRF, f. 05, op. 15, p. 111, d. 100, l. 11.
52 Litvinov to Aleksandrovskii, no. 314/L, secret, 25 Nov. 1935, AVPRF, f. 05, op. 15, p. 111, d. 100, ll. 12–13; and Litvinov to Aleksandrovskii, no. 372/L, secret, 26 Dec. 1935, ibid., l. 14.
53 Potemkin to Krestinskii, no. 489, secret, 11 Nov. 1935, AVPRF, f. 010, op. 10, p. 60, d. 148, ll. 212–15.
54 Ostrovskii to Litvinov, no. 233, very secret, 19 Nov. 1935, AVPRF, f. 0125, op. 17, p. 111, d. 1, 262–257 (published in *SRO*, II, 34–8).
55 Excerpt from Vinogradov's *dnevnik*, "Meeting with Colonel Kowalewski …," no. 238, very secret, 20 Nov. 1935, AVPRF, f. 05, op. 15, p. 109, d. 72, ll. 144–8.
56 Excerpt from Vinogradov's *dnevnik*, no. 262, secret, 30 Nov. 1935, AVPRF, f. 05, op. 15, p. 109, d. 72, ll. 150–1.
57 Vinogradov to Litvinov, no. 284/s, very secret, 24 Dec. 1935, AVPRF, f. 05, op. 16, p. 121, d. 97, l. 29.
58 Roland Köster, German ambassador in Paris, no. 1161, 18 Nov. 1935, *DGFP*, C, IV, 825–9.
59 Köpke's memorandum, 28 Nov. 1935, *DGFP*. C, IV, 849–51.
60 Potemkin to Krestinskii, no. 5346, secret, 26 Nov. 1935, AVPRF, f. 0136, op. 19, p. 164, d. 814, ll. 119–22.
61 Memorandum by Neurath [German foreign minister], 25 June 1935, *DGFP*, C, IV, 255–6; Köster to German foreign ministry, no. 1188, 27 Nov. 1935, ibid., 859–62; and Köster to German foreign ministry, no. 1223, 18 Dec. 1935, ibid., 925–6.
62 Köster to German foreign ministry, no. 827, 27 July 1935, *DGFP*, C, IV, 493–6.
63 Excerpt from Litvinov's *denvnik*, "Meeting with Alphand, secret, 29 Nov. 1935," AVPRF, f. 0136, op. 19, d. 814, p. 164, ll. 2–3.

64 Potemkin to Litvinov, highest priority, 22 Nov. 1935, *DVP*, XVIII, 562–4; Potemkin to Litvinov, immediate, 27 Nov. 1935, ibid., 567–8; Litvinov to Potemkin, 4 Nov. 1935, ibid., 667; and Litvinov to Maiskii, no. 289/L, secret, 4 Nov. 1935, AVPRF, f. 05, op. 15, d. 16, p. 106, ll. 35–7 .
65 Litvinov to Potemkin, no. 341/L, secret, 26 Nov. 1935, AVPRF, f. 010, op. 10, p. 60, d. 148, ll. 223–4.
66 "Mme Félix Decori, Navachine, Dimitri …," P/5047, Préfecture de police, 11 Aug. 1923, AN F7 12952; and Anne Martin-Fugier, *La bourgeoise* (Paris: Grasset, 1983).
67 Carley, "Five Kopeks," 46–7.
68 Potemkin to Litvinov, no. 527, secret, 11 Dec. 1935, AVPRF, f. 010, op. 10, p. 60, d. 148, ll. 225–31.
69 Litvinov to Potemkin, no. 366/L, secret, 19 Dec. 1935, AVPRF, f. 010, op. 10, p. 60, d. 148, ll. 233–4.
70 "Conversation of the ambassador with Alphand," no. 13, secret, Potemkin, 10 Jan. 1936, AVPRF, f. 0136, op. 20, d. 828, p. 167, ll. 18–11.
71 Excerpt from Neiman's *dnevnik*, "Record of conversation with the counsellor of the French embassy Payart," secret, 21 Dec. 1935, AVPRF, f. 0136, op. 19, p. 164, d. 814, ll. 29–31.
72 "Conversation with Mandel [on 27 Dec. 1935]," secret, Potemkin, 10 Jan. 1936, AVPRF, f. 0136, op. 20, p. 167, d. 828, ll. 4–3.
73 Litvinov to Potemkin, no. 3507/L, secret, 3 Jan. 1936, AVPRF, f. 05, op. 16, p. 123, d. 119, ll. 1–2.
74 Potemkin to Litvinov, no. 34, secret, 11 Jan. 1936, AVPRF, f. 05, op. 16, p. 123, d. 120, ll. 1–5.
75 Ibid.
76 Alphand to Laval, no. 275, 2 July 1935, MAÉ URSS/1059, 122–5.
77 Carley, "Five Kopeks," 47.
78 Potemkin to Litvinov, no. 34, secret, 11 Jan. 1936, AVPRF, f. 05, op. 16, p. 123, d. 120, ll. 1–5.
79 Ibid.
80 Litvinov to Potemkin, 13 Jan. 1936, *DVP*, XIX, 26–7.
81 Record of conversation with Alphand, Litvinov, 14 Jan. 1936, *DVP*, XIX, 27–8.
82 Alphand to Laval, nos. 15–16, 14 Jan. 1936, *DDF*, 2[e], I, 69.
83 Litvinov to Stalin, no. 3517/L, secret, 13 Jan. 1936, AVPRF, f. 05, op. 16, p. 114, d. 1, ll. 9–13.
84 Litvinov to Stalin, no. 3556/L, secret, 22 Feb. 1936, AVPRF, f. 05, op. 16, p. 114, d. 1, ll. 61–5.
85 Excerpt from Potemkin's *dnevnik*, "Conversation with Laval," no. 48, secret, 25 Jan. 1936, AVPRF, f. 0136, op. 20, p. 167, d. 828, ll. 27–19.
86 Potemkin to Litvinov, no. 36, personal, secret, 18 Jan. 1936, AVPRF, f. 05, op. 16, p. 123, d. 120, ll. 34–8, and "Conversation with the minister of post and telegraph Mandel [on 17 January]," no. 51, secret, 25 Jan. 1936, ibid., ll. 44–55.

87 Potemkin to Litvinov, unnumbered, personal letter, 20 Jan. 1936, AVPRF, f. 05, op. 16, p. 123, d. 120, ll. 42–3.

15 Collapse in London: The Failure of the Anglo-Soviet Rapprochement, 1936

1 Rose, *Vansittart*, 271.

2 Kenneth Young, ed., *The Diaries of Sir Robert Bruce Lockhart, 1915–1946*, vol. 1 (London: Macmillan, 1973), 329.

3 Manchester, *Caged Lion*, 166.

4 Collier's minute, 19 Dec. 1935, N6255/7/38, TNA FO 371 19450; minutes by Sargent, 17 Jan. 1936, and Vansittart, 17 Jan. 1936, N6642/76/38, TNA FO 371 19460; and Sargent to Vansittart, 17 Jan. 1936, ibid.

5 "Discussion with Eden, 6 January 1936," no. 8, Maiskii, secret, AVPRF, f. 05, op. 16, p. 117, d. 23, ll. 7–10; Maiskii's telegram, immediate, 6 Jan. 1936, *DVP*, XIX, 13–14; and Eden to Chilston, no. 11, 6 Jan. 1936, N120/20/38, TNA FO 371 20338.

6 Vansittart's minute, 7 Jan. 1936, N120/20/38, TNA FO 371 20338; and memorandum by Collier, 7 Jan. 1936 N125/20/38, ibid.

7 Sargent to Vansittart, 9 Jan. 1936, N425/20/38, TNA FO 371 20338.

8 Collier's minute, 25 Nov. 1936, N5715/187/38, TNA FO 371 20347.

9 Eden's minutes, 15 Jan. 1936 & 10 Jan. 1936, N479/20/38, TNA FO 371 20338.

10 Minutes by Stanhope and Cranborne, 14 Jan. 1936, TNA FO 371 20338.

11 Vansittart's minutes, 9 & 15 Jan. 1936, TNA FO 371 20338.

12 Memorandum by Collier, 23 Jan. 1936, N425/20/38, TNA FO 371 20338.

13 Stanhope's minutes, n.d. & 14 Jan. 1936, N425/20/38, TNA FO 371 20338.

14 "Discussion with Vansittart, 9 January 1936," no. 34/s, Maiskii, secret, AVPRF, f. 05, op. 16, p. 117, d. 23, ll. 27–30.

15 "Discussion with Austin Chamberlain, 22 January 1936," no. 38/s, Maiskii, secret, AVPRF, f. 05, op. 16, p. 117, d. 23, ll. 19–26.

16 Maiskii, *Dnevnik*, I, 137–8, entry of 30 Jan. 1936.

17 Eden to Chilston, no. 56, 30 Jan. 1936, N622/20/38, PRO FO 371 20339; and Litvinov (Paris) to NKID, immediate, 31 Jan. 1936, *DVP*, XIX, 57.

18 Colin A. Edmond, British consul, Geneva, from Eden, no. 8 LN, 21 Jan. 1936, C452/92/62, TNA FO 371 19879; and minutes by Sargent, 23 Jan. 1936, and Collier, 29 Jan. 1936, ibid.

19 Vansittart's minute, 1 Feb. 1936, N515/187/38, TNA FO 371 20346.

20 "Notes of meeting held in the Secretary of State's room at the Foreign Office on February 3rd, 1936 …," C979/4/18, TNA FO 371 19885; minutes by Wigram, 4 Feb. 1936, and Eden, 10 Feb. 1936, C835/4/18, TNA FO 371 19884; and Phipps, no. 29 saving, 15 Feb. 1936, & minutes, N923/187/38, TNA FO 371 20346.

21 Collier to Chilston, secret, 5 Feb. 1936, N803/20/38, TNA FO 371 20339; and minutes by Collier, 10 Feb. 1936 & Sargent, 21 Feb. 1936, N756/187/38, TNA FO 371 20346; and Collier to Oliphant, 24 Feb. 1936, ibid.

22 "Record of a conversation … with … [Duff] Cooper," Maiskii, 5 Feb. 1936, *DVP*, XIX, 62–4; "Discussion with Eden, 11 February 1936," no. 73/s, Maiskii, secret, AVPRF, f. 05, op. 16, p. 117, d. 23, ll. 52–9 (published in *DVP*, XIX, 73–80); and Eden to Chilston, no. 76, 11 Feb. 1936, N833/20/38, TNA FO 371 20339.

23 "Record of a conversation … with … Collier," Maiskii, 13 Feb. 1936, *DVP*, XIX, 86–8; Maiskii, *Dnevnik*, I, 138–9, entry of 10 Feb. 1936; Collier's minute, 14 Feb. 1936, N833/20/38, TNA FO 371 20339; and Collier to Browett, Board of Trade, 14 Feb. 1936, N856/20/38, ibid.

24 Sargent's minute, 2 Jan. 1936, C1/1/17, TNA FO 371 19855.

25 Minutes by Eden, 29 March 1936, N1840/1298/38, TNA FO 371 20352 and Sargent, 2 March 1936, C1081/4/18, TNA FO 371 19886; report by Colonel E.O. Skaife, British military attaché in Moscow, 20 Jan. 1936, 26pp., N752/287/38, TNA FO 371 20348; and Keith Neilson, " Pursued by a Bear: British Estimates of Soviet Military Strength and Anglo-Soviet Relations, 1922–1939," *Canadian Journal of History* 28, no. 2 (1993): 210–12.

26 Sargent's minute, 2 March 1936, C1081/4/18, TNA FO 371 19886.

27 "S. of S.," Sargent, 19 Feb. 1936, N833/20/38, TNA FO 371 20339.

28 Minutes by Sargent & Vansittart, 1 Feb. 1936 and Eden, 3 Feb. 1936, C573/92/62, TNA FO 371 19879; and Oliphant's minute, 20 Feb. 1936, N833/20/38, TNA FO 371 20339.

29 Chilston, no. 96, 10 Feb. 1936, N880/20/38, TNA FO 371 20339; and minutes by Collier, 19 Feb. 1936 & Eden, 28 Feb. 1936, ibid.

30 Eden to Phipps, private, 28 Feb. 1936, N1693/20/38, TNA FO 371 20339.

31 "Soviet Union, Annual Report, 1935," Chilston, 31 Jan. 1936, N871/871/38, TNA FO 371 20352.

32 Maiskii to Litvinov, no. 42/s, secret, 10 Feb. 1936, AVPRF, f. 05, op. 16, p. 117, d. 23, ll. 89–93.

33 Ibid.

34 Oliphant's minute, 19 Feb. 1936, N880/20/38, TNA FO 371 20339.

35 Maiskii to Litvinov, no. 47/s, secret, 16 Feb. 1936, AVPRF, f. 05, op. 16, p. 117, d. 23, ll. 37–40.

36 Maiskii to NKID, 8 March 1936, *DVP*, XIX, 128–9; Litvinov to Maiskii, 9 March 1936, ibid., 130; Maiskii to Litvinov, 10 March 1936, ibid., 134; and Cranborne's untitled record of conversation with Maiskii, 10 March 1936, C1716/4/18, TNA FO 371 19890.

37 Harold Nicolson, *Dairies and Letters, 1930–1939* (New York: Altheneum, 1966), 248–54.

38 "Discussion with the President of the Board of Trade, Runciman, 2 April 1936," no. 118/s, Maiskii, secret, AVPRF, f. 05, op. 16, p. 117, d. 23, ll. 112–16 (published in *DVP*, XIX, 207–11).

39 Martin Gilbert, *Prophet of Truth: Winston S. Churchill, 1922–1939* (London: Minerva, 1990), 723.

40 "Discussion with Churchill, 3 April 1936," no. 119/s, Maiskii, secret, AVPRF, f. 05, op. 16, p. 117, d. 23, ll. 117–23 (published in *DVP*, XIX, 211–17); and Maiskii to NKID, cc. Stalin, et al., no. 6041, rigorously secret, immediate, 3 April 1936, AVPRF, f. 059, op. 1, p. 220, d. 1582, ll. 165–6, RF, World War II, 1936.
41 Litvinov to Maiskii, no. 3596/L, secret, 19 April 1936, AVPRF, f. 05, op. 16, p. 117, d. 26, ll. 1–3.
42 Maiskii to Litvinov, no. 122/s, secret, 7 April 1936, AVPRF, f. 05, op. 16, p. 117, d. 23, ll. 102–11.
43 Litvinov to Maiskii, no. 3596/L, secret, 19 April 1936, AVPRF, f. 05, op. 16, p. 117, d. 26, ll. 1–3.
44 Maiskii to Litvinov, dispatch not numbered, personal, secret, 24 April 1936, AVPRF, f. 05, op. 16, p. 117, d. 23, ll. 130–3.
45 Litvinov to Maiskii, no. 3614/L, secret, 4 May 1936, AVPRF, f. 05, op. 16, p. 117, d. 26, ll. 4–6.
46 Litvinov to Maiskii, no. 25444, immediate, rigorously secret, 25 April 1936, AVPRF, f. 059, op. 1, p. 221, d. 1586, l. 148, RF, World War II, 1936; "Discussion with Eden [28 April1936]," no. 154/s, Maiskii, secret, 9 May 1936, AVPRF, f. 05, op. 16, p. 117, d. 23, ll. 141–8; Maiskii's telegram, immediate, 28 April 1936, *DVP*, XIX, 248–50; and Eden to D. MacKillop, British chargé d'affaires in Moscow, no. 247, 28 April 1936, C3231/4/18, TNA FO 371 19904.
47 "Record of a conversation … with … Vansittart," Maiskii, 13 May 1936, *DVP*, XIX, 264–6; and, e.g., minutes by Vansittart, 26 March 1936, C2390/4/18, TNA FO 371 19898; 15 April 1936, C2487/4/18, ibid.; and 17 May 1936, C3677/4/18, TNA FO 371 19905.
48 Collier's minutes, 29 May 1936, N2828/307/38, TNA FO 371 20349 & 11 July 1936, N3215/20/38, TNA FO 371 20340.
49 Minutes by Collier, 13 May 1936; Vansittart, 18 May 1936; and Eden, 21 May 1936, N2514/16/38, TNA FO 371 20338.
50 Maiskii to Litvinov, no. 149/s secret, 9 May 1936, AVPRF, f. 05, op. 16, p. 117, d. 23, ll. 151–5.
51 Chilston, no. 637, 20 Nov. 1936, N5715/187/36, TNA FO 371 20347; and Collier's minute, 19 Feb. 1936, N911/187/38, TNA FO 371 20346.
52 Minutes by G.P. Labouchere, 24 Nov. 1936; Collier, 25 Nov. 1936; and Vansittart, 28 Nov. 1936, N5722/307/38, TNA FO 371 20349.
53 Gaines Post Jr., *Dilemmas of Appeasement: British Deterrence and Defense, 1934–1937* (Ithaca, NY: Cornell University Press, 1993), 255.
54 Nicolson, *Diaries*, 273, quoting Tory M.P. Henry Channon; Richard Lamb, *The Drift to War, 1922–1939* (London: Bloomsbury, 1991), 192; Post, *Dilemmas*, 106–7; and Maurice Cowling, *The Impact of Hitler: British Politics and British Policy, 1933–1940* (London: Cambridge University Press, 1975), 147.
55 Sargent's minute, 15 Oct. 1936, C7262/92/62, TNA FO 371 19880.

56 See, e.g., Lord Halifax, Foreign Secretary, to Sir M. Peterson, British representative in Spain, no. 800, 5 Oct. 1939, C15821/15/18, TNA FO 371 22985; "First Month of the War," Leeper, 4 Oct. 1939, C16151/15/18, ibid.; untitled memorandum, secret, FO, 19 Oct. 1939, C16324/15/18, ibid.; and Sargent's minutes, 11 Oct. 1939, C16573/15/18, ibid.

57 Gladwyn Jebb's minute, 16 March 1936, C1558/4/18, TNA FO 371 19888.

16 Good News, Bad News: The Fall of Laval and the Abdication of France, 1936

1 Alphand, nos. 36–40, 25 Jan. 1936, MAÉ, *Bureau du chiffre, télégrammes, à l'arrivée de Moscou, 1936.*

2 Litvinov (Paris) to NKID, immediate, 31 Jan. 1936, *DVP*, XIX, 57; and Eden to Chilston, no. 56, 30 Jan. 1936, N622/20/38, TNA FO 371 20339.

3 Excerpt from Potemkin's *dnevnik*, "Conversation with Léger [on 29 January]," no. 68, secret, 11 Feb. 1936, AVPRF, f. 05, op. 16, p. 123, d. 120, ll. 68–71.

4 Ibid.

5 Litvinov (Paris) to NKID, immediate, 1 Feb. 1936, *DVP*, XIX, 58.

6 "The narkom's conversation with Léger [on 1 February]," no. 66, secret, 11 Feb. 1936, AVPRF, f. 05, op. 16, p. 123, d. 120, ll. 52–6.

7 "Notes sur les conversations de Paris (30 janvier-8 février 1936)," secret, *DDF*, 2e, I, 221–7.

8 "The narkom's conversation with Flandin [on 2 February]," no. 67, secret, 11 Feb. 1936, AVPRF, f. 05, op. 16, p. 123, d. 120, ll. 57–63.

9 "Notes sur les conversations de Paris (30 janvier-8 février 1936)," secret, *DDF*, 2e, I, 221–7.

10 Noël to Flandin, no. 94, *confidentiel, réservé*, 2 Feb. 1936, *DDF*, 2e, I, 179–80.

11 Alphand, no. 55, 8 Feb. 1936, *DDF*, 2e, I, 216.

12 Excerpt from Potemkin's *dnevnik*, "Conversation with Bastid," no. 71, secret, 11 Feb. 1936, AVPRF, f. 05, op. 16, p. 123, d. 120, ll. 72–3.

13 Excerpt from Potemkin's *dnevnik*, "Conversation with Flandin [on 8 February]," no. 73, secret, 11 Feb. 1936, AVPRF, f. 05, op. 16, p. 123, d. 120, ll. 74–7.

14 Corbin, no. 104, 10 Feb. 1936, *DDF*, 2e, I, 136–40.

15 Excerpt from Potemkin's *dnevnik*, "Conversation with Paul-Boncour [on 10 February]," no. 74, secret, 11 Feb. 1936, AVPRF, f. 05, op. 16, p. 123, d. 120, ll. 78–9.

16 *Journal officiel de la République française. Débats parlementaires, Chambre des députés*, 12 & 13, 18 Feb. 1936.

17 Litvinov to Stalin, no. 3533/L, secret, 13 Feb. 1936, AVPRF, f. 16, p. 114, d. 1, ll. 30–2.

18 "The Franco-Soviet Accord and French Reactionaries," *Pravda*, 15 Feb. 1936.

19 Alphand, no. 71, 17 Feb. 1936, MAÉ, *Bureau du chiffre, télégrammes, à l'arrivée de Moscou, 1936.*

20 Excerpt from Potemkin's *dnevnik*, "Conversation with the *député* Torrès [on 17 February in his office]," secret, 26 March 1936, AVPRF, f. 0136, op. 20, p. 167, d. 828, ll. 78–76.
21 *Journal officiel de la République française. Débats parlementaires, Chambre des députés*, 20 Feb. 1936.
22 Litvinov to Stalin, cc. Molotov, no. 3543/L, secret, 19 Feb. 1936, AVPRF, f. 16, p. 114, d. 1, l. 42.
23 Litvinov to Stalin, cc. Molotov, Voroshilov, Ordzhonikidze, no. 3547/L, secret, 22 Feb. 1936, AVPRF, f. 16, p. 114, d. 1, ll. 43–4; and Litvinov to Potemkin, 23 Feb. 1936, *DVP*, XIX, 98–9.
24 Potemkin to Litvinov, 24 Feb. 1936, *DVP*, XIX, 99.
25 Potemkin to NKID, high priority, 26 Feb. 1936, *DVP*, XIX, 102–3.
26 *Journal officiel de la République française. Débats parlementaires, Chambre des députés*, 25 & 27 Feb. 1936.
27 Alphand, nos. 91–2, 28 Feb. 1936, *Bureau du chiffre, télégrammes, à l'arrivée de Moscou, 1936.*
28 Potemkin to Krestinskii, no. 105, secret, 27 Feb. 1936, AVPRF, f. 05, op. 16, p. 123, d. 120, ll. 88–96.
29 Litvinov to Potemkin, no. 3566/L, secret, 4 March 1936, AVPRF, f. 05, op. 16, p. 123, d. 119, ll. 4–5.
30 Bullitt to Hull, 7 March 1936, *Foreign Relations of the United States*, 1936, I, 212–13.
31 Alphand, nos. 113–17, 8 March 1936, *DDF*, 2[e], I, 438–9.
32 Maiskii, nos. 4384, 4388, 4391, cc. Stalin, et al., rigorously secret, immediate/highest priority, 8 March 1936, AVPRF, f. 059, op. 1, p. 220, d. 1582, ll. 105–8, RF, World War II, 1936.
33 Litvinov to Maiskii, cc. Molotov, et al., no. 3159, rigorously secret, 9 March 1936, AVPRF, f. 059, op. 1, p. 221, d. 1586, l. 73, RF, World War II, 1936.
34 Excerpt from Potemkin's *dnevnik*, "Conversation with Flandin [on 9 March]," no. 115, secret, 12 March 1936, AVPRF, f. 05, op. 16, p. 123, d. 120, ll. 109–13.
35 Litvinov (London) to NKID, immediate, 13 March 1936, *DVP*, XIX, 137–8.
36 Litvinov (London) to NKID, high priority, 14 March 1936, *DVP*, XIX, 142–3.
37 Litvinov (London) to NKID, immediate, 18 March 1936, *DVP*, XIX, 162.
38 Vansittart to Sir George R. Clerk, British ambassador in Paris, no. 73, by telephone, immediate, 18? March 1936, C2026/4/18, TNA FO 371 19894.
39 Memorandum by Vansittart, "Seen by S. of S.," 14 March 1936, C1858/4/18, TNA FO 371 19891.
40 Clerk, no. 145, 17 March 1936, C1989/4/18, TNA FO 371 19893.
41 Untitled memorandum by Eden, 24 March 1936, C2338/4/18, TNA FO 371 19897.
42 Wigram's minute, 18 March 1936, C1989/4/18, TNA FO 371 19893.
43 Untitled memorandum by Sargent, 16 March 1936, C2134/4/18, TNA FO 371 19895.

44 Sargent's minute, 19 March 1936, C2048/4/18, TNA FO 371 19894.
45 See, for example, Keith Neilson, "Orme Sargent, Appeasement and British Policy in Europe, 1933–39," *Twentieth Century British History* 21, no. 1 (2010): 1–28.
46 "Record of Conversation between the French Ambassador and Sir R. Vansittart," Vansittart, 13 March 1936, C1833/4/18, TNA FO 371 19891.
47 Colonel Frederic Beaumont-Nesbitt, British military attaché in Paris, to Clerk, no. 12, 20 March 1936; and Vansittart's minute, 30 March 1936, C2203/4/18, TNA FO 371 19896.
48 Excerpt from Potemkin's *dnevnik*, "Conversation with Laval [on 15 March]," no. 122, secret, 26 March 1936, AVPRF, f. 05, op. 16, p. 123, d. 120, ll. 135–8.
49 Excerpt from Potemkin's *dnevnik*, "Conversation with Mandel [on 18 March, *chez* Mandel]," no. 124, secret, 26 March 1936, AVPRF, f. 05, op. 16, p. 123, d. 120, ll. 123–8 (published in *DVP*, XIX, 162–6).
50 Excerpt from Potemkin's *dnevnik*, "Conversation with Sarraut [on 19 March]," no. 125, secret, 26 March 1936, AVPRF, f. 05, op. 16, p. 123, d. 120, ll. 129–34 (published in *DVP*, XIX, 174–8).
51 Duroselle, *Décadence*, 176.
52 Memorandum by Vansittart, 8 Dec. 1936; and Vansittart's minute, 11 Dec. 1936, C8892/4/18, TNA FO 371 19916.
53 Litvinov (London) to NKID, immediate, 19 March 1936, *DVP*, XIX, 172–3.
54 Litvinov (London) to Stalin, immediate, 21 March 1936, *DVP*, XIX, 179.
55 Krestinskii to Litvinov, immediate, special cipher, 22 March 1936, AVPRF, f. 059, op. 1, p. 221, d. 1586, l. 91, RF, World War II, 1936.
56 Litvinov to NKID, immediate, 19 March 1936, *DVP*, XIX, 172–3.
57 Krestinskii to Potemkin, 22 March 1936, *DVP*, XIX, 182–3.
58 Litvinov (Paris) to NKID, 28 March 1936, *DVP*, XIX, 734n55.
59 Potemkin to Krestinskii, no. 129, secret, 26 March 1936, AVPRF, f. 05, op. 16, p. 123, d. 120, ll. 139–49 (published in *DVP*, XIX, 189–95).

17 Epilogue

1 Alphand, nos. 163–5, 4 April 1936, *DDF*, 2^{e}, II, 45.
2 Litvinov to Maiskii, no. 3596/L, secret, 19 April 1936, AVPRF, f. 05, op. 16, p. 117, d. 26, ll. 11–13; and Litvinov to Maiskii, no. 3614/L, secret, 4 May 1936, ibid., ll. 4–6.
3 François-Poncet to Flandin, no. 485, secret, 17 March 1936, *DDF*, 2^{e}, I, 577–9.
4 Tim Bouverie, *Appeasement: Chamberlain, Hitler, Churchill and the Road to War* (New York: Tim Duggan Books, 2019), 90.
5 Maiskii to NKID, cc. Stalin, *et al.*, no. 6338, rigorously secret, immediate, 9 April 1936, AVPRF, f. 059, op. 1, p. 220, d. 1582, ll. 177–8, RF, World War II, 1936.
6 Excerpt from Potemkin's *dnevnik*, "Conversation with Herriot [on 21 April in Lyon]" no. 192, secret, 26 April 1936, AVPRF, f. 0136, op. 20, p. 167, d. 828 (sub-file no. 1), ll. 124–120.

7 Excerpt from Potemkin's *dnevnik*, "Conversation with Flandin [on 28 April at the Quai d'Orsay]," no. 238, secret, 11 May 1936, AVPRF, f. 05, op. 16, p. 123, d. 120, ll. 187–92.

8 Ibid.

9 Litvinov to Potemkin, no. 3613/L, secret, 4 May 1936, AVPRF, f. 05, op. 16, p. 123, d. 119, ll. 10–11.

10 Haslam, *Spectre of War*, 381.

11 Litvinov to Maiskii, no. 3614/L, secret, 4 May 1936, AVPRF, f. 05, op. 16, p. 117, d. 26, ll. 4–6.

12 For example, see Eugen Weber, *The Hollow Years: France in the 1930s* (New York: Norton, 1994), 150–81.

Bibliography

Unpublished Documents

France
Archives nationales, Paris
Ministère des Affaires étrangères, Paris
Service historique de l'Armée de terre, Château de Vincennes
Great Britain
The National Archives of Great Britain, Kew, Surrey
University of Birmingham
Russian Federation
Arkhiv vneshni politiki Rossiiskoi Federatsii (AVPRF), Moscow
Vtoraia Mirovaia voina v Arkhivnykh dokumentax, Prezidentskaia Biblioteka imeni B. N. El'tsina (https://www.prlib.ru/collections/1298142)
United States
National Archives, Bethesda, Maryland
Franklin D. Roosevelt Presidential Library, Hyde Park, NY
Bullitt Papers, Yale University

Published Documents and *Dnevniki*

Documents diplomatiques français, 1re série, 13 vols. Paris: Imprimerie nationale, 1964–84; 2e série, 19 vols. Paris: Imprimerie nationale, 1963–86.
Documents on British Foreign Policy, 2nd series, 19 vols. London: HM Stationery Office, 1947–84; 3rd series, 9 vols. London: HM Stationery Office, 1949–57.
Documents on German Foreign Policy, series C, 7 vols.; series D, 13 vols. London, Paris, & Washington, DC: Government Printing Office, 1949–56.
Dokumenty i materialy po istorii sovetsko-chekhoslovatskikh otnoshenii, vol. 3, *iiun' 1934g.-mart 1939g.* Moscow: Nauka, 1978.
Dokumenty i materialy po istorii sovetsko-pol'skikh otnoshenii, vols. 6–7, *1933–1943gg.* Moscow: Nauka, 1969–73.

Dokumenty vneshnei politiki SSSR, 26 vols. Moscow: Politizdat, 1958–.
Kollontai, Aleksandra M., *Diplomaticheskie dnevniki, 1922–1940*. vol. 2. Moscow: Academia, 2001.
Lubianka: Stalin i VChK-GPU-OGPU-NKVD, ianvar' 1922–dekabr' 1936. Moscow: Publisher: Izd. "Materik", 2003.
Maiskii, Ivan Mikhailovich. *Izbrannaia perepiska s rossiiskimi korrespondentami*. 2 vols. Moscow: Nauka, 2005.
– *Dnevnik diplomata: London, 1934–1943*. 3 vols. Moscow: Nauka, 2006–9.
Moskva-Berlin: Politika i diplomatiia Kremlia, 1920–1941, 3 vols. Moscow: Nauka, 2011.
Moskva-Rim: Politika i diplomatiia Kremlia, 1920–1939. Moscow: Nauka, 2002.
Moskva-Tokio: Politika i diplomatiia Kremlia, 1921–1931. 2 vols. Moscow: Nauka, 2007.
Moskva-Vashington: Politika i diplomatiia Kremlia, 1921–1941. 3 vols. Moscow: Nauka, 2009.
Narinskii, Mikhail M., N.E. Kleimenova, and S.A. Skliarov. *Sovetsko-Pol'skie otnosheniia v 1918–1945gg*. 4 vols. Moscow: Aspent Press, 2017.
Politbiuro Tsk RKP(b) i Evropa: Resheniia "Osoboi Papki," 1923–1939. Moscow: Rosspen, 2001.
Politbiuro Tsk RKP(b)-VKP(b) i Komintern, 1919–1943, Dokumenty. Moscow: Rosspen, 2004.
Rossiia i SShA: Ekonomicheskie otnosheniia, 1917–1941. 2 vols. Moscow: Nauka, 1997–2001.
Sovetsko-Amerikanskie otnosheniia, 1934–1939, Dokumenty. Moscow: Izd. "Materik," 2003.
Sovetsko-Amerikanskie otnosheniia, Gody nepriznaniia, 1927–1933. Dokumenty. Moscow: Izd. "Materik," 2002.
Sovetsko-Rumynskie otnosheniia, 1917–1941, 2 vols. Moscow: Mezhdunarodnye Otnosheniia, 2000.
SSSR-Germaniia, 1932–1941. 2nd ed. Moscow: IstLit, 2019.
Stalin i Kaganovich, Perepiska, 1931–1936gg. Moscow: Rosspen, 2001.
Ul', Mattias, Vladimir Khaustov, and Vladimir Zakharov, eds. *Glazami razvedki. SSSR i Evropa, 1919- 1938 gody: sbornik dokumentov iz rossiiskikh arkhivov*. Moscow: IstLit, 2015.

Books and Articles

Adamthwaite, Anthony. *France and the Coming of Second World War, 1936–1939*. London: Routledge, 1977.
– *Grandeur & Misery: France's Bid for Power in Europe, 1914–1940*. London: Hodder Arnold, 1995.
Alexander, Martin S. *The Republic in Danger: General Maurice Gamelin and the Politics of French Defence, 1933–1940*. Cambridge: Cambridge University Press, 1992.

Alphand, Hervé. *L'Étonnement d'être*. Paris: Fayard, 1977.

Andrew, Christopher. *Secret Service: The Making of the British Intelligence Community*. London: Sceptre, 1987.

Banac, Ivo, ed. *The Diary of Georgi Dimitrov, 1933–1949*. New Haven, CT: Yale University Press, 2003.

Beevor, Antony. *The Battle for Spain: The Spanish Civil War 1936–1939*. London: Penguin, 2006.

Bejan, Cristina A. *Intellectuals and Fascism in Interwar Romania: The Criterion Association*. London: Palgrave, 2019.

Bell, P.M.H. *France and Britain, 1900–1940: Entente & Estrangement*. London: Longman, 1996.

Bennett, Edward M. *Franklin D. Roosevelt and the Search for Security: American-Soviet Relations, 1933–1939*. Wilmington, DE: Scholarly Resources, 1985.

Berstein, Serge, and Jean-Jacques Becker. *Histoire de l'anti-communisme, 1917–1940*. Paris: Orban, 1987.

Blatt, Joel, ed. *The French Defeat of 1940: Reassessments*. Oxford: Berghahn, 1998.

Bouverie, Tim. *Appeasement: Chamberlain, Hitler, Churchill, and the Road to War*. New York: Tim Duggan Books, 2019.

Brogan, D.W. *The Development of Modern France, 1870–1939*, 2 vols. Gloucester, MA: Peter Smith, 1970.

Broué, Pierre. *Histoire de l'Internationale communiste, 1919–1943*. Paris: Fayard, 1997.

Brower, Daniel R. *The New Jacobins: The French Communist Party and the Popular Front*. Ithaca, NY: Cornell University Press, 1968.

Bullitt, Orville H., ed. *For the President, Personal and Secret: Correspondence between Franklin D. Roosevelt and William C. Bullitt*. Boston: Houghton Mifflin, 1972.

Burgwyn, H. James, Italian Foreign Policy in the Interwar Period, 1918–1940. Westport, CT: Praeger, 1997.

Cairns, John C. "March 7, 1936, Again: The View from Paris." In Hans W. Gatzke, ed., *European Diplomacy between Two Wars, 1919–1939*, 172–89. Chicago: Quadrangle, 1972.

Calvitt Clarke, Joseph. *Russia and Italy against Hitler: The Bolshevik-Fascist Rapprochement of the 1930s*. Westport, CT: Greenwood Press, 1991.

Carew, Joy Gleason. *Blacks, Reds, and Russians: Sojourners in Search of the Soviet Promise*. New Brunswick, NJ: Rutgers University Press, 2008.

Carley, Michael Jabara. *Revolution & Intervention: The French Government and the Russian Civil War, 1917–1919*. Montreal: McGill-Queen's University Press, 1983.

– "Five Kopecks for Five Kopecks: Franco-Soviet Trade Relations, 1928–1939." *Cahiers du monde russe et soviétique* 33, no. 1 (1992): 23–58.

– "End of the 'Low, Dishonest Decade': Failure of the Anglo-Franco-Soviet Alliance in 1939." *Europe-Asia Studies* 45, no. 2 (1993): 303–41.

– "Down a Blind-Alley: Anglo-Franco-Soviet Relations, 1920–1939." *Canadian Journal of History* 29, no. 1 (1994): 147–72.

– "Fearful Concatenation of Circumstances: the Anglo-Soviet Rapprochement, 1934–1936." *Contemporary European History* 5, no. 1 (1996): 29–69.
– "Prelude to Defeat: Franco-Soviet Relations, 1919–1939." *Historical Reflections* 22, no. 1 (1996): 159–88.
– *1939: The Alliance that Never Was and the Coming of World War II*. Chicago: Ivan R. Dee, 1999.
– "Episodes from the Early Cold War: Franco-Soviet Relations, 1917–1927." *Europe-Asia Studies* 52, no. 7 (2000): 1275–305.
– "Behind Stalin's Moustache: Pragmatism in Early Soviet Foreign Policy, 1917–1941." *Diplomacy & Statecraft* 12, no. 3 (2001): 159–74.
– "Resurgent France or Decadent France: War Origins Once Again." *Canadian Journal of History* 37, no. 2 (2002): 311–17.
– "Soviet Foreign Policy in the West: 1936–1941: A Review Article." *Europe-Asia Studies* 56, no. 7 (2004): 1080–92.
– "An Eye on France from the Soviet Embassy on the rue de Grenelle, 1924–1940." *Diplomacy & Statecraft* 17, no. 2 (2006): 295–346.
– "1933–39: La drôle d'avant guerre et l'alliance de la dernière chance." *Histoire(s) de la dernière guerre, 1939–1945: au jour le jour* 1 (2009): 14–20.
– *Silent Conflict: A Hidden History of Early Soviet-Western Relations*. Lanham, MD: Rowman & Littlefield, 2014.
– "Who Betrayed Whom? Franco-Anglo-Soviet Relations, 1932–1939." In C. Koch, ed., *Gab es einen Stalin-Hitler-Pakt? Charakter, Bedeutung und Deutung des deutsch-sowjetischen Nichtangriffsvertrages vom 23. August 1939*, 119–37. Frankfurt am Main: Peter Lang, 2015.
– "Who Was Iosif Vissarionovich Stalin?" *Europe-Asia Studies* 67, no. 7 (2015): 1030–44.
– "Once Burnt, Twice Shy: The Failure of Mutual Assistance against Nazi Germany, 1933–1935." *Istoriia/История* (Moscow) 3, no. 89 (2020). DOI: 10.18254/S207987840009129-0.
– "Pochti ne sluchilos': Heveroiatnyi velikii soiuz v vtoroi mirovoi voine (1929-1942)." *Kontsept* (Moscow) 5, no. 1 (2021): 75–95.
Carr, E.H. *The Twilight of the Comintern, 1930–1935*. London: Pantheon, 1982.
Carswell, John. *The Exile: A Life of Ivy Litvinov*. London: Faber & Faber, 1983.
Cassella-Blackburn, Michael. *The Donkey, the Carrot, and the Club: William C. Bullitt and Soviet-American Relations, 1917–1948*. Westport, CT: Praeger, 2004.
Charmley, John. *Churchill: The End of Glory*. Toronto: Macfarlane, Walter & Ross, 1993.
Chubar'ian, A.O., ed. *Evropa mezhdu mirom i voinoi, 1918–1939*. Moscow: Nauka, 1992.
Churchill, Winston S. *The Gathering Storm*. Boston: Houghton Mifflin, 1948.
Colton, Joel. *Léon Blum: Humanist in Politics*. New York: Knopf, 1966.
Colvin, Ian. *Vansittart in Office*. London: Victor Gollancz, 1965.

Coulondre, Robert. *De Staline à Hitler, souvenirs de deux ambassades, 1936–1939.* Paris: Hachette, 1950.

Cowling, Maurice. *The Impact of Hitler: British Politics and British Policy, 1933–1940.* London: Cambridge University Press, 1975.

Craig, Gordon A., and Felix Gilbert. *The Diplomats*. 2 vols. New York: Atheneum, 1965.

D'Agostino, Anthony. *The Rise of the Global Powers: International Politics in the Era of the World Wars*. Cambridge: Cambridge University Press, 2012.

Dallin, Alexander, and F.I. Firsov, eds. *Dimitrov & Stalin, 1934–1943: Letters from the Soviet Archives*. New Haven, CT: Yale University Press, 2000.

Dalton, Hugh. *The Fateful Years: Memoirs 1931–1945*. London: Frederik Muller, 1957.

Davies, Sarah, and James Harris. *Stalin's World. Dictating the Soviet Order*. New Haven, CT: Yale University Press, 2014.

Dessberg, Frédéric. *Le triangle impossible: Les relations franco-soviétiques et le facteur polonais dans les questions de sécurité en Europe (1924–1935)*. Brussels: Peter Lang, 2009.

Deutscher, Isaac. *Russia after Stalin*. London: Hamish Hamilton, 1953.

– *Stalin: A Political Biography*. New York: Vintage, 1960.

– *Trotsky*. 3 vols. New York: Vintage, 1954–63.

Di Biagio, Anna. "Moscow: The Comintern and the War Scare, 1926–28." In Silvio Pons and Andrea Romano, eds., *Russia in the Age of Wars, 1914–1945*, 83–102. Milan: Feltrinelli Editore, 2000.

Dockrill, Michael, and Brian McKercher, eds. *Diplomacy and World Power: Studies in British Foreign Policy, 1890–1950*. Cambridge: Cambridge University Press, 1996.

Dullin, Sabine. "Les Diplomates soviétiques à la Société des Nations." *Relations internationales* 75 (1993): 329–43.

– "Le Rôle de Maxime Litvinov dans les années trente." *Communisme* 42/43/44 (1995): 75–93.

– *Des hommes d'influences: Les ambassadeurs de Staline en Europe, 1930–1939*. Paris: Payot, 2001.

Dunn, Dennis J. *Caught between Roosevelt and Stalin: America's Ambassadors to Moscow*. Lexington: University Press of Kentucky, 1997.

Du Réau, Elisabeth. *Édouard Daladier, 1884–1970*. Paris: Fayard, 1993.

Duroselle, Jean-Baptiste. *La Décadence, 1932–1939*. 3rd ed. Paris: Imprimerie nationale, 1985.

Eden, Anthony. *Facing the Dictators*. Boston: Houghton Mifflin, 1962.

Foglesong, David, S. *America's Secret War against Bolshevism: U.S. Intervention in the Russian Civil War, 1917–1920*. Chapel Hill, NC: University of North Carolina Press, 1995.

Fujii, George. "H-Diplo Roundtable XXII-18 on Snyder, *The Road to Unfreedom: Russia, Europe, America*." Review by Joseph Kellner, H-Diplo, 21 December 2020. https://networks.h-net.org/node/28443/discussions/6990543/h-diplo-roundtable-xxii-18-snyder-road-unfreedom-russia-europe#_Toc59206493.

Gamelin, Maurice. *Servir*. 3 vols. Paris: Plon, 1946.

George, Margaret. *Warped Vision: British Foreign Policy, 1933–1939*. Pittsburgh: University of Pittsburgh Press, 1965.

Gilbert, Martin. *Prophet of Truth: Winston S. Churchill, 1922–1939*. London: Minerva, 1990.

Glantz, Mary E. *FDR and the Soviet Union: The President's Battles over Foreign Policy*. Lawrence: University Press of Kansas, 2005.

Gorlov, Sergei A. *Sovershenno sekretno, Moskva – Berlin, 1920–1933: Voenno-politcheskie otnosheniia mezhdu SSSR i Germaniei*. Moscow: Institut vseobshchei istorii RAN, 1999.

Gorodetsky, Gabriel, ed. *The Complete Maiskii Diaries*. 3 vols. Translated by Tatiana Sorokina and Oliver Ready. New Haven, CT: Yale University Press, 2017.

Guelton, Frédéric. "Les relations militaires franco-soviétiques dans les années trente." In Mikhail Narinskii, Élisabeth du Réau, Georges-Henri Soutou, and Alexandre Tchoubarian, with the collaboration of Christophe Réveillard, *La France et l'URSS dans l'Europe des années 30*, 61–72. Paris: Presses de l'Université de Paris-Sorbonne, 2005.

Harris, James. "Encircled by Enemies: Stalin's Perceptions of the Capitalist World, 1918–1941." *Journal of Strategic Studies* 30, no. 3 (June 2007): 513–45.

Harvey, John, ed. *The Diplomatic Diaries of Oliver Harvey, 1937–1940*. London: Collins, 1970.

Haslam, Jonathan. *Soviet Foreign Policy, 1930–33: The Impact of the Depression*. New York: St. Martin's Press, 1983.

– *The Soviet Union and the Struggle for Collective Security in Europe, 1933–39*. New York: St. Martin's Press, 1984.

– *The Soviet Union and the Threat from the East, Moscow, Tokyo and the Prelude to the Pacific War*. Pittsburgh: University of Pittsburgh Press, 1992.

– *The Spectre of War: International Communism and the Origins of World War II*. Princeton, NJ: Princeton University Press, 2021.

Herndon, James S., and Joseph O. Baylen. "Col. Philip R. Faymonville and the Red Army, 1934–43." *Slavic Review* 34, no. 3 (1975): 483–505.

Herriot, Édouard. *Jadis: D'une guerre à l'autre, 1914–1936*. Paris: Flammarion, 1952.

Irvine, William D. *French Conservatism in Crisis: The Republican Federation of France in the 1930s*. Baton Rouge, LA: Louisiana State University Press, 1979.

Jackson, Peter. *France and the Nazi Menace: Intelligence and Policy Making, 1933–1939*. Oxford: Oxford University Press, 2000.

James, Robert Rhodes, ed. *Chips: The Diaries of Sir Henry Channon*. London: Weidenfeld & Nicolson, 1967.

Jansen, Sabine. *Pierre Cot: Un antifasciste radical*. Paris: Fayard, 2002.

Jeanneney, Jules E. *Journal politique, septembre 1939–juillet 1942*. Paris: Armand Colin, 1972.

Jędrzejewicz, Wacław, ed. *Diplomat in Berlin, 1933–1939: Papers and Memoirs of Józef Lipski*. New York: Columbia University Press, 1968.

–, ed. *Diplomat in Paris, 1936–1939: Papers and Memoirs of Juliusz Łukasiewicz*. New York: Columbia University Press, 1970.

Jones, Gareth. "The Arrest of the British Engineers." Margaret Siriol Colley. Accessed 28 September 2002, https://www.garethjones.org/margaret_siriol_colley/metrovik_trial.htm#_ednref12.

Jones, Thomas. *A Dairy with Letters, 1931–1950*. London: Oxford University Press, 1954.

Ken, Oleg N. *Collective Security or Isolation? Soviet Foreign Policy and Poland, 1930–1935*. St. Petersburg: Evropeiskiy Dom, 1996.

– "M.S. Ostrovskii i sovetsko-rumynskie otnosheniia (1934–1938gg.)." In *Rossiia v XX veke: Sbornik statei k 70-letiiu rozhdeniia chl.-kopp. RAN prof. V. A. Shishkina*, 336–50. St. Petersburg: n.p., 2005.

Ken, Oleg N., and A.I. Rupasov. *Politbiuro TsK VKP (b) i otnosheniia SSSR s zapadnimi gosudarstvami*. St. Petersburg: Evropeiskii Dom, 2000.

Kennedy, Paul. "Appeasement." In Gordon Martel, ed., *The Origins of the Second World War Reconsidered*, 140–61. Boston: Allen & Unwin, 1986.

Khlevniuk, Oleg V. *Master of the House: Stalin and his Inner Circle*. New Haven, CT: Yale University Press, 2009.

Khormach, I.A. *SSSR-Italiia. 1924–1939 gg*. Moscow: Institut rossiiskoi istorii RAN, 1995.

– *Vozvrashchenie v mirovoe soobshchestvo: bor'ba i sotrudnichestvo Sovetskogo gosudarstva s Ligii natsii v 1919–1934 gg*. Moscow: Kuchkovo pole, 2011.

– *SSSR v Lige natsii, 1934–1939 gg*. Moscow: Tsentr Gumanitarnykh Initsiativ, 2017.

Korotkov, A.V., et al., eds. *Na prieme u Stalina: Tetradi (zhurnaly) zapisei lits, priniatykh I. V. Stalinym (1924–1953gg)*. Moscow: Novyi khronograf, 2008.

Kotkin, Stephen. *Stalin: Waiting for Hitler, 1929–1941*. London: Allen Lane, 2017.

Kudryashov, Sergei V., ed. *SSSR-Germaniia, 1933–1941*. Moscow: Vestnik Arkhiva Prezidenta Rossiiskoi Federatsii, 2009.

Lacroix-Riz, Annie. *Le Choix de la défaite: les élites françaises dans les années 1930*. Paris: Armand Colin, 2006.

Lamb, Richard. *The Drift to War, 1922–1939*. London: Bloomsbury, 1991.

Lenoe, Matthew E. *The Kirov Murder and Soviet History*. New Haven: Yale University Press, 2010.

Lih, Lars T., Oleg V. Naumov, Oleg V. Khlevniuk, L. Kosheleva, L. Rogovaia, V. Lelchuk, and V. Naumov, eds. *Stalin's Letters to Molotov*. Translated by Catherine A. Fitzpatrick. New Haven, CT: Yale University Press, 1995.

Lukes, Igor, *Czechoslovakia between Stalin and Hitler: The Diplomacy of Edvard Beneš in the 1930s*. Oxford: Oxford University Press, 1996.

Lungu, Dov B. *Romania and the Great Powers, 1933–1940*. Durham, NC: Duke University Press, 1989.

Maiolo, Joseph. "Anglo-Soviet Naval Armaments Diplomacy before the Second World War." *English Historical Review* 133, no. 501 (2008): 351–78.

Maiskii, Ivan M. *Who Helped Hitler*. London: Hutchinson, 1964.

– *Vospominaniia sovetskogo diplomata, 1925–1945 gg*. Moscow: Nauka, 1971.

Manchester, William. *The Caged Lion: Winston Spencer Churchill, 1932–1940*. London: Cardinal, 1989.

Manevy, Raymond. *Histoire de la Presse, 1914–1939*. Paris: Éditions Corréa, 1945.

Manne, Robert. "The Foreign Office and the Failure of Anglo-Soviet Rapprochement." *Journal of Contemporary History* 16, no. 4 (1981): 725–55.

Martel, Gordon, ed. *Origins of the Second World War Reconsidered*. 2nd ed. New York: Routledge, 1999.

–, ed. *The Times and Appeasement: The Journals of A.L. Kennedy, 1932–1939*. Cambridge: Cambridge University Press, 2000.

Martin-Fugier, Anne. *La bourgeoise*. Paris: Grasset, 1983.

Mazower, Mark. *Dark Continent: Europe's Twentieth Century*. New York: Vintage, 1998.

McDermott, Kevin, and Jeremy Agnew. *The Comintern: A History of International Communism from Lenin to Stalin*. New York: St. Martin's Press, 1997.

McKercher, B.J.C., ed. "Robert Vansittrat and an Unbrave World, 1930–37." Special issue, *Diplomacy & Statecraft* 6, no. 1 (1995).

McMeekin, Sean. *Stalin's War: A New History of World War II*. New York: Basic Books, 2021.

Mel'tiukhov, Mikhail I. *17 Sentiabria 1939. Sovetsko-pol'skie konflikty 1918–1939*. Moscow: Veche, 2009.

– *Pribaltiiskii platsdarm v mezhdunarodnoi politike Moskvy [1918–1939 gg.]*. Moscow: Algolritm, 2015.

Meltz, Renaud. *Alexis Léger dit Saint-John Perse*. Paris: Flammarion, 2008.

– "Lorsque le Quai d'Orsay dictait des articles: la fabrication de l'opinion publique dans l'entre-deux-guerres." *Relations internationales* 154 (2013): 33–50.

– *Pierre Laval. Un mystère français*. Paris: Perrin, 2018.

Micaud, Charles. *The French Right and Nazi Germany, 1933–1939*. New York: Octagon Books, 1964

Middlemas, Keith. *Diplomacy of Illusion: The British Government and Germany, 1937–1939*. London: Weidenfeld & Nicolson, 1972.

Millman, Brock. *The Ill-Made Alliance: Anglo-Turkish Relations, 1934–1940*. Montreal: McGill-Queen's University Press, 1998.

Miner, Steven Merritt. *Between Churchill and Stalin: The Soviet Union, Great Britain, and the Origins of the Grand Alliance*. Chapel Hill, NC: University of North Carolina Press, 1988.

– "His Master's Voice: Viacheslav Mikhailovich Molotov as Stalin's Foreign Commissar." In G.A. Craig and F.L. Loewenheim, eds., *The Diplomats, 1939–1979*, 65–100. Princeton, NJ: Princeton University Press.

Morozov, Stanislav V. *Polk'sko-chekhoslovatskie otnosheniia 1933–1939*. Moscow: Izd. Moskovskogo Universiteta, 2004.

Morrell, Gordon W. *Britain Confronts the Stalin Revolution: Anglo-Soviet Relations and the Metro-Vickers Crisis*. Waterloo, ON: Wilfrid Laurier University Press, 1995.

Narinski, Mikhail, Elisabeth Du Réau, Georges-Henri Soutou, and Alexandre Tchoubarian. *La France et l'URSS dans l'Europe des années trente*. Paris: Presses de l'Université de Paris-Sorbonne, 2005.

Neilson, Keith. "Pursued by a Bear: British Estimates of Soviet Military Strength and Anglo-Soviet Relations, 1922–1939." *Canadian Journal of History* 28, no. 2 (1993): 189–221.

– "Stalin's Moustache: The Soviet Union and the Coming of the War." *Diplomacy & Statecraft* 12, no. 2 (2001): 197–208.

– *Britain, Soviet Russia and the Collapse of the Versailles Order, 1919–1939*. Cambridge: Cambridge University Press, 2006.

– "Orme Sargent, Appeasement and British Policy in Europe, 1933–39." *Twentieth Century British History* 21, no. 1 (2010): 1–28.

Nekrich, Aleksandr M. *Pariahs, Partners, Predators: German-Soviet Relations, 1922–1941*. New York: Columbia University Press, 1997.

Nezhinskii, L.N., ed. *Sovetskaia vneshniaia politika, 1917–1945gg.: Poiski novykh podkhodov*. Moscow: Mezhdunarodnye Otnosheniia, 1992.

– *V interesakh naroda ili vopreki im?: Sovetskaia mezhdunarodnaia politika v 1917–1933 godakh*. Moscow: Nauka, 2004.

– *Puti i pereput'ia sovetskoi mezhdunarodnoi politiki v 1934–1941 gg*. Tula: Grif i K, 2008.

Nicolson, Harold. *Diaries and Letters, 1930–1939*. New York: Altheneum, 1966.

Noël, Léon. *L'Agression allemande contre la Pologne*. Paris: Flammarion, 1946.

Parker, R.A.C. *Chamberlain and Appeasement: British Policy and the Coming of the Second World War*. London: Macmillan, 1993.

Paul-Boncour, Joseph. *Entre deux guerres: souvenirs sur la IIIe République*. 3 vols. Paris: Plon, 1946.

Peden, G.C. *British Rearmament and the Treasury, 1932–1939*. Edinburgh: Scottish Academic Press, 1979.

– *Churchill, Chamberlain, and Appeasement*. London: Cambridge University Press, 2023.

Pertinax, André Géraud. *Les Fossoyeurs*. 2 vols. New York: Éditions de la Maison Française, 1943.

Phillips, Hugh D. *Between the Revolution and the West: A Political Biography of Maxim M. Litvinov*. Boulder, CO: Westview Press, 1992.

Pinals, Robert S. "Louise Bryant: An Adventurous Life and Painful Death from Dercum's Disease." *The Pharos* (Winter 2019): 21–3.

Pons, Silvio. *Stalin and the Inevitable War, 1936–1941*. London: Frank Cass, 2002.

Pons, Silvio, and Andrea Romano, eds. *Russia in the Age of War, 1914–1945*. Milan: Feltrinelli, 2000.

Post, Gaines Jr. *Dilemmas of Appeasement: British Deterrence and Defense, 1934–1937*. Ithaca, NY: Cornell University Press, 1993.

Resis, Albert, ed. *Molotov Remembers: Inside Kremlin Politics, Conversations with Felix Chuev*. Chicago: Ivan R. Dee, 1993.

Roberts, Geoffrey. "A Soviet Bid for Coexistence with Nazi Germany, 1935–1937: The Kandelaki Affair." *International History Review* 16, no. 3 (1994): 466–90.

– *The Soviet Union and the Origins of the Second World War: Russo-German Relations and the Road to War, 1933–1941*. London: Macmillian, 1995.

Robertson, James C. "The Hoare-Plan." *Journal of Contemporary History* 10, no. 3 (1975): 433–64.

Roman, Meredith L. *Opposing Jim Crow: African Americans and the Soviet Indictment of U.S. Racism, 1928–1937*. Lincoln: University of Nebraska Press, 2012.

Rose, Norman. *Vansittart: Study of a Diplomat*. London: Heinemann, 1978.

Rowse, A.L. *Appeasement: A Study in Political Decline, 1933–39*. New York: Norton, 1963.

Safonov, V. P. *SSSR, SShA i Iaponskaia agressiia na Dal'nem Vostoke i Tikhom Okenae, 1931–1945 gg*. Moscow: Moscow: Institut rossiiskoi istorii RAN, 2001.

Schuker, Stephen A. "France and the Remilitarization of the Rhineland, 1936." *French Historical Studies* 14, no. 3 (1986): 299–338.

– "Two Cheers for Appeasement." Paper presented at the Society for French Historical Studies Conference, Boston, MA, March 1996.

Scott, William Evans. *Alliance against Hitler: The Origins of the Franco-Soviet Pact*. Durham, NC: Duke University Press, 1962.

Service, Robert. *Stalin: A Biography*. Cambridge, MA: Belknap Press, 2004.

Sevost'ianov, G.N. *Moskva-Vashington: Diplomaticheskie otnosheniia, 1933–1936*. Moscow: Nauka, 2002.

– *Moskva-Vashington: Na puti k priznaniiu, 1918–1933*. Moscow: Nauka, 2004.

Shaw, Louise Grace. *The British Political Elite and the Soviet Union, 1937–1939*. London: Routledge, 2003.

Sheinis, Zinovy. *Maksim Litvinov*. Moscow: Izd. Politicheskoi Literatury, 1989.

Sherwood, John Michael. *Georges Mandel and the Third Republic*. Stanford, CA: Stanford University Press, 1970.

Sheviakov, A.A. *Sovetsko-Rumynskie otnosheniia i problema evropeiskoi bezopasnosti, 1932–1939*. Moscow: Nauka, 1977.

Shirer, William L. *Berlin Diary: The Journal of a Foreign Correspondent, 1934–1941*. New York: Knopf, 1941.

– *The Collapse of the Third Republic: An Inquiry into the Fall of France in 1940*. New York: Simon & Schuster, 1969.

Shura, Patrick. "O'Neill's Strange Interlude and the 'Strange Marriage' of Louise Bryant." *The Eugene O'Neill Review* 30 (2008): 7–20.

Sipols, V. Ia., *Vneshniaia politika Sovetskogo Soiuza, 1933–1935gg*. Moscow: Nauka, 1980.

– *Diplomaticheskaia bor'ba nakanune vtoroi mirovoi voiny*. Moscow: Mezhdunardnye Otnosheniia, 1989.

Souvarine, Boris. *Stalin*. New York: Longmans, Green & Co., 1939.
Stedman, Andrew David. *Alternatives to Appeasement: Neville Chamberlain and Hitler's Germany*. London: I.B. Tauris, 2011.
Stamsell, Christine. "Louise Bryant Grows Old." *History Workshop Journal* 50, no. 1 (2000): 156–80.
Steiner, Zara. *The Lights that Failed*. Oxford: Oxford University Press, 2005.
– *The Triumph of the Dark*. Oxford: Oxford University Press, 2011.
Strang, G. Bruce, ed. *Collision of Empires: Italy's Invasion of Ethiopia and its International Impact*. New York: Routledge, 2013.
Strang, William. *Home and Abroad*. London: A. Deutsch, 1956.
Szembek, Jean. *Journal, 1933–1939*. Paris: Plon, 1952.
Tabouis, Geneviève. *They Called Me Cassandra*. New York: Charles Scribner's Sons, 1942.
Taylor, A.J.P. *The Origins of the Second World War*. Middlesex: Penguin, 1964.
– *English History, 1914–1945*. New York: Oxford University Press, 1965.
– *1939 Revisited*. London: German Historical Institute, 1981.
Thompson, Neville. *The Anti-Appeasers: Conservative Opposition to Appeasement in the 1930s*. Oxford: Oxford University Press, 1971.
Torrès, Henry. *Pierre Laval*. Toronto: Oxford University Press, 1941.
Trotskii, Lev Davidovich. *Stalin*. New York: Stein & Day, 1967.
– *My Life*. New York: Pathfinder Press, 1970.
Tucker, Robert C. *Stalin as Revolutionary, 1879–1929*. New York: W.W. Norton, 1973.
– *Stalin in Power: The Revolution from Above, 1928–1941*. New York: Norton, 1990.
Ulam, Adam B. *Expansion and Coexistence: The History of Soviet Foreign Policy, 1917–1967*. New York: Frederick A. Praeger, 1968.
Uldricks, Teddy J. "A.J.P. Taylor and the Russians." In Gordon Martel, ed., *The Origins of the Second World War Reconsidered*, 2nd ed., 162–86. New York: Routledge, 1999.
– "War, Politics and Memory: Russian Historians Reevaluate the Origins of World War II." *History and Memory* 21, no. 2 (2009): 60–82.
Vaïsse, Maurice. "Les Militaires français et l'alliance franco-soviétique au cours des années 1930." In *Forces armées et systèmes d'alliances: Colloque international d'histoire militaire et d'études de défense nationale*, vol. 2, 689–704. Paris: Foundation pour les études de défense nationale, 1983.
Vansittart, Robert G. *The Mist Procession: The Autobiography of Lord Vansittart*. London: Hutchinson, 1958.
Varey, David. "The Politics of Naval Aid: The Foreign Office, the Admiralty, and Anglo-Soviet Technical Cooperation, 1936–37." *Diplomacy & Statecraft* 14, no. 4 (2003): 50–68.
Veeder, V.V. "The Lena Goldfields Arbitration: The Historical Roots of Three Ideas." *International and Comparative Law Quarterly* 47, no. 4 (1998): 747–92.
Vershinin, Alexander. "'My Task Is to Get into the French Army': Soviet Strategy and the Origins of Soviet-French Military Cooperation in the 1930s." *Journal of Strategic Studies* 44, no. 5 (2021): 685–714.

– "SSSR i Krasnaia armiia glazami voennogo attashe Frantsii E. Mendras 1933–1934gg." *Noveishaia istoriia Rossii* 11, no. 3 (2021): 686–704.

Vidal, Georges. "Le PCF et la défense nationale à l'époque du Front populaire (1934–1939)." *Guerres mondiales et conflits contemporains* 215 (2004): 47–73.

– *Une alliance improbable. L'armée française et la Russie soviétique, 1917–1939*. Rennes: Presses Universitaires de Rennes, 2015.

Viola, Lynn. *Peasant Rebels under Stalin: Collectivization and the Culture of Peasant Resistance*. New York: Oxford University Press, 1996.

Volkogonov, Dimitri. *Staline*. Paris: Flammarion 1991.

Wark, Wesley K. *The Ultimate Enemy: British Intelligence and Nazi Germany, 1933–1939*. Ithaca, NY: Cornell University Press, 1985.

Watson, Derek. "Appeasement Revisited." *International History Review* 17, no 3 (1995): 545–62.

– *Molotov: A Biography*. London: Palgrave, 2005.

Weber, Eugen. *Action Française: Royalism and Reaction in Twentieth-Century France*. Stanford, CA: Stanford University Press, 1962.

– *The Hollow Years: France in the 1930s*. New York: Norton, 1994.

Weinberg, Gerhard. *The Foreign Policy of Hitler's Germany: Diplomatic Revolution in Europe, 1933–1936*. Chicago: University of Chicago Press, 1970.

– *The Foreign Policy of Hitler's Germany: Starting World War II, 1937–1939*. Chicago: University of Chicago Press, 1980.

West, Nigel. *The A to Z of British Intelligence*. Langham, MD: Rowman & Littlefield, 2009.

Williams, Andrew J. *Trading with the Bolsheviks: The Politics of East-West Trade, 1920–1939*. Manchester: Manchester University Press, 1992.

Wilson, Joan Hoff. *Ideology and Economics: U.S. Relations with the Soviet Union, 1918–1933*. Columbia, MO: University of Missouri, 1974.

Young, Kenneth, ed. *The Diaries of Sir Robert Bruce Lockhart, 1915–1946*. 2 vols. London: Macmillan, 1973.

Young, Robert J. *In Command of France: French Foreign Policy and Military Planning, 1933–1940*. Cambridge, MA: Harvard University Press, 1978.

– "French Military Intelligence." In Ernest R. May, ed., *Knowing One's Enemies: Intelligence Assessment before the Two World Wars*, 271–309. Princeton, NJ: Princeton University Press, 1985.

– "A.J.P. Taylor and the Problem with France." In Gordon Martel, ed., *The Origins of the Second World War Reconsidered*, 2nd ed., 97–118. New York: Routledge, 1999.

– *Power and Pleasure: Louis Barthou and the Third French Republic*. Montreal: McGill-Queen's University Press, 1991.

– *France and the Origins of the Second World War*. New York: St Martin's Press, 1996.

Index

Abyssinian crisis: Anglo-Soviet relations and, 409, 459; Britain and, 401, 410, 417–18, 455, 472–3; France and, 401; Hoare-Laval plan, 415, 416, 417, 448–9, 507; League of Nations and, 398, 413, 471; Litvinov on, 469–70; outbreak of, 7, 506; question of sanctions, 403–4; Soviet Union and, 394, 395–400, 402–5, 410, 414, 416–17
air pact proposal, 344, 347, 350–1, 353, 362
Aleksandrovskii, Sergei S.: conversations with Beneš, 385, 386, 387, 388, 389; diplomatic career of, xv; Litvinov's dispatches to, 363, 441; Soviet-Czechoslovak mutual assistance pact and, 426
Alexander I, king of Yugoslavia: assassination of, 190
Alphand, Charles, xv, 361; on Barthou, 170; contacts among Soviet officials, 177; diplomatic reports of, 192, 245–6, 251, 348, 476, 477; on Eastern Pact, 190, 344, 354; on Eden's visit to Moscow, 319; Franco-Soviet relations and, 129, 131–2, 134–5, 191, 248, 249, 375–6, 380, 452, 477, 491; on French papers, 424; Krestinskii and, 436; Litvinov's meeting with, 146, 177, 183, 192–3, 352, 354, 427, 482, 509; mission to Moscow, 125; on Polish foreign policy, 111, 160; on political situation in France, 449; Potemkin and, 449; Rhineland crisis and, 495; on rumours about ousting of Litvinov, 242; Russophile views of, 476; Stomoniakov and, 129, 168–9; support of Laval, 448
American Communist Party, 39, 48
American Federation of Labor (AFL), 36, 37
Amtorg Trading Corporation, New York, 35, 36–7, 42, 43, 211, 218
Andreichin, G.I., 48
Anglo-German naval agreement, 332–3, 393, 409–10, 413, 480, 506
Anglo-Soviet relations: Abyssinian crisis and, 409; Anglo-German naval agreement and, 393; Anglo-Japanese relations and, 294; British domestic politics and, 66, 474; British press on, 287; Comintern and, 299, 460, 462; communist propaganda and, 266, 293, 421–2, 464; diplomatic recognition of the USSR, 4; Eden's visit to Moscow, 309–19; exchange of military attachés, 291; Germany and, 311–12, 456–7, 464, 465; Hoare-Maiskii exchange, 406; Lena Goldfields dispute, 281, 286, 291, 293;

Anglo-Soviet relations (*cont.*)
loan question, 418–20, 456–9, 461–3, 473–4, 491; mutual assistance pact, 352; new triple entente idea, 461, 464, 470; "pebbles" in the road of, 323–5; Politburo resolution on, 263; rapprochement, 262–333, 449–50, 455–6, 458, 462, 463, 483; realism in, 315, 316; reimbursement of the tsarist debts, 420–1; Rubinin-Charles discussion of, 266–7; Soviet press on, 313–14; tensions in, 69, 81; trade, 65–6, 88–9, 96, 101–2, 265–6; tsarist legacy in, 17–18. *See also* Metro-Vickers Affair
Antonov-Ovseenko, Vladimir A., xv; Jean Payart and, 141; meetings with Polish politicians, 34, 153; on Nazi-Polish non-aggression pact, 154–5; at odds with Moscow, 117–18; on Polish-German relations, 115–16, 122; Stomoniakov's polemic with, 31, 33, 113–14, 115, 161, 252
Aras, Tevfik Rüştü, 334, 492
Arciszewski, Mirosław, xv, 433, 443, 444, 445
Arcos (All-Russian Co-operative Society) raid, 266
Ashton-Gwatkin, Frank, xv, 274, 333, 420
Attolico, Bernardo, 363
Austria, xx, 161, 468, 470, 471, 473, 486; German threat to, 249, 250, 288, 290, 319, 363, 408, 417, 442, 445; guarantee of independence of, 335, 346; Nazi coup d'état attempt in, 259–60
Austria-Hungary, 117, 385

Baldwin, Stanley, xv, 91, 342; Abyssinian crisis and, 394, 418; meeting with Maiskii, 394; meeting with Ovey, 90; reputation of, 455; on Soviet interest in India, 394–5; speeches in the House of Commons, 71, 76, 83; Vansittart and, 307, 308; view of Germany, 332, 475, 510
Balkan Entente (Greece, Turkey, Yugoslavia, and Romania), 336, 347, 354, 362, 368, 371, 372, 389–90, 474
Baltic states: French assistance to, 174, 175, 185; German policy towards, 34, 179–80; question of security of, 159, 162, 314–15, 356, 362, 379
Banque de France, 19, 134, 150, 451
Bargeton, Paul, 169, 173, 174, 254, 360, 361, 377, 390, 476
Barlow, Lester, 45
Barthou, Louis: assassination of, 190–1, 506; Baltic region security and, 356; career of, xv, 166, 170, 337; Dovgalevskii and, 170; Eastern Pact and, 173, 378; foreign policy of, 245, 360, 479, 505; Geneva talks with Litvinov, 174–5, 176; Moscow press on, 248–9; on Polish foreign policy, 253; talks to Beck, 189–90; visit to London, 182–3, 286; visit to Warsaw, 186
Basdevant, Jules, 374, 375, 377, 390, 476
Bastid, Paul, 482, 489, 490, 491
Bayonne, France, 151–2
Beaverbrook, William Maxwell Aitken, Baron: on Anglo-German naval agreement, 332; attitude to the USSR, 325, 326; business of, 325; on danger from Germany, 326–7; Maiskii and, 325–7, 332, 412; on policy of isolation, 412
Beck, Józef: attitude to Anschluss, 174; background of, 117; Barthou talks to, 189–90; Bullitt's meeting with, 208; foreign policy of, 31, 112, 114–17, 340, 429–30, 507; on German rearmament, 153–4; on Hitler's relations with Poland, 182; on idea of Eastern Pact, 335–6, 363, 364; Laval's meeting with, 348, 506; on League of Nations, 157; on Litvinov-Laval protocol, 257; Litvinov's meetings

with, 156, 157–9, 175, 349, 427; on Nazi Germany, 157, 159, 160, 482; photographs of, 117, *158*; political career of, xv; on Soviet entry into the League of Nations, 187; visit to Berlin, 430; visit to Moscow, 156–60, 161, 186, 207–8
Belgium: map of, 494; security guarantees to, 141, 142, 172, 379, 380, 460, 468, 469, 480, 498, 500
Beneš, Eduard, xv, 261, 358; Aleksandrovskii's conversation with, 385, 386, 388; background of, 384–5; Eastern Pact and, 335, 363; on Eden, 387–8; foreign policy of, 384, 388–9; pro-Soviet policy of, 372, 426, 434; relations with Laval, 386–7, 442, 506; on security of Eastern Europe, 385–6; Titulescu and, 387; view of Poland, 507; visit to Moscow, 426
Berson, Jan (Otmar), 252
Berthelot, Philippe, xv, 14, 18, 19, 20, 28
Besedovskii scandal, 14–15, 38
Bessarabia, 337, 339, 428, 433, 440
Bethmann-Hollweg, Theobald von, 146
Bevan, Aneurin, 325
Big Five powers, 268
Black Americans: invitation to Moscow, 47–9, 63
Black and White (film project), 47–9
Blum, Léon, xv, 376, 511, 513, 514
Bogdanov, Petr A.: Cooper and, 49; Del'gas affair and, 38; diplomatic reports of, 41, 44, 50, 51; on FDR, 50; Litvinov's mission to Washington and, 62; testimony before Fish Committee, 36–7, 38; on US-Soviet trade, 40, 42–3
Bolshevik Revolution, 13
Boothby, Robert, 266, 291–2, 297
Borah, William E., 39, 41
Brailsford, Henry Noel, 263
Bressy, Pierre, 189
Brest-Litovsk, Treaty of, 484
Briand, Aristide, xv, 15–16, 19–20, 28
Brinon, Fernand de, xv, 510
British Broadcasting Corporation (B.B.C.), 421
British Chambers of Commerce, 422
British Communist Party, 263, 411, 421
British Defence White Paper (1935), 355
Bruce Lockhart, R.H., 13, 455
Brüning, Heinrich, 45, 250
Bryant, Louise, 195–6
Bukharin, Nikolai I., xv, 6
Bukovina, 433
Bulgaria, xxi, 435–6
Bullitt, William C.: background and education of, 195, 196; daughter of, 196–7; departure to Vladivostok, 240; diplomatic career of, xv, 51–2, 61, 195, 196–7; FDR and, 196, 235, 236; on Franco-Soviet pact, 146; Il'inskii and, 197; on Japan's foreign policy, 198, 208, 213–14; Kalinin's conversation with, 198; Krestinskii's talks with, 215–18, 219; Litvinov's negotiations with, 56–62, 197, 198, 200, 202–3, 209–11, 213, 215, 220–1, 225–8, 231, 236–40, 243–4, 493; meetings with the NKID officials, 198; Molotov's meeting with, 238; on Nazi Germany, 198; Paul-Boncour and, 203; reports of, 200, 212; Rubinin's meetings with, 209, 215–18, 219, 237; Skvirskii's meeting with, 51, 235–6; on Soviet-Japanese relations, 207; State Department instructions to, 237; TASS interview, 197; telegram to Hull, 236; US-Soviet trade negotiations and, 204, 207–12, 226–34, 235–40; visit to Paris, 203; visit to the Kremlin Wall, 200; visit to Warsaw, 208; Voroshilov's conversation with, 200–2, 227–8; Wiley and, 240–1; writings of, 196
Burcă, Ecaterina, 336
Buré, Émile, 125
Burgin, Leslie, 297, 298, 300

Caillaux, Joseph, 448
Cambon, Roger, 184
Campbell, Ronald, 380–1
Carol II, king of Romania, 433, 441, 443, 444, 479, 480
Carr, E.H., 274
Cayrol, Robert, 125, 126, 135–7
Cazalet, Victor, 419
Cerruti, Vittorio, 446
Cesianu, Konstantin, 488
Chamberlain, Austen, 289, 459–60, 461, 468, 469, 473
Chamberlain, Neville, xv, 90, 294, 298, 455
Charles, Noel, 266–7, 291
Chautemps, Camille, xv, 152
Chiappe, Jean, 165
Chicherin, Georgii V., *5*, 6, 276
Chilston, Aretas Akers-Douglas, Lord: on Anglo-Soviet relations, 287, 291, 302, 333, 422; on British loan to Moscow, 420; on communist propaganda, 464; diplomatic career of, xv, 269; Eden's visit to Moscow and, *317*, 319; meeting with Litvinov, 276–7; meeting with Maiskii, 272; on Soviet security policy, 270
China: relations with Japan, 213, 459
Churchill, Clementine, 329
Churchill, Winston Spencer: on Anglo-German naval agreement, 413; on Anglo-Soviet relations, 266, 289, 329, 414, 420, 422–3, 455, 508; anti-Nazi views of, 330, 354, 467–8, 469; on containment of Japan, 398; on danger of new world war, 412; on domestic situation in England, 331–2; on Far East policy, 330–1, 414; on Hoare-Laval affair, 422; idea of Anglo-Franco-Soviet defensive alliance, 331; on League of Nations, 413–14; Maiskii and, 329–32, 412–14; personality of, 329, 330; political career of, xv, 420; on Soviet foreign policy, 331
Clemenceau, Georges, 345
Clerk, George, 355, 361, 362, 381–2, 497
Cold War, 8
Collier, Laurence: on Anglo-Soviet relations and, 265, 277, 293–4, 422, 455–6, 457, 461–2, 465, 473; on British "complaisance" towards Hitler, 475; on British relations with Japan, 298; conversations with Maiskii, 269, 274; diplomatic career of, xv, 271; dispute between Sargent and, 321, 322; on Franco-Soviet pact, 320; on Litvinov-Ovey exchanges, 87–8; Metro-Vickers crisis and, 77, 86, 87–8, 103; Rhineland crisis and, 466; on Soviet foreign policy, 288
Colville, David John, 103
Comintern, 176; anti-fascist policy, 400, 449, 477; British view of, 457, 458, 460, 462, 464; Congress in 1935, 477; decline of, 7; establishment of, 4; financing of, 26–7, 239; interference in French affairs, 453; propaganda of, 265, 269, 304, 457, 458; Soviet foreign policy and, 6–7; subsidies for communist press from, 323; support of popular fronts, 464
Cooper, Duff, 462
Cooper, Hugh L.: advice to Soviet diplomats, 50–1; on anti-American propaganda, 47; career of, 44, 49; FDR and, 50; personal irritation with Moscow, 46–7; racism of, 47, 48, 49
Corbin, Charles: on Anglo-Soviet relations, 288, 352, 483; conversations with Maiskii, 286, 463, 495; criticism of, 327; diplomatic career of, xv; Laval's instructions to, 254, 357; Rhineland crisis and, 495; on Tory Sovietphobia, 290; Vansittart and, 498
Cot, Pierre: on Franco-Soviet relations, 130, 133, 137, 508; Litvinov-Laval protocol and, 257; political career of, xvi, 123, 131, 514; resignation of,

165, 169; as source of information for Moscow, 126; speech in Geneva about European security, 125; visit to the USSR, 131, 132
Cranborne, Robert Arthur, Viscount, xvi, 457, 466, 476
Cudahy, John, 214, 429
Curtius, Julius, 109
Czechoslovakia: First World War and, 385; Franco-Soviet Pact and, 441–2; independence movement, 385; insecure position of, 388–9, 407–8, 442; relations with France, 506; relations with Germany, 384; relations with Poland, 389, 434; relations with the USSR, 384, 389–90, 426–7; Sudeten territories, 384
Czechoslovak-Soviet mutual assistance pact, 381, 389–90, 426

Daily Express, 310, 325
Daily Mail, 83, 301, 310, 327
Daily Worker, 264, 323
Daladier, Édouard: attitude to the communists, 510; fall of cabinet of, 134, 136; foreign policy of, 137, 510, 512; Franco-Soviet relations and, 250, 488; Germanophilia of, 111, 130, 203; government of, 29, 151, 152–3, 164–5; planned meeting with Hitler, 140; political career of, xvi, 454, 513–14; Stavisky scandal and, 165
Dalimier, Albert, 152
Danubian Pact, 346
Davtian, Iakov Kh.: Anatole de Monzie and, 434–5; background of, 162–3; on Beck's foreign policy, 363, 429, 430–1; diplomatic career of, xvi, 162, 163, 339; Eden's meeting with, 363; on Franco-Polish relations, 434–5; photographs of, 163; on Poland's position on Eastern Pact, 183; on Polish relations with Czechoslovakia, 434; on Soviet-Polish relations, 430–1, 432; Stomoniakov's instructions to, 163–4
Decori, Magdeleine, 448
Dejean, François, 20, 30, 123
Delbos, Yvon, xvi, 482, 492, 514
Del'gas, Vasilii V., 38–9
Deutscher, Isaac, 9, 22
Dimitrov, Georgi, 7
Dirksen, Herbert von, xix, 28, 105, 106–7, 109–11, 118–20, 122
Divil'kovskii, Ivan A., 207
Dniepr dam, 44, 47
Dollfuss, Englebert, 259, 287
Dominic, Pierre, 125
Doriot, Jacques, 367
Doumergue, Gaston, 165, 174, 245, 246–7, 249
Dovgalevskaia, Nadezhda I., 17
Dovgalevskii, Valerian S.: Anatole de Monzie and, 29; Comintern and, 26; conversations with Paul-Boncour, 138, 142, 168; diplomatic career of, xvi, 14–15; discussions of Franco-Soviet relations, 18, 20, 26, 123, 142–3, 146–7, 151, 164; education of, 14; French communists and, 26; illness and death of, 183; Kutepov affair and, 15–16; meeting with Berthelot, 19; mistrust of the French, 374
Duranty, Walter, 226
Duroselle, Jean-Baptiste, 260, 382, 504
Dzhugashvili, Iakov I., 23
Dzhugashvili, Nadezhda S., 23
Dzhugashvili, Svetlana I., 23
Dzhugashvili, Vasilii I., 23
Dzhugashvili, Vissarion, 22

Eastern Pact (Eastern Locarno): Baltic states and, 314; British position on, 182–4, 283, 284, 301, 302, 304–5, 308, 319–20, 335, 341–3, 347, 350–1, 352–4, 386, 394; failure of, 505; Franco-English discussion of, 306, 354;

Eastern Pact (Eastern Locarno) (*cont.*)
Franco-Polish discussion of, 189–90; Franco-Soviet consultations on, 351–2; French position on, 257–8, 286, 334–5, 347–8, 354–5, 366, 369, 370–1; German position on, 181, 186, 189, 250–1, 305, 314, 341, 344, 347, 350, 351, 363–4; guarantor of, 183; idea of, 174; Italian position on, 369; Litvinov-Laval discussion of, 253–4, 255; London negotiations on, 341–3; mutual assistance provisions, 339, 347, 350, 352–53, 370; Paris consultations on, 348; Polish position on, 183, 186, 189–90, 258, 335–6, 340, 349–50, 363–4; Romanian position on, 336, 369; Soviet position on, 343–5, 346–437, 501
Eden, Anthony: on Abyssinian crisis, 418, 472–3; Anglo-Soviet relations and, 316, 461–2, 465, 469, 474, 483, 503; British communists' criticism of, 410; on British loan to Moscow, 421, 473; on British public opinion, 472; on British relations with France, 358, 474; on Eastern Pact, 305, 358; Franco-Soviet negotiations and, 362; on German foreign policy, 470, 472; on Hitler's peace plan (1936), 471; on Hoare-Laval plan, 472; meeting with Laval, 358, 360; meetings with Beneš, 363, 387–8; meetings with Maiskii, 295, 304–5, 313, 410–11, 456–7, 470, 471–2; political career of, xvi, 319, 477, 503; relations with Vansittart, 271, 288, 313, 455; reputation of, 455; Rhineland crisis and, 495, 496, 503, 508; on Soviet propaganda, 411, 464; in Warsaw, 363
Eden, Anthony, and visit to Moscow: arrival in Moscow, *317*; goal of, 314; historic importance of, 310–11, 315; impact of British rapprochement with Germany on, 311–12; meeting with Stalin and Molotov, 318–19; meetings with Litvinov, 316–19, *318*; plans for, 307–8, 309, 313, 357; "propaganda" issue, 318; question of the Baltics and, 314; Soviet publicity of, 309–10; stop in Berlin, 316; stop in Paris, 358
Edward VIII, king of Great Britain, 461, 465
Egorov, Aleksandr I., xvi, 150, 177, 201
Ehrenburg, Il'ia G., 378
Elliot, Walter, xvi, 295
Entente Powers, 4
Europe: in 1930s, map of, xx–xxi, *428*
Evening Standard, 325

Far East: international relations in, 294, 296
fascism in Europe, 3, 109, 191, 192, 340, 400, 402, 404, 512–13
Faure, Paul, 511, 514
Faymonville, Philip R., 234, 235
Feldman's story, 258–9
Finland: Soviet security proposal to, 159, 162
First World War, 5, 28, 30, 129, 295, 385, 415, 497, 505, 508
Fish, Hamilton, 35, 43, 201
Fish Committee: Bogdanov's testimony before, 36–7, 38; final report of, 41; formation of, 35–6; investigation of Amtorg, 40–1; Skvirskii's testimony before, 39–40
Fitzmaurice, Gerald, 70, 77–8
Flandin, Pierre-Étienne: on 1936 French elections, 511–12; Alphand's letters to, 476, 477; Eastern Pact and, 341, 342, 344; foreign policy of, 245, 511; Franco-Soviet relations and, 19, 355, 378, 476, 483, 489, 490–3; on Germany, 480; on Italy's participation in collective security, 481; Litvinov and, 480, 502; on Poland, 348, 481–2; political career of, xvi, 245, 334, 513; Potemkin and, 480, 490, 511–12; Rhineland Crisis and, 496–7, 503; on Spanish Civil War, 515

Foreign Office, Great Britain: Abyssinian crisis and, 411, 417–18; Anglo-Soviet relations and, 265, 268–70, 291, 297, 305; communist propaganda and, 421; correspondence with ambassadors, 397; Eastern Pact and, 184; Franco-Soviet relations and, 184–5, 321, 381, 382–4; intervention into B.B.C. broadcast, 421–2; note to Hitler, 311, 312; opposition to Soviet collective security, 319–21; policy change, 464–5; position on Eastern Locarno, 283; question of British loan to Moscow and, 418–19, 420; relations with Germany, 352; reservations about the Soviet Union, 185, 297; social events at, 274, 275; Soviet entry into the League of Nations and, 284

France: attitude towards communists in, 424–5; banks, 451; colonies of, 169; East European allies of, 424–54; elections of 1936, 510–11, 512; far-right leagues, 10; fascism in, 166–7, 509, 510; Great Depression in, 17; political instability, 150, 151, 152–53, 164–7, 245–6, 445, 449, 450, 511, 513; relations with Britain, 268, 348–9, 403–4, 500–1; relations with Czechoslovakia, 360, 362, 506; relations with Germany, 28–9, 193, 245, 246, 256–7, 446, 505; relations with Italy, 260, 507; relations with Poland, 113, 252–3, 257, 348–9, 434–5; relations with Romania, 506; Rhineland crisis and, *494*, 508, 509; Socialist-Communist alliance, 191; social unrest, 168, 191, 509; Soviet informants in, 334, 335, 346, 365–6; Soviet press on, 11; Tardieu-Weygand group, 256, 257

Francis I, king of France, 249, 253, 484, 488

Franco-Czech-Soviet pact of mutual assistance, 360, 362

François-Poncet, André, 446, 447, 492, 493, 509–10

Franco-Soviet mutual assistance pact: British position on, 357, 358, 380–2, 384, 461, 468, 495–6; debates on ratification of, 442, 445, 448, 450, 453–4, 478, 480, 482–92, 496, 498, 507, 509; French position on, 360–2, 370, 377, 378, 379, 491, 506; Germany and, 384, 482–3, 484, 502; international importance of, 495; Litvinov's promotion of, 362–5, 369–70, 377–80, 425; negotiations of, 334, 340, 355, 371, 372–3, 375–6, 380, 390; political struggle over, 442–3; press coverage of, 376, 377, 487–8; reference to The Hague tribunal, 501; revisions of, 372, 373–4, 375, 379, 390; right-wing critics of, 484–5; signing of, 382, *383*, 389; Soviet position on, 372, 374, 379, 487, 489–90, 493

Franco-Soviet relations: Besedovskii scandal and, 14–15; Britain and, 184, 372; collective security issue, 140–2; Doumergue cabinet and, 175–6; downturn of, 476, 477–8, 506; economic dispute, 17–20, 133–4, 150, 339, 448, 451; exchange of aviation experts and military attachés, 123–4, 134; French political and social crisis and, 152–3, 166–7, 168, 246–7, 251–2, 509; Germany and, 123–4, 245, 246, 249, 252, 295; Herriot and, 28–9, 130–1; Kutepov affair and, 15–17; Litvinov-Laval protocol and, 257–8; military cooperation issue, 258, 390–1; mutual assistance initiative, 142–3, 169; non-aggression pact, 26–8, 29, 30; Paul-Boncour and, 29–30; "policy of the night lamp," 11; rapprochement, 29–30, 31, 128–32, 146–7, 148, 166, 254, 505; Sarraut government and, 482; Soviet entry into League of Nations and, 187; Soviet press on, 150;

Franco-Soviet relations (*cont.*)
Soviet trade mission in, 16; Stavisky scandal, 151–2, 164–5; tsarist debts issue, 21, 484, 489; wives diplomacy, 17
French Communist Party: Comintern's support of, 26, 27, 192, 193; elections of 1936, 511, 512; growth of, 449; relation with socialists, 357, 447; Soviet ties with, 26–7
Front populaire: Comintern and, 453; electoral campaigns, 445, 510, 511, 512, 513; Franco-German relations and, 447; government of, 513–15; growing strength of, 424, 449; organization of, 167; Soviet influence of, 513

Gaboriaud, Léo, 346, 454, 476
Gamelin, Maurice, xvi, 124, 126, 128, 498, 508
Garat, Joseph, 152
Garvin, James L., 267–8, 335
Gazeta Polska (newspaper), 33, 252
Gel'fand, Lev B., 66–7, 68
General Motors, 44–5
Geneva protocol, 370, 371
George V, king of Great Britain, 461, 477
Germany: air pact proposal and, 344, 350, 353; anti-Soviet attitudes, 109, 118–19, 120–1; blood purge of Ernst Röhm, 290; Brüning government, 45; Eastern European policy, 255–7, 290, 347, 350, 351, 363–4, 473; expansionism of, 283; Franco-Soviet relations and, 123–4, 245, 246, 249, 252, 295, 303; League of Nations and, 358; militarist policy, 139–40, 310, 311, 315–16, 466; rearmament of, 153–4, 162, 250, 251, 268, 360, 365, 480; reintroduction of conscription, 310, 355, 360, 368; relations with Britain, 290, 332, 352, 356, 359, 459, 460, 465, 475, 480, 510; relations with Czechoslovakia, 384; relations with Italy, 259–60; relations with Japan, 252; relations with Poland, 111, 112, 186, 255–6, 482, 507; remilitarization of Rhineland, 466–7, 470, 493; Saar reunification with, 300–1; Soviet relations with, 4, 9, 106, 144–7, 150–1, 153, 252, 359–60, 508; violation of international treaties, 478, 480, 493. *See also* Soviet-German relations
Girshfel'd, Evgenii V., xvi, 334, 346
Goebbels, Joseph, 121, 162
Gosplan (the State Planning Committee), 220–1
Great Britain: anti-Soviet agenda, 65; collective security system, 262; Conservative foreign policy, 289–90; Eastern Pact and, 341–3, 350–1; fear of Nazi Germany, 265, 324, 326, 327; Franco-Soviet pact and, 461, 468; German-Soviet hostility and, 358–9; Labour foreign policy, 65–6, 310, 321–2; labour movement, 263–4; League of Nations and, 418; military spending, 309; Peace Ballot, 333; political situation in, 357, 359; public opinion of the USSR, 268–9; relations with France, 268, 348–9, 403–4, 500–1; relations with Germany, 290, 311–12, 331–3, 335, 348–9, 352, 356, 359, 413, 459, 460, 465, 475, 480, 510; relations with Italy, 319; relations with Japan, 294, 465; Rhineland crisis and, 466–8, 495, 500–1, 502–3; Soviet press on, 276–7. *See also* Anglo-German naval agreement; Anglo-Soviet relations
Great Depression, 10, 42
Great War. *See* First World War
Grosvald, Olgerd, 185
Guernut, Henri, 492
Guimier, Pierre, 487

Hague arbitration, 499
Hailsham, Douglas Hogg, Viscount, 90, 91, 306, 419
Halifax, Edward Wood, Earl of, xvi, 324
Hankey, Maurice, 475
Hardy, Oliver, 305
Haslam, Jonathan, 513
Herbette, Jean, xvi, 11, 14, 16–17, 20, 79, 80
Herriot, Édouard: on Anglo-French relations, 404; anti-German views, 354, 362; on Doumergue cabinet meeting, 175–6; Franco-Soviet relations and, 28–30, 130, 170, 253, 257, 260, 373, 378, 382, 488–9, 491–2, 501, 505; on Laval's foreign policy, 260–1; Papen and, 145; political career of, xvi, 166, 167, 345, 513; Potemkin and, 374, 375, 454, 510; prediction of war, 3, 510–11; reputation of, 346; resignation of, 454, 476; return to power, 28; Rhineland crisis and, 503–4; Rozenberg and, 170–1; support of Paul-Boncour's initiative, 150; Tabouis and, 334; tour of the USSR, 130–1, 132
Hertzfeld, Harry, 16
Hilton Young, Edward, 323–4
Hindenburg, Paul von, 288
Hitler, Adolf: 1932 presidential elections, 28; Baltic policy, 180; cartoon against, 325; foreign policy of, 139, 145–6, 157, 250, 301, 356, 368, 369, 479, 502; hypocrisy of, 301, 309, 335; meeting with Simon, 316; *Mein Kampf*, 3, 53, 105, 106, 139, 145; opposition to Eastern Pact, 368, 369; post-Rhineland "Peace Plan," 470–1; Rhineland Crisis and, 466, 493, 495; rise to power, 3, 7, 31, 105, 288, 505, 511; speech in the Reichstag, 106
Hoare, Samuel: Abyssinian crisis and, 415, 507; anti-Bolshevism of, 324; British loan to Moscow and, 421; Churchill and, 331; on European affairs, 328; influence of, 455; Maiskii and, 328, 332, 394, 406; political career of, xvi, 306, 324, 477; promotion of British loan to Moscow, 420; resignation of, 449
Hoare-Laval affair, 415, 416, 417, 448–9, 455, 472, 507
Hodža, Milan, 442
Hoover, Herbert, xvi, 35, 41
Hudson, Robert, 297, 298, 300
Hugenberg, Alfred, 103, 110, 113, 118, 119
Hughes, Langston, 47
Hull, Cordell: Bullitt's correspondence with, 226; meetings with Litvinov, 53–4, 55, 56; political career of, xvi, 51; on Soviet loans, 233; Troianovskii and, 214–15, 229, 231, 233; US-Soviet negotiations and, 212–13, 218, 220, 225, 232, 243
L'Humanité (newspaper), 376, 453

Iaroslavkaia, Marianna E., 127
Il'inskii, Ia. S., 196, 197
India: British concern of Soviet interest in, 394–5
Ioffe, Adol'f A., 127, 163
Italo-Abyssinian War. *See* Abyssinian crisis
Italy: foreign policy, 259–60, 319, 335, 403, 506, 507; invasion of Abyssinia, 7, 394, 400; population of, 395; potential anti-Nazi coalition and, 415
Izvestiia (newspaper), 33, 81, 150, 156, 265, 276, 307, 354, 486

Japan: British policy towards, 294, 414, 465; FDR's view of, 62; foreign policy of, 46, 198, 202, 203, 268, 282; invasion of China, 213, 397, 459
Joffre, Joseph, 497
Jones, Gareth, 80, 95
Journal de Genève, 416
Journal de Moscou, 143, 440, 445

Kagan, Samuil B., 87, 88–9, 458
Kaganovich, Lazar M.: on Anglo-Soviet relations, 288; criticism of the NKID, 21, 25; influence of, 153; Litvinov's policies and, 29, 43–4, 251, 400, 403; political career of, xvi; as Stalin's loyalist, 24, 45; US-Soviet negotiations and, 53, 224, 241, 242
Kalinin, Mikhail I., 51–2, 198, 201, 251
Karakhan, Lev M.: at dinner in honour of Voroshilov, 179; diplomatic career of, xvi, 228; efforts to discredit Ovey, 80–1; meeting with Bullitt, 198; meetings with Stalin, 81; Nadolny and, 148–9; negotiations with Patek, 25
Kelley, Robert F.: anti-Soviet views of, 39, 207; *Black and White* film controversy and, 48; career of, xvi, 207; meeting with Troianovskii, 229; proposal of "gentleman's agreement," 206, 208, 209, 210, 212
Kennan, George F., 197
Kennedy, A.L., 283, 303
Kerenskii debt, 56, 57, 209, 216, 218, 220–2, 225, 230, 236, 238
Kerillis, Henri de, 191, 259, 345
Kerr, Philip (Lord Lothian), 301, 302
Khinchuk, Lev M., 109, 110, 145–6, 180–1
Kolchak, Aleksandr V., 278
Köster, Roland, 446–7
Kotkin, Stephen, 23
Kowalewski, Jan, xvi, 443, 444, 445, 482
Krestinskii, Nikolai N.: on Baltic protocol, 179; on British loan, 420; on British policy towards Germany, 311–12; Bullitt's talks with, 207, 208, 215–21, 234; conversation with Ivy Ledbetter Lee, 46; correspondence with Potemkin, 358, 375, 501–2; at dinner in honour of Voroshilov, 179; diplomatic career of, xvi, 107–8, 109; Dirksen and, 105, 106, 118–20, 122; on Eastern Locarno, 501; education of, 108; on Franco-Soviet relations, 29, 123–4, 128, 501–2; on German-Polish relations, 115; on German rearmament, 139–40; on Herriot, 28; idea of Soviet concessions to the US, 229–30; instructions to Troianovskii, 212, 225, 230–1, 233; on Laval, 261; Laval's visit to Moscow and, 390; Litvinov's letters to, 103; meetings with Stalin, 81, 354; on Metro-Vickers Affair, 67, 77, 96; Nadolny and, 144, 148; on Ovey, 80–1; photograph of, *108*; political career of, xvi, 108; on Soviet entry into the League of Nations, 138–9; on Soviet-German relations, 107, 110, 118–19, 120; on Soviet-Polish rapprochement, 113; Stalin and, 109; on subsidy to British press, 263, 264; support of Trotskii, 108–9; on US-Soviet "gentleman's agreement," 219
Kutepov affair, 15–17

Labonne, Eirik, 476
LaFollette, Robert, Jr., 50
Laroche, Jules: diplomatic career of, xvi; on Eastern Pact, 182, 348; on Polish rapprochement with Germany, 155; on Soviet-Polish relations, 112, 185, 186
La Rocque, François de, 256
Lasteyrie, Charles, 484
Lattre de Tassigny, Jean de, 125, 135–7, 339
Laurel, Stan, 305
Laval, Josée, 367
Laval, Pierre: Abyssinian crisis and, 401–2, 415, 447, 507; anti-communism of, 176, 365, 447; Aubervilliers and, 176, 177, 193, 246, 359, 360, 367, 368, 376, 377; background and education of, 367; British opinion of, 345; on Catholic Church, 392; on Comintern, 26, 27, 453; Eastern Pact negotiations and, 257–8, 341–4, 347, 350, 351, 358,

364, 366, 369; Franco-Soviet Pact and, 360–1, 372–3, 375, 378, 379–82, *383*, 390, 437, 442–3, 445, 461, 506; French Communist Party and, 357; influence of, 436; Köster and, 446–7; on Little Entente, 365; "little steps" of, 259–60; Litvinov's meetings with, 253–4, 255, 257, 335, *341*, 370; "Monsieur Zigzag," 358, 360, 361, 370, 424, 433; Mussolini and, 260, 400–1, 409; personality of, 367–8, 371–2; at Piłsudski's funeral, 424; political career of, xvi, 175, 193, 245, 357, 361, 367; Potemkin's meetings with, 355, 357, 359–61, 370–1, 375, 447, 498–9; press attacks against, 376; relations with Britain, 404, 409; relations with Germany, 246, 250, 253, 254, 256, 442, 446–8, 510; relations with Italy, 403; relations with Poland, 348, 443; relations with the Soviet Union, 18, 177, 193, 340–1, 448, 451–2; resignation of, 476, 493, 507; Rome accords and, 260, 335; Simon and, 306; Stalin and, *391*, 391–2; Titulescu and, 361; on tsarist debts, 390; visit to Moscow, 357, 359, 390

League of Nations: Abyssinian crisis and, 395, 396, 398, 413, 471; British opinion on, 413, 414–15, 418; Council meetings, 496, 503; declaration of Italy as aggressor, 400; France's reliance on, 472; Germany and, 122, 140, 358; great powers in, 459–60; Rhineland Crisis and, 495; Soviet policy towards, 164, 271–2, 288, 402–3; vice-president's election, 398–9; weakness of, 111, 157, 455, 468, 472, 501. *See also* Soviet entry into the League of Nations

Lebrun, Albert, 125, 346, 510

Lee, Ivy Ledbetter, 41, 43, 46

Leeper, Reginald A., xvii, 100–1, 102, 262–3, 455, 466

Léger, Alexis: Abyssinia agreement and, 415; background of, 135; on collective security, 142; Dovgalevskii and, 142–3, 151, 164; Eastern Pact negotiations, 172–3, 345, 347; Franco-Soviet negotiations, 132, 135, 172, 355, 375, 376, 377, 378, 382, 476, 478–9, 504; Litvinov and, 478, 479, 502; political career of, xvii, 135; Potemkin and, 361, 369, 374, 375, 452, 479; Rhineland Crisis and, 497; Rozenberg and, 172, 173; on Soviet entry into the League of Nations, 169

Leméry, Henri, 348

Lena Goldfields concession, 281, 286, 291, 293

Lenin, Vladimir I., 5, 195

LeTrocquer, Yves, 492

Lipski, Józef, 113, 115, 154, 182

Lithuania, 163, 168, 179, 189, 256, 327, 349, 408, 410, *428*

Little Entente (Czechoslovakia, Romania, Yugoslavia), 301, 368, 398, 468, 496, 499; conference in Ljubljana, 387; Eastern Pact and, 334; France and, 365; Franco-Soviet rapprochement and, 132, 334, 335, 358, 362, 389–90; Poland and, 31, 114, 186; Romania and, 336; Soviet relations with, 110, 143, 187, 343, 344; weakness of, 364–5

Litvinov, Maksim M.: Abyssinian crisis and, 395–6, 400, 404–5, 414, 416–17, 469–70; air pact proposal, 251, 344, 351; on Anglo-German naval agreement, 332, 333; on Anglo-Soviet relations, 81, 277, 288, 299–300, 315, 506; anti-Nazi attitude, 103, 104, 319, 332, 349–50, 364, 506; approach to Soviet foreign policy, 9, 25–6, 141–2, 304; background and education of, 11–12;

Litvinov, Maksim M. (*cont.*)
Balkan policy, 435–6; on Baltic countries, 6, 106, 116, 151, 159, 178–80, 314, 356; on British foreign policy, 97, 98, 357, 396, 397–8, 405–6, 474–5; Chicherin and, 6; on Churchill, 468; collective security policy, 141, 250–1, 354, 481, 501; conflict with Troianovskii, 204–5, 211–12, 222–6, 228–9, 241, 242; on dealing with go-betweens, 84–5; on definition of an aggressor, 111; diary of, 15, 76; Dovgalevskii's dispatches to, 164; Eastern Pact negotiations and, 183, 343–5, 351–2, 358; Eden's visit to Moscow and, 314, 316–19, 477; on exchange of military attachés with Britain, 291; Far Eastern policy, 242; on Franco-Italian relations, 260; Franco-Soviet relations and, 11, 18, 26–8, 128–32, 142, 150, 203, 242, 251–2, 362–5, 369–70, 372–3, 374, 375, 376, 377–80, 382–3, *383*, 425, 439, 448–9, 481, 486–7, 489, 493, 509; on French Communist Party, 26–7; on French elections, 512, 513; on French political instability, 136, 166, 192, 245; on Front populaire, 513; Geneva trips, 218, 335, 340; at George V's funeral, 461, 477; on German foreign policy, 145, 181–2, 250, 316–17; on German-Polish relations, 159, 175; gift to FDR, 215; on Hitler, 8, 470–1, 479; on Hoare-Laval plan, 449; idea of triple entente, 461; illness of, 207, 208, 269; instructions to Maiskii, 269, 279, 299–300, 304, 396–7, 405–6; instructions to Ostrovskii, 437, 439, 440; instructions to Potemkin, 351, 354–5, 362–3, 364, 380, 436, 452, 512; instructions to Rozenberg, 253; on Japanese threat, 202, 203; Kaganovich and, 25; on Kerenskii debt, 221–2, 227; on Laval's policies, 261, 447–8, 452–3; on League of Nations, 111, 187, 188–9, 202, 271–2, 398–9; marriage of, 12, 13; on *Mein Kampf*, 145–6, 148, 149–50, 151, 182; Metro-Vickers Affair and, 67, 70–84, 86, 87–8, 90, 95–104; mission to Berlin, 122, 133; on national defence, 177; on Nazi campaign against Jews, 63; on Nazi-Polish relations, 155, 156, 158–9; on negotiations between the Locarno powers, 496; negotiations with Laval, 242, 253–4, 255, 257, *341*, 370, 378–9, 390; Neurath and, 105–6, 122, 133, 181–2; Papen's proposals and, 28–9; personality of, 202, 227, 513; photographs of, *5*, *12*, *158*; Polish-Soviet relations and, 25–6, 154, 160, 161, 162, 176, 427, 429, 507; political career of, xvii, 6, 13; relations with Politburo, 49, 58, 379–80; reports to Stalin, 24, 178, 205, 223, 250–1, 343–4, 350, 356, 362, 383, 452–3, 489; reputation in the West, 43–4; revolutionary pseudonyms of, 11–12; Rhineland crisis and, 493, 495, 508, 509; rumours about ousting, 242, 251; on Saar problem, 301, 335; scapegoating of, 240; on Soviet and English press, 276–7; on Soviet-German relations, 109–11, 148, 359; speculation about future war, 3; speech in Geneva, 1934, *188*; speech to the Central Committee, 147; Titulescu and, 337, *338*, 387, 437, 440; on tsarist debts, 224; Twardowski and, 121–2, 147; US-Soviet negotiations and, 52–3, 203, 211, 212, 238, 239, 244; Wiley and, 208, 241, 242; Wilson and, 254–5; at World Disarmament Conference, 111; at World Economic Conference, 99–100

Litvinov, Maksim M., and meetings:
with Alphand, 192–3, 352, 427, 452, 482; with Barthou, 174–5, 176, 191;

with Beck, 157–9, 175, 427; with Beneš, 372, 384; with Bullitt, 195, 200, 201, 202–4, 208–11, 215, 220–1, 225, 226, 236, 237–40; with Chilston, 276–7, 291; with Dirksen, 106–7, 109–11; with Edward VIII, 461; with Flandin, 496; with Herbette, 16–17; with Leeper, 262–3; with Léger, 479; with Łukasiewicz, 154, 156; with Mussolini, 139; with Nadolny, 144–5, 147–51, 180; with Ovey, 71–2, 75–81; with Pole, 99–100; with Simon, 102, 103, 306; with Stalin, 81, 95, 354, 370, 377

Litvinov, Maksim M., and mission to Washington: debt-loan negotiations, 59–62, 63; discussion of mutual assistance, 54, 139; FDR and, 53–4, 60–1, 62–3, 130–2, 134, 194, 203, 205–6, 208, 211, 214, 219–20, 224, 230, 231, 238; financial issues, 55, 56, 57; "gentleman's agreement" with Roosevelt, 60, 61, 130–2, 134, 194, 203, 205–6, 208, 211, 214, 219–20, 224, 230, 231, 238, 505; guidelines for negotiations, 52–3; Kerenskii debt issue, 56, 57, 59; negotiations with Hull, 53–4, 55; outcome of, 505; Politburo and, 58; political issues, 62–3; religious rights issue, 54, 55, 58, 60, 62, 63; Roosevelt's eleven points, 56–7; Soviet concessions, 224–5; Stalin and, 52, 58, 60, 61–2

Lloyd, George Ambrose, Baron, 276, 282

Lloyd George, David, xvi, 195, 279, 327

Locarno Pact, 172, 362, 389, 485; German violation of, 478, 480, 493, 495. *See also* Eastern Pact

Loizeau, Lucien, 436

Loraine, Percy, 268–9

Low, David, 325

Low, Ivy, 12, 13, 75

Luftwaffe, 310, 311, 355, 360

Łukasiewicz, Juliusz: diplomatic career of, xvii; on Eastern Pact, 190; Litvinov and, 116, 154, 156, 160, 349–50, 429; on Soviet-Polish relations, 160–1, 252; Stomoniakov and, 113, 161, 430

Lunarcharskii, Anatolii V., 147

Lupescu, Elena, 339

MacDonald, Ishbel, 275

MacDonald, Ramsay: authorization for Simon's trip to Moscow, 307, 308; Eastern Pact and, 301; foreign policy of, 91, 269; Metro-Vickers crisis and, 100; political career of, xvii; at Stresa Conference, 319; travels of, 71, 83

Macmillan, George A., 84–5, 86

Maiskaia, Agniia A., 267, 280, 458

Maiskii, Ivan M.: on Abyssinian crisis and, 394, 397; on alliance against Germany, 474; on Anglo-Franco-Soviet entente, 461, 464, 470; on Anglo-German relations, 313, 357, 393–4, 412, 465; Anglo-Soviet rapprochement and, 88–9, 263–7, 272–7, 285–6, 287, 288, 289, 291, 316, 334, 411, 506; approach to bargaining, 89; background and education of, 277–8; on British foreign policy, 265, 302–3, 474; on British loan to the USSR, 419, 420, 456; on British position on the League of Nations, 418; on British press, 83; confrontation with Hudson and Burgin, 300; on Conservative Party, 289–90; contacts and acquaintances of, 279, 324–5, 406; diplomatic career of, xvii, 43, 262, 278–9; disagreements between Litvinov and, 396–7; on disarmament policy, 284; dispatches to Moscow, 83–4, 284, 285; on Eastern Pact, 283, 295, 301, 352–3, 471;

Maiskii, Ivan M. (*cont.*)
on Eden's visit to Moscow, 309–10; on European security, 292; Foreign Office and, 87, 274, 275, 465; on Franco-Polish relations, 348; on French foreign policy, 472; on Germany, 283, 284, 513; on Hitler's peace plan, 323, 470; on Hoare-Laval plan, 417, 458; on India, 394–5; on Japan's foreign policy, 281, 284, 293; Krestinskii's correspondence with, 390; on Labour Party, 310; on lack of information from Moscow, 97; language skills of, 278; on Laval, 355; letter to Eden, 422–3; Litvinov's communications with, 43, 280–1, 300, 383; Litvinov's opinion of, 97; meeting with Baldwin, 394; meeting with Chilton, 272; meeting with Cooper, 462; meeting with Garvin, 267–8; meetings with Austen Chamberlain, 459–60; meetings with Churchill, 329–32, 412–14, 467; meetings with Collier, 86–7, 269, 273; meetings with Eden, 295, 304–5, 410–11, 456–7, 470, 471–2, 507; meetings with Hoare, 328, 394, 406; meetings with Lady Vansittart, 275, 279–80, 281, 307, 465; meetings with Lord Beaverbrook, 325–7, 332, 412; meetings with Macmillan, 84–6; meetings with Marshall, 84–6, 89; meetings with Simon, 91–4, 274–5, 292–3, 295, 300, 304–5; meetings with Strang, 273–4; meetings with Vansittart, 276, 279–88, 295–9, 300, 307–9, 312–13, 321–3, 343, 357, 382, 384, 393–5, 406–8, 458–9; meetings with Young, 323–4; Metro-Vickers affair and, 77, 82–7, 90–1, 289; on Ovey, 83, 90; photograph of, 278; on reimbursement of the tsarist debts, 420; Rhineland crisis and, 466–7, 469, 495; Russian Civil War and, 278; on Simon's visit to Moscow, 306, 307; socialist views of, 277; on Soviet entry into the League of Nations, 272; on Soviet foreign policy, 281, 292, 294; on Soviet press, 293; on Soviet public opinion, 281; on Stalin's meeting with Laval, 391; on subsidy to British press, 263, 264–5; on triple entente, 466–7

Manchuria, 45, 63, *199*, 396, 397

Mandel, Georges: background of, 345; Nazi invasion of France and, 508, 514; negotiation of Franco-Soviet pact and, 371, 378, 404, 454, 488; political career of, xvii, 345–6, 450, 476, 513; Potemkin and, 450, 499–500; Rhineland Crisis and, 503–4

Manuil'skii, Dmitri Z., 282

Margerie, Roland de, 342–3, 345

Marshall, Arthur, 65, 84–5, 86, 89

Masaryk, Jan, xvii

Massigli, René, 372, 388, 389, 425, 497

Matignon accords, 514

Matuszewski, Ignacy, 117

Maurin, Louis, 373

McMeekin, Sean, 509

Mein Kampf (Hitler): dissemination of, 145–6, 268; on Eastern policy, 146, 250, 318, 508; FDR on, 53; Litvinov on, 106, 145–6, 148, 149–50, 180, 182; publication of, 3, 105

Meltz, Renaud, 173, 415

Memel, 179, 327, 408, 417, *428*, 471

Mendras, Edmond: career of, xvii, 123; at dinner with Voroshilov, 177; on fear of Nazi-Japanese alliance, 139; on Franco-Soviet relations, 126, 132, 146, 169, 176; on Nadolny, 181; on Poland, 253, 507; reputation of, 125–6; on Soviet foreign policy, 251; on Stalin's influence on Litvinov, 364

Menzhenskii, Viacheslav R., 127

Mercier, Ernest, 492

Metro-Vickers Affair, 66–104; aftermath of, 96–9; appeals for clemency, 97, 98; arrests in Moscow, 66–8; British embassy's reaction on, 66–7, 68–9; British public opinion on, 74, 101; business community and, 101; escalation of, 69–75; Foreign Office and, 69–70, 77–8, 81, 85, 103–4; Gel'fand's statement on, 68–9; impact on Anglo-Soviet relations, 506; Litvinov-Ovey exchanges over, 70–3, 75–81, 88; Litvinov-Simon meeting on, 101–2; Maiskii and, 77, 82–4; OGPU investigation of, 94–95; question of embargo and, 102–3; resolution of, 98, 101–4, 262; sentences, 95–6; TASS communiqué about, 80, 83; trial, 91–6; Vansittart's instructions on, 67, 70

Mezhlauk, Valerii I., 51

MI6 (British Secret Intelligence Service), 15

Miedziński, Bogusław, 33–4, 112, 117, 252

Mikoian, Anastas I., xvii, 36, 37

Molotov, Viacheslav M.: Comintern declaration, 400; Eden's visit to Moscow and, 318–19; on Hitler's plan of conquest of the USSR, 318; influence of, 153; on issue of loans and debts, 238; on Litvinov, 251, 403; meeting with Bullitt, 238; Nazi policy and, 29; on Ovey, 302; political career of, xvii; on Rapallo policy, 120; as Stalin's loyalist, 24; US-Soviet negotiations and, 53, 224, 242

Monzie, Anatole de, 29, 166, 434–5, 476

Moore, R. Walton: career of, xvii, 207, 232; meeting with Troianovskii, 229; on Rubinin, 209; telegram for Bullitt, 237; US-Soviet negotiations and, 214, 221, 223, 232–3

Morgenthau, Henry, Jr., 51, 59, 61, 62, 63, 194, 206

Moskauer Rundschau (newspaper), 143

Mounsey, George A., xvii, 297, 315

Mussolini, Benito: anticipation of war, 3; cartoon against, 325; Eastern Pact and, 369; foreign policy of, 141, 400, 506; meeting with Litvinov, 139, 141; negotiations with Laval, 260, 400–1; political career of, xvii; relations with Germany, 259–60; response to Austrian coup, 259; Rome accords and, 335; at Stresa Conference, 319

Nadolny, Rudolf: on Baltic protocol, 179; conversations with Voroshilov, 149, 179, 181; diplomatic career of, xvii, 144; German-Soviet relations and, 144, 145; isolation in embassy, 178; on Litvinov's influence, 153; meetings with NKID leadership, 144, 147–51, 178, 180; proponent of Rapallo, 144; resignation of, 181; on Soviet relations with France, 148

National Socialist German Workers' Party (NSDAP), 3, 10, 178

Nazi Brownshirts (*Braunhemden*), 10, 109, 150

Nazi-Polish non-aggression pact, 154, 155, 157

Neiman, Aleksei F., 449, 450

Neurath, Konstantin von, 105–6, 122, 133, 151, 181–2

New Leader, the, 263, 264

New York Chamber of Commerce, 42, 51

New York Times, the, 226, 242

Nicolson, Harold, 466

Niessel, Henri Albert, 126

Nixon, F.H., 102

NKID (People's Commissariat for Foreign Affairs), 3; Abyssinian crisis and, 398; budget, 453; criticism of, 21, 25; defectors from, 15; Eastern Pact and, 429; Franco-Soviet relations and, 31, 251, 370; intelligence gathering, 334, 358, 365–6;

NKID (People's Commissariat for Foreign Affairs) (*cont.*)
Metro-Vickers Affair and, 68; Polish policy, 164, 429; subsidy to foreign press, 264
Noël, Léon, xvii, 346, 430, 481, 482
Novaia Zhizn (newspaper), 12

OGPU (Soviet secret police), 15
Oliphant, Lancelot: Anglo-Soviet negotiations and, 77, 86, 265, 266, 277, 300; on matter of "Germany v. Russia," 463–4, 475; Metro-Vickers crisis and, 103; on Soviet foreign policy, 465
Orde, C.W., 320
Orlicz-Dreszer, Gustaw Konstanty, 259
Ostrovskii, Mikhail S.: connection in French defence ministry, 125; dinner with de Lattre and Cayrol, 135–7; diplomatic career of, xvii, 124, 338–9; education of, 124; with embassy staff in Bucharest, *438*; language skills of, 339; letter to Voroshilov, 126; Litvinov's instructions to, 437–8, 439, 440; on Polish-Romanian relations, 433; reports on situation in Paris, 125–7
Osuský, Štefan, xvii, 492
Ovey, Edmond: "Big Seven" and, 90–1; conversations with Rubinin, 70, 73–4; diplomatic career of, xvii; meetings with Litvinov, 71–2, 75–81; Metro-Vickers Affair and, 67, 68, 69–71, 73, 74, 76, 83, 88, 90; resignation of, 79; return to London, 81; Soviet attempt to discredit, 80–1; on Soviet foreign policy, 19
Ozerskii, Aleksandr V., 102

Papen, Franz von, 28, 45, 145
Patek, Stanisław, 25, 26
Paul-Boncour, Joseph: background of, 29–30; Eastern Pact negotiations, 347–8, 351, 370; on German-Polish negotiations, 111; meeting with Bullitt, 203; meetings with Dovgalevskii, 138, 142, 146–7, 151, 153, 164; meetings with Litvinov, 130, 134; mutual assistance initiative, 141, 150, 479; political career of, xvii, 29, 152, 165, 448, 476, 513; Rhineland crisis and, 496; on Soviet entry into League of Nations, 138–9, 140–1; support of Franco-Soviet rapprochement, 30, 134–5, 146–7, 169, 202, 350, 354, 478, 484, 492, 493, 505, 508
Payart, Jean, xvii, 141, 191, 345, 361, 449, 450
Péri, Gabriel, xvii, 485–6, 487, 488, 489, 493, 508, 514
Pertinax (André Géraud), xvii, 335, 345, 346, 376, 514
Pétain, Philippe, 487, 511
Phillips, William, 55, 63
Phipps, Eric, 315, 458, 459, 461–2
Piatakov, Iurii L., 201
Piétri, François, 488
Piłsudski, Józef: anticipation of war, 3; foreign policy of, 31, 34, 155–6, 163, 174, 252, 257; funeral of, 392, 424; on Laval, 256; military and political career of, xvii; personality of, 338; Soviet-Polish war and, 24
Podol'skii, Boris G., 432
Poincaré, Raymond, xvii, 18, 28, 150, 483, 484
Poland: anti-Soviet attitudes in, 20–1, 161, 163–4, 252, 271, 340, 431; change of government in, 432; Eastern Pact and, 335, 349, 363–4; elitist society, 117; international influence of, 385; possibility of "fourth partition" of, 507; relations with Czechoslovakia, 434; relations with France, 252–3, 257, 348–9, 443–6; relations with Germany, 113–16, 153–4, 157–62, 174, 186, 202, 207–8, 252, 257, 258–9, 431–2, 445,

482, 507; relations with Romania, 338, 433–4, 445; Soviet ambassadors in, 162–3; Soviet intelligence reports on, 186, 258–9; Soviet interest in rapprochement with, 31–2, 33–4, 432, 505; as spoiler of collective security, 185. *See also* Soviet-Polish relations
Pole, Felix, 84, 87, 99–100
Polish Corridor, 112, 155, 157, 182, 255, *428*, 433
Polish-German non-aggression pact, 207–8, 507
Politburo: on Abyssinian crisis, 417; approval of new policy on France, 143; collective security policy, 151, 363; on concessions to the Americans, 242; directives on Czech-Soviet mutual assistance, 389–90; directives on Eastern Pact, 351, 370; directives on Franco-Soviet pact, 376–7; Litvinov's reports to, 379–80; resolution on Anglo-Soviet relations, 263
Pollitt, Harry, 421, 422
Poncet, André François, 140
Pope, Frederick, 48–9, 51
Potemkin, Vladimir P.: on Anglo-French relations, 502–3; background of, 247; consultations on Eastern Pact, 343–4, 345, 346–7; diplomatic career of, xvii, 247, 425; on elections in France, 510; on French foreign policy, 424, 442, 502; on French government, 481; on The Hague initiative, 500; on Laval, 340–1, 358, 447; Litvinov's instructions to, 351, 354–5, 362–3, 380, 436; meeting with Sarraut, 500; meeting with Titulescu, 368; meetings with Alphand, 477; meetings with Flandin, 480, 490, 511–12; meetings with Herriot, 260–1, 374, 375; meetings with Laval, 350, 355, 357–8, 359–61, 369, 370–1, 375, 376, 390, 453, 498–9; meetings with Léger, 346–7, 369, 374, 452, 479; meetings with Mandel, 450, 499–500, 502; meetings with Paul-Boncour, 347, 348, 350, 484; photograph of, *248*; Politburo directives to, 370; political contacts of, 345, 346, 448, 453; promotion of Franco-Soviet rapprochement, 335, 362, 371, 374–5, 446, 448, 450–2, 478, 483–4, 487, 490, 491–2; Rhineland crisis and, 510; on Sadoul project, 358; on Soviet-German relations, 105; travels to Geneva, 402, 403; view of Poland, 507
Pravda (newspaper), 14, 107, 113, 150, 276, 486, 487
Pressard, Georges, 152
Proudhon, Pierre-Joseph, 246
Putna, Vitovt K., 291

Quilici, Francois, 415

Radek, Karl B.: career of, xviii; conversation with Miedziński, 33; criticism of Litvinov, 231; discussion of Polish-Soviet relations and, 115–17; on French foreign policy, 251; prediction of war, 146; on Soviet foreign policy, 103, 188; "The Hissing of Fascist Vermin," 179; tour of Poland, 111–12; on Treaty of Versailles, 107
Radziwiłł, Janusz F., 160
Ramseyer, Christian William, 36
Rapallo, Treaty of: decline of, 115; diplomatic effect of, 4; German position on, 121, 144; importance of, 9; termination of, 147, 151, 505
Rathenau, Walther, 109
Reed, John: *Ten Days that Shook the World*, 195
Reynaud, Paul, xviii, 126
Rhineland: map of, *494*; remilitarization of, 466–7, 508

Rhineland crisis: British position on, 495, 499, 500–1, 508; French position on, 493, 498, 500–1, 503–4, 508, 510; German diplomacy and, 498–9; international reaction to, 495–9, 502–3, 509; League of Nations' reaction to, 493; Soviet position on, 504
Ribbentrop, Joachim von, xix, 408
Röhm, Ernst, 283
Rollin, Henri, 346, 453
Romania: collective security policy, 445–6; Eastern Pact and, 336; relations with France, 336, 506; relations with Poland, 338, 433–4, 445. *See also* Soviet-Romanian relations
Rome accords, 260
Roosevelt, Eleanor, 53
Roosevelt, Franklin D. (FDR): 1932 presidential election, 50; Barlow's ties with, 45; domestic problems, 214; foreign policy of, 48–9, 52, 62–3, 239, 505; on Hitler's *Mein Kampf*, 53; negotiations with Litvinov, 53–4, 55, 56, 57, 59–60; polio therapy, 59; reputation of, 214
Rosenberg, Alfred, 145, 149, 151, 182, 250, 268
Rothermere, Harold Sidney Harmsworth, Viscount, 473
Rowse, A.L., 301
Rozenberg, Marcel' I.: background and education of, 127; diplomatic career of, xviii, 127, 247, 334, *338*; Franco-Soviet relations and, 124, 126–7; on German danger, 29, 44; on Laval, 246; Litvinov's instructions to, 174, 253; marriage of, 127; meeting with Barthou, 174; meeting with Doumergue, 246–7, 248; meeting with Herriot, 170–1; meeting with Léger, 172–3; meeting with Payart, 361; photograph of, *128*; reports on situation in France, 132–3, 137, 140, 166–7
Rozengol'ts, Arkadii P., xviii, 42
Rubinin, Evgenii V.: on Anglo-Soviet relations, 291; diplomatic career of, xviii; Eastern Pact negotiations and, 348; meetings with Bullitt, 209, 215–18, 219–20, 237; meetings with Noel Charles, 266–7; meetings with Ovey, 70, 71, 73–4; trip to Washington, 214; on US-Soviet negotiations, 229
Runciman, Walter, 90, 91, 92, 93, 419, 466–7
Russian Christians: Archbishop of Canterbury's prayer for, 323
Russian Civil War, 278
Rydz-Śmigły, Edward, 112

Saar plebiscite, 300–1, 315, 335
Sadoul, Jacques, 358, 361
Salengro, Roger, 515
Sargent, Orme Garton: Anglo-Soviet relations and, 320–1, 455–6, 461, 463, 477, 483; on British loan to Moscow, 420, 421; on Comintern propaganda, 457, 462; on Eastern Pact, 319–20; on Franco-Soviet relations, 321, 380, 384, 425; political career of, xviii; on relations with Germany, 406, 463, 465; Rhineland crisis and, 497–8
Sarraut, Albert: anti-communism of, 169; cabinet of, 476, 478, 512–13, 514; Franco-Soviet Pact and, 490, 492, 493, 506; The Hague initiative, 500; Litvinov and, 502; political career of, xviii, 454; position towards Germany, 511; Rhineland Crisis and, 499, 503
Schacht, Hjalmar, 442
Schulenburg, Friedrich Werner von der, xix, 301, 365
Schweisguth, Victor-Henri, xix, 441

Second World War, x, xi, 3, 8, 15, 475
Semenov, Nikolai A., xviii, 258, 259
Seymour, H.J., xviii, 275
Shakhty affair, 66, 67
Sheinmann, A.L., 15
Shirer, William, 165
Shliapnikov, Aleksandr G., 223
Shtein, Boris E., xviii, 337, 384, 416
Shtern, David G., xviii, 110
Simon, John: Anglo-Soviet relations and, 269, 287, 292, 296, 300, 306; on British embargo, 89; on communist propaganda, 293; conversations with Maiskii, 274–5, 292–3, 295; diplomatic career of, xviii, 66; disagreements with Vansittart, 280, 307–8; Franco-Soviet negotiations and, 355, 380, 382; instructions to Campbell, 380; invitation to visit Moscow, 306, 355; letter to Chilston, 287; Litvinov's suspicion of, 370; meeting with Hitler, 316; meeting with Lady Vansittart, 279; meeting with Laval, 306; meeting with Litvinov, 102; meetings with Maiskii, 91–4, 279, 304–5; Metro-Vickers Affair and, 91, 98, 100; negotiations on Eastern Pact and, 185, 301, 305, 342; Paris mission (1935), 306; pro-Japanese position, 293, 294; on Soviet entry into the League of Nations, 187, 286; travels of, 83; on universal security agreement, 369; visit to Berlin, 313, 356, 357, 358
Sinclair, Archibald, 412
Skvirskii, Boris E.: on Bogdanov's testimony, 37; Bullitt's talk with, 52, 235–6; conversations with US government, 50–1, 234–6; diplomatic career of, xviii, 194; on diplomatic recognition of the USSR, 43; on Fish Committee, 41; Litvinov's opinion on, 204–5; reports of, 35, 36, 50, 51, 52; on Soviet-American trade, 40, 42; testimony before Fish Committee, 39–40
Sokolin, Vladimir A., 365–6, 367, 368, 371–2, 491
Sokolnikov, Gregorii Ia., xviii, 198
Soviet-American relations: American business and, 46, 51; Bullitt's role in, 51–2, 207–12; debts-credits negotiations, 205–6, 213, 231–3, 234–5, 240, 244; establishment of, 194; evolution of, 44, 46–7, 51–3, 228, 505–6; FDR and, 50–2, 63–4; Japan and, 198; Kerenskii debt issue, 209, 216, 218, 220, 230; negotiations in Moscow, 212–18, 240–3; negotiations in Washington, 53–64, 221–2, 243–4; policy of non-recognition, 35; propaganda issue in, 47–8; Soviet concessions, 224–5, 229–30; trade, 35, 36, 41–2
Soviet-Czechoslovak mutual assistance treaty, 381, 389–90, *426*
Soviet entry into the League of Nations, 288; British position on, 269–70, 287, 289; discussions of, 174, 186–8, 202, 268; French position on, 138–9, 140–1, 169, 187, 269–70, 286; proposal of, 138–9
Soviet foreign policy: evolution of, 19; in the Far East, 202, 294; Germany and, 9; historiography, 508–9; NKID and, 6; Stalin and, 7, 304; traditional approach in, 436; Western historiography on, 7–8, 9
Soviet-French guarantee pact. *See* Franco-Soviet Treaty of Mutual Assistance
Soviet-German relations, 4, 105–7, 109, 110, 118–19, 501
Soviet-Italian relations, 139, 403, 505
Soviet-Japanese war, 162, 169
Soviet-Polish non-aggression pact, 25–6, 31, 158, 161, 162
Soviet-Polish relations: change of Polish government and, 432; cultural exchange, 161;

Soviet-Polish relations (*cont.*)
evolution of, 21–32, 33–4, 111–12, 113–16, 153–4, 158–9, 160, 429, 431–2; exchange of diplomatic missions, 160–1; German factor in, 113, 114–15, 430–1; incident with Łukasiewicz's chauffeur, 432–3; mistrust in, 427, 429; peace and security declaration, 116; territorial claims, 20
Soviet-Polish War, 24, 363
Soviet-Romanian relations, 20–1, 34, 337–40, 427, 437–41, 480, 482
Soviet Union: American business in, 44–5; anti-American propaganda in, 47; collective security policy, 7, 144, 151, 505, 507, 508; collectivization, 9, 43; dissolution of, 8; export, 36; fear of Nazi aggression, 303–4; First Five-Year Plan, 9; French press on, 191–2; government decision-making, 104; industrial development of, 9–10, 43, 201, 292; propaganda, 323; Purges, 23; railways in, 201; *troika,* 24, 242; Western relations with, 13, 20
Soviet Vakhtangov Theatre Company, 161
Spain: Civil War, 7, 515; fascist dictatorship, 512; Popular Front government, 512
SS *Washington* (steamship), 205
Stalin, Iosif V.: on agreement with Czechoslovakia, 389; background of, 21–5; at banquet with Bullitt, 201–2; in British historiography, 8; as businessman, 44–5; Eastern Pact and, 354, 363; Eden's visit to Moscow and, 318–19; education of, 22; family of, 23; foreign policymaking, 7, 25–6, 177, 187, 288; inner circle of, 21, 24, 241, 378; instructions to Litvinov, 52, 345, 364, 398, 399, 402, 403, 487, 489–90, 501; Kremlin log of meetings of, 242; Laval and, *391,* 391–2, 506; on League of Nations, 399; Litvinov's reports to, 25–6, 81, 247, 250, 251, 343–4, 350, 356, 362, 370, 377; marriages of, 23; on pact with the Pope, 392; personality of, 23–4; photographs of, *22*; on Poland, 24, 154, 156, 164, 391, 507; political career of, xviii; pseudonyms of, 23; revolutionary activities of, 22–3; on Roosevelt's eleven points, 52, 56–7; on Soviet-German relations, 153; on special rights for American citizens, 56; speech at 17th Party Congress, 153, 156; struggle for power, 5, 24; support for Troianovskii, 224, 229, 230; Trotskii and, 23–4; US-Soviet negotiations and, 42, 52, 55–6, 58, 231
Stanhope, James Richard Stanhope, Earl, 421, 457–8
Stavisky scandal, 151–2, 164–5, 166
Steiger, Boris S., 99, 103
Stimson, Henry, 48, 49
Stojadinović, Milan, 441, 443
Stomoniakov, Boris S.: background of, 32; on Beck, 160, 431; diplomatic career of, xviii, 32; on Eastern Pact, 190, 348; instructions to Davtian, 163–4; meeting with Bullitt, 198; meeting with Nadolny, 178; meeting with Stalin, 354; meetings with Alphand, 129, 168–9; meetings with Łukasiewicz, 156, 161, 430; photograph of, *33*; on Poland, 31–2, 34, 252, 432, 507; polemic between Antonov-Ovseenko and, 113–14, 115; revolutionary activities of, 32; on Soviet-Polish relations, 111, 161
Strang, William: on Anglo-Soviet relations, 273; conversations with Maiskii, 272, 273–4; diplomatic career of, xviii; Metro-Vickers crisis and, 66–7, 68, 89–90, 94, 95, 98, 99
Stresa Conference, 319, 332, 369, 371, 372
Stresa Front, 394, 417, 435, 450, 458
Stresemann, Gustav, 109, 155
Sudeten territories, 384, 445

Suleiman the Magnificent, Sultan of Turkey, 249, 253, 484, 488
Surits, Iakov Z., xviii, 193, 252
Szembek, Jan, 185, 348

Tabouis, Geneviève, xviii, 334–5, 340, 346, 371, 376, 415, 416, 453
Taittinger, Pierre, 485, 486
Talleyrand, Charles-Maurice de, 429
Tannery, Jean, 451
Tardieu, André, 27, 28, 30, 166, 256
Tătărescu, Gheorghe I., xviii, 434
Taylor, A.J.P., 8, 416; *Origins of the Second World War*, 416
Le Temps (newspaper), 346, 424, 453
Těšín district, 155, 162
Thomas, J.H., 90, 91
Times, the, 283, 284, 287, 291, 301–3, 305, 306, 327, 393, 406, 483
Tissier, Gustave, 152
Titulescu, Nicolae: anti-German position of, 337–8, 439–40; background of, 336–7; on collective security, 492; contacts with Potemkin, 346, 361, 368; Eastern Pact and, 334, 369, 370, 371, 373; King Carol II and, 441; meeting with Ostrovskii, 441; personality of, 339; policy towards the Soviet Union, 336, 337–40, 358, 362, 387, 480, 508; Polish policy and, 433, 434, 507; political career of, xviii; pressure on Laval, 506; pro-Italian views of, 261; quarrel between Beneš and, 387; relations with Litvinov, 337, *338*, 387, 427, 440, 498; relations with Ostrovskii, 339; Rhineland crisis and, 496; on Romanian-Soviet rapprochement, 437, 438, 439; visit to Moscow, 437; on Yugoslavia, 480
Torrès, Henri, 448, 484, 487, 488, 503
Trans-Siberian Railway, 201, 240, 385
Triple Entente, 246, 461
Troianovskii, Aleksandr A.: background of, 194; claim of meeting with Stalin, 241–2; debt-loan negotiations, 62, 214, 231, 233, 420; diplomatic career of, xviii, 61, 166, 204–6; English-language skills of, 194; on Kerenskii debt, 221–2; Krestinskii's dispatches to, 233, 234; letter to Stalin, 224; meeting with FDR, 214–15; meeting with Molotov, 241; meetings with Hull, 213, 214–15, 229, 233–4; meetings with Kelley, 229, 233–4; meetings with Moore, 229, 233–4; meetings with Wiley, 240–3; negotiations with the State Department, 214, 223, 224; personality of, 243; photographs of, 194–5; proposals of the "gentleman's agreement," 206; on publication of a Soviet procurement plan, 221; relations with Litvinov, 204–5, 215, 221, 222–6, 241; return to Washington, 243–4; Stalin's support for, 229, 230; trip to Moscow, 240–3
Trotskii, Lev D., xviii, 5, 23–4, 390
Trudeau, Justin, 9
Tukhachevskii, Mikhail N., xix, 365, 461, 477, 483
Twardowski, Fritz von, 120, 121–2, 146–7, 148, 150

Ulam, Adam, 509
United States: anti-communism, 35; economic crisis, 36; Johnson Act, 203, 206, 208, 210, 211; Moscow consulate in, 237; public opinion on European affairs, 255; racism in, 49; Soviet friends and foes in, 43–4. *See also* Soviet-American relations
US Export-Import Bank, 209, 210, 212, 214, 216, 218, 221, 228, 237
USSR. *See* Soviet Union
US State Department, 235, 236–7, 244, 489

Valentino, Arone di, 402, 403, 405, 416
Vallat, Xavier, 484–5, 486, 488
Vansittart, Robert Gilbert: on Abyssinian crisis, 415, 417–18, 459, 507; on aggression against Czechoslovakia, 407–8; on Anglo-French agreement, 303; on Anglo-German naval pact, 409–10; attitude to communists, 271; on British loan to Moscow, 420, 422, 473; on British parliamentary elections, 407; on British policy in the Far East, 282, 296, 297; on defence of Belgium, 498; diplomatic career of, xix, 270, 299, 353; disagreements with Simon, 307–8; on Eastern Pact, 302, 308, 320, 386; on Eden's visit to Moscow, 309, 322–3; education of, 270; on Flandin, 497; on Foreign Office policy, 283–4; on Franco-Soviet alliance, 320; on French foreign policy, 408–9; on Germany, 283, 286, 299, 300, 301, 302, 319, 353, 473, 510; on Hitler's *Mein Kampf*, 283; on Hoare-Laval plan, 458; on Japan, 282, 286, 299, 300; on Labour foreign policy, 303, 321–2; on Laval, 408; on Maiskii, 82, 279; marriages of, 270; meetings with Maiskii, 275, 276, 279–88, 295–9, 307–9, 312–13, 321–3, 343, 357, 382, 384, 393–5, 406–7, 411, 458–9, 461; Metro-Vickers affair and, 67, 70, 74, 101, 103; photographs of, 270, 271; promotion of Anglo-Soviet relations, 269, 275–6, 277, 287, 288, 294, 298–9, 302, 315, 334, 352–4, 390, 393, 409, 457, 462–3, 465, 506, 508; realpolitik of, 271; reputation of, 455; Rhineland crisis and, 466, 500–1; on Soviet entry into the League of Nations, 271, 286; on Soviet foreign policy, 303–4, 456; on Soviet press, 284; split between Sargent and, 381; subordinates of, 271; writings of, 270–1
Vansittart, Sarita, 270, 275, 279–80, 284, 285, 307, 329, 458, 465
Veinberg, Khaim S., 242
Ventsov, Semen I., xix, 123, 126, 128
Versailles, Treaty of, 4, 319, 355, 356, 394, 468, 480, 493
Vinogradov, Boris D., xix, 482; article in the *Journal de Moscou*, 440, 445; conversations with Kowalewski, 443–5
Voroshilov, Kliment E., 241, 242; conversations with Bullitt, 200–1, 227–8, 231; dinners at the French embassy, 177; meeting with Nadolny, 149, 179, 181; on payment of war debts, 227–8; on Polish relations with Germany, 177–8; political career of, xix; as Stalin's loyalist, 24; support of Litvinov's policies, 251
Vyshinskii, Andrei Ia., 95

Waley, S.D., 419
Webb, Beatrice, 279
Wellesley, Victor, 291, 300
Western colonialism, 7
Weygand, Maxime, 125, 136–7, 253, 339, 404
White Russian émigrés, 16
Wigram, Ralph, 271, 320, 411, 466, 497
Wiley, John, xix, 189, 205–6, 208, 212, 240, 241–3
Wilson, Hugh, 254–5
Wilson, Woodrow, 51, 195
Wood, Olivier, 267
World Disarmament Conference, 111
World Economic Conference, 99, 110

Zay, Jean, xix, 514
Zetkin, Clara, 119
Zhdanov, Andrei A., 242
Zinoviev, Grigorii E., 6
Zinoviev Letter, 65, 266

www.ingramcontent.com/pod-product-compliance
Lightning Source LLC
LaVergne TN
LVHW010354080826
844660LV00016B/970/J

* 9 7 8 1 4 8 7 5 4 4 4 1 6 *